# THE PETER TOWNSEND READER

*Edited by The Policy Press*

*Section editors*
Alan Walker
David Gordon
Ruth Levitas
Peter Phillimore
Chris Phillipson
Margot E. Salomon
Nicola Yeates

This edition published in Great Britain in 2010 by

The Policy Press
University of Bristol
Fourth Floor
Beacon House
Queen's Road
Bristol BS8 1QU
UK

t: +44 (0)117 331 4054
f: +44 (0)117 331 4093
e: tpp-info@bristol.ac.uk
www.policypress.co.uk

North American office:
The Policy Press
c/o International Specialized Books Services
920 NE 58th Avenue, Suite 300
Portland, OR 97213-3786, USA
t: +1 503 287 3093
f: +1 503 280 8832
e: info@isbs.com

© The Policy Press 2010

British Library Cataloguing in Publication Data
A catalogue record for this book is available from the British Library.

Library of Congress Cataloging-in-Publication Data
A catalog record for this book has been requested.

ISBN 978 1 84742 404 4 paperback
ISBN 978 1 84742 405 1 hardcover

Cover design by Robin Hawes
Printed and bound in Great Britain by Hobbs the Printers, Southampton

# Contents

Contents

# Note for readers

To allow accurate citations, table numbering in each of the chapters has been kept as it was given in the original sources. Where references have been given as notes, the original style has been retained, but notes have been renumbered and placed as endnotes to the chapter.

All effort has been made to insert missing references but some sources missing from the originals have not been possible to identify or locate. Peter surely would have remembered what they were.

All royalties from the sale of this reader will be donated to Child Poverty Action Group and Disability Alliance.

# Acknowledgements

Sage Publications for permission to reproduce extracts from 'Guerrillas, subordinates and passers-by', *Journal of Critical Social Policy*, 1981, vol 1, no 2 (Chapters 2 and 3); and 'Absolute and overall poverty: the 1995 Copenhagen approach to the fulfilment of human rights', *Global Social Policy*, 2006, vol 6, no 3 (Chapter 8).

The Fabian Society for permission to reproduce 'The 2009 Minority Report on the World Bank', www.fabiansociety.org.uk, 2009 (Chapter 9).

Palgrave and the International Labour Organization for permission to reproduce 'Investment in social security: a possible UN model for child benefit', Chapter 7 in *Building decent societies*, 2009 (Chapter 11).

The London School of Economics and Blackwell Wiley for permission to reproduce 'Measuring poverty', *British Journal of Sociology*, 1954, vol 5, no 2 (Chapter 13); and 'The meaning of poverty', *British Journal of Sociology*, 1962, vol 13, no 2 (Chapter 14).

Cambridge University Press for permission to reproduce extracts from 'Deprivation', *Journal of Social Policy*, 1987, vol 16, no 2 (Chapter 17).

Harvester Wheatsheaf and David Piachaud for permission to reproduce extracts from 'Theoretical disputes about poverty', Chapter 6 in *The international analysis of poverty*, 1993 (Chapter 18).

New Statesman for permission to reproduce 'The truce on inequality', *New Statesman*, 26 September 1959 (Chapter 21); 'How the rich stay rich', *New Statesman*, 1 October 1976 (Chapter 23); 'The disabled need help', *New Society*, 28 September 1967 (Chapter 50); and 'We have a fair way to go', *New Statesman & Society*, 25 March 1994 (Chapter 57).

*The Times* for permission to reproduce 'Poverty: has the welfare state failed?', *The Times*, 9 March 1971 (Chapter 22); and 'An aid scale for disabled children', *The Times*, 23 January 1973 (Chapter 45).

Child Poverty Action Group for permission to reproduce 'The pursuit of equality', *Poverty*, 1983 (Chapter 24); 'A matter of class', *Poverty*, Winter 1986/7 (Chapter 25); and *A policy to establish the legal rights of low income families*, 1969 (Chapter 52).

BMJ Publishing Group for permission to reproduce 'The rich man in his castle', *British Medical Journal*, no 309, 24 December 1994 (Chapter 27); and 'Better benefits for health: plan to implement the central recommendations of the Acheson Report', *British Medical Journal*, no 7185, 13 March 1999 (Chapter 34).

Elsevier for permission to reproduce extracts from 'Inequality in the health service', *The Lancet*, vol 303, no 7868, 15 June 1974 (Chapter 31).

Baywood Publishing for permission to reproduce extracts from 'Individual or social responsibility for premature death?', *International Journal of Health Services*, 1990, vol 20, no 30 (Chapter 33).

Oxford University Press for permission to reproduce 'The anxieties of retirement', *Occupational Medicine*, 1955, vol 5, no 1 (Chapter 36), and to kind staff at the Society of Occupational Medicine who located a complete copy of the article.

The Centre for Policy on Ageing, the British Society of Gerontology and Cambridge University Press for permission to reproduce extracts from 'The structured dependency of the elderly', *Ageing & Society*, 1981, vol 1, no 1 (Chapter 38); and 'Policies for the aged in the 21st century', *Ageing & Society*, 2006, vol 26, no 2 (Chapter 39).

Townsend Centre for Poverty Research, University of Bristol, for permission to reproduce extracts from *New pensions for old: The key to welfare reform*, 1999 (Chapter 40).

The Disability Alliance for permission to reproduce extracts from *Poverty and disability*, 1987 (Chapter 51).

The International Labour Organization for permission to reproduce extracts from *The right to social security and development*, Discussion Paper 18, 2007 (Chapter 53).

New Left Review for permission to reproduce 'Persuasion and conformity: an assessment of the Borrie Report on social justice', *New Left Review*, 1995, no 213, Sep/Oct (Chapter 55).

All effort has been made to obtain permission for the remaining extracts for which copyright was not already held or reverted to Peter Townsend or held by the publisher.

# Notes on the section editors

**David Gordon** is Director of the Townsend Centre for International Poverty Research and Professor of Social Justice in the School for Policy Studies, University of Bristol. His expertise is in poverty and poverty-related research, social justice and criminal justice matters. He has been involved in extensive research into inequalities in health and the fair allocation of government expenditure and has published numerous publications on poverty and inequality, including *Breadline Europe* and *World poverty*, both edited with Peter Townsend (The Policy Press, 2000 and 2002).

David is also experienced in the analysis of social statistics and in particular the Census, and has more than ten years' experience of studying disability in childhood and the definitions of disability.

**Ruth Levitas** has been Professor of Sociology at Bristol since 2001, and a member of the Department of Sociology at Bristol since 1979.

She is predominantly known for her work on utopianism and on social exclusion. Her research interests in the first field cover the history of oppositional and utopian thought, the relationship between utopia and social theory, utopia as a method in the social sciences, utopia and music, and utopia, history, memory and place. In May 2010 she takes up a Leverhulme Research Fellowship to complete work on a book on *The imaginary reconstitution of society: Utopia as method*.

She has also written widely on contemporary political ideologies and discourses, as well as on New Labour, poverty, inequality and social inclusion and exclusion. Her recent work on social exclusion in collaboration with colleagues in the School for Policy Studies and elsewhere has focused on conceptualisation and measurement. It includes research funded by the Joseph Rowntree Foundation, the Social Exclusion Unit and The Social Exclusion Task Force. She is co-founder and immediate past Chair of the Utopian Studies Society Europe. She is also Vice-Chair of the William Morris Society, a charity founded in London in 1955.

Ruth's key publications include *The ideology of the new right* (Polity Press, 1986), *The concept of utopia* (Philip Allan, 1990 and Peter Lang 2009), *Interpreting official statistics* (edited with Will Guy, Routledge, 1996), *The inclusive society? New Labour and social exclusion* (Macmillan, 1998 and 2005) and *Poverty and social exclusion in Britain* (edited with Christina Pantazis and David Gordon, The Policy Press, 2006).

**Peter Phillimore** is professor of social anthropology at Newcastle University, in the School of Geography, Politics and Sociology. He studied anthropology at Edinburgh and Durham, and holds a PhD from the latter based on fieldwork in Kangra, in northern India, where he researched kinship and marriage and the shepherding economy of the pastoralist Gaddi. His first research post was at the University of Bristol, where he worked with Peter Townsend for four years on two projects researching health and inequality in the north-east of England. He has been at Newcastle University since 1988.

His research with Peter Townsend led to an interest in environmental health and environmental politics. His subsequent research has been in these two areas – the anthropology of health and the anthropology of the environment – on which he has published widely, most recently on comparative research in major chemical centres in Scotland and Germany. He is now leading part of an EU project on health policies and practices relating to diabetes and chronic heart disease in Syria, Tunisia, Turkey and Palestine.

**Chris Phillipson** has held the post of Professor of Applied Social Studies and Social Gerontology, at the University of Keele since 1988. Chris established the Department of Applied Social Studies and Social Work in 1988 and headed the Department until 1996. He has been Dean of Research for the Faculty of Social Sciences and served as Pro-Vice Chancellor for the University (2005-2009). He was also founding Director (1986-1997) of the Centre for Social Gerontology.

His research has been in the field of ageing where he has led a number of research programmes investigating issues relating to pre-retirement education, family and community life in old age, problems of social exclusion, and issues relating to urbanisation and migration. He has published extensively on age-related matters and his books include: *Reconstructing old age* (Sage, 1998), *Social theory and social ageing* (co-authored, McGraw-Hill, 2003), *Social networks and social exclusion* (co-edited, Ashgate, 2004), *Ageing, globalisation and inequality* (co-edited, Baywood, 2006) and *Futures of old age* (co-edited, Sage, 2006). His co-edited *Handbook of social gerontology* will be published by Sage in 2010.

Chris is a past-President of the British Society of Gerontology and a former Vice-Chair of the Training and Development Board of the Economic and Social Research Council. He has been a visiting Professor to universities in Japan and the USA. He is a Founding Fellow of the British Society of Gerontology and an Academician of the Academy of Social Sciences.

**Margot E. Salomon** is Senior Lecturer at the Centre for the Study of Human Rights and Law Department, London School of Economics and Political Science. Her research interests address the legal dimensions of world poverty, human rights and the international political economy, and third generation rights, with forthcoming research focusing on human rights and climate change.

Margot is a consultant to the UN Office of the High Commissioner for Human Rights on extreme poverty and human rights and on the right to development, a Member of the International Law Association's Committee on the Rights of Indigenous Peoples, and coordinator of the LSE's inter-departmental research group on Globalization, Poverty and Responsibility.

Recent publications include: 'Poverty, privilege and international law: the Millennium Development Goals and the guise of humanitarianism', *German Yearbook of International Law* (2008); *Global responsibility for human rights* (Oxford University Press, 2007) and *Casting the net wider: Human rights, development and new duty-bearers* (edited with A. Tostensen and W. Vandenhole, Intersentia, 2007).

Margot received a PhD in international law from the LSE, an LLM from University College London, and holds degrees from the University of Amsterdam and Concordia University in Montreal.

**Alan Walker** joined the Department of Sociological Studies at the University of Sheffield in 1977 and has been a Lecturer, Senior Lecturer and Reader in Social Policy. He was appointed Professor of Social Policy in 1985 and was Head of Department from 1988 to 1996. He directed the £3.5 million ESRC Growing Older Programme, 1999-2004, and the UK National Collaboration on Ageing Research, 2001-2004. He is currently Director of the £22 million ESRC, EPSRC, BBSRC, MRC and AHRC New Dynamics of Ageing Programme and is also Director of the European Research Area in Ageing and spends most of his time on research and postgraduate supervision.

Alan's research interests span a wide range in social analysis, social policy and social planning. He is a specialist in social gerontology and, with two colleagues in the Netherlands, is responsible for developing the concept of social quality, chairing the European Foundation on Social Quality, based in Amsterdam. He has published more than 30 books, over 200 reports and more than 300 papers in scholarly journals and edited volumes, and this work has been published in more than 20 languages. His recent publications include *Understanding quality of life in old age* (Open University Press, 2006) and *Social policy in ageing societies* (with Gerhard Naegele, Palgrave 2009).

Alan is a founding Academician of the Academy for Learned Societies in the Social Sciences. He was given lifetime achievement awards in 2007 by both the Social Policy Association and the British Society for Gerontology.

He has also been active in the UK voluntary sector for many years and co-founded the Disability Alliance with Peter Townsend in 1974. He is also currently Patron of the National Pensioner's Convention.

**Nicola Yeates** is Senior Lecturer in Social Policy at the Open University and an Honorary Senior Research Fellow at Dublin City University. Her intellectual concerns broadly lie with transnational and global processes and their implications for social policy as a field of academic study and as a practice.

Nicola has published extensively in the areas of globalisation, migration and social policy, including *The global social policy reader* (The Policy Press, 2009), *Globalising care economies and migrant workers*, (Palgrave, 2009), *Understanding global social policy* (The Policy Press, 2008) and *Globalization and social policy* (Sage, 2001). She is co-editor of the journal *Global Social Policy*, and is on the editorial board of *Transformations: Irish Race, Migration and Social Transformation Review*.

She is Founder and Director of Academic Studies of the Social Welfare Summer School, Department for Social Development (Belfast) and Department for Social and Family Affairs (Dublin), and has been an academic tutor for the Department for Work and Pensions Social Policy Summer School, King's College, Cambridge, since 1998.

# Introduction

Peter Townsend was one of the world's greatest social scientists. His career spanned seven decades during which time he was not only hugely prolific but also wrote, in different styles, for a wide range of audiences: from scientific journals and books to newspapers, campaign literature and advice guides. No matter which audience he was addressing, his writing was always beautifully crafted, crystal clear and entirely without conceit. This book brings together, for the first time, selections of his writing across the whole spectrum of his remarkable career.

The idea for this reader was conceived while Peter was still alive and he was involved closely in its development. After producing his mammoth publication list as part of his 80th birthday celebrations and final retirement from LSE, The Policy Press felt that a reader covering each aspect of his written work, much of which was not readily available, would be an appropriate introduction to this intellectual giant for new generations of students in sociology, social policy and related subjects. Peter was delighted with and enthusiastic about this project but, sadly, was not able to see it through. The original plan was for him to write an introductory essay but, obviously, that plan had to be abandoned. There can be no attempt here to construct a chapter in his name or to try to shadow his imagined intentions. He was an original thinker and, no doubt, would have surprised and excited us with his insights and wisdom. Moreover there are very few who can match the quality of his prose. Nor is this the place for obituaries: several have been published (*The Guardian*, 9 June 2009; *The Times*, 11 June 2009; *The Independent*, 13 June 2009) and there are numerous accolades from colleagues and former students.[1] Instead this short substitute introduction addresses one simple question: why should students continue to read Peter Townsend even though some of his major publications date from the 1950s and 1960s, and the (ill-conceived) pressure on them to refer to only the most recent sources grows ever stronger?

As a quick glance at the contents of this volume will demonstrate the scope of Peter's analytical compass was truly remarkable. Moreover this was not the result of any inability to focus but quite the opposite. Rather than being an intellectual gadfly, he had the rare power to see the connections between social problems, such as the influential causative role of social class and status differences in structuring society to the benefit of some and the disadvantage of others. In an era of academic specialisation this is a highly distinctive and valuable perspective that students should be encouraged to emulate to avoid the dangers of analytical myopia and overspecialisation. He was also a master tactician and would seize opportunities to advance arguments aimed at achieving social justice, such as his early career switch from qualitative to quantitative methods (which led to heated debates with, among others, his close friend Dennis Marsden) and the adoption of a human rights perspective later in his professional life.

Even more amazing than the breadth of his research is its depth. In each of his major fields, highlighted in this reader, he made seminal contributions. He is best known for his path-breaking work on poverty, from the 1950s to the present century, but he was also a founder of the sociology of later life or social gerontology, producing four landmark texts before the age of 40. The extracts in this book therefore provide easily accessible insights into not only one of the largest academic corpuses in the social policy field but also one of the most impressive in quality terms. In addition it is one of the most influential in both academic and policy circles.

The Townsend heritage sampled in the following pages is compelling too because it represents his unique career as a public intellectual. He embodied the commitment, to paraphrase Marx, to not just understand society but to change it as well. Thus he combined theoretical analysis and empirical research with political campaigns aimed at improving society. Some may be daunted by the prospect of emulating this extraordinary multi-talented phenomenon, who would not be? However this should not obscure the central message of his life's work, that the force of well marshalled evidence and persuasion should be directed at trying to combat injustices, nor the specific examples for students provided by each of his major skills in research, quantitative and qualitative, social theory, policy analysis and campaigning. If we cannot hope to match him on all fronts we can profit from close observation of particular elements of his portfolio and then perhaps commit a fraction of the lifelong energy he displayed to one or more of them.

Each section of the reader provides plenty of examples of his theoretical insights. He trained as an anthropologist and sociologist and employed those skills to both narrate and theorise various social issues such as poverty, disability and old age. The essential lesson here is the necessity not just to describe but also to understand why various social problems occur. In terms of empirical research his approach is a model for any novice researcher. Regardless of whether it was qualitative (*The last refuge*; see Chapter 37) or quantitative (*Poverty in the United Kingdom*; see Chapters 16 and 47) he adopted the same rigorous, grounded stance, painstakingly analysing every variable and building his theory and policy proposals on the basis of the evidence. It is because of this serious workmanlike dedication, as well as his analytical and literary flair, that he was able to produce so many classic texts in both quantitative and qualitative research. With regard to policy analysis he was a widely acknowledged master, as many of the following extracts illustrate. He would forensically dissect arguments and subject them to withering scrutiny and cross-examination (see for example Chapter 18), always quoting evidence to support or deny the case being made. Students wanting to hone their analytical skills can dip into any of the reader's sections where there are many rich rewards to be found.

Students of social policy and sociology should be particularly interested in this collection because he was a leading exponent of both. In addition he was one of the few to try to connect them (see Section I). His view was that social policy must be underpinned by a sociological perspective because it is 'social' policy. In other words it is concerned centrally with social structures, social relations and social formations (groups, institutions, governments) and not only with the role of the state. This key message has enduring relevance for contemporary students of social policy who should beware of over-emphasising the formal institutions conventionally defined as social policy ones.

As Richard Titmuss asserted, students of social policy have a special duty to make explicit their values and Peter was always very clear about his. He was an avowed campaigner for social justice. He worked within the Fabian tradition for over 60 years and is identified as one of its leading exponents. This means the careful gathering of evidence-based arguments in order to 'tell the truth to power'. Although this approach to social change has been criticised as being very top-down, expert-led and reformist, even its strongest adversaries would acknowledge, albeit grudgingly for some, that such reformism has a place and that Peter was one of its most dogged practitioners. As a fully signed-up public intellectual he was a leading campaigner with regard to child poverty, disability and pensions. He co-founded the Child Poverty Action Group in 1965 and the Disability Alliance in 1974 and, over the whole of his professional career, he was active in the campaign for better old age pensions.

The readings in this book include several of his campaigning documents (for example Chapters 9, 12, 40, 52), because, on the one hand, they represent a major aspect of his life's work and, on the other, they are often seminal contributors to twentieth century social policy. Examples include his major, defining inputs to the struggle to end child poverty, the campaign for a comprehensive disability income and the battle for decent pensions to prevent poverty in old age. These are not peripheral but central contributions to social policy over the past five to six decades. There is much in this body of campaigning literature on which present day reformers can draw and there is inspiration too, not just in the words but in the deeds. He was a rather successful campaigner on several fronts: sheltered housing for older people, de-institutionalisation of people with mental health problems, the introduction of Attendance Allowances, increases in child benefits and the current child poverty reduction target are some examples. While he was not always the sole motivator of policy change to affect these major social reforms, which improved the living standards and well-being of hundreds and thousands of people, he was certainly a vital and prominent voice among them and often a rallying post for others bent on the same cause. Since his death a large number of people and organisations, national and international, have acknowledged warmly their enormous debt to Peter. He was truly a giant in each of his chosen fields.

In the rich and varied readings that follow, each introduced by experts knowledgeable in the particular topic and about this work, you will find both challenge and inspiration, as well as some of the finest writing in social science that you are ever likely to encounter. This reader also comprises an historical overview of the development of social research and social policy over the second half of the past century and the first decade of this one that all of the editors hope will be a long-lasting and invaluable resource.

*Alan Walker*

## Endnote

[1] See for examples those on the websites of the London School of Economics and Political Science (www2.lse.ac.uk/socialpolicy/PeterTownsendTribute.aspx), the University of Bristol (www.bris.ac.uk/poverty) and the *Generations Review* (www. britishgerontology.org/09newsletter3/news_reviews5.asp).

# Section I

# Sociology and social policy

*Edited by Alan Walker*

# Introduction

Peter Townsend read philosophy and social anthropology at Cambridge (in the 1940s, there was no sociology course). He sharpened his sociological skills subsequently during a postgraduate fellowship at the Free University in Berlin. Following research posts and a teaching position at LSE he was appointed as the first Professor of Sociology at the new University of Essex in 1963, at the age of 35. He created a department which was unique in terms of its breadth and quality, including disciplinary backgrounds as diverse as social anthropology, social history, social psychology, geography, philosophy, classics and the natural sciences as well as sociology and social policy. He was a passionate advocate of sociology and saw as one of its main roles the provision of evidence to inform progressive social change. Unfortunately the discipline became rather introspective following the cultural turn and, consequently, it has lost much of the policy orientation that he sought to encourage. Nonetheless, as noted by Joan Busfield (2009) he made a major contribution to the development of sociology in Britain.

His dedication to social change was one reason why he never wrote a textbook on sociology or social policy. For him these disciplines were not purely academic but also public pursuits which should be focused on 'telling truth to power'. He was also completely disinterested in the material rewards that large textbook sales might generate. Thus, there is no work of reference that sets out at length Peter's sociological approach to social policy. This is a real pity because he laid the foundations for it but never built on them in a concerted way. Instead his contributions in the field of sociology and social policy take two main forms.

First of all he insisted on the inseparability of social policy and sociology. This is a view that is not shared by the mainstream of either discipline and, in my view, diminishes both of them. He made a powerful case, including a foundation sociological definition of social policy. The extracts in this section will be devoted mainly to this dimension. His second major contribution was represented by his extensive sociological analyses of social policy issues. In other words, he did social policy in sociological terms. Thus his policy-related research on ageing, disability, globalisation, health inequalities, poverty and social exclusion was, in fact, sociological research from a policy perspective. His definitions of poverty, disability and so on are sociological definitions and his methods are sociological. Readers are advised to approach other sections in this volume in that light, and it is there that his most important work on sociology and social policy will be found (see, for example, **Chapters 5, 14, 26, 38** and **49** in this volume). Here the emphasis is on the sociology of social policy.

## The separation of sociology and social policy

Peter Townsend discussed his sociological approach to social policy most fully in a lecture to the Department of Sociology at the University of Aberdeen in 1973. A revised version was published as 'Sociology and social policy' in the book of the same name in 1975. In the opening part of this chapter he takes issue with both sociology and social policy for allowing the separation of the two: criticising the former for pretending to be value free or having over-optimistic theories of social change and the latter for its narrow concentration on welfare administration. For him social policy should be conceived and studied as an aspect of sociology, as the opening paragraphs of **Chapter 1** make clear. He returned to this theme in 1981 in the second issue of *Critical Social Policy* pointedly titled 'Guerillas, subordinates and passers-by'. The extract in **Chapter 2** comes from this article and emphasises the common historical roots of both sociology and social policy as well as some of the reasons for the neglect of social policy by sociologists and the narrow focus of social policy.

## The definition of social policy

The argument for a fusion between sociology and social policy was a bold one in the 1970s because, as **Chapter 2** describes, the two disciplines had developed along different paths. Subsequent entrenchment by the two professions means that this case is even harder to make today than 30 years ago. It is when we consider his sociological definition of social policy, however, that the full extent of the unnecessary restriction on both disciplines, caused by their separation, may be realised. The end of **Chapter 1** focuses on this definition. The path-breaking and potentially liberating nature of this definition, in terms of the rationale by which social institutions and groups are created or steered to enable preservation or development, can only be grasped by reference to the prevailing contemporary definitions of the subject. Marshall for example described social policy as 'the policy of governments with regard to action having a direct impact on the welfare of citizens, by providing them with services or income' (1967, p 6). The contrast could not be starker: while Marshall focuses very narrowly on state action to promote well-being or welfare, Townsend links and extends greatly Titmuss's (1958) analyses of the social division of welfare to create a conception of social policy that is not tied to government action and encompasses both positive and negative intentions. As he noted, 'Government policy is no more synonymous with social policy than government behaviour is synonymous with social behaviour' (Townsend, 1975, p 3). This potentially opened up a path towards the analysis of social policy in much broader terms than either hitherto or contemporaneously. In practice this would mean more emphasis on the structural causes of inequality and other social problems and less on the specific remedies institutionalised by governments or promised by oppositions. Although he did not develop further this conceptual framework for social policy Peter did devote his professional life to the sociological analysis of structural inequalities. Also, his initial sociological account of social policy raised questions about the nature of the adjective 'social' in social policy which contributed substantially to later work on 'social quality' (Walker, 1984; Beck et al, 1998).

Lest it be thought that this discussion of social policy definitions is purely historical it is worth quoting a key contemporary source on the subject. Social policy is

> based upon a distinct empirical focus – support for the well-being of citizens provided through social action…. So social policy refers both to the activity of policy-making to promote well-being and to the academic study of such actions. (Alcock, 2008, p 3)

This definition of the subject owes more to Marshall than Townsend. While some may lament the survival of the former's limited conception of social policy and its role, and also the failure to explore the scope and meaning of specifically social as opposed to other policies, there is no doubt that the latter's approach is challenging to operationalise. Peter himself recognised the potential disadvantages, as well as the advantages, of his proposed sociological analysis of social policy (**Chapter 1**).

## The sociology of social policy

The third extract in this section (**Chapter 3**) provides a sociological critique of social policy. In it Peter delineates the conservative influences on social policy such as bureaucracy and the control of official statistics and professionalism. In both cases power is wielded to preserve the status quo, prevent radical change or deny the excluded access to resources. He also includes the rich and especially their self-interest as a major source of restriction on the current scope of social policy (further discussion on this topic can be found in **Section IV** by Ruth Levitas with reference to his paper 'Underclass and overclass' [Townsend, 1993]).

In a subsequent pamphlet *The rise of international social policy* he outlines the case for social policy with an international focus to be integral to all universities. Again the case is a sociological one in which he insists that "the analysis of social policy and the predominant institutions of policy are at the heart of sociological theories of social change and evolution" (1995, p 11). The final extract (**Chapter 4**) comes from this paper.

There is no doubt about the considerable extent to which the discipline of social policy addresses Peter Townsend's research, especially in the fields of poverty, inequality and health. In social gerontology he is regarded as a foundation researcher (Walker, 2009). The failure of sociology and social policy – the two disciplines he so successfully straddled – to take forward Peter's pioneering contributions to the sociological understanding of social policy is a major shortcoming of both.

## References

Alcock, P. (2008) 'The subject of social policy' in P. Alcock, M. May and K. Rowlingson (eds) *The student's companion to social policy*, Oxford: Blackwell, pp 3-10.

Beck, W., van der Maesen, L. and Walker, A. (eds) (1998) *The social quality of Europe*, Bristol: The Policy Press.

Busfield, J. (2009) Letter published in *The Guardian*, 10 June.

Marshall, T.H. (1967) *Social policy in the twentieth century*, London: Hutchinson.

Titmuss, R.M. (1958) *Essays on 'the welfare state'*, London: Unwin Books.

Townsend, P. (1975) *Sociology and social policy*, London: Allen Lane.

Townsend, P. (1981) 'Guerrillas, subordinates and passers-by: the relationship between sociologists and social policy', *Critical Social Policy*, vol 1, no 2, pp 22-34.

Townsend, P. (1993) 'Underclass and overclass: the widening gulf between social classes in Britain in the 1980s', in M. Cross and G. Payne (eds) *Sociology in action*, London: Macmillan, pp 91-118.

Townsend, P. (1995) *The rise of international social policy*, Bristol: The Policy Press.

Walker, A. (1984) *Social planning*, Oxford: Blackwell.

Walker, A. (2009) 'Peter Townsend (1928-2009)', in *Ageing & Society*, vol 29, pp 1007-13.

# 1

# Sociology and social policy

The separation of the study of social policy from sociology is, I believe, wrong. It arises in part because the concept of social policy, perhaps unconsciously for political reasons, has been confined narrowly by many scholars and others to that of welfare administration: in part because the pursuit of sociology has been wrongly believed by many to be 'value free'; and in part because many sociologists have adopted unduly optimistic and facile theories of social change. Unlike Marx, they have been concerned to trace the progress of the achievements of modern society rather than its inadequacies and have concentrated more on the problems of social order and equilibrium than on those of the identification and exploration of social change. While social problems have formed part of the university curriculum they have been examined in an over-generalized way, usually from a functionalist standpoint, which does not explain incidence or degree and offers no indication of the mechanisms by which they might be reduced or eliminated. Theories of change have been insufficiently exact to furnish clear and inescapable implications for policy.

The study of social policy is the study of the means whereby societies prevent, postpone, introduce and manage changes in structure. According to the customary, if supercilious, distinction ordinarily made, such study is therefore not an applied but a 'pure' social science. It is as necessary as the study of social structure to the development and exposition of theories of social change.

[...]

An extended conception of social policy has a number of disadvantages and advantages. It covers so many activities that there are difficulties in arranging component information as well as ideas into comparable form. Even if attention is concentrated upon different government activities they are hard to relate. For example, only in recent years have there been any official attempts to show the respective contributions made by gross earnings, direct and indirect taxation, and direct and indirect benefits of the social services to the distribution of income.[1] The first publication of the annual *Social Trends* in 1970 was a significant development, but the series has not yet given much impression of reflecting a broader conception of social policy or even an 'objective' conception of social policy. A lot more work

---

Extracts (pp 1-2, 4-7) from Townsend, P. (1975) *Sociology and social policy*, London: Allen Lane.

remains to be done if the social effects of any change in levels of earnings, taxation or social services are to be traced in detail.[2] Again, it is hard to compare government services with equivalent activities of industry and voluntary and private bodies. Little statistical information is collected and issued routinely about the latter and rarely is it presented in a form which is comparable with government statistics. The existing fragmentation is very understandable. Civil servants and local authority officials are employed primarily to administer services for which they are publicly accountable. It is natural that they should concentrate on these services and give little heed to those outside their jurisdiction, and that statistical output and other information should reflect the history and administrative organization of government. It is also natural that the public should have been encouraged to concentrate their attentions on 'public' services which are not only so defined but financed directly by them through taxation and administered directly by government servants. There is therefore wide agreement in principle that extensive information should be made available about these 'public' services. But it is also natural that so-called 'private' industry should be reluctant to produce some kinds of corresponding information about the welfare services of industry. That might appear to be encroaching upon public responsibilities, demonstrate too clearly how privileges are conferred on certain sections of personnel and assist competitors. It would be difficult too to get information produced in a standardized form. So even if we were to attempt to adopt a broad policy perspective it could not be sustained without great difficulty. The problem of converting society's definition of the scope and categories of social policy into one which is broader and functionally more consistent is huge. Again and again, through lack of appropriate information and of the efforts and agreement to produce it, the task is likely to be frustrated. The structure of inequality frustrates attempts even to document it. Discussion in academic journals as well as the mass media will tend to revert to more reassuring administrative concepts and will concentrate on areas about which there is information.

A related disadvantage is that the policy analyst will be overwhelmed by the sheer magnitude of his task. Any attempt to invest a conception with elaborate sub-divisions of meaning and a very broad range of subject matter is bound to cause strain. It is difficult to preserve a sense of balance and context, not only because of the lack of good statistical data for many parts of the conception, but because so much knowledge is brought into play and, moreover, needs to be graded and weighed. For example, in reducing poverty is fiscal policy more important than price control, or employment policy more important than social security? Different government agencies, and non-government as well as government agencies, serve similar social objectives. Criteria have to be evolved to settle the list of agencies which are contributing, and the degree to which they are contributing, to specific social objectives. When the information which is circulating about agencies varies in amount and accessibility this is extraordinarily difficult. And the conception becomes more difficult to communicate. Many laymen feel they can at least come to terms with experts who are talking about a set of centrally or locally administered welfare services – within which are included education, health, social security, housing and the care of children, the disabled and the old. It is an interest or a commitment which they can respect, even when it does not seem to be ideologically paramount. But a social policy analyst who is as much preoccupied with the social benefits of possible extensions of the public ownership of industry as he is with improving the housing facilities of the aged, or with the social benefits of a different earnings or tax structure as he is with transformations of social security, may appear to them to be more elusive, and perhaps more disconcerting. Too easily he can give the impression of being some kind of intellectual imperialist, gobbling up areas of expertise believed previously to be remote from his interests and competence.

Against these disadvantages, which have to be conceded, certain advantages have to be recognized. Social realities, and especially inequalities, are more likely to be perceived by rulers and ruled. Improvements in state unemployment insurance might be more than counter-balanced by an increase in structural unemployment leaving more families living in conditions of deprivation. So the student of social policy must seek knowledge about the structural causes of, and remedies for, unemployment as well as about the means of meeting the needs of those who are unemployed. Selective increases in indirect taxation may wipe out hard-won improvements in levels of low pay, pensions or family allowances. So the social effects of different tax policies have to be disentangled. The extension of employers' welfare benefits in kind for high-income groups may quickly neutralize the effects of the introduction of a more progressive system of taxation. Or again, the gradual development of private systems of welfare for privileged groups of the population, whether in education, medical care, housing or pensions, may undermine equality of rights, benefits or opportunities that governments fondly believe have been introduced through state legislation. So employer welfare cannot be ignored.

Policy analysts must therefore depend on a broad sociological perspective about both objectives and means. Social policy is best conceived as a kind of blueprint for the management of society towards social ends: it can be defined as *the underlying as well as the professed rationale by which social institutions and groups are used or brought into being to ensure social preservation or development.* Social policy is, in other words, the institutionalized control of services, agencies and organizations to maintain or change social structure and values. Sometimes this control may be utterly conscious, and consciously expressed by government spokesmen and others. Sometimes it may be unspoken and even unrecognised.

In this sense of the term, then, all societies have social policies. In identifying the different policies of the developing and advanced societies the sociologist may gradually call attention to the fact that policy analysis is independent of planning. The difference is essentially one between a subjective orientation, even when that is expressed collectively by a community, a city or a nation, and one that strives to be objective. Policy analysis is the task of unravelling and evaluating the policy of society, or, more correctly the policies of different social groups and agencies, with government and industry being the predominant agencies in advanced industrial societies. Planning, by contradistinction, is best conceived as the search for alternative policies. It is the definition of goals on the basis of measured needs among (and between) populations and the development of a rational strategy and of appropriate means to fulfil those objectives most quickly. This begs further questions about choosing goals, measuring needs, defining what is rational and what is appropriate, but ... a planning perspective can be regarded as arising from the analysis of social conditions, with inequality and deprivation as the guiding concepts. A 'plan' may be adopted and put into effect as policy, but it is normally distorted in the process by the subjective interpretations and emphases of government and officials, concessions to interest groups and limitations imposed by external forces. Whether 'planning' and research units of local and central government and universities are planning units in an objective sense of the word rather than instruments of social policy is very doubtful. Their detachment or impartiality is of dubious validity, if only because the influences upon them of the research foundations, professions, universities or employing departments to which in some measure they owe allegiance.

I said above that there may not be a single social policy but rather the policies of different social groups, overlapping each other in the objectives and methods which they adopt, and one or sometimes two of the groups (state and industry, or state and church) being predominant. They are controlled by public and professional perceptions of their functions and usually operate much less independently than their directors realize. Social policy is the rationale by which societies are steered towards social ends, and the rationale according to which different ends are combined together and weighed. Policy depends on a definition of needs that are perceived rather than measured, and upon administrative agencies or services that have been set up and have become familiar, rather than alternative agencies or services that might be created. It also depends, it may be said, on a concept of social change as it is perceived within society rather than as something absolute or 'objective'. So the policy analyst has to remember that the discussion of social problems is biased, whether in Parliament, the press, government publications or even the social science journals. There are intellectual fashions in each phase of history when some problems are illuminated and others ignored, and this applies, though in different degrees, to all the contending interest groups of the policy system. It also applies to the perception of strategies.

### References

[1] Marshall, T.H., *Social Policy in the Twentieth Century*, Hutchinson, 2nd ed., 1967, p.6 (also see p. 166)

[2] Beales, H.L., *The Making of Social Policy in the Nineteenth Century*, Hobhouse Memorial Lecture, no. 15, O.U.P., 1946; Carr, E.H., *The New Society*, 1951; Polayani, K. *The Great Transformation*, 1944; Bruce, M., *The Coming of the Welfare State*, Batsford, 1961; Robson, W.A., *The Welfare State*, Hobhouse Memorial Lecture, no. 26, O.U.P., 1957; Gregg, P., *The Welfare State*, Harrap, 1967.

# 2

# Origins of sociology and social policy

This article argues that a concern with social policy must be central rather than peripheral to sociology. Some sociologists wrongly regard policy analysis as inconsequential, or as an applied subject; others subordinate scientific to conventional, and highly restricted, interpretations of the concept. Both thereby fail to play a positive role in explaining how society came to be what it is and how it could be changed for the better. The role of the state in engineering social structure, particularly social stratification, and in controlling the direction of social change has been, as a consequence, underestimated. This article reviews in outline the history and future of the study of social policy.

1834 would be an appropriate year to choose to begin any account of the foundations of British sociology. It was the year of the Report of the Commission on the Poor Law, or the year when the 'liberal democratic' state might be said to have taken a giant stride along the road of calculated social oppression, and also, as Philip Abrams has reminded us, the year of the foundation of the Statistical Society.[1] The two are not unconnected. On the one hand, the new industrial and urban forces which had been unleashed by rapid industrialisation and economic and political aggrandisement, and which included entrepreneurs, planners, builders, administrators and the new professionals, needed to come to terms with the traditional governing forces represented by landowners, gentry and the ancient professions, and define what kind of emergent society was desirable, including a labouring class dependent for subsistence upon their compliance with low wages and poor conditions of work. Ruling elites were obliged, in short, to develop a more concerted social policy by virtue of their interest in profit and imperialism.

On the other hand, new forms of information, communication and control were required to serve that goal, and better statistics, especially official statistics, was one of the instruments. The development of the Statistical Society set in train a huge industry of fact gathering, through Blue Books, social histories and social surveys and administrative compilations of statistics which exerted a major influence on the whole course of the social sciences in Britain and of sociology in particular. There were other

---

Extract (pp 22-24) from Townsend, P. (1981) 'Guerrillas, subordinates and
passers-by: the relationship between sociologists and social policy',
*Critical Social Policy*, vol 1, no 2, pp 22-34.

influences of a restrictive kind. The question is how far, as a consequence, British sociology has become an instrument of the state and is or is not intellectually obsequious to ruling values. Let me be plain. These examples serve a deliberate purpose. From the end of the nineteenth century social policy came to be interpreted restrictedly in relation to the management of social casualties and the provision of basic rights to education and housing or a national minimum.[2] The churches and voluntary organisations played no little part in this process but later on sociologists were also responsible for accepting such a limitation on their theoretical predispositions. This is a fascinating problem to be explained. The Poor Law Report and the subsequent Amendment Act stand so recognisably as instruments of social policy that they afford a reference point by which we might trace, and perhaps explain, the historical constriction of the meaning of social policy. But there is an academic and not just a national history to be written. The encroachment of administrative perspectives, including statistical conventions, upon a small and weak profession subordinated part of it to conventional values, causing them to serve established views and interests directly, through acceptance of research briefs and studies and hence social problems defined by the governing class, but also indirectly, by withdrawing from studies of the making of social policy on such spurious grounds as that these were 'applied' studies or were not central sociological problems. The functions of sociology itself came to be narrowly defined. The emergence of what I choose to call an 'integrated' sociology was frustrated. The role of the state and of state institutions in social structure, action and change was underestimated and even ignored. The social values implicit in the management of the economy and in the administration of the country were taken for granted and rarely identified, still less explained or questioned.

## The concept of social policy as applied to 1834 and 1980

In a short article I can do no more than introduce these large themes. I shall devote most of this article to illustrating how the study of social policy came to be restricted and go on to consider how the functions of sociology may be more flexibly and radically defined. All societies come to formulate and pursue social objectives, and the means by which they do this constitutes the subject matter of the study of social policy. There are, of course, different ways of expressing the matter generally. Social policy could be said to be the institutionalised control of services, agencies and organisations to maintain or change social structure and values.[3] This could be argued to be an internally coherent and scientific interpretation of the term. I put it this way because more is involved than the central and local administration of social services in the modern industrial state. We are concerned with the creation, modification or reproduction of social institutions like class and the family, and therefore with generalised and not just particularised law, with the development and modification of custom and values and not just the organising principles and practices of statutory services, and with the control and allocation of wealth and income, and how that is legitimised, and not just the adjustment of resources once received in the name of 'redistribution'. This conceptual issue is of great political as well as sociological importance today, as it has been in the past.

Let me contrast 1834 and 1980. The Poor Law Commission of 1832-34 reflected the view of ruling elites that poverty was necessary in order to motivate the poor to work. They adopted the 'less eligibility' principle – that the poor on relief should not be in a situation as eligible as the poorest in work.[4] But how could they justify to themselves and not only to others the harsh treatment of the poor who were not in work? They *believed* that pauperism, a condition of moral defect, applied to many of the selfsame poor. An individualistic explanation for poverty was developed. Some people were the deserving poor: they were victims of individual misfortunes like illness or disablement. But others were undeserving: they were drunks, improvident or feckless. And once this reasoning was applied to people who were not in work it could also be applied, if less directly, to the low paid and the working classes generally. Either they lacked the personal strengths and skills to attain high earnings or they frittered their money away and needed the constant threat of poverty to keep them at work. The literature on the Poor Law is voluminous, and 1834 seems to be sufficiently distant historically to allow people to take a more critical and detached judgement of events than they are of corresponding events today. No one doubts that the Poor Law Amendment Act was part of the making of social policy. But, equally, no one doubts that it contributed powerfully to the future structure of society, as well as the management of the economy. Its repercussions were felt in every factory and house. Today there are, of course, those who look back into the recesses of 1834 and later years simply to trace the foundations of health and welfare services and social security.[5] But the interpretation of social policy which their inquiries claim to represent is manifestly inadequate. 1834 involves much more than an historical juncture from which can be dated a number of developments in income relief, health, education and welfare. The administration of the new Poor Law underpinned a *laissez-faire* capitalist economy and a highly stratified society and was fundamental to the whole social structure. It linked a severe conception of virtue with access to, and conditions of, work, and embodied the principle which elsewhere I have summarised as 'conditional welfare for the few'.[6] Far from softening the harshness of society it reinforced and even extended it. It was the copingstone of social policy at that time.

## Endnotes

[1] P. Abrams, *The Origins of British Sociology: 1834-1914*, Chicago and London: The University of Chicago Press 1968, p.vi.

[2] Zsusa Ferge is one of the few sociologists who have reflected this view. 'Social policy has emerged historically as a palliative or corrective instrument intended to cope with imminent social problems endangering the status quo.' Z. Ferge, *A Society in the Making: Hungarian Social and Societal Policy 1945-75*, Harmondsworth: Penguin 1979, p.50.

[3] A discussion of the concept will be found in my *Sociology and Social Policy*, Harmondsworth: Penguin 1975, especially chapter 1. A more recent illustration of the use of the concept in the analysis of social structure will be found in a paper entitled 'The structured dependency of the elderly: a creation of social policy in the twentieth century', which I published in *Ageing and Society*, vol.1, no.1, 1981.

[4] 'The first and the most essential of all conditions, a principle which we find universally admitted, even by those whose practice is at variance with it, is, that [the pauper's] situation on the whole shall not be made really or apparently so eligible as the situation of the independent labourer of the lowest class'. *Report from His Majesty's Commissioners for Inquiring into the Administration and Practical Operation of the Poor Laws*, London: Fellowes 1834, p.228.

[5] While the new Poor Law could be said to date from 1834 it was of course the culmination of a long process of administrative experiment and adaptation. It represented a victory of one set of tough-minded over another set of more tender-minded values in the countrywide administration of poor relief.

[6] P. Townsend, *Poverty in the United Kingdom*, Harmondsworth: Penguin 1979, chapter 2.

# 3

# Guerrillas, subordinates and passers-by

## Official statistics, committees of enquiry and research

In maintaining departmental power and cohesion, senior administrators in the bureaucracy are not always conscious of the steps they take to obstruct or divert radical change. They adopt a variety of methods. One is in controlling the scope, nature and form of presentation of official statistics. Outside bodies are heavily dependent upon central departments for their knowledge of social conditions and problems. Few people yet appreciate the subtle influences which civil servants exert upon statistical output, including matters of substance as well as presentation, which might appear to be contentious. This is no more malign than the way individuals or families present themselves, and their images of society to outsiders.[1] Statistics are devised, collected and circulated, for example, to show departmental actions in a favourable light, relate new events to customary interpretations of political and social activity and define national needs and objectives in conformity with government views about available resources. In his presidential address to the Royal Statistical Society on 7 November 1979, Sir Claus Moser drew a distinction between political or administrative 'interference' with statisticians in the Government Statistical Service and matters which threatened the professional 'integrity' of statisticians.[2] He believed that interference was regrettable but inevitable. Thus the administrative and political machine decided what statistics to collect and issue. He gives as examples the cancellation of the 1976 census of population and 'the unwillingness of successive governments to permit the linking of statistical and administrative data across departments'. Questions of integrity were questions of lesser importance, like the release dates of particular series of statistics and the reservations that had to be kept in mind in the publication of particular figures. His interpretation of the limited part that professional statisticians can play in 'civilising' government will be regarded by many as only realistic; but I wonder whether he accepts

Extract (pp 27-31) from Townsend, P. (1981) 'Guerrillas, subordinates and passers-by: the relationship between sociologists and social policy', *Critical Social Policy*, vol 1, no 2, pp 22-34.

for them a too subordinate role. I find surprising his apparent willingness to leave to others the ongoing responsibility for redefining the scope of, and priorities in, statistical work.[3] Professional statisticians are also inclined to exaggerate the importance of advances in technical dexterity and even the sheer quantity of statistical output. I believe this is to mistake absolute or historical for relative criteria of 'progress'. The value of statistical output has to be judged in relation to the needs of present society and not the technically inferior output of a previous era.

Bureaucracies are often miserly in providing information, not just to the public but also to independent committees of enquiry. Even when a royal commission, government committee or working party persist in seeking sensitive information from the officials who are supposed to serve them, so that it can be published, that information will often be denied to them. Action on requests is delayed beyond the point of usefulness, or the requests get lost in the system, or innocuous versions of what has been requested are given, or the requests are obtusely misunderstood, or polite excuses are made about the difficulties of time, expertise of lower ranks, uncooperativeness of other departments or authorities or cost. The analogies between personal and organisational behaviour have to be remembered. An organisation will tend to give favourable accounts of its own work and hold perceptions of society which reflect beliefs which predominate among its senior membership. This reconstruction of reality deserves close analysis. But the reconstruction of reality can take more assertive forms. Civil servants are a very solid presence at many meetings of government committees and working parties where 'independent' views are intended to prevail. They will have advised about terms of reference and recruitment of members, and provide the secretariat who normally do a great deal more than simply copy out the views of the members of the committee.

All this begins to explain how social scientists depend upon the conceptualisations and practices of administrative elites for the definition of a large part of their subject matter and may also be influenced in interpreting policy questions. Bureaucracies also play important roles in research, particularly in commissioning what is done, whether and how access by research workers is to be allowed and what data and types of methodology will remain available. The establishment and growth of intelligence, statistical and research units in government departments (and now, through corporate planning and information and research units of social service departments, in local authorities) might be interpreted as a deliberate assertion of ascendancy over outside, especially academic, expertise but also lay opinion. The civil service has been quick to appreciate that access to and deployment of technical expertise is one of the modern roads to power. The Treasury and the Centre for Administrative Studies, followed by the Departments of Education and Employment, seized on the importance of output budgeting and programme budgeting in the late 1960s[4] and nearly all the major departments now draw on units of their own instead of outside advisers.

## Bureaucratic aggrandisement

Current trends in control over statistical information, technical expertise, sources of advice and scientific research might be said to lend support to a thesis of bureaucratic aggrandisement. Among key evidence which can be considered is the recent history of the Chief Scientist's Committee of the DHSS. When the academic members of that committee protested that the committee was an ineffectual rump and that the real decisions about research were being taken by the research liaison groups, over which the department wielded very tight control, the eventual result was the winding up, in late 1978, of that committee. Another instance would be control over surveys of national scope. It is increasingly supposed that national information about social conditions must be provided by government – through the processes of everyday administration, the national census and annual or occasional social surveys. I believe that that assumption represents a threat to the understanding of social realities as well as indirectly a threat to freedom of inquiry and speech. The Family Expenditure Survey, the General Household Survey and the National Food Survey, for example, are annual national surveys which cost a great deal, and there are single or occasional national surveys like those on the elderly, family income and unemployment.[5] This work is reputable and thorough and sometimes, as at the OPCS, a tradition of high standards of 'house' research are achieved. But the limitations in the conception and implementation of the research are insufficiently recognised. Annual and ad hoc surveys come under strong central control and are rarely susceptible to external academic influence of a substantial kind.[6] Administrative and hence conservative perceptions of their functions come to dominate their management. In tracing bureaucratic encroachment on the areas of responsibility of social scientists, the implications of subordination, both in the sense of research being relegated to highly specialised, peripheral or local questions and professional allegiance being committed, directly or indirectly, to the bureaucracy, are disturbing. The implication of this argument is that more conscious efforts have to be made, in the interests of developing scientific knowledge in the widest sense and not only in the interests of national planning and democratic accountability, to establish genuinely independent and generously financed research centres. The relative subservience of research interests to bureaucratic interests will otherwise continue to restrict the interpretation of the role of social policy.

## Professionalism

For reasons analogous to those I have given about the bureaucracy, the analysis of professionalism also produces criticisms of conventional interpretations of social policy. The proportion of the male labour force who are professionals has grown rapidly. The number of male professionals dwarfs the number of female professionals relatively as well as absolutely. The professions arrogate resources to themselves and are not simply of preeminent occupational status. They are active and not just passive elites in a hierarchy. The active side of their assertion of status is to contribute powerfully to social policy and to the models which society develops of its own future. This can be seen every day in the influence of hospital consultants within the health services, and in reproducing inequality. Professionals have been playing an increasing part in social service organisations, fostering the decline of local government and the evolution of managerial hierarchies. In a study of the development of social work, Noel Parry and José Parry have called attention to a hybrid form of organisation in the social services of professions working within the bureaucracy, or the 'bureau-professional'.[7] And in a study of professionalism Larson points out that the rise of the professions inaugurated

> a new form of structural inequality: it was different from the earlier model of aristocratic patronage, and different also from the model of social inequality based on property and identified with capitalist entrepreneurship ...The conditions of professional work have changed, so that the predominant pattern is no longer that of the free practitioner in a market of services but that of the salaried specialist in a large organisation.[8]

One of the major problems of professionalism is the induction through social policy of dependence among large sections of the population. There is a fine line between public service and imperious rule in professional activity, which deserves very careful examination and understanding. The undemocratic, inegalitarian and even antisocial aspects of professionalism need to be better related to the overall evolution of social policy.

## The contributions of the rich to social policy

Just as professionalism as well as bureaucracy have been underestimated as major forces for conservatism in social policy so the different contributions of the rich to the making of social policy are underestimated. In a recent work on poverty I came to stress how *active* is the defence and promotion by the rich of their resources and interests.[9] This affords part, but only part, of the explanation of inequality and hence of poverty. Another part of the explanation is the contribution they make to form and style of living of emerging society. The rich not only benefit from the economic and social system, and exploit it, they actively shape its standards or values and the attitudes which are struck about the changes which should or should not be made in its structure. They set fashions which become the styles sought after by the mass of the population. They foster the values which preserve their own status and which induce deference.

More exactly they play a very active part, especially in their professional, administrative and managerial capacities, both in defining public services and in redefining standards of deprivation or need. They influence public perceptions of what conditions should be regarded as unacceptable and what minimum standards of life should be conceded in deciding desert. In *Economy and Society*[10] Weber developed the idea that status groups could impose their way of life on society through domination of the educational system. In some respects he overestimated their independence or autonomy. It could be argued that he did not sufficiently acknowledge the dependence of these groups upon the generalised class to which they are affiliated. Patronage, and especially honours, for example, still count for a great deal in British society. In other respects he underestimated their autonomy. Their capacity to establish conditions of dependence among the mass of the population, to confuse and dominate through their powers to interpret knowledge, develop technical jargon, control procedures affecting the application of social regulations, are among the examples I have in mind, and not only their capacity to manage their own remuneration and reinforce wide inequalities. Some such thesis seems to me to be necessary to explain the persistence of marked inequality and poverty in democratic socialist societies (despite the claims which are made for the welfare state in those societies) and also in state socialist societies.

## The problem of acquiescence

More than they may realise, sociologists are steeped in the general values of professionalism and corporatism – or the modern version of bureaucracy. Through their professional practice as well as their position in bureaucratic organisations, they become accommodated to prevailing, orthodox views of the scope, functions and content of social policy. I am suggesting therefore that any detailed historical study of the relationship between sociology and social policy is bound to reveal the extent to which sociologists (and other social scientists) have acquiesced with conventional definitions and assessments of the achievements of social policy. There are some histories of the welfare state, for example, in which the governing classes' definition of social policy is taken at face value and the marvels of legislative social 'progress' are reverently listed.[11] Most people working within both sociology and social administration are more critical than that, but formerly restricted and indeed uncritical assumptions are only now being broadened. Thus, in the earlier post-war period T.H. Marshall[12] and even John Goldthorpe[13] adopted relatively conventional definitions of the scope of social policy and as a consequence interpreted social progress over-optimistically. Marshall certainly modified later editions of his book *Social Policy* (though not as radically as he might have done) and Goldthorpe has moved much closer to the 'integrative' position which I have urged in this article.

But *acquiescence*, including perspectives which allow reasoned criticism with relatively mild implications for social outcomes, is a problem which remains to be resolved. For all Marshall's approval of a social policy which has bestowed citizenship rights and a national minimum, Britain remains a society in which the richest ten per cent (not just the richest one per cent or even five per cent) enjoys a standard of living, after allowing for dependencies, of nearly ten times the poorest ten per cent, and the situation is now getting a lot worse. This illustrates how much more critical need to be the criteria of social conditions by which conceptions and outcomes of social policy have to be checked.

A broader conceptualisation of social policy is necessary to unravel some of the accepted sociological problems of stratification and order. It could also be said to be the central concept for theories of social change. During the last decade an increasing number of British sociologists have come to recognise this. In part this has been due to the welcome, if belated, extension of Marxist work, particularly on the state, but also on selected areas of policy – such as housing. I am thinking especially of the work of those like O'Connor, Gough, Ginsburg, Cynthia Cockburn, Pat Thane, and Noel Parry and his colleagues.[14] But there are features of their work which remain as yet relatively undeveloped. One is in bringing out the relationship between policy and structure – particularly the effects on the dispersion of standards of living among the working class through a mixture of wage, employment, taxation and social service policies. Another is the position of minorities – like the elderly and the disabled as well as racial minorities – in relation to social policies. A third is the explanation of variations in patterns of inequality among different capitalist societies, but also between capitalist and state socialist societies, in relation to their social policies. While it is useful to concentrate attention on the form of central and local administration of services in capitalist societies, there are other sources of social control and inequality than the 'state' in this sense. As Ferge has demonstrated, many of the problems of non-capitalist societies are comparable, if not always as extreme. There are an increasing number of self-reflective works by sociologists about the research that they do and the professional positions they adopt in relation to social policy as conventionally understood.[15] In one compilation Ray Pahl, for example, writes about his role in the late 1960s and early 1970s as one of the assessors to the panel for the Greater London Development Plan Inquiry.[16] This is a rounded and yet provocative account of the sociologist's role and potentialities and provides a good example of the greater willingness of sociologists in Britain than in the United States[17] to rethink the relationship between sociology and policy. Pahl sets out some of the putative roles which sociologists might find themselves in when working for a government department or local authority – such as (i) the gatekeeper to the literature; (ii) the filterer of the literature; (iii) an advocate of a focus of interest, like housing; (iv) the social statistician; (v) the managerialist/technocrat; (vi) the demystifier; (vii) the legitimator, and so on. Many of these are facilitating or subordinate roles. At one point he writes:

> Anyone who becomes involved with policy-making must be prepared to be a social engineer to some extent. My friends and colleagues assumed that I would use my position to argue for some radical or progressive policy which those without the benefit of sociological understanding could not otherwise see. I have often heard it argued that if more sociologists were involved in the process of government 'better' decisions would be made. My experience is that arguing intervention with interventionists is not easy.

The germ of an alternative formulation of objectives, content, programming and evaluation of policy seems to be touched upon here but not followed through. The sociologist can relate what his employer conceives of as social policy to what, implicitly as well as explicitly, it may really be. And from analysis of social conditions and institutional infrastructure he can derive some of the elements at least of alternative policy. It is for reasons such as these that I believe the sociologist can play a less passive, and more constructive, role as a professional adviser.

**References**

[1] There is a growing literature on official statistics by sociologists. See, for example, A. Cicourel, *Method and Measurement in Sociology*, New York: Free Press 1964; J.D. Douglas, *The Social Meaning of Suicide*, Princeton: Princeton University Press 1967; P. Townsend, 'Politics and the statistics of poverty', *Political Quarterly*, vol.43, no.1, January–March 1972; B. Hindess, *The Use of Official Statistics in Sociology*, London: Macmillan 1973; J. Irvine, I. Miles and J. Evans (eds), *Demystifying Social Statistics*, London: Pluto Press 1979; R. Thomas, *Do Statistics Influence Policy?* Milton Keynes: O.U.P. 1980. Some social scientists believe the criticisms of official statistics are in many respects unfair and exaggerated, and regard this fashion in sociology as a form of philistinism. See, for example, M. Bulmer, 'Why don't sociologists make more use of official statistics?', *Sociology*, vol.14, no.4, Nov. 1980.

[2] Sir C. Moser, 'Statistics and public policy', *Journal of the Royal Statistical Society*, Series A (General) vol.143, part 1, 1980.

[3] To be fair, Sir Claus goes on to argue that government statisticians should give more attention to the analysis and interpretation of statistics and 'an integrated framework of social data'.

[4] See the series of occasional papers based on the Centre for Administrative Studies, published by the Treasury from 1967; Department of Education, *Output-Budgeting for the DES: Report of a Feasibility Study*, London: HMSO 1970 and J.J. Hughes, *Cost Benefit Aspects of Manpower Retraining*, Department of Employment, 1970.

[5] For example, A. Hunt, *The Elderly at Home*, OPCS, London: HMSO 1979.

[6] There are exceptions. In the mid-sixties, after representations had been made to the then National Assistance Board by social scientists, the annual reports of the board were expanded to give much fuller information derived from sample analyses. Similarly, there was a considerable improvement in both the quantity and quality of information about supplementary benefits published in the mid 1970s by the Supplementary Benefits Commission, under its chairman, Professor David Donnison.

[7] N. Parry, M. Rustin and C. Satyamurti (eds), *Social Work, Welfare and the State*, London: Edward Arnold 1979, chapter 2.

[8] M.S. Larson, *The Rise of Professionalism: A Sociological Analysis*, Berkeley and London: University of California Press 1977, pp.xvi-xvii.

[9] P. Townsend, *Poverty in the United Kingdom*, Harmondsworth: Penguin 1979, chapter 9.

[10] M. Weber, *Economy and Society: An Outline of Interpretive Sociology*, Berkeley: University of California Press 1978, vol. 2, especially chapter 9.

[11] For example, M. Bruce, *The Coming of the Welfare State*, London: Batsford 1961.

[12] T.H. Marshall, *Social Policy*, London: Hutchinson, 2nd ed. 1967.

[13] J. Goldthorpe, 'The development of social policy in England, 1800-1914' in *Transactions of the Fifth World Congress of Sociology*, vol. IV, 1962.

[14] J. O'Connor, *The Fiscal Crisis of the State*, London: St. James Press 1973; I. Gough, *The Political Economy of the Welfare State*, London: Macmillan 1979; C. Cockburn, *The Local State*, London: Pluto Press 1977; P. Thane, *Origins of British Social Policy*, London: Croom Helm 1978; N. Parry, *et. al.*, *op. cit.*

[15] C. Bell and H. Newby, *Doing Sociological Research*, London: Allen & Unwin 1977; M. Bulmer (ed), *Social Policy Research*, London: Macmillan 1978.

[16] R. Pahl, 'Playing the rationality game: the sociologist as a hired expert', in C. Bell and H. Newby, *ibid*.

[17] For example, in a recent paper James Coleman has adopted an extraordinarily limited view of the role of sociology — first to conduct social policy research 'to inform policy in a narrow sense or to inform societal actions in a broader sense' (like

experiments on negative income tax and housing allowances) and second 'about the way in which sociology can inform action in society'. He explains 'insofar as sociological analysis is seen as having a role in the functioning of society [it] is in providing the feedback information that allows redirection of social action'. He found little in the writings of Marx, Weber and Durkheim, or other early sociologists, about the social role of sociological analysis. The possibility that social policy might cover more than governments choose to specify, or that sociologists might analyse social conditions both to criticise existing policies and develop alternative goals, priorities or policies is scarcely broached. J. Coleman, 'Sociological analysis and social policy', in T. Bottomore and R. Nisbet (eds), *A History of Sociological Analysis*, London: Heinemann 1979.

# 4

# The rise of international social policy

[...]

Social policy analysis draws on a range of sociological, political and economic theories to explain how policies have come to be framed and developed, and why they operate in the way that they do. There are laws and bodies of regulations to be studied and understood, histories of experience and of professional, administrative and political organisation and practice to be mastered, and causes of social problems and influences upon policy to be carefully and comprehensively analysed. [...]

In debating questions of organisation it is therefore useful to hold a conception of the scope of the subject. Certainly the thrust of developments came originally from national interest in clarifying and explaining problems to do with social management. We think of unemployment, poverty, sickness and disability, and the vulnerability of young children and the elderly. There was a demand for expert study. Social institutions were developed to respond to the problems. In many respects the welfare state was built as a system like a casualty service, to repair and mend victims of industrialisation, urbanisation and social change.

## Changing conceptions of social policy

Although some of the[se] themes, ironically, are much like those addressed in the nineteenth century, the explanations of causes, and therefore the remedies that are being and have to be given attention, are changing fast. The intellectual base of the subject is being broadened. This has to be recognised in any new discussion about the place of the subject in a university.

The steps in the argument so far presented deserve to be summarised. In universities the problem-orientated nature of the subject of social policy propelled *academic* interest in:

- the history of the development of the welfare state;
- the enormous scale, as measured by expenditure, of personnel and clients, patients, pupils, students, tenants or beneficiaries of the subject matter in national life;

Extract (pp 9-12) from Townsend, P. (1995) *The rise of international social policy*, Bristol: The Policy Press.

- the production and evaluation of evidence about the handling and outcome of trends in social problems;
- the tracking of a huge range of relevant, and rapidly growing, legislation and regulation;
- the theoretical underpinning of understanding on the one hand and policy on the other (struggling all the time to take account of the implications of the latest developments – as in the 1980s of, for example, feminism, monetarism, post-modernism and structural adjustment theory).

Because of the scale and complexity of these things it made sense to concentrate academic research and teaching in a single department, even when social scientific analysis depended also on specialised complementary work in sociology, political science, economics and other disciplines. That also made sense to those who take the view that the strongest intellectual affinity is with, or within, sociology. I maintain that the analysis of social policy and of the predominant institutions of policy are at the heart of sociological theories of social change and evolution. [...]

There are two principal reasons for the strengthening of social policy in the university. One is broadly theoretical – the subject used to be conceived of as an applied subject, and it also tended to be restricted to services dealing with specific social problems. Both of these assumptions are now outmoded, or at least seriously questioned. On the one hand, policies have complex histories and tend to acquire a life of their own, much like the policy institutions producing and managing them. Questions about dependent and independent variables in the equations are more complex. And, especially in recent years, social policies can be demonstrated to have had effects that have *deepened*. Even less than formerly can the evolution of the welfare state be interpreted as being one of linear progression. Policies propel major social changes that have bad and not only good effects and therefore lie at the heart of theoretical analysis and discussion.

Comparative and international research is also exposing the traditional study of social services as a very restricted vision of social development. It is not simply social services, but fiscal systems, labour markets, administrative bureaucracies, professions, banking systems and financial organisations that are relevant. Nowadays all of these are primarily international or cross-national. Paradoxically this wider view of development has been spawned by theorists of monetarism, during the high tide of that creed, and by the ideologues of the New Right.

Another way of expressing the theoretical change is to acknowledge the shift from casualty to preventive thinking. For most of the twentieth century social policy has been more concerned with damage than with prevention, with ill-health rather than with health. However, the intellectual challenge to construct cities or services for hardworking and committed individuals as well as communities in order to prevent serious problems from arising, and thereby provide alternative models of explanation for present disorders provides a larger and more complex agenda. It is an agenda that patently has so far eluded western governments. In such an agenda precedence would be given to 'structural' *theories* in explaining social conditions and trends – and therefore to 'structural' *plans* in developing government policies.

Bourdieu is one of those who is acutely sensitive about the relationship between what is political and what is scientific. He takes the view that sociology is not yet a unified scientific field on a world scale. Sociology, he says, is torn by

> two discrepant logics: the logic of the political field, in which the force of ideas is mainly a function of the power of the groups that take them to be true; and the logic of the scientific field which, in its most advanced states, knows and recognises only the 'intrinsic force of the true idea'. [In the political field certain propositions must be taken into account because people who] muster a lot of social power would like them to be true. (Bourdieu, 1991, p 376)

What has become of such interest to sociologists is the way in which ideology colours the treatment of scientific evidence and also the construction of scientific theory. By extension, in this academic debate the international is being linked to the ideological *and*, of course, to the theoretical. [...]

**Reference**
Bourdieu, P. (1991) 'Epilogue on the possibility of a field of world sociology', in P. Bourdieu and J.S. Coleman (eds), *Social theory for a changing society*, New York: Westview Press, Russell Sage Foundation.

# Section II

# From welfare state to international welfare

*Edited by Nicola Yeates*

# Introduction

Although perhaps best known for his campaigns to improve the conditions of the poorest people in the UK, Peter Townsend's work was framed by an international perspective from the earliest days. Indeed, some two decades before the landmark study *Poverty in the United Kingdom* was published in 1979, Peter was immersed in locating the scale and meaning of poverty and family change across a diverse range of rich and poor countries and drawing on international evidence to argue in favour of egalitarian social provision (via education and family allowances).[1] By the 1960s he had already published in Italian and Dutch, and was presenting research papers at conferences in continental Europe and the US, authoring reports for the United Nations and was involved in the international committee on poverty research of the World Congress of Sociology. The extensive geographical scope of Peter's early work extended beyond the advanced economies of Western Europe and North America, to include the transition economies of post-Soviet Eastern Europe and the 'developing' countries of Africa, Asia and South America.

Pre-dating by some three decades the 'globalist' scholarship that finally emerged outside Marxian social science in the 1990s, Peter was examining the international context of the scale and meaning of world poverty. He productively combined the insights of structuralist schools of global sociology with the institutional focus of sociological and social policy analyses to relate poverty in a range of countries to the wider global context. While calling for detailed studies of poverty, inequality and social polarisation nationally, the 'domestic' and the 'international' were for him inseparable realms of scientific analysis and political action. Thus, national systems of social stratification and forces of social polarisation necessarily had to be related to the wider international context, including processes of policy formation in cross-border spheres of governance. In this he was an unacknowledged pioneer of the scholarly and policy realm that has since become known as global social policy.

The first reading in the section (**Chapter 5**), 'Measures and explanations of poverty in high income and low income countries' (1970), provides an early exposition of overarching and enduring themes in Peter's work: the interpretive value of cross-national comparative and development-oriented empirical research into world poverty, together with the role of scientific studies in informing practical policy making. This empirical focus never lapsed into mindless empiricism, however; he was clear that robust explanatory frameworks were required to interpret trends in world poverty. Peter cogently sets out an "approach to development and stratification that can help in explaining how poverty arises and is perpetuated in low income and high income countries" (p

30). His scepticism of the value of the canon of sociological theory gravitating around industrialisation, modernisation and 'development' as explanations of global inequality and poverty drew him to radical schools of the sociology of development (such as the work of André Gunther Frank) to emphasise how "systems of international social stratification and [national] social stratification interact to produce poverty". Here as in later work (such as **Chapter 6**) he was clear about the role of the advanced economies in perpetuating poverty in low-income countries and their responsibility to eradicate it. And he was equally as clear about the necessity of connecting poverty at home and abroad, a view best articulated by the following eloquent statement: "A wealthy society which deprives a poor country of resources may simultaneously deprive its own poor classes through maldistribution of those additional resources" (Townsend, 1993, p 42).

Peter was not a prisoner of conventional intellectual or political boundaries: empirical and normative arguments, research and policy debates, and national and international action were skilfully woven together. His indignance at the massive and growing scale of world poverty led him to argue for better scientific understandings of the phenomenon to provide a sound basis of collective political action. Guided by the principle that "[p]overty is not just a lack of resources required to live a normal life. It is a lack of resources used, and felt to be rightly used, by the rich" (Townsend, 1970, p 45; **Chapter 5**), entitlements across the social scale must, he argued, be addressed. As the first extract makes clear, this meant extending and strengthening social security, employer and other social provision at the same time as curtailing the privileges of more prosperous sections of society through, for example, restrictions on high salaries, progressive taxation, and the elimination of substantial private ownership. Over the years Peter's prescriptions for necessary actions to address social polarisation and poverty were extended, but his commitment to the establishment of fairer systems of distribution and redistribution never waned.

From the 1990s Peter's internationalism focused squarely on the 'new' global context of social development. **Chapter 6** (1993) and **Chapter 7** (2002) reiterate the argument that poverty in any one country can be neither understood nor acted upon solely by reference to that country alone. The enduring themes of his work all find a place here, namely the need for: a scientifically acceptable universal meaning and measurement of poverty; comprehensive cross-national empirical research studies to map the impacts of social change on living standards; structuralist theoretical frameworks that relate poverty in rich and poor countries to the wider international context of social development; and concerted international action on poverty. **Chapter 6** pays especial attention to the rise of global markets, and the role of international organisations and transnational corporations (TNCs) in shaping national economies and the distribution of national resources. These cannot, he argued, with any justification be confined merely to the background context of social policy analyses of poverty, inequality and social polarisation. Dedicating in **Chapter 6** attention to problems of European social policy he calls for a strategy not only of regulatory and policy reform but of democratisation more generally. Always with an eye to the development context, he highlights the shameful participation of the UK and other EU countries in forging a version of European integration that worsens the terms of trade and labour for developing countries and propels processes of social polarisation within the EU. Here, too, the power of TNCs, many of which command incomes exceeding the GDP of many countries in the world, must also be curtailed as part of any progressive strategy of democratisation, regulation and redistribution.

Peter was clear that such strategies need to be pursued through transnational policy fora such as the EU, UN, IMF and World Bank as well as at the national level. Indeed, Peter recognised that a progressive national/UK politics of poverty necessarily has to engage with the poverty policies of these international organisations. The failure of these organisations to adopt a more progressive stance, to establish what Peter called an 'international welfare state' that sets in its sight fairer levels of distribution and redistribution in rich and poor countries alike, would, as he rightly predicted, mean adding hundreds of millions of people to those billion and a half already impoverished (**Chapter 8**).

While the European and international communities have been slow to embrace democratic and other elements of progressive policy reform, Peter could at least take heart from developments in the area of the internationalisation of poverty methodology. If there was already some satisfaction to be had at the EU's adoption of his relative concept of poverty, he was especially heartened by the UN World Summit for Social Development's Copenhagen Declaration (1995) whose agreement of an overall definition of poverty, applicable in high- and low-income countries he declared a 'breakthrough' (**Chapter 9**). Peter was clear that the UN's adoption of this definition was a necessary start to serious efforts to assess – and take action against – world poverty on a global and scientific basis. He did have certain misgivings about the declaration and action programme, however: "[c]ommitments about national action to meet basic needs and reduce inequalities remain unacceptably vague. References to redistributive taxation do not begin to address the need to set up a substantial and effective cross-national system. Nor is any recognition displayed of the need to address distribution and not just redistribution, by introducing some policies and minimum wage legislation to move in the direction of a more principled and equitable distribution of earned income" (Townsend and Donkor, 1996, p 41).

If Peter had certain misgivings about the UN Copenhagen Declaration and programme for action, he was scathing in his criticism of the World

Bank (**Chapters 7, 8, 9**). Not only was its absolutist notion of poverty outdated, but its operationalisation of a poverty measure at one dollar or less per day was shockingly arbitrary and irrational. In addition, the Bank's policy approach to poverty and social development was a major hindrance in the fight against world poverty. First, despite the World Bank's talk of social investment and protection, most of its resources are diverted away from it. Its lending record on social protection amounts to less than five-hundredths of one per cent of world GDP, and its total lending is less than one percent of the income of the world's top 500 companies. Second, the Bank's failure to lead the fight against world poverty is not just a question of the Bank's lack of commandable resources or the political will or agency: it is a question of the very nature of the Bank's poverty policy. These, Peter argues, bear a close resemblance to a globalised poor law, reliant as they are on economic growth, investment in education and 'safety-net' welfare benefits for the very poor. In conducting disastrous policies informed by neoliberal ideology, the Bank – and its rich country financiers – are, he argues, responsible for the increase in world poverty over the years. In its enunciation of a neoliberal approach to tackling poverty, the World Bank symbolised to Peter a major global obstacle in the construction of a progressive global and national politics and policy of international welfare.

Never shying away from the opportunity to articulate the steps necessary to tackle poverty comprehensively, Peter called for a thorough review of the work of the Bank and its reorientation to meet the UN's Millennium Development Goals on poverty, namely a human rights-based approach to collectivism, economic and social planning, public service and social protection. A bold step indeed, but the scale of Peter's ambitions and assessment of the work to be done can be seen in the 'Manifesto: international action to defeat poverty' (**Chapter 10**). Setting out eighteen major steps, including implementing existing human rights conventions and introducing new enforceable rights, introducing new legal powers to govern TNCs and the disbursement of development assistance, strengthening tax systems and instituting new cross-border taxes, democratising global and regional institutions and developing comprehensive action plans for equalising resources between as well as between countries, this global social policy manifesto brings in one place together many of the reform proposals articulated across Peter's work. In the debate between those who wish to abolish global institutions and those who wish to reform them, Peter was on the side of the latter. But he was no co-optee. He was clear that the democratisation of these institutions necessitated modernised, coherent governance structures and policy coordination with an enhanced emphasis on Keynesian, development-oriented social and economic planning.

While despairing of the World Bank, Peter was heartened by the more progressive, human rights-based approaches of UNICEF, International

Labour Organization (ILO), United Nations Development Programme (UNDP) and the UN High Commission on Human Rights. The focus of his work during the latter years of his life came to be framed by a human rights perspective to anti-poverty research and action, and he worked in conjunction with these UN social agencies. Part of the team commissioned by UNICEF to undertake the first international survey of child poverty in the developing world using the Copenhagen poverty definition (Gordon et al, 2003), Peter went on to develop the global social policy implications of this work in conjunction with UNICEF and the ILO in particular (Townsend, 2008). **Chapter 11**, taken from his final book (Townsend, 2009), outlines the value of a human rights approach to child poverty, which he argues "shifts the focus of debate from the personal failures of the 'poor' to the failures to resolve poverty of macro-economic structures and policies of nation-states and international bodies". Clear that addressing child poverty requires institutionalising universal social (security) protection rather than the 'social safety-nets' approach favoured by international organisations like the World Bank, his attention turns to practical ways of achieving this. In particular, he outlines a new source of international financing to eliminate child poverty. In keeping with his argument that TNCs bear responsibility for world poverty, he argues that corporate social responsibility frameworks need to be made mandatory for them to be meaningful, and that new legal frameworks are needed to hold TNCs accountable and to compel them to fund social insurance or tax-funded benefits in low-income countries. Building on proposals for a 'Tobin Tax', an international levy on currency transfers, he argues that revenue raised from this could feasibly be used to promote universal social security provision for children and categorical benefits for severely disabled children.

Across his life's work, Peter's comparative, empirical and development-oriented work on the international dimensions of the scientific measurement, politics and policy of poverty reflected his unequivocal understanding that there are common global and not just national or local trends and causes of social polarisation and that common/collective actions/solutions are required to the poverty and inequality it generates. A firm believer in the possibilities of scientific approaches to the study of and political action on poverty, he was as committed to the eradication of world poverty wherever it was manifested. This commitment was not, however, merely one borne of a 'detached' social scientist, for it also reflected his political alignment with leftist social analysts and reformers for whom events and conditions abroad and international solidarity were as important as issues of social structures and policies 'at home'. Indeed, Peter was a true cosmopolitan – he made no distinctions between the worth of human lives based on national or social origin. An articulate and passionate supporter of scholarly and political campaigns for a coherent global social policy based on equality, universalism and human rights, his commitment to a materialist analysis of poverty and his advocacy of social planning, though unfashionable in certain leftist intellectual quarters and unpopular among the political right, found him many more friends and allies globally.

## Endnote

[1] For example: 1957 'Family relationships: methods and the study of the old person', in *The need for cross-national surveys of old age*, International Association of Gerontology, report of a conference in Copenhagen in 1956; also in Mens en Maatschappijm Tweemaandel I jka Tijdschript, Amsterdam; and in *Longevita*, Milan, with the title 'Metedo per lo studio dell anzio in famiglia, March; 'Poverty in Western Countries' 1964 paper to colloquium organised by the Bureau de Recherches Sociales and held under the auspices of UNESCO; 'The scale and meaning of poverty in contemporary western society' in P. Townsend, J. Berliner, S. Miller and E. Clague (eds) (1965) *Dependency and Poverty*, Colloquia 1963-1964, The Florence Heller School for Advanced Studies in Social Welfare, Waltham, MA, Brandeis University; 'The argument for comprehensive schools' in E. Hillman (ed) (1966) *Essays in local government enterprise*, vol 3, London, Merlin; 'Family relationships of the aged in the United States, Denmark and Britain' in *Proceedings of seminars 1961-1965* (1966) Duke University Council of Gerontology, and published in 1968 as *Old people in three industrial societies* (co-edited with E. Shanas, D. Wedderburn, H. Friis, P. Milhoj and J. Stehouwer) Routledge/Atherton, London/New York); 'Social policy: international ideas', *New Statesman*, 25 September 1969: 479-80 (Source: Peter Townsend Complete List of Publications 1948-2008, www.bris.ac.uk/poverty/ Background_files/townsend%20publications%2048-08.pdf).

## References

Gordon, D., Nandy, S., Pantazis, C., Pemberton, S. and Townsend, P. (2003) *Child poverty in the developing world*, Bristol: The Policy Press.

Townsend, P (ed) (1970) *The concept of poverty*, London: Heinemann.

Townsend, P. (1979) *Poverty in the United Kingdom: A survey of household resources and standards of living*, Harmondsworth: Penguin.

Townsend, P. (1993) *The international analysis of poverty*, Hemel Hempstead: Harvester Wheatsheaf.

Townsend, P. (2002) 'Poverty, social exclusion and social polarisation: the need to construct an international welfare state', in P. Townsend and D. Gordon (eds) *World poverty: New policies to defeat an old enemy*, Bristol: The Policy Press.

Townsend, P. (2008) *The abolition of child poverty and the right to social security: A possible UN model for child benefit?* A report to the ILO, GTZ and DfID, London: Lulu Press.

Townsend, P. (2009) 'Investment in social security: a possible UN model for child benefit?', in P. Townsend (ed) (2009) *Building decent societies: Rethinking the role of social security in development*, Geneva/Basingstoke: ILO/Palgrave.

Townsend, P. and Donkor, K. (1996) *Global restructuring and social policy: The need to establish an international welfare state*, Bristol: The Policy Press.

# 5

# Measures and explanations of poverty in high income and low income countries

A fifth of the population of the United States, the wealthiest nation in the world, were officially described in 1964 as living in conditions of poverty.[1] Yet the United States, with only 6 per cent of its population, accounts for nearly a third of the world's Gross National Product in real terms. This is nearly twice as much as all the so-called developing countries put together, excluding China.[2] Moreover, some families in the United States with ten times the real income per person of that in the poorest developing countries are adjudged to be in poverty.[3] Can this paradox be explained? Is there a coherent theoretical framework which will relate statements about poverty in affluent with that in developing societies? The view taken in this chapter is that needs which are unmet can be defined satisfactorily only in terms relative to the society in which they are found or expressed. Distinctions hitherto made between 'absolute' and 'relative' poverty, or between 'basic' and 'cultural' needs are argued to be unreal upon analysis. Needs which are believed to be absolute or basic can be shown to be relative. Poverty must be regarded as a general form of relative deprivation which is the effect of the maldistribution of resources. [...]

The view put forward is therefore that the description, analysis and explanation of poverty in any country must proceed within the context of a general theory of stratification as applied to social systems and sub-systems on a continuum ranging from the household or family at one extreme through local communities and national societies to world society at the other. But this is easier said than done. If good theory is to be developed, three groups of studies upon which a great deal of attention has been recently concentrated need to be deliberately related. These are (a) studies of differences between countries in their degree of development or modernization, which help us to understand their poverty; (b) studies of the form of social stratification within countries; and (c) studies of the scale and

---

Extracts (pp 1–16, 30–45) from Townsend, P. (1970) 'Measures and explanations of poverty in high income and low income countries: the problems of operationalising the concepts of development, class and poverty', Chapter 1 in *The concept of poverty: Working papers on methods of investigation and life-styles of the poor in different countries*, London: Heinemann, pp 1–45.

nature of poverty in advanced industrial societies. We are still at a very early stage in our understanding of the manifestations and causation of poverty and for historical reasons some of the most relevant work in the social sciences has been undertaken in isolated compartments. The relationship between the concepts of development, class and poverty will be explored in this chapter for heuristic purposes. [...]

## Development and international social stratification

The comparative study of total societies has been given considerable impetus in recent years because of the emergence of new nation-states, the interests of the big powers in geographical spheres of influence and the promotion of 'development' by the United Nations to combat 'world poverty'. The very existence of the United Nations and of many other international agencies, such as UNESCO, ILO and FAO, promotes comparison and national self-consciousness and has had a profound influence as much upon academic pursuits as upon social and political perspectives. The United Nations has itself begun to issue extremely valuable compendia of national statistics. One study examined the relative standing of 74 countries according to income, health, nutrients and food consumption and literacy.[4] In recent years a growing number of cross-national economic, political and social studies have been published.[5]

One consequence of cross-national comparison is, as Table 1 suggests, that a basis for explanation and for practical policy-making can be laid. Not only may 'stages' of economic and social development be hypothesized; at any one time nation-states can be ranked according to their economic activity, social structure and possession of different resources. Some countries are wealthier, or have a larger population, a lower mortality rate, relatively more men under arms and more young people in higher education than others. Their position in the world economic order, or their power or prestige, can be regarded as superior. Social scientists have seized upon the possibilities offered by modern methods of data-collection to present ambitious comparisons between countries as a basis for theories of development.

Some of the efforts being made in this direction by social scientists may be misplaced, however. There are various problems in producing theories of development. There is the uneven quality of basic information; the unconscious ideological or technical bias in the selection of those parts of the economic and social systems of different countries which are felt to be relevant to 'development'; the difficulty of deciding what *weight* should be given to different parts of the economic and social system at different stages of development; and finally the difficulty of deciding whether there are definite stages of development and whether different nations follow roughly the same or widely different paths of development. First, basic information – essential statistics are just not available for some developing countries [...]. The lack of statistics about some matters means, of course, that these matters get too little attention in national and international discussion. When statistics do exist for developing countries, they are often unreliable. Population statistics for Nigeria, for example, have recently been revised upwards and are still recognized to be subject to a considerable margin of error. Such difficulties as these are very great and must not be underestimated. Perhaps the random sample survey has been insufficiently exploited in some countries, especially in Africa and Asia.[6]

As well as the lack of quantitative information over many aspects of social and economic life there is, second, the problem of selecting the criteria according to which comparisons between countries can be made. It can be argued that there is a kind of bias in the selection of the variables which are felt to be relevant to development. The criteria of comparison which are adopted in all studies tend to favour western-style 'consumption' societies. Non-monetary resources other than the distribution of agricultural land tend to be overlooked. Cinema attendance and ownership of radios take precedence over measures of direct participation in local cultural events. Urbanization rates have more significance than living space or playing space for children. Unpaid services reciprocated within the family and the community do not feature among the indicators of 'development'. Neither is there a place for measures of social integration, such as low prevalence, say, of individual isolation. One author notes that 'recreation, funerals, religious services, domestic service and indigenous medicine, provided outside the market sector in a peasant economy and sometimes included in national income and sometimes not, ought to be fully included in a comparison with a country where these items are automatically part of income because they are within the market factor'.[7] All the factor analyses and regression equations in the world cannot make good the crudity of the information that is available, nor objectify the western-style cultural and economic ideology that underlies the whole approach.

Whether development is defined restrictedly in terms of economic variables alone or broadly to cover economic, social and political variables there is a problem not only of selecting the variables, but also of relating variables of different weight, many of which may not be quantifiable. If a broad definition is adopted, how would the indicator for higher education, as in Table 1, for example, be weighed with that for number of inhabitants per physician? [...] It would [also] be very difficult to define the shelter, whether in terms of cubic footage or of facilities, needed by a family, without taking account of social norms about the sharing of beds and rooms by people of different sex, age and consanguinity. It would be difficult to define nutritional needs without taking account of the kinds and demands of occupations and

## Table 1: Stages of economic and political development (Russett *et al*)

| Stages | Numbers of countries | GNP per person (1) | Per cent of population which is urban (living in towns 20,000+) | Per cent of population which is literate | Numbers in higher education per 100,000 population | Inhabitants per physician | Per cent of population voting in major elections | Numbers of radios per 1,000 population |
|---|---|---|---|---|---|---|---|---|
| I 'Traditional Primitive' Societies | 11 | 56 | 6 | 13 | 27 | 46,100 | 30 | 12 |
| II 'Traditional Civilisations' | 15 | 87 | 10 | 24 | 86 | 22,200 | 49 | 20 |
| III 'Transitional' Societies | 31 | 173 | 21 | 42 | 165 | 5,400 | 41 | 56 |
| IV 'Industrial Revolution' Societies | 36 | 445 | 34 | 77 | 386 | 1,600 | 69 | 157 |
| V 'High Mass-Consumption' Societies | 14 | 1,330 | 45 | 98 | 650 | 900 | 78 | 352 |
| **Selected Nations** | | | | | | | | |
| I Laos | | 50 | 4 | 17 | 4 | 100,000 | – | 8 |
| II Libya | | 60 | 18 | 13 | 49 | 5,800 | – | 8 |
| II Nigeria | | 78 | 10 | 10 | 4 | 32,000 | 40 | 4 |
| III Thailand | | 96 | 8 | 68 | 251 | 7,500 | – | 6 |
| III Philippines | | 220 | 13 | 75 | 967 | 5,600 | 55 | 22 |
| III Mauritius | | 225 | 27 | 52 | 14 | 4,500 | – | – |
| IV Hungary | | 490 | 37 | 97 | 258 | 650 | 93 | 231 |
| IV Puerto Rico | | 563 | 32 | 81 | 1,192 | 2,200 | 73 | – |
| V West Germany | | 927 | 55 | 98 | 528 | 798 | 87 | 319 |
| V France | | 943 | 30 | 96 | 667 | 1,014 | 89 | 282 |
| V United Kingdom | | 1,189 | 67 | 98 | 460 | 935 | 78 | 289 |
| V United States | | 2,577 | 52 | 98 | 1,983 | 780 | 64 | 948 |

(1) Estimates converted at current exchange rates into US dollars.

*Source:* Russett, B. M., and Alker, H. R., Deutsch, K. W., Lasswell, H. D., *World Handbook of Political and Social Indicators*, New Haven and London, Yale University Press, 1964.

of leisure time pursuits in a society. Recent sociological and other studies have shown how tenuous are definitions of absolute needs.[8]

A final problem that is involved in ranking countries according to certain criteria and comparing them is that of appearing to represent 'stages' of development. Let us consider certain lesser objections before turning to a fundamental objection. At what point can a society be called 'developed'? Is there a logical continuum through all stages or are there discontinuities or thresholds which separate quite different kinds of economic and social activity? It can be argued that societies in Stages I and V (see Table 1) are so different in their resources and organization that it may be difficult to find common criteria of comparison. To meet this objection it has been suggested that it may be more appropriate to outline 'short span' operational criteria to apply to groups of societies within limited ranges. A series of overlapping measures would still permit detailed study within a general theory of development.

Even if a continuum of development is assumed, the path of development is by no means smooth or consistent. Let us consider certain problems of detail. Through the various stages of development, as crudely represented in Table 1, there seems to be a rapid increase in GNP per person and in the proportions of the population that are urbanized, literate and receiving higher education, while there is a sharp decrease in the number of persons depending on a single physician. In the broadest terms these and other variables 'form a quite consistent cluster indicating the state of a nation's economic growth'.[9] But there are marked deviations, as the lower half of the table shows. For its GNP per person and its low rate of urbanization Thailand has remarkably high rates for literacy and higher education, and the ratio of physicians to population is relatively favourable. The difference between the Philippines and Mauritius in the proportion of the population receiving higher education is enormous and, at the next stage of development, that between Puerto Rico and Hungary is also large. The special situation in the Philippines and Puerto Rico no doubt owes much to prolonged American cultural domination. But these examples in themselves show that profiles of achievement vary and may be difficult to explain.'[10]

Rather than throwing doubt on the hypothesis of a continuum of development it has been suggested that disequilibrium in ranking may indicate high rates of development for the societies in question.[11] The effort of trying to restore equilibrium is thought to result in increased growth. This theory has prompted intensive study of the effects of investing disproportionately in one sector of the economy, or institution such as, higher education. However, the correlation between GNP per person and higher education enrolment, unlike that between GNP per person and primary and secondary education or literacy, is quite low.[12]

But the more we study stages, component variables and the weighting of component variables of development, the more we are led to question the assumptions that are made about the nature of development. Not only is it difficult to fit certain countries in any continuum, even if it is presumed that some of them miss certain stages of development entirely. It is also difficult to treat two countries as being so independent of each other that the second can be said to represent the predictable future state of the first. It is like suggesting that as an inevitable result of economic growth the poorest man in the United States or Britain will one day live and behave just like the richest man in that society. In each case a simple connection is overlooked. The privilege of the one and the deprivation of the other are directly related.

Rostow, for example, posits five stages of development (rather like the five stages adopted from Russett *et al* in Table 1): traditional society, pre-conditions for take-off, take-off, the drive to maturity and the age of high mass-consumption[13] as if societies which had entered the final stage had achieved it largely without help and as if societies in the first two stages had never experienced anything different. Yet any attempt to document these stages from world history encounters awkward facts. India was de-industrialized. In Africa the slave trade plundered social resources long before colonialism did so again. In Latin America the high civilizations of the Incas and Aztecs were obliterated. Many of the societies now acknowledged to be highly developed were capitalized at the expense of those which have remained underdeveloped. In many important respects it would be fair to conclude that the structure of underdevelopment has been created by centuries of association with the mercantile and colonialist nations. It would be naïve in the extreme not to recognize that western countries may have much to gain economically and politically even today from the poverty of the so-called developing countries though they may also have a lot to lose by policies of exploitation. Theories of development may unwittingly safeguard western ideology.[14]

The relationships between societies must therefore be seen in terms of a system of international social stratification. [...]

In relation to a system of stratification there are three conceptions of development. First, all societies advance equally and uniformly; mobility is nil and the form of stratification remains constant. Second, some societies are mobile; they improve their rank *vis-á-vis* others but the form and dispersion of stratification remains constant. Third, there is a convergence of rank; more societies may cluster in the middle ranks or the form of stratification may change in that the number of ranks may be reduced. Most theories of development implicitly adopt the first of these conceptions.

Development is usually interpreted as a process maximizing economic growth, and GNP per person the indicator of that growth. GNP per person is often used also as a measure of comfort or wellbeing. But it is a measure of production rather than of welfare. The United States has the largest GNP per person but has neither the highest life expectancy nor the lowest infant mortality rate. By selecting GNP per person as the ultimate criterion of advanced development and international status a distorted view of the world is presented. The selection of such a measure inevitably discriminates against the developing countries; for example, agricultural products and consumption from the land tend to be under-reported.[15] But the question of favouring industrial as compared with agricultural economies is perhaps an incidental one. Precedence is given to economic institutions and the products from the economic system. Other national activities and achievements, such as the redistribution of wealth, the development of social services, the integration of racial minorities and the minimization of violent acts against the person, are correspondingly accorded smaller value. The narrowly economic view of development can, of course, be challenged. Development can be conceived alternatively as a process achieving balanced economic and social well being.[16] This demands the formulation in detail of social objectives and of criteria by which indicators of degrees of success in attaining objectives may be combined. At the least it means that societies low in rank according to GNP may be ranked higher in social development than, say, the United States and West Germany.

The implications of all this for the study of world poverty are far-reaching. Some societies are desperately poor more because wealthier societies are continuing to follow policies of protecting their own special interests than because the poor societies lack technology and special skills which they need to learn or be taught to develop. What we need to study are the different systems which control the accumulation and unequal distribution of resources: trade, overseas investment, political relations and military alliances and campaigns. The degeneration or depression of regions, nations and sections of nations into conditions of deprivation can then be traced. The 'stages of growth' theory of development implies that the poverty of poor nations is relieved as their economies grow. It implies that the poverty of traditional societies is natural and encourages them to be patient until the preconditions for take-off and industrialization are established. Yet this is no more convincing than the corresponding theory, which held widespread currency throughout the West in the decade or more following the Second World War, that poverty *within* societies is gradually eliminated as their economies grow. For the United States provides living testimony of the falsity of this proposition.

[…]

The United States Social Security Administration measure of poverty is of greater purchasing value than the United Kingdom 'national assistance' standard[17] but has an approximately similar relationship to average wage levels. Both standards represent very much higher living standards than those experienced by the mass of the populations of the poorest developing countries. When measures of poverty are devised for the populations of these countries they are sometimes found to represent higher standards of living than can be secured by *average* wage rates. For example, Professor E. Batson, Director of the School of Social Science and Social Administration, University of Cape Town, devised a Poverty Datum Line which furnished 'the barest minimum upon which subsistence and health can theoretically be achieved'. When applied at the time to Kenya and Tanganyika it was found to be higher than average wages. The Tanganyika Territorial Minimum Wages Board found that it exceeded average cash earnings of African workers and preferred to adopt other criteria as guidelines for recommendations about minimum wages.[18] There are other examples of the misapplication of western standards of need to the deprived nations, and there are few reliable studies of the components of living standards. Standards of need tend to be unrealistic and lack a consistent theoretical perspective. They are not worked out in relation to the nations to which they are applied. Rarely in agricultural societies are non-monetary resources adequately investigated and assessed. We must conclude that two standards of poverty are required, 'nation-relational' and 'world-relational', which are both conceived in terms of systems of national and international stratification.

## The form of stratification within countries

There are important forms of stratification within societies which need to be delineated as precisely as forms of international stratification. Yet there is astonishingly little attempt to provide exact measurement. It is rather significant, for example, that many of the indicators used in comparing societies are expressed in averages or per 1,000 population.[19] The equalization of resources is given very little attention and is certainly not regarded as the hallmark of a highly developed society. Yet it could be so regarded if a 'convergence' rather than an 'infinitely hierarchical' or 'stages of growth' theory of development is preferred.

There are different kinds of variations in income distribution within countries. There are regional variations which are extremely important in some countries, such as Nigeria, Pakistan, Italy, and Yugoslavia.[20] There are also variations according to occupation, education and dependency. In general, some societies can be said to have a more equal distribution of income than others, as Table 3 shows, but there are few income data for the poor countries and considerable doubt has been cast on the validity of the data relating to income distribution for some of the wealthier countries.[21] Moreover, the Gini index of inequality, which furnishes the basis for Table 3, is extraordinarily crude and conceals some types of 'skewed' distribution. In both advanced and developing countries there are few official data about the 'incomes' of those who are not tax–paying wage or salary earners.

**Table 3:** Income distribution after taxes: Gini index of inequality (Russett *et al*)

| Country | Index of Inequality | Year | Per cent of income earned by the top 10 per cent of earners |
|---|---|---|---|
| West Germany | 0.432 | 1950 | 34 |
| Guatemala | 0.423 | 1948 | 43 |
| Ceylon | 0.407 | 1953 | 37 |
| Denmark | 0.396 | 1952 | 29 |
| El Salvador | 0.393 | 1946 | 43 |
| Netherlands | 0.388 | 1950 | 33 |
| Sweden | 0.388 | 1948 | 29 |
| United States | 0.373 | 1956 | 29 |
| India | 0.350 | 1956 | 33 |
| United Kingdom | 0.318 | 1955 | 26 |
| Norway | 0.313 | 1950 | 26 |
| Australia | 0.277 | 1956 | 30 |

*Source:* Russett, B. M., *et al*, *World Handbook of Political and Social Indicators*, New Haven and London, Yale University Press, 1964, p. 247.

It is particularly difficult to compare the different layers of wealth or of income of different countries. The data which are available are rarely comprehensive in the sense that they cover entire national populations; they are insufficient in the sense that they are based on narrow definitions of income and of wealth, and they are over-generalized in the sense that different types of income units and households and a wide range of income levels are often lumped together in analysis. Table 4 gives another example of the rough results that are all that can be obtained from existing data. The 5 per cent of persons with highest incomes had 37 per cent of total income in Mexico, 31 per cent in Ceylon, 29 per cent in Argentina and the Philippines, but around 20 per cent in the United States, Denmark, India and the United Kingdom. By contrast the 60 per cent of persons with lowest incomes had around a third of total personal income in the United States, the United Kingdom and India but only 25 per cent in the Philippines and only 21 per cent in Mexico. While there is some support from Tables 3 and 4 for the conclusion that incomes tend to be distributed more unequally in the low than in the high income countries there are some interesting puzzles in the statistics and the pattern is by no means consistent.[22] It should be stressed that important variations are concealed by sweeping comparisons of the kind that have so far been made in international studies and more sophisticated studies are badly needed.[23]

[...]

**Table 4:** Percentage of total personal income received by the five per cent of persons in the population with highest incomes and by the sixty per cent with lowest incomes

| Country | Five per cent with highest incomes | Sixty per cent with lowest incomes |
| --- | --- | --- |
| Mexico, 1957 | 37 | 21 |
| Ceylon, 1963 | 31 | 28 |
| Philippines, 1961 | 29 | 25 |
| Argentina, 1961 | 29 | 30 |
| Puerto Rico, 1953 | 23 | 30 |
| United Kingdom, 1951-2 | 21 | 33 |
| India, 1953-7 | 20 | 36 |
| Denmark, 1952 | 20 | 30 |
| United States, 1950 | 20 | 32 |

*Sources:* United Nations, *Economic Survey of Asia and the Far East 1966, Part 1, Aspects of the Finance of Development*, March, 1967; United Nations, Economic Commission for Europe, *Economic Survey of Europe*, 1956; Ohja, P. D., and Bhatt, V. V., 'Pattern of Income Distribution in an Underdeveloped Economy: A Case-Study of India,' *The American Economic Review*, Vol. LIV, No. 5, September, 1964; Reyes, P. S., and Chan, T. L., 'Family Income Distribution in the Philippines', *The Statistical Reporter*, Vol. 9, No. 2, 1965, p. 30; United Nations, *Economic Bulletin for Latin America*, Vol. 11, No. 1, April, 1966.

## The analysis of poverty in low income countries

[...] The accelerating collapse of colonialism since the war, the spread of post-colonial nationalism, the geometric rise of population in many countries and the fumbling moves towards a world order have all played their part in arousing the public's interest in the problems of development and modernization. The early pages of this chapter have described the response to the need that has been felt for information and an interpretative framework. There are many ways in which comparisons such as those illustrated in Table 1 can be extended – not just additional single indicators like marriage rates, numbers of children per woman of childbearing age and so on but carefully worked out types of family and community groupings, value-systems, patterns of ritual and political systems. [...] It is important to have separate concepts of social and economic development (or at least a well integrated concept of social and economic development) to help redress present western ideological bias in the selection, application and interpretation of indicators. But it is important also to remember that a set of statistical indicators can only provide part, if a helpful part, of an overall interpretative framework. I shall try to suggest how certain concepts and measures might be applied in analysing poverty in low-income countries.

Let us reconsider first the theme of development. Table 1 carries the implicit assumption that if a nation can climb up a stage or two this represents progress. Differences in achievement at a moment in time can be represented as earlier and later stages of development. (Some of the same overtones attach to the upper strata in a system of social stratification: if an individual can advance himself by his own efforts through social mobility this represents progress.) As discussed above ... a view of development can be very misleading both analytically and ideologically (though, of course, value can be wrung out of detailed structural comparison).

[...]

Both high and low income countries are a mixture, though to a differing degree, of traditional and modern elements. In many low income countries the most startling visual and physical contrasts are cheek by jowl – American cars and primitive rickshaws, Sandhurst-trained Nigerian Army officers and street beggars, government offices in new skyscrapers and corrugated-roofed shanty towns. Yet in all high income countries there are strong traces of the past – villages, landed estates, rural preservation societies, folk-dancing, religious and political rituals, social courtesies. These images are suggested for a deliberate theoretical purpose. Too often extreme analytic polarizations have plagued our attempts to compare different societies – 'modern' and 'primitive', 'developed' and 'underdeveloped', 'industrial' and 'agrarian'. We are encouraged to feel that they are so far removed at either end of a long spectrum, like chalk and cheese, that there is little that is alike (and the divergent history of anthropological theory and fieldwork, on the one hand, and of sociological theory and field work on the other, help to preserve the illusion). Almost inevitably corresponding ideas of superiority and inferiority are encouraged, however much they may be denied or qualified.

All this expresses, in effect, profound scepticism of the value of much sociological theory of industrialization, modernization and development.[24] Like Rostow's theory of stages of economic growth, both the historical and contemporaneous evidence about different societies tends to be insufficiently sought and digested.[25] There are primary relationships (e.g. between parents and grandparents within the family) and traditional customs and practices which are an important part of modern society. Every modern society has a traditional one inside it. As Professor Almond has argued, we need dualistic models *rather than* monistic ones and developmental *as well as* equilibrium models if we are to understand differences between societies and the processes of social and political change.[26] More constant reference needs to be made to empirical reality by theorists than it has in the past.[27] Like development, world poverty cannot adequately be explained or understood, therefore, by applying any of the 'stages of growth', 'diffusionist' or 'structural differentiationist' models of development.

## Nationalism and development

There are certain factors which are of particular value in revealing the present direction being taken by low income societies, which help also to explain the existence of poverty among them. Why is nationalism rampant? Whether we look at the republics of Latin America, the new African states, at India or Indonesia, or even China, nationalism is strong and dynamic – though of course it takes a number of different forms. It is a response conditioned by contact with western countries. It is not the nationalism of old states like Ethiopia, Liberia, and the former kingdom of Dahomey in Africa, or of the Mogul Empire in India. Old-style nationalism was founded on submission to a common ruler, who was recognized to occupy a position at the apex of a social and political hierarchy. The adoption of political equality, with elaboration of the individual's legal and social rights, distinguished modern nation-states from preceding monarchies. Nationalism almost seems to be a requirement if the States are to survive and if economic aims are to be achieved. [...]

Nationalism can in some ways be represented as indispensable to the actual achievement of higher standards of living, while largely continuing existing stratification, or, more related to the concept of poverty put forward in this chapter, the hierarchy of privilege and deprivation.

When we remember that the great majority of people in the low income countries are engaged in subsistence agriculture and live in villages which are relatively self-contained economic units, we can begin to understand the almost inevitable link between nationalism and economic development. Some writers see its function as the *transference* of primary loyalties from the village or kinship group to the larger society[28] but, in keeping with the *dualistic* approach [...], I believe it is better viewed both as a broadening or an extension of loyalties and a means of safeguarding the security of élites and enhancing their status, by consolidating political and social control and establishing their independence of foreign dominating powers.

## Social and political élites

The withdrawal of the occupying power completely transforms the lives of some nationals. Although some may have held high positions formerly, others suddenly find themselves projected from subordinate positions as, say, clerks or itinerant students into positions of power. There is a tendency to take over the salaries, the attitudes of superiority and even to some extent the styles of life of colonial administrators. Some new leaders are very youthful. This is not social mobility: it is 'pitchfork' upward mobility. The former administrative hierarchy has an inheritance effect.

Contact with high income countries also has many subtle effects. Here is the new state comparing itself not only with its neighbours in the third world but with former colonial powers and other heavily industrialized countries. The international agencies reinforce a system of social stratification among nations, with nominal equality of status but wide, and widening,[29] inequality of wealth. The humbling ratios of the kind described in Table 1, average incomes, mortality rates and literacy rates, are brought embarrassingly into the light of day. Small wonder that one response of the low-income country is an over-assertive nationalism and a determination to insist on the rights of national equality. Status at international meetings and in the dealings with advanced countries is jealously watched. Wherever possible political and administrative leaders emulate their counterparts in western countries. Moreover, many of them have been educated in the United States or Europe and when they become lawyers, business managers, doctors, administrators and political leaders they expect broadly commensurate living standards. Long periods without contact with family and community of origin also lead some of them to a kind of dissociation of attitude which tends to confirm the seclusion of élites rather than élites attempting to pursue policies of social integration. Traditional control of ethical values is weakened. Again, before independence there is often a cluster of, say, African or Asian élites gathering around the European administrators, traders and settlers, expecting to take over the same positions.

All this results in the extreme wealth and exceptionally high salaries of many élites. If there is greater inequality of wealth in low income than in high income societies (and this remains to be firmly established) then it may be primarily the result of prolonged contact with colonial or high income countries. The wealth and power of some élites, as in India, may have been 'artificially' maintained or increased before independence, and afterwards emulation of élites in high income countries, combined with trading, political and professional contacts, may perpetuate the disparity. A year after independence Dahomey spent 60 per cent of its budget on the salaries of Government personnel. In Nigeria, as the Morgan Report on Wages and Salaries revealed, Ministers and managing directors were recently drawing between £3,500 and £10,000 while unskilled workers in the State sector were earning an average of £50 to £60 a year. The latter, of course, were better off than many peasants and agricultural workers.

> On top of their salaries Ministers were given houses specially built at a cost of £32,000 each. They also pay no electricity, telephone or water charges; they get a basic car allowance of £80 a month and when on an official trip they are also paid 1s. 3d. a mile. In addition they get cheap petrol from Public Works Department pumps ... Senior Civil Servants and officials of Corporations fare little worse.[30]

[...]

The social characteristics of the élites, tend, therefore, to place them apart from and on top of the mass of the people. The middle class tends to be small. One additional reason for this is that before independence and in some states long afterwards commercial activity has been in the hands of alien groups: for example, Indians in South and East Africa, Indians and Chinese in South-East Asia and Lebanese and Jews in North Africa. Table 7 gives a vivid illustration of the comparative wealth of Europeans and Asians in Africa and shows how small are the middle income groups. The number of African income–units with much less than £120 a year is, of course, underestimated in the table. Many families working on the land pay no tax.[31]

**Table 7:** Percentage of Taxpayers of Different Race in Kenya, According to Income

| Income | Europeans | Asians | Arabs and Somalis | Africans | All races |
|--------|-----------|--------|-------------------|----------|-----------|
| Over £200 | 96.0 | 85.9 | 5.1 | 1.6 | 8.4 |
| £161-£200 | 0.5 | 2.4 | 2.7 | 1.2 | 1.3 |
| £120-£160 | 2.3 | 3.6 | 7.1 | 3.7 | 3.7 |
| Under £120 | 1.2 | 8.1 | 85.1 | 93.5 | 86.5 |
| Total | 100 | 100 | 100 | 100 | 100 |
| N= | 25,245 | 47,221 | 21,957 | 846,806 | 941,229 |

*Note:* The total number of taxpayers was 941,229. The total population was estimated to be 8,485,000 in that year.
*Source:* Data compiled by the Kenya Government and cited in Due, D. F., *Taxation and Economic Development in Tropical Africa*, Cambridge, Mass., Massachusetts Institute of Technology Press, 1963, p. 81.

## A wage-earning working class and development

Let us take a third important factor in the contemporary explanation of poverty in low income countries – a small but growing wage-earning industrial class. In many countries the proportion of wage-earners is still very small. The number of peasants and of cash-crop workers is usually large. Socially and financially the rift between these two groups is considerable and in many countries appears to be growing.[32] It is difficult to argue that, in general, peasants constitute a politically conscious class. They share similar conditions and styles of life, but they rarely act in any concerted fashion in defence of their interests and engage in wider political activity. But wage-earners in many of the new states are a clamant minority, and are either firmly integrated with the government's interests (for example, trade unions have long been part of one-party government in Tunisia and Ghana) or are won over by generous wage-concessions (for example, the 1964 general strike in Nigeria). They form an embryonic class. This tends to be rather more heterogeneous than European counterparts, often because of the large number of short-term migrant workers (who may work up to five years before returning to the country), seasonal workers who alternate between wage-earning and subsistence agriculture, and part-time wage-earners who live on the land and work also as part-time cultivators. [...]

There are various degrees of combination between land/tribal and urban/industrial ties. When, as in East London, large numbers of workers settling temporarily or permanently in one area of the city come from a single tribe, social relationships are an intermingling of the two. When, as in the towns of the Zambian copper-mining area, the migrant workers are drawn from a wide variety of tribal groups, in this case over 70, a more conventional pattern of urban relationships emerges. But in many countries the small size and the instability of the wage-earning industrial class should be remembered. There is a lot of part-time casual work and a good deal of unemployment. Moreover the land still dominates. In all the African States south of the Sahara only South Africa has more than 7 per cent of its population in cities of 100,000 or more. None of the new African States has more than 15 per cent of its population in towns of 5,000 or more. African wage-earners rarely form more than 15 per cent of the adult male labour force, although in Tanzania, Kenya and the Congo the figure ranges from a fifth to a third.[33] Less than 20 per cent of the population of India and Ceylon and only 10 per cent of that of Pakistan is categorized as urban.

But the relative advantage of the urban wage-earner should be kept in mind. It is not simply the fact that he obtains a disproportionate share of increases in national income and has, by African standards, a good income. Many undertakings give him well-cooked and balanced meals and some issue rations to his family as well. When so large a part of the population is malnourished, high productivity depends on giving special privileges to the wage-earning class.[34] Standards of living in agricultural regions may even be depressed so that an urban wage-earning class may be established.

## Poverty and development

The structural developments I have described have the effect of introducing a more hierarchical, or similarly hierarchical, form of social stratification, with the consequence of increasing, or at least perpetuating, poverty. There is the rural poverty of large sections of the population who live on the margins of dietary sufficiency and some of whom struggle for survival. The arrival of nationhood, the extension of systems of communication and the growth of urban areas contributes to the deepening of their poverty. But what are conditions like? There are great difficulties in establishing the true resources and in particular the nutritive content of the diet of many peoples in the agricultural regions. The Food and Agriculture Organization has made recommendations that the average daily calorie intake for a man should be around 3,000. Most experts consider that fewer than 2,500 represents under-nourishment, under 2,000 acute shortage and around 1,500 famine. But while the food supply in Bolivia, Chile, Peru and Ecuador does not reach 2,000 calories a day, Josue de Castro, for example, argues that this is in fact supplemented to a greater extent than is usually assumed by home production and 'natural' foodstuffs which are peculiar to particular areas.[35] In the period immediately before the harvest, when stocks of food are low, the intake drops in some areas of Africa below 1,000 calories a day. Where the diet appears to be on the borderline of sufficiency, as among the Senoufo, special account may have to be taken of the quite frequent festival days. The average daily ration here was found to rise as a result from 2,586 calories a head to 2,750. In one fertile district on the lower Senegal river a careful year's investigation by one team from the Organization for Research into Food and Nutrition in Africa showed an average daily intake per person of 2,175 calories.[36] These are the kinds of problems that arise in attempting any exact measurement of malnutrition in these areas. Moreover, care has to be taken not to assume that the prevalence of deficiency diseases such as kwashiorkor, beriberi, scurvy, pellagra, glaucoma and anaemia are due solely to a shortage of food. While populations sometimes escape widespread deficiency diseases they can also invite them because of their food customs. Kwashiorkor, which is primarily protein deficiency, may become common because it is believed that rich meats are bad for children, not because there is a scarcity of meat as such. Beriberi would not be so prevalent if highly milled rice was not so popular. And the slender margins of nutritional sufficiency of some people in these areas can be lost in a drought, by the repressive act of an overlord, by the introduction of less nutritious commercial foodstuffs and by the influx of refugees.

The poverty of the people in these agricultural regions is a resigned or compliant poverty, or at least, so it has seemed in the past. With limited social horizons and reference points, it is not surprising that they find it difficult even to conceive of vastly improved standards of living. But the establishment of nation states and the ideology of nationalism are changing all this, and introducing a second form of poverty. There is the miserable poverty of those in the cities and towns whose share of national resources, whose conditions of life and whose opportunities are far below either average real, or average computed, resources. In addition to the shortage of simple foodstuffs the insanitary squalor of shanty town conditions is imposed upon them. Knowledge of the gross disparities between élites, regular wage-earners and agricultural workers in standards of living and career opportunities is gradually percolating through to the rural areas. Men and families are attracted temporarily or permanently to the towns. The new wage-earners are jealous of their pay and their security. The movement into the urban centres is bigger than growth of capacity to provide employment, and population increase makes the problem worse. As a consequence there are large groups of destitute families and individuals living in shanty towns, many of whom hope they are on their way up the income and social scales, others of whom, after continued disappointments, still find compensations in urban life. [...]

[...] This kind of poverty is a direct and inevitable consequence of the overall social structure – a creation of relative wage-earning prosperity, which is concentrated in the cities, of subsistence farming in the rural regions, of 'pedestal' élites and of nationalist ideology.

## Accounting for poverty

The thesis of this chapter has been that systems of international social stratification and social stratification interact to produce poverty. We started with a puzzle: does it make sense to say there are considerable numbers of people in poverty in the United States when they can buy far more than the masses of the population in, say, Asia, Africa or Latin America? I have tried to show that it is in attempting to give a systematic and comprehensive answer to this question that we can begin to put concepts and theories of poverty in both high income and low income countries on to a secure footing. [...] [T]he poverty of deprived *nations* is comprehensible only if we attribute it substantially to the existence of a system of international social stratification, a hierarchy of societies with vastly different resources in which the wealth of some is linked historically and contemporaneously to the poverty of others. This system operated crudely in the era of colonial domination, and continues to operate today, though more subtly, through systems of trade, education, political relations, military alliances and industrial corporations. A wealthy society which deprives a poor country of resources may simultaneously deprive its own poor classes through maldistribution of those additional resources.

[T]he poverty of individuals and of families is related to the form of social stratification within nations. Such stratification tends to be based on the distribution of resources, which is understood in a much broader sense than income, and includes five categories: cash income, capital assets and three systems of benefits in kind – employment benefits, public social service benefits and private benefits. The distribution of these resources is governed by principles defining the recipients and scale of allocation. Thus, the distribution of cash income depends on the operation of a number of sub-systems – for example, the wage system, the social security system, income from rent, interest and dividend systems and the occupational pension system, cash income being adjusted overall by the fiscal system. It is the differential interaction of these principal systems and their sub-systems which accounts for the arrangement of the population in strata with different resources. A family might rank high on one system but low on another. Another family might rank low on all systems. The application of rank equilibrium theory to such examples helps to operationalize the necessary concepts of partial and total poverty.

Poverty is [...] defined in terms of relative deprivation (understood in an objective and not, as by some sociologists, a subjective sense) and two steps have to be taken to identify it. One is to show exactly how resources are distributed among a population and by what different ranking systems. The other is to show what diets, activities and living conditions are customary in society as a whole from which the poor tend to be excluded. Much more information from both high income and low income countries is required before these steps can be traced in any detail and before theory can be developed very far.

[...]

This approach to theory does, of course, have direct implications for action. [...] The elimination of poverty requires not the reform, education or rehabilitation of the individual or even, bearing in mind a major strategy of the American war on poverty, the creation of more opportunities of upward mobility for the individual. It requires reconstruction of the national and regional systems by which resources are distributed, or, alternatively, the introduction of additional systems which are universalistic and egalitarian. Systems which are confined either to the rich (like the ownership of land or of stocks and shares) or to the poor (like public assistance and free school meals) tend towards privilege on the one hand, and disprivilege on the other. They separate society into more rigidly defined strata.

Given this analysis of poverty there can be no single remedy. Poverty can be reduced by introducing and strengthening systems of social security (particularly family allowances, allowances for fatherless families and pensions for the old and disabled); by extending (through legislation) employer benefits in kind to all employees; by developing free community welfare services for all; but also by restricting the privileges of the prosperous sections of society – partly by restricting excessively high salaries among élites and by maintaining a strong system of progressive taxation, but also diffusing wealth by the elimination of substantial private ownership. These policies have positive value in breaking down rigid attitudes about human superiority and inferiority, which is required if the dominant wage–system is to become more egalitarian. The restraints placed on élites by, for example, the Tanzanian Arusha Declaration, suggest one strategy.[37] Poverty is not just a lack of resources required to live a normal life. It is lack of resources in fact used, and felt to be rightly used, by the rich.

### References

[1] Economic Report of the President of the United States for 1964, Washington D.C., US Government Printing Office, 1964; Orshansky, M., 'Counting the Poor: Another Look at the Poverty Profile', *Social Security Bulletin,* Vol. 28, January, 1965.

[2] See, for example, Lagos, G., *International Stratification and Underdeveloped Countries,* Chapel Hill, University of North Carolina Press, 1963, p. 4.

[3] The poverty line used by the US Social Security Administration in 1963 ranged from $1,500 a year for a person living alone to about $700 a head for large families. See Orshansky, M., *op. cit.* Despite difficulties in comparing these amounts with income per person in developing countries (see in particular the difficulties in estimating GNP listed by Russett, B. M., *et al, World Handbook of Political and Social Indicators,* New Haven and London, Yale University Press, 1964, pp. 149-151) it is clear that the line represents a standard of living which is several times greater than the average standard in the poorest countries.

[4] United Nations, *Report on the World Social Situation,* New York, 1961.

[5] See, for example, Ginsberg, N., *Atlas of Economic Development,* Chicago, 1961; Lerner, D., *The Passing of Traditional Society,* The Free Press, Glencoe, Ill., 1958; Deutsch, K. W., 'Social Mobilization and Political Development', *American Political Science Review,* Vol. 55, September, 1961; Miller, S. M., 'Comparative Social Mobility', *Current Sociology,* Vol. 9, 1960; Almond, G. A., and Coleman, J. S., *The Politics of the Developing Areas,* Princeton, Princeton University Press, 1960; Cutright, P., 'National Political Development: Measurement and Analysis', *American Sociological Review,* Vol. 28, April, 1963; Russett, B. M., *et al, op. cit.;* and Drewnowski, J., and Scott, W., *The Level of Living Index,* United Nations Research Institute for Social Development. Report No. 4, Geneva, September, 1966.

[6] See, for example, Mitchell, R. E., 'Survey Materials Collected in the Developing Countries: Sampling, Measurement and Interviewing Obstacles to Intra- and Inter-National Comparisons', *International Social Science Journal,* Vol. XVII, No. 4, 1965.

[7] Usher, D., *Rich and Poor Countries: A Study in Problems of Comparisons of Real Income,* London, Institute of Economic Affairs, 1966, p. 17.

[8] See, for example, Townsend, P., 'The Meaning of Poverty', *British Journal of Sociology,* September, 1962 [Chapter 14 in this volume]; Franklin, N. N., 'The Concept and Measurement of "Minimum Living Standards"', *International Labour Review,* April, 1967.

[9] Russett, B. M., *et al, op. cit.,* p. 288.

[10] In a valuable analysis of a large number of Afro-Asian and European nations Robertson and Tudor have shown that rank disequilibrium (i.e. the extent to which a nation, or unit, is high-ranking on some dimensions, e.g. income and education, and not on others, e.g. newspapers) is in practice common among the nations of the world; that this disequilibrium tends to be greatest for those nations in the middle or the upper-middle of the total ranking (mainly but not entirely in correspondence with a simple mathematical model); but that some nations, like Malaysia and Turkey, diverge strikingly from 'expected' degrees of disequilibrium. They call for further study of such rank divergence. Robertson, R., and Tudor, A., 'The Third World and International Stratification: Theoretical Considerations and Research Findings, *Sociology,* January, 1968.

[11] Galtung, J., and Höivik, T., 'On the Definition and Theory of Development with a View to the Application of Rank Order Indicators in the Elaboration of a Composite Index of Human Resources,' UNESCO, Warsaw, December, 1967.

[12] Russett, B. M., *et a?, op. cit.,* p. 288.

[13] Rostow, W. W., *The Stages of Economic Growth, A Non-Communist Manifesto,* Cambridge, Cambridge University Press, 1962.

[14] This theme is elaborated trenchantly and caustically in one of the best critical analyses of theories of development by Frank, André G., 'Sociology of Development and Underdevelopment of Sociology', *Catalyst* (State University of New York in Buffalo), No. 3, Summer, 1967.

[15] For some of the difficulties in the valuation of subsistence output, see Prest, A. R., *Public Finance in Underdeveloped Countries,* London, Weidenfeld and Nicolson, 1962, Appendix 1, 'The Valuation of Subsistence Output'.

[16] See, for example, Drewnowski, J., *Social and Economic Factors in Development,* United Nations Research Institute for Social Development, Report No. 3, Geneva, February, 1966. Attempts have been made to distinguish development from 'modernization'. Lagos, for example, regards the modernization of a society as the process of insuring 'a regular flow of innovations within its social system'. Lagos, *op. cit.,* p. 243. Nettl and Robertson have argued that 'modernization' is the crucial concept, to which the concepts of development and industrialization should be subordinated. 'Modernization is the process whereby national elites seek successfully

to reduce their atimic status and move towards equivalence with other "well-placed" nations. The goal of equivalence is not a fixed but a moving target. . ..' Nettl, J. P., and Robertson, R., 'Industrialization, Development or Modernization', *British Journal of Sociology*, Vol. XVII, No. 3, September, 1966.

[17] Abel-Smith, B., and Townsend, P., *The Poor and the Poorest: A New Analysis of the Ministry of Labour's Family Expenditure Surveys of 1953-4 and 1960*, London, Bell, pp. 16-20.

[18] *Report of the Territorial Minimum Wages Board, Tanganyika,* Dar es Salaam, printed by the Government Printer, 1962. See also, United Nations, *Assistance to the Needy in Less-Developed Areas,* Department of Economic and Social Affairs, New York, United Nations, 1956, pp. 19-21.

[19] Of the 75 indicators used in Russett, *et al, World Handbook of Political and Social Indicators,* only three are measures of dispersion.

[20] According to the Government of Pakistan's *Third Five Year Plan,* the top 5 per cent of income earners had 22 per cent of total income in Karachi in 1959-60, compared with 14 per cent and 11 per cent respectively in rural West Pakistan and East Pakistan.

[21] See, for example, Titmuss, R. M., *Income Distribution and Social Change,* London, Allen & Unwin, 1962.

[22] There are alternative estimates for income distribution in India which are much closer to those for Ceylon. Government of India Planning Commission, *Report of the Committee on Distribution of Income and Levels of Living,* Part I, February, 1964, Statement 2, p. 27.

[23] See, for example, Lydall, H., and Lansing, J. B., 'A Comparison of the Distribution of Personal Income and Wealth in the United States and Great Britain', *American Economic Review,* Vol. XLIX, March, 1959; and Wedderburn, D., 'The Financial Resources of Older People: A General Review', in Shanas, E., Townsend, P., Wedderburrs, D., Friis, H., Milhøj, P., and Stehouwer, J., *Old People in Three Industrial Societies,* New York and London, Atherton and Rourledge, 1967.

[24] A good example of the failure of latter-day functionalists, for example, to adapt theoretical models of change to the increasing volume of historical and contemporary evidence is the section on 'Changing Family Relations' in Smelser, N. J., 'Processes of Social Change', in Smelser, N. J. (ed), *Sociology: An Introduction,* New York, John Wiley, 1967, pp. 720-722.

[25] See, for example, the criticisms of Hoselitz, Parsons and others in Frank, A. G., *op. cit.*

[26] Almond, G. A., and Coleman, J. S. (eds), *op. cit.,* pp. 20-25.

[27] Such reference will also help to moderate over-enthusiastic attempts to adapt formal techniques in economics to the construction of sociological theories of development. It would be wrong to make out that there is a 'positive' sociology which can 'predict' development in any strict sense. We can only hope to show specific probable connections between variables within a general descriptive context,

as Leibenstein and others have argued. See, for example, Leibenstein, H., 'What Can We Expect from a Theory of Development', *Kykios,* Fasc 1, Switzerland, 1966.

[28] For example, Hoselitz, B. F., 'Nationalism and Economic Development', in Feinstein, O. (ed), *Two Worlds of Change,* New York, Doubleday Anchor Books, 1964, pp. 256-257.

[29] Economic inequality between countries is in certain senses widening. See Myrdal, G., *Economic Theory and Underdeveloped Regions,* London, Methuen University Paperbacks, 1963.

[30] Bulloch, J., 'Nigerian Anger at Leaders' Rich Living', *Sunday Telegraph,* 21st June 1964, quoted by Davies, I., *African Trade Unions,* Harmondsworth, Penguin Books, 1966, PP. 127-128.

[31] The differences between the races in South Africa are even more extreme. In 1959-60 only 16 of the 43,780 persons in South Africa having an income of more than $5,600 were Africans. Only one of the 5,938 persons with an income of more than $14,000 was African. It is estimated that the income *per capita* of the European population since the war has been more than ten times as much as that of the African population. United Nations, *Economic Survey of Africa: Vol. 1, Western Sub-Region,* 1966, P. 178.

[32] Sample survey data cited in the Tomlinson Report, for example, show that 85 per cent of families in the low rainfall zone of South Africa in the 1950s received an income of less than $56 (including the value of subsistence output and cash from migrant labourers). Since the average size of a South African family is over six, average income *per capita* must be around $10 in that zone. Yet GNP *per capita* for South Africa as a whole was over $300 at this time.

[33] Coleman, J. S., 'Sub-Saharan Africa', in Almond, G. A., and Coleman, J. S., *The Politics of the Developing Areas,* Princeton, Princeton University Press, 1960, pp. 271-275.

[34] Employers estimate that productivity can rise by as much as 30 per cent, and that labour turnover and absenteeism are reduced to small dimensions by providing meals to workers and families. Drogat, N., *The Challenge of Hunger,* London, Burns and Oates, 1962, pp. 52-53. Nonetheless, this kind of paternalism is not universal. Many urban workers depend solely on wages only, and these wages are insufficient to obtain adequate diets. See, for example, the description of men working from Nairobi on the Kenya-Uganda railway, some of whom had no midday meal and little to eat in the mornings. UNESCO, *Social Aspects of the Industrialisation and Urbanisation of Africa to the South of the Sahara,* 1956, p. 152.

[35] de Castro, J., *Hunger in Brazil,* p. 57.

[36] Drogat, N., *op. cit.,* pp. 65-80.

[37] The following are extracts from the resolution agreed by the Tanzanian National Executive committee at Arusha, January, 1967:

No TANU or government leader should...

- hold shares in any company

- receive two or more salaries

- hold directorships in any privately-owned enterprises

- own houses which he rents to others.

A 'leader' was defined to include ministers, members of parliament, senior officials, councillors and civil servants of high and medium grade.

# 6

# The international analysis of poverty

## The changing world map of poverty

[…] Poverty is deep-seated in many rich and not only poor countries and seems destined to get worse in both groups of countries unless scientific means are mobilised to fully explain current trends, and international action is taken collaboratively to counter them. If poverty is to be fully understood so that it can be defeated or reduced, myopic and piecemeal preoccupation with particular cultural and regional meanings of the word, arising from misconceived theory and ideology, has to be relinquished. Instead, 'poverty' has to be given scientifically acceptable universal meaning and measurement. It has also to be explained primarily in terms of the huge influence of international developments – the policies of international agencies and global corporations and the institutions of the world's economy and trade – on social class and on style as well as conditions of life in every country. All of this applies to poverty in a wide variety of rural and urban areas of the United States, Ethiopia, India, France and the United Kingdom no less than it does to the most wretched areas of the cities of New York, Addis Ababa, Calcutta, Marseilles and Manchester.

## The perils of narrow individualism

… [T]here has been a long intellectual tradition justifying severe inequality. At the same time, on grounds which have to be shown to be specious, there has been a parallel tradition of thought excusing, upholding and reinforcing the conditions which are experienced by the poor. They are represented as bringing those conditions upon themselves, or as lacking the qualities or skills to deserve anything different. The quarrel with these two insidious traditions is as relevant to world society at the end of the twentieth century, and therefore present-day conditions in Peru, Nigeria, Indonesia and Bangladesh in the 1990s, as it was to Elizabethan or Victorian England.

However, the school of thought involves more than the legitimation of inequality on the one hand and of widespread poverty on the other.

---

Extracts (pp 3, 6-17, 22-25, 101-6, 112, 236-40, 242-3, 246-50, 252) from Townsend, P. (1993) *The international analysis of poverty*, Hemel Hempstead: Harvester Wheatsheaf.

It involves the identification of the causes of poverty in individuals and local groups. The causes of poverty are believed to rest overwhelmingly in individual and sub-cultural defects and dispositions. Responsibility is deflected from states and national and multinational economic, administrative and legal organisations to individuals and groups – especially racial groups. Little or no attention is given to the interacting consequences for families of national and multinational policies to do with employment, taxation, housing, social security and public services. Instead of structural factors and state laws and policies prominence is given in analysis of individual and sub-cultural factors. One seems to go with the other. What is exploited is popular readiness to assign blame for poverty to individuals or families, or alternatively to minority groups. Laissez-faire individualism and the legitimation of racial discrimination are in fact the intellectual sources of this tradition.

## Absorbing the importance of comparative analysis

The intellectual quarrel about the interpretation of poverty is not only historical, theoretical and ideological. It is comparative too. In recent years many people have argued that it is Third World and not First World poverty which matters. While understandable, this view can be dangerously diversionary. Because national income in the rich countries is many times larger than in the poor countries members of the former are tempted to dismiss the severity of conditions experienced by the poorest in their own countries in the belief that they have food enough and access enough to a variety of modern facilities. At the same time they respond sympathetically to reports and pictures of the raw scarcities of sub-Saharan Africa and other deprived regions. People who react in this way ignore common (international) causes of impoverished conditions in the two places. They also ignore respects in which poverty in a rich society takes forms which can be as bad as, if not worse than, those in a poor society. And the problem becomes far less immediate to, and more remote from, them. They are relatively uninvolved; they do not consider they have much responsibility for those conditions. Although sensitive observers strive to work for understanding and improvement it is difficult for them to behave other than as intellectual *voyeurs*. They turn away from societies in which they can exert influence to others where they can merely watch.

## Extreme variations in poverty across the world

This is where the discussion has to become acutely methodological, comparative and empirical, and not just critical of mainstream theoretical and intellectual tradition. Our capacity to deal with poverty depends on giving equal and simultaneous attention to meaning, measurement, explanation and policy analysis. Table 1.1 illustrates the varied pattern requiring explanation. Poverty is not the same as inequality. Although the two have to be distinguished, they are connected. In the present state of knowledge it is easier to compare sections of the population, regions and countries on some measured interpretation of resources or income than it is on some measured interpretation of poverty. Although major improvements still remain to be made to the former it satisfies some of the requirements of consistency. The latter is more problematic.[...] A measure of poverty must apply not just to the low end of the resource or income distribution, but must also involve the selection of criteria applying to a threshold of income at which needs are not met or there is a disproportionate risk of severe or multiple deprivation.

Table 1.1 also illustrates another key feature of poverty analysis [...]. In dealing with the international statistics of poverty the differences *between* populations but also *within* populations have to be expressed. An acceptable theory of one has to be an acceptable theory of the other too. How can the pattern of world poverty be explained? The difference between rich and poor countries in command over income is vast. More than 160 countries are now listed in the information provided routinely by UN agencies. In allowing for variations in size, differences in aggregate income are usually expressed per person. For the countries of western and northern Europe, North America and some of the strongest oil-powers of the Middle East the average person's income, when standardised according to exchange rates, is as much as 50 times that found in the countries of the Far East, like India, Pakistan and Bangladesh, and the countries of Africa, like Mozambique, Somalia, Mali and Ethiopia. Thus, GNP per person was US $12,510 for the industrialised countries but only US $230 for the 'least developed countries' in 1988 (as defined by the UN General Assembly). This suggests a ratio of 54:1.

However, comparisons expressed by using exchange rates can be very misleading. Cash economies are variable in their scope, and exchange rates can be unhelpful in measuring the value of goods and services that are available in different countries. The UN International Comparison Project (ICP) has sought to develop comparable international measures of real GDP using purchasing power parities (PPP) instead of exchange rates as conversion factors. These are expressed in international dollars. The consequence of this revaluation has been to diminish the gap in income between rich and poor countries. Thus the income of the industrialised countries was revalued at PPP $14,350 and of the least developed countries at PPP $720 per person in 1988. This produces a ratio of 20:1 – notably smaller than the exchange rate ratio. The measured difference between rich and poor countries is still very great but not as extreme as initially suggested.

**Table 1.1:** Average annual income per person (and of richest 20 per cent and poorest 20 per cent) (measured in international dollars) and per cent in poverty

|  | Real GDP per person (PPP$)[1] (1988) | Richest 20 per cent[2] | Poorest 20 per cent[3] | Per cent population below poverty line[4] |
|---|---|---|---|---|
| US | 19,850 | 41,565 | 4,662 | (13) |
| Canada | 17,680 | 35,454 | 5,027 | (15) |
| Sweden | 14,940 | 27,419 | 5,944 | -- |
| Germany | 14,620 | 28,200 | 4,943 | (10) |
| Hong Kong | 14,010 | 32,934 | 3,783 | -- |
| Japan | 13,650 | 25,618 | 5,944 | -- |
| France | 13,590 | 27,586 | 4,271 | (16) |
| UK | 13,060 | 25,806 | 3,789 | (18) |
| Italy | 13,000 | 26,780 | 4,441 | (15) |
| Spain | 8,250 | 16,603 | 2,858 | (19) |
| Ireland | 7,020 | -- | 2,817 | (19) |
| Hungary | 5,920 | 9,599 | 3,225 | -- |
| Korea | 5,680 | -- | 1,893 | 16 |
| Venezuela | 5,650 | 14,308 | 1,329 | -- |
| Mexico | 5,320 | 16,300 | 1,360 | -- |
| Malaysia | 5,070 | 12,953 | 1,154 | 27 |
| Yugoslavia | 4,860 | 10,407 | 1,482 | -- |
| Brazil | 4,620 | 14,469 | 554 | -- |
| Syria | 4,460 | -- | 1,301 | -- |
| Argentina | 4,360 | -- | 1,553 | -- |
| WORLD | 4,340 | -- | -- | -- |
| Costa Rica | 4,320 | 11,789 | 714 | -- |
| Poland | 4,190 | 7,366 | 2,029 | -- |
| Colombia | 3,810 | 10,100 | 762 | -- |
| Panama | 3,790 | 10,500 | 715 | 25 |
| Thailand | 3,280 | 10,600 | 1,050 | 30 |
| Peru | 3,080 | 7,200 | 616 | -- |
| Jamaica | 2,630 | 6,472 | 700 | 80 |
| Botswana | 2,510 | 7,420 | 314 | 51 |
| Guatemala | 2,430 | 6,682 | 637 | 71 |
| Morocco | 2,380 | 4,692 | 1,168 | 37 |
| Philippines | 2,170 | 5,141 | 588 | 58 |
| Sri Lanka | 2,120 | 5,954 | 510 | -- |
| Egypt | 1,930 | 4,900 | 819 | 23 |
| Indonesia | 1,820 | 3,763 | 803 | 39 |
| Pakistan | 1,790 | 4,078 | 695 | 30 |

**Table 1.1:** continued

| | Real GDP per person (PPP$)[1] (1988) | Richest 20 per cent[2] | Poorest 20 per cent[3] | Per cent population below poverty line[4] |
|---|---|---|---|---|
| Cote d'Ivoire | 1,430 | 3,768 | 355 | 28 |
| Kenya | 1,010 | -- | 191 | 44 |
| Ghana | 970 | 2,159 | 315 | 44 |
| India | 870 | 1,802 | 353 | 48 |
| Bangladesh | 720 | 1,336 | 373 | 86 |

*Source:* United Nations Development Programme (1991), Tables 17 and 38, United Nations Development Programme (1992), Technical Note Table 2.3, EUROSTAT (1990), Ross, D.P., and Shillington, R. (1989), Sarpellon, G. (1992).

*Notes:*

(1) Instead of using exchange rates to compare cross-national living standards, measures of income in local currencies have been converted on an internationally comparable scale using **purchasing power parities**. This conversion factor improves the 'real' comparability of international income data but is not ideal, because supplementary measures of the value of income in kind and unwaged services are not available.

(2) Measures of income distribution are taken from one of the years between 1979 and 1989, depending not only on their availability but also, in the case of the richer countries, on the selection in fact made by the international agencies. Thus, for the poor countries illustrated in the table this information applies to one of the years in the mid- and late 1980s; for the rich countries the year selected was 1979 or a year in the early 1980s (see UNDP, 1992, p. 96; World Bank, 1992, p. 227)

(3) Strictly the UNDP provide these data in relation to GNP in exchange rate dollars. However while GDP per person in 'purchasing power parities' is little different in some countries from GNP per person in exchange rate dollars (eg, US, UK, Italy and Ireland) the former is usually three times greater than the latter in designated 'developing' countries. In absence of contrary evidence, I have assumed that the conversion from one to the other applies equally to the poorer and richer ends of the distribution within countries.

(4) The 'poverty line' is defined as 'that income level below which a minimum nutritionally adequate diet plus essential non-food requirements are not affordable'. Figures in brackets illustrate results from latest national surveys in rich countries based on measures linked directly or indirectly to subsistence.

However, this is only a modest start in improving comparability. The value of home production, unpaid family and community services, freely available natural resources, and location as well as environment, are among the complex issues requiring investigation and evaluation. Oversimplification of measurement can mislead those who produce policies as well as those whose job it is to interpret and explain world patterns. On the other hand, technical sophistication is used by elites to establish their ascendency in debates about the interpretation of, as well as action upon, the 'facts'. Some of the documentary work of the United Nations Development Programme in the early 1990s is setting a constructive example. At least the efforts to establish a common basis of international information holds out the prospect of uncovering well-documented examples of advantages which poor countries hold over their rich counterparts.

## Third world destitution

Many millions in the Third World are living at standards which can be described only as those of utter destitution. This can be easily seen by comparing countries at the head and foot of Table 1.1. In 1988 the United States had an income per person approximately 28 times that of Bangladesh. Even the poorest 20 per cent of the United States population had an income per person six times higher than the Bangladesh average.

[...]

There are countries with fewer resources even than Bangladesh. In 1988 16 were listed in the UN Development Programme with fewer resources per person. For many of the poor countries there are no reliable measures of the distribution of income or even of their aggregate resources. And this problem applies particularly to countries in turmoil as a consequence of military occupation, radical change of government, civil war and famine, or a mixture of these events. In the early 1990s the breakup of Yugoslavia, the desperate loss of life in Somalia, the instability created by the warring factions in Afghanistan, the transformation of the Soviet Union into 15 republics, and the plight of the Kurds and the Shi–ite Moslems in Iraq following the Gulf War provide examples of rapid impoverishment of many millions of people. Such dramatic events are often ignored in constructing theories of poverty. Yet they are symptomatic of the swings of fortune which can stabilise in forms of long–lasting oppression or dependency (reminiscent, say, of colonialism and feudalism). They also illustrate again how powerful are the structural forces lurking even in the most orderly of societies which perpetuate extreme poverty and inequalities.

Similarly, the collapse of previously well–regulated cities with the onset of riots, or the continuing abrasive effects of conflict between minorities, as in Northern Ireland, or even with the rapid growth of homelessness and unemployment, are also symptomatic of a sudden rise in the percentage of the population found to experience poverty, and have to be incorporated into general theories of trends. Again, local or regional turbulence of this kind tends to be discounted in country-wide explanations of poverty. To seek reasons can be instructive. Theories which depend primarily on long–term biological, psychological or sub-cultural dispositions of individuals, like those of Martin Anderson (1978), Charles Murray (1984 and 1990) and Milton Friedman (1962), cannot accommodate sea-changes in the pattern of material living standards of a population.

Table 1.1 is intended to illustrate two other features of global living standards. The second and third columns show the incomes, for one of the years between 1979 and 1989, of rich and poor at either end of the spectrum in each country. Each population is divided into fifths. A fifth is of course a substantial section of any population. [...]. The difference between the richest fifth and the poorest fifth is considerable in all countries. But the poor in rich countries share living standards with considerable sections of the populations of the poorest countries. Fifty million people in the United States have little more income than the world's average and less in fact than large sections of the populations in countries like Sri Lanka, the Philippines, Morocco and Egypt. The same applies to other countries of the OECD.

Similar paradoxes apply to measures of poverty, although, because they are less comprehensive or consistent, they cannot be demonstrated quite so categorically. In the fourth column of Table 1.1 measures of the extent of poverty in middle-income and poor countries are reproduced. So far as possible these are measures of income below which 'a minimum nutritionally adequate diet plus essential non-food requirements are not affordable' (UNDP, 1992, pp. 208-9).

I have put corresponding figures for the richer countries in brackets, not because they are less reliable, but to warn that they so often seem to depend in practice on a more rigorous interpretation of subsistence and hence budgetary need. The United States measure, for example, represents a long tradition of estimating the costs of meeting minimum dietary needs, but which accepts that to cover these costs the measure has to allow for non-food costs in nearly the same proportion as found in practice to be allocated in low-income budgets. The point is not inconsequential, and might be applied to Third World measures.

The figures given for the EC countries are based on a poverty line of half average disposable household expenditure. Although that is a relative measure, a number of commentators call attention to its correspondence with subsistence standards constructed in particular countries. As one commentator points out, the approach 'is consistent with viewing poverty in terms of exclusion from the minimum acceptable way of life of the country in which the person lives' (Nolan, 1992, p. 34). [...]

Despite the reservations which have to be made about the comparability of measures of poverty all the international agencies agree that poverty is less prevalent in industrial countries. For example,

> Some 1.4 billion of the world's 5.3 billion people live in poverty. Other estimates suggest that including those living 'along the subsistence margin' with only minimal necessities increases the number of poor to nearly two billion. (UNDP, 1992, p. 17)

About 1.2 billion of the total 1.4 billion are in the developing countries, but 200 millions are in the industrial countries, including about 30 millions in the United States and 100 millions in the former USSR and Eastern Europe (UNDP, 1991, pp. 23-6).

## Dual policy control

Since the rich countries possess the greatest influence over the world's economy and, through their connections with international organisations and multi-national companies, over the global distribution of resources, they hold the key to the changes taking place in the distribution of incomes *within* as well as *between* countries and the percentage of each population found to be in poverty. In general, their advantage has not changed in recent decades, despite development and financial aid programmes drawn up according to prevailing anti-poverty and development theory and despite the adoption of what are conceived to be noble objectives on the part of international organizations.

On certain criteria inequalities have widened and material and social deprivation worsened. Thus, GNP per person grew on average in industrial countries between 1965 and 1989 by 2.4 per cent each year but remained static (or more strictly grew by a tiny 0.1 per cent) in least developed countries (UNDP, 1992, p.37). And within some at least of the richest countries inequalities have widened and poverty increased within their own territories. Yet they are powerful beyond as well as within their own boundaries. Put very simply, they direct the international organisations controlling distribution and redistribution between countries. And they also largely, if decreasingly, control distribution and redistribution of resources within their own territories. This can be characterised as 'dual policy control'. Explanations of poverty in the world must therefore deal centrally with this duality – part national, part international.

## Poverty and inequality in rich countries

Accordingly, Table 1.2 concentrates attention on two countries: the richest country in the world and one which is a representative example of industrial and economic powers of the second rank. Statistical information about trends, inequality and poverty for these two countries is comparatively full. The most striking fact about the United States and the United Kingdom is the sharp increase in inequality in both. My thesis is that rapidly increasing access to international markets, combined with increasing control of the domestic labour market has led to the depression of the incomes of the poor at the same time as the enlargement of the incomes of the rich.

[…]

In both the United States and the United Kingdom the after-tax income of the richest 1 per cent increased even more dramatically, during the 1980s, by three-fifths and by three-quarters respectively. Although polarisation in these two countries has been exceptional, the trend has also been reported for other industrial countries. What has to be better recognised is the shift of capital assets to the richest groups in the population. The 'increase in the real value of wealth-holdings' (Good, 1990, p. 146) has been an important source of enhanced power for the very rich, in addition to their higher real incomes, despite little apparent change in the percentage distribution of marketable wealth.

[…]

The trend in the fortunes of the rich has to be linked firmly with trends in poverty and with the restructuring of the world's economy. It is no accident that the 'underclass' has fared badly while the 'overclass' has been enriched. Both developments have common sources. Between 1979 and 1989, as Table 1.2 shows, the share of 'adjusted family income' going to the poorest 20 per cent of households in the United States fell from 6.4 per cent to 5.6 per cent and real average income (at 1989 values) from 5,536 to 5,420 dollars (representing a percentage fall of 2.1). There was an even sharper decline for families with children. […] Organisations like the National Commission to Prevent Infant Mortality had recommended urgent action to deal with the tragically high levels of infant mortality, and a report on behalf of UNICEF had concluded that a quite modest package of new policies could in fact transform the situation of many children in poverty in the United States (Danziger and Stern, 1990). There is little doubt about the increase in extent and severity of poverty in a decade. In 1990 over 30 millions in the US, or about 13 per cent, were reported to live below the poverty line.

In the same years the share of total after-tax income of the poorest 20 per cent in the United Kingdom also fell, from 9 per cent to 8 per cent even when incomes are rearranged to take account of family size and composition in a formula approved by the government (DSS, 1992). As the lower part of Table 1.2 also shows, there was no gain at all in their disposable income, and in fact there was a fall in the income of the poorest 10 per cent (Hansard, 16 July 1992, and see notes to Table 1.2). […] The statistics issued from the DSS have been greatly delayed and selective in coverage, and measurement (DSS, 1988a and b; 1990a and b; 1992 […]). One report of a substantial rise in lower levels of income turned out to be an error.

[…]

## National and international policies

… [A] necessary basis of the argument for national planning is the argument for international planning. Up to the present time this has attracted even less

**Table 1.2** Trends in income in real terms of richest and poorest 20 per cent in the US and the UK (standardised for household size and composition) 1979-1989

| Country | Share of total disposable income | | | |
|---|---|---|---|---|
| | 1979 | 1989 | Change in percentage share | Ratio richest/ poorest |
| United States[1] | | | | |
| Richest 20% | 39.0 | 42.1 | +3.1 | 7.5 |
| Poorest 20% | 6.4 | 5.6 | -0.8 | |
| United Kingdom | | | | |
| Richest 20% | 36 | 42[2] | +8 | 5.2 |
| Poorest 20% | 9 | 8[2] | -1 | |
| Average annual disposable income per person (in 1989 dollars/pounds) | | | | |
| United States[1] | $ | $ | Increase or decrease | Per cent |
| Richest 20% | 33,883 | 40,811 | +6,928 | +20.4 |
| Poorest 20% | 5,536 | 5,420 | -116 | -2.1 |
| United Kingdom | £ | £ | | |
| Richest 20% | 13,156 | 18,460[3] | +5,304 | +40.3 |
| Poorest 20% | 4,212 | 4,212[3] | 0 | 0 |
| (Poorest 10%) | 3,640 | 3,432[3] | -208 | -5.7 |

*Sources:* United States: Committee on Ways and Means, US House of Representatives (1992), pp. 1356, 1379 and 1383. United Kingdom: Central Statistical Office, *Social Trends* 22, 1991, London, HMSO, Table 5.19 (equivalised disposable income). Written answers to Parliamentary Questions, Hansard 16 July 1992, EUROSTAT (1990), Room (1990).

*Notes:*
(1) Standardisation for household size but not composition (in the US but not the UK adjustments in ranking incomes are made by number of persons, but not by age of children, if any).
(2) 1988.
(3) 1988-9 (in government publications the two years are amalgamated).

notice than national planning. [...] One of the problems is to relate national with international policy analysis. Any account of the pattern of international poverty, as illustrated in Table 1.1, must draw on the nature and effect of aid policies. The rich countries have failed to reach the internationally agreed target of 0.7 per cent of GNP for official development assistance (ODA). The Scandinavian countries and the Netherlands are the exceptions but their resources are small, compared with the United States, Japan and the four most populous states of the EC. The commitment to international redistribution is far smaller than to national redistribution. It has also declined substantially rather than increased – particularly in the wealthiest society on earth, the US, and in other rich countries like the UK and Australia, as Table 1.3 shows. 'Aid' is increasingly recognised across the world to be an unhappy euphemism. The rules and practices of the World Bank, the IMF and the commercial banks have tied the poor countries to neo-colonial policies as well as debt-servicing which has crippled their resources and their capacity to take countervailing action to relieve their own poverty. Responsibility for this outcome rests with the international agencies and the rich countries has been documented over many years (Payer, 1974, 1982 and 1991; Hayter, 1981; Hayter and Watson, 1985; Hunt, 1989; Hancock, 1989 [...]). Eugene Black, a former President of the World Bank who died in 1992 once said

> Our foreign aid programs constitute a distinct benefit to America business. The three major benefits are (1) foreign aid provides a substantial and immediate market for United States goods and services, (2) foreign aid stimulates the development of new overseas markets for US companies, (3) foreign aid orients national economics towards a free enterprise system in which US firms can prosper. (Quoted in Hayter, 1981, p. 83)

Another revealing statement was made by President Nixon in his 1968 presidential campaign: 'Let us remember that the main purpose of American aid is not to help other nations but to help ourselves.'

**Table 1.3** Per cent of the national resources of rich countries committed to overseas development assistance

| | Overseas development assistance – percent GNP per person | | | |
| --- | --- | --- | --- | --- |
| | 1960 | 1970 | 1980 | 1990 |
| Norway | 0.13 | 0.33 | 0.90 | 1.17 |
| Sweden | 0.06 | 0.41 | 0.85 | 0.90 |
| Netherlands | 0.38 | 0.60 | 0.90 | 0.93 |
| Denmark | 0.11 | 0.40 | 0.72 | 0.93 |
| Canada | 0.16 | 0.41 | 0.47 | 0.44 |
| Australia | 0.40 | 0.59 | 0.52 | 0.34 |
| Japan | 0.22 | 0.23 | 0.27 | 0.31 |
| UK | 0.56 | 0.42 | 0.43 | 0.27 |
| USA | 0.56 | 0.31 | 0.24 | 0.19 |

*Source:* United Nations Development Programme (1991), p. 53. United Nations Development Programme (1992), p. 198.

International planning needs to be transformed from a jaundiced preoccupation with financial aid and debt servicing to international minimum wage rates, regulation of work conditions, and domestic taxation to assist people and services in other countries.

## International forces determining structural trends

[...] I have traced the disparities within as well as between countries and shown that in rich and poor countries the problems of poverty often continue to be as bad as ten or more years previously, or are even becoming worse. The policies of international agencies and the activities of multinational companies in fact lie behind the problem in the 1990s of social polarisation and even more endemic poverty. It is a remorseless further segmentation of population into the haves and have-nots, and the development on a substantial scale of Third World conditions in First World territories. Familiar social networks and relationships are unravelling and are taking disconcerting forms – like the dependency among poorer groups induced by professionalisation of the prosperous and rich. It is accompanied by stronger police and bureaucratic controls of minorities, refugees and migrants, partly prompted by rising levels of crime and violence and the retreat of middle classes into high-security enclaves.

This polarisation is beginning to be seen in Europe not so much as an exceptional aberration resulting from the ideologies in government of President Reagan and Prime Minister Thatcher, whereby expenditure on public services and the poor was reduced, public utilities and services privatised, business deregulated, the powers of the trade unions reduced and the enterprise culture lauded, but as the early consequences of a new and much more powerful multinationalism. This is the problem which [I seek] to highlight. International agencies like the World Bank and the IMF have policies of social control whose effects, whether in the 15 new republics of the Commonwealth of Independent States, Afghanistan or the Philippines are certainly not redistributive. The European Community is more 'workerist' or 'economistic' than it is concerned with the total interests of member populations. The EC was instigated to serve free-market principles and has a very long way to go to remedy the 'democratic deficit' and the weakness of institutions like the Social and Regional Funds and the Anti-Poverty Programme. It is more creature than regulator of the international market.

A number of global corporations now have resources substantially larger than most nation-states. Labour markets are more unequal; conditions, including wages, of manual and poorer non-manual workers in the rich countries and not just the Third World are becoming subject to downward pressures and re-casualisation; large-scale unemployment, which had been abolished in some if not all welfare states, is now returning, and national governments are becoming less 'interventionist' because they are subject themselves to the manipulative powers of global corporations and international agencies alike. Why else is redistribution (and fairer distribution) such a feeble political issue in both the US and the UK when all the evidence shows it to be the prime international as well as national problem?

This has been due partly to the collapse of manufacturing employment, the reappearance of casual labour, the emergence of many vulnerable small businesses in response to heavy long-term unemployment, the consequences of privatisation and deregulation in the loss of employment rights in the upward swing of injury and accident rates, the fall in young people's earnings, the growth of homelessness and the resort to theft, and theft with violence. It has been due to the application of successive cuts in social security and the erosion of the necessary basis for successful family activity and productive work. Cross-national evidence confirms that former assumptions about 'trickle-down' of resources must be severely questioned, and even reversed (for example Newman and Thomson, 1989).

[...]

## A theory of poverty

[...]

A [structural] approach [to poverty] must be global, institutional and class-based. I mean that if we have to explain the variations in poverty between different countries we have to explain not merely the unequal distribution of income in its most comprehensive sense but the continuing development of an interrelated set of national cultures or styles of life. The rise and maintenance of forms of social discrimination in law and in the institutions of society has to be laid out. [...]

International institutions do more than provide a context in which this development takes place. They initiate, guide, influence and determine as well. A full account has also to be given of the national as well as international institutions which (i) produce, disseminate and control resources and (ii) establish the norms of social association and activity. And the two-way relationship between these institutions and different layers or classes of international and national populations has to be spelt out.

The functioning of international institutions is a necessary part of the explanation not just of the poverty of what is called the Third World but of poverty within both rich and poor nation-states. At the end of the Second World War the United States was one of the two dominant world powers. This is symbolised by the establishment of the headquarters of the United Nations in New York. The Western powers met at Bretton Woods in New Hampshire in 1944 and set up two instruments for international financial and monetary control: the International Bank for Reconstruction and Development, now known as the World Bank, to provide loans to assist the reconstruction of Europe and Japan, and for the Third World, and the International Monetary Fund to be the regulator of currencies, promoting stable exchange rates and providing liquidity for the free flow of trade. Both of these were established in Washington. The Marshall Plan and what later became known as the Organisation for Economic Co-operation and Development helped to fulfil the plans for the reconstruction of Europe. A parallel organisation, The Council for Mutual Economic Assistance – also known as Comecon – which consisted of the Eastern powers, was established in Moscow.

The analysis of the financial arrangements between nation-states and the rules by which trade can be continued, has to begin with the description of the structure and control of the network of such international organisations. The United Nations and related agencies were developed to deal with different aspects of international poverty – the World Health Organization, the International Labour Organization, the United Nations Educational, Scientific and Culture Organization and so on. Money talks, and the origins and staffing and financing of these organisations helped to explain not only how the pattern of world trade is supervised and disciplined but how world resources are distributed, and wealth is produced at the expense of the poor. In the broadest terms, the various alliances between nation-states, in conjunction with their respective military power, underwrite and institutionalise these inequalities in the distribution of resources.

Until the late 1980s many of the accounts of Third World poverty gave insufficient attention to this international power structure (exceptions were Hoogvelt, 1982; and Hayter, 1981). The first report of the Brandt Commission provided an example. In conformity with most development theory of the 1960s and 1970s it assumed that nation-states are predominantly autonomous. Thus

> the governments and people of the South have the primary responsibility for solving many of their own problems; they will have to continue to generate most of their resources by their own efforts, and to plan to manage their own economies. Only they can ensure that the fruits of development are fairly distributed inside their countries, and that greater justice and equity in the world are matched by appropriate reforms at home. (Brandt Report, 1980; pp. 41-2)

Analytically, this assumption picks up and reinforces the individualistic theories of poverty within nation-states. The victim is blamed. The causal responsibility of the rich is neglected.

The Brandt Commission recognised that there is a crisis of confidence in the world and that new measures are required to prevent the gap between rich and poor countries widening. But their recommendations, namely of more aid, a more powerful voice for the poor countries in trade and the fixing of commodity prices and the establishment of new monetary institutions designed to diminish dependence, can be said to have been unrealistic when compared with the existing distribution of military and financial resources in the world. In some ways the policies recommended were no more than the reformulation of policies which had been tried in the past and failed. The analysis might be said to have avoided the principle issues of the origins of world poverty and to have led to recommendations for change which would not have made much difference to the status quo. That is not to say that such proposals should not be supported if there is no other analysis or policy which has any prospect of attracting political favour and support. Often policy-making is the process of choosing the lesser of different evils.

Criticisms have grown since the late 1980s. Even within the United Nations itself those associated with the UN Development Programme are now beginning to offer critical discussion of aid programmes and especially debt financing (UNDP, 1992). But this has to be balanced with a move on the part 'the World Bank and the International Monetary Fund to a position of financial orthodoxy, and greater subservience on the part of agencies of the UN to the rule of market forces.

The second important element in an 'institutional' theory of poverty is the internationalisation of industry. Transnational corporations have become a major force in the world and some of the biggest are establishing a kind independence of control from any single nation-state. Half the 100 wealthiest powers in the world are transnational corporations and not nation-states. Exxon and Standard Oil, for example, have larger budgets than does Switzerland or Saudi Arabia. A third of all trade can now be traced as being between the different subsidiaries or divisions of the transnational companies rather than between nations. Their power is exercised in the relocation of manufacturing industry in countries of the Third World – like Brazil and South Korea. Labour is cheap and new forms of technology make it possible to restrict the range of skills which have to be taught to, and practised by, partly skilled workers. The manufacture of some products can be divided between countries, so ensuring freedom from national take-overs. Improvement in communications and the development of international professional management makes possible the complex juggling of these huge companies. By switching production from the rich countries to overseas subsidiaries they have weakened the local bargaining power of trade unions.

The emergence of the EC is not unconnected with the growth in fortune of such companies. The European Community has paved the way for the abandonment of tariffs, the liberalisation of trade, the free movement of capital and the relative decline of special subsidies for poor regions. Thus, the European Commission discouraged member states from pursuing certain internal regional policies and has sought to restrict the size of financial inducements offered (Armstrong, 1978). Regional groupings like the EC have been taking over certain powers from national governments to control national economies – without the same mechanisms of union and democratic accountability, and with proportionately fewer resources committed to ameliorative social policies.

The influence of international organisations and transnational corporations upon national economies and upon the distribution of national resources also requires a larger share in any theory of poverty than it has attracted hitherto. For example, a considerable part of the rise in unemployment in Britain is attributable to the relocation of industrial production overseas and the redirection of financial investment to Europe and elsewhere.

Nationally, it is important in explaining the scale and severity of production to examine factors controlling not merely production but the social distribution of employment, and the institutions which govern the allocation of wealth and income. The key factors include the national level of employment; the institutions which govern the inheritance and accumulation of wealth including its scale and distribution; and the institutions which shape and change the wage system, as well as those which govern the scope and rates of the social security system. This helps to explain the distribution of resources.

A second strand of analysis is required to explain how human needs are socially created (which resources are required to satisfy). The state enacts laws, produces regulations and encourages conformist behaviour, which defines 'citizenship' and therefore defines the needs of people in their capacity as citizens. The obligations and expectations naturally carry an implication of cost in order that they be fulfilled. Similarly, the employer fixes the terms and conditions of employment, with some overview from the state, so that the obligations and expectations attached to the 'work role' and therefore the needs of workers may be defined. But people do not only play the roles of citizen and worker. The same line of analysis can be pursued with the roles they play in the community, the family, among friends, as consumers, homemakers and so on. The terms and conditions which define people's membership of groups, and the customs and conventions which they observe naturally as a consequence, also define their needs. At all levels of human association there are powerful forces seeking to influence the specification of what it means to be a member of society and observe social customs and advantages. The state takes an active interest in levels of education, training and skill. Commercial organisations influence patterns of consumption and the performance of family and neighbourly roles. The professions also have high expectations of their clients and set exacting standards of compliance for those who consult them.

It is in following this line of analysis that the full implications of existing class structure can be seen. Thus, the rich are not only the favoured recipients of the allocative mechanisms of society. They play a positive function in at least two respects. They reinforce their own financial power by securing their interests in the financial institutions which reproduce unequal distribution of wealth and income. Second, through the initiatives of the market and also the professions and senior administration they influence and to a large extent construct the national style of living which is to prevail. So the elaborate system of classes is maintained not just by the institutionalised differentiation of the wage system and social security but by the differentiated expression of nationally approved styles of living which class positions denote. People *act* by virtue of class position and not only reflect *status*.

[…]

A structural or institutional theory of poverty would imply radical programmes not just of international aid to Third World countries but the opportunities to develop new forms of manufacturing industry and agricultural production. International action would be required to regulate, and change the pattern of ownership of transnational corporations. Nationally, a more positive approach would have to be taken towards social planning, and especially the coordination of economic and social policies. Instead of the redistributive mechanisms of the social services, emphasis would be placed on the allocative mechanisms of the economy – a fairer distribution of wealth, the withdrawal of the right to inherit vast wealth; the introduction of a less unequal wage system, including a maximum as well as a minimum wage; the extension of incomes to those, especially women, who undertake work which is unpaid; and enlargement of the rights of citizens to participate in the establishment of the institutions and services of the local community. Ideas like 'social planning', 'public service' and 'public ownership' would be rehabilitated.

This kind of strategy envisages a growing need for collaborative international action to reduce global poverty and inequality. It envisages a creative or preventive role for social policy rather than a casualty treatment role. It involves opposition to discrimination in the operation and practice of all institutions. These are the relatively new objectives which can be distilled from the analysis of the current predicaments of international poverty.

[…]

## The prospects for European social policy

### The colonial inheritance

Part of the problem of our present relations with Europe can be traced to the history of the British Empire. During the last two decades new work on the colonial period (for example, Roxborough, 1979; Wallerstein, 1979; Warren, 1980; Frank, 1981; Hoogvelt, 1982; Seers, 1983; Amin, 1990) has caused many observers to look back with fresh understanding upon the international trading and military domination or exploitation of many millions of people, which formed the basis of a system of social and economic inequality that has survived until the present day. The work of dependency and other radical theorists of world development goes on to show that this inequality is being reinforced by the national and international financial, political and trading institutions which have been taking the place of colonial structures (Payer, 1974; Hayter, 1981; Hayter and Watson, 1985). This does of course help us to explain and understand the predicament of the Third World. That kind of retrospective analysis has great value in constructing lessons which may be drawn for the future.

But the consequences for other parties to this relationship, and particularly for the world's former leading colonial power, Britain, may not yet have been properly understood. There are always disadvantages to the rich and not only to the poor when poverty is manufactured. This applies particularly when the form rather than the substance of power is relinquished by the rich. I mean there are social problems for the UK in occupying the lonely status of having been the world's foremost colonial power – for example arrogant self-regard and of maintaining a vast network of ruling or dominant institutions at home as well as overseas.

Once independence was conferred upon country after country in the post-war years itinerant colonial administrators returned. Many were accustomed to privileges and power of a kind impossible for them to now emulate. There were tens of thousands of British men and women with as good education, and more relevant work experience, as themselves. They were frequently ill-fitted to their surroundings and resentful in expressing extreme views. Yet they were a recognisable element of the UK's nationalism and therefore of its stance towards policy. […] The influence of ex-colonials was only one of the consequences of the abandonment of colonial rule. Perhaps internal domestic equality was harder to achieve. Certainly the evolution from Empire to Commonwealth and the history of the Atlantic Alliance were two national experiences which made far more difficult the development of close working relations with member countries of the European Community.

[…]

During the early post-war decades colonialist assumptions helped to reinforce class inequalities at a time when most countries were experiencing some equalisation of class structure. [...] From being a pioneer of world industrialisation in the early nineteenth century and of the welfare state at the end of that century it came a little hard for representatives of the UK to recognise, or admit, that by the late twentieth century it was some way down the rankings of industrialised countries and an 'also-ran' among welfare states. [...]

This colonial inheritance also had an effect on the construction of welfare state institutions and the public perception of the welfare state. Because it was a world imperial power the UK's introduction of welfare in the first half of the twentieth century was closely watched everywhere and widely imitated, or dutifully taken over by dependent colonies. In particular Beveridge's 1942 plan for social security and the Labour Government's introduction in 1948 of the National Health Service were seen as pioneering measures of vast social importance. But the scale and impact of these changes, and their relevance to social development as a whole seems now to have been exaggerated, and certainly the momentum was not sustained under successive governments.

[...] Nonetheless, for many years after the 1939 war there remained in the UK considerable complacency about the welfare state on Right and Left, and widespread disposition on either flank, for different reasons, to exaggerate its scale. We may wryly conclude that the colonial tradition, and especially its invocations of 'greatness' or supremacy helped to maintain not just the illusions of power but also the illusions of welfare.

[...]

## The reluctant Europeans

If the colonial inheritance is one relatively unrecognised influence upon the UK's own social development and policies, Europeanisation is another. The British appear to be the reluctant Europeans. They are Europeans primarily because of economic imperatives. They are reluctant because of the standoffishness induced not only by the imperial tradition but by the traditions of a distinctively class society and one with strong North American connections.

[...]

Much has been made of the UK's ambivalent membership of Europe. It joined later and experienced the economic disadvantages of late but also grudging membership. In their frustration some observers have renewed their appeals for a return to UK sovereignty. The suggestion is that we preserve the capacity to decide our own destiny rather than submit to the collective political decisions of our European partners. This is a mistaken analysis. Class privilege or wealth is in some respects being dressed up as sovereignty. The UK's elites want to resist the threats, as they see it, of a more participative style of business management, stronger public services, greater regulation of the labour market, better social insurance. Old-style class management is preferred to new-fangled European interdependence. But proponents of this view, and their European partners, may be underestimating the remorseless erosion in fact of sovereignty – the fast-growing multinational companies and the general evolution of international market institutions within or behind the evolution of Europe. It is arguable that these pose much bigger threats to social stability in the UK and the rest of Europe alike.

There is a paradox in the behaviour of the present government. On the one hand that government has been responding more swiftly, and more radically to international market forces than any of its European neighbours. This may explain its objections to the attempts by the majority of the members of the European Community to maintain old-style welfare states during the restructuring of the European economy.

On the other hand, it is promulgating an old-fashioned belief in the independence of the nation-state, when such independence is far less viable than ever it was. This may explain its indifference to external causes of new, or deepening, social problems at home, and its ignorance of the need for new strategies and policies which involve European institutions to meet UK as well as continental problems. The question is not whether, but how, to live together. Collective values, collective relationships and collective organisation, have become more necessary just at the time when the Government has been telling us they matter less.

[…]

## The Social Charter

One example of the problem [of developing adequate European social policies] is the debate raging around the Social Charter. In judging the meaning and likely effects of the Social Charter its genesis has to be explained. From the beginning the European Community was what might be called 'economistic'. The objectives and programmes of the Community were governed by relatively short-term economic values. It has to be seen as an organisation seeking to enhance its wealth and its power in relation to the rest of the world. In exchange for the scrapping of national controls like import duties and tariffs among members prosperity could be guaranteed by extending the internal market to all members of the new club and by confronting countries outside with tougher conditions of trade. The freedom of trade was followed closely by free movement of capital and this allowed multinational companies to grow rapidly. It meant also the proliferation of a network of international agencies, including banks, which were no longer so dependent upon the country of origin. [...]

The 'social' was always marginal to the development. This is illustrated by the Social Charter itself – which is workerist rather than collectivist in orientation ([...] Leibfried, 1991). But, to do justice to the original six members, certain social assumptions – like collective bargaining, worker consultation and fairly high levels of support for dependent sections of the population – were taken for granted, though it must be emphasised that this was not so much planned as already provided by the individual welfare states of continental Europe. This gave a basis for consensus in taking decisions on behalf of competitive aggrandisement. But it has not been enlarged by EC measures and constitutional provisions. [...]

There were three major stages in this entire European development. Obstacles to market operations on the part of large corporations and multinational companies were swept away. Second, forms of democratic accountability were, by comparison with the political institutions of individual member states, meagre. And, third, few commitments were made to social developments, services or costs. These three now represent massive problems not just for the European idea itself, but for each of the member countries. They pose the daunting challenge which instruments like the Social Charter are intended to meet.

Let me briefly illustrate the three. First, obstacles to market operations were swept away. To serve the objectives of fair competition the Rome Treaty sought the removal not just of national tariffs but of national subsidies and regulatory devices. This suits multinational companies in various ways. There is the problem of transferring some control of prices from the state to the multinational companies (Murray, 1987). This has far- reaching effects in reducing national independence and control of the national economy. It also means that pricing of components of production can be varied to maximise profit and minimise taxation and other forms of control.

There is the problem of creating greater inequality of employment between regions and of eroding existing employment rights. Since 1979 the UK Government has consistently pursued a policy of deregulation. The Chancellor of the Exchequer, Nigel Lawson, said that the object of policy was to 'remove obstacles to the effective working of markets in general and of the labour market in particular' (*Hansard*, 1985, col. 792). But 'part time employment at low rates of pay, self-employment and various forms of casual work have also increased at the expense of full-time regular employment.' There had been a 'widening of pay inequalities and a lowering of labour standards', the 'removal of the legal floor of rights to wages and employment', and the 'inducement, through the tax and social security system, of low wage employment' (Deakin and Wilkinson, 1989, p. 1).

[…]

After measures to introduce easier market operations the second stage of European development can be said to have been marked by the establishment of relatively weak and contradictory forms of democratic accountability. This can be said to have indirectly enhanced the powers of the market. Forms of democracy long-developed by individual member states assumed lesser importance once EC institutions began to operate. Democratic accountability is badly served by EC institutions. […] The piecemeal development of democratic structures is now believed by some observers to be a major obstacle to desirable European development (Lodge, 1991a and 1991b; Meehan, 1987). […]

Whatever the prospects of democratic reform in the short term, the internationalisation of the market during the last three decades has not been matched by the evolution in Europe of adequate forms of democratic accountability and control. […]

Another revealing example is the growing importance attached by the EC to the principle of 'subsidiarity'. This is the principle that action should not be taken at EC level if it can be taken as effectively at a lower level. […] Subsidiarity is the pretence of restoring sovereignty. Having removed the power of nation-states to act effectively to protect interests threatened by multinational corporations and agencies the EC is now turning back difficult issues to member states and leading them to believe they can exercise powers when such powers are hollow or are at most very weak. […]

The third stage in this evolutionary process has been the meagre backing for social development. The social is even more problematic than the economic and the political. European social policies are already skimpy. The Social Fund is much more narrowly based than originally intended and is limited to measures to relocate and retrain the European unemployed only. […] Few observers expect the Social Charter to have much influence on differential earnings, and even less on the adequacy of social security benefits (see, for example, Blackwell, 1990, pp. 364 and 375). […] The entire anti-poverty programme of the EC is less than the social services budget of the county of Avon, where I live.

There is every reason therefore to regard EC developments with dismay. To begin addressing twenty-first century social problems three major transformations are required: constitutional reform to enable democracy to operate coherently; constitutional reform to confer human and social rights; and legislation on social development and organisation, with corresponding upwards surge in budgetary provision. None of these things have much hope of early fulfilment. Our problem is that as the European Community grows in power – it is mainly a negative power to dismantle the national welfare states without much guarantee of what is to be put in their place. […] The creation of an international welfare state is going to be a very long haul indeed.

## Worker participation in multinationals

If these are the three biggest structural problems what might be done to meet them? Perhaps the most difficult step would be to establish a viable policy for multinationals. The problem is not just one of finding the means of regulating or controlling them. What now has to be added is worker or democratic participation in management. This has become critically important because the state can no longer be expected to be able to police companies, or intervene to the same extent on behalf of workers, especially to achieve full, or relatively full employment, when they become multinational in organisation and character.

[...]

One possibility is the reform of national company laws. The problem here is the impracticality of controlling a company in only one of the 20 or 30 countries in which it might be operating. Efforts have nonetheless been made in EC programmes to encourage 'harmonisation' in this sense. The UK has repeatedly frustrated the programme designed to offer different types of workers one at least of several models of consultation and participation.

[...]

An alternative proposal is to set up European companies under a standard Community law which would apply to all countries in which the company operated, including the one in which it is based. This multinational law might gradually apply to companies extending their operations or proposing mergers with transnational companies. The problem is how to concert political authority to enact enforceable laws in the first place, and secure the objectives of worker participation and social responsible management.

[...]

Little progress has been made with accountability. In Britain there seems to be greater interest in Bills or Charters of individual rights than in concerting democratic authority to challenge if not tame the international market. The Labour Party has declared that unless parliamentary power lost at the national level is replaced at the EC level there will be a 'democratic deficit'. [...] The real problem is to seek a change of direction in the construction of policy. [...] The political challenge is to seek links between national and supra–national agencies – and, indeed to go beyond the EC to meet some of the needs and interests of Third World representatives. Innovations in political consultation, representation and participation are required.

[...] The internationalisation of the UK's social policy is the greatest priority. If it does not take place our politicians will become largely helpless observers of [...] remorseless social polarisation and mass impoverishment [...].

## References

Anderson, M. (1978) *Welfare: The political economy of welfare reform in the United States*, Stanford, CA: Hoover Institution.

Armstrong, H.W. (1978) 'Community regional policy: a survey and critique', *Regional Studies*, vol 12.

Blackwell, J. (1990) 'The EC Social Charter and the Labour Market in Ireland', in *The Single European Market and the Irish Economy*, Dublin, pp 350-80.

Brandt, W. (Chairman) (1980) *North-South: A programme for survival*, London: Pan Books.

Central Statistical Office (1991) *Social Trends*, London: HMSO.

Committee on Ways and Means, US House of Representatives (1992) *Overview of entitlement programs, 1992 Green Book*, Washington, DC, US Government Printing Office.

Danziger, S. and Stern, J. (1990) *The causes and consequences of child poverty in the United States*, Special Sub-series: Child Poverty in Industrialised Countries, UNICEF International Child Development Centre, Florence: UNICEF.

Deakin, S. and Wilkinson, F. (1989) *Labour law, social security and economic inequality*, London: Institute of Employment Rights.

DSS (1988a) Social Services Select Committee: *Benefit levels and a minimum income*, London: Department of Social Security.

DSS (1988b) 'The measurement of living standards for households below average income', *Reply to the Government to the Fourth Report from the Select Committee on Social Services*, Cm 523, London: HMSO.

DSS (1990a) *Households below average income: A statistical analysis 1991-87*, London: Government Statistical Service, July.

DSS (1990b) *The measurement of living standards for households below average income*, Cm 1162, London: HMSO.

DSS (1992) *Households below average income: A statistical analysis 1979-88/9*, Government Statistical Service, London: HMSO.

EUROSTAT (1990) *Poverty in figures*, Luxembourg: EC Statistical Office.

Frank, A.G. (1981) *Crisis in the third world*, London: Heinemann.

Friedman, M. (1962) *Capitalism and freedom*, Chicago, IL: University of Chicago Press.

Good, F.J. (1990) 'Estimates of the distribution of personal wealth', *Economic Trends*, October, pp 137-57.

Hancock, G. (1989) *Lords of poverty: The power, prestige and corruption of the international aid business*, London: Macmillan.

Hayter, T. (1981) *The creation of world poverty*, London: Pluto Press.

Hayter, T. and Watson, C. (1985) *Aid: Rhetoric and reality*, London: Pluto Press.

Hoogvelt, A.M.M. (1982) *The third world in global development*, London: Macmillan.

Hunt, D. (1989) *Economic theories of development*, Hemel Hempstead: Harvester Wheatsheaf.

Leibfried, S. (1991) 'Europe's could-be social state: social policy and post-1992 European integration', Presentation to a conference in Ann Arbor, Michigan, on Europe after 1992, 6-7 September 1991.

Lodge, J. (1991a) *The democratic deficit and the European Parliament*, Discussion Paper No 4, London: Fabian Society.

Lodge, J. (1991b) 'European Union and the democratic deficit', *Social Studies Review*, March, pp 149-53.

Meehan, E. (1987) 'Women's equality and the European Community', in F. Ashton and G Whitting (eds) *Feminist theory and practical policies*, Bristol: School for Advanced Urban Studies, pp 42-70.

Murray, C. (1984) *Losing ground: American social policy, 1950-1980*, New York, NY: Basic Books.

Murray, C., with Field, F., Brown, J.C., Walker, A. and Deakin, N. (1990) *The emerging British underclass*, London: Institute of Economic Affairs, Health and Welfare Unit.

Murray, R. (ed) (1987) *Multinationals beyond the market: Intra-firm trade and the control of transfer pricing*, Harvester Studies in Development, in association with the Institute of Development Studies, University of Sussex, Hemel Hempstead: Harvester Wheatsheaf.

Newman, B.A. and Thompson, R.J. (1989) 'Economic growth and social development: a longitudinal analysis of causal priority', *World Development*, pp 461-71.

Nolan, B. (1992) 'The European Community's poverty measures', *Radical Statistics*, 51.

Payer, C. (1974) *The debt trap: The IMF and the Third World*, Harmondsworth: Penguin.

Payer, C. (1982) *The World Bank: A critical analysis*, MRP.

Payer, C. (1991) *Lent and lost: Foreign credit and third world development*, London: Zed Books.

Ross, D.P. and Shillington, E.R. (1989) *The Canadian fact book on poverty – 1989*, Ottowa/Montreal: Canadian Council on Social Development.

Roxborough, I. (1979) *Theories of underdevelopment*, London: Macmillan.

Sarpellon, G. (1992) 'Presidente Commissione d'Indagine sulla Poverta e l'Emarginazione', *Secondo Rapporto sulla Poverta in Italia*, Milan: Franco Angeli.

Seers, D. (1983) *The political economy of nationalism*, Oxford: Oxford University Press.

United Nations Development Programme (1991) *Human development report, 1991*, Oxford/New York, NY: Oxford University Press.

United Nations Development Programme (1992) *Human development report, 1992*, Oxford/New York, NY: Oxford University Press.

Wallerstein, I. (1979) *The capitalist world economy*, Cambridge: Cambridge University Press.

Warren, W. (1980) *Imperialism, pioneer of capitalism*, London: New Left Books.

World Bank (1992) *World development report*, Oxford: Oxford University Press.

# 7

# The need to construct an international welfare state

During the last half-century, the conventional wisdom has been that poverty can be diminished automatically through economic growth. This has got to change. During the next half-century, the world's most fundamental problem – as agreed by the biggest international agencies and a growing number of governments – is that wealth and poverty are becoming increasingly polarised, and that a different priority has to be followed.
[...]

## Building on international agreement

[I]f we are to adopt practical policies to reduce the two problems of poverty and social exclusion, we need to be clear about how to distinguish them, as well as how they are to be applied cross-nationally, rather than erratically and variously in different cultures. I say 'erratically' because the links between country- or region-specific definition and international definition have neither been investigated thoroughly nor justified – even when we can acknowledge that the research in question is helpful in understanding some internal conditions. 'Erratically' also, because the absence of scientific precision makes for political ambiguity – the great escape for holders of wealth. 'Erratically' too in relation to the international agencies. Here the World Bank's adoption of the crude criterion of $1 per day at 1985 prices for the poorest countries, $2 per day for Latin America, and $4 per day for the transitional economies, without regard to the changing conditions of needs and markets, affronts science as it affronts reasoned development of priorities in international policies. In 1997, UNDP topped this absurdity by suggesting that the US criterion of $14.4 per day might be applied to the Organisation for Economic Co-operation and Development (OECD) countries (UNDP, 1997).

If measurement is arbitrary and irrational, it is impossible either to concoct the right policies for the alleviation or eradication of poverty, or monitor

Extracts (pp 3, 5-6, 9-19) from Townsend, P. (2002) 'Poverty, social exclusion and social polarisation: the need to construct an international welfare state', in P. Townsend and D. Gordon (eds) *World poverty: New policies to defeat an old enemy*, Bristol: The Policy Press, pp 3-24.

their effects closely. The World Bank persists broadly with the anti-poverty approach of the 1960s, despite continuing evidence of that approach's failure. Thus, following reports in the early 1990s (for example, World Bank, 1990, 1993), there was little sign in the Bank's reports of the mid- and late 1990s of a change in the threefold strategy that continued to be stated time and again:

- broad-based economic growth;
- development of human capital;
- social safety nets for vulnerable groups (World Bank, 1996, 1997a, 1997b, 1997c; Psacharapoulas et al, 1997).

Each of these three requires detailed exposition, documentation and discussion.

The job of social policy analysis is to keep alive alternative strategies and policies that seem to fit the account of global problems and needs. For purposes of illustration, one alternative strategy might consist of:

- equitable tax and income policies;
- an employment creation programme;
- regeneration or creation of collective, or 'universal', social security and public social services;
- accountability and a measure of social control of transnational corporations and international agencies.

There are no signs yet of a debate taking place about the merits of even two alternative strategies, or sets of policies, to establish beyond reasonable doubt which alternative is the most successful – or indeed popular in democratic terms – in reducing poverty and contributing to social development.

We are dealing here with a strategy that has become the conventional wisdom and that wields extraordinary influence throughout the world. We are compelled to elucidate the international social impact of recent models of monetarist theory and neoliberalism.

The discussion of these doctrines cannot be conducted in (over)generalised terms. We have to examine the text and outcomes of international agreements…. We have to review scientific evidence about key issues, such as economic growth. For example, does the empirical evidence that growth is 'trickle-up' oblige us to abandon the blithe assumptions about 'trickle-down' that have been taken for granted for many years (Newman and Thomson, 1989)?

[…]

## Explaining polarisation

### Defective structural adjustment policies

What are the reasons for this structural change? There is an international analysis that has to be tied in with nationally circumscribed investigation. What has to be accepted is the increasing impact of international developments on national subgroups and local populations. I mean that exposition of familiar problems to do with gender, ageing, disabilities, and families with children, for example, now displays overriding international determinants. I mean also that local problems, such as conflict on inner city housing estates, drugs, closure of local factories, and unsatisfactory privatisation of local services, are generated or enlarged by global market and other international factors.

Among the major policies of the international agencies, national governments and transnational corporations, for which a powerful consensus had been built up during the 1980s and 1990s, are the stabilisation, liberalisation, privatisation and welfare targeting and safety net programmes adopted as a result of the worldwide influence of monetarist theory. For example, the so-called *stabilisation and structural adjustment programmes*, that were advocated and supported by the international agencies, have entailed the reduction of subsidies on food, fuel and other goods, retrenchments in public employment, cuts in public sector wages and other deflationary measures. This not only generates recession, but also distributional outcomes which, as Cornia has argued (1999, pp 11-12) are adverse in the poorer countries compared with industrialised countries, where wage systems are strongly institutionalised and self protecting, and where long-established social security provides a better cushion for downturns in the economy. Policies to cut public expenditure, and target welfare on the poorest (for example through means testing and the introduction of healthcare charges), have increased inequality and perpetuated poverty, especially in countries where, because of globalised trade and growing influence of transnational corporations, there has been a particularly rapid concentration of wealth.

In recognising what policies have brought about greater inequality within and between countries we have to understand the similarity of the programmes influencing developments throughout the world, at the same time as we recognise that they are calculated to vary in extent and force in different regions. The terminology is not always consistent. Governments as well as international agencies are often eager to adopt new names for conformist (rather than 'convergent') policies, especially when evidence that they are not working begins to accumulate.

In a remarkable shift from its long-standing policies, the World Bank has admitted that poverty has tended to increase during recessions in sub-Saharan

Africa, Eastern Europe, and Latin America and not to decrease to the same extent during economic recoveries. Examples were given in a report showing that "crises and recessions may result in irreversible damage to the poor: malnutrition or death from starvation (in extreme cases) and lower schooling levels" (World Bank, 1999, p 109). Higher food prices in the stabilisation programme in Côte d'Ivoire and elsewhere are cited. "Sudden fluctuations in income or food availability can be fatal to already malnourished children." Consequences include lower IQ, retarded physical growth, mental disabilities, lower resistance to infections, and associated problems like dropout from schools (World Bank, 1999, p 103; see also Huther et al, 1997).

Greater sensitivity to the encroachments of poverty also helps to explain the reactions of the international agencies to the financial crisis in East and South East Asia. The magic wand of liberalisation and structural adjustment programmes could no longer be waved, as it had been in Latin America and Africa and then in Eastern Europe and the Commonwealth of Independent States (and in similar strategic form in the industrial countries). The World Bank expected poverty rates, especially in Indonesia, to rise very sharply. Revealingly, the Bank no longer emphasises privatisation and extreme targeting. At one point it even suggests that the possible remedies in a difficult situation "include waiving charges for the poor and extending health care to workers dismissed from their jobs" (World Bank, 1999, p 109).

## The concentration of hierarchical power

Due to deregulation and privatisation by governments, often at the behest of international agencies, control of labour markets has veered away from states and towards transnational corporations. Paradoxically, states in which the headquarters of the biggest transnational corporations are located have acquired greater power to influence global economic developments. The G7, or G8, has exerted influence on the development of world trade (for example through the World Trade Organization and the Multilateral Investment Agreement), and the management of debt.

Therefore, in trade the emphasis on exports from the poorer countries was supposed to favour rural agricultural production and diminish poverty, by removing the imbalance between rural and urban living standards. This has not worked, partly because of the low wages induced by cash cropping, and the corresponding substitution of employed labour and technology for subsistence farming. This has also had a knock-on weakening effect on the vitality of urban markets. In many countries, self-sufficiency in growing a range of crops has given way to a precarious dependence on sales from the export of those crops to finance the purchase of imports at affordable prices. Transnational companies have exceptional power to cut the costs of what they buy and raise the costs of what they sell.

The growth of transnational companies is one of the greatest economic and social changes of the late 20th century. Only 25 countries of the world are now listed as having larger GDP than the annual value of the sales of the biggest transnational corporation – General Motors. The top ten transnational corporations (General Motors, Ford Motor, Mitsui, Mitsubishi, Itochu, Royal Dutch Shell Group, Marubeni Sumitomo, Exxon and Toyota Motor) have bigger sales than the GDP of Malaysia, Venezuela and Colombia, and some of them more than Saudi Arabia, South Africa, Norway, Greece and Thailand. New Zealand's GDP is dwarfed by the sales of each of these corporations, and Australia accounts for only about three times the value of the average sale of all ten (UNDP, 1999, pp 32, 184-7).

The social policies of transnational corporations take at least two forms. On the one hand their internal policies, in relation to their senior staff and permanent and temporary workers scattered through subsidiary companies in many different countries, have to be explained. On the other, the larger role they play in contributing to social change, by influencing developments in world trade, government taxation and redistribution and investment, as well as recommendations for privatisation, also has to be explained (ILO, 1989; Lang and Hines, 1994; Deacon et al, 1997; Hoogvelt, 1997; Kozul-Wright and Rowthorn, 1998).

There are serious shortcomings in both national and international company and social law in relation to transnationals. While capable of contributing positively to social development, one review found that few of them were doing much of consequence. The activities of some were positively harmful (Kolodner, 1994). Recent books on transnational corporations (for example, Korten, 1996) have been assembling a case that governments and international agencies are going to find hard to ignore.

One feature of mergers between companies and the absorption of workforces overseas into the subsidiaries of corporations is not just the extension of the labour force accountable to management, but the elaboration as well as extension of the hierarchy of pay and rights in the corporation. There are many layers in workforces consisting of scores of thousands, sometimes hundreds of thousands, of employees working full-time, part-time, permanently and temporarily in 50, 60 or even more countries. Salaries at the top have been elevated, those at the bottom depressed.

[…]

The evolving hierarchy comprises new occupational sets, ranks and classes, involving housing and locality, and not simply workplace. Ideas of supra- and subordination are played out internationally as well as nationally and locally, and are carried over from one context to the other. This evolving hierarchy is also reflected in the development of the interrelationships of states and international agencies – by means of disproportionate representation among senior personnel, origins of finance for research, and responsibility for the publication of statistical and other information to the media. There are different senses in which social stratification is becoming strongly internationalised.

## Privatisation

The international financial agencies have been eager to encourage privatisation. They argue that:

- it would enhance global market competition;
- it would weaken the intervening role of the state and reduce government taxation, so that public expenditure in general, and public services in particular, would cost less;
- private companies would have greater freedom to manage their affairs as they wanted.

However, the agencies have thereby adopted a very narrow interpretation of the economic good, and have tended to ignore the fact that economic development is an integral part of social development.

World Bank advocacy of privatisation is explicit or implied in almost every published report of recent years – even in relation to poverty. A key text for the Bank's position was published in 1997. Its author, Pierre Guislain, is a development specialist who has advised many African countries on their privatisation programmes. The book (Guislain, 1997) covers a lot of ground and is testimony to the accelerating scale across the world of privatisation. However, its attempts to be dispassionate are not successful. The arguments especially for public service and cooperative companies are largely absent, and there are no conclusions about the balance that might be struck between the public and private sectors in particular contexts and according to particular objectives. There is a strange indifference to the historical reasons for the growth of public ownership and the welfare state. Certainly there is no dispassionate argument about alternative strategies.

Another Bank report looks at privatisation in different countries and the rapid growth of equity markets in these same countries (Liebermann and Kirkness, 1998). The book interprets the process favourably. Privatisation is said to 'kick-start' newly created capital markets, such as those in Central and Eastern Europe and the Commonwealth of Independent States. It can 'awaken' moribund markets in Egypt and much of Latin America. Examples of well-publicised privatisation programmes in Argentina and Mexico are compared with the less well-known 'achievements' in Egypt, Morocco and Peru. "There are many more privatisations to come in developing and transition economies" (Liebermann and Kirkness, 1998).

In the analysis of many experts, much is made of the necessity of financial deregulation and the privatisation of insurance and the pension funds in order to create the right market conditions. The conflict of public interest in relation to the historical establishment of social insurance (for good reasons) is not discussed.

The rapid growth of privatisation is not, even now, widely appreciated. In 1989 the gross annual revenue from the process was estimated to be $25 billion. In 1994 and 1995 annual revenue reached $80 billion. Over five years $271 billion were generated. By the mid–1990s the developing and 'transition' countries accounted for much of the revenue. Guislain concludes that privatisation is "likely to remain a key policy instrument in many countries for decades to come" (1997, p 3; see also Lieberman and Kirkness, 1998).

Assets have often been sold extraordinarily cheaply, by market standards. Academic reviews, as in the UK, have failed to demonstrate evidence of privatisation being successful in terms of growth and price. There are examples either way (see, for example, Parker and Martin, 1997).

### The shortcomings of targeting and safety nets

In developing their structural adjustment programmes, first in Latin America and Africa, and then in the 'transition' countries of Eastern Europe and the former Soviet Union, the IMF and the World Bank tried to balance the unequal social consequences of liberalisation, privatisation and cuts in public expenditure with proposals to target help on the most vulnerable groups in the population. For some years, and still to a large extent today, this has been presented within the principle of means testing. Even if coverage was poor, large sums of money would be saved if the 'almost poor' were no longer subsidised by public funds.

Therefore, a report for the IMF (Chu and Gupta, 1998) seeks to pin responsibility on the transition countries for a failure to transform universal services into targeted and partly privatised services. Unfortunately, this report also reveals serious amnesia about the institutional history of the introduction of legislation establishing public services and social security in particular (see, for example, pp 90-2, 111-12). Ways in which former universal provisions might be modified to allow market competition to grow but not create penury among millions were not seriously considered.

IMF loan conditions demanding lower government expenditures in the poorest countries have led to sharp reductions in general social spending at a time when the poorest fifth of the population in those countries have been receiving only about half their share of education and health expenditures – thus making access worse. This is evidence drawn from the IMF's own studies (IMF, 1997), which shows that "the poorest three-fifths of these nations are being excluded from whatever social 'safety net' exists for education, health, housing and social security and welfare" (Kolko, 1999, p 56).

However, loan conditionalities affect economic security in other ways. There are cuts in the number of government employees and in their salaries, and there are private sector cuts and lay-offs, both of which are designed to raise cost-effectiveness in the world's export markets. Price subsidies for commodities such as bread and cooking oil are cut. Higher value added taxes that are advocated are regressive on income distribution.

In December 1987, the IMF introduced a new stage of its existing structural adjustment programme – the 'Enhanced Structural Adjustment Facility' (ESAF). Of the 79 countries eligible for these ESAF loans – on condition they complied with the IMF in setting "specific, quantifiable plans for financial policies" – 36 had done so. Since World Bank aid also depends on fulfilling IMF criteria there is intense pressure on governments to accede. Critics have now concluded that countries which stayed out of the ESAF programme "began and remained better off by not accepting its advice". Those accepting the programme "have experienced profound economic crises: low or even declining economic growth, much larger foreign debts, and the stagnation that perpetuates systemic poverty". The IMF's own studies provided "a devastating assessment of the social and economic consequences of its guidance of dozens of poor nations" (Kolko, 1999, p 53).

The problem applies sharply to rich and not only poor countries. The biggest struggle of the coming years is going to be between restriction of social security, or 'welfare', largely to means-tested benefits. Those who have assembled evidence for different European countries over many years (for example, van Oorschot, 1999) point out that such policies are poor in coverage, administratively expensive and complex, provoke social divisions, are difficult to square with incentives into work, and tend to discourage forms of saving. What is notable is the recent tempering of World Bank and other agency reactions. It is now conceded that targeting can include 'categorical' policies affecting vulnerable or disadvantaged groups in the population. The prime example of this shift in policies is the social crisis in Eastern Europe and the former Soviet Union (UNDP, 1998).

The World Bank has itself begun to offer grudging concessions. "Safety nets are programmes that protect a person or household against two adverse outcomes: chronic incapacity to work and earn (chronic poverty), and a decline in this capacity from a marginal situation that provides minimal means for survival; with few reserves (transient poverty)." Although social insurance programmes constitute the most dominant form of cash transfer in most countries of Eastern Europe and the former Soviet Union, and provide relief for the poor in the formal sectors, these programmes are not addressed here because issues pertaining to pensions were the focus of a recent World Bank policy study (Fox, 1994 as reported in World Bank, 1997a, pp 2-3).

This is a revealing qualification. When structural adjustment programmes began to be applied in the early 1990s to Eastern Europe and the former Soviet Union, it was clear they would compound the problems of poverty, following liberalisation. Social insurance, and social security generally, were a substantial part of the institutional infrastructures of these states, and the collapse of industry might have led to some external efforts to maintain at least a residual system in order to protect people, especially children, the disabled and the elderly, from the worst forms of destitution and even starvation. Unhappily World Bank and IMF teams lacked expertise in such institutions. They were also influenced by a prevailing ideology of the 'short, sharp shock' following the collapse of communism. An additional factor was that social security systems were weak if not non-existent in the poorest developing countries, and the possibility that structural adjustment as applied to those countries was inappropriate in Eastern Europe.

From an anti-poverty perspective one analyst of events in the former Soviet Union concludes:

> Consideration of social policy has hitherto been dominated by fiscal considerations, which has led to radical proposals for reform of the pension and benefits systems which would have devastating consequences if they did not work as intended. The dependence of many households on age-related pensions and the inability of the majority of wage-earners to support even one dependant make the preservation of the real value of retirement pensions and the restoration of the real value and regular payment of child benefit much the most effective anti-poverty measures in a context in which the introduction of means-tested social assistance is completely unrealistic. (Clarke, 1999, p 240)

A report from UNDP is the most explicit concession yet to the need for change in development policies (UNDP, 1998). In describing the growth of poverty in the early 1990s in Eastern Europe and the former Soviet Union this concedes the strengths of the former institutions of social security.

> Policy-makers attempted to create a relatively egalitarian society free from poverty. Socialist income policy was based upon two main objectives: 1) To ensure a minimum standard of living for all citizens; and 2) To achieve a relatively flat income distribution. (1998, p 90)

Governments regulated overall salaries and fixed minimum wages high enough to ensure a basic standard of living.... At the core of the social security systems were work-related contributory insurance programmes. The public came to expect that most social benefits would depend upon work-related factors such as years spent on the job and wages earned.... Social insurance schemes were comprehensive. Pensions, like employment, were virtually guaranteed.... Social insurance itself covered numerous exigencies, including accidents, sickness, parental death and child birth.... Overall, means-tested social benefits were almost non-existent, representing on average less than 1% of GDP. This was due largely to the inefficiency and high administrative costs associated with means-testing programmes.

> The *socially inclusive* advantages of these schemes was recognised. Therefore, pension programmes "became a kind of contract between generations, whereby people invested their efforts in the collective welfare and were rewarded by a guarantee of supplemental income.... Because social assistance allowances are very low in all transition countries, moving pensions towards means-tested social assistance programmes would push practically all pensioners into poverty" (UNDP, 1998, pp 108-9).

All in all, this is the first substantial acknowledgement from any of the international agencies I have read in the last ten years that the 'socialist welfare state' actually had certain strengths (see, in particular, UNDP, 1998, pp 92-3). What is striking is that the authors go on to claim there is a consensus for active labour market policies and work for social benefits as necessary components of the social insurance system. "At the core of welfare policy ... there must also be a comprehensive social insurance scheme that compensates all people in time of need" (UNDP, 1998, p 105). Funding should be both public and private forms of 'Pay-As-You-Go'. "Categorical benefits should be offered to all in need, or at least to all those near or below the poverty line. It is very important to avoid providing support only to the 'poorest of the poor' while neglecting the relatively poor" (UNDP, 1998, p 105). This plea for group or 'categorical' benefits in place of means-tested benefits was qualified by a recognition that some such benefits could be conditional in different ways.

## Conclusion: the invention of the international welfare state

Where does this analysis lead? [...] An alternative international strategy and set of policies concerned with arresting the growth of inequality and radically reducing poverty has been outlined.... The 1995 World Summit on Social Development in Copenhagen provides a good precedent of the model of theory, strategy and policy that we are seeking to develop (UN, 1995). However, it will be evident [...] that, despite its strengths, the Copenhagen Agreement and Programme of Action, failed to address, or illustrate, the key explanatory concept of social polarisation [...] in its necessary relationship with concerns about growing poverty and social exclusion.

What elements might [an] overall international strategy include? First, unless a scientific consensus is achieved in operationally defining, and measuring, international forms of poverty and social exclusion, the fact that the defeat of poverty worldwide has been put at the top of the international agencies' agenda will turn out to be empty rhetoric. Perhaps one hope is to build on the 1995 World Summit agreement to measure, and monitor, agreed definitions across countries of 'absolute' and 'overall' poverty (Gordon et al, 2000; Gordon and Townsend, 2000)

Second, unless, the *policy-related causes* of poverty and social exclusion are properly traced and publicised in relation to structural trends in all societies, we will find it difficult to discriminate effectively between what are the successful, unsuccessful and even counterproductive measures working towards, or against, the agreed objectives.

Third, since poverty and social exclusion can neither be traced nor explained except in the context of the structural changes embodied in social polarisation, it is this phenomenon that has to be explained.

The effect of policies that have been tried has to be clarified. The *stabilisation and structural adjustment programmes* of the 1980s and 1990s are alleged to have contributed to growing inequality. Policies contributing to the *institutionalisation of unequal power* are argued to deepen that process. Far more attention has to be given to the entire hierarchical *system*, and especially rich institutions and rich individuals at the top. The international agencies, regional associations and national governments must begin to analyse the extraordinary growth of transnational corporations, and ask what reasonable limits can be placed upon their powers. All that has happened so far is that agencies such as OECD have issued 'guidelines' exhorting corporations to be socially responsible. The International Labour Organization (ILO) has gone further. In 1977 its governing board put forward a declaration. This sought to exert influence upon governments, concluding that gradual reinforcement could pave the way for "more specific potentially binding international standards", turning codes of conduct into "the seed of customary rules of international law" (ILO, 1989). Policies contributing to the occupational structures or systems of transnational companies seem to deserve special examination.

Agencies have tended to be shy of relating observed impoverishment or unemployment to the policies of transnational corporations. And they have not been keen on self-examination either. Their growing role in shaping social as well as economic development badly needs critical examination. This has sometimes been provided by outside observers (Payer, 1982, 1991;

Deacon et al, 1997; Hoogvelt, 1997) but needs to be addressed institutionally by governments and the agencies themselves.

*Privatisation* policies are a key element. They have been initiated and encouraged by the international agencies, but without much attention being paid to the problems of creating a much weaker public sector. Some of the biggest transnational corporations have adopted a 'Big Brother' relationship with the public sector. This could damage national identity and cohesion and divide society. Research is needed, for example, to systematically compare the performance of the public and private sectors in different fields, and recommend what is the right mix (as well as how the two might be reconstituted).

Policies representing the principles, or ideologies, of *targeting and safety nets* also deserve better assessment. There are grave doubts that they provide the right strategy to compensate for the inequalities and impoverishment induced by liberalisation and the enhanced power of markets. The international agencies are beginning to recognise that, as policy, means testing is neither easy to introduce nor successful. The advantages of modernised social insurance, for developing as well as industrialised countries, are beginning to earn renewed international interest. This is a sign of hope.

There are of course new policies that have to be found as well as existing policies that deserve to be abandoned or corrected if the damaging structural trend of social polarisation is first to be halted, and then turned round. There seem to be two stages. At the first stage the whole critique has to be pulled together and made more forceful. This includes the reformulation of the measurement of poverty, social exclusion and unemployment. It includes insistence on the monitoring and determined fulfilment of international agreements. And it includes the mobilisation of new coalitions or alliances across countries – of parties, unions, campaigning groups and voluntary agencies – to question the conventional wisdom and promote alternative strategies. At the second stage measures for international taxation, regulation of transnational corporations and international agencies, reform of representation at the UN, and new guarantees of human rights, including minimal standards of income, have to be introduced and legally enforced.

New legal and political institutions for social good in a global economy have to be built. A start would come with new international company and taxation law, combined with the modernisation and strengthening of social insurance and more imaginative planning and investment in basic services, such as health and education, so that they reflect international and not just national or regional standards.

This amounts to calling for an *international* welfare state (Townsend, with Donkor, 1996). One hundred years ago, different governments, including those of Britain and Germany as well as of smaller countries like New Zealand and Norway, responded to the manifest problems of poverty in those days. There were innovations which led to the establishment of national welfare states and a more civilised form of economic development.

Early in the 21st century the prospect of even greater social self-destruction, experienced as an accompanying feature of social polarisation, looms before us – unless urgent countervailing measures are taken. Collaborative scientific and political action to establish a more democratic and internationalised legal framework to protect human living standards has become the first priority.

## References

Chu, Ke-Y. and Gupta, S. (eds) (1998) *Social safety nets: Issues and recent experiences*, Washington, DC: IMF.

Clarke, S. (1999) *New forms of employment and household survival survival in Russia, Coventry and Moscow*, Coventry/Moscow: Centre for Comparative Labour Studies, University of Warwick/Institute for Comparative Labour Relations Research.

Cornia, G.A. (1999) *Social funds in stabilisation and adjustment programmes*, Research for Action 48, Helsinki: UNU World Institute for Development Economic Research.

Deacon, B. with Hulse, M. and Stubbs, P. (1997) *Global social policy: International organisations and the future of welfare*, London: Sage Publications.

Gordon, D. and Townsend, P. (eds) (2000) *Breadline Europe: The measurement of poverty*, Bristol: The Policy Press.

Gordon, D., Adelman, A., Ashworth, K., Bradshaw, J., Levitas, R., Middleton, S., Pantazis, C., Patsios, D., Payne, S., Townsend, P. and Williams, J. (2000) *Poverty and social exclusion in Britain*, York: Joseph Rowntree Foundation (www.bris. ac.uk/poverty/pse/).

Guislain, P. (1997) *The privatization challenge: A strategic, legal and institutional analysis of international experience*, Washington, DC: World Bank.

Hoogvelt, A. (1997) *Globalisation and the postcolonial world: The new political economy of development*, Basingstoke, Hampshire and London: Macmillan.

Huther, J., Roberts, S. and Shah, A. (1997) *Public expenditure reform under adjustment lending: Lessons from the World Bank Experience*, World Bank Discussion Paper no 382, Washington, DC: World Bank.

ILO (International Labour Organization) (1989) *The ILO tripartite declaration of principles concerning multinational enterprises and social policy – Ten years after*, Geneva: ILO.

Kolko, G. (1999) 'Ravaging the poor: the International Monetary Fund indicted by its own data', *International Journal of Health Services*, vol 29, no 1, pp 51-7.

Kolodner, E. (1994) *Transnational corporations: Impediments or catalysts of social development?*, Occasional Paper no 5, Geneva: World Summit for Social Development, UNRISD.

Korten, D.C. (1996) *When corporations rule the world*, London: Earthscan Publications.

Kozul-Wright, R. and Rowthorn, R. (1998) *Transnational corporations and the global economy*, Helsinki: UNU World Institute for Development Economic Research.

Lang, T. and Hines, C. (1994) *The new protectionism: Protecting the future against free trade*, London: Earthscan Publications.

Lieberman, I.W. and Kirkness, C.D. (eds) (1998) *Privatisation and emerging equity markets*, Washington, DC: World Bank and Flemings.

Newman, B. and Thomson, R.J. (1989) 'Economic growth and social development: a longitudinal analysis of causal priority', *World Development*.

Parker, D. and Martin, S. (1997) *The impact of privatisation*, London: Routledge.

Payer, C. (1982) *The World Bank: A critical analysis*, New York, NY: Monthly Review Press.

Payer, C. (1991) *Lent and lost: Foreign credit and Third World development*, London and New Jersey: Zed Books.

Psacharapoulos, G., Morley, S., Fiszbein, A., Lee, H. and Wood, B. (1997) *Poverty and income distribution in Latin America: The story of the 1980s*, World Bank Technical Paper no 351, Washington, DC: World Bank.

Townsend, P. with Donkor, K. (1996) *Global restructuring and social policy: An alternative strategy: Establishing an international welfare state*, International Seminar on Economic Restructuring and Social Policy, sponsored by UNRISD and UNDP, United Nations, New York, 1995, Bristol: The Policy Press.

UN (United Nations) (1995) *The Copenhagen Declaration and Programme of Action: World Summit for Social Development*, New York, NY: UN.

UNDP (United Nations Development Programme) (1997) *Human development report 1997*, New York and Oxford: Oxford University Press.

UNDP (1998) *Poverty in transition*, Regional Bureau for Europe and the CIS, New York, NY: UNDP.

UNDP (1999) *Human development report 1999*, New York and Oxford: Oxford University Press.

van Oorschot, W. (1999) *Targeting welfare: On the functions and dysfunctions of means-testing in social policy*, Research in Europe Budapest conference on developing poverty measures.

World Bank (1990) *World development report 1990: Poverty*, Washington, DC: World Bank.

World Bank (1993) *Implementing the World Bank's strategy to reduce poverty: Progress and challenges*, Washington, DC: World Bank.

World Bank (1996) *Poverty reduction and the World Bank: Progress and challenges in the 1990s*, Washington, DC: World Bank.

World Bank (1997a) *Safety net programs and poverty reduction: Lessons from cross-country experience*, Washington, DC: World Bank.

World Bank (1997b) *Poverty reduction and the World Bank: Progress in fiscal 1996 and 1997*, Washington, DC: World Bank.

World Bank (1997c) *World development report 1997: The state in a changing world*, Washington, DC and New York, NY: Oxford University Press.

World Bank (1999) *Global economic prospects and the developing countries 1998/99: Beyond financial crisis*, Washington, DC and New York, NY: Oxford University Press.

# 8

# 'Absolute' and 'overall' poverty: the 1995 Copenhagen approach to the fulfilment of human rights

Among the innovations agreed by 117 countries in the 1995 *Copenhagen Declaration and Programme of Action* was the preparation of national anti-poverty plans based on measures in all countries, rich and poor, of 'absolute' and 'overall' poverty. The aim was to link, if not reconcile, the difference between First and Third World conceptions, allow more reliable comparisons to be made between countries and regions, and make easier the identification of acceptable priorities for action. In developing anti-poverty strategies, the 1995 World Summit agreement was a breakthrough.

With the passing years the need for this has become more apparent. In the 21st century there is increasing concern about the slow progress in reducing mass poverty in the world and the remorseless increase in inequalities between countries and within countries. This trend is destabilizing many societies and sits uncomfortably with the multiplying expressions and commitments on the part of nearly all governments for universal human rights. The Copenhagen example shows how the two can begin to be brought together.

The problem is not just one of international political will and agency. The President of the World Bank put poverty eradication at the top of the Bank's agenda in the 1960s. By the 1990s, the Bank admitted that progress had been fitful, if not negative, and that a fresh commitment had to be made (e.g. World Bank, 1996). New strategies were duly announced, but there was little significant departure from the Bank's arbitrary and insufficient measure of a dollar per person per day or from its prescriptions for action – namely economic growth, investment in education and restricted and low-cost welfare payments to the very poor.[1]

The UN's expressed aim of halving world poverty by 2015 will not be achieved, or even approached.[2] Governments with a decreasing share of world resources also find themselves with decreasing room for policy manoeuvre at a time when the international agencies continue to expect them to solve their huge domestic economic and social problems.

---

Townsend, P. (2006) '"Absolute" and "overall" poverty: the 1995 Copenhagen approach to the fulfilment of human rights', *Global Social Policy*, vol 6, no 3, pp 284-7.

To a growing number of social scientists, the problem is not conventional domestic policy prescription, and conformity with Bank precepts, or edicts. The nature and priorities of policy have to be identified more precisely by means of authoritative measurement of severe conditions, and also of the impact of existing policies.

The idea of poverty has to be extricated from political ideology. An internationally comparable and indeed scientific meaning can be sought in the form of a threshold of income needed in different countries to escape multiple material and social deprivation, incapacity and premature death rather than a threshold of income narrowly concerned with the physical and nutritional needs of human beings outside their social context.

The World Summit for Social Development in 1995 highlighted the problems in rich and poor countries of poverty and social exclusion. The report called for 'the substantial reduction of overall poverty and the eradication of absolute poverty ... Each country should develop a precise definition and assessment of absolute poverty' (UN, 1995: 60–1).

Absolute poverty is defined as 'a condition characterised by severe deprivation of basic human needs, including food, safe drinking water, sanitation facilities, health, shelter, education and information. It depends not only on income but also on access to services' (UN, 1995: 57).

Overall poverty takes various forms, including

> lack of income and productive resources to ensure sustainable livelihoods; hunger and malnutrition; ill health; limited or lack of access to education and other basic services; increased morbidity and mortality from illness; homelessness and inadequate housing; unsafe environments and social discrimination and exclusion. It is also characterised by lack of participation in decision–making and in civil, social and cultural life. It occurs in all countries: as mass poverty in many developing countries, pockets of poverty amid wealth in developed countries, loss of livelihoods as a result of economic recession, sudden poverty as a result of disaster or conflict, the poverty of low–wage workers, and the utter destitution of people who fall outside family support systems, social institutions and safety nets. (UN, 1995: 57)

On behalf of UNICEF, a Bristol/London School of Economics (LSE) research team tracked down survey data for 1.2m people in 46 countries in 2003, increased to 2.4m in 73 countries by 2005, and produced the first reliable report on the extent of 'absolute' poverty as recommended in the 1995 Copenhagen report, that is, severe or extreme material and social deprivation – among children – in the developing world (Gordon et al.,

2003; UNICEF, 2005). This paves the way for the staged integration of comparable data on the two-level poverty measure worldwide.

The driving force behind this international work is 'universalism' – the need to analyse social and economic conditions on a global and scientific basis to understand cause, but also priority action. [...]

Mounting acceptance throughout the world of human rights is the prime illustration of 'universalism' and puts pressure on all countries accordingly to recast development policies and eliminate poverty.[3] Human rights have come to play a central part in discussions about economic and social development, and the various instruments have been ratified by the great majority of governments in the world. A key lesson from the divergent historical experience of 'developed' and 'developing' countries is to put into practice the fundamental rights to social security, including social insurance, and an 'adequate' standard of living. The rights are enshrined in Articles 22 and 25 of the Universal Declaration of Human Rights; 9 and 11 of the International Covenant on Economic, Social and Cultural Rights; and, 26 and 27 of the Convention on the Rights of the Child.

The impact of social security systems in the Organisation for Economic Co-operation and Development (OECD) countries over more than 100 years best illustrates the gathering importance of these rights.

Since 2000, the strengths of universal public social services and social protection or security payments have begun to be recognized, partly at the instigation of international organizations such as the International Labour Organization and UNICEF. Recognition of the strengths in particular of social insurance and 'categorical' non-contributory minimum income payments also described as tax-financed group benefits, on behalf of children, disabled people and the elderly may follow. The urgent reformulation of development policies to reduce poverty may then be welcomed – and bring tangible success.

The strength of a universalist, human rights, approach to social security is in turning to future advantage what, after extraordinary struggle, proved to be a highly successful strategy in the past. Working people responded to extreme individual need by combining in collective interest to contribute creatively to economic development and the alleviation of the poverty of others in their midst. Collective protest and action led to the social good – often by the extension of the ideas of representative democracy and citizen participation.

### Endnotes

[1] For example, Ravi Kanbur, the prime mover of the World Bank's development report on poverty in 2000, was reported to have resigned because he was 'believed to have wanted to emphasise that economic growth alone will not be enough to

reduce poverty and that it will also require equal emphasis on redistributive tax and spending policies' (Atkinson, 2000).

[2] Thus, the Bank admitted 'the number of poor people has risen worldwide, and in some regions the proportion of poor has also increased' (World Bank, 1999: 25). See also the statement of goals, including halving world poverty by 2015 (World Bank, 2000: 8).

[3] The use of the human rights framework to construct more effective anti-poverty policies is illustrated in Townsend and Gordon (2002), especially Chapters 14 and 17.

## References

Atkinson, M. (2000) 'Poverty row author quits World Bank', *Guardian*, 15 June.

Gordon, D., Nandy, S., Pantazis, C., Pemberton, S. and Townsend, P. (2003) *Child poverty in the developing world*, Bristol: The Policy Press.

Townsend, P. and Gordon, D. (2002) *World poverty: New policies to defeat an old enemy*, Bristol: The Policy Press.

UN (1995) 'The Copenhagen Declaration and Programme of Action', World Summit for Social Development, 6–12 March, New York, NY: United Nations.

UNICEF (2005) *State of the world's children in 2005*, New York, NY: UNICEF.

World Bank (1996) *Poverty reduction and the World Bank: Progress and challenges in the 1990s*, Washington, DC: World Bank.

World Bank (1999) 'Entering the 21st century: World Development Report 1999–2000', Washington, DC/Oxford: World Bank/Oxford University Press.

World Bank (2000) *World Development Indicators*, Washington, DC: World Bank.

# 9

# The 2009 Minority Report on the World Bank

*What would the Webbs do in 2009? In this article Peter Townsend adopts the Webbs' authoritative style of planning and applies some of the precepts they used to challenge the failed poor laws and domestic poverty in 1909 to the global poverty that faces us in 2009.*

In present conditions I believe the Webbs would see that 2009 offers an extraordinary opportunity to re-establish some of the values expressed in 1909 in relation to new policies. I am thinking in particular of human rights and John Maynard Keynes. Today the problem is not just regulation or reconstruction of banks – but of other global institutions, and particularly the World Bank. In debate, we have to be conscious always of alternative strategies, and advocate what is, in the circumstances, best.

The World Bank has failed to diminish poverty in the developing world. That failure is surely a contributory factor in the unprecedented 2008 collapse of the global financial system. Getting rich quick has meant exploiting many millions on the lowest incomes and failing to satisfy their basic human rights. And this can be ascribed to the reach and dominance of neoliberal economic ideology in the last 40 years.

This ideology germinated in 1944 with Hayek's Road to Serfdom. Despite being treated for decades as an arch conservative whose views could not be taken seriously, and despite the postures of organisations created in his name, like the Institute for Economic Affairs in the UK in the 1950s and 1960s, his free market position was given a shot in the arm by the Chicago School of economists and in particular by Milton Friedman.

Monetarism gained adherents and prospered. The objective of a free global market gathered momentum. The collapse of the Soviet Union and the protracted period of power exercised by the Republican Party in the United States through the election triumphs of Nixon, Reagan, Bush senior and Bush junior gave a fillip to neoliberal economic policies. This led inevitably to the stark inequalities produced by public expenditure cuts, privatisation, smaller and less progressive taxes, anti-union legislation, and free trade in the interests of Western-based global corporations.

---

Townsend, P. (2009) 'The 2009 Minority Report on the World Bank', published online at fabiansociety.org.uk, London: The Fabian Society.

The World Bank has served its masters dutifully and effectively. Its influence is all-pervasive. But lingering extreme poverty on a huge scale and realisation of the deep faults in the banking system invites an urgent review of the Bank's work.

The failure to advise effectively about world poverty is the most compelling example. Since 2000 the primary goal of the United Nations to halve world poverty by 2015 has been at odds with the reality of unremitting social polarisation and degrading mass poverty. There have been a growing number of reports reliably documenting both. The World Bank has nonetheless persisted with its discriminatory measure of poverty and its selective and unsuccessful policies.

## Measurement failures

For many years the World Bank made claims of a steady decline in the scale of poverty. But gradually the decline – even on the Bank's figures – looked slow and halting and the Bank's technical expertise was convincingly questioned. Economists have savaged the technical updating of the dollar-a-day poverty line from year to year, and the way that poverty line was translated into the equivalent purchasing power in the currency of each particular country. Thus, Kakwani and Son (2006) show that if the poverty line up to 2005 had been pitched at a level of $1.50 instead of $1.08 in the mid- and late 1990s to allow for the true, and properly weighted, levels of inflation around the world, the count of those in severe poverty would have been much larger. Absolute poverty in the world would have been 36 per cent and not 21 per cent in 2001 – raising the total numbers by 800 millions to little short of 2 billions.

The second measurement fault is more fundamental. The Bank's practice since 1985 has been to restrict the measure of a 'poverty line' to material needs and not include social needs – such as people's needs to meet the costs of going to work and their obligations to family and society. In the early 1990s the Bank stated repeatedly that these were the two necessary elements in the measure of poverty (World Bank, 1990, p.26; and see also World Bank, 1993a, 1993b, 1996, 1997, 2000, and 2001). By the World Bank's own authority, the scale of world poverty must have been routinely under-estimated ever since.

For half a century the Bank has obstructed the development of a measure of poverty that is international and scientific. The UN initiative at the Copenhagen World Summit in 1995 – which would have begun to allow rich and poor countries to be compared – was ignored. In 2008 two researchers at the Bank stated that "richer countries tend to adopt higher standards of living in defining poverty" and that the Bank has "aimed to apply a common [sic] standard, anchored to what poverty means in the world's poorest countries" (Chen and Ravallion, 2008, p.2).

The measure is circular as well as discriminatory. Current very low income is treated as equivalent to minimum income need. But how can the choice of a threshold of poverty or a poverty 'line' be validated? In principle the scientific approach would be to choose criteria other than income to examine in order to provide acceptable evidence of a threshold of income that satisfies need. One such alternative is the collection of representative household information about multiple material and social deprivation. An appendix gives an example of the use that can be made of existing cross-national surveys to derive reliable indicators.

The World Bank authors finally admitted in 2008 that the celebration of the apparently sharp decline in poverty that the Bank claimed again and again in the 1990s and early 2000s had been "premature": the results had been biased and based on "rather crude price surveys" for just 10 countries (ibid, p.3). The quantity but not quality of items had been priced. Poverty in China was underestimated, they say, by 300 millions.

But old habits die hard. For the World Bank's researchers to admit some necessary technical adjustments, and accept minor retrospective adjustments in the figures they had published in the past is not the same as admitting the big mistakes that had been made for decades in Bank methodology. They have failed to establish a reliable basis for measuring trends in poverty in developing countries that genuinely allows for inflation. Thus, the researchers do not discuss what inflation index applies best to developing countries. They do not withdraw the $1.08 figure for inflation between 1985 and 1993 of a poverty line of $1.00 per person per day in 1985 in favour of the more appropriate $1.50 testified by critics. And this refusal of course affects the choice of the figure for 2005. The World Bank's spokesmen say the "new international poverty line" for 2005 follows "the same definition used in our past work, namely that the line should be representative of the national lines found in the poorest countries" (ibid, pp 3, 9–10). But arbitrary choice of the number of countries and arbitrary selection of a threshold of income is not selection according to pecuniary need.

## World Bank policies

Along with the UN and all international organisations, the Bank has upheld economic growth, debt relief and overseas aid as the primary instruments of global anti-poverty strategy. More recently fairer trade, through reform of the WTO, has been added. But different policies on behalf of these four objectives have not been examined closely to reveal what are the specific effects of each of them on the scale and distribution of continuing poverty. Policies developed in their name are relatively indiscriminate and poorly designed in their distributional effect upon population poverty. Without detailed evidence of policy delivery these strategies can be regarded only as empty shells. Success depends on whether a sufficient share of additional cash income and income in kind from these sources happens to reach the poor, and quickly. Their intentions are not always clear and their consequences left uncharted. The blithe assumption that they are good in themselves has not yet been replaced with resolute determination to ensure that policies in their name are pro-poor.

From the 1980s the World Bank has followed a three-fold strategy to reduce poverty: broad-based economic growth; development of human capital through education; and safety-nets for vulnerable groups. But investment in children's education can only begin to have an effect on the poverty rate years later, if at all, when the children become working adults – while the dire effects of poverty are ever-present. And 'safety-nets' that comprise concessions for the extreme poor through selective policies disguise the tiny scale of the commitment of resources to these policies and therefore to a problem that in many countries affects the majority of the population.

The Bank has not contributed much to the diminution of extreme poverty. In 2005 it lent approximately $22 billion but only $2.4 billion (10 per cent) was for social protection (Hall, 2007). The largest lending was for financial and private sector development and two other large allocations for urban development and environmental and natural resource management – these three making up half the Bank's programme. The sum for social protection is less than five-hundredths of one per cent of world GDP and is dwarfed by the sum spent each year by each of the rich countries on social protection (or social security) alone. Thus, the UK Department of Work and Pensions spent the equivalent of $210 billion in 2005, compared with the World Bank's total loans for social protection in the entire world of $2.4 billion.

The latest news carries an even worse indictment. In 2008 the Bank committed less than half of what it had committed in 2005 to social protection – 4 per cent of the total of $24.7 billion in the year – i.e. $0.9 billion, compared with $2.4 billion in 2005 (World Bank, 2008b).

The Bank's action remains deliberately puny and has done little to change the entrenchment of free market policies: one analyst concluded that social policy had been condemned to a "residual category of safety nets" (Tendler, 2004, p.119).

Yet as much as two-thirds of the poverty that would otherwise exist in the rich countries has been ruled out by the development of their social security systems. While public expenditure on social protection, more properly named social security (such as on child benefit, sickness and disability benefit and pensions for the elderly) has continued to increase (nearly 14 per cent of GDP in 2005) in the average OECD country, it is between 1 per cent and

3 per cent in most low income countries: for example, 1.5 per cent in India (Townsend, 2007, p.9, and see also ILO, 2001). Because the redistributive mechanisms of social security are not in place, even for groups who cannot be expected to gain earnings through employment, there cannot be effective 'trickle-down' from economic growth.

Overseas aid for the extreme poor in the developing countries is also miserly. The total of all the Bank's lending throughout the world each year has reached $25billion (World Bank, 2008a, 2008b) – less than half the average annual income of each of the biggest 500 global corporations (Fortune Magazine, 2008). At the top Wal-Mart has annual revenue of $379 billion and Exxon Mobil $373billion - each of them 15 times greater than the World Bank's total lending. The Bank's lending represents less than 1 per cent of the annual income of the top 500 global corporations.

The Bank has done a far better job in concealing its deterrent 'poor law' policies and the relatively puny scale of resources committed than those who concocted or sought to implement the 1834 Poor Law Act. The Webbs of 1909 would be rising up in fury.

## The World Bank and Keynesian post-war recovery

What would have been the alternative, successful, strategy for the World Bank to pursue during the last three decades? It would have been drawn from a different theory of economic and social development than that of the Chicago School of monetarism and then of neoliberalism. Keynes argued for a kind of world central bank or 'Clearing Union' that created a deposit of new currency for every country in the world which it could count on at times of difficulty to pay creditor governments. The big countries would create a giant fund from which countries in demonstrable financial adversity could draw – up to a sizeable minimum level – without strings. Up to that minimum level they would not have to justify their policies. His was a successful precedent during the eerily similar depression years of the 1930s and the years anticipating post-war reconstruction. He believed too in the creation of jobs rather than market incentives and the protection of the unemployed and other poor by social security. His say-so was a factor lurking behind the promulgation and acceptance of the Beveridge Report – which spurred different countries into acts of redistribution of a major kind. His strategy deserves fresh examination.

After 1944 the Bretton Woods institutions turned out to be a pale shadow of Keynes' intentions. Total resources provided for them were less than a third of what he advised. Countries were not awarded an allocation. They had to contribute to the total Fund to be eligible for membership and hence have the opportunity to apply for loans – to which stringent conditions could be attached. Membership was conditional rather than universal; debtors had less independence, aid had strings, and the US remained predominantly in charge of those strings.

In the pages above the desolate outcome has been sketched. The consequences of neoliberal economic thought are to be found everywhere. "Behind [the World Bank] are the economic strategies of the G8 nations and the virtually unaccountable multinational corporations. The Bank is not a humanitarian agency and its analysts usually evaluate its operations on the economic principle of efficiency. Yet growing inequality is literally a matter of life and death to many millions of people" (Turshen, p.131).

## Transformation of the World Bank

The World Bank has helped to implant neoliberal ideology among governments, corporations and consumers, weakened the state and reinforced economic inequality and gross destitution. In 2009 its resonance has a hollow ring. As a vehicle with capacity to influence organisations world-wide by employing a large number of internationally informed and intelligent people, it has been driven by the wrong forces subservient to that neo-liberal philosophy. It advocates disastrous policies, lends with discriminatory conditions, and has little experience or resources to invest grants directly in jobs, services and people.

Altogether it has the wrong policies and ignores human rights.

Action has to be governed by motives of job creation, public service, staged international planning, accountable leadership, and collective organisation of social security and other social services.

The largest global corporations and international agencies (including the banks and insurance corporations, which in 2006-7 made up 100 of the 500 largest corporations) would attract praise by committing a very small percentage of their growing resources to social security and a larger percentage to minimum rights to wages and employment conditions in the low income countries. That would mean keeping track of activities in subsidiaries and sub-contracted employment, and extending rights to those workers. New international company law (Townsend and Gordon, 2002), and more effective international taxation, would be necessary components. 'Corporate social responsibility' would thereby acquire meaning.

For example global corporations could add one or two per cent of wage costs in different countries towards a universal child benefit to help banish malnutrition, poverty and premature child death, and also encourage more schooling and access to health care. Employer contributions towards domestic social insurance schemes in the OECD countries could be extended to employer operations in the low-income countries.

The creation of jobs locally and nationally would be paramount, building on some positive policies of present government. By singling out green forms of energy replacement, subsidies for domestic manufacture and farming, and expansion of some of the primary social services the lines of an employment strategy less dependent on imports would be evident.

The strategy offers the possibility of satisfying the principal UN millennium goal of eliminating poverty, and slowing or halting runaway social polarisation; a start in the necessary reconciliation of market globalisation and public ownership and control; a principled series of stages in the fulfilment of human rights; and a feasible way of properly internationalising development.

# 10

# Manifesto: international action to defeat poverty

1. **Introduce and develop schemes to fulfil fundamental right to social security** (Article 22 of the Universal Declaration of Human Rights). To be implemented by introducing or extending social security and especially public provision of social insurance and/or basic income for all citizens.

2. **Legally enforce right to adequate standard of living** (Article 25 of the Universal Declaration of Human Rights). To be implemented by adoption of state-defined minimum earnings in conjunction with state-defined minimum cash benefits for those not in paid work, including the equivalent value of benefits (goods and services) in kind.

3. **Introduce or strengthen legal right to child benefit** (Articles 25 and 27 of the Convention on the Rights of the Child). Provision to be made for every child of a monthly cash benefit, or the equivalent in value included of goods and services, which is universally adequate, to surmount material and social deprivation.

4. **All developed countries to adopt legally binding minimum level of 1% GNP overseas development assistance.** To be introduced first by the EU, immediately in the case of some member states, and in stages by the poorer member states, and extended to all OECD countries.

5. **Establish universal right of access locally to publicly provided basic health care and education services** (with reference to Articles 21, 25 and 26 of the Universal Declaration of Human Rights, but also such objectives as agreed by governments at the Copenhagen World Summit for Social Development [of 1995]). The purpose here is to clarify and give tangible support for the provision in all countries of a network of geographically accessible institutions and services, and check annually about introduction and coverage. National plans to be underwritten jointly by governments and the UN. Easy access to safe drinking water and sanitation must be included in the provision within a defined number of years of "equal access to public service" (Article 21).

---

Townsend, P. and Gordon, D. (2002) 'Appendix A: Manifesto: international action to defeat poverty', in P. Townsend and D. Gordon (eds) *World poverty: New policies to defeat an old enemy*, Bristol: The Policy Press.

6.  **Provide temporary and permanent public housing units for homeless people and people living in seriously substandard accommodation.** The aim must be to prioritise the housing needs of the poorest 10% of the population by means of national and local ownership and administration of minimally adequate standard accommodation. The needs of immigrant, asylum-seeking and resident families must be balanced fairly in the programme.

7.  **The UN with other international agencies and national governments to agree action plan for staged greater equalisation of resources within and between countries** (with particular reference to Commitment 2 of the Copenhagen World Summit for Social Development). Just as the 1945 target of 0.7% GNP for overseas development assistance on the part of the developed countries will be replaced by a 1.0% target (see Manifesto 4), every government will adopt an upper limit of income inequality; for example, a standard of 0.4 on the Gini coefficient.

8.  **Extend measures for full employment and set up an International Full Employment Agency** (Article 23 of the Universal Declaration of Human Rights). Where unemployment and under-employment is most severe and extensive, the UN – in agreement with governments – must devise plans to curb the scale of job losses and promote alternative employment. This will be funded, along with child benefit (see Manifesto 3) by the new international financial transactions tax (see Manifesto 12). Action against specific violations of human rights, like the eradication of child labour and of the abuse of street children, will be a key part of the new agency's role.

9.  **Agree a new operational specification of fair trade.** Representatives of each world region to agree the terms of a framework plan, to be endorsed by a majority of the UN and agreed in stages over 10 years. This will necessarily involve removal of protective agricultural subsidies in rich countries to allow fair trade and the subsequent removal of tariffs and other barriers to trade on the part of poor countries. Domestic food production and a fair price standard for food commodities produced in the developing countries to become rules operated by the World Trade Organisation.

10. **Introduce new international company law.** The priority must be the introduction of a new international law requiring transnational corporations (TNCs) to curb anti-social activities and curb excessively high profits from poor countries.

11. **Rebuild and/or strengthen tax administration.** Taxation systems to be introduced and strengthened where necessary, and to be answerable to representatives of national electorates, who should have

independent powers to monitor policies and outcomes. Monitoring by an independent international inspectorate will also become necessary.

12. **Introduce an international financial transactions tax to be administered by the UN.** In the first instance a tax at a rate of 0.2% would be payable on all currency exchanges at banks and currency exchange offices. Half of the gross revenue would be administered by the UN to subsidise the establishment of child benefit in developing countries.

13. **Reconstitute international financial agencies.** Membership to be automatically open to all countries, funded by an agreed percentage of national GDP, for example 0.3%, with equal regional representation on governing councils and committees, and five-year circulation of chairmanship. Terms of reference to be subject every five years to majority vote at the UN.

14. **Transnational prospectus to be agreed.** Each TNC will be required to draw up policy statements both for employees (including employees in subsidiary companies), and for countries in which the TNC has operations of significant scale. The former to include specification of employment conditions and rights for all types of employees. The latter policy statement to be subject to approval by a consultative body representing the TNC, the national electorate in the 'headquarter' country and the governments of the countries from which overseas profits are derived (one third representation each).

15. **Further democratisation of the UN.** Representation of populous countries, and of the poorest 100 countries, to be increased on UN committees, especially powerful economic and social committees. The objective will be to progress in stages to equal representation of regions by population size.

16. **To establish strong regional policy alliances.** Collaborative working relationships between regional or global non-government organisations (NGOs) and governments must be introduced and strengthened, as part of improved democratisation. The UN must play a leading role, and the provision of a legal framework is one option.

17. **To agree an international poverty line.** An international poverty line that defines a threshold of income (including the value of income in kind) – ordinarily required in different countries to surmount material and social deprivation – must be a priority. The defined line will be subject to demonstrable scientific, not politically convenient, consensus.

18. **To monitor the success of anti-poverty policies.** Further steps to be taken to fulfil the agreements of the Copenhagen World Summit for Social Development of 1995, and to regularise the publication of

annual anti-poverty reports by governments, but also by the UN and the other principal international agencies. This process must involve regular evaluation of the quantitative contribution of different national and cross-national policies to reduce poverty.

# 11

# Investment in social security: a possible UN model for child benefit?

We live in a world where children are accorded priority emotionally and politically. Five of the eight Millennium Development Goals (MDGs) of the UN are directed at children: one is to eradicate extreme poverty and hunger, another to drastically reduce under-five mortality, a third to reverse the spread of HIV/AIDS, malaria and other diseases, and the fourth and fifth to ensure full and gender-equal schooling (UN, 2000 [...]). Yet international leaders have conceded that declared progress is too slow to meet the goals by 2015.

The policies offered to protect children's welfare have been ineffective (UNICEF, 2004, 2005) – most are over-generalized and indirect or selectively helpful only to very small numbers. Children's social security is not defined precisely but often wrapped up in the 'family' or 'household' benefits to which their parents may or may not be entitled. The scale of their rights to income in developing countries has still to be defined, categorized for different age-groups in different locations, and endorsed by representative government.

Previous chapters have shown the viability and affordability of social security in national economies, and illustrated promising initiatives in middle- and low-income countries to accelerate the growth of social security systems. This chapter aims to take three steps further: (1) to focus on children, who have greater risk of being in poverty than adults and no opportunity to contribute to their own social security; (2) to pin down the nature and causes of child poverty to improve policy-effectiveness; and (3) to demonstrate that international funds have to be found, and can be found quickly, to match national resources to meet child poverty directly. I will discuss;

- the consequences of poverty and multiple deprivation for child survival and health;
- child rights as the appropriate framework for measurement, analysis and the construction of policy;

Townsend, P. (2009) 'Investment in social security: a possible UN model for child benefit?', in P. Townsend (ed) *Building decent societies*, Basingstoke: Palgrave for the International Labour Organization, pp 151-66.

- the need to reveal the extent of international responsibility for funding anti-poverty strategies;
- the recent disappointing history of international finance; and, as the most practical alternative,
- the use of a currency transfer tax to build up a UN Investment Fund for child benefit.

## The consequences of child poverty and multiple deprivation

A special investigation for UNICEF found that 56 per cent of children in developing countries – 1.2 billion – experienced one or more forms of severe deprivation, over half of them (674 million) at least two forms of severe multiple deprivation like total absence of toilet facilities, lack of nearby clean water, malnutrition and extreme overcrowding and poor shelter (Gordon et al., 2003; UNICEF, 2005). This is more potent evidence of child poverty than the (very crude, and unreliable) estimates by the World Bank of the numbers of children in households with less than US$1 per capita per day.[1] Over 10 million children in developing countries die each year, mainly from preventable causes, including malnutrition, pneumonia, diarrhoea, measles and malaria. Poverty, whether measured by household income or multiple material and social deprivation, and early child mortality, are intertwined. The World Health Organization (WHO) found that as many as seven out of every ten childhood deaths can be attributed to these five causes or their combination. Three in every four children seen by health services are suffering from at least one of these conditions. Many of these deaths could be prevented using readily available medical technologies at comparatively little cost and many more by providing resources for shelter, clean water, sanitary facilities, food and fuel. Thus, the free issue of mosquito nets, as illustrated in one initiative in different areas of Kenya (Rice, 2007), can dramatically reduce rates of malaria among children. Again, public provision of shelter, food and sanitary facilities and basic income as well as access to services for those widowed or orphaned by HIV/AIDS can save many from miserable existence and early painful death (Akwanalo Mate, 2006). The number of children in sub-Saharan Africa orphaned by HIV/AIDS is expected to rise to 15.7 million, or a quarter of all children, by 2010 (UNICEF, 2007: 42). Globally, 1,800 children are newly infected every day by HIY/AIDS (UNICEF, 2005: 16).

The accumulating studies of enforced child deprivation are calling sharp attention to mass violations of child rights that for many children maintain, and for some increase, the risks of survival (Pemberton et al., 2007). For health professionals this has led recently to fuller acknowledgement of the positive relationship between human rights and health (Gruskin et al., 2007;

R. MacDonald, 2007; T. H. MacDonald, 2007; Pemberton et al., 2005; Singh et al., 2007).

The WHO and other international agencies have been unable until now to distinguish rates of child mortality and malnutrition in richer and poorer households. The use in representative country surveys of questions about assets owned by households has led to a breakthrough.[2] In Table 7.1 I have drawn from the WHO's *World Health Statistics* 2007, in which it has proved possible for the first time to measure ownership of assets, albeit crudely, to compare children in the poorest 20 per cent with the richest 20 per cent of households in the country. In countries where there is mass poverty it should be noted that asset impoverishment may still apply to some among the richest 20 per cent. Table 7.1 shows that 58 per cent of under-fives in the poorest 20 per cent of households in India, compared with 42 per cent in sub-Saharan Africa and 36 per cent in Latin America, are physically stunted for their age, compared with 27 per cent, 23 per cent and 4 per cent, respectively, in the richest 20 per cent of households. Mortality rates of under-fives in the poorest households in these three regions are also disproportionately high, being 14 per cent, 16 per cent and 9 per cent respectively. And, as another indicator, 72 per cent, 46 per cent and 34 per cent of one-year-olds in the poorest households in these three regions have been found not to have been immunized against measles.

Data for individual countries in the three regions are to be found in the Appendix to this chapter. The highest percentages of children found to be stunted in sub-Saharan Africa (50 per cent or more) were in Rwanda, Malawi, Chad, Zambia and Madagascar. The highest percentage in Latin America was 65 in Guatemala. In India this percentage must have been matched or exceeded in some deprived areas.

**Table 7.1** Child mortality and poor health conditions, three regions (%)

| Indicator | India | Sub-Saharan Africa (25 countries) | Latin America (8 countries) |
|---|---|---|---|
| Under-5s stunted for age | | | |
| – poorest 20% | 58 | 42 | 36 |
| – richest 20% | 27 | 24 | 4 |
| Mortality under-5 years | | | |
| – poorest 20% | 14 | 16 | 9 |
| – richest 20% | 5 | 10 | 4 |
| 1-yr-olds not immunized against measles | | | |
| – poorest 20% | 72 | 46 | 34 |
| – richest 20% | 19 | 22 | 16 |

*Source:* WHO (2007)

## Using child rights to construct policies to defeat child poverty

Using human rights as a methodology to pin down major patterns of development and assess policy is of growing importance. For the first time *multiple* deprivation as reflected in numerous statements in a number of the human rights treaties can be expressed in precise statistical and empirical terms using random but coordinated national surveys, namely the Demographic Health Surveys (DHS) and the Multiple Indicator Cluster Surveys (MICS) which have been and are being conducted in countries covering more than 85 per cent of the developing country populations. Beginning in the last decade a practicable method of constructing a measure of the economic and social conditions of small and large populations, so that they can be compared, has evolved. For example, during 2002-8 one research team based at the University of Bristol has been able to produce the first reliable global estimates for children, young people and all adults (Gordon et al., 2003; Gordon et al., 2009; UN, 2009).

The methodology draws on the analytical frameworks of the human rights treaties. Human rights have come to play a central part in discussions about economic and social development, and have been ratified by the great major-ity of governments in the world. There are rights to income and to social security enshrined in Articles 22 and 25 of the Universal Declaration of Human Rights; 9 and 11 of the International Covenant on Economic, Social and Cultural Rights; and 26 and 27 of the Convention on the Rights of the Child. But in the Convention on the Rights of the Child there are also elaborate injunctions to protect children from malnutrition, maltreatment, neglect, abuse and exploitation and ensure they are not deprived of access to clean water, sanitary facilities, shelter, health care services, education and information: governments are enjoined to 'recognize the right of every child to a standard of living adequate for the child's physical, mental, spiritual, moral and social development' (Article 27 and also see Articles 13, 17, 19, 20, 23, 24, 26, 28, 31, 32, 34, 37 and 39).

The statements, ratified by nearly all of the 191 nation-states in the world, allow single but also multiple measures or indicators of the denial or fulfilment of the specified rights to be devised and tracked. Social science therefore has a considerable role to play in coordinating the collection and analysis of such evidence and evaluating policy impact.

There are two particular arguments in favour of using this methodology in relation to poverty and social security. First, all the human rights treaties allow multiple indicators of violations of those rights to be constructed. The UNCRC, for example, does not contain an explicit human right to freedom from poverty. However, statements about the conditions of material and social deprivation underlying poverty and characterizing ill health, as specified above, occur in a number of different articles of the CRC, and have become the subject of national and international survey investigation. The rights are interrelated, and therefore deliberate action to fulfil a particular right is relevant to the realization of other rights. So the progressive realization of human rights will depend on the prior clustering of rights. Policies designed to implement a particular right have to be tested in relation to the outcomes for other rights. This is the source of scientific confirmation of the problem to be addressed, and of greater public confidence in policies designed to deliver human rights.

Second, human conditions are rarely one thing or the other – either good or bad. For example, there is under-nourishment but also extreme malnutrition. There is poverty but also extreme poverty. Empirical inquiry can trace a continuum from one extreme to the other, and thresholds of severity of conditions experienced by humans found. The advantage of empirical surveys of population conditions is that moderate needs can be distinguished from severe or extreme needs and doubts about over-generalized evidence removed. Another advantage is that by measuring severity as well as multiplicity of condition cause can be more exactly unravelled and priorities for remedial policy demonstrated. There is a gradient or continuum ranging from complete fulfilment to extreme violation of rights – for example on the continuum ranging from 'good health' to 'poor health/death' (see Gordon et al., 2003: 7–8). Courts make judgments in individual cases about this gradient to establish the correct threshold at which rights have been either violated or fulfilled. Correspondingly, scientists and policy-analysts can demonstrate the point on the gradient at which there are severe or extreme violations, so that grey areas of the interpretation of mild or moderate violation can be set aside, and governments and international agencies persuaded that there are grounds for institutional action.

The language of rights therefore changes the analysis of world conditions and the discussion of responsible policies. It shifts the focus of debate from the personal failures of the 'poor' to the failures to resolve poverty of macro-economic structures and policies of nation-states and international bodies (agencies such as the WTO, World Bank, IMF and UN, but also the most powerful transnational corporations (TNCs) and alliances of groups of governments). Child poverty cannot then be considered as a parental problem or a local community problem but a 'violation of rights' that nation-states, and international agencies, groups of governments and TNCs have a legal and institutional obligation to remedy (Chinkin, 2001). And violations of the rights of children to health, including problems like malaria and HIV/AIDS, would more easily be seen to be socio-structural problems and not only medical or health care problems.

Two 2007 examples may be given. The free issue of mosquito nets to selected populations (as in Kenya) can dramatically reduce rates of malaria among children (Rice, 2007). The problem is the scale of the issue – so that the children's needs are covered universally – rather than a small-scale scheme piloted by NGOs or governments in a few selected areas. Second, public provision of shelter, food and sanitary facilities and basic income as well as access to services for those widowed or orphaned by HIV/AIDS can save many from miserable existence and early painful death. This includes many among the nearly 16 million children, orphaned in sub-Saharan Africa by HIV/AIDS. Resources have to be mobilized for population care and especially material resources that directly reach children (Akwanalo Mate, 2006). Again, the problem is to ensure universal coverage so that children in extreme need do not slip through grudgingly devised nets.

## International responsibility for funding

### Trans-national corporations

Who is responsible for ensuring these policies are universal? The argument developed here is that TNCs and the international agencies can work wonders by committing a tiny percentage of their growing resources to social security in the low-income countries, and also by moving towards acceptance of minimum standards of monthly or weekly income on the part of wage-earners and those not in paid employment who are entitled to social security.

Both the OECD and ILO have issued guidelines on 'corporate social responsibility' (ILO, 2001; OECD, 2001). Both organizations have sought to fill a growing gap left upon the termination by the UN in the early 1990s of substantial monitoring and reporting of the trends in TNC practices. In 2003 the UN produced draft norms on the responsibilities of TNCs and other business enterprises with regard to human rights. It may be the first document to place human rights at the core of its mandate (UN, 2003; Vagts, 2003: 795; and see De Schutter, 2006) but it remains a generalized draft. The guidelines issued by the OECD and ILO are not yet attracting vigorous debate. The desirability of universal rules of practice for TNCs and international agencies is missing from much current commentary and analysis.

The growing bargaining power of the TNCs in headquarter locations in the rich countries is creating social and economic disequilibrium. This 'institutional hierarchy of power' has to be taken seriously. Recent failures of privatization schemes, and of major TNCs such as Enron, WorldCom, ImClone, Credit Suisse First Boston, Hollinger International, Adelphi Communications, Martha Stewart Living Omnimedia and parts of the financial services industry, provide lessons that have to be learned and acted upon internationally to restore structural stability. Recurring reports of instances of corporate corruption have paved the way for calls for collective approaches to be made through law and regulation (for example Hertz, 2001; Hines, 2001; Hudson, 1996; Korten, 1996; Kozul-Wright and Rowthorn, 1998; Lang and Hines, 1993; Madeley, 1999; Scott et al., 1985; Sklair, 2001; Watkins, 2002) that go a lot further than the minimal and highly variable expressions so far of the unenforceable appeals for the observance of 'corporate social responsibility' – as contained in the OECD and ILO guidelines or in the UN's Corporate Citizenship Initiative, 'the Global Compact', launched in June 2000.

Low-income countries are heavily dependent on trade with corporations with far larger resources than they possess. Through subsidiaries and sub-contractors controlled from far away they are restricted in the employment that can be found, the wages that can be charged, the taxes that can be raised and the conditions of life that have to be protected for national populations. The poorest countries have too few resources to make swift headway in reducing poverty and creating real opportunities for enterprise on behalf of the great majority of their populations (see for example Watkins, 2002). The hierarchy of power is illustrated by elaborate stratification of wages, conditions of work and access to social security from the executive boards of TNCs in the United States, Japan, Germany and the United Kingdom through to the 70 or 100 countries in which they operate. There has been a huge upsurge in trans-national resources without corresponding modernization of company law to adapt to the new social conditions and responsibilities for economic and social development and impose particular obligations on corporations.

Through its Tripartite Declaration of Principles concerning Multinational Enterprises and Social Policy, first adopted in 1977, the ILO has sought to encourage governments to reinforce corporate responsibility to pave the way for more specific potentially binding international standards, turning codes of conduct into the seed of customary rules of international law (ILO, 2001c). The problem is that as they stand these guidelines have no teeth and are not routinely publicized and discussed. Observance is voluntary and not dependent on national or international sanctions or law. Some corporations and companies are concerned about their image and good name, and are prepared to moderate their practices, and profits, in consideration of the rights of their workers. Others take advantage of non-existent or inconsistent law.

A starting point might be an agreement about children. One serious and continuing embarrassment for many TNCs are charges that children are involved in extreme forms of labour by sub-contractors and subsidiaries in locations remote from TNC headquarters (ILO, 2005). There is evidence of children as young as 7 who are involved in producing paving stones, foot-balls, clothing and carpets, operating with dangerous pesticides and other chemicals, digging trenches, picking cotton and working in mines – often for

10 or more hours a day. A common corporation plea is that illegal practices, or violations of child rights, along the production line were unintended and unknown, and abhorrence of such practices by headquarters would now be passed down the chain of command. The problem is that the conditions of payment and the standards expected of the finished product are imposed. These inevitably affect incentives and lead to extreme practices. Accountability for such practices could be ensured by legal and other means – particularly through monitored reports and statistics for which headquarter organizations must be held routinely responsible (in the same way as nation-states) and that would have to be submitted for public scrutiny. Agreement reached by the UN and TNCs about their accountability for severe deprivation among children engaged in forms of bonded labour connected with their trade represents one useful future development.

Perhaps the key element in taking such a step would be to concentrate on company responsibility for social security. In the late nineteenth century and throughout the twentieth century employers came to accept provision of a 'social wage' as a condition of making profit. Laws were enacted to provide for temporary and long-term unemployment, and contributions by employers for illness and disability and other dependencies of family members, especially children, were expected. There were insurance payments for specific contingencies and taxes to meet shifts in economic conditions that could not be predicted. The social wage was one of the rules of economic operation that became widely accepted. New global conditions in the twenty-first century have transformed that responsibility and a new legal and social responsibility for impoverished conditions in low-income countries has to be accepted throughout the hierarchy of power exerted by headquarters corporations. The income rights of children could lie at the core of discussions to make globalization work socially.

Employers who were expected or compelled in the OECD countries at early stages of the industrial revolution to make substantial contributions to social protection were national rather than trans-national employers. People with hard-earned professional skills built on minimum standards of living and universal access to public social services were not at that time tempted overseas from national service or careers in the national economy, and neither were they given extensive opportunities to leave chosen countries of domicile. Cross-border social security is one burning question for the twenty-first century, but only one example of the urgent need to develop basic universal social security.

Children have been placed at the centre of this analysis. Trans-national employers can add, or be obliged to add, 1 or 2 per cent of wage costs in different countries for a child benefit to help banish malnutrition, poverty and premature child death, and also encourage more schooling. At the same time, extreme forms of child labour would become less necessary as well as made illegal. Standard contributions towards social insurance for sickness, disability, bereavement and ageing, or represented in new taxes, could follow. The question of social protection or social security in the national interest has become one of social protection in the *international* interest.

## International agencies

What cannot be disregarded in this discussion of children's needs is inter-national funding. The responsibility of the UN and other agencies in funding social security, especially child benefit, requires urgent review. What conclusions can be drawn from present international funding, and how much of that funding actually reaches children in extreme poverty? When questions are asked about global, as distinct from national, anti-poverty mea-sures, international agencies stress the importance of three sources of aid economic growth, debt relief and overseas aid. Box 7.1 summarizes these sources and criticisms of these sources of aid remain largely unanswered. Added lately as a fourth element of international anti-poverty strategy has been fairer trade, through reform of the WTO. In practice all four measures are principally dependent on the big economic powers, including TNCs, in the modern global economy. In working out what this means for children we need to understand that the four types of international funding are rel-atively indiscriminate and unpredictable in their distributional effect upon populations. Success depends on whether a sufficient share of additional cash income and income in kind from these sources happens to reach the poor and how quickly.

---

### Box 7.1: The current orthodox funding strategy for low-income countries

The strategy has been threefold:
- Broad-based economic growth
- Debt relief
- Overseas aid

Drawing on evidence of the trends over 30 years, the outcome of this strategy can be judged unsuccessful for several reasons:
- 'Trickle-up' growth
- Conditionality policies for loans
- Cost-recovery policies in basic social services
- Cuts in public expenditure
- Lack of social security systems
- Excessive privatization
- Unregulated globalization and unequal terms of trade
- Enhancement of the power of the global 'triumvirate' (G8, TNCs and international framework agreements)

---

The absence of social security systems in many low-income countries means that 'trickle-down' from economic growth, or indeed most forms of overseas aid and debt relief, does not arise. These forms of funding have 'indirect' social outcomes. They are intended to reach the poorest, but measures of trends in extreme poverty, and not only the lack of investigative precise follow-up, cast doubt on the intended outcome. The over-generalized, and indirect, strategy has contributed to the failure to reduce poverty, especially child poverty.

What different forms of funding have been examined? The scale of resources to be made available has now become an acute problem. In September 2000 the lack of significant progress in reducing poverty, together with severe delays in implementing funding agreements, led the UN General Assembly to ask for a rigorous analysis of the advantages, disadvantages and other implications of proposals for developing new and innovative sources of funding'. A panel was set up under the chairmanship of Ernesto Zedillo and its report was issued in 2001 (UN, 2001).

On the question of scale the Zedillo panel estimated conservatively that an additional US$50 billion was required annually to reach the MDGs. The World Bank estimated that additional overseas development aid (ODA) of US$60 billion over 2003 allocations would be needed in 2006, and US$83 billion by 2010 (World Bank, 2005: 162). These estimates were unrealistically low, since they depended on making up the incomes of population below $1 a day and not on the relatively indiscriminate indirect funding provided by economic growth, overseas aid, debt relief and fairer trade. Instead, the necessary increase in ODA was projected as US$20 billion for 2006 and US$50 billion for 2010 – and even these underestimates leave a gap of more than US$30 billion. By that year the total is estimated to reach an average of 0.36 per cent GNI (OECD, 2005) but 'it is not clear that this is realistic' (Atkinson, 2005: 6). The Netherlands, Denmark, Sweden, Norway and Luxembourg are the only countries to have reached the UN's 0.7 target for ODA. In 2004 the United Kingdom stood at 0.36 per cent and the United States 0.16 per cent.

By 2003 the UN inquiry about alternative funding had lost momentum. A parallel inquiry by the Helsinki-based World Institute for Development and Economic Research (WIDER) was mapping out alternative sources of funding (see Box 7.2). Because the UN process had offered little guidance the alternatives were presented cautiously in 2004 (Atkinson, 2004). The seven alternatives are of course different in scale as well as likely support. The International Finance Facility (IFF) was planned to reach a flow of US$50 billion for 2010-15. Private donations, i.e. from NGOs, totalled US$10 billion in 2003, and might be increased, but on past evidence it is unlikely that in the foreseeable future they will provide the predominant share of the resources needed. They can be expected to fill only a small proportion of the funding gap. The creation by the IMF of Special Drawing Rights has been opposed by the United States and since any new issue has to be approved by an 85 per cent majority, the United States alone can veto progress. The two most promising alternatives for serious examination seem to be a global environment tax and a currency transfer tax (CTT). The former is usually illustrated by a tax on hydrocarbon fuels with high carbon content – or by a tax on airline travel. The 'Tobin' tax alternative is a tax on foreign currency transactions (covering different types of transaction – spot, forwards, swaps, derivatives and so on).

## Box 7.2 New sources of development finance

1. Global environment taxes.
2. Tax in currency flows (for example Tobin).
3. New 'special drawing rights'.
4. International Finance Facility (UK govt.).
5. Private development donations.
6. Global lottery or premium bonds.
7. Increased remittances from emigrants.

*Source:* Atkinson (2004)

Both these taxes have been vigorously opposed on economic grounds. As Atkinson has pointed out, both need not necessarily be of a scale to warrant hostility, and could be reduced even further to produce substantial funds without adverse reactions in different markets. A small-scale initiative could of course be criticized, on the one hand, for failing to reduce global warming or pollution, and on the other hand, for failing to reduce currency speculation. But even small-scale taxes could produce substantial sums for international investment in development and the elimination of poverty. Such an investment could also be used to partially fund investments in a social security system by low-income countries. Even a tiny CTT of 0.02 per cent is estimated by Atkinson to raise US$28 billion, and a small energy tax twice this sum – giving figures from three to five times the value of all private donations.

The energies of international bodies were diverted from consideration of the CTT. Two new issues were brought up in 2003. First was the possible creation of an international tax organization. After the United Nations International Conference on Financing for Development in Mexico in March 2003, the Zedillo panel recommended creating within the UN an agency called the International Tax Organization (ITO) and an 'adequate international tax source' for global spending programmes.[3] Second was to explore how multinational business might promote strong domestic private sectors in the developing world. (In June 2003 a Commission on the Private Sector and Development, co-chaired by Ernesto Zedillo, was convened by UNDP at the request of Kofi Annan to recommend 'how to promote strong domestic private sectors in the developing world as a key strategy towards the achievement of the Millennium Development Goals'.[4] There was no reference back to the simplicity and affordability of a single form of international tax in relation to that aim. In particular, the commission looked at how multinational business can become a supportive partner for local entrepreneurs in the developing countries. The discussion of these issues at the world conference in Davos in 2004 was inconclusive. The case for a CTT was effectively kicked into touch.

## A currency transfer tax: new resources for child benefit and social security

Since the mid-1990s there has been a groundswell of support for the Tobin tax, particularly in Europe,[5] as a source of international finance for aid and economic stabilization.

James Tobin put forward the idea of such a tax first in 1972 and then it was resurrected in UNDP's Human Development Report for 1994. The rate of tax lately suggested is in the range 0.1 to 0.5 per cent of currency transactions. If applied universally a tax of 0.1 per cent on all currency transactions, including the charge for changing different currencies for travellers, was estimated in 2002 to be likely to raise $400 billion a year (see Townsend and Gordon, 2002: 369) – or five times higher than the low target of debt relief and aid advocated for low-income countries by the international financial agencies and members of the G8.

Eighty per cent of exchange transactions currently involve only eight industrialized countries (with the United Kingdom and the United States accounting for about 50 per cent). Eighty-eight per cent of transactions also take place between five currencies: the dollar, the pound sterling, the euro, the yen and the Swiss franc.[6] Thus, agreement among a bare majority of the G8 countries would be sufficient to ensure large-scale implementation at a first stage.

The key question is taxation for what? In the first years of the millennium progress in implementing international taxation to pump-prime social security systems has made very little progress. In 2002 the General Assembly of the UN considered a report prepared at the instigation of Kofi Annan. The Zedillo panel (the UN High-Level Panel on Financing for Development) had been appointed in 2001, as stated above,[7] to 'recommend strategies for the mobilization of resources required to accelerate equitable and sustainable growth in developing countries as well as economies in transition, and to fulfil the poverty and development commitments enshrined in the UN

Millennium Declaration'. The Zedillo panel reported an annual shortfall of US$15 billion for the provision of global public goods, in addition to the extra US$50 billion per year needed to meet the MDG targets. A number of governments had been pressing for consideration of the recommendation by James Tobin of a currency transfer tax. Thus, a 2002 report from the Federal Ministry of Economic Cooperation and Development in Bonn explained that the tax was feasible and could even be introduced right away by the OECD or EC countries.[8] The European Parliament carried out a feasibility study, with France, Germany and Belgium in favour, and the Vatican coming round to acceptance. Outside the European Union, Canada also offered its active consent. Poor countries saw the Tobin tax as something which rich countries could implement straightaway,[9] a domestic taxation control that had very small financial drawbacks for the donors but large benefits for the potential recipients. At a UN conference on 'Finance for Development' in April 2002 in Monterrey, Mexico, a number of countries pressed for the CTT. The report to be submitted to the General Assembly was signed by 113 countries, but innovative mechanisms of financing were given only one paragraph and were left open for further consideration.

The Zedillo report had described the merits of a CTT as 'highly controversial' and concluded that 'further rigorous study would be needed to resolve the doubts about the feasibility of such a tax'. The Zedillo authors claimed to have examined a range of proposed mechanisms including a carbon tax, a currency transactions tax, and a new allocation of Special Drawing Rights (SDRs), concluding that 'new sources of finance should be considered without prejudice by all parties involved'.

However, there is no evidence that the issues were examined in any depth. Surprisingly the Zedillo panel made no attempt to consider alternative practicable models of the Tobin tax, and to compare them, or to deal with the difficulties said to be involved in implementing such a tax. They did not compare its merits with other methods of raising funds for overseas development, or give persuasive estimates of costs and outcome. The uses to which the tax might be put or what social benefits might be derived were not discussed.

A CTT of 0.2 per cent, compared with a standard fee of 2 or 3 per cent charged by firms for currency exchange at airports, would raise US$280 billion. A start would be feasible for those OECD countries prepared to introduce a CTT for travellers. Compared with an existing charge of 2 or 3 per cent, it seems likely that the travelling public would accept an additional charge for an international investment tax of 0.2 per cent. The social use of such a tax also deserves searching investigation. This has not, hitherto, attracted any attention.

Like a corporation 'tax' of 1 per cent of turnover a currency transfer tax could directly benefit children. The potential use of the tax was not considered by Tobin when introducing his idea in 1972, nor in the 1990s when publicity was again attracted to his proposal and, despite the terms of reference agreed by the Zedillo panel, the idea was not given serious attention in 2001 or subsequently. Interpreted and administered in the name of the world's impoverished children, for example, the tax could have considerably more public appeal and therefore potential acceptance. The proceeds of a tax – introduced severally or collectively by the richest countries – could be used to set up an international investment fund for children. Following its initiative in introducing the MDGs the United Nations would be the obvious international organization to administer the fund. A universal benefit for children, in cash or in kind, would attract worldwide support. It could prove to be not just a salvation for the world's children, but regain public respect for the work of the international agencies on world social development and the fulfilment of the MDGs.

Grants from that fund to governments could be made conditional on, say, payments by each government and by the UN of 50 per cent of the cost of the programme, as well as evidence of payment. The scheme would be monitored by a representative UN committee as well as individual governments.

This chapter has pointed up the fragile condition of a fifth of the world's children and has sought to recommend a change of strategy to bring resources directly to children, and to seek substantial funding from international bodies. The current threat to global economic and social development because of the financial downturn obliges the largest economic powers, international agencies and TNCs to reconsider their agreed commitments and obligations to human rights in all parts of the world. The governments of the 'developed' countries have to consider sharing the responsibility for the establishment and emergency reinforcement of social security systems to meet declared goals to eliminate world poverty. It is not just administrative know-how and domestic taxation that count, but also participatory international funding.

The use of a currency transfer tax for universal child benefit would immediately improve the life chances of hundreds of millions of children, and pave the way for the emergence of social security systems in low-income countries on a scale that will eventually compare with that of the OECD countries and therefore radically reduce mass poverty.

The priority recommendation is for an international child benefit that once administratively in place has a direct and immediate effect in bolstering family purchasing power and reducing child poverty. Because the circumstances of countries differ widely a new child benefit would necessarily take a variety of forms and be introduced progressively. It could be a weekly allowance in cash or kind for children under a given age – say 10, or 5, or infants under 2. A low birthweight baby allowance is an example of a measure that could be applied in rich and poor countries alike. The scheme could be phased in, depending on available resources – maybe starting with infants – so long as it is introduced country- or district-wide. Conditional cash transfer schemes that have started in recent years, especially in parts of Latin America and Africa, could be merged or treated as preliminary or complementary stages of a process of rapid extension of entitlement to all children.

A second priority recommendation is a categorical child benefit for severely disabled children. Whether parents are in paid employment or not, the costs of caring for a severely disabled child often account for family poverty. And the market does not recognize this form of dependency. While some forms of congenital or disabling long-term illness may be declining there are the disabling conditions of the major problems of the last two decades, like HIV/AIDS, oil, nuclear and chemical pollution, and armed conflict, including landmines.

**Endnotes**

1. There is good reason to question whether the World Bank had technically achieved accurate updating of its 1985 $1 per person per day poverty line (see for example Kakwani and Son, 2006; Pogge and Reddy, 2003; Wade, 2004) and why the admitted insufficiency of the threshold had not been made good in later research, as promised by the Bank in the early 1990s (see especially Townsend, chapter 14 in Townsend and Gordon, 2002).

2. There are now two principal sources of standardized cross-national survey data Demographic Health Surveys (DHS) and Multiple Indicator Cluster Surveys (MICS), the latter sponsored by UNICEF.

3. Report of the High-Level Panel on Financing for Development, 28 June 2001, UN Headquarters, New York.

4. Mr Kofi Annan, Secretary-General of the United Nations: Address to the World Economic Forum, Davos, Switzerland, 23 January 2004.

5. For example, a report commissioned by the Federal Ministry for Economic Cooperation and Development, Bonn, concluded that the Tobin tax is feasible and does not need global ratification, but could be started by OECD or EU countries: 'On the Feasibility of a Tax on Foreign Exchange Transactions' January 2002).

6. Jean-Marie Harribey, Professeur de Sciences Economiques et Sociales at l'Universite Montesquieu-Bordeaux IV, France, *The Seven Mistakes of the Opponents to 'the Tax'* (2002), published by the Scientific Committee of ATTAC.

7. Report of the High-Level Panel on Financing for Development, 28 June 2001, UN Headquarters, New York.

8. See Federal Ministry for Economic Cooperation and Development (2002), 'On the Feasibility of a Tax on Foreign Exchange Transactions', Bonn.

9. See *The View from the South on the Tobin Tax*, Afrodad BFA, REPERES, www.ppp.ch for a really good overview of where African countries stand on the Tobin tax.

## References

Akwanalo Mate, F. (2006) *Children's property and inheritance rights: Experience of orphans affected by HIV/AIDS and other vulnerable orphans in Africa*, London: Department of Social Policy, London School of Economics.

Atkinson, A.B. (ed) (2004) *New sources of development finance*, UN-WIDER, Oxford: Oxford University Press.

Atkinson, A.B. (2005) 'Global political finance and funding the Millennium Development Goals', Jelle Zijlstra Lecture 4, Wassenar, Netherlands Institute for Advanced Study in the Humanities and Social Sciences (NIAS).

Chinkin, C. (2001) 'The United Nations Decade for the Elimination of Poverty: what role for international law?', *Current Legal Problems*, 54, pp 553-89.

De Schutter, O. (2006) *Transnational corporations and human rights*, Oxford: Hart.

Gordon, D., Nandy, S., Pantazis, C., Pemberton, S. and Townsend, P. (2003) *Child poverty in the developing world*, report to UNICEF, Bristol: The Policy Press.

Gordon, D., Nandy, S., Pantazis, C. and Pemberton, S. (2009) *Global estimates of adult and child poverty*, Bristol: The Policy Press.

Gruskin, S., Mills, E.J. and Tarantola, D. (2007) 'History, principles and practice of health and human rights', *The Lancet*, 370, pp 9585.

Hertz, N. (2001) *The silent takeover: Global capitalism and the death of bureaucracy*, London: William Heinemann.

Hines, C. (2001) *Localization: A global manifesto*, London: Earthscan.

Hudson, E. (ed) (1996) *Merchants of misery: How corporate America profits from poverty*, Maine, NE: Courage.

ILO, (2001) *The ILO tripartite declaration of principles concerning multinational enterprises and social policy*, 3rd edn, Geneva: ILO.

ILO (2005) *Social protection as a productive factor*, GB.294/ESP/4, November, Geneva: ILO.

Kakwani, N. and Son, H.H. (2006) *New global poverty counts*, Working Paper No 20, Brasilia: UNDP International Poverty Centre.

Korten, D.C. (1996) *When corporations rule the world*, London: Earthscan.

Kozul-Wright, R. and Rowthorn, R. (1998) *Transnational corporations and the global economy*, Helsinki, Finland: UNU World Institute for Development Economic Research.

Lang, T. and Hines, C. (1993) *The new protectionism*, London: Earthscan.

MacDonald, R. (2007) 'An inspirational defence of the right to health', *The Lancet*, 370, pp 379-80.

MacDonald, T.H. (2007) *The global human right to health: Dream or possibility?*, Oxford: Radcliffe Medical Publishing.

Madeley, J. (1999) *Big business, poor people: The impact of transnational corporations on the world's poor*, London and New York, NY: Zed Books.

OECD (2001) *The OECD guidelines for multinational enterprises 2001: Focus: Global instruments for corporate responsibility*, Paris: OECD. (First adopted 1976 and amended 1991.)

OECD (2005) 'DAC members' net ODA 1990-2004 and DAC Secretariat simulations of net ODA in 2006 and 2010', OECD website, 12 September.

Pemberton, S., Gordon, D., Nandy, S., Pantazis, C. and Townsend, P. (2005) 'The relationship between child poverty and child rights: the role of indicators', in A. Minujin, E. Delamonica and M. Komarecki (eds) *Human rights and social policies for children and women: The MICS in practice*, New York, NY: UNICEF/New School University.

Pemberton, S., Gordon, D., Nandy, S., Pantazis, C. and Townsend, P. (2007) 'Child rights and child poverty: can the international framework of children's rights be used to improve child survival rates?', *Plos Medicine*, vol 4, no 10, pp e307 (www. plosmedicine.org).

Pogge, T. and Reddy, S. (2003) *Unknown: The extent, distribution and trend of global income poverty*, www.socialanalysis .org.

Rice, X. (2007) 'Net givaway halves Kenya's child deaths from malaria', *The Guardian*, 17 August.

Scott, J., Stokman, F.N. and Ziegler, R. (1985) *Networks of corporate power*, Cambridge: Polity Press.

Singh, J.A., Govender, M. and Mills, E.J. (2007) 'Do human rights matter to health?', *The Lancet*, 370, pp 9586.

Sklair, L. (2001) *The transnational capitalist class*, Oxford: Basil Blackwell.

Townsend, P. and Gordon, D. (2002) *World poverty: New policies to defeat and old enemy*, Bristol: The Policy Press.

UN (United Nations) (2001) *Report of the high-level panel on financing for development*, 28 June, New York, NY: UN.

UN (2003) *Economic, social and cultural rights: Norms on the responsibilities of transnational corporations and other business enterprises with regard to human rights*, Economic and Social Council, Commission on Human Rights, New York, NY: UN.

UN (2009) *Youth development indicators*, Department of Economic and Social Affairs, Expert Group, New York, NY: UNDESA.

UNDP (United Nations Development Programme) (2000) *Overcoming human poverty: UNDP poverty report 2000*, New York, NY: UNDP.

UNICEF (2004) *The state of the world's children 2005*, New York, NY: UNICEF.

UNICEF (2005) *The state of the world's children 2006*, New York, NY: UNICEF.

UNICEF (2007) *State of the world's children 2008*, New York, NY: UNICEF.

Vagts, D.F. (2003) 'The UN norms for transnational corporations', *Leiden Journal of International Law*, vol 16, pp 795-802.

Wade, R.H. (2004) 'Is globalization reducing poverty and inequality?', *International Journal of Health Services*, vol 34, no 3, pp 381-414.

Watkins, K. (2002) *Rigged rules and double standards: Trade, globalization and the fight against poverty*, New York, NY: Oxfam International (www.marketradefair.com).

World Bank (2005) *World development report 2005*, Washington, DC: World Bank.

# Section III

# Poverty

*Edited by David Gordon*

# Introduction

Professor Peter Townsend was the greatest social scientist of the 20th century. He made seminal contributions to the study of inequalities in health, disability, social care of the elderly, human rights, domestic and international social policy. He is, however, best known for his lifelong work which revolutionised both the theory and practice of poverty research and resulted in a paradigm shift.

In the early 1950s, most academics and politicians believed that poverty should be defined and measured in terms of people's minimum needs for physical subsistence and that it had effectively been eradicated in the UK by the welfare state. In 1952, in his early twenties, Peter Townsend wrote 'Poverty: ten years after Beveridge' (**Chapter 12**) which reviewed developments since the publication of the Beveridge Report and argued that poverty had not been eradicated as many had claimed.

Townsend's ideas about the concept and measurement of poverty were crystallised in two important papers published in the *British Journal of Sociology*: 'Measuring poverty' (Townsend, 1954; **Chapter 13**) and 'The meaning of poverty' (Townsend, 1962; **Chapter 14**). Townsend showed that poverty was not absolute and static but both relative and dynamic:

> Poverty is a dynamic, not a static concept… Our general theory, then, should be that individuals and families whose resources over time fall seriously short of the resources commanded by the average individual or family in the community in which they live … are in poverty. (1962, pp 219 and 225)

In 1965, Peter Townsend and Brian Abel-Smith produced *The poor and the poorest*, an empirical analysis of the 1953–54 and 1960 Family Expenditure Surveys, which proved that poverty remained both persistent and widespread. Extracts from the introductory chapters to this book are reproduced as **Chapter 15**.

## Peter Townsend and the paradigm shift in poverty research

Peter Townsend's work so completely changed public perceptions about poverty that it is often hard for younger students in the 21st century to believe that in the 1950s most people genuinely believed that poverty no longer existed in Britain. The impact of Townsend's work was succinctly described by Ken Coates and Richard Silburn:

It was not until the beginning of the sixties that the small group of people who had consistently maintained that there was still a serious problem of material poverty began to make a serious impact on public opinion. As early as 1952, Peter Townsend, the most distinguished and persistent student of contemporary poverty, raised doubts about the validity of Rowntree and Lavers' conclusions. At the time Townsend was working for the independent research organization, Political and Economic Planning (P.E.P.), and in their bulletin *Planning* he challenged the validity of Rowntree's minutely calculated subsistence scales, from which he deduced his poverty line. Townsend argued that the list of items deemed to be a 'necessary expenditure' was too narrow, and urged a more realistic appraisal of 'necessaries'. Two years later he returned to this theme in the *British Journal of Sociology*, where he suggested that calculations of essential expenditure should not be based upon the prejudices of research workers or other experts who claim to know how other people's money should best be spent, but upon actual spending patterns of working class groups. He recognizes here that spending habits are not 'rational' (in a strict economic sense), but take place in the context of a social system which applies certain pressure upon its, members…. Finally and most significantly, in December 1965 came 'The Poor and the Poorest' by Professor Brian Abel Smith and Peter Townsend…. The authors showed that, in 1953, 7.8 per cent of the population was living in poverty and the proportion was growing, so that, by 1960, 14.2 per cent of the population was affected. (Coates and Silburn, 1970, pp 29-30)

Townsend argued conclusively that no 'absolute' definition of poverty, related to either subsistence or basic needs, was scientifically valid. Poverty could only be objectively and scientifically defined and measured using his 'theory of relative deprivation'. This theory was comprehensively explained in his seminal 1,200-page book *Poverty in the United Kingdom* (Townsend, 1979). The opening paragraph is the most important ever written about poverty and is so well known that many academics can recite it by heart – particularly the final two sentences:

Poverty can be defined objectively and applied consistently only in terms of the concept of relative deprivation. That is the theme of this book. The term is understood objectively rather than subjectively. Individuals, families and groups in the population can be said to be in poverty when they lack the resources to obtain the types of diet, participate in the activities and have the living conditions and amenities which are customary, or at least widely encouraged or approved, in the society to which they belong. Their resources are so seriously below those commanded by the average individual of family that they are in effect, excluded from ordinary living patterns, customs and activities. (p 31)

Extracts from the rest of this chapter make up **Chapter 16**.

Townsend believed subsistence and basic needs definitions of poverty to be inadequate as they failed to acknowledge people's social roles and obligations. In all societies, people require resources to mark births, deaths and to give presents on special occasions such as birthdays and marriage and on religious festivals. These social obligations are as important and sometimes more important than people's physical and material needs. For instance, parents will sometimes go hungry or without heating in order to be able to buy their child a birthday present.

Townsend's careful scientific research was so influential that it resulted in a paradigm shift in the understanding of poverty. In December 1984, the European Commission adopted a definition of poverty for policy purposes which is effectively identical to that proposed by Peter Townsend:

> the poor shall be taken to mean persons, families and groups of persons whose resources (material, cultural and social) are so limited as to exclude them from the minimum acceptable way of life in the Member State in which they live. (EEC, 1985)

Thus, Townsend's work directly influenced European anti-poverty policies, which help improve the living conditions of 550 million people in 27 EU member countries to this day.

Townsend's methodological research, particularly the *Poverty in the UK* survey, created the measurement of poverty through combining indicators of resources and deprivation in order to identify a scientifically valid poverty line. He later elaborated on both the concept and measurement of deprivation in a key 1987 paper in the *Journal of Social Policy* (Townsend, 1987) which was based on his experience of undertaking the first ever nationally representative poverty survey in the UK in 1968–69 (Poverty in the UK Survey) and the Booth Centenary Survey of Life and Labour in London in 1985 (**Chapter 17**).

This research resulted in two major theoretical disputes between Townsend and his critics during the 1980s which still form the basis of many undergraduate texts on poverty. Firstly, David Piachaud reviewed *Poverty in the UK* in *New Society* (Piachaud, 1981) and argued that Townsend had failed to measure poverty scientifically and indeed that the scientific measurement of poverty was impossible. Amartya Sen, in an exchange in *Oxford Economic Papers*, argued that, contrary to Townsend's belief, there was an irreducible absolutist core to poverty (see Sen, 1983, 1985). Townsend summarised the key arguments from both sides of these disputes in Chapter 6 of one of his major books *The international analysis of poverty* (Townsend, 1993); his responses are included in this volume as **Chapter 18** (see also **Chapter 6**).

In 1987, working with Peter Phillimore and Alastair Beattie on the geography of health inequalities, Townsend developed the first theory based deprivation index (**Chapter 19**) ,which could be calculated using 1981 small area Census data – the eponymous 'Townsend Deprivation Index'. The deprivation index consisted of four variables (unemployment, lack of access to a car, social and private renting, and overcrowding) and had such great explanatory power that it became the most widely used Census deprivation index in health geography research.

During the 1990s and the early years of the 21st century, Townsend increasingly focused his research on international poverty issues, particularly, extending the coverage of social security to all people, effective social controls on transnational corporations and the use of international agreements on human rights as effective anti-poverty policy tools (Townsend and Gordon, 2002; see **Chapter 10** in this volume). For example, Peter Townsend and his colleagues were funded by UNICEF to produce the first ever scientific estimates on the extent and nature of child poverty in developing countries, within the framework provided by the UN Convention on the Rights of the Child. The conclusions and policy recommendations from this report (Gordon et al, 2003) are reproduced in **Chapter 20**.

Townsend's empirical work showed that poverty was a pervasive structural phenomenon rather than due to the fecklessness or 'bad' behaviours of the 'poor'. Targeting regeneration interventions at the poorest slums or housing estates could never effectively eradicate poverty; profound changes were required to the structures in society which caused poverty. He argued that the causes of poverty could only be adequately understood in relation to the power and privilege of the 'rich'. Internationally, this required knowledge about the structures of society which served the interests and maintained the power of both national and international elites and transnational corporations. Poverty could only be effectively eradicated if some power and resources were redistributed from the 'rich' to the 'poor'. Townsend criticised academics, successive Labour Governments and UN organisations for failing to engage with this 'problem of riches'. He quoted fellow Fabian, R.H. Tawney, approvingly:

"Nothing could be more remote from Socialist ideals than the competitive scramble of a society which pays lip service to equality, but too often means by it merely equal opportunities of becoming unequal." He warns against "the corrupting influence of a false standard of values, which perverts, not only in education, but wide tracts of thought and life. It is this demon – the idolatry of money and success – with whom, not in one sphere alone but in all, including our own hearts and minds, Socialists have to grapple." (quoting from Tawney, 1964)

Peter Townsend did not only create new knowledge, he then acted upon it. He did not just understand the world, he changed it. He helped to found both the Child Poverty Action Group (CPAG) and the Disability Alliance organisations whose advocacy and campaigning work have helped improve thousands of lives. Peter also worked effectively with politicians and policy makers, such as UNICEF and the International Labour Organization (ILO), to improve the human rights of poor adults and children, including campaigning for a global child benefit, as a means to reduce poverty.

UNICEF acknowledged the debt they owed to him with the following tribute shortly after his death:

> Peter Townsend will be missed by UNICEF, but even more by the millions of poor children around the world, who never heard his voice, but whom he never forgot either in his research or in his advocacy, nor, most importantly, in his heart. Yet his voice will echo beyond his lifetime, and continue to influence efforts to end child poverty, in the rich and the poor world. (UNICEF, 2009)

Peter Townsend's final lecture, was an e-lecture on social policy and poverty to South African MSc students. Unfortunately, they did not have time to thank Peter before he died. The students have now sent a short and poignant farewell:

> *Hamba Kahle – 'Go well' Champion of the Poor.*

### References

Abel-Smith, B. and Townsend, P. (1965) *The poor and the poorest: A new analysis of the Ministry of Labour's Family Expenditure Surveys of 1953–4 and 1960*, London: Bell.

Coates, K. and Silburn, R. (1970) *Poverty: The forgotten Englishman*, Harmondsworth: Penguin.

EEC (1985) *On specific community action to combat poverty*, Council Decision of 19 December 1984, 85/8/EEC, *Official Journal of the EEC*, 2/24.

Gordon, D. , Nandy, S., Pantazis, C., Pemberton, S.A. and Townsend, P. (2003) *Child poverty in the developing world*, Report for UNICEF, Bristol: The Policy Press.

Piachaud, D. (1981) 'Peter Townsend and the Holy Grail', *New Society*, September, p 421.

Sen, A. (1983) 'Poor, relatively speaking', *Oxford Economic Papers*, No 35, August.

Sen, A. (1985) 'A sociological approach to the measurement of poverty: a reply to Professor Peter Townsend', *Oxford Economic Papers*, No 37, November.

Tawney, R.H. (1964) 'Socialism and freedom', *Dissent*, vol 11, no 2.

Townsend, P. (1952) 'Poverty: ten years after Beveridge', *Planning*, vol XIX, no 34, pp 21–40.

Townsend, P. (1954) 'Measuring poverty', *British Journal of Sociology*, vol 5, no 2, pp 130–7.

Townsend, P. (1962) 'The meaning of poverty', *British Journal of Sociology*, vol 13, no 3, pp 210–27.

Townsend, P. (1979) *Poverty in the United Kingdom: A survey of household resources and standards of living*, Harmondsworth: Penguin.

Townsend, P. (1987) 'Deprivation', *Journal of Social Policy*, vol 16, no 2, pp 125–46.

Townsend, P. (1993) *The international analysis of poverty*, Hemel Hempstead: Harvester Wheatsheaf.

Townsend, P. and Gordon, D. (eds) (2002) *World poverty: New policies to defeat an old enemy*, Bristol: The Policy Press.

Townsend, P., Phillimore, P. and Beattie, A. (1988) *Health and deprivation: Inequality and the North*, London: Croom Helm.

UNICEF (2009) 'UNICEF mourns death of Professor Peter Townsend', Press Release, 15 June 2009, New York, NY; UNICEF.

# 12

# Poverty: ten years after Beveridge

"The basic purpose of the social security scheme is freedom from want." *Beveridge Report*, para. 17.

It is now ten years since the publication of the report on *Social Insurance and Allied Services*, known more familiarly by the name of its author Sir William (now Lord) Beveridge. This famous report had one chief purpose, which is summarised in the quotation [above]. Has this purpose, to build up in Britain efficient and permanent defences against poverty, been fulfilled in the ten years that have passed? If success has been achieved, is it complete or only partial?

Before the war, and especially in the 1930s, a number of investigations were made into the nature and incidence of poverty in Britain, as well as the means of reducing it. Since the war, there has been only one investigation of a comparable kind, the third Social Survey of York, which attracted considerable attention when it was published in 1951. The results of this survey have been widely quoted as proof that poverty has been largely eliminated in Britain, an interpretation not wholly intended by the authors. But there is reason to doubt both the results of this survey and the interpretations placed upon them. The implications for national assistance, national insurance, and other social measures concerned with the maintenance of standards of consumption are therefore important.

But the problem of the extent of poverty in Britain today and the adequacy of social measures as a defence against it cannot be fully examined without answering two prior questions. What is meant by poverty? What information and methods are available for fixing a poverty standard, which may be used both by investigators in charge of social surveys and by administrators in determining the level of social payments? This broadsheet is chiefly concerned with these two questions, which are basic to all others about social security.

Townsend, P. (1952) 'Poverty: ten years after Beveridge', *Planning*, vol XIX, no 344, pp 21–40.

## Defining poverty

No exact definition of poverty is given in the Beveridge report, except indirectly in the detailed account it gives of subsistence standards. Elsewhere[1] Lord Beveridge has stated: "Want is defined as lack of income to obtain the means of healthy subsistence – adequate food, shelter, clothing and fuel." The standard cannot be made an absolute one, as has been recognized by economists, at least since the days of Adam Smith:

> "By necessaries I understand, not only the commodities which are indispensably necessary for the support of life, but whatever the custom of the country renders it indecent for creditable people, even of the lowest order, to be without." *The Wealth of Nations*, Bk 5. Chap. 2. Part 1, 1776.

There is inevitably a strong social, not to say subjective element in any definition of poverty. Opinions differ not only about the quantities of goods required to achieve "healthy subsistence" but also about some of the goods themselves.

The starting-point must be to enquire both what has been regarded as a minimum standard of consumption of food, clothing and shelter, and how people actually lay out their incomes on these items. It will be found that standards vary, not only according to sex and age, but also regionally, occupationally and from one period to another. These variations do not mean that it is impossible to arrive at a standard of subsistence which may be used both as a measure of the number of people in want and of what help a particular individual or family may require. Social investigators and administrators alike are obliged to apply such a standard. A form of averaging is unavoidable. The danger at one extreme comes from believing that there is some absolute standard of human needs which can be made the basis of a scientifically designed system of social security payments and allowances. The danger at the other extreme comes from making a series of inspired guesses which result in a standard that is completely arbitrary.
[...]

## The Beveridge Report

In his report on *Social Insurance and Allied Services* Lord Beveridge was not aiming to measure the amount and kind of poverty in the country, as were the social surveys, but to find a standard on which to base social security payments. However, his estimation of subsistence standards is instructive in that a much clearer idea of the methods involved is given than in the social surveys.[2]

He based his allowance for food on the diets provided by the League of Nations Technical Commission and the British Medical Association. This followed former practice. In his allowances for clothing, fuel and light and household sundries he did not attempt to re-price former standards or accept the type and price of the goods observed to be purchased by the lower working classes, as had been done in several social surveys, but based his judgements largely on the Ministry of Labour enquiry of 1937–38 into working-class household budgets.

In the case of clothing, for example, Beveridge fixed the allowance for a man and wife at 3s. a week on the grounds that the average expenditure of 4s. 10½d. by a working-class couple was "above the subsistence requirement, since (it) relates to households which are living above the minimum", and that "in none of the social surveys undertaken in various towns before the war was the weekly cost of clothing for men and women together put as high as 3s." The latter statement is not strictly correct; for example, the 1936 York survey gave a figure of 4s. 9d. for man and wife, and as has been pointed out above, most of the other surveys based their allowances on the first survey of York in 1901. Clothing "needs", determined as they are by social conventions which reflect changing economic circumstances, can scarcely be said to have remained unaltered from 1901 to 1938 and the 1940s. In the main, Beveridge fixed a certain sum for clothing needs on the ground that the average working-class expenditure was well above it.

The allowances for fuel, light and household sundries was also based on the Ministry of Labour budget enquiry of 1937–38. The average expenditure of a two-person family among industrial households on fuel and light was 4s. 10d. and of the poorest two-person families 3s. 7d. Beveridge's estimate for fuel, light and household sundries was accordingly put at 4s. for two adults.

The social surveys before the war had invariably and unavoidably allowed for the actual rent paid by each family in calculating the income required for subsistence needs. Rent provided Beveridge with an almost insurmountable difficulty. Despite the variations in the rent paid in different regions of the country, e.g. 7.6 shillings in Scotland and 16.0 shillings in London for the average industrial household, and the variations within any given locality, Beveridge was inclined to make a fixed allowance so that the subsistence standard and, accordingly, the rates of insurance benefit, could also be so fixed. He argued that the principle of a flat rate of insurance contributions leading to a flat rate of benefit was simpler to administer and was easier to defend than any other.

Finally, Beveridge allowed a "margin" of 2s. a week for a man and woman together with 1s. 6d. for a man or a woman separately in his subsistence standard. This allowance covered "inefficiency in purchasing".

For retired persons Beveridge made a smaller allowance for food and clothing, on the ground that their requirements were less, and he slightly increased the allowance for fuel and light. It is interesting to note that old people were expected to spend more on clothing than children.

**Table III:** Beveridge subsistence standard (as a basis for insurance benefit)

| | Food | | Clothing | | Fuel, light and sundries | | Margin | | Rent | | Total | |
|---|---|---|---|---|---|---|---|---|---|---|---|---|
| | *s.* | *d.* | *s.* | *d.* | *s.* | *d.* | *s.* | *d.* | *s.* | *d.* | *s.* | *d.* |
| Single man | 7 | 0 | 1 | 6 | 2 | 6 | 1 | 6 | 6 | 6 | 19 | 0 |
| Single woman | 6 | 0 | 1 | 6 | 2 | 6 | 1 | 6 | 6 | 6 | 18 | 0 |
| Man and wife | 13 | 0 | 3 | 0 | 4 | 0 | 2 | 0 | 10 | 0 | 32 | 0 |
| Average child | 6 | 0 | [0] | 10 | [0] | 3 | – | | – | | 7 | 1 |
| Retired man | 6 | 0 | 1 | 4 | 3 | 0 | 1 | 6 | 6 | 0 | 17 | 10 |
| Retired woman | 5 | 6 | 1 | 4 | 3 | 0 | 1 | 6 | 6 | 0 | 17 | 4 |
| Retired couple | 11 | 6 | 2 | 8 | 5 | 0 | 2 | 0 | 8 | 6 | 29 | 8 |

[...]

## Standards and actual expenditure

The discussion of the Beveridge Report has thrown emphasis on the importance of looking at the way poorer people spend their money if a subsistence standard is to be built up. This has always been borne in mind by those trying to arrive at such a standard. Nevertheless, there has invariably been a great difference between the standards proposed and the actual expenditure of poorer groups. Investigators have usually justified this by saying the sum required to purchase the goods composing a subsistence standard is adequate *provided it is spent efficiently*. This argument deserves much closer scrutiny than it has received in the past. It may be that some purchases, previously excluded from subsistence standards, should have been included. It may be that people do not know what goods are "necessary" and where they can be obtained cheaply. Or it may be that many spending habits are determined by the conventions of the lowest stratum of society and by economic and social measures, such as rationing and indirect taxes, currently adopted by the community as a whole. All this is quite apart from individual habits and inclinations, which are usually thought of first when discussing "unnecessary" and "inefficient" spending. It is important to consider briefly some of these points.

First, the question of how great a difference there is between the way people spend their money and subsistence standards can be settled by examining statistics on the expenditures of the lowest income groups. When this is done ... it is clear that the way people living on low incomes actually spent their money in 1938 was very different from that proposed in the standards set by Rowntree and Beveridge. Beveridge's total subsistence allowance was roughly the same as the actual expenditure of the lowest expenditure group, and, as this group was a very small one, Beveridge's standard cannot be described as generous. Among all families expenditure on "other items" was substantial.

From some studies of pre-1939 budgets of families with children[3] a further point is clear. Families with children getting an equivalent income in 1938 to the total Beveridge subsistence allowance were spending it in a manner very different from that recommended by Beveridge. For example, a man and wife with two children at this level of income were spending 10-15 per cent less on food than Beveridge thought necessary. With three or four children the food deficiency was even greater. The larger the family the less it followed the pattern of necessary spending suggested by Beveridge. Of households in the 50s. expenditure group, in 1938, families with three children spent only 2s. 11d. more on food than childless families and actually spent less on meat, bacon, fish, fruit and vegetables. In all the expenditure groups an unexpected similarity was found in the proportions devoted to food, clothing, drink and other items, by families of different sizes. *A change in income had far more importance for the structure of the budgets than the addition of even three children.* This indicates, among other things, that people are unwilling, or unable, to change the pattern of their spending habits drastically when their family circumstances change.

In considering the justifiability of the wide difference between the standards and actual spending, the "other items" sum presents the main problem. In estimating subsistence needs should it be ignored, as in the Beveridge Report, or accounted for, as in Rowntree's 1936 Survey of York? The former was concerned with the basis of benefit payments, the latter with a yardstick of poverty, and this difference of purpose must be borne in mind. But whatever the reasons for maintaining that a man needs less when he is old, sick or unemployed than when he is employed, the question of deciding the level of social payments comes *after* the question of deciding the relationship between a subsistence standard and actual patterns of expenditure.

The problem centres on what is to be considered "necessary" and what is not. Once some items are included in the standard on the grounds that they are "conventionally" necessary, for instance clothing and household sundries, it is difficult to decide where to draw the line. Are tea, handkerchiefs, haircuts and cigarettes equally "necessary" in the conventional sense? On re-examination of family budgets, certain items are found in budgets of all lower income groups, and usually much the same is spent on them, e.g. trade union and burial club subscriptions, soap, other cleaning and toilet materials, newspapers, postage, hairdressing and laundry. Such items have rarely, some of them never, found a place in previous subsistence standards, and yet it would be reasonable to enquire whether their claim to a place is not as great as the generally accepted items, such as clothing and fuel.

Many people might be inclined to include these items but to exclude others, such as luxury foods, beer and tobacco, and entertainment. But it can be argued that although some families may spend nothing on tobacco, and others never go to the cinema, almost all poor families spend a proportion of their incomes on one or more "luxuries" of this kind. On this view, if no allowance is made in a subsistence standard for this kind of spending, which would cover holidays, entertainment, drink and tobacco, the standard would bear no relation to actual habits, and spending on the more essential items, such as food and fuel, would be skimped.

No general guidance on this problem can be given. All that the investigator can do at this point is to show what part these items play in the budgets of poorer families.

## Subsistence and rising prices

In preceding sections the discussion has centred on the questions of measuring poverty and establishing a subsistence standard. Once a standard is fixed it is useful to know how it can be revised from year to year as prices and incomes change. The difficulties of doing this have been largely neglected and yet the problem of revising the standard has an important bearing, not only on keeping track of subsistence requirements, but on social payments. Such payments will be considered in the next section.

In the absence of regular budget surveys the best that can be done to revise existing standards is to apply suitable cost of living indices. Most authorities agree, bearing in mind the various subsistence standards and the standard proposed by Lord Beveridge, that an index based on the first five items in the Ministry of Labour Interim index gives the fairest reflection of the cost of meeting subsistence needs, namely food, rent, clothing, fuel and light and household durable goods, omitting miscellaneous goods, services, drink and tobacco. The present Minister of National Insurance suggested in Parliament recently that some such index as this is used by the National Assistance Board.

[...] [T]he cost of paying for subsistence needs has risen faster than working class prices as a whole in recent years, particularly in the last year. The cost of meeting subsistence needs has in fact more than doubled since

1938, having risen by 114 per cent if rent is included, and by 128 per cent if rent is excluded.

Such an index should not be used without questioning its validity. After all, the goods covered by the Ministry of Labour index are not only those considered to be necessary to subsistence, and the real rise in the costs of meeting subsistence may have been under- or over-estimated. This can be checked only by comparing the index with regular studies of the cost of maintaining subsistence. These do not exist, but there are thorough and practical data on a human needs diet contained in the half-yearly papers written by Miss T. Schulz of the Oxford University Institute of Statistics. [...]

Miss Schulz and Rowntree are the only investigators who have issued figures of the cost of human needs diets based on actual surveys since the war and deserve to be taken seriously. Their work indicates how far price indices have understated actual rises in the costs of subsistence.

A subsistence index is the most reliable instrument in estimating the changes in the cost required to meet needs, but this itself has tended in recent years to underestimate the actual rise, at least as regards food. In order to provide enough information to put a value on present subsistence needs a new standard or base-line would have to be devised. For this insufficient material is at present available.

## The official view of subsistence needs

Having discussed the Beveridge subsistence standard and the methods involved in bringing a subsistence standard up to date, it is of value to see how far social payments have conformed to a standard of needs in recent years. The rates paid under national assistance represent the Government's view of what it costs to pay for the needs, and the benefit rates paid under national insurance have been claimed by Governments since the war to be related, more or less, to Beveridge's principle of a subsistence basis for insurance payments. Although it can be argued that the Beveridge standard was a tough one, this was the standard which influenced the official view of what it cost to meet needs, and it is important to have some idea of how social payments today compare with Beveridge's standard [...].

It must be emphasised that the adjustment made to the original Beveridge scales is a minimum adjustment, on the basis of indices which themselves have been shown in the previous section to understate the actual rise in the cost of subsistence needs. No precision is claimed for the figures, but no way can be seen of making them lower. Insurance payments for all but retired persons were about 10 per cent below the Beveridge standard in 1948 and in January 1952 were about 30 per cent below. For retired persons, payments were about 8 per cent below the Beveridge standard in 1948, 15 per cent in 1950, 9 per cent in October 1951 and 16 per cent in January 1952.

The relationship between the rates of insurance benefits and those of national assistance has changed greatly in recent years. In 1948 the sums payable by the National Assistance Board were fixed slightly below benefits though the difference was not as large as recommended by Beveridge, who would have made the two differ by the amount of rent allowed. The rent paid in each individual case of payment by the Board is added on to the rate of assistance. At present the scale of assistance is 15-20 per cent higher than the scale of insurance benefits, except for pensioners. The new scales proposed for the latter part of 1952 reduce the difference to 8 or 9 per cent. Nevertheless, the fact that assistance payments will be 8 to 9 per cent above insurance payments, *despite* the exclusion of an allowance for rent in the fixed payments, is some measure of the extent by which insurance payments fail to reach a level of needs.

This point is confirmed by the increases in the number of current payments by the National Assistance Board. The number of current allowances paid out under national assistance, excluding non-contributory old age pensions, was 842,000 in July 1948, 1,157,000 in December 1949, 1,350,000 in December 1950, and 1,461,00 in December 1951 (in February 1952 the total passed 1½ millions). Thus the numbers increased by 169 thousand in the second half of 1948, by 146 thousand in 1949, by 193 thousand in 1950, by 111 thousand in 1951 and by 44 thousand in the first three months of this year. However, some part of the increase would be accounted for by the fact that some people do not realise at once that they can apply for assistance.

The conclusion to be drawn from these data seems to be that the benefits conferred under the National Insurance scheme have been increasingly inadequate in recent years in providing for the necessities of subsistence, even in the stringent Beveridge sense of "subsistence". And, as has been pointed out recently in *The Times*[4], the new insurance benefits will in no sense represent a return to the subsistence basis of the Beveridge Report. There is even some doubt over the application of the more modest principle of making payments roughly sufficient for needs without including provision for rent. An increasing number of people seem to be applying for national assistance in order to meet their needs.

In practice, the subsistence basis of insurance payments has been abandoned. This poses one of the most serious questions that must be faced when the quinquennial review of the National Insurance scheme is presented to Parliament in 1954: should the subsistence standard be restored? And if so, which standard? A great deal of fresh information is required for a satisfactory answer.

## Conclusion

In 1943, surveying the Beveridge Report, P E P endorsed the author's view that "... the State's duty is to ensure to all citizens a minimum income sufficient for their 'human needs' in all the main contingencies of life..." and went on, "To provide less than a subsistence minimum is indefensible; to provide more is unnecessary, possibly dangerous".[5]

Few people have ever seriously questioned Beveridge's principle; but if this principle is to be applied, "a subsistence minimum" must be given a much clearer meaning than it has at present. This must be done before the numbers of people in poverty, and the extent to which they are in need, can be measured accurately, and before any assessment can be made of the effectiveness of particular social measures in diminishing poverty.

An attempt has been made in this broadsheet to describe the steps that are involved in arriving at such a minimum. It is evident that there is not enough information available to enable a satisfactory subsistence standard to be worked out.

Much of the missing information could be furnished by the proposed enquiry by the Ministry of Labour into family budgets. Since its chief purpose is to provide facts for a revision of the index of retail prices, it is important to emphasise the types of information which this enquiry could contribute to the formulation of a subsistence standard. It is not enough to know the average spending a head in particular income groups, as was given in the report on the previous budget enquiry made in 1937–38. Spending must be broken down not only by family size but also by income group, so that the spending patterns of childless families can be compared with those of families with children in the same and different income groups.

The enquiry could also provide useful information about the spending of particular sub-groups such as the aged, families with infants, those receiving insurance benefits and those receiving national assistance. It would then be possible to see how social payments are used and to get a clearer idea of the needs of different groups in the population. A specialized study revealing how people's spending reacts to unavoidable new claims on their incomes, or to changes in income, would do even more to show what things people forgo in the event of sickness, unemployment or other of the "main contingencies of life".

The scope of the proposed enquiry is still under discussion. In any event its results are unlikely to be ready before the end of next year at the earliest: consequently they will not be available for the first quinquennial review of the National Insurance scheme. The need for such information is set out in the 1946 Act itself, which lays down (S.40) that: "... The Minister shall review the rates and amounts of benefits in relation ... to the circumstances at the time of insured persons in Great Britain, including in particular the expenditure which is necessary for the preservation of health and working capacity…" It is difficult to see how the Minister can adequately relate benefits to subsistence needs without the necessary budget data. If it is impossible to get the results of a national enquiry in time, then a few smaller enquiries into the spending of sub-groups of the population, such as the aged and those receiving national assistance, should be started without delay.

But the necessary facts, when collected, do not automatically provide a justifiable subsistence standard. Knowing what people actually spend does not explain what they ought to spend. A number of decisions have to be made about the type of goods and services necessary for subsistence in modern society, and in what quantities they are necessary. Hitherto, in the various social surveys and in the Beveridge Report, the bases of such decisions have not been critically examined and few attempts have been made to judge their probable effects.

There is no absolute standard to which reference can be made. It is true that in the case of food, which forms by far the largest single item in a subsistence budget, judgement is aided by the results of investigations into nutritional needs. But given these, there is still no fixed amount which can be said to be needed by every man, woman and child. A woman may require some 17 per cent fewer calories than a man, but her need of certain vitamins is no less, while the need of a pregnant woman for many nutrients is greater than that of a man. It is clear that age, occupation and the composition of the family are of great importance in deciding what kind of food expenditure is needed.

Nevertheless useful average figures which take these qualifications into account can be evolved, provided also that reference is made to the expenditure on food in the lowest income groups as revealed by budget data; expenditure which is influenced by factors such as rationing, taste, standardization of products and what is currently available on the market, as well as "nutritive needs".

For items other than food the use of family budget data is the only practical way of limiting the arbitrariness of judgements. For these items it is necessary to know the average amounts spent on various goods by families in the lower income groups, and the make-up of family budgets in these income groups. This knowledge would help to relate a subsistence standard to actual spending habits. It is also essential to know, for example, not only the average spending of the aged poor, or families with three or four children, but also how far individual spending ranges from the average. These figures could be modified by examining the use of particular commodities; for instance, the purchase of individual garments and their life, or what is the minimum sum required to keep one coal fire going through winter.

There is a strong argument for adding a few specific items, such as postage, shaving and hairdressing, laundry, contraceptives, sanitary towels, certain subscriptions, soap and other cleaning materials, to the list of necessaries usually adopted in a standard (clothing, fuel and light and household sundries), on the ground both that they occupy a consistent place in family budgets and that, by conventional standards, they might also be regarded as "necessary".

There remain two problems in arriving at a standard. At what level should the "necessary" spending on all these items be fixed? And should items not listed above, such as entertainment, holidays, drink and tobacco, be excluded from the subsistence standard? (The Government subsidizes tobacco for old age pensioners, and thus virtually recognizes this as a necessary item in some budgets.) A guide to answering both these questions, particularly the second, which was discussed [above] would be provided by more information about rigidities in patterns of spending, the effects of rationing and indirect taxes, and the social prestige influence ("keeping up with the Joneses") on spending. But in the last resort, decisions must be based on contemporary views about the lowest living conditions that are tolerable in the community.

Once an agreed subsistence standard is determined, the methods by which the Government can ensure that no one falls below it are open to argument. During recent years national insurance has probably been less of a guarantee of this than it is apt to be imagined. Increased wages, full employment, and the food subsidies have done much more than insurance benefits to reduce poverty in Britain. This is partly because these factors affect everyone whereas insurance benefits only affect a minority, and partly because, as has been shown, the Beveridge principle of tying benefits to a subsistence standard has been abandoned in practice.

This departure may or may not be a retrograde step. It can be argued that the principle of flat rate benefits is inconsistent with maintaining benefits at subsistence level, and it may be decided for various reasons that insurance benefits need not be maintained at this level. Other ways of preventing poverty may be preferred. But whatever the policy, a carefully determined subsistence standard is essential for the measurement of its success.

**Endnotes**

[1] *Full Employment in a Free Society*, 1944, p. 17.

[2] pp. 76-90.

[3] "The Economic Position of the Family", Memorandum to the Royal Commission on Population by J. Hajnal and A.M. Henderson. "Variations in Working Class Family Expenditure", J.L. Nicholson, *Journal of the Royal Statistical Society*, Vol. XCII, Part IV. "The Cost of a Family", A.M. Henderson, *The Review of Economic Studies*, 1949-50.

[4] "Social payments", *The Times*, April 17 and 18, 1952.

[5] After the Beveridge Report, *Planning*, No 205, April 20, 1943.

# 13

# Measuring poverty

One of the basic aims of social policy in the years immediately following the war was the elimination of poverty. In order to find how far this aim has been realized there must be adequate inquiries from time to time in the form of social surveys which adopt certain definite standards of measurement. In the ten years preceding the war at least ten surveys of the extent and causes of poverty in particular areas were carried out. In the nine years since the war only one study of this type has been published. This in itself may be an indication that the problem of poverty is less pressing than it was, but, on the evidence of a single study, we cannot claim much detailed knowledge about the living conditions of poorer people, or about the effects of the new social security services. The aim of this article is to consider on what basis this knowledge may be acquired in the future. I will discuss briefly the standards used in measuring poverty in the past, and in the course of this will argue for an entirely different approach.

The standard selected is important not only to the research worker intent on measuring the extent of poverty or general living conditions in any locality. A standard of a similar kind has been used in framing social policy. Social security benefit payments are intended to be related to a rough standard of subsistence, and this relation will have to be considered when the quinquennial review of the social security scheme is presented to Parliament in the near future. It is therefore appropriate to examine what is meant by a subsistence or poverty standard.

The sociological study and measurement of poverty in this country dates from the pioneering work of Charles Booth and B. Seebohm Rowntree at the end of the last century.[1,2] In introducing his study Rowntree said,

> The families living in poverty may be divided into two sections:
>
> (1) Families whose total earnings are insufficient to obtain the minimum necessaries for the maintenance of merely physical efficiency. Poverty falling under this head may be described as "primary" poverty.

Townsend, P. (1954) 'Measuring poverty', *British Journal of Sociology*, vol 5, no 2, pp 130-7.

(2) Families whose total earnings would be sufficient for the maintenance of merely physical efficiency were it not that some portion of it is absorbed by other expenditure, either useful or wasteful. Poverty falling under this head may be described as "secondary" poverty.

The "minimum necessaries for the maintenance of merely physical efficiency" were calculated by estimating the nutritional needs of adults and children and by translating such needs into quantities of different foods and hence into money terms, and by adding on to these figures certain minimum sums for clothing, fuel and household sundries, according to the size of family. The poverty line for a family of five was, food 12s. 9d., clothing 2s. 3d., fuel 1s. 10d., household sundries 10d., totalling 17s. 8d. per week. Rent was treated as unavoidable outlay and was added to this sum. A family was considered to be in poverty if its total income fell short of the poverty line plus rent. The studies that followed in the next forty years adopted the same approach and although there were some minor alterations, the standards used for measuring poverty were broadly the same, adjusted according to change in prices, as that used by Rowntree in 1899.[3, 13] In the 1930s a standard applicable to 1899 and converted by means of a price index based on articles purchased in 1904 was taken to be the best method of measuring poverty.[4, 14] By and large the changes in the conditions of life brought about in the intervening years were ignored.

In 1936 Rowntree made a second survey of York, in the course of which he used a more generous standard of poverty. This differed in degree, but not in kind, from the standard used at the end of the last century. The list of necessaries was lengthened to include compulsory insurance contributions, trade union subscriptions, travelling to and from work, and personal sundries such as a daily newspaper, a little stationery, and a few other odds and ends. A similar list was adopted in his and G.R. Lavers' Third Survey of York, *Poverty and the Welfare State*, 1951. A discussion of these standards and of those used in earlier surveys will be found in "Poverty: Ten Years after Beveridge".[15]

In considering all these poverty standards in detail, one cannot help feeling that they are too arbitrary. If clothing, money for travel to work and newspapers are considered to be "necessaries" in the conventional sense, why not tea, handkerchiefs, laundry, contraceptives, cosmetics, hair-dressing and shaving, and life insurance payments? Are we indeed so sure that a list of necessaries must exclude cigarettes, beer, toys for children, Christmas gifts and cinema entertainment? The question of what were regarded or what ought to have been regarded as necessaries was very rarely raised in any of the surveys.

In attempts to reduce the arbitrariness of the standard some investigators had tried to find out the actual spending of families on certain items. In 1899 and 1936 Rowntree based his allowances for clothing and fuel and light on information and opinions passed on to him by "a large number of working people", though in 1936 he admitted that in arriving at an allowance for personal sundries "I was forced to rely largely on my own judgment", and in both years his findings on the food consumption and expenditure of 18 and 28 families respectively did not affect his formulation of the poverty line. In the third survey of York in 1950 Rowntree found out the spending of 29 women on clothing and household sundries, and of 32 men on clothing and fuel and light. In the last case, for example, the amounts to be included in the poverty standard for women's and children's clothing and for household sundries were based on the average expenditure of three women whose expenditure on these items was the smallest of those from whom information was obtained. Finding out the expenditure of the poorest families on clothing, fuel and light and household sundries is perhaps a less arbitrary method of compiling a standard, but why should these items be selected from budgets for consideration and not others as well? And secondly, does the average expenditure of those who spend least on clothing or fuel provide a standard of what people *need to spend* on such items to be out of poverty?

The most defensible constituent of the poverty line has always been the amount allocated to food. Experts on nutrition have worked out the average nutritive needs of broad classes of the population, in terms of calories, proteins, vitamins, iron, calcium and so on. These needs, as stated earlier, can be translated into quantities of different foods and from foods into money terms. The diet, as derived, gives adequate nutrition at the lowest possible cost, and demands considerable knowledge of the most nutritious and cheapest foods on the market. It may well be argued that few families have the knowledge or opportunity to attain such a standard. In a study of the diets of 28 families in different income groups in his 1936 survey of York Rowntree said:

> It is true that, at 1936 prices, a family of five could be adequately fed for this sum (20s. 6d.), but ... the housewife must possess an unusual amount of knowledge of the nutritive value of different foodstuffs. Among the 28 families, some of which were very poor, not one succeeded in selecting a dietary anything like as economical as that used in our minimum standard of living (p. 173).[a]

The same point applies to the half-yearly papers on the cost of a "human needs" diet, which stem from the standard used by Rowntree in 1936, written by Miss T. Schulz of the Oxford University Institute of Statistics.[b]

If indeed few working-class families attain this standard, then it may not be a practicable one to use in measuring poverty.

The main fault in the standards used has been their lack of relation to the budgets and customs of life of working people. Many who are considered to be above the poverty line because their income exceeds the total cost of meeting basic needs do, in fact, spend less on the individual items included in the standard – food, clothing, fuel and light and household sundries – simply because they spend money on other things. This can be illustrated by comparing the poverty standards used immediately before the war (and the subsistence standard outlined in the Beveridge Report) with the budgets of poorer families in 1938, details of which were collected by the Ministry of Labour.[16] Lord Beveridge, for example, arguing for a subsistence standard similar in kind to the poverty lines used in the surveys before the war, allowed a man, wife and three small children 53s. 3d. a week at 1938 prices, including 31s. for food (58 per cent of the total). But in 1938 families of the same size with roughly the same total income were spending less than 22s. on food (41 per cent of the total income).[c] How those on the borderline of poverty ought to spend their money is a very different thing from how they do spend their money. It would be unrealistic to expect them, as in effect many social investigators have expected them, to be skilled dieticians with marked tendencies towards puritanism.

In all the definitions of poverty in the social surveys there is the implication that many poor people ought to limit their spending to a short list of "necessaries" laid down by those in charge of the surveys and that if they did not do this they were in poverty only through their own fault. "Our definition is such that a family is deemed to be in poverty if the joint income of the members, *supposing it were all available and wisely spent*, would not suffice to purchase for them the necessaries of life…" (p. 148, *Social Survey of Merseyside* [my italics]). Many critics fastened on to the large numbers in what Rowntree called "secondary" poverty as evidence of the need for moral regeneration, and said that these people lacked merely strength of will to pull themselves out of poverty. It was not appreciated that many in this class would have needed virtues of self-denial, skill and knowledge not possessed by any other class of society, if they were to spend their money as it was thought they should spend it.

Judgments of one social class on another are notoriously untrustworthy and things which are treated as necessaries by one group may not be so regarded by another. A few drinks in a pub on a Saturday night after watching the local football match may be as necessary, in the conventional sense, to membership of the poorest stratum of society as a Savile Row suit and business meetings over lunch at the Savoy to membership of a wealthier stratum of society. Recent experience of the effects of unemployment in the cotton towns in Lancashire showed that when incomes were reduced from a full wage to an unemployment insurance allowance many families were apt to cut down on things such as meat and fruit in order not to forgo an occasional visit to a cinema or football match.[17] In considering the spending habits of poorer people, it seems that due regard must be paid to the conventions sanctioning membership of their community, to the influence of economic and social measures currently adopted by society as a whole, such as rationing, welfare foods services, food subsidies and indirect taxes, and to the standards encouraged by advertisers,[d] the press, the B.B.C. and the Church.

## A new standard

The pattern of spending among poor people is largely determined by the accepted modes of behaviour in the communities in which they live, and these, in turn, are determined to some extent by the practices adopted by the society as a whole through central and local government. A yardstick for measuring poverty can only be devised in the light of knowledge about family budgets. How can this be done with the least arbitrariness?

One improvement was suggested in a study of a Birmingham community, carried out in 1939 and published in 1942.[13] In this study poverty was measured in two ways: (i) by comparing net income (i.e. total income less rent, compulsory insurances, and fares to and from work) with an assumed minimum standard of expenditure on food, fuel, light, clothing and cleaning materials; and (ii) by comparing with a minimum standard of expenditure on food the balance out of housekeeping money theoretically available for food, after paying the assumed minimum on non-food items in (i) plus voluntary insurances and regular hire-purchase instalments. The first, the usual type of measurement adopted in social surveys, was said to take "less account of actualities" and the second was "a more realistic measure of the standard of sufficiency of the family". But it was acknowledged that both these methods could be criticized, though the second to a lesser extent, for "ignoring certain types of necessary expenditure, such as that on household utensils, medical treatment, and holidays, as well as expenditure on tobacco, beer, newspapers, and recreation, which are, to say the least of it, customary" (p 47).

The second method, although open to many of the criticisms expressed above, gives prominence to expenditure on food as a criterion of poverty. In future, it would seem reasonable to accept such a criterion, with certain qualifications, simply because nutritional needs are more susceptible of measurement than clothing, fuel and other needs.

The following procedure might be justifiable in future surveys: (i) The collection of data relating to the food consumption and expenditure as well as the income of working-class households; (ii) The comparison of this data, assembled according to constitution of household and income group, with a scale of nutritive needs, such as that in the Report of the Committee on Nutrition of the British Medical Association, 1950; (iii) The isolation, from all those securing minimum nutrition, of, say, the 25 per cent in the various household groups who achieve it on the smallest incomes, or rather, the smallest incomes less one or two fixed involuntary overheads, such as rent and compulsory insurances. The average total expenditure of these households, less the overheads, according to their different sizes, can be taken as the poverty line.

Such a standard may be justified on the ground that it is, in fact, attained by a fair proportion of working-class people, and is therefore realistic. It would obviate the need for subjective decisions about the sums of money required for clothing, fuel and light and so on. Inevitably, a subjective element remains, and this is involved in the choice of the proportion of working-class households whose members have an adequate diet and whose spending is to be considered in fixing the standard. But this element need not be obtrusive, particularly if the choice is made with full knowledge of the budgetary patterns of different families, and with full knowledge of the dispersion, and the reasons for the dispersion, around the budgetary mean of each income and household group.

Part of the information essential to the application of this method is already obtained in the course of the Nationals Food Survey. The latest Report on this, for 1951,[18] analyses the adequacy of diet by social class, but the classes are rather broadly defined,[e] and the diet and expenditure of those in the lowest income group is not set out in any detail. A great deal of information about family budgets will issue from the new survey of household expenditure being made at present by the Ministry of Labour. It is to be hoped that this will be tabulated by household size and constitution, for each income group.

It is true that the method suggested is basically a method of measuring the extent of malnutrition not attributable to wasteful spending, but I think it would give the fairest index of poverty, particularly if the results gained by its use were correlated with other findings based on standards of overcrowding, household amenities, education and so on.

## The level of benefit payments

The different approach which has been urged has an important bearing on the standards adopted in social policy for benefit payments. Lord Beveridge, in his *Report on Social Insurance and Allied Services*, formulated a subsistence standard very similar to the poverty lines used in the social surveys before the war, as a reasonable way of fixing benefit rates. This was generally regarded as the "central idea" of the Beveridge Plan.[19, 20] Lord Beveridge has himself reaffirmed this point in recent months. The National Assistance scales are determined by means of a similar standard, and although the National Insurance scales fall short of the Beveridge standard, they are still in principle related to it. Neither the Labour nor the Conservative Party has explicitly abandoned this principle. Whether, in fact, the subsistence basis for benefit payments should be accepted by the nation in the future is one of the fundamental questions that will have to be faced by Parliament next year when the quinquennial review of social security is considered. The adoption of a true subsistence minimum would add greatly to the costs of the scheme. It is true that in recent years an increasing number of people have received wages during sickness and have entered superannuation schemes, and income from the social security services in times of adversity may therefore be less important now than it was. For short periods of unemployment or sickness people seem to manage quite well, because, apart from insurance payments, they frequently get deferred wages, trade union allowances and P.A.Y.E. refunds, and need to purchase few items of clothing or household materials. (Large families should not be included in this category.) There would appear to be a case for two scales, one for a short and one for a long period of need. It may be true, too, that payments to the old should be lower than those to other people in continuing need, but this is a matter for further inquiry. In any event, the acceptance of a standard such as the pre-war poverty line or the Beveridge subsistence minimum implies that poor working-class people should and could live as social scientists and administrators think they should live. There has been little attempt to discuss the distinction between "luxuries" and "necessities" in terms of economic and social sanctions for spending behaviour, nor in terms of individual and class differences. And there has been no attempt to distinguish between the humanly attainable and the desirable in the pattern of family budgets.

I have tried to set out the difficulties of arriving at a satisfactory standard for measuring poverty, which can be used in social surveys, and the difficulties of eliminating class judgments from that standard. The conclusion seems to be that the problem of whether or not a family is in poverty is best decided by finding whether its expenditure, save for one or two involuntary overheads, such as rent and compulsory insurances, is less than that which actually secures minimum nutrition for a large number of working-class families.

### References

[1] London: *Life and Labour of the People in London*, Charles Booth.

[2] York: *Poverty: A Study of Town Life*, B.S. Rowntree.

[3] A Survey of Five Towns: *Livelihood and Poverty*, A.L. Bowley and A.R. Burnett-Hurst, 1915, and *Has Poverty Diminished ?* A.L. Bowley and Margaret H. Hogg, 1925.

[4] London: *New Survey of London Life and Labour*, 1930-5.

[5] Merseyside: *Social Survey of Merseyside*, ed. D. Caradog-Jones, 1934.

[6] Southampton: *Work and Wealth in a Modern Port*, P. Ford, 1934.

[7] Sheffield: *A Survey of the Standard of Living in Sheffield*, A.D.K. Owen, 1934.

[8] Miles Platting (Manchester): *Poverty and Housing Conditions in a Manchester Ward*, John Inman, 1934.

[9] Plymouth: *A Social Survey of Plymouth*, 1935.

[10] York: *Poverty and Progress*, B.S. Rowntree, 1941.

[11] Bristol: *The Standard of Living in Bristol*, H. Tout, 1938.

[12] Six Towns: *Men Without Work*, A report made to the Pilgrim Trust, 1938.

[13] Kingstanding (Birmingham): *Nutrition and Size of Family*, M.S. Soutar, E.H. Wilkins and P. Sargant Florence, 1942.

[14] "A New Calculation of the Poverty Line", R.F. George, *Journal of the Royal Statistical Society*, 1937.

[15] "Poverty: Ten Years After Beveridge", *Planning*, No. 344, August 4, 1952.

[16] *Weekly Expenditure of Working Class Households in the United Kingdom in 1937-38*, Detailed Tables, July, 1949.

[17] "Social Security and Unemployment in Lancashire", *Planning*, No. 349, December 1, 1952.

[18] "Domestic Food Consumption and Expenditure, 1951", *Report of the National Food Survey Committee*, 1953.

[19] *England's Road to Social Security*, Karl de Schweinitz, 1943.

[20] "After the Beveridge Report", *Planning*, No. 205, April 20, 1943.

**Endnotes**

[a] In the *New Survey of London Life and Labour*, Vol. VI, p. 320, discussing working-class culinary and dietetic standards, Miss F.A. Livingstone argued that full weight must be given "to all the handicaps and difficulties, such as cramped space, absence of storage, defective water supply or cooking apparatus, and the severe limitation of time arising from other pressing duties", besides working-class "habits and prejudices".

[b] In a summary of her studies Miss Schulz said: "It needed, indeed, exceptional knowledge of food values as well as considerable skill in cooking for the adequate nutrition of a family to be attained at the figures of cost computed by us since 1941." *Human Needs Diets from 1935 to 1949*, Bulletin of the Oxford University Institute of Statistics, October, 1949.

[c] Based on data in "The Cost of a Family", A.M. Henderson, *The Review of Economic Studies 1949-50*, Vol. XVII (2).

[d] "To (the advertiser) a bride is not a young woman on the edge of a great adventure; she is a conditioned consumer who, by buying the right cosmetics and right brassiere has captured her man and who, when she returns from her honeymoon, will go into the grocer's and automatically recite those branded names which have been the most loudly dinned into her ears for the last twenty-one years." *The Shocking History of Advertising*, E. S. Turner, 1952, p. 12.

[e] The sample was divided into the following income groups: £20 and over per week (1 per cent of the population), £13-£20 (2 per cent), £8-£13 (13 per cent), £4 10s.-£8 (64 per cent), and under £4 10s. per week (20 per cent).

# 14

# The meaning of poverty

The belief that poverty has been virtually eliminated in Britain is commonly held. It has been reiterated in parliament and the press and has gained authority from a stream of books and papers published by economists, sociologists and others in the post-war years.[1]

In the main the proposition rests on three generalizations which are accepted as facts. The first is that full employment, combined with larger real wages and the enormous increase in the numbers of married women in paid employment, has brought prosperity to the mass of the population. The second is that there has been a marked redistribution of income from rich to poor and, indeed, a continuing equalization of income and wealth. And the third is that the introduction of a welfare state has created a net – though some prefer to use the metaphor a featherbed – which prevents nearly all those who are sick, disabled, old or unemployed from falling below a civilized standard of subsistence. Each of these generalizations needs to be examined carefully. We might, for example, ask whether a population of the present size, with 400,000 registered unemployed, constitutes a society with 'full employment'; or whether to the official numbers of the unemployed, we should add many thousands of married women, handicapped persons and persons of pensionable age who do not register with employment exchanges, but who would take certain forms of paid work, particularly light or sheltered work, if it was available. Again, we might ask whether post-war Britain justifies the epithet of a 'welfare' state in relation either to contemporary needs and resources or to the social services which existed during and before the war.

But perhaps the crucial concepts embedded in these three generalizations which should give us pause are those of 'prosperity', 'equality' and 'subsistence'. I cannot attempt to deal comprehensively with these elusive concepts. I shall merely try to say something about the meaning of 'subsistence', which appears to govern much contemporary thought about the subject of poverty. My main thesis is that both 'poverty' and 'subsistence' are relative concepts and that they can only be defined in relation to the material and emotional resources available at a particular time to the members either of a particular society or different societies.

---

Townsend, P. (1962) 'The meaning of poverty', *British Journal of Sociology*, vol 13, no 3, pp 210-27.

The state of almost dazed euphoria which seems to have overtaken social scientists in the late 1940s has gradually given way to a more lively, if cautious, examination of the peripheries of the welfare state and even of a few of its nerve centres. Dr. J.H. Sheldon's revelations about the state of chronic sick hospitals in the Birmingham region,[2] Mr. Peter Marris' study of widows in East London,[3] Mr. Merfyn Turner's account of life in lodging-houses,[4] Dr. John Wing's and Mr. George Brown's detailed analyses of conditions in some mental hospitals,[5] Miss L.A. Shaw's and Mrs. M. Bowerbank's description of the hardship experienced by families whose breadwinners die or are ill[6] and Mrs. Harriet Wilson's description of the economic stress experienced by problem families[7] comprise just a few of the revealing studies which have been published in recent years. As a result of such work and of public interest in the problems of some groups in the population – for example, homeless families and gypsies – there has been greater readiness in the last few years to concede the existence at least of 'residual' poverty.

## The numbers in poverty, according to the standard of subsistence

But what are the dimensions of poverty? Everything turns on the precise meaning given to the term. Charles Booth and Seebohm Rowntree each developed a rough definition towards the end of the nineteenth century and the latter's was broadly followed, with various modifications, in a series of surveys during this century. In 1941 Lord Beveridge was guided by these in working out benefit rates to be paid under the new scheme of social security to be introduced after the war. Even today the amounts paid in national insurance benefits and national assistance allowances derive what logic they have from his approach. Beveridge leaned heavily on Rowntree's work.

In 1950, with G.R. Lavers, Rowntree undertook his third and final survey of the City of York.[8] Whatever criticisms we might make of its methods it listed the levels of income said to be needed by different types of households to keep clear of poverty. For example, an income of £5 0s. 2d. per week, excluding rent, was said to be needed by a family consisting of man and wife and three children, and £1 13s. 2d. by an unemployed or retired woman living alone. The chief conclusion was that 1½ per cent of the total population of York was in poverty in 1950, compared with 18 per cent in the similar, but not identical, survey of 1936. Most of this small group were retirement pensioners.

Even accepting the methods used, would the conclusion have been as true of the whole country as many people supposed at the time? The Ministry of Labour carried out a detailed survey of the expenditure (and income) of a random sample of nearly 13,000 households in the United Kingdom during 1953 and the early weeks of 1954. These households comprised some 41,000 persons. A report was published in 1957[9] but this did not allow more than intelligent guesses to be made about the number and type of households falling below certain levels of expenditure. Lately, with the help of the Ministry, my colleagues and I have had an opportunity of studying the results in more detail and particularly the distributions of expenditure. We adjusted Rowntree's income standards according to the rise in prices between 1950 and 1953, and then applied them to the budget data collected by the Ministry.[10] We found that 5.4 per cent of the households, comprising 4.1 per cent of the persons in the sample, were in poverty, according to Rowntree's criteria. Another 10.6 per cent of persons were living at a standard lower than 40 per cent above the poverty line. Altogether 14.7 per cent of the persons in the sample were in poverty or near-poverty. Applied to the whole population these figures would suggest that there were 2.1 million persons in poverty, and another 5.4 million only marginally better off, giving a total of 7½ millions.

The rather lower subsistence standard of the National Assistance Board was also applied to these data. In 1953 the ordinary amounts payable by the Board were 35s. for a single householder, 59s. for husband and wife, and amounts ranging for children and other dependants in the household from 11s. to 31s., according to their age. Usually the actual rent paid by the household could be added to these amounts. For each type of household in the Ministry of Labour sample of 1953-4, we worked out the minimum sum which it would normally receive in adversity from the National Assistance Board. The total expenditure of each household was then compared with the national assistance rate. We found that 2.1 per cent of households, comprising 1.2 per cent of the total persons in the sample, had an average weekly expenditure below the basic national assistance rates plus rent and that another 6.6 per cent of persons had less than 40 per cent above these rates. Altogether 10.1 per cent of households and 7.8 per cent of persons were living at a standard less than 40 per cent above the basic national assistance rates. Some details are shown in Table 1.

These figures may under-represent the proportions in poverty in the United Kingdom at that time. In its report the Ministry points out that persons aged 61 or more were under-represented in the sample by about a quarter[11] and our scrutiny of the data also suggested that there was some under-representation of the sick. It is after all understandable that poor persons, particularly those who are aged or sick, may find it more difficult than other persons to keep detailed expenditure records for a period of three weeks. With this important reservation, the figures imply that almost 4 million persons in the United Kingdom were in 1953-4 living below, or less than 40 per cent above, the national assistance level. Twenty-nine per cent of these were children under the age of 16 (about a third of whom were children under 5). As would be expected, a large proportion of the total, in fact nearly half consisted of elderly persons or couples living alone. Another substantial proportion consisted of households in which the head was sick or unemployed. But what may be surprising to some is that over a third were living in households where the head was working full-time, as shown in Table 2. Most of these were people living in households containing three, four or more children.

**Table I:** Percentage of Households and Persons Living close to National Assistance Levels (national sample surveyed by the Ministry of Labour, 1953-4)

| Total household expenditure as percentage of national assistance scale rate plus rent | Households % | Persons % |
| --- | --- | --- |
| Under 90 | 1.09 | 0.48 |
| 90-99 | 1.02 | 0.72 |
| 100-119 | 3.56 | 2.85 |
| 120-139 | 4.43 | 3.77 |
| 140-159 | 5.02 | 5.13 |
| 160 and over | 84.88 | 87.04 |
| Total | 100 | 100 |
| Number in sample | 12,911 | 41,090 |

**Table 2:** Percentage of Persons Living in Households with Total Expenditure close to National Assistance Levels, According to Employment Status of Head

| Employment status of households | Percentage of persons living in households with total expenditure of less than 40 per cent above national assistance rates plus rent |
| --- | --- |
| Working full-time | 34.5 |
| Working part-time | 3.6 |
| Unemployed | 5.3 |
| Sick | 7.2 |
| Retired | 49.4 |
| Total | 100 |
| Number in sample | 3,224 |

The data showed that the poorest persons in the United Kingdom consist chiefly of old persons and members of large families.

The reasons for drawing a line at a level of 40 per cent above the basic national assistance rates are important and should be explained. First, in deciding entitlement to assistance the Board disregards certain kinds and amounts of income, and of savings. For example, in 1953, earnings up to

20s. a week and superannuation up to 10s. 6d., or a disability pension up to 20s. could be wholly disregarded, as also could war savings up to £375 or other capital up to £50. A substantial proportion of national assistance beneficiaries receive some income which is disregarded by the Board. There is also a reasonable presumption that its officers ignore gifts of money and small allowances, as for example from children to retirement pensioners, which are nonetheless reflected in the expenditure of the latter. They also probably ignore small windfalls such as occasional gifts from charitable organizations and winnings from the football pool companies.

Second, the Board often adds certain small amounts to its basic benefits, at the discretion of its officers, for special needs, to take account of expenditure on special diets in old age and sickness, laundry, fuel and domestic help. Thus, in 1954 some 621,000 of the allowances or over a third of the total number, were increased by an average amount of 5s. 3d. per week. The Board also makes single grants for exceptional needs and repays prescription charges. Of course, to calculate an average figure to allow for all these grants or disregards and add it to the basic rate would be difficult as well as unrealistic.

These points may be put in a more practical way. From the 1953-4 sample we found that the expenditure of persons living alone who were dependent wholly or partly on national assistance averaged 27 per cent, and of married couples, 44 per cent, above the basic assistance rate. If therefore we aim to find out how many people are living below, at, or just above the standard of living actually attained by national assistance recipients, it would appear to be justifiable to take the criterion of 40 per cent above the basic rates. It should be remembered, of course, that the expenditure of a substantial number of households in the sample was several hundred per cent larger than the national assistance rates and that the expenditure of the average household was around 260 per cent of these rates.

It must be emphasized that by no means all of those living around the national assistance level in 1953-4 were receiving it. A large number were in households primarily dependent on the earnings of the head. Another large number were in households primarily dependent on insurance benefits. The Ministry of Labour data suggested that a group of households depending on social insurance benefits, not wages, and representing about 900,000 persons in the population, were living at a standard which, *prima facie*, might have allowed a very large number of them to qualify for supplementary allowances from the National Assistance Board. Moreover, substantial numbers of persons in households with an expenditure of more than 40 per cent higher than the level were nonetheless receiving some assistance. Some of these were pensioners living alone. A large number were pensioners living, usually with children, in households primarily dependent on a wage. Some were persons receiving the higher rates payable to those suffering from tuberculosis and blindness. To summarize, it would appear that in

1953-4 there were, in the United Kingdom, (i) approximately, 1,350,000 retirement pensioners and their dependants; (ii) approximately 900,000 widows, disabled, sick, handicapped and other persons, including members of their families, primarily dependent on other forms of social security, and (iii) 1,750,000 other persons primarily dependent on wages, *all 4 million of whom were living in households with a total expenditure less than 40 per cent above national assistance scale rates plus rent.*

There were also (iv) approximately 600,000 retirement pensioners (and their dependants) and (v) approximately 700,000 other persons who were actually receiving or dependent on a national assistance allowance of some kind, although the total expenditure of the households in which they lived was 40 per cent or more above the basic assistance rates. This gives a total of approximately 5,300,000 persons.

Such analyses as I have described need to be presented in detail. We hope to publish these shortly, not only for the year 1953-4, but also for 1960.[12]

## The problem of defining 'subsistence' and 'adequate' nutrition

But is this approach to the question of defining the nature and extent of poverty good enough? The income standards applied above to the Ministry budget data are determined by the rather special meaning that has been given to the term 'subsistence'. In 1901 Seebohm Rowntree stated that families living in poverty were those 'whose total earnings are insufficient to obtain the minimum necessaries for the maintenance of merely physical efficiency'.[13] He drew up a list of necessities under the headings of food, clothing, fuel and household sundries, and estimated how much it would cost to buy them. Other students of the subject afterwards adopted a similar approach.

Many people have been uneasily aware of the problems of defining necessities like housing, clothing, or fuel and light. A family might maintain its physical efficiency just as well in a caravan, a Nissen hut or even a railway waiting room as in a three-bedroom council house. It could go to bed early and spend nothing on electricity. It could salvage wood from the neighbourhood rather than buy coal, and scrounge clothing from the W.V.S. or the Salvation Army. The bread-winner might be more physically efficient if he walked to work and saved train fares. We could go on interminably debating such issues and it is evident that any standard we might adopt must be an arbitrary or conventional one.

But uncertainty about such matters has been excused because the definition of a family's food requirements has always been supposed to be more scientifically certain, and food, from the beginning of this century onwards, has remained the most vital component of the measure of subsistence or poverty.

Shrewdly, and originally, Rowntree saw at the end of the nineteenth century that the work of nutritionists could be used in social surveys of populations to illuminate, more objectively than in the past, the living standards of poor families. Excluding rent, the amount allocated for food in his poverty standard for a family of man and wife and three children accounted for 72 per cent of the total.[14] He leaned heavily on the work of an American nutritionist, Atwater, in fixing on the nutrients required by adults and children. Broadly speaking, what he did was to select, from conflicting data, figures of the number of calories and amount of protein thought to be required by an average man, translate these nutritional components into a standard diet and thence into the cost of purchasing such a diet. Yet the determination of the income needed to purchase minimum nutrition has always been a hazardous exercise.

[...]

The first step in the traditional approach to the question of defining and measuring poverty is difficult enough. The next steps become more difficult still. Having obtained estimates of nutritional requirements the investigator seeks to translate these into the cheapest possible diet. From his knowledge of nutritional values and market prices he might tend to produce a diet giving prominence to potatoes, cabbage, bread, margarine and cooking fat, cheese, and fish such as herrings. Purely on nutritional and financial grounds he would be led perhaps to exclude from the diet meat, citrus fruit, tinned vegetables, frozen foods, sweets, chocolates, and fish and chips. But already we can begin to see how unrealistic this procedure might be. Should an allowance for sweets be made in the diet? The same energy value could be provided by sugar or jam and at cheaper cost. But can we ignore the fact that nearly all households are accustomed to eating sweets as a regular, if perhaps marginal, part of their diet? Surely it is important to take account of eating habits which have endured for generations and which have their physiological as well as their psychological consequences. And it is also important to remember that housewives living on low incomes are influenced in making their purchases of foodstuffs not only by the tastes of their families and friends but also by commercial advertising. They are educated to take account of the virtues of particular brands and particular forms of packaging. We cannot assume that they are well informed about the nutritional content of certain foods and where to obtain them most cheaply, nor can we assume, if they are, that they are actuated only by the need to maintain the physical efficiency of those in their households. Tea is an even better example, for it has little or no nutritional value. Should any allowance be made for this in the minimum diet? Drinking tea is a widespread custom in Britain. But to say that it is 'customary' may also mean that it is 'necessary', and in two senses. It may be psychologically necessary, in the same sense that a habit-forming drug is necessary. Individuals have grown up to accept and expect it. Second, it serves an important social function. When a neighbour or a relative calls, a housewife will often make a cup of tea. True, in another society she might prepare coffee or open a bottle of wine, but this is what she will generally do in Britain. The reciprocation of small gifts and services, and sharing the enjoyment of them, is one of the most important ways in which an individual recognizes and maintains his social relationships.

This line of analysis suggests that we cannot depend solely on a narrow interpretation of 'physical efficiency' or nutritional value in choosing a list of necessary foodstuffs. But this is not the only difficulty. Are the foodstuffs on the list everywhere available? The list also has to be priced. How far should some allowance be made for variation in prices between different districts of a country or even of a town? Indeed, could some items on the list be obtained not by buying them in markets or shops, but by growing them more cheaply in gardens or allotments?

Rowntree and others who carried out surveys of poverty were aware of some of these difficulties but tended to skate over them, eschewing anxious discussion and depending on crude methods which, even for their time, could have been bettered. Rowntree, for example, referred in his first and possibly his finest book to the different calorific value of the diet required by men and women and by children of different ages and yet made no allowance for such differences in the standard which he used in measuring poverty. Like other students of poverty, he sought to produce a simple and uniform standard which would be relatively easy to compare with household income. But this was done at the price of neglecting wide variations in nutritional and other needs. Social and economic truths can often be blurred or concealed in inquiries which depend on an over-assiduous application of the law of averages.

The advantages of hindsight can always mislead us into being unduly severe in our judgments of men of distinction who pioneer difficult paths. Rowntree, Booth, Bowley and others did much to awaken Britain's social conscience and reveal the deprivations of the poor. But we have allowed our respect for their vision and methods to dull the critical sensibilities which we need to investigate modern society.

## The need for a new approach

Although other evidence would be needed to provide a conclusive argument, perhaps enough has been said to suggest that the study of poverty has not developed theoretically during the course of this century. One mistake has been to narrow attention largely to the preservation of physical efficiency, whatever that may mean, and by implication to assume that the physical efficiency of individuals can be divorced from their psychological well-being and the organization and structure of society. Another has been to draw up a list of basic necessities, translate them into a certain income, and call this 'subsistence'. All students of poverty have in fact made some concessions to psychological and social needs and conventions, but they have tended to write as if their subsistence standards consisted of a list of absolute necessities which could be applied irrespective of time and place, rather as if a fixed yardstick could be devised and measured against a given population, whether in 1900, 1930 or 1950, and whether in York, London, Sicily or Calcutta. Poverty is a dynamic, not a static, concept. Man is not a Robinson Crusoe living on a desert island. He is a social animal entangled in a web of relationships at work and in family and community which exert complex and changing pressures to which he must respond, as much in his consumption of goods and services as in any other aspect of his behaviour. And there is no list of the absolute necessities of life to maintain even physical efficiency or health which applies at any time and in any society, without reference to the structure, organization, physical environment and available resources of that society. [...]

The sciences of economics and sociology sometimes seem to be imprisoned within narrow specialisms which discount the flesh and blood, and the problems, of ordinary life. Partly as a consequence, serious misconceptions about the nature and direction of our society are commonly held.

## The level of income in relation to levels of nutrition

A new approach might be developed from a number of different directions. First, despite all criticisms, more imaginative use could be made of nutritional studies. [...] To establish a minimum income standard is meaningless unless we also show that there are some families with that income who do in fact secure a defined level of nutrition. This fundamental criticism could be made of nearly all studies of poverty.

[...]

## Fluctuations in living standards over life

Second, the living standards of individuals might be studied in relation to the standards those individuals had previously experienced. In common speech we often say that a man is poor or in poverty because he has 'fallen down in the world'. Our reference point is some previous standard of living. A man who experiences a drastic fall in income when he retires, becomes sick or disabled, or is forced to take a much less well-paid job, is often described in this way, whether he falls from £3,000 to £1,000 a year, or £10 to £5 a week. He cannot go on living in his accustomed manner, and has to move to a smaller house, give up a car, reduce his expenditure on food or forgo new clothes and house furnishings. It would be illuminating to study how people manage in certain adversities and whether sharp fluctuations in living standards are common experiences.

This kind of study would amount to a revival of interest in the 'life cycle of poverty', referred to in the past by some social scientists, but never properly explored.[15] It would offer a means of finding out what individuals actually treat as expendable budget items and what as necessities. A few pilot studies have shown that when household income falls, say, from £10 to £5 a week, the members of the household take a very different view from that of moralists and economists of what goods and services they must continue to buy.[16]

## Relative insufficiencies of income and wealth

Third, in an important sense, poverty could be defined on the basis of the number of households or families of certain types having a total income of less than, say, half or two-thirds of the average. As Professor Galbraith has said, 'People are poverty-stricken when their income, even if adequate for survival, falls markedly behind that of the community.'[17]

The studies of income distribution that have been carried out since the war are inadequate for this purpose, because they rest chiefly on statistics produced by the Board of Inland Revenue. Many economists treat these statistics with awe and believe they offer conclusive evidence not only of greater redistribution of income in post-war, as compared with pre-war, years, but also of a continuing equalization of income and wealth.[18] In fact they have been of diminishing value as a general guide to relative standards of living in Britain. The Board's figures refer to a haphazard mixture of individuals and tax units, and are not re-worked in terms of households or families. They relate to a narrow definition of income. Comparisons over time do not take account of sharp changes in the demographic structure of the population. As Richard Titmuss emphasizes in an important new work, the statistics are increasingly presenting a 'delusive picture of the economic and social structure of society'.[19]

[...]

All this suggests why we need to devise more sensitive indicators of the living standards enjoyed by different sections of the population.[20] Perhaps more use might be made of the concepts of 'average disposable income per head',[21] or 'average household income' for different types of household. A possible definition of poverty might be developed on the basis of measuring how many households or families of certain types have a total income of less than, say, 50 per cent or 66 per cent of the average.[...]

## Inequitable distribution of housing, medical, educational and other resources

Fourth, more study might be given to the distribution of non–monetary resources among individuals and families comprising the population. Some families with relatively large incomes might be obliged to live in slum houses or send their children to grossly over-crowded schools. They might therefore be 'poor' only in certain limited respects. We must remember that to some extent the concept of 'poverty' is independent of that of income. The housing standards enjoyed by different classes and types of household might be carefully described. Account would be taken of facts such as that in 1951, there were 2½ million homes without piped water, 3 million without a w.c. and 6 million without a bath; and that in 1958 about 150,000 people in England and Wales, other than gypsies, were living in caravans, often because they could not get a house.[22] [...] Many other examples could be given. To achieve point and precision such internal comparisons would have to be placed in context and related to the allocation of resources as between different regions of the country and as between public and private services. There is considerable evidence of the co-existence of poverty and plenty and of stark contrasts between public squalor and private opulence.

## Inequitable distribution of international resources

Finally, the development of theories of poverty and deprivation cannot be based solely on studies in Britain. It has always been evident that what most people would call poverty in one society would be comparative affluence in another. To give one vivid example, the standard of living chosen by Rowntree in 1899 to define poverty in York was certainly at least two or three times higher than the average standard enjoyed today by the populations of such countries as India, Pakistan, Indonesia and Bolivia.

## Relative deprivation

The vague concept of 'subsistence' is an inadequate and misleading criterion of poverty, partly because it does not have the scientific objectivity sometimes claimed for it, but also because it is essentially a static concept. It tends, with the passing of time, to become devalued, like money. By going on using it we have convinced ourselves that there is almost no poverty in Britain. In fact there seems to be a substantial amount, and more, by any reasonable criterion, than we care to admit. Of course we are more prosperous than were our grandparents 50 years ago. That is a claim which can be made by each generation and one, no doubt, which our grandchildren will be making 50 years hence. But this is a different matter from eliminating poverty. One can no more proclaim the abolition of want than the abolition of disease. Poverty is not an absolute state. It is relative deprivation. Society itself is continuously changing and thrusting new obligations on its members. They, in turn, develop new needs. They are rich or poor according to their share of the resources that are available to all. This is true as much of nutritional as monetary or even educational resources. Our general theory, then, should be that individuals and families whose resources, over time, fall seriously short of the resources commanded by the average individual or family in the community in which they live, whether that community is a local, national or international one, are in poverty.

**Endnotes**

[1] See, for example, the reference to 'the virtual elimination of primary poverty', by Mr. J. M. Kirk, the chairman of the National Food Survey Committee, in his preface to the Annual Report of the Committee, *Domestic Food Consumption and Expenditure: 1958*, London, H.M.S.O., 1960.

[2] J.H. Sheldon, *Report to the Birmingham Regional Hospital Board on its Geriatric Services*, Birmingham Regional Hospital Board, 1961.

[3] P. Marris, *Widows and their Families*, London, Routledge & Kegan Paul, 1958.

[4] M. Turner, *Forgotten Men*, London, National Council of Social Service, 1960.

[5] See, for example, G.W. Brown and J.K. Wing, 'A Comparative Clinical and Social Survey of Three Mental Hospitals', *Sociology and Medicine, Studies within the framework of the British National Health Service, The Sociological Review*, Monograph No. 5, 1962.

[6] L.A. Shaw, 'Living on a State-Maintained Income – I', *Case Conference*, March 1958; and M. Bowerbank, 'Living on a State-Maintained Income II', *Case Conference*, April 1958.

[7] H.C. Wilson, 'Problem Families and the Concept of Immaturity', *Case Conference*, October 1959.

[8] B.S. Rowntree and G.R. Lavers, *Poverty and the Welfare State: A Third Social Survey of York dealing only with Economic Questions*, London, Longmans, 1951.

[9] Ministry of Labour and National Service, *Report of an Enquiry into Household Expenditure in 1953-4*, London, H.M.S.O., 1957.

[10] The study was carried out in collaboration with Dr. Brian Abel-Smith, and with the full-time assistance of Mrs. Caroline Woodroffe. In preparing this paper I have also benefited from help and advice given by Mrs. Vivien Sober, Dr. Royston Lambert and Mr. Tony Lynes. Because of complexities in the way the data were arranged we found that our resources did not allow us to scrutinise the figures of expenditure extracted from information relating to every household in the sample. We confined ourselves to all those in the low and middle income groups, and selected a one-in-four sample of these. This procedure introduces a further element of possible sampling error to the error already recognized and discussed

by the Ministry in its report of the results of the survey. But in view of the size of the national sample studied in 1953-4 this is not likely to have invalidated the broad results.

[11] *Report … into Household Expenditure*, op. cit., p. 12.

[12] Although at the time of writing we have still to analyse in full the information obtained from the Ministry of Labour Family Expenditure Survey in 1960, our counts show that 4 per cent of the population were living below the basic national assistance rates plus rent, 5 per cent less than 20 per cent above those rates and a further 5 per cent less than 40 per cent above, giving a total of 14 per cent, equivalent to about 7½ million persons in the population. It is, however, difficult to compare in detail the 1953-4 and 1960 results, because the former are based on total expenditure, while the latter are based on total income, less tax and national insurance contributions. The 1953-4 income data were not reliable enough for detailed analysis. We used definitions of income and expenditure which were broadly comparable but it is well known that budget surveys tend to produce under-estimates of household income and, to a lesser extent, over-estimates as well as under-estimates of certain kinds of household expenditure. In comparing the results for 1953-4 with those for 1960 differences in size of sample and methods of inquiry must also be remembered. Certain data about the 1960 survey is also given in a paper by Dorothy Cole Wedderburn on the evidence of poverty in Britain, which is to be published shortly in *The Sociological Review*. This paper, and another by Brian Abel-Smith, completed an interdependent series of three given at the 1962 conference of the British Sociological Association.

[13] B.S. Rowntree, *Poverty: A Study of Town Life*, London, Macmillan, p. 86.

[14] In the war, when Beveridge looked to Rowntree and others for guidance in deciding what rates should be paid in the new system of social security, the minimum income thought to be sufficient for subsistence for a family of five included an amount for food which represented 72 per cent of the total (rent excluded).

[15] See, for example, H. Tout, *The Standard of Living in Bristol*, 1938.

[16] For example, Political and Economic Planning, *Social Security and Unemployment in Lancashire*, No. 349, 1 December 1952.

[17] J.K. Galbraith, *The Affluent Society*, London, Hamish Hamilton, 1958, p.252.

[18] See, for example, H.F. Lydall, 'The Long-Term Trend in the Size Distribution of Income', *Journal of the Royal Statistical Society*, 1959, Vol. 122, Part I; F.W. Paish, 'The Real Incidence of Personal Taxation', *Lloyds Bank Review*, January 1957; and D. Seers, *The Levelling of Incomes since 1938*, 1951.

[19] R.M. Titmuss, *Income Distribution and Social Change: A Study in Criticism*, London, Allen & Unwin [1962].

[20] In making the rather inadequate comments in these paragraphs, I am grateful to Richard Titmuss for allowing me to draw on his new study.

[21] As adopted in T. Lynes, *National Assistance and National Prosperity*, Occasional Papers on Social Administration, No. 5, Welwyn, The Codicote Press, 1969.

[22] Ministry of Housing and Local Government, *Caravans as Homes*, Cmd. 872, London: H.M.S.O., 1959.

# 15

# The poor and the poorest

## Introduction

Two assumptions have governed much economic thinking the Britain since the war. The first is that we have "abolished" poverty. The second is that we are a much more equal society: that the differences between the living standards of rich and poor are much smaller than they used to be.

These assumptions are of great practical as well as theoretical importance. They form the background to much of the discussion of social and economic policy. But are they true? The findings of the survey carried out in 1950 in York by Rowntree and Lavers were encouraging.[1] They seemed to confirm expert as well as popular supposition. The absence of mass unemployment, the steady increase in the employment of married women, the post-war improvements in the social services and the increase in real wages all seemed to point unequivocally to the virtual elimination of poverty, at least as it had been understood in the nineteen-thirties.

Second, the authors of a number of studies of income distribution have found a levelling of incomes in 1938.[2] Indeed, many recent writers have concluded not only that there is less inequality of income in post-war as compared with pre-war Britain, but that the process of levelling continued during the nineteen-fifties.[3] The data produced be economists seemed merely to confirm what had been implied by the maintenance after the war of high rates of taxation, by the competition for labour in a society with relatively full employment and by the general increase in the number of persons with professional, managerial and technical skills. Both assumptions seemed to be strongly founded.

The direct evidence is nonetheless ambiguous, to say the least. Since 1945 the Rowntree-Lavers survey has been the only one conducted explicitly to find the incidence of poverty.[4] This survey was extremely limited in conception and the report left many questions unanswered.[5] The studies of the distribution of income are also far from being conclusive. This is largely because the data provided by the Board of Inland Revenue, on which they are based, have become of less value as the years have passed, as Professor

---

Chapters 1 and 2 from Abel-Smith, B. and Townsend, P. (1965) *The poor and the poorest: A new analysis of the Ministry of Labour's Family Expenditure Surveys of 1953–54 and 1960*, London: Bell.

Richard Titmuss has shown in a recent analysis.[6] Not only do the statistical data comprise a haphazard mixture of individuals and tax units, but they are based on a narrow definition of income which omits certain important categories – particularly the different forms of capital appreciation (a major source, if not *the* major source, of the wealth of the rich in the nineteen fifties and sixties). The statistics also omit many forms of indirect income, mainly benefits in kind, which have been of growing importance in contributing to the living standards enjoyed by many sections of the population. (These are usually called 'fringe' benefits – an epithet which may have misled a number of otherwise discerning economists.) The incomes described by the Board of Inland Revenue in the early 1960s represent a smaller proportion of real incomes than the income described in the pre-war reports.

What changes, however, have taken place in the resources of the richest 5 per cent or 1 per cent of the population and the poorest 20 per cent? Information about the rich is sparse. It has always been difficult to make scientific calculations of their true wealth and recent developments in tax laws and in tax avoidance techniques have not made these calculations any easier. The loss, or partial loss, of estates by some wealthy traditionalists may be more than balanced by the acquisitions of a new class of property speculators. Very little is known about the composition of the wealthiest 5 per cent and the figures published by the Board of Inland Revenue of their taxable income may be serious underestimates of their real income, even according to the Board's definition of income. We need to develop better ways of measuring "net accretion of economic power" in the financial year.[7] Until a really intelligent analysis of Inland Revenue information is produced and until a major empirical study of the rich is carried out by sociologists or economists, or both, assertions about changes in the income of the wealthiest minority will be limited to little more than crude aggregate estimates and speculations about the meaning of certain forms of conspicuous consumption – such as investments in houses and yachts in the Bahamas or, to take a very different example, investment in charitable foundations at home.

Equally, there is very little hard information about the changes in the economic condition of the poor. Some statistical information is given by the Ministry of Pensions and the National Assistance Board about the numbers and kinds of persons receiving income security benefits.[8] However, it is difficult to relate the statistics of people receiving different benefits and we know far too little about those receiving no benefits or reduced benefits. It is even more difficult to relate this information to the statistics on wages and incomes issued by the Ministry of Labour and the Board of Inland Revenue. Economists generally have refrained from attempting to do so.

The concluding statements of those who have studied income distribution are usually reached by comparing the incomes of the very rich and those around the median in society. For example, Mr. H. F. Lydall's statistical tables cover the first, fifth, tenth, twentieth and fiftieth percentiles. As Mr. J. Utting pointed out during a professional discussion of Mr. Lydall's paper, it "deals wholly with the top 50 per cent of the income distribution – and the main part of it is concerned with the top 20 per cent. I am equally interested to see what has happened to the bottom 50 per cent, who are of major importance from the point of view of social policy, although their impact upon many aspects of the national economy is very much less than that of people at the top".[9] In reply, Mr. Lydall said "I accept this criticism in principle and agree that much more thought is needed about this matter. But the real difficulty is the lack of data on the lower incomes, especially for pre-war... The true situation can only be revealed by means of sample surveys in which the lowest income groups are covered equally with others."

But how telling are these criticisms? It would of course be possible to give a long historical account of the various economic and social changes in Britain since the war. Even though there are considerable difficulties in measuring these changes in precise qualitative terms there is no doubt that the purchasing power of manual workers and of social security beneficiaries has increased substantially. There is also no doubt that during the past 20 years the number of persons holding the traditionally better-paid professional, managerial and skilled manual occupations has continued to increase relative to those in the semi-skilled and unskilled manual occupations – at least according to the traditional definition of 'skill'. Given the pattern of wage- and salary-levels that has existed in this country, the number and proportion of incomes in the middle ranges have tended to increase as a consequence. But beyond statements such as these it is difficult to go. The precise nature of changes in income distribution are obscure. Moreover, every generation tends to exaggerate its achievements. Those living in post-war Britain were particularly anxious to show that they had broken decisively with the past. Everyone wanted to erase the bitter memories of the thirties. By the 1950's, both major political parties had a vested interest in making the creation of the 'Welfare State' seem a greater change than it actually was. Both wanted to gain political credit for introducing it, and the Labour Party in particular wanted to gain or sustain electoral popularity because of its legislative programme of 1945-51. It was difficult for its members to tolerate criticism of its achievements or even talk about them without exaggeration. The Conservative Party had a two-fold motive – first to gain the credit for the original inspiration of the Welfare State but secondly to show that it had become unnecessarily extravagant. Middle-class anxieties about the 'burden' of taxation could be legitimated by the belief that welfare had become excessive. Certain types of information could be interpreted according to these various attitudes.

There are many features of social belief and value which deserve fuller explanation than we can attempt here. In particular the general assumption that economic and social progress has been sharper and faster than it has actually been is a sociological phenomenon of the first importance which it would be instructive to analyse. Our point is, first, that society has tended to make a rather sweeping interpretation of such evidence as there is about the reduction of poverty and the increase in equality since the war and, secondly, this evidence is a lot weaker than many social scientists have supposed. Basically, its weakness derives from conceptual rather than technical inadequacy, particularly in the sense that the measures of need and of income that have been used are more appropriate to a static than to a dynamic society.

A fresh approach is therefore called for. As a first step the income and expenditure surveys carried out by government and outside bodies, usually University departments, are likely to prove to be the most promising source for revising or obtaining information about developments in the post-war years and currently. The reports of these are tantalisingly silent on the two assumptions described at the beginning of this paper. They tell little about social conditions. They do not contain analyses of the circumstances of the poorest households in the sample in relation to conventional definitions of subsistence. Nor do they compare such households with wealthy or average households of similar or different composition. In fairness to those carrying out such surveys, they were not intended to do so. But the data could nevertheless be re-analysed in this way.

This was the starting point of the present inquiry. Our object was to secure evidence about poverty and inequality. Rather than seek immediately to launch a time-consuming and expensive survey we felt that every effort should first be made to explore existing information. The basic data collected by interviewers in previous national studies should be available for the kind of analysis in which we were interested. In the event we found it would be possible to study the data collected by the Ministry of Labour in two sample surveys of the United Kingdom, the first carried out in 1953–54 and the second in 1960.[10] [...]

## Methods and definitions

Our purpose, therefore, was to attempt to find out from the surveys carried out by the Ministry of Labour the number and characteristics of persons with low levels of living. We also wished to study the differences in levels of living that existed among households of similar size and composition. In this chapter we set out in some detail the methods, and the reasons for the methods, that we adopted.

It is important to bear in mind that the surveys of income and expenditure undertaken for the Ministry of Labour have had rather different objects. Chiefly they have aimed to supply data for the compilation and revision of retail price indices. The price index which covered the period of 1914 to 1947 was based on fewer than 2,000 budgets collected in 1904. During 1937-38, the Ministry conducted a larger survey of expenditure of working class households,[11] but the war started before much could be done with the results. The next index, which was introduced in June 1947, followed the recommendations of the Cost of Living Advisory Committee, appointed in 1946. The committee was conscious that the budget patterns of the population had changed markedly during and immediately after the war and, although obliged to make use of the 1937-38 data, felt that the index which they had worked out should be regarded as an 'interim' one "to serve as a temporary expedient until a new full-scale inquiry into household expenditure could be undertaken to provide an up-to-date weighting basis for a new index".[12] In 1951 the Advisory Committee recommended that such an inquiry should be started as soon as possible and it was accordingly undertaken in 1953-54. Advance information allowed the Committee to compile a new index in 1955 and the government introduced it in January 1956. A full report was published in 1957.[13]

This was a large-scale inquiry. A sample of 20,000 households was drawn throughout the United Kingdom and nearly 13,000 of these co-operated and provided records of their expenditure during a three-week period. Interviewing began on 26th January, 1953, and continued into the early weeks of 1954. In the introduction to its report, the Ministry says, "Although the provision of a weighting basis for a price index is one of the most important uses of a household expenditure inquiry, there are also many other purposes for which such an inquiry is valuable. In such fields as national income studies, market research, nutritional studies, and many other branches of social and economic science, the need for detailed information about family expenditure is constantly recurring. For this reason it was decided that the new inquiry should take a comprehensive form, covering a sample of the whole community in order to obtain information of a more general character about the pattern of expenditure of households outside the groups where wages or salaries were likely to be directly related to a new index."[14]

### Supplementary objects of the official surveys

Before this inquiry began, the Cost of Living Advisory Committee had recommended "Smaller-scale inquiries at frequent intervals thereafter".[15] The continuous Family Expenditure Survey, as it is known, was put into operation in 1957, and summary reports have been published fairly quickly.[16] The fullest description of its methods is to be found in a paper by Kemsley.[17] The survey now serves a variety of needs. Its primary purposes is to provide a basis for the annual revision of the base weights of the index of retail prices. But now it is also intended to satisfy three special needs of the Central Statistical Office:

> … first, to provide estimates of personal expenditure on consumer goods and services to supplement the sources used in compiling the official estimates to national income and expenditure, which are published quarterly; second, to enable studies to be made of the relationship between the income and the pattern of expenditure of different groups of households, classified by size and type – this demand analysis (as it has been termed) is intended to provide information about the various factors which influence the demand for different commodities; third, to enable estimates to be made of the amounts paid in different forms of direct and indirect taxation, and the value of the benefits obtained from subsidies, national insurance and the various social services by households at different levels classified by size and type. This analysis will show the incidence of particular taxes and benefits on different groups of households.[18]

The second and third are clearly of considerable importance to those interested in income distribution and tax policy. A series of special tabulations was first published in 1962, showing the impact of taxes and social service benefits on different groups of households.[19]

As mentioned earlier, the data which we have used for this study were those collected for the years 1953–54 and 1960. The inquiry for the second of these two years was much smaller than that for 1953–54. While the 1953–54 inquiry, as mentioned earlier, obtained information from 13,000 households among a total of 20,000 who were asked to co-operate, the 1960 inquiry collected information from 3,540 households among a total of about 5,000 who were approached. The interviews were spread throughout the calendar year 1960. We hoped also to include the year 1962, but found that the system of processing had become mechanised so that it would have been a much more laborious task to re-classify the data in the form needed for this study. Some essential information (for example about the ages of children in the household) had not been summarised in a way which allowed us to categorise individual households.

## Defining poverty

In planning our method of work, our first step was to choose one or more measures of low levels of living to be used as indicators of 'poverty'. Many attempts have been made to define 'poverty lines' for use in Britain in studies conducted in the past. The pioneer work on this problem was undertaken by Charles Booth and Seebohm Rowntree before the end of the last century. Rowntree was the first to attempt a really precise definition. He estimated the cost of buying the 'necessities' which he calculated were needed by different types of family to maintain physical efficiency. He then counted the families whose total income was insufficient to enable them to purchase these necessities. These were the families he described as living in 'poverty'. In time his approach became widely accepted, first by social scientists and later by the government. During the last war, when devising a new system of income security, Lord Beveridge recognised the advantages of this 'subsidence' standard and the government accepted his reasoning.[20] The rates paid by the National Assistance Board after the war conformed closely to the Beveridge standard, which in turn bore a close resemblance to the standard which had been used by Rowntree in his second survey of York in 1936.[21] Since 1948 the real value of these rates has been increased.[22] In recent years some account has been taken of the increase in the real level of living of the rest of the community.

In the post-war years, Rowntree produced a further definition of 'poverty' which he used for the third survey of York which, in conjunction with G. R. Lavers, he undertook in 1950. In this survey he used a rather more generous definition of 'subsidence' that he has used either in 1936 or 1899. A modest sum was included for conventional needs. As a proportion of wages, on the other hand, his new standard was more stringent than those used for the earlier studies. In 1899, Rowntree's standard for a family of five approximated to 79 per cent of average manual earnings; in 1936 it was 69 per cent and in 1950, 60 per cent.[23] Nevertheless, an attempt had been made to produce an interpretation of the meaning of subsidence appropriate to the more prosperous post-war world.

Other approaches have been suggested to the problem of defining 'poverty'. The allowance for nutritional needs in the subsistence standard has always appeared to be more objective than the allowance for clothing, warmth and other needs. For many years Rowntree's human needs diet has been brought up to date and re-priced for certain types of family.[24] It would, of course, be possible to look again at budget surveys to find which families failed to spend the necessary sum on food and then compare their total incomes with those of other families. Or, as a more precise development from this approach, it would be possible to explore the data collected by the Ministry of Agriculture in its national food surveys,[25] which could be used to identify those families which failed in at least one particular to reach the nutritional levels recommended by the British Medical Association and, again, compare their total incomes (and the proportion spent on food) with those of other families surveyed and with national data about the distribution of incomes. The difficulty about this approach is that inadequate diet represents a somewhat narrow interpretation of poverty.[26]

## National assistance rates as a measure of poverty

We did not adopt this approach. Nor did we ourselves attempt to produce new definitions of 'subsidence' or 'poverty' to be applied to the data for the two separate years which we were studying. Such an attempt would have required new empirical investigations which were beyond our resources. The principal measure of 'poverty' which we use in this paper is the level of living of National Assistance Board applicants in each year which is being studied. In the case of the year 1953-54 we also use the Rowntree-Lavers standard developed for their 1950 study of York, revised for changes in prices between 1950 and 1953-54. We did not attempt to apply this standard to the 1960 data, partly because of the difficulty of making reliable price adjustments over this longer period and partly because we felt that Rowntree would have devised a higher 'poverty level' for 1960 had he been alive to undertake a further study in that year.

Whatever may be said about the adequacy of the National Assistance Board level of living as a just or publicly approved measure of 'poverty', it has at least the advantage of being in a sense the 'official' operational definition of the minimum level of living at any particular time. In using it we do not intend to imply that we ourselves consider either that this level of living is an appropriate measure or that the households of different composition living at the national assistance standard have comparable levels of living.

The level of living of National Assistance Board applicants cannot be defined with precision. The expenditure incurred by households with the same composition who receive grants from the Board varies widely. There are many reasons for this variation. First, some resources of applicants are 'disregarded' when the level of grant is calculated. In 1953, earnings up to 20s. per week and superannuation of up to 10s. 6d. per week, or a disability pension of up to 20s. per week, could be wholly disregarded. War savings up to the value of £375 and other capital up to £50 could all be ignored. At the end of that year there were in fact 110,000 beneficiaries, each with capital other than War Savings amounting to £75 or more, 48,000 with superannuation, 101,000 with charitable or voluntary payments, 48,000 with disability or dependants' war pension and 78,000 with some earnings.[27] It is likely also that the Board's officers overlook modest allowances made by relatives or friends, such as those received by retirement pensioners from their children. And they usually overlook occasional gifts in cash and kind.[28] The full rates are therefore often paid to persons who possess other resources amounting to a pound or two a week.

Second, an applicant may be granted more than the basic scale. Small additional allowances and grants are often made to beneficiaries, particularly the sick and retired, for special needs. There may be a continuing allowance for extra fuel, a special diet, laundering or domestic help, etc.; or exceptional grants may be paid for clothing and shoes or bed-linen. Again, charges for prescriptions could be met. In December 1953, some 574,000 allowances, or a third of the total number, were increased by an average amount of 5s. 0d. per week. Single payments for exceptional needs during the year amounted to over £500,000 and repayments of charges for prescriptions, spectacles and dentures to over £1 million.

Third, higher basic rates are available for the blind and certain persons suffering from respiratory tuberculosis or its after-effects. Eighty-nine thousand persons were receiving these higher rates in December 1953. For all these reasons the level of living of persons receiving national assistance could be higher than that provided by the basic scale. There are, however, some applicants who are given grants which provide them with an income below that of the basic scale. They include applicants who are believed not to be genuinely seeking work, who have voluntarily left their employment, or whose normal earnings (less tax, national insurance contributions, etc.) if they were working would be smaller than a grant at the basic times. This 'wage stop' is applied to about a third of the unemployment applicants with children. National assistance cannot be paid to those in full-time work.

Many of these regulations result in wide variations in the level of living of households receiving national assistance grants. Some people depend of savings, or other sources of income which could be disregarded, while others may have sources of income or stocks of capital which they fail to disclose to the Board. It is at least clear that the average level of living of persons receiving national assistance has been considerably above the level of the basic rates of the National Assistance Board in the years since 1948. For the purpose of this study we considered the possibility of averaging the disregarded income and the additional allowances and grants and adding this figure to the basic rates. We felt that this would be rather unreal and decided instead to express our findings as percentage variations from the basic rates. We distinguish three groups: those whose resources fell below even the basic national assistance scales, those whose resources were less than 20 per cent above the scales, and those whose resources amounted to less than 40 per cent of these scales. We chose this last figure when we found that there were many households receiving national assistance whose level of living was 40 per cent or more above the basic rates.[29] In some but not all cases, the household consisted of one assistance applicant (e.g. retired parent) living with a family which had a level or living considerably above the national assistance level.

There are many different sizes and types or household and basic national assistance rates had be worked out for each type of household for comparison with the level of living of the household. In 1953 a single householder was normally entitled to 35s. and a married couple 59s. The rates for children varied according to age. All these rates are set out in Appendix 1 [Appendices are not reproduced in this volume]. In applying them to the Ministry of Labour data, certain assumptions had to be made in cases where the information collected in the survey was not sufficiently exact to indicate which National Assistance payment should be applied. These assumptions are also set out in Appendix 1. They are one reason why the figures presented in this study are not precisely accurate.

In addition to the basic scale, national assistance applicants are given a grant for their housing costs.[30] Normally this is equal to the weekly cost of housing, but in some cases a lower grant is given when the rent is held to be 'not reasonable in the circumstances'. We added the actual housing expenditure to the assistance scale calculated for each household and then calculated how far the level of living of that household diverged from its basic national assistance scale plus actual housing cost.

In Appendix 2, we show the subsistence standards used by Rowntree in 1950 for some of the commoner types of household, together with our estimate of this standard in 1953 prices. The price index used was that devised by Mr. T. Lynes for certain low income households. It is estimated that between October 1950 and July 1953, prices rose by between 25 per cent and 29 per cent depending on the composition of the household.[31]

It should be appreciated that in using the national assistance rates current in each of our two years as the principal measure of low levels of living we are not applying the same absolute measure to each year. The national assistance scales provided a higher real level of living in 1960 than in 1953-54. Nor have we attempted to show in 1960 the number of persons and households who fell below the absolute levels of our 1953-54 standard. The approach which we have adopted follows from the principle that the minimum level of living regarded as acceptable by a society increases with rising national prosperity.[32]

Between 1953-54 and 1960 the basic assistance scale for a single householder increased by 43 per cent. Between July 1953 and July 1960 the Ministry of Labour index of prices increased by about 20 per cent, while Mr. Lynes' indices for low income households (excluding housing) as mentioned earlier, increased by between 25 and 29 per cent depending on the type of household.[33] Thus the basic assistance rates increased more than prices, however the movement of the latter is measured.

It is more relevant to the concept underlying our present study to see how the assistance scales have changed in relation to the general level of living in the community. Between 1953 and 1960, average industrial earnings increased by 52 per cent[34] and personal income per head increased by 51 per cent.[35] These increases were greater than those of the basic assistance scales (excluding housing) which amounted to 43-44 per cent. Between 1953 and 1960 housing costs as a whole increased by 43 per cent.[36] The increase was greater for low income households, as during this period there were important changed in rent control legislation which particularly affected low income households. Between 1953 and 1960, the average rent (as defined by the National Assistance Board) of national assistance applicants increased by 68 per cent. By adding this average rent to the basic national assistance scales operative in 1953 and 1960 for households consisting of a single householder and a couple living alone and weighting these two categories of household by the proportions found among national assistance applicants in 1953-54,[37] we found that the basic national assistance scales *including* the actual rent of national assistance applicants increased by 49 per cent between 1953 and 1960.

Thus, when the large increase in rent payments found among national assistance applicants is taken into account, between 1953 and 1960 the level of living provided by the basic scales of National Assistance Board increased slightly less than the general level of living in the United Kingdom. Compared to average levels of living, our measure was also slightly lower in 1960 than in 1953-54.

It appears also that the level of living of those actually receiving national assistance changed in proportion to the level of basic grants provided by the Board. In other words the average income of applicants from other sources increased in proportion to their income from the Board. These other sources included exceptional needs grants, discretionary assistance, state pensions and allowances, earnings, private pensions, unearned income, etc. From information published in the Reports of the National Assistance Board, it can be calculated that the average income per recipient from these sources increased by 49 per cent between 1953 and 1960.

## The samples

As mentioned earlier there were nearly 13,000 respondents to the 1953-54 survey we started by drawing a random sub-sample of 25 per cent to reduce the amount of clerical work which would have been involved if we had attempted to examine statistical summaries for all respondents.

Comparisons with other data indicated that in some respects the respondents to the surveys were not representative of the population. First, in both the years, the proportion of children was 12-13 per cent greater than would have been expected from national figures. Second, the 1953–54 sample included only 80 per cent and the 1960 sample only about 91 per cent of the numbers of aged persons that would be expected. Third, the 1953–54 sample included only about 60 per cent of the number of households with sick heads which could be expected in private households from national figures. A similar figure cannot be calculated for 1960 as the relevant question was not asked in that year.

Consistent with the under-representation of both the aged and the sick was a considerable under-representation of households receiving national assistance in 1953–54. While we would have expected to have found 11 per cent of households receiving national assistance in 1953, we only identified 6.3 per cent. In the case of the 1960 sample, we did not manage to calculate the total number of households receiving national assistance. We did however find 8.5 per cent households with national assistance compared with 11.2 per cent in the total population.

The households in the survey which were known to be receiving national assistance were on average slightly larger than the average of families covered by assistance grants. The reason was the under-representation of the elderly and the over-representation of families with children. Thus while in both 1953 and 1960 adults represented about 84 per cent of persons covered by regular grants from the National Assistance Board, we found in both the years studied that adults accounted for between 75 and 80 per cent of the persons dependent on assistance.[38]

In general, therefore, the figures which are given in the following chapters considerable underestimate the number of households and persons with low levels of living. The understatement is greater in the case of the 1953–54 figures than in the case of the 1960 figures. This is one reason why direct comparison between the data which we present for the two years cannot be made with precision.

### Data used to calculate the low levels of living

A further and possibly more important reason for the lack of precise comparability between the figures presented later for the two years arose out of the problem of choosing income or expenditure as the measure of low levels of living. In the case of the 1953–54 survey, figures were available showing the *actual* income and the total expenditure of the household during the three weeks of the survey, but we were advised by those in charge of the Ministry survey that the income data were not reliable enough for detailed analysis. In some instances rough estimates appear to have been made.[39] From examining the data, however, it was clear that the expenditure figures gave the more reliable indication of the normal level of living of the household. Accordingly we adopted the expenditure basis for the analysis of the 1953-54 material. We used a very wide definition of expenditure, including mortgage and other payments concerned with housing, life assurance, pension contributions, contributions to savings clubs and holiday clubs and sums deposited in savings banks – but not income tax and national insurance contributions. A number of calculations had to be made for each household in reaching a figure of total expenditure and in relating it to the special national assistance rate.

By the time the 1960 survey was undertaken, the questions on income had been extended. Information on the respondents' *actual* income during the period of the survey was more reliable and information could also be put together to derive respondents' *normal* income. Figures for income which were 'temporarily' (i.e., for less than 13 weeks) low or high were ignored. The change was officially believed to have considerably reduced the divergence between income and expenditure figures and to have allowed income groupings to be more realistic.[40] However, the total and sub-totals of expenditure of each separate household were no longer calculated. Expenditure on different items was added and averaged for aggregates of households only. We lacked the time and resources to calculate individual household expenditure for many hundred households by adding up each item of expenditure recorded on many different sheets and thus present comparable findings for the two years. This was disappointing, since we had embarked on an analysis of the 1953-54 data before we had secured permission to examine the 1960 data and hoped to carry out a full analysis according to expenditure as well as income. But it could not be helped and at the time we were encouraged by the progress that had been made in reducing the discrepancy in these surveys between income totals and expenditure totals. The concept of 'normal income' was closer to what we intended to mean by level of living.[41]

Thus we adopted income a basis for the analysis of the 1960 data. We made adjustments to the totals so that the definition conformed as closely as possible to the wide definition of expenditure adopted for 1953-54 referring to all forms of income less tax and national insurance contributions. The Ministry's definition of income does not include withdrawals from savings, gains from the sale of houses, cars and other assets or legacies and other 'windfalls'. In estimating total income, information for a previous period of up to twelve months has to be obtained.

## The problem of interpreting changes in the amount of poverty

The results we obtained for the two years proved difficult to compare not only because methods of sampling and analysis and the representativeness of the sample differed to some extent but because expenditure formed the basis of measurement in the first year and income in the second. No one knew what was the precise relationship between the two. When we came to set out the results we realised that there was scope for controversy about the change that appeared to have taken place between 1953-54 and 1960 in the general extent of poverty. We therefore decided to modify our original decision and obtain information about the *expenditure* of a small sub-sample of households in 1960. This information would at least show the broad relationship between income and expenditure among low-income households in 1960 and allow conclusions to be reached on the general change between 1953-54 and 1960 in the proportion of the population living at low levels.

Appendix 4 describes the results of this special analysis of the expenditure of the sub-sample of households. A total of 152 households in four income groups, £3-£6, £6-£8-£10, £10-14 per week, was selected and, by using serial numbers, each item of expenditure was traced. Their total expenditure was then compared with their total income. The Ministry of Labour had itself carried out a special analysis of the expenditure of the 60 households with incomes of less than £3 per week and this information was also made available to us.

We were thus able to prepare estimates for 1960 of the proportions of the population living below or just above the national assistance 'standard' on the basis of expenditure data referring to a period of two weeks as well as on the basis of 'normal' income.

## Relationship between income and expenditure

The exercise described in Appendix 4 which seemed to have been forced upon us by the logic of research strategy had a more revealing, or more puzzling, outcome than we had expected. It raised a number of questions about the relationship between income and expenditure which have serious implications for an understanding of the extent and meaning of poverty. These must be mentioned briefly, since they are described in subsequent chapters.

Social scientists have been aware for many years that in household expenditure and income surveys average expenditure, as recorded, substantially exceeds income. Table 1 gives an example from one of the most recent of the surveys carried out for the Ministry of Labour and shows that the proportionate excess is greatest for the lowest income group but is still notable for all other income groups except the highest, where average expenditure falls to slightly below average income.

The phenomenon was discussed in a paper by Cole and Utting, which used particularly detailed data collected in Cambridgeshire, published in 1956.[42] Even when dissaving was taken into account they found that the trend shown in the last column of Table 1 is a common feature of expenditure and income surveys. They concluded that expenditure tends to be overstated but income understated. In their Cambridgeshire inquiry they estimated that expenditure was too high by about five per cent and income too low by about ten per cent.

**Table 1:** Average gross income and average gross expenditure of different household income groups in the United Kingdom, 1963*

| Income per week | Average gross income (shillings) | Average gross expenditure (shillings) | Expenditure as per cent of income |
|---|---|---|---|
| Under £4 | 66 | 110 | 167 |
| £4 but under £6 | 97 | 117 | 120 |
| £6 but under £10 | 156 | 198 | 127 |
| £10 but under £15 | 252 | 288 | 114 |
| £15 but under £20 | 349 | 392 | 112 |
| £20 but under £25 | 447 | 488 | 109 |
| £25 but under £30 | 551 | 591 | 107 |
| £30 but under £40 | 681 | 762 | 112 |
| £40 or more | 1,181 | 1,144 | 97 |

*Note:* *Ministry of Labour, *Family Expenditure Survey, Report for 1963*, London, HMSO, 1965, Table 2.

What are the reasons for the overstatement of expenditure? Individuals keeping records or reporting information tend to try to impress and to provide as many positive answers as possible. They also telescope time and attribute expenditure to the more recent past than the facts justify. If records are kept for two weeks or more, expenditure in the first week is always higher, on average, than the second, third or fourth weeks. This is called '*the end-period effect*'.[43] There appears to be some exaggeration of expenditure on 'necessities' and under-reporting on 'luxuries' – especially drink, but also cigarettes and tobacco, meals out, ice cream, chocolates and sweets. (There is some reason for supposing that expenditure incurred by children is not always reported.) There may also be some unwitting double-counting of expenditure by husband and wife (each of whom separately keep records for the Ministry of Labour) which cannot always be picked up during clerical checks. Finally, estimates of some expenditure incurred irregularly over the year may be inflated by extrapolation from the last payment (e.g., a quarterly fuel bill). When wages and prices are changing rapidly it is difficult to put together information referring to different periods over a year.[44]

Income tends to be understated for a variety of reasons. First of all, it is difficult to trace certain sources of income – particularly windfalls. Money given to children and adults by their relatives, income from goods sold, occasional earnings in evenings or weekends, lump sums paid on certain insurance policies, return of money on overpaid bills and rebates from slot meter payments for gas and electricity are a few examples. Possible sources of income are so various that it is difficult in an interview to cover them all. Small sources of income can be easily overlooked. Second, the definition of income may be relatively narrow and details of some types of income may not be collected. In the annual surveys carried out by the Ministry of Labour, income does not include withdrawals from past savings, proceeds from the sale of houses, cars, furniture or other capital assets, or receipts from legacies, maturing insurance policies or other windfalls.[45] Third, certain kinds of income appear to be considerably understated, particularly by the highest income groups. Income from rent, dividends and interest and from self-employment are examples. However, although part of the problem may be due to the same kind of deliberate under-reporting that might be encountered by the tax authorities, some of it seems to be due to the difficulty of establishing accurate figures without complex enquiry. Finally, income information usually relates to periods further in the past than expenditure information. For example, professional income and the weekly equivalents of bonuses paid to employees are based on the previous twelve months. Since expenditure information mainly relates to the previous 14 days it is evident that in a period of rising prices the income given for a particular household may fall short of its expenditure.

Quite how all these and other factors apply to the lowest income groups is still largely conjectural. Practically no special analyses have been made, except of aggregated data. As Appendix 4 shows, however, the discrepancies for some households between their total income and their total expenditure are so large as to justify a special inquiry.

There are some other problems too. For example, is 'current' or 'normal' income or expenditure the criterion of a family's standard of living? No doubt we must decide the answer to this question according to the motives and purposes of the inquiry, but an example will help to show what kind of conceptual difficulties arise. A man who is unemployed may have a low income but his expenditure might still nearly reflect the wage he was receiving, say, five weeks previously. His last week's wage at work may have been spread out over the first two or three weeks of unemployment, he may have received an income tax rebate, he may have received payments from a trade union or he may have relied on various forms of temporary 'credit' or loans. Yet he is also using up the financial and psychological 'reserves' which most other people in society retain and in certain important senses is much worse off.

There is further a problem of representation. The poor tend to be under-represented in income and expenditure surveys. They have difficulties in keeping records. Their educational or intellectual level may be low; their homes and their days may be crowded with children; or they may be old or sick. It is difficult at present to decide whether or not certain categories of poor people, and exactly how many, tend to be left out of family expenditure surveys.

Fresh intensive research on small samples of households is likely to contribute substantially towards an understanding of these problems of a surplus of expenditure over income, fluctuating living standards and non-representation. Some research on these lines will be carried out at the University of Essex and the London School of Economics under the auspices of the Rowntree Trust. Until such work is completed it will be difficult to use family expenditure survey data to define *precisely* the scope and nature of poverty or low levels of living in modern society.

[...]

## Endnotes

[1] Rowntree, B. S., and Lavers, G. R., *Poverty and the Welfare State: A Third Social Survey of York dealing only with Economic Questions*, London, Longmans, 1951.

[2] Seers, D., *The Levelling of Incomes since 1938*, Oxford, Blackwell, 1951; Carter, A. M., *The Redistribution of Income in Post-War Britain*, New Haven, Yale University Press, 1955; Paish, F.W., "The Real Incidence of Personal Taxation", *Lloyds Bank Review*, 43, 1957, p. 1; Lydall, H. F., "The Long-Term Trend in the Size Distribution of Income", *Journal of Royal Statistical Society*, Series A (General), 122, Part 1, 1959, p. 1.

[3] "A Study of the period 1938-57 reveals a continuous trend towards greater equality in the distribution of allocated personal income... For the future, unless there is a catastrophic slump, the trend towards equality is likely to continue, though probably not as fast as in the past twenty years." Lydall, H. F., *ibid*, p. 34.

[4] The Social Science Department of the University of Liverpool has recently been carrying out a study in that city.

[5] For example, it is unlikely that the working-class districts of the city of York – the area chosen for the survey – contained a representative number of the nation's low-income families. Indeed the authors themselves virtually admit this. "...We may safely assume that from the standpoint of the earnings of the workers, York holds a position not far from the median, among the towns of Great Britain... There are no large industries... where wages are exceptionally low." *Op.cit.,* p. 6. The report is short and does not give an adequate account of methods of sampling and obtaining income data. For a discussion of these and other criticisms, see Political and Economic Planning, *Poverty: Ten Years After Beveridge*, Planning, XIX, No. 344, 1952.

[6] The statistics are increasingly presenting a "delusive picture of the economic and social structure of society". Titmuss, R. M., *Income Distribution and Social Change*, London, Allen & Unwin, 1962, p. 168.

[7] The phrase was used in a memorandum of dissent by a minority of the Royal Commission on Taxation. The minority pointed out the narrowness of the Board's definition of income. "In fact no concept of income can be really equitable that stops short of the comprehensive definition which embraces all receipts which increase an individual's command over the use of society's scarce resources – in other words, his 'net accretion of economic power between two points of time'." *Report of the Royal Commission on Taxation*, Cmd. 9474, 1955, p. 8.

[8] For example, the number of weekly allowances currently paid by the National Assistance Board was 1,694,000 in June 1953 and 1,793,000 in June 1960.

[9] Utting, J., discussing Lydall, H. F., *op.cit.*, p. 42. See also Paish, F.W., *op.cit.*, particularly pp. 9-15.

[10] A preliminary account of the results of analysing the data for the first year are to be found in Townsend, P., "The Meaning of Poverty", *British Journal of Sociology*, Vol. XIII, No. 3, Sept. 1962. A similar type of analysis for 1960 is reported by Wedderburn, D., "Poverty in Britain Today. The Evidence", *Sociological Review*, Vol. 10, No. 3, 1962.

[11] Ministry of Labour, *Weekly Expenditure of Working-Class Households in the U.K. in 1937-38*, London, Mimeographed, 1949. Some statistical summaries were published in the *Ministry of Labour Gazette*, December 1940, and January and February 1941.

[12] Ministry of Labour and National Service, Cost of Living Advisory Committee, *Report on Proposals for a New Index of Retail Prices*, Cmd. 9710, London, HMSO, 1956, p. iii.

[13] Ministry of Labour, *Report of an Enquiry into Household Expenditure in 1953-54*, London, HMSO. 1957.

[14] Ministry of Labour, *Report of an Enquiry into Household Expenditure in 1953-54*, p. 2.

[15] Ministry of Labour, *Interim Report of the Cost of Living Advisory Committee*, Cmd. 8328, London, HMSO, 1951, p. 2.

[16] Selected tables are usually published first in the *Ministry of Labour Gazette*. See also Ministry of Labour, *Family Expenditure Survey*, Reports for 1957-59, 1960-61, 1962, 1963 and 1964, London, HMSO, 1961, 1962, 1963, 1964 and 1965.

[17] Kemsley, W. F. F., "Expenditure Surveys: Descriptions of the Sample, Fieldwork Procedure and Response Rate," in the *Report of the Committee of Inquiry into the Impact of Rates on Households* (The Allen Report), Cmnd. 2582, London, HMSO, 1965, Appendix 2.

[18] Report for 1957-59, *ibid.*, p. 1. For an interesting account of the origins and methods of the survey, see Fowler, R. F. and Moss, L., "The Continuous Budget Survey in the United Kingdom", *Family Living Studies: A Symposium*, Geneva: International Labour Office, 1961.

[19] "The Impact of Taxes and Social Service Benefits on Different Groups of Household", in *Economic Trends*, No. 109, published for the Central Statistical Office by HMSO, November 1962. See also "The Incidence of Taxes and Social Service Benefits in 1961 and 1962", *Economic Trends*, No. 124, February 1964; and Nicholson, J. L., *Redistribution of Income in the United Kingdom in 1959, 1957 and 1953*, London, Bowest & Bowes, 1965.

[20] Government spokesmen were somewhat ambivalent about the basis of national insurance payments, for although these were broadly intended in time to equal the real Beveridge standard, in fact they fell below it in 1948 and succeeding years.

[21] Rowntree, B. S., *Poverty and Progress*, London, Longmans, 1941. For a discussion of Beveridge's standard and its relation to National Assistance rates, see Lynes, T., *National Assistance and National Prosperity*, Occasional Papers on Social Administration, No. 5, London, Bell, 1962; and also PEP, *Poverty: Ten Years After Beveridge*, Planning, Vol. XIX, No. 344, 1952.

[22] Lynes, T., *ibid.*, pp. 36-41.

[23] "In 1899, the average wage of the male heads of families was 27s. 5d... In 1936 it was 63s. 0d." Rowntree, B. S. *Poverty and Progress*, *op. cit.*, p. 452. No comparable figure was given in the report on the 1950 survey, and we have taken the figure of average weekly industrial earnings for October of that year – 150s. 5d.

[24] See the papers written over many years by Miss T. Schulz in *Oxford University Bulletin of Statistics*.

[25] The information available in these surveys is discussed in Lambert, R., *Nutrition in Britain, 1950-60* in Occasional Papers in Social Administration No. 6, Bell, London, 1964.

[26] For a discussion of this approach in relation to that used by Rowntree and others, see Townsend, P., "Measuring Poverty", *British Journal of Sociology*, Vol. V, No. 2, June 1954.

[27] *Report of the National Assistance Board for the year ended 31st December, 1953*, London: HMSO, pp. 8-9 and 37.

[28] If a recipient of assistance has *regular* help in kind to a significant extent, say a hundredweight of coal a week, the Board put a cash value on it and treat it in the same way as a regular cash allowance from a similar source. Their officers ignore 'little things' though they may be regular, and also gifts, whether in cash or in kind, which are only occasional. In practice it is the occasional gift which is the more common kind of help. (We are indebted to Mr. T. Lynes for this information taken from a personal communication with the Board.)

[29] We are not able to give a precise estimate from our data of how far the level of living of the average national assistance applicant varies from the basic scale. Nearly a sixth of household receiving national assistance have other members who are not on national assistance. In such households it was not possible to distinguish persons dependent on national assistance and it would have been unreal as well as impractical to try and separate the level of living of those on assistance from

those not on assistance. Households of one person receiving national assistance obviously consisted of assistance recipients alone. In 1953-54 we found the average expenditure of one person households receiving national assistance was 26 per cent higher than the basic national assistance scale plus rent. Owing to the different procedure used in handling the 1960 data a comparable calculation has not been made for that year.

[30] No rent is granted to applicants under 18 years of age.

[31] Appendix 2.

[32] "Determination of what is required for reasonable human subsidence is to some extent a matter of judgment; estimates on this point change with time, and generally, in a progressive community, change upwards." *Social Insurance and Allied Services* (The Beveridge Report), Cmd. 6404, London, HMSO, 1942, p. 14.

[33] Lynes, T. *op. cit.* p. 31.

[34] Calculated by averaging the April and October figures for each year as given in the *Ministry of Labour Gazette*.

[35] Calculated from *National Income and Expenditure 1963*, pp. 4-5.

[36] *National Income and Expenditure 1963*, p.23.

[37] In making this calculation, we have assumed that only one adult dependant was living with each applicant and we have ignored child dependants. The inclusion of the latter would tend to reduce the figure of 49 per cent as rent would become a lower proportion of the basic scale.

[38] There were a number of large households with various amounts of income from different sources and the number of children dependent on assistance sometimes had to be estimated. Adults accounted for 75 per cent in both years of *all* persons in households listed as deriving any income from national assistance. There is one further point about the national assistance figures to which attention must be drawn. The average size of households receiving national assistance was 2.27 in 1953-54 and 1.99 in 1960. An analysis of the figures showed that in 1953-54 about 40 per cent of these households were one person households compared with 54 per cent in 1960. On the other hand, 36 per cent and 23 per cent respectively were two person households. From examination of the appropriate National Assistance Board report we would have expected to find about 40 per cent of one person households in 1960. Though information is not available in the Report of the National Assistance Board for 1953 from which a similar calculation could be made for that year, we would be surprised if the figure was very different.

[39] For example, an estimated income range, e.g., £3-£6, was given for approximately one in ten of the households for which expenditure data had been collected.

[40] *Family Expenditure Survey, Report for 1960 and 1961*, London, HMSO, 1962, p. 2.

[41] The chief problem in using the concept of 'normal' income is that it tends to take no account of *average* reductions brought about by temporary interruptions

during a year of earnings because of sickness, unemployment or short-time working – quite apart from additions brought about by occasional windfalls or gifts. The Ministry of Labour regards an income as 'temporary' if it has not been received for the previous thirteen weeks.

[42] Cole, D. and Utting, J. E. G., "Estimating Expenditure, Saving and Income from Household Budgets", *Journal of the Royal Statistical Society*, Series A, General Vol. 119, Part IV 1956, pp. 371-73.

[43] Kemsley found that expenditure in the first week was about 7 per cent higher than in weeks two and three. Kemsley, W. F. F., "The Household Expenditure Enquiry of the Ministry of Labour: Variability in the 1953-54 Enquiry", *Applied Statistics*, Vol. X, 1961, pp. 117-35.

[44] There may be other reasons for error. For example, interviewers collecting information in the Ministry of Labour's surveys are instructed not to allow records of expenditure to be kept until all members of a household are present. Holidays at the expense of relatives or friends (with a saving of expenditure during certain days or weeks of the year) are not allowed for. Yet this kind of hospitality is common. On the day of the Census 1961, there were more than half a million 'visitors'. There were also nearly 250,000 households with all their members temporarily absent. *Census, 1961, England and Wales, Housing Tables, Part II*, Tenure and Household Arrangements, Table 19, London, HMSO, 1965.

[45] Ministry of Labour, *Family Expenditure Survey, Report for 1963*, London, HMSO, 1965.

# 16

# Concepts of poverty and deprivation

## Concepts of poverty and deprivation

Poverty can be defined objectively and applied consistently only in terms of the concept of relative deprivation. […] The term is understood objectively rather than subjectively. Individuals, families and groups in the population can be said to be in poverty when they lack the resources to obtain the types of diet, participate in the activities and have the living conditions and amenities which are customary, or are at least widely encouraged or approved, in the societies to which they belong. Their resources are so seriously below those commanded by the average individual or family that they are, in effect, excluded from ordinary living patterns, customs and activities.

The consequences of adopting this definition will be illustrated to bring out its meaning. For example, research studies might find more poverty, according to this definition, in certain wealthy than in certain less wealthy societies, although the poor in the former might be better off, according to some criteria, than the poor in the latter. Again, despite continued economic growth over a period of years, the proportion of the population of an advanced industrial society which is found to be in poverty might rise. Certainly some of the assumptions that are currently made in comparing and contrasting the more developed with the less developed societies, and in judging progress in overcoming poverty in affluent societies, would have to be revised. In the United States, for example, the assumption that the prevalence of poverty has been steadily reduced since 1959 may have to be abandoned, principally because the definition upon which prevalence is measured is rooted in the conceptions of a particular moment of history and not sufficiently related to the needs and demands of a changing society. The US government adopted a standard which was misconceived, but showed, for example, that the number of people in poverty declined from 22.4 percent (or 39.5 million) in 1959 to 12.5 per cent (or 25.6 million) in 1971,[1] and 11.6 per cent (or 24.3 million) in 1974.[2] Students of income distribution in the United States were coming to appreciate by the late 1970s that the standard of living was seriously misleading.[3]

---

Extracts (pp 31–60) from Townsend, P. (1979) *Poverty in the United Kingdom: A survey of household resources and standards of living*, Harmondsworth: Penguin.

The definition also has implications for policy which should be recognised at the outset. Although all societies have ways of identifying and trying to deal with their problems, the social sciences are having an increasing influence upon decision-makers, both in providing information and implicitly or explicitly legitimating action. An important example in the history of the formulation of social policies to deal with poverty is the definition of the subsistence standard in the Beveridge Report of 1942. Beveridge adapted the definition used in measuring poverty by Seebohm Rowntree, A. L. Bowley and others in their studies for different communities in Britain, and he argued that this was the right basis for paying benefits in a social security scheme designed to abolish want.[4] For thirty years the rationale for the level of benefits paid in the British schemes of national insurance and supplementary benefit (formerly National Assistance) has rested upon the arguments put forward in the early years of the Second World War. No attempt has yet been made to present an alternative rationale, although benefits have been increased from time to time in response to rises in prices and wages. A clear definition allows the scale and degree as well as the nature of the problem of poverty to be identified, and therefore points to the scale as well as the kind of remedial action that might be taken. Such action may involve not just the general level of benefits, for example, but revision of relativities between benefits received by different types of family.

## Previous definitions of poverty

Any attempt to justify a new approach[5] towards the definition and measurement of poverty, so that its causes and means of alleviation may be identified, must begin with previous definitions and evidence. The literature about both poverty and inequality are closely related and need to be considered in turn. Any explanation of the fact that the poor receive an unequal share of resources must be related to the larger explanation of social inequality. We will consider definitions, evidence about poverty and related evidence about inequality.

Previous operational definitions of poverty have not been expressed in thoroughgoing relativist terms, nor founded comprehensively on the key concepts of resources and style of living. The concern has been with narrower concepts of income and the maintenance of physical efficiency. Among the early studies of poverty, the work of Seebohm Rowntree is most important. [...] He defined families whose 'total earnings are insufficient to obtain the minimum necessaries for the maintenance of merely physical efficiency as being in primary poverty'.[6] [...]

Nearly all subsequent studies were influenced deeply by this application of the concept of subsistence. With minor adaptations, a stream of area surveys of poverty based on Rowntree's methods was carried out in Britain, especially between the wars.[7] Rowntree himself carried out further studies in York in 1936 and 1950.[8] [...]

But the standards which were adopted proved difficult to defend. Rowntree's estimates of the costs of necessities other than food were based either on his own and other's opinions or, as in the case of clothing, on the actual expenditure of those among a small selection of poor families who spent the least. Does the actual expenditure of the poorest families represent what they *need* to spend on certain items? Neither in his studies nor in similar studies were criteria of need, independent of personal judgement or of the minimum amounts actually spent on certain goods, put forward.

[...]

A number of points in the argument can be examined critically. First, and most important, the index is not redefined periodically to take account of changing customs and needs. In one of her influential articles Mollie Orshansky writes, 'Except to allow for rising prices, the poverty index has not been adjusted since 1959.' Between 1959 and 1966, 'the average income of 4-person families had increased by 37 per cent but the poverty line by only 9 per cent'.[9] Yet the same writer had pointed out earlier that 'social conscience and custom dictate that there be not only sufficient quantity of food but sufficient variety to meet recommended nutritional goals and conform to customary eating patterns'.[10] In a rapidly developing society like the United States, dietary customs and needs are liable to change equally rapidly and estimates of need must be reviewed frequently. Otherwise the risk is run of reading the needs of the present generation as if they were those of the past. Foods are processed differently, and presented from time to time in new forms, whether in recipe or packaging. Real prices may rise without any corresponding improvement in nutritional content. In the Unites States as well as Britain household expenditure on food has increased faster than prices in the last ten or twenty years, but regular studies of nutrition have shown little change in nutritional intakes. This evidence provides the minimum case for raising the poverty line between two points in time by more than the rise in prices.[11] [...]

Secondly, nutritional needs are narrowly defined. The cost of buying a minimally adequate diet, providing families restrict the kind and quality of their purchases and exercise skill in preparing as well as in buying food, is worked out.[12] [...] While it may seen to be reasonable to average nutritional requirements, empirical studies of diets in relationship to incomes and activities have to be undertaken to demonstrate whether that procedure is in fact as reasonable as it purports to be.

Finally, the question of finding criteria for needs other than food is dodged by estimating food costs and then taking these as a fixed percentage of the total budget stated to be necessary. The percentage varies for households of different size and is lower for farm families than for other families. How, therefore, are the percentages chosen? Essentially they are a reflection of actual consumption, or, more strictly, consumption in the mid 1950s.[13] But again, although actual behaviour is more relevant than an arbitrarily defined category of 'poor', it cannot be regarded as a criterion of need. This remains the nagging problem about the entire procedure. All that can be conceded is that at least the United States method makes more allowance (although out of date) for conventional distribution of a poverty budget between food, fuel and clothing and other items, than the Rowntree method, which expected poor families to adopt a distributional pattern of spending quite unlike other families.

[...]

Socio-economic measures cannot rest only on imaginable or even politically acceptable, but must also rest on demonstrable, definitions of social conditions. These may be difficult to apply consistently. There are bound to be difficulties and disadvantages in any approach that is developed. In the final analysis, a definition of poverty may have to rest on value judgements. But this does not mean that a definition cannot be objective and that is cannot be distinguished from social or individual opinion.

[...]

Two conclusions might be drawn form this brief historical review of attempts, especially in Britain and the United States, to define poverty. The first is that definitions which are based on some conception of 'absolute' deprivation disintegrate upon close and sustained examination and deserve to be abandoned. Poverty has often been defined, in the words of an OECD review, 'in terms of some absolute level of minimal needs, below which people are regarded as being poor, for purpose of social and government concern, and which does not change through time'.[14] In fact, people's needs, even for food, are conditioned by the society in which they live and to which they belong, and just as needs differ in different societies so they differ in different periods of the evolution of single societies. Any conception of poverty as 'absolute' is therefore inappropriate and misleading.

The second conclusion which might be drawn is that, though the principle definitions put forward historically have invoked some 'absolute' level of minimum needs, they have in practice represented rather narrow conceptions of relative deprivation and deserve to be clarified as such.[15]

## The limitations of the evidence of poverty

I shall now briefly review available evidence about poverty. It is certainly voluminous, but also incomplete and inconsistent. Most of it is indirect, in the sense that particular aspects of poverty, such as bad-quality housing, homelessness, overcrowding and malnourishment, the hardship of the unemployed, aged, sick and disabled and the severity of some working conditions rather than actual income in relation to community living standards have been described and discussed. One tradition is the polemical, comprehensive account of working and living conditions, as, for example, in some of the writing of Engels, Masterman and Orwell.[16] Another is the painstaking official commission of inquiry, ranging, for example, from the 1844 Report of the Commission of Enquiry into the State of Large Towns to the 1965 Report of the Milner Holland Committee on Housing in Greater London.[17] A third is the punctiliously specific research study.

[…]

But the underlying task of developing a definition of poverty in operational terms which can be applied in different countries and regions, and which can permit measurement of a kind sensitive enough to show the short–term effect on the numbers in poverty of, say, an increase in unemployment, an unusually large increase in process, or the stepping–up in value of social security benefits, is still in an early stage. This remains true to despite a longish history of empirical work in some countries.[18] Even recent work reflects continuing reliance on the subsistence approach, despite appreciation of its inadequacy.[19] Recent quantitative analyses in different countries of the extent of poverty can be compared. In 1966 the British Ministry of Social Security found that 160,000 families with two or more children, or 4.1 per cent of such families, were living on incomes lower than the prevailing basic rates of national assistance.[20] In the same year, the US Social Security Administration, using a more generous definition of adequacy, found that 13.6 per cent of all households with children (15.6 per cent with two or more children) and 17.7 per cent of all households were poor.[21] In 1966 in Melbourne, 4.8 per cent of families with children (6.1 per cent of families with two or more children) and just over 7 per cent of all households were found to be in poverty.[22] But although the last of these three 1966 surveys copied methods used in the United States to estimate what incomes for families of different size were equivalent, they each adopted a national or conventional and not independent standard. […] In each case, standards which had already proved to be politically acceptable rather than other standards were invoked. […]

In calling attention to the fact that much of the evidence about poverty depends on measures which are built, in the final analysis, on conventional judgement or experience rather than on independent criteria, such evidence must not be discounted. If there are national standards of need, expressed through public assistance scales, a minimum wage or child endowment, knowing the number of people having incomes of less than these standards none the less represents valuable information. Such information can also be collected for different definitions of poverty which are in practice made by a society or by different groups within a society and those which depend on alternative and more scientific criteria.

[…]

## Poverty and inequality

Any preliminary outline of available evidence about poverty must include evidence about inequality. For many countries there is a considerable amount of evidence about unequal distribution of incomes, for example, the proportion of aggregate incomes taken by the poorest 10 per cent or 20 per cent of income recipients. In one wide-ranging review, Harold Lydall found that the countries distributing employment income most equally were Czechoslovakia, Hungary, New Zealand and Australia. Those distributing them most unequally were Brazil, Chile, India, Ceylon and Mexico. […]

The methods that have been used to compare the distribution of income in different countries can be criticized on grounds that they are so crude as to be misleading. For example, the ranking of so-called developed and developing countries according to a measure of inequality, such as the Gini coefficient, can change remarkably if alternative measures, such as the standard deviation of logarithms or coefficient of variation, are used.[23] The rankings are sufficiently diverse to throw profound doubt on the accepted conclusion that inequality is greater in the developing countries. As Atkinson points out, nearly all the conventional measures are insensitive to whether or not inequality is more pronounced near the top rather than near the bottom of the distribution.[24] What is at stake is the concept of equality. An attempt is made in Figure 1.1 to bring out the ambiguities in present conceptions. In Country A, the total range of the distribution of income is not as wide as in Country B, but 97 per cent of the population of B are concentrated over a narrower range of income. In which country is income distribution more unequal? Equality might be taken to mean the range of the distribution being narrow, or a high proportion of population being concentrated around the mean, or a very small proportion of population being found much below the mean. As Professor Atkinson points out, 'The degree of inequality cannot, in general, be measured without introducing social judgments.'[25]

[…]

Apparent differences between countries in inequalities of income distribution might be wholly explained by the differential use by sections of the population of such resources. Inevitably we are driven to develop a more comprehensive definition of income and collect more comprehensive data on which to build theory. Better information about accepted styles of living in different countries is also required. The same relative level of command over resources in each of two countries might permit minimal participation in such styles in one but not in the other.

**Figure 1.1:** Illustration of the distribution in incomes in two countries

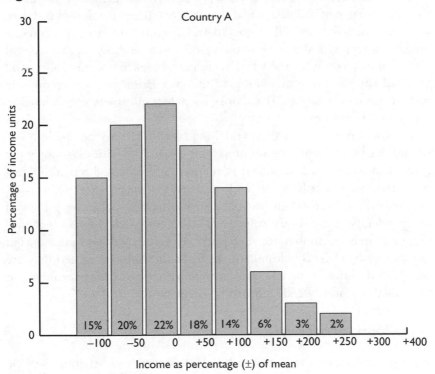

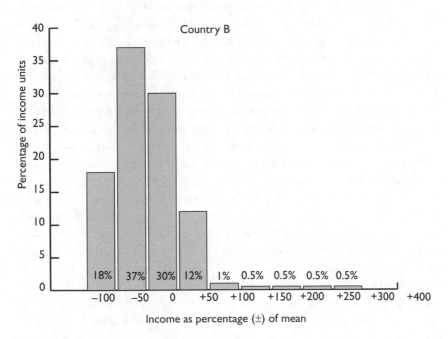

Theories and data are, of course, interdependent. Bad theories may not just be the consequence of bad data, but also give rise to the collection of bad data, or at least the failure to collect good data. Economic theories of inequality tend to misrepresent the shape of the wood, and in endeavoring to account for it, fail to account for the trees. Sociological theories of inequality tend to avoid any specific examination of the correlation between economic resources and occupational status or styles of life, and are, as a consequence, unnecessarily diffuse.

Information about poverty and inequality tends to be shaped and permeated by conventional opinion, and certainly decisions about what is or is not collected and how it is analysed and reported rest ultimately with governments rather than with independent social scientists in most countries. [...] Even when comparable information could be produced independently in a country substantial resources would be required, and these are rarely committed for such purposes either by the governments in question or by charitable foundations. When they are committed they are usually committed to people who are sympathetic to the government or to its methods of data collection and presentation.

## Three forms of deprivation

Present national or social conceptions of poverty tend therefore to be inadequate and idiosyncratic or inconsistent, and the evidence which is collected about the phenomenon seriously, incomplete. A new approach to both the definition and measurement of poverty is called for. This depends in part on adopting some such concept as 'relative deprivation'. As already argued, a fundamental distinction has to be made between actual and socially perceived need, and therefore between actual and socially perceived poverty – or more strictly, between *objective* and *conventionally acknowledged* poverty. All too easily the social scientist can be the unwitting servant of contemporary social values, and in the study of poverty this can have disastrous practical consequences. He may side with the dominant or majority view of the poor. If, by contrast, he feels obliged or is encouraged from the start to make a formal distinction between scientific and conventional perspectives, he is more likely to enlarge knowledge by bringing to light information which has been neglected and create more elbow-room for alternative forms of action, even if, in the end, some colouring of scientific procedure by social attitudes and opinion or individual valuation is inescapable.[26] At least he is struggling to free himself from control and manipulation by the values which prevail within the constrictions of his own small society, social class or occupational group. Without pretending that the approach offered in these pages, or any alternative approach, can escape the exercise of judgment at key stages, it may open the way to cross-national usage and limit the element of arbitrariness.

On the one hand we have to examine the different elements which go to make up living standards at a point of time and how they vary over time, and on the other the sectional and collective interpretations of, or feelings about, such living standards. Throughout a given period of history there may be no change whatever in the actual inequalities of wealth and of income, and yet social perceptions of those inequalities and of any change in them may become keener. Alternatively, substantial changes in the structure of incomes in society may occur without the corresponding perception that such changes are taking place.

The distinction [between actuality and perception] may also encourage sociologists to pay more attention to actuality than many have paid hitherto. The term 'relative deprivation' was coined originally by Stouffer and his colleagues,[27] and elaborated valuably first by Merton and then by Runciman,[28] to denote *feelings* of deprivation relative to others and not *conditions* of deprivation relative to others. Yet the latter would be a preferable usage since differences in conditions between men underlie social structure and values, are not at all easy to define and measure, and may in fact be obscured by social belief. Little or no attempt has been made to specify and measure conditions of deprivation which some people experience relative to others in recent work, perhaps because such conditions are recognized to be complex phenomena requiring elaborate and patient fieldwork to identify precisely. The description and analysis of these conditions is important in many, different ways. For example, a group of skilled manual workers may feel deprived in relation to a group of office staff, and it may be observed that their take-home earnings may be as high, or higher, than the salaries of the office staff. Before jumping too readily to an assumption that subjective and objective states are out of line, more information has to be given about pay and conditions. We have to establish what are the inequalities in actual working conditions, security of employment, promotion prospects and fringe benefits and, in addition, the extent to which some workers may be excluded from sharing in the conditions available either to other groups of workers in the same industry, or workers comparable to themselves in other industries. It is surely impossible to assess the importance of subjective deprivation as an explanatory variable independent of assessing actual deprivation.

[…]

So the social scientist has to collect evidence about (a) objective deprivation, (b) conventionally acknowledged or normative deprivation, and (c) individual subjective or group deprivation. The distinction between the second and third is in some ways a matter of degree. The former represents a dominant or majority valuation in society. The latter may reflect the views held by different kinds of minority group. There are various possibilities.

Some individuals may feel poor, especially by reference to their previous situations in life, even when they are neither demonstrably poor nor acknowledged to be poor by society. Some retired middle-class persons, for example, have an income which is more than adequate according to either objective or conventional standards, but which is inadequate according to their own customary or expected standards. A group of manual or professional workers who have earnings considerably higher than the mean may feel poor by reference to other groups.

There are alternative ways which are open to the social scientist of defining and measuring conventionally acknowledged or normative deprivation. In the course of history, societies develop rules about the award of welfare payments and services to poor families. These rules can be said to reflect the standard of poverty conventionally acknowledged by these societies. The rates of payment under public assistance laws, for example, represent a contemporary social standard. The extent to which people in different societies in fact fall below national standards can be investigated, as in one study in Britain.[29] Similarly, societies use minimum housing standards; whether of overcrowding or amenities. These standards tend to be changed from time to time in response to political pressures. They represent conventional or elitist values rather than standards the non-fulfillment of which represents objective deprivation.[30]

Each of the three types of deprivation deserves thorough documentation and measurement, as a basis for explaining social conditions, attitudes and behaviour. But by trying to separate subjective and collective views about poverty from the actual conditions which constitute the problem, we are led to define both subjective and objective states and their relationships rather more carefully.

## Concepts of relativity

The idea of 'the relativity' of poverty requires some explanation. The frame of reference in adopting this approach can be regional, national or international, although until formal ties between nation states are stronger, or global corporations even more strongly entrenched, the international perspective is unlikely to be given enough emphasis. The question is how far peoples are bound by the same economic, trading, institutional and cultural systems, how far they have similar activities and customs and therefore have similar needs. Needs arise by virtue of the kind of society to which individuals belong. Society imposes expectations, through its occupational, educational, economic and other systems, and it also it creates wants, through its organization and customs.

This is easy enough to demonstrate for certain commodities. Tea is nutritionally worthless, but in some countries is generally accepted as a 'necessity of life'. For many people in these countries drinking tea has been a life-long custom and is psychologically essential. And the fact that friends and neighbours expect to be offered a cup of tea (or the equivalent) when they visit helps to make it socially necessary as well: a small contribution is made towards maintaining the threads of social relationships. [...]

Clothing is another good example. Climate may determine whether or not any soft forms of protection are placed over the body, and how thick they are, but social convention, itself partly dependent on resources available, determines the type and style. Who would lay down a scale of necessities for the 1970s for young women in Britain consisting of one pair of boots, two aprons, one second-hand dress, one skirt made from an old dress, a third of the cost of a new hat, a third of the cost of a shawl and a jacket, two pairs of stockings, a few unspecified under-clothes, one pair of stays and one pair of old boots worn as slippers, as Rowntree did in 1899?[31]

But convention is much more than ephemeral fashion. It is a style of living also governed by state laws and regulations. Industry conditions the population not only want certain products and services, but to put up with certain disservices. The Public Health and Housing Acts and regulations control sanitation, the structure, size and layout of housing, streets and shops. A population becomes conditioned to expect to live in certain broad types of homes, and to heat and furnish them accordingly. Their environment, and the expectations of society around them, create their needs in an objective as well as a subjective sense. [...] Laws and norms are in delicate interdependence with need.

[...]

If poverty is relative cross-nationally or cross-culturally, then it is also relative historically. It is relative to time as well as place. Needs which are a product of laws and social norms must change as new legislation is passed, social organizations grow and coalesce, automation develops and expectations change. Within a generation the possession of a television set in Britain has changed from being a doubtful privilege of a tiny minority to being an expected right of 95 per cent of the population. But this is only one example. [...] The attenuation of public transport services is brought about in some areas by the development of private transport and, if private transport becomes the norm, that can only be at greater real cost per family. Two or three weeks' summer holiday away from home is another social revolution of the mid twentieth century which, now that it has become a majority convention, adds to the needs which the average family is expected to meet.

Laws and not only conventions and structures also change the character of family needs. For example, by raising the school leaving age Parliament has imposed new obligations on families to support children for one year longer. With economic growth, though not necessarily in direct proportion to such growth, the needs which a family is expected to meet also increase. Standards rise subtly, sometimes imperceptibly, as society itself adapts to greater prosperity and responds to the changes demanded by industry, consumers, educationists and the professionals. Certainly no standard of sufficiency could be revised only to take account of changes in prices, for that would be to ignore changes in the goods and services consumed as well as new obligations and expectations placed on members of the community. Lacking an alternative criterion, the best assumption would be to relate sufficiency to the average rise in real incomes.

There is one further important elaboration. If needs are relative to society, then they are also relative to the set of social sub-systems to which the individual belongs. This seems to suggest that a different definition of poverty is required of every society, or indeed every relatively autonomous community. But this tends to ignore the marked interrelationship of many communities within regional and national economic, political, communication, welfare and other systems. Members of ethnic minorities can often be said to participate in commonly shared rather than exclusive activities. They use the common system of transport, work in multiracial occupations, go to multiracial schools which broadly subscribe to national cultural values, and generally adapt in many ways to the conventions and styles of life of the national society. Many of their needs will therefore be the same as of persons who are not members of such minorities and the same as of persons who are members of other minorities. But to some extent their resources will be different and their activities and beliefs relatively autonomous. A national definition of need, and more particularly of poverty, will to that extent not apply to them. [...]

It would be wrong, however, to call attention only to the possible divergence of racial or ethnic sub-systems from the social system as a whole. There are differences between rural and urban communities and even between different urban communities which would compel different overall definitions of their needs. The difficulty of allowing properly for the income in kind of the country dweller (such as home-grown vegetables, free or cheap fuel, and tied accommodation), but also the lack of facilities available to the town or city dweller, especially if he is young (for example, entertainment, choice of shops and choice of indoor as compared with outdoor work) are reasonably well recognized. Inevitably both would have to be taken into account in any sophisticated investigation of poverty, not just in qualifying the results of any measure but also in applying that measure.

## Style of living

A distinction must therefore be made between the resources which are made available by society to individuals and families and the style of life with which they are expected, or to which they feel prompted, to conform. [...] Any attempt to define this style and represent it in some form of operational index, so that the conformity of a population can be measured statistically, is bound to be rough and ready. One kind of analogy could be drawn with the Retail Price Index. The price index does not show how much the cost of living may have changed between two dates for any particular family or section of the population, but only in broad terms for society as a whole. There are difficulties in applying it to retirement pensioners or to the poor generally and to different regions. Techniques have to be developed so that applications to certain groups can be qualified; or a modified index, such as the index for retirement pensioners, is developed. But nonetheless it represents a useful point of departure and a means of accumulating, and generalizing, knowledge.

## Stratification and resources

What principles must therefore govern the attempt to obtain better information? The conditions and numbers of the poor relative to others in society are to be identified. The population must be ranked in strata according to a criterion of inequality. But the criterion of cash income is inadequate. There are groups in the population with considerable income in kind, such as farmers and smallholders. There are people with small cash incomes but considerable assets, which elevate their standards of living. There are people with identical wages or salaries who differ greatly in the extent to which fringe benefits from employers add substantially to their living standards. There are people with identical cash incomes who differ greatly in the support they may obtain from free public social services, because, for example, they live in different areas.

Living standards depend on the total contribution of not one but several systems distributing resources to individuals, families, work-groups and communities. To concentrate on cash incomes is to ignore the subtle ways developed in both modern and traditional societies for conferring and redistributing benefits. Moreover, to concentrate on income as the sole criterion of poverty also implies that relatively simple adjustments, as might be made in a single scheme for negative income tax, will relieve it.

A plural approach is unavoidable. Thus, the list given below shows the types of resource arising from the principal systems of resource distribution. Even a fleeting reference to the different systems in society which distribute and redistribute resources, such as the wage system, insurance and banking, social security and services like the National Health Service, may suggest that poverty is the creation of their complex interrelationship, or perhaps, more fundamentally, of the values and norms upon which they rest or which they continuously reinforce. The practical implication is that the abolition of poverty may require comprehensive structural change in not one but several institutional systems. The problem is to establish, first, the part that the different types of resource play in determining the overall standards of living of different strata in the population, and secondly, which of the systems underlying the distribution of that resource can be manipulated most efficiently to reduce poverty. The list is as follows:

1. *Cash income:*
   (a) Earned.
   (b) Unearned.
   (c) Social security.
2. *Capital assets:*
   (a) House/flat occupied by family, and living facilities.
   (b) Assets (other than occupied house) and savings.
3. *Value of employment benefits in kind:*
   (a) Employers' fringe benefits; subsidies and value of occupational insurance.
   (b) Occupational facilities.
4. *Value of public social services in kind:*
   Including government subsidies and services, e.g. health, education and housing but excluding social security.
5. *Private income in kind:*
   (a) Home production (e.g. of smallholding or garden).
   (b) Gifts.
   (c) Value of personal supporting services.

To obtain full information about all these types of resource for a representative cross-section of households is an ambitious but necessary task. [...]

One of the purposes of combining the ranking of resources in different dimensions would be to allow *total* and *partial* poverty to be distinguished. If resources are distributed by different institutional systems, then it follows that while some people may lack a minimal share of any of these resources, there will be others who lack a minimal share of one or two of these types of resource but have a substantial share of others. [...]

Another advantage is to trace more clearly the differences between *temporary* and *long-term* poverty. The distribution of resources changes over time. People are promoted within the wage system; they change jobs, and become unemployed or sick; they obtain new dependants. Clearly there may be major changes in the possession of resources both in the long term, over the entire life-cycle, but also in the short term, from month to month and even week to week. [...] A proportion of the population may always have been poor, but a much larger proportion have had occasional or periodic but not continuous experience of poverty.

A larger proportion still have lived or are living under the constant threat of poverty and regard some of the resources flowing to them, or available to them, as undependable. For the purposes of understanding the experience of poverty and the development of good policy, it is most important to find whether the over-confident division of the population into 'we the people' and 'they the poor' has to be modified.

Inequality, however, is not poverty. Even if inequalities in the distribution of resources are successfully identified and measured, those in the lowest 20 per cent or 10 per cent, say, are not necessarily poor. For example, the 20 per cent with the lowest incomes in Sweden are not so badly placed as the corresponding 20 per cent in the United States.[32] Some criterion of deprivation is required by which a poverty line may be drawn and the numbers and characteristics of persons and families in the population who fall below the line estimated. It may be hypothesized that, as resources for any individual or family are diminished, there is a point at which there occurs a sudden withdrawal from participation in the customs and activities sanctioned by the culture. The point at which withdrawal 'escalates' disproportionately to falling resources could be defined as the poverty line. It would be difficult to gain information about all customs and activities which make up the style of living which predominates in society, or which can be distilled, as a kind of common denominator, from the overlapping styles of different groups and classes. Instead information could be obtained for a random selection of common activities (common in the sense either that they are followed by over half the population, or at least are approved and are widespread). These would comprise an index. It should be stressed that no one indicator alone could be sufficient. Sometimes particular social customs are observed or not observed for reasons which are locked, for example, in special factors of personality or group religion. All that can be claimed is that a *pattern* of non-observance may be conditioned by severe lack of resources.

Let me set out in a little more detail the reasoning behind these statements. Just as I have argued that a wider concept of 'sources' should replace 'income' in the study of inequality and poverty, so I would argue that 'style of living' should replace 'consumption' (or more narrowly still, 'nutritional intakes') in determining what levels in the ranking of resources should be regarded as constituting deprivation. Some care is required in establishing the meaning of the concept of style of living, for it has been used in sociology in many different senses. For Weber, stratification by economic class and status could both be represented by style of living. 'Status honour is normally expressed by the fact that a special style of *life* can be expected from all who wish to belong to the circle.'[33] But Veblen and more recently sociologists such as Warner developed the concept into a system of what amounts to supercilious and derogatory distinctions in society. Everyone, or nearly everyone, was supposed to hold similar views about what was good and desirable. Modern studies have begun to break down this unrelieved picture of a uniformly acquisitive, materialistic, consumer society, and a number of community studies in particular have shown that there are not just enclaves of traditional working-class culture but highly developed and pervasive styles of community living.[34] Tom Burns suggests that, in contemporary urban society, the principle of segregation is more and more strictly followed. In any large town or city there are social areas 'representing important expressive aspects not only of the income but of the occupations, social proclivities, educational background, and social pretensions of the people who live in them – or rather of the kind of people who are supposed to live in them'. In suburbs, neighbourhoods and even blocks of flats there were, he continued, groupings of young married couples, middle-aged people, the retired or bachelor girls and men. Consumption was the expressive aspect of style of life, and 'style of life has developed a much greater significance as a mode of organizing individual behaviour and leisure, careers and, therefore, as a form of social structure.... Individuals do organize their lives in terms of a preferred style of life which is expressed concretely in terms of a pattern of consumption ranging from houses, and other consumer durables, to clothing, holidays, entertainment, food and drink.'[35]

Style of life is made up of very widely and very restrictedly shared elements. This must always have been so for reasons of cultural self-confidence and social control as well as individual and local community self-respect. But the mix for any particular section or group in society may be different and may change over time. There are types of behaviour which are nationally sanctioned, and even upheld in law, affecting working hours and conditions, child care, marital relations, spending and so on. There are public corporations and departments which endeavour to provide recognizably uniform services throughout the country. There are trade unions, which encourage their membership to adopt a nationally cohesive outlook and not diverse and perhaps contradictory branch opinions and activities. There are symbols of nationhood, like the Royal Family, the British policeman, a village green, a love of animals or of cricket, which are repeatedly invoked in family or local rituals. And through the mass-communication industries – television, newspapers, popular magazines, the cinema and advertising – the cultural norms of society are both reflected and modified. The mass media help to standardize the kinds of leisure-time pursuits, child-rearing practices, manners and language which certain wide sections of the population will feel it is appropriate for them to adopt.

There are subtle gradations of styles of living ramifying through society as well as different mixes of national and local styles for different communities and ethnic groups. Different classes may engage in similar types of activity, such as going on a holiday or holding a birthday party for children, but do them differently. In developing an operational definition of style of living it is therefore necessary to distinguish (a) types of custom and social activity practiced or approved, and home, environmental and work conditions enjoyed or expected by a majority of the national population; (b) the types of custom and social activity practised or approved by a majority of people in a locality, community, class, racial group, religious sect or work group; and (c) the specific content and manner of individual and group expression of both national and local customs or practices. It is hypothesized that, with a diminishing level of resources, people will engage less fully in the national 'style of living'. At relatively low levels of resources people find they are unable to enjoy a wide representation of consumer goods, customs and activities and are able to enjoy only cheaper versions of some goods, customs and activities. The range is reduced proportionately to falling levels of resources. The reduction is more gradual than the diminishing resources would suggest, because of the need to maintain social cohesion or integration. Through state, industry, community, church and family, means are found, for example, through mass production and the mass media, to satisfy and integrate the relatively hard up. But at still lower levels of individual and family resources, economical forms of social participation become impossible to provide. People's participation in the national style of living diminishes disproportionately. [...]

## Conclusion

[...] Historically, the most influential definitions [of poverty and inequality] have been those which have been expressed in terms of some absolute level of minimum needs, below which people are regarded as being poor, and which does not change through time. However, conceptions of poverty as 'absolute' were found to be inappropriate and misleading. People's needs, even for food, are conditioned by the society in which they live and to which they belong, and just as needs differ in different societies, so they differ in different periods of the evolution of single societies. In practice, previous definitions have represented narrow conceptions of relative deprivation – sometimes associated only with what is necessary for the physical efficiency of the working classes. A fuller conception of relative deprivation needs to be adopted and spelt out.

The social scientist is very frequently the victim of normative values, and his perceptions and measures tend to be permeated by them. But if he feels obliged to make a distinction, as I have suggested, between subjective, collective and objective assessments of need, then first he becomes much more aware of the forces which are controlling his own perceptions, and secondly he becomes that much more prepared to break with the conventions that restrict and trivialize his theoretical work.

I have suggested two steps that might be taken towards the objectification of the measurement of poverty. One is to endeavour to measure all types of resources, public and private, which are distributed unequally in society and which contribute towards actual standards of living. This will tend to uncover sources of inequality which tend to be proscribed from public and even academic discourse. It will also lay the basis for comparisons between conditions in different societies. The other is to endeavour to define the style of living which is generally shared or approved in each society, and find whether there is, as I have hypothesized, a point in the scale of the distribution of resources below which, as resources diminish, families find it particularly difficult to share in the customs, activities and diets comprising their society's style of living.

But this does not leave measurement value-free. In the last resort the decisions which are taken to define the exact boundaries of the concept of resources and weigh the value of different types of resource have to be based on judgment, even if such judgment incorporates certain criteria of number and logical consistency. And decisions have to be taken about all the different ingredients of 'style of living', their relative importance and the extent to which they can be reliably represented by indicators used as criteria of deprivation by social scientists. Values will not have been eliminated from social research. But at least they will have been pushed one or two stages further back and an attempt made to make measurement both reproducible and more dependent on externally instead of subjectively assessed criteria.

It will be some time before theory and methodology can be put on to a respectable scientific footing. The problem of poverty has attracted a lot of concern, and also justifiable anger. Many of the attempts to document and explain it have been grounded in limited national and even parochial, not to say individualistic, conceptions. Until social scientists can provide the rigorous conception within which the poverty of industrial societies and the Third World can both be examined, and the relationship between inequality and poverty perceived, the accumulation of data and the debates about the scale and casual antecedents of the problem will in large measure be fruitless.

**Endnotes**

[1] *Social Indicators, 1973*, the 1970 Manpower Report of the President, Social and Economic Statistics Administration, US Department of Commerce, Government Printing Office, Washington DC, 1974. See Table 5.17 in particular. The 1970 Manpower Report of the President by the US Department of Labour solemnly traces, like many other reports emanating from the US government, and also papers and books by social scientists, the fall in poverty during the 1960s and early 1970s. But since a fixed and not updated poverty line has been applied at regular intervals, this fall is scarcely surprising. The same trend could have been demonstrated for every industrial society in the years since the war and, indeed for nearly all periods of history since the Industrial Revolution.

[2] *The Measure of Poverty*, A Report to Congress as Mandated by the Educational Amendments of 1974, US Department of Health, Education and Welfare, Washington DC, April 1976, p. 13.

[3] Schorr, A. L. (ed.), *Jubilee for our Times: A Practical Program for Income Equality*, Columbia University Press, 1977, pp. 15-16

[4] *Social Insurance and Allied Services* (The Beveridge Report), Cmd 6404, HMSO, London, 1942.

[5] It is only in the sense that the implications and applications do not appear to have been spelled out systematically and in detail. The line of thought has been put forward by many social scientists in the past. For example, Adam Smith wrote, "By necessities I understand, not only the commodities which are indispensably necessary for the support of life, but whatever the custom of the country renders it indecent for creditable people, even of the lowest order, to be without." He gave as examples linen shirts and leather shoes which "the established rules of decency have rendered necessary to the lowest rank of people". However, beer and ale, in Great Britain, and wine, even in the wine countries, were not necessities because "custom nowhere renders it indecent for people to live without them." See *The Wealth of Nations*, Ward, Lock, London, 1812, p. 693 (first published 1776).

[6] Rowntree, B. Seebohm, *Poverty: A Study of Town Life*, Macmillan, London, 1901. Charles Booth's major work in London between 1887 and 1892 was on a larger scale but employed a cruder measure of poverty. See his *Life and Labour of the People in London*, Macmillan, London (17 volumes published in 1903; first volume on East London originally published 1889).

[7] See, for example, Bell, Lady F., *At the Works*, Nelson, London, 1912; Davies, M., *Life in an English Village*, London, 1909; Reeves, P., *Round About a Pound a Week*, London, 1914; Bowley, A. L., and Burnett-Hurst, A. R., *Livelihood and Poverty, A Study in the Economic and Social Conditions of Working Class Households in Northampton, Warrington, Stanley, Reading and Bolton*, King, London, 1915; Bowley, A.L. and Hogg, M.H. *Has Poverty Diminished?*, London, 1925; *New Survey of London Life and Labour*, London, 1930–35; Soutar, M.S., Wilkins, E.H. and Florence, P., *Nutrition and Size of Family*, London, 1942.

[8] Rowntree, B. S., *Poverty and Progress,* Longmans, Green, London, 1941; Rowntree, B. S. (with Lavers, G. R.), *Poverty and the Welfare State,* Longmans, Green, London, 1951.

[9] Orshansky, M., 'Who Was Poor in 1966?', *Research and Statistics Note,* US Department of Health and Education and Welfare, 6 December 1967, p. 3. The 1970 Manpower Report of the President puts the same point in rather a different way: 'Whereas in 1959 the poverty threshold represented about 48 per cent of the average income of al four-person families, in 1968 it represented only 36 per cent.'

[10] Orshanksy, 'Counting the Poor: Another Look at the Poverty Profile', *Social Security Bulletin*, vol. 28, January 1965, p. 5.

[11] Between 1960 and 1968, average expenditure per head in Britain on food increased by about 6 per cent more than prices, but the energy value of nutritional intakes by only about 1 per cent and calcium by less than 3 per cent. However, there is no satisfactory comprehensive index for nutritional intakes. See Ministry of Agriculture, *Household Food Consumption and Expenditure: 1968*, HMSO, London, 1970, pp. 8, 57 and 64; *Household Food Consumption and Expenditure: 1966*, HMSO, London, 1968, pp. 9 and 84.

[12] 'All the plans, if strictly followed, can provide an acceptable and adequate diet but – generally speaking – the lower the level of cost, the more restricted the kinds and qualities of food must be and the more skill in marketing and food preparation that is required' – Orshansky, 'Counting the Poor', p. 5.

[13] Orshansky herself quoted a Bureau of Labour Statistics Survey for 1960-61, showing that food represented only 22 per cent of the expenditure of a household of three people, for example, compared with 31 per cent in the 1955 survey. Acknowledging that the percentage had decreased, she stated that this 'undoubtedly reflect[ed] in part the general improvement in real income achieved by the Nation as a whole in the 6 years which elapsed between the two studies'. Had the later percentages been adopted, the poverty line would have been $1400 to $1500 higher for a family of three persons, for example, and the total number of families in poverty would have been at least half as many again. See Orshansky, 'How Poverty is Measured', p.9. The percentage chosen is a further instance of the rigidity of poverty measurement. In the last hundred years the proportion of the family budget spent on food has fallen steadily in the United States, Britain, Japan and other rich countries, and tends to be higher in countries which have a lower income per capita than the USA. See, for example, *Social Policy and the Distribution of Income*, pp. 53-6.

[14] The review tacitly acknowledges the intellectual weakness of this approach. See Organization for Economic Cooperation and Development, *Public Expenditure on Income Maintenance Programmes,* Studies in Resource Allocation No. 3, Paris, July, 1976, pp. 62-4.

[15] A good example of continuing ambivalence about 'absolute' and 'relative' standards is a review in the mid 1970s of trends in poverty in relation to evidence form the Family Expenditure Survey for the years 1953 to 1973. The fact that Rowntree and others did not in practice apply the same 'absolute' standard at different dates

is documented, but the authors never quite come to terms with that fact, either theoretically or operationally, and find why an 'absolute' definition cannot be sustained. While appearing to wish to keep both options open, they seem to come down in favour of an 'absolute' approach. Thus, under a subheading entitled, 'The Decline of Poverty', in the Conclusions, A. D. Smith writes, 'Our principle finding on the extent of poverty is that, on the basis of a constant 1971 absolute living standard, numbers in poverty declined from about a fifth of the population in 1953/4 to about a fortieth in 1973. A fall by a factor of eight in only twenty years is a notable improvement. But in relative terms we found little change: the net income of the poorest fifth percentile was about the same proportion of the median income on both years, so that the decline in numbers in poverty so measured reflects essentially the growth of the economy rather than a redistribution of income'. See Smith, A. D., 'Conclusions', in Fiegehen, G. C., Lansley, P.S., and Smith, A. D., *Poverty and Progress in Britain 1953-73*, Cambridge University Press, 1977, p. 111.

[16] Compare, for example, Engels, F., *The Condition of the Working Class in England*, Panther Books, London, 1969 (first published 1845); Masterman, C., *The Condition of England*, Methuen, London, 1960 (first published 1909); and Orwell, G., *The Road to Wigan Pier*, Penguin Books, Harmondsworth, 1962 (first published 1937).

[17] Report of the Committee on Housing in Greater London (The Sir Milner Holland Committee), Cmnd 2605, HMSO, London, 1965.

[18] American work of a systematic kind could be said to date from Dubois, W.E.B., *The Philadelphia Negro*, first published in 1899 (reissued by Schocken, New York, 1967). The early work in England of Booth and Rowntree in the 1880s and 1890s prompted a succession of studies in towns and cities. See, for example, Bowley and Burnett-Hurst, *Livelihood and Poverty;* Caradog Jones, D., *Social Survey of Merseyside*, Liverpool, 1934; Tout, H., *The Standard of Living in Bristol*, Bristol, 1938, as well as Rowntree's own subsequent work. Much the same approach was followed by Professor Geoffrey Batson in South Africa, 1941-4 and 1945. For a review of English studies, see Political and Economic Planning, *Poverty: Ten Years after Beveridge*, Planning No. 344, 1952. For a general review of surveys using the subsidence standard of measurement, see Pagani, A., *La Linea Della Poverta,* Collana di Scienze Sociali, Edizioni ANEA, Milan, 1960.

[19] For example, a long series of studies in South Africa and Central Africa have adopted the Poverty Datum Line, developed by Batson on the basis of Rowntree's and Bowley's work. Modern research workers have a wry appreciation of its shortcomings. See Maasdorp, G., and Humphreys, A. S. B. (eds.), *From Shanty Town to Township: An Economic Study of African Poverty and Rehousing in a South African City,* Juta, Capetown, 1975.

[20] Ministry of Social Security, *Circumstances of Families*, HMSO, London, 1967, p. 8.

[21] Orshansky, 'Who Was Poor in 1966', Table 4. In Canada, a similar kind of approach to that used in the United States produced an official estimate of 3.85 million people in poverty in 1967, or about a quarter of the population. The proportion was highest in the Atlantic Provinces. See a brief prepared by the Department of National Health and Welfare for presentation to the Special Committee of the

Senate on Poverty, The Senate of Canada, *Proceedings of the Special Senate Committee on Poverty*, 24 and 26 February 1970, pp. 18–19 and 62.

[22] Estimated from Table 7.5 in Henderson, R. F., Harcourt, A., and Harper, R. J. A., *People in Poverty: A Melbourne Survey*, Cheshire, Melbourne, 1970, p. 117. Also see Henderson, R. F., Harcourt, A., Harper, R. J. A., and Shaver, S., *The Melbourne Poverty Survey: Further Notes on Methods and Results*, Technical Paper No. 3, Institute of Applied Economic and Social Research, University of Melbourne, May 1972. A further, national, survey of incomes on the basis of this work was carried out in August 1973 by the Australian Bureau of Statistics. This found a rather higher percentage in poverty (10.2) than just in the city of Melbourne (7.3), which was broadly similar to the study of 1966. See *Poverty in Australia*, Interim Report of the Australian Government's Commission of Inquiry into Poverty, March 1974, Canberra.

[23] For example, see Russett, B. M., *et al.*, *World Handbook of Political and Social indicators*, Yale University Press, 1964; Kuznets, S. 'Quantitative Aspects of Economic Growth of Nations: VIII Distribution of Income by Size', *Economic Development and Cultural Change*, 11 January 1963.

[24] Atkinson, A. B., 'On the Measurement of Inequality', *Journal of Economic Theory*, September 1970, pp. 258–62.

[25] Atkinson, A. B., *The Economics of Inequality*, Clarendon Press, Oxford, 1975, p. 47.

[26] Gunnar Myrdal is well aware of this problem and describes it in broad terms. 'The scientists in any particular institutional and political setting move as a flock, reserving their controversies and particular originalities for matters that do not call into question the fundamental system of biases they share…The common need for rationalization will tend…to influence the concepts, model and theories applied; hence it will also affect the selection of relevant data, the recording of observations, the theoretical and practical inferences drawn explicitly or implicitly, and the manner of presentation of the results of research.' He argues that 'objectivity' can be understood only in the sense that however elaborately a framework of fact is developed the underlying set of values premises must also be made explicit. 'This represents an advance towards the goals of honesty, clarity and effectiveness in research…It should overcome the inhibitions against drawing practical and political conclusions openly, systematically and logically. This method would consequently render social research a much more powerful instrument for guiding rational policy formation.' See Myrdal, G., *Objectivity in Social Research*, Duckworth, London, 1970, pp. 53 and 72. Of course, this does not absolve the social scientist for giving the grounds for the values he adopts for, as Alvin Gouldner has aptly argued, it 'betrays smugness and naïveté. It is smug because it assumes that the values that we have are good enough: it is naïve because it assumes that we known the values we have.' See Gouldner, A., 'The Sociologist as Partisan: Sociology and the Welfare State', in Douglas, J. D. (ed), *The Relevance of Sociology*, Appleton-Century-Crofts, New York, 1970, p. 136.

[27] Stouffer, S. A., *et al.*, *The American Soldier*, Princeton, 1949.

[28] Merton, R. K., *Social Theory and Social Structure* (revised ed), Glencoe, Illinois, *1957;* Runciman, W. G., *Relative Deprivation and Social Justice*, Routledge & Kegan Paul, London, 1966. Runciman's work is particularly valuable, not just because he

expounds the practical relevance of the concept to contemporary problems, such as wage bargaining, but because he shows its relevance to the analysis of political behaviour generally. A new edition of his book, with the addition of a postscript, was published by Penguin Books in 1972.

[29] This was a secondary analysis of income and expenditure data. The social or normative standard of poverty was discussed and applied and the number and characteristics of people living below that standard identified. The authors did not claim that this was an objective or an ideal definition of poverty – though their work was sometimes subsequently misinterpreted as such. See Abel-Smith, B., and Townsend, P., *The Poor and the Poorest,* Bell, London, 1965. For a similar approach, see Ministry of Social Security, *Circumstances of Families,* HMSO, London, 1967.

[30] The present definition of overcrowding adopted by the Registrar General is 1½ persons per room. A 'bedroom standard' of overcrowding has been devised which makes greater provision for family norms about the age and sex of children who share rooms. A 'minimum fitness' standard for housing was also worked out by the Denington Committee. See Ministry of Housing, Central Housing Advisory Committee, *Our Older Homes: A Call for Action,* HMSO, London, 1966.

[31] Rowntree, *Poverty: A Study of Town Life,* pp. 108-9 and 382-4.

[32] They have about 6 per cent of pre-tax income, compared with about 4 per cent in the United States. The top quintile have about 43 per cent compared with 46 per cent. See Lydall, H., and Lansing, I. B., 'A Comparison of the Distribution of Personal Income and Wealth in the United States and Great Britain', *American Economic Review,* March 1959; United Nations, *Economic Survey of Europe in 1956,* Geneva, 1957, Chapter IX, p. 6.

[33] Gerth, H., and Mills, C.W., *From Max Weber: Essays in Sociology,* Oxford University Press, 1946, p. 187.

[34] See, for example, Willmott, P., and Young, M., *Family and Class in a London Suburb,* Routledge & Kegan Paul, London, 1960; Stacey, M., *Tradition and Change: A Study of Banbury,* Oxford University Press, 1960.

[35] Burns, T., 'The Study of Consumer Behaviour: A Sociological View', *Archives of European Sociology,* VII, 1966, pp. 321-2.

# 17

# Deprivation

Deprivation may be defined as a state of observable and demonstrable disadvantage relative to the local community or the wider society or nation to which an individual, family or group belongs. The idea has come to be applied to conditions (that is, physical, environmental and social states or circumstances) rather than resources and to specific and not only general circumstances, and therefore can be distinguished from the concept of poverty. For purposes of scientific exposition and analysis both ideas are important and their relationship has to be clarified.

Deprivation takes many different forms in every known society. People can be said to be deprived if they lack the types of diet, clothing, housing, household facilities and fuel and environmental, educational, working and social conditions, activities and facilities which are customary, or at least widely encouraged and approved, in the societies to which they belong (Townsend, 1979, p.413). They fall below standards of living which can be demonstrated to be attained by a majority of the national population or which are socially accepted or institutionalised. Objective and socially approved conventions do not always coincide and the difference between the two is an important matter for enquiry. These two approaches are explicit or implicit in many studies. There is also a third 'standard' of deprivation. People may not fall below the majority's standard of living but they may fall below what could be the majority's standard – given a better redistribution of resources or a reorganisation of institutions in that society. This last approach tends to be adopted more readily in studies of countries in the Third World than in the First World (ibid, p.413).

The idea that deprivation takes a variety of forms is widely agreed. A recent review of the entire programme of work on the 'cycle' of deprivation, financed by the Social Science Research Council in the United Kingdom, concluded 'In using the term deprivation, then, we are essentially referring to the wide range of states or categories of deprivation' (Brown and Madge, 1982, p.39). An earlier study had taken the view that deprivation covers 'all the various misfortunes people can suffer in society'. These involve conditions and experiences 'becoming more unacceptable to society as a whole ...The word deprivation, as it is commonly used, appears to imply a situation that is unacceptably below some minimum standard, even though more general inequality may be accepted as at least inevitable, if not desirable.

---

Townsend, P. (1987) 'Deprivation', *Journal of Social Policy*, vol 16, no 2, pp 125-46.

If inequality can be seen as a hill, deprivation is a ravine into which people should not be allowed to fall' (Berthoud, 1976, pp.175, 180).

Some aspects of national life are better known and researched than others. Thus, the literature on slums or bad housing is huge. The undesirability of walls penetrated by damp and rooms infested with cockroaches, or accommodation too small for its occupants, is widely accepted. Some of the effects of these conditions on health have also been systematically exposed. One of the latest studies shows the increased risk to people living in prefabricated homes of contracting various respiratory diseases, because fungae develop from condensation on inside concrete walls and respiratory ailments are passed on by means of their spores. In this particular instance housing 'deprivation' can be shown to have scientific force as well as popular acceptance. But that does not mean it takes a simple form.

[...]

Public concepts of deprivation cannot, however, be understood only according to some scale of scientific discovery and representation. They are socially 'structured' – through a process of familiarity and indifference, advocacy and repetition in social experience and discourse. Interest groups strive to convert them into vehicles carrying their own views and concerns and this can have distorting effects. Concepts like inequality, class, poverty and deprivation may tend to become concepts predominantly about the situation or condition of men than about that of women, especially when put into operational form. Today, any mature consideration of the problems of sexism, racism or ageism, for example, shows that such ideas can be gender blind, or colour blind, or age blind. The needs of some groups are suppressed in thought and meaning and not simply neglected in fact.

What may be discerned in mapping out the scientific future of the subject is the desirability of distinguishing between 'material' and 'social' deprivation. People may not have the material goods of modern life or the immediately surrounding material facilities or amenities. On the other hand, they may not have access to ordinary social customs, activities and relationships. The latter are more difficult to establish and measure, and the two sets of conditions may be difficult in practice to separate.

[...]

In ordinary speech people recognise the problems of those who lead restricted or stunted social lives and they feel sorry for them or criticise those who appear to impose restrictions upon them. The concept of 'social deprivation' provides a useful means of generalising the condition of those who do not or cannot enter into ordinary forms of family and other social relationships. However, it has to be admitted that operational measures of that concept are much less developed than of the corresponding concept of material deprivation (for illustration see Bulmer, 1984).

If a primary distinction can therefore be made between material and social deprivation, then subcategories of both of these concepts can also be distinguished. This is helpful in explaining social conditions and particularly in explaining paradoxes of the apparent coexistence of prosperity and deprivation. Thus, if there are different forms of deprivation then some people will experience multiple deprivation and others only a single form of deprivation. This has a number of logical and predictable consequences. It will be difficult to disentangle the relative importance of different forms of deprivation on health, personality and social pathology. Measures of deprivation are still too rough and ready and depend on the use of particular indicators, whose scope and representativeness is greatly, if often unwittingly, exaggerated. Empirically the pattern of deprivation will include many paradoxes. People with prosperous home conditions will be deprived at work, and vice-versa.

Some people who are materially deprived will be less socially deprived than their conditions would lead observers to expect.

It follows from this that the scientist must consider deprivation as the darker side of the entire lifestyle of a people. He or she has to be aware of all forms of production, consumption, behaviour and status and to consider exclusion or withdrawal from that pattern as a major possible explanation of individual and social pathology. Any specialised examination of a single form of deprivation has to be placed in a more general context of explanation.

'Objective' deprivation in these senses therefore amounts not just to the scientific observation and measurement of events and conditions which are registered on the public's consciousness, but those too which are not. Part of the social scientist's affiliation to 'objectivity' depends on his or her conscious detachment from the social or political consensus developed by state and other institutions. In degree or kind the social scientist must always be on the look-out for what is not yet publicly known or recognised.

[…]

Subjectively acknowledged deprivation is also important in itself. The wide ranging and multiple characteristics of objective deprivation make it hard to pin down to everyone's satisfaction. There is considerable scientific controversy, not least because of the emphasis on individual aetiology within prevailing social scientific and medical theories. In this situation enlightenment may partly depend on prevailing social perceptions and not only scientific evaluation of deprivation. What does the majority of the population, and not just scientific observers, think about deprivation? One step in persuading central and local authorities to accept the existence and extent of certain needs is to find whether a large number, or indeed a majority, of people, recognise those needs. In some studies this approach dominates. Thus,

Deprivations are loosely regarded as unsatisfactory and undesirable circumstances, whether material, emotional, physical or behavioural, as recognised by a fair degree of societal consensus. Deprivations involve a lack of something generally held to be desirable – an adequate income, good health etc. – a lack which is associated to a greater or lesser extent with some degree of suffering ... (Brown and Madge, 1982, p.39).

Individual views, and the views of particular groups in the population, may of course be out of line with conventional or majority opinion. But that in itself adds interest and a fresh dimension to the prospective analysis.

Theoretically, therefore, deprivation can be conceived to be objective, or as subjective in two senses – as collectively or socially perceived, and as individually perceived. All three versions of the concept have value in the exposition and analysis of social structure and social change.

The corresponding meaning of poverty remains to be clarified. The different approaches to the concept have been discussed in detail (Townsend, 1979) and are being vigorously debated at the present time. [...]

This conceptualisation has a number of advantages. People can experience one or more forms of deprivation without necessarily being in poverty. People with the same resources may display a different relationship to forms of deprivation. And people with fewer resources than others may be much more likely to experience forms of deprivation even when their resources remain considerably above the 'poverty line'. However, it is assumed in this conceptualisation that at a certain point in descending the scale of income or resources deprivation is likely to grow disproportionate to further loss of resources and that this 'threshold' properly marks the beginning of a state of objective poverty. Thus, while people experiencing some forms of deprivation may not all have low income, people experiencing multiple or single but very severe forms of deprivation are in almost every instance likely to have very little income and little or no other resources.

## Operational measures

[...]

One example of the operational definition of deprivation is the list of eight indicators of urban deprivation put forward by the DOE (1983). These are:

1. Percentage of economically active persons who are unemployed.
2. Percentage of households defined as overcrowded.
3. Percentage of households with single parent family.
4. Percentage of households lacking exclusive use of two basic amenities.

5. Percentage of pensioners living alone.

6. Percentage population change.

7. Standardised mortality rate.

8. Percentage of households in which the head was born in the New Commonwealth or Pakistan.

The Department carefully points out that these indicators 'do not cover all facets of urban deprivation ... However, it is reasonable to assume that areas which do not appear deprived on the eight indicators examined in this analysis are unlikely to have high overall levels of deprivation' (DOE, 1983, p. 3). That may be true, but it would be reassuring if enquiries in depth were to be made in even a small cross section of areas in an endeavour to measure 'total' deprivation so that the virtues of different combinations of selected indicators could be evaluated. There is one logical consequence of this procedure which the Department does not appear to examine at all. It is that the use of these eight indicators produces a rather different ranking of areas than does a different number and combination of indicators. This is by no means inconsequential, if only because large grants from the Government are at stake.

[...]

Indicators of deprivation are sometimes direct and sometimes indirect, sometimes representing conditions or states and sometimes representing victims of those conditions or states. From a sociological perspective it is important to distinguish between the measurement of deprivation in different areas and the kind of people experiencing that deprivation. Otherwise there is a danger of treating age, ethnicity and single parenthood as causes of the phenomenon under study. It is wrong in principle to treat being black or old and alone or a single parent as part of the definition of deprivation. Even if many such people are deprived it is their deprivation and not their status which has to be measured. And many people having that status are demonstrably not deprived.

[T]he objective of better 'coherence' is also achieved by specifying different forms of deprivation, as considered above. Perhaps the most useful conceptual distinction is between material and social forms of deprivation – one involving the material apparatus, goods, services, resources, amenities and physical environment and location of life, and the other involving the roles, relationships, functions, customs, rights and responsibilities of membership of society and its subgroups. However, the latter is rarely at issue in current operational definitions of deprivation, except perhaps implicitly in high rates of residential change (residential and social insecurity); high rates of pensioners living alone (social isolation); high proportions of migrants or ethnic minorities (again, social isolation or at least social discrimination); and high proportions of one parent families (absence of a necessary family member or partner). Even in attempting to classify these items the need for explicit clarification of the functions being served by particular indicators becomes apparent. [...]

The following forms of deprivation were separately classified in a study of multiple deprivation in relation to income in the United Kingdom (Townsend, 1979, pp. 1173–1176):

*Material Deprivation*
    1. Dietary deprivation (6 indicators);
    2. Physical and mental health (5);
    3. Clothing (4);
    4. Housing (8);
    5. Household facilities (9);
    6. Environment (5);
    7. Work (conditions, security and amenities) (12).
*Social Deprivation*
    8. Social – family activities (4);
    9. Social – social support and integration (4);
    10. Social – recreational (2);
    11. Social – educational (1).
Material and Social Deprivation: All 11 above (60).

[C]are has to be taken that a particular indicator really is relevant to the form of deprivation it purports to measure. A good example is the use of census information to pick out households lacking two 'basic' household facilities (that is, exclusive use of a bath and indoors WC). This or something like it has been used frequently as a surrogate for poor housing. But, as reports from committees of medical practitioners described by Professor Jarman make clear (Jarman, 1984, p.1590), this is no longer appropriate, since many council estates in the poorest areas have these amenities and yet reveal many features of thoroughly run down and bad housing.

[T]he representativeness of the selected indicators of either 'material' or 'social' deprivation, when combined together, would need if possible to be demonstrated. [...] One problem would be to try to counter bias in the selection of indicators and the emphasis given to groups of them in the overall index. Measures used socially tend to be 'structured'. They can be unwittingly discriminatory, as for example by gender or colour. This can happen if more of the selected items in the measure of deprivation apply to men than to women or cover the situation of whites better than blacks.

One attempt to meet some of these problems within the limits of available statistics has been to define material deprivation in terms of the following indicators:

1. Unemployment. Percentage of those of economically active age who are unemployed.
2. Overcrowding. Percentage of households which are overcrowded.
3. Lack of resources. Percentage of households lacking a car.
4. Lack of resources and residential insecurity. Percentage of households not being home buyers or owners.

[...]

## A 1985-6 measure of multiple deprivation

A more elaborate attempt to meet the problems of defining multiple deprivation operationally was made in a survey of a random sample of the adult population of Greater London (Townsend, with Corrigan and Kowarzik, 1987). Two general points should be explained to clarify the procedure. First, it was assumed that in principle the items listed in any definition of material and social deprivation should represent all aspects of the material and social conditions of life. For various, mainly practical, reasons, it is impossible to apply this principle comprehensively, although it is possible to cover large areas of experience in interviews which are prolonged.

Second, it was assumed that the definition should be 'objective' rather than subjective: the items to be selected were to be indicators of conditions, relationships and behaviour rather than of attitudes or beliefs, important though it may have been to establish independently the nature of those attitudes or beliefs against which conditions and behaviour could be compared. Again, this principle is difficult to fulfil in interview conditions. Sometimes, as in the case of housing and environment, information provided by individuals can be confirmed or substantiated by observation. In other cases information has to be taken on trust. Inevitably there are grey areas where it is not easy to sort out fact from opinion. There are elements in any broad enquiry about actual states or conditions which depend more than would be desirable upon the subjective perceptions of people being interviewed.

It should also be added that as well as seeking to establish deprived conditions, experiences and behaviour the aim was also to invite people to select items which they considered to be 'necessary'. Although a correlation between actual and socially perceived necessities was expected to be established as a result of this approach some differences were also anticipated. Not all conditions of life treated as necessities are perceived as such.

The types of deprivation incorporated into the survey questionnaire were as follows:

*Material Deprivation*
    Dietary
    Clothing
    Housing
    Home facilities
    Environment
    Location
    Work (paid and unpaid).
*Social Deprivation*
    Rights to employment
    Family activities
    Integration into community
    Formal participation in social institutions
    Recreation
    Education

[...]

Two further points should be emphasised. The sample interviewed in Greater London were invited for most of these indicators to say whether or not they believed them to be 'necessary in today's conditions', that is, necessary to them as individuals. Majority opinion on the elements believed to be necessary to present day living standards can therefore be compared with majority circumstances and behaviour. Second, the interviews include a large number of questions about forms of subjective deprivation. The relationship between objective and subjective deprivation can therefore be extensively explored.

## Conclusion

This paper argues that deprivation is as important a concept as poverty to the analysis of social conditions. It has attracted more and more attention in recent years, but is not yet being treated very coherently. While coherence is never easy to achieve the current scientific and professional literature provides a good basis for review to attempt to improve matters.

The concept has to be distinguished from poverty. People can be said to be deprived if they lack the material standards of diet, clothing, housing, household facilities, working, environmental and locational conditions and facilities which are ordinarily available in their society, and do not participate in or have access to the forms of employment, occupation, education, recreation and family and social activities and relationships which are commonly experienced or accepted. If they lack or are denied resources to obtain these conditions of life and for this reason are unable to fulfil membership of society they can be said to be in poverty. The first turns on the level of conditions or activities experienced, the second on the incomes and other resources directly available.

Second, any operational definition of the concept needs to be based on a principle of comprehensiveness. Scientific generalisations about deprivation should depend on inquiries into all aspects of the material and social conditions of life of a people, unearthing conditions which are ignored or not even perceived, and properly representing those which are underestimated, as well as reproducing those which are popularly accepted or approved. Of course this is easier said than done. The practical difficulties are considerable. However, they are no more considerable than many other scientific problems, like the exploration of the universe, or the structure of DNA. Many of the sophisticated statistical treatments of deprivation in recent years in Britain rest on flimsy foundations. The restricted indicators from the census – and rarely other sources – have been uncritically accepted as the only quantitative measures on offer. Instead, more thought needs to be given by scientists and governments to the kind of research which will produce better representations of the phenomenon.

Third, a case is made here for drawing a distinction between material and social deprivation. The former is much more highly developed in the literature (for example, slum conditions in housing) than the latter. I believe this has led to misplaced priorities. The problems of isolation, fears to venture into the community, bereavement, withdrawal from family or other social relationships, the breakdown or building up of community support, discrimination against minorities and lack of opportunities for education or employment, tend to be poorly or imprecisely identified and rarely put together in terms of their distribution among the population.

Again, despite some conceptual and practical difficulties, a distinction has also been drawn between objective and subjective forms of deprivation. Within subjective deprivation a difference between the summation of the attitudes of individuals and the dispositions or organised representations of particular social groups can be identified. Each of these can profitably be explored for the purpose of generating explanations of the trends in experience of deprivation.

Finally, this paper has called particular attention to the distinction between the measurement of deprivation in different areas and the kind of people experiencing that deprivation. In much current practice, for example that of the Department of the Environment, there is a kind of double counting. Deprivation is counted, but so are specific groups like pensioners living alone, ethnic minorities and one parent families. This distorts the findings about the extent of differences between areas or communities and, it can be argued, has led to misallocation of government resources for deprived regions and areas.

## Appendix: An illustrative index of multiple deprivation

A survey of poverty and the London labour market was carried out from late 1985 to late 1986. One of the principal objects was to measure the extent of multiple forms of deprivation. Operationally a distinction was drawn between material and social deprivation and a division was made into 13 specific types of deprivation. A total of 77 indicators or groups of indicators was selected (with a total maximum score of 94). These are set out below:

### Material deprivation

1. *Dietary deprivation*
   i. At least one day in last fortnight with insufficient to eat;
   ii. No fresh meat or fish most days of week (alternative formulation for vegetarians);
   iii. No special meal or roast most weeks;
   iv. No fresh fruit most days;
   v. Short of food on at least one occasion in last 12 months to meet needs of someone in family.
2. *Clothing deprivation*
   i. Inadequate footwear for all weathers;
   ii. Inadequate protection against heavy rain;
   iii. Inadequate protection against severe cold;
   iv. No dressing gown;
   v. Fewer than three pairs socks/stockings in good repair;
   vi. Bought secondhand clothing in last 12 months.
3. *Housing deprivation*
   i. No exclusive use of indoor WC and bath or shower;
   ii. External structural defects;
   iii. Internal structural defects;
   iv. No electricity;
   v. All rooms not heated winter evenings;
   vi. Housing not free of damp;
   vii. Housing not free of infestation;
   viii. Poor state of internal and/or external paintwork and decoration;
   ix. Poor access to accommodation;
   x. Overcrowded (fewer rooms – excluding kitchen and bathroom – than persons);
   xi. No spare room for visitor to sleep.

*4. Deprivation of home facilities:*
 i. No car;
 ii. No television;
 iii. No radio;
 iv. No washing machine;
 v. No refrigerator;
 vi. No freezer;
 vii. No electric iron;
 viii. No gas or electric cooker;
 ix. No vacuum cleaner;
 x. No central heating;
 xi. No telephone;
 xii. Lack of carpeting in main rooms.

*5. Deprivation of environment*
 i. No garden;
 ii. Nowhere for children under five to play safely outside;
 iii. Nowhere for children aged five to ten to play safely nearby;
 iv. Industrial air pollution;
 v. Other forms of air pollution;
 vi. Risk of road accidents around home;
 vii. Problem of noise from traffic, aircraft, building works.

*6. Deprivation of location*
 i. No open space (like park or heath) within easy walking distance;
 ii. No recreational facilities for young people or older adults nearby;
 iii. No shops for ordinary household goods within 10 minutes' journey;
 iv. Problem of litter and debris in local streets;
 v. Doctor's surgery or hospital outpatients' department not within 10 minutes' journey.

*7. Deprivation at work*
 i. Poor working environment (polluted air, dust, noise, vibration and high or low temperature – maximum score of 9);
 ii. Stands or walks about more than three-quarters of the working day;
 iii. Works 'unsocial hours';
 iv. Either poor outdoor amenities of work; or poor indoor amenities at work (maximum score of 10).

*7a. Alternative series on deprivation at work*
 (for people not answering questions applying to paid employment and who have shown they undertake at least 20 hours unpaid work altogether caring for children, sick or disabled or elderly persons in the household or elsewhere):

i. Repeat of total score for housing deprivation (item 3 above
– maximum score of 11);

ii. No central heating (4 x. above: repeat score if necessary);

iii. No telephone (4 xi. above: repeat score if necessary);

iv. Worked 50 or more hours in last week (unpaid work but also
including any paid work).

v. Air pollution (items 5 iv. and 5 v. above)

vi. Repeat the total score for locational deprivation (item 6 above
– maximum score 5).

## Social deprivation

8. *Lack of rights in employment*
    i. Unemployed for two weeks or more during previous 12 months;
    ii. Subject to one week's termination of employment or less;
    iii. No paid holiday;
    iv. No meals paid or subsidised by employer;
    v. No entitlement to occupational pension;
    vi. Not entitled to full pay in first six months of sickness;
    vii. Worked 50 or more hours previous week.

9. *Deprivation of family activity*
    i. Difficulties indoors for child to play;
    ii. If has children, child has not had holiday away from home in the
    last 12 months;
    iii. If has children, child has not had outing during the last 12
    months;
    iv. No days staying with family or friends in previous 12 months;
    v. Problem of the health of someone in family;
    vi. Has care of disabled or elderly relative.

10. *Lack of integration into community*
    i. Being alone and isolated from people;
    ii. Relatively unsafe in surrounding streets;
    iii. Racial harassment;
    iv. Experiences discrimination on grounds of race, sex, age, disability
    or sexual orientation;
    v. In illness no expected source of help;
    vi. Not a source of care or help to others inside or outside the
    home;
    vii. Moved house three or more times in last five years.

11. *Lack of formal participation in social institutions*
    i. Did not vote at last election;
    ii. No participation in trade union or staff association, educational
    courses, sport clubs or associations, or political parties;

iii. No participation in voluntary service activities.

*12. Recreational deprivation*

i. No holiday away from home in last 12 months;

ii. Fewer than five hours a week of specified range of leisure activities.

*13. Educational deprivation*

i. Fewer than 10 years' education;

ii. No formal qualifications from school or subsequent educational courses or apprenticeships.

Material and Social Deprivation: Total indicators or groups of indicators 77 (with a maximum total score of 94).

**References**

Berthoud, R. (1976) *The disadvantages of inequality: A study of social deprivation,* A PEP Report, London: MacDonald and Janes.

Brown, M. and Madge, N. (1982) *Despite the welfare state,* London: Heinemann.

Bulmer, M. (1984) 'Local inequality: sociability, isolation and loneliness as factors in the differential provision of neighbourhood care', Paper presented to the Social Administration Association Conference, University of Kent.

Department of the Environment (1983) *Urban deprivation,* Information Note No 2, London: Inner Cities Directorate, Department of the Environment.

Jarman, B. (1984) 'Underprivileged areas: validation and distribution of scores', *British Medical Journal,* no 289, pp 1587-92.

Townsend, P. (1979) *Poverty in the United Kingdom: A survey of household resources and standards of living,* Harmondsworth: Penguin Books.

Townsend, P. with Corrigan, P. and Kowarzik, U. (1987) *Poverty and the London labour market: The third London survey, interim report,* London: The Low Pay Unit.

# 18

# Theoretical disputes about poverty

*This chapter reproduces theoretical exchanges about poverty in the late 1980s, starting with David Piachaud's commentary on* Poverty in the United Kingdom *in 1981 in* New Society, *and Peter Townsend's reply. This is followed by a summary of a lecture by Amartya Sen, a rejoinder from Peter Townsend, and an extract from a relevant paper by Maghnad Desai and Anup Shah – all in* Oxford Economic Papers. *An attempt has been made to represent the key arguments. Readers are referred to the full version of the papers to place these extracts or summaries in context (Piachaud, 1981; Sen, 1983 and 1985; Townsend, 1981 and 1985; Desai and Shah, 1988).*

*Among the themes are those repeatedly considered by social scientists: conceptions of absolute versus relative deprivation; the advantages and disadvantages of 'subsistence' and of 'relative deprivation' as governing ideas; the viability of a 'culture' of poverty; the relationship between inequality and poverty; the operational measurement of 'relative deprivation' as a criterion of poverty, as well as the measurement of income or resources; and the possibilities in analysis of the 'ideas' of capabilities and commodities rather than those of relative deprivation and needs in understanding poverty. In addition, attention is called to the underlying differences of approach between economics and sociology.*

## Part 1: David Piachaud – Poverty in the United Kingdom

Townsend suggests two steps 'towards the objectification of the measurement of poverty'. The first is:

> To endeavour to measure all types of resources, public and private, which are distributed unequally in society and which contribute towards actual standards of living. This will uncover sources of inequality which tend to be proscribed from public and even academic discourse.

---

Chapter 6 (pp 113–38) Townsend, P. (1993) 'Theoretical disputes about poverty', Chapter 6 from Townsend, P. (1993) *The international analysis of poverty*, Hemel Hempstead: Harvester Wheatsheaf.

It is certainly true that economists have in the past tended to talk about money incomes and their distribution, as though they were all that mattered. In recent years, economists have expanded their horizons to take in rather more of the real world (despite those who think that economics is a branch of mathematics), and there is increasing research on inequality of wealth and income in public services. But non-economists like Titmuss and Townsend led the way. The extension of the concept of income to embrace a wider range of resources, public as well as private, is important and uncontentious.

But Townsend's second step towards an 'objective' measurement of poverty is

> to endeavour to define a style of living which is generally shared or approved in each society, and find whether there is … a point on the scale of the distribution of resources below which, as resources diminish, families find it particularly difficult to share in the customs, activities and diets comprising their society's style of living.

Thus Townsend attempted to 'provide an estimate of objective poverty on the basis of a level of deprivation disproportionate to resources' – an index of relative deprivation. How he did this, and whether it stands up to examination, are my central concerns here.

First, how was it constructed?

> A list of 60 indicators of the 'style of living' of the population was built up. This covered diet, clothing, fuel and light, home amenities, housing and housing facilities, the immediate environment of the home, the characteristics, security, general conditions and welfare benefits of work, family support, recreation, education, health and social relations…. The indicators can be expressed as indicators of deprivation – for example, lacking that amenity or not participating in that activity. By applying the indicators to individuals and families, a 'score' for different forms of deprivation can be added up: the higher the score the lower the participation.

He then compiled a 'provisional' deprivation index, based on the 12 characteristics which are set out in Table 6.1. His next step was to consider the relationship of score on the deprivation index to income. Taking the mean deprivation index for different income groups, he found a clear relationship with income.

**Table 6.1:** Townsend's deprivation index

| | Characteristic | % of population |
|---|---|---|
| 1. | Has not had a week's holiday away from home in the past 12 months | 53.6 |
| 2. | (Adults only) Has not had a relative or friend to the home for a meal or snack in the last 4 weeks | 33.4 |
| 3. | (Adults only) Has not been out in the last 4 weeks to a relative or friend for a meal or snack | 45.1 |
| 4. | (Children under 15 only) Has not had a friend to play or to tea in the last 4 weeks | 36.3 |
| 5. | (Children only) Did not have a party last birthday | 56.6 |
| 6. | Has not had an afternoon or evening out for entertainment in the last two weeks | 47.0 |
| 7. | Does not have fresh meat (including meals out) as many as four days a week | 19.3 |
| 8. | Has gone through one or more days in the past fortnight without a cooked meal | 7.0 |
| 9. | Has not had a cooked breakfast most days of the week | 67.3 |
| 10. | Household does not have a refrigerator | 45.1 |
| 11. | Household does not usually have a Sunday joint (3 in 4 times) | 25.9 |
| 12. | Household does not have sole use of four amenities indoors (flush WC; sink or washbasin and cold-water tap; fixed bath or shower; and gas or electric cooker) | 21.4 |

*Source:* Townsend (1979)

Townsend continued:

> So far, we have been able to show a relationship between diminishing income and increasing deprivation. But is there evidence of the existence of a 'threshold' of income for different types of household, below which people are disproportionately deprived? The evidence from this survey is inconclusive, but suggests such a threshold may exist.

The indication that a threshold may exist is derived from the following steps. First, Townsend adjusted incomes for household size by expressing them as proportions of the supplementary benefit scale rate for that household. Second, he grouped households by this adjusted income level, and estimated the most common value of the deprivation index for each group – technically called the 'modal value'. Third, he plotted this modal value against the income level (expressed in logarithmic form), as shown in the figure below.

**Figure 6.1:** Model deprivation by logarithm of income as a percentage of supplementary benefit scale rates

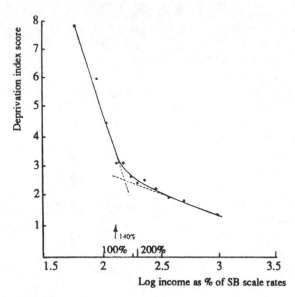

Source: Townsend (1979)

From this, he concluded: As income diminishes from the highest levels, so deprivation steadily increases, but below 150 per cent of the supplementary benefit standard, deprivation begins to increase swiftly. He establishes a relative deprivation standard of poverty which was 'at levels higher than the prevailing supplementary benefit standard, especially for households with children and households with disabled people'. Using this relative deprivation standard, he estimates that 25 per cent of households are living in poverty. This compares with 7 per cent in poverty, defined in terms of the state's supplementary benefit standard.[...]

The first problem arises with the components of Townsend's deprivation index, as set out in Table 6.1. It is not clear what some of them have to do with poverty, nor how they were selected. Some of the components may certainly have a direct link with poverty – the holiday components may certainly have a direct link with poverty – the holiday (item 1), the evening's entertainments (6), the refrigerator (10) and the household amenities (12). But other components – fresh meat (7), cooked meals (8), cooked breakfast (9) and Sunday joint (11) – may be as much to do with tastes as with poverty. Not having a cooked breakfast, for example, is often a remedy for overindulgence on other occasions.

Still other components – involving adults or children providing or attending a meal or party (items 2 to 5) – are often linked with poverty. But if such arrangements are fully reciprocated, a person may entertain and be entertained by a relative or friend at no net cost (indeed, economies of scale may make this more economical). There is thus no prior reason why many of the components of the deprivation index should bear any relationship to poverty. Townsend's index offers no solution to the intractable problem of disentangling the effects of differences in tastes from those of differences in income. That certain characteristics are related to income level tell us something about people's behavior and social and cultural differences. But it might tell us little or nothing about deprivation.

The second problem arises from the diversity of the results. As I noted earlier, Townsend showed that the mean deprivation index rose as income fell. But this mean score concealed the extent of the variation between people at the same income level.[...] If all the components of the deprivation index were ambiguous indicators of some form of deprivation, then you might argue that those on high incomes with high deprivation scores are, despite their incomes, deprived. But this is not the case. A large part of the variation in deprivation scores in merely due to diversity in styles of living wholly unattributed to poverty. *There can be no doubt that Townsend's provisional deprivation index is of no practical value whatsoever as an indicator of deprivation.*

The third problem with Townsend's approach is on the question of whether there is a *threshold* below which the deprivation index increases sharply. Here the problem is, alas, rather technical. His use of modal values of deprivation index scores, and of logarithmic income scale are questionable. As his own diagram shows, the scores follow a curve, not the two straight lines he imposed. Townsend has not used any test that would satisfactorily establish whether a threshold (at about 150 per cent of supplementary benefit levels) exists.

He concludes: 'With qualifications both about measurement and sample size, the evidence suggested that there existed a threshold of deprivation for certain types of household at low levels of income'. He has striven to find such evidence, because it is fundamental to his central hypothesis. But on the basis of what he presents, my own conclusion is: *There is at present no satisfactory evidence to suggest that there is any such threshold of deprivation.*

Thus, there are serious problems with Professor Townsend's measure of deprivation. There are also problems with his basic conception. One implication of his hypothesis that the poor 'are deprived of the conditions of life which ordinarily define membership of a society' is that the poor form a separate social group. Poverty is still with us – and a lot needs to be done about that – but it no longer conforms to a picture of Dickensian destitution, with the pauper in a pitiable state. *There is a continuum from great wealth to chronic poverty and along that continuum a wide diversity of patterns of living. The poor in Britain are worse off than others; but for the most part, they are members of society, not outcasts.* The combination of the two factors – that there is diversity in styles of living, and that poverty is relative – mean that you would *not*, in fact, expect to find any threshold between the poor and the rest of society. Townsend's hypothesis that such a threshold would exist is intrinsically implausible.

The most strange and unsatisfactory feature in Townsend's conception of relative deprivation is the emphasis on style of living. His deprivation index concerns itself with a number of primarily private aspects of behavior. He does not include in his index more social aspects, such as deprivation at work, of environment, of public services. He does discuss these extensively elsewhere in his study; but the emphasis in his deprivation index on style of living serves to narrow, rather than broaden, the concept of relative deprivation.

It is an unsatisfactory feature of any conception of relative deprivation that, even if all inequality of incomes were removed, there would still be relative deprivation as long as people behaved differently. Taken to its logical conclusion, only when everyone behaved identically would no one be defined as deprived. Townsend's index of relative deprivation cannot cope with diversity.

It is no indicator of deprivation that someone chooses to stay at home, eating salads and uncooked breakfasts. But all these personal choices are 'extraordinary', and so add to the score on Townsend's relative deprivation index. But as patterns of living become more diverse, it becomes steadily harder and less useful to think in terms of 'ordinary membership of society'.

What surely matters most is the choice a person has, and the constraints he or she faces. To *choose* not to go on holiday or eat meat is one thing: it may interest sociologists but it is of no interest to those concerned with poverty. To have little or no *opportunity* to take a holiday or buy meat is entirely different.

The study of styles of living is essentially about outcomes – how people choose to behave given the choices open to them. As Townsend found, it reveals a wider diversity of behavior. But what is of much more importance is the level of resources a person has, and the opportunities this affords. *The reason for tackling poverty is not to create uniformity, but to push back the constraints and increase choice and freedom.*

Townsend acknowledges, in fact, that his measurement of poverty is not wholly objective. For example, 'decisions have to be taken about all the different ingredients of "style of living".' But it is clear, nonetheless, that he is *seeking* an objective measure:

> Until social scientists can provide the rigorous conception within which the poverty of industrial societies and the third world can both be examined, and the relationship between inequality and poverty perceived, the accumulation of data and the debates about

the scale and causal antecedents of the problem will be in large measure fruitless.

## Inequality is not poverty

On this he is, I believe, not only destined to eternal frustration, but also profoundly wrong. Social scientists can describe the inequality of resources within and between countries as objectively as possible. But *inequality is not the same as poverty*. The term 'poverty' carries with it an implication and moral imperative that something should be done about it. The definition by an individual, or by a society collectively, of what level represents 'poverty', will also be a value-judgment. Social scientists have no business trying to preempt such judgments with 'scientific' prescriptions.

Questioning Peter Townsend's emphasis on styles of living in his conception of poverty and his measure of deprivation, is not (as I have acknowledged) to question that poverty is a relative concept, or that there is real poverty in the United Kingdom. Nor is it to accept that the state's poverty standard, the supplementary benefit level, is adequate. But it is to question the bold claim with which he starts his study: 'Poverty can be defined objectively and applied consistently only in terms of the concept of relative deprivation.'

We can learn much from the attempt, which is in line with Peter Townsend's massive contribution, over the years, to understanding social policy. But he has not substantiated his claim of scientific objectivity, any more than the knights of old found the Holy Grail.

*Some of the points expressed here are taken up in a later paper by David Piachaud (1987) 'Problems in the Definition and Measurement of Poverty',* Journal of Social Policy, *vol 16, no 2 pp 147-64.*

## Part 2: Peter Townsend's reply

There appear to be bigger differences between David Piachaud and myself about the nature and severity of poverty than I would have supposed. It is no good papering over the differences, because they represent not just a divergence of scientific exchanges but a difference about the changes required in policy to deal with the phenomenon – not only in Britain but in the so called 'South' or Third World. To a large extent the differences are attributable to the gulf which exists between modern variants of neoclassical orthodox economics, with its individualistic and conformist basis, and the material and often radical basis of much present sociology.

Like 'inequality' and 'order', 'poverty' is one of the major concepts of the social sciences required to understand and explain society and inform its management. For many years it was treated rather casually and as relatively unproblematic, and David Piachaud seems to be tempted to follow this path, because he did not attempt to deal with it in an analytical way.

Like other concepts, however, 'poverty' can be given different meanings by professions, governments and bureaucracies. One of the tasks of the social scientist is to bring out how concepts tend to be the creatures of the arbitrary exercise of power; and to look beyond them to a more democratic representation of interests in the meanings that they are given, and to the even more elusive pantheon of scientific 'objectivity'.

Part of my purpose in writing *Poverty in the United Kingdom* [Townsend, 1979] was to call attention to the elitist and subjugatory ways in which the concept has been, and is, defined and applied. After every qualification is dutifully listed, the familiar 'subsistence' basis of the concept used in Britain and in other countries, especially those associated with the colonial tradition, can be shown to represent a narrow view of human needs which has played its part in legitimating meagre treatment of the poor and the perpetuation of severe inequality.

The cloudier, if slightly broader, concept of 'basic needs' is similarly playing its part in legitimating the continuation of impoverished conditions in the Third World....

While reality may be inaccessible except through interpretation, it is necessary to make a distinction between the two. Only through the pursuit of objective social science can we properly appreciate the indoctrinated quality of our social perceptions. This is a paradox with which those who study poverty will have to live, and which David Piachaud fails to address. Whatever we may *mean* by 'poverty', there are people whose resources are so low that they bear the observable and 'objective' marks of multiple deprivation, including ill-health or disability and the risk of early death....

## A social conception of need

Poverty is a function of two things. As I tried to summarise these (p. 917):

> In all societies, there is a crucial relationship between the production, distribution and redistribution of resources on the one hand, and the creation of sponsorship of style of living on the other. One governs the resources which come to be in the control of individuals and families. The other governs the 'ordinary' conditions and expectations attaching to membership of the society, the denial or lack of which represents deprivation. The two are in constant

interaction and explain at any given moment historically both the level and extent of poverty.

David Piachaud plays down the difficulties of the first, saying that 'the extension of the concept of income to embrace a wider range of resources, public as well as private, is important and uncontentious'.

That final word is astonishing. If it were uncontentious, would it not be hard to explain why administrative and professional elites have resisted the collection of information on the augmentation of living standards through the selected allocation of wealth and employer welfare benefits in kind? In our poverty survey, the research team made the collection of this information one of its priorities. A theory of poverty necessarily depends in part on a theory of wealth.

A similar point about relativity and structural determinism has to be made when we turn to 'deprivation'. We have to describe the roles which people are expected to play and the customs, amenities and activities which they are expected to share and enjoy as citizens, in order to discern and measure forms and degrees of deprivation. An understanding of the latter depends on making a prior analysis of the former, which, for want of a better term, I called 'style of living' in my book.

In developing a theory of poverty, it is as important to understand the generation of new styles of living, establishing norms, amenities and customs from which categories of poor may be excluded – as it is to understand the generation and distribution of resources, which enable people to participate in those self-same styles of living.

Needless to say, it was impossible in a single national survey to undertake a comprehensive examination of styles of living, or of multiple forms of deprivation. Indicators were chosen on the basis of knowledge of previous studies to which one or both of these concepts seemed to apply. [...]

[Piachaud] comments on the rather rough nature of the correlation between deprivation and income, quoting figures which show that few with high incomes were substantially deprived, and some with low incomes were found not to be deprived. Such a distribution depends, at the margins, on definitions of household, income, regularity of income, and coverage of chosen indicators of deprivation; and those who have undertaken social, particularly income, surveys will know the problems.

His objections to certain indicators are inconsistent, and not theoretically grounded. He suggests that some forms of behaviour represent individual 'tastes', which are unrelated to poverty. But three of the four examples he picks were in fact found to correlate strongly with diminishing income and even more with diminishing resources. The items included in the index were highly intercorrelated, as were the great majority of the full list of 60 indicators.

The evidence shows a close relationship between different forms of deprivation, including ill–health, and also that there is a much stronger material or economic basis than hitherto supposed for what has come to be dismissed as 'diversity of taste'. This is of immense theoretical and practical importance, and governed a number of the conclusions reached in the book, both about the causes of poverty and about the structural changes to remedy it.

A final question involves the tentative idea of a 'threshold' of income. Is diminishing income uniformly correlated with increasing deprivation, or is there a threshold of income, for different income units or households, below which deprivation increases disproportionately? The findings of the survey were suggestive but inconclusive, as the book states. David Piachaud believes that such a threshold is implausible.

However, there is evidence of people pulling out of roles, responsibilities, customs and shared activities, below certain levels of income. Thus, with diminishing income, people restrict the nature of, say, a summer holiday, but below some level of income decide not to have a holiday at all. Among poor families, children are absent from school on days when they are supposed to turn up with sports clothing or contributions for a school outing. When they are too poor, pensioners no longer go to a pub to share drinks with their friends.

### Shutting themselves off

Some people avoid one form of deprivation only by submitting to others. Some families maintain household amenities, and meet some of the needs of their children, only by shutting themselves off from their neighbours and from friendship at work. We can see many of these responses among the rapidly growing number of unemployed.

Contrary, then, to David Piachaud, 'relative deprivation', together with an operational version of a deprivation index, is of considerable practical value, in developing a theory of poverty and hence social policy. On the basis of the national evidence, I would reject his view that poverty *'no longer* (my italics) conforms to a picture of Dickensian destitution, with the pauper in a pitiable state', and, elsewhere in his article, that the poor are 'not outcasts'.

This is fundamentally to misperceive the relativity of the condition of poor people. They are living in the society of the 1980s rather than that of 1840–70; and in this context the conditions of some at least are as bad, or worse, than those which Dickens observed more than a hundred years ago.

On the basis of the approach I have discussed, those having their incomes paid under the supplementary benefit and national insurance schemes can be shown to be deprived; and a strongly buttressed case for substantially raising, and legitimating, the level of these payments can be presented.

(This is a case to which, incidentally, the former Supplementary Benefits Commission, to their credit, and others have also contributed.) Moreover, the evidence about the distribution of wealth and of other resources also shows that higher payments can in principle be comfortably financed. These are two particular and perhaps practical outcomes of the attempt to apply 'relative deprivation' in a national study.

## Part 3: Amartya Sen – Poor, Relatively Speaking (summary of 1983 lecture)

*In his Geary lecture, published in* Oxford Economic Papers *in 1983, Amartya Sen commented at length on discussions calling attention to the 'relativity' of poverty and he argued for the retention of an 'absolutist' conception – albeit in a sense different from other commentators. He put forward a theoretical perspective based primarily on a conception of 'capability'. A summary of his argument follows.*

*He began his paper by agreeing with social scientists like Peter Townsend (1962) and Dorothy Wedderburn (1962) who had shown that large sectors of the British population remained deprived in misery in the 1960s and the battle against poverty was far from over. They had opened up the question of how poverty lines should be determined.*

*But he questioned the abandonment of the idea of 'absolute' need. There were two defects in the arguments for abandonment presented by Townsend (1979, pp. 17-18). Absoluteness of needs was not the same thing as their 'fixity over time'. Under an absolutist approach, the poverty line was a function of some variables, and there was no 'a priori' reason why these variables might not change over time. Second, there was a difference between achieving relatively less than others, and achieving absolutely less because of falling behind others. People's ability to enjoy an uncrowded beach might depend on them knowing about that beach when others did not, so that the absolute advantage they would enjoy – being on an uncrowded beach – would depend on their relative position – knowing something that others did not. They wanted to have that information not to do relatively better than others but to do absolutely well.*

*In 'more rigidly relativist' views held by other authors (Fiegehen, Lansley and Smith, 1977) the gains shared by all the population tended to be discounted. This was implicit in poverty lines defined as half the median income in society, for example. Somewhere in the process of refining the crudities of Charles Booth's and Seebohm Rowntree's old-fashioned criteria of poverty, an essential characteristic of poverty (its absoluteness) had been abandoned, with 'some imperfect representation of inequality as such' being substituted.*

*Another flawed relativist approach, according to Sen, was the policy definition of poverty – whereby the amounts for which people were eligible under social security laws were treated as a poverty line. The problem was that this definition went 'well beyond reflecting the cut-off point of identified poverty'. For one thing it reflected what was feasible. Levels of eligibility might be reduced. This would change the numbers in poverty even if there was no other change. And other aims than the reduction of poverty might be numbered among the considerations of politicians and administrators in deciding those levels. None of the relativist views could therefore serve as an adequate theoretical basis for conceptualising poverty. There was 'an irreducible absolutist core in the idea of poverty'. One element of this was starvation and hunger. If these existed, no matter what the relative picture looked like, poverty must exist. This applied to other aspects of living standards. Thus, Adam Smith called attention to the fact that an eighteenth-century Englishman had to have leather shoes to be able to avoid shame. It was not a relative question of being less ashamed than others but to not be ashamed at all – an* absolute *achievement.*

*What was an alternative approach to the question of measuring living standards? The right focus was neither commodities, nor characteristics, nor utility, but a person's 'capability' (Sen, 1981, 1983). Commodity ownership did not explain what a person could do. Thus, a bicycle was a commodity, but it had the characteristic of transportation, which gave someone the* capability *to function.*

*This central focus allowed the dispute about absolute and relative standards of poverty to be sorted out. 'At the risk of oversimplification, I would like to say that poverty is an absolute notion in the space of capabilities but very often it will take a relative form in the space of commodities or characteristics.' (Sen, 1983)*

*Sen argued that there was no conflict between the irreducible absolutist element in this notion of poverty and the 'thoroughgoing relativity' to which Townsend referred, if the latter were interpreted as applying to commodities and resources. 'If Townsend puts his finger wrong, this happens when he points towards the untenability of the idea of absolute needs.' Of course, needs varied between one society and another, but they involved a different bundle of commodities and higher real value of resources fulfilling the* same *general needs. He believed that Townsend was, in fact, estimating the varying resource requirements of fulfilling the same absolute need of being able to 'participate in the activities of the community'.*

*In a poor community the commodities or resources needed to participate in community activities might be very little indeed. Poverty was primarily concerned with the commodity requirements of fulfilling nutritional needs and perhaps some needs of being clothed, sheltered and free from disease. This was the world of Charles Booth or Seebohm Rowntree in the nineteenth-century or early twentieth-century London or York, and that of poverty estimation today, say, in India. For richer communities, however, the nutritional and other physical requirements (like clothing) were typically already met, and the needs of communal participation – while absolutely no different in the space of capabilities – would have a much higher demand in the space of commodities and that of resources. Relative deprivation, in this case, was nothing other than a relative failure in the commodity space – or resource space – having the effect of an absolute deprivation in the capability space (p. 162).*

*The varying commodity requirements of meeting the same absolute need applied not merely to avoiding shame from failing to meet conventional requirements, and not being able to participate in the activities of the community, but also to a number of other needs. In a car-owning society, public transport services might be poor, so that a carless family might be* absolutely *poor in a way that it might not have been in a poorer society. Again, widespread ownership of refrigerators and freezers in a community might affect the structure of food retailing, thereby making it more difficult to make do without having these facilities.*

*In conclusion, Sen stated that there remained a good case for an absolutist approach to poverty, but that such an approach should be linked with the notion of 'capability'. Capabilities differed from both commodities and characteristics, on the one hand, and utilities on the other. The capability approach shared with John Rawls the rejection of the utilitarian obsession with one type of mental reaction, but differed from Rawls' concentration on primary goods by focusing on the capabilities of human beings rather than characteristics of goods they possess.*

*An 'absolute approach in the space of capabilities' translated into a 'relative approach in the space of commodities, resources and incomes' when considering capabilities, for example avoiding shame from failure to meet social conventions, participating in social activities, and retaining self-respect.*

*Inequality remained important. While poverty could be seen as a failure to reach some absolute level of capability, the issue of inequality of capabilities was important in its own right in discussing public policy.*

## Part 4: Rejoinder – Peter Townsend

In his paper Professor Amartya Sen takes issue with part of my work on poverty. Unfortunately he does not correctly represent my approach to the concept and, as a consequence, fails to provide fair criticism of the treatment of 'relative deprivation' by myself and others as a quite distinct example of the relativist views of poverty which he argues comprehensively against in the first part of the paper. He gives very confused grounds for retaining an 'absolute' core to the meaning of poverty and makes an insufficient case for treating 'capability' as a key concept in the analysis of trends in living standards. I will discuss these matters in turn. My discussion follows the structure of Professor Sen's paper. Some readers may prefer to skim through the first section to reach the general issues considered in the second and third sections of the rejoinder.

### Misrepresentation of 'relative deprivation' approach

First, Professor Sen quotes from a criticism of mine of the idea of absolute need. This passage from my work reads as follows:

> A thorough-going relativity applies to time as well as place. The necessities of life are not fixed. They are continuously being adapted

and augmented as changes take place in a society and in its products. Increasing stratification and a developing division of labour, as well as the growth of powerful new organisations, create as well as reconstitute need.

Professor Sen says that this line of reasoning suffers from two general defects. He objects first that absoluteness of needs is not the same thing as their fixity over times and goes on 'Even under an absolutist approach, the poverty line will be a function of *some* variables, and there is no a prior reason why these variables might not change over time'. Professor Sen is saying something different from the majority of those who uphold an 'absolutist' perspective. While generally they take an absolute standard and apply it on subsequent occasions in the same form but updated for change in prices only, he suggests that an *absolute* poverty line might change with time according to certain variables (he does not say *which* variables). But in making a vague concession in the direction of relativism he does not perceive the importance, as argued in the passage of mine quoted and in a variety of other contexts in the literature on poverty, of adopting a scientific conceptualisation which *both* allows comparisons to be made through time about changes in conditions within a single society *and* differences in conditions between different societies at a simultaneous moment of time. That is what the 'relative deprivation' conceptualisation attempts to do.[1] His analysis cannot be said to be addressed to this problem.

The second 'general defect' which attributed to my line of reasoning is that I do not recognise that 'there is a difference between achieving relatively less than others, and achieving absolutely less because of a falling behind others'. I have some difficulty grasping what Professor Sen is driving at, particularly since he immediately goes on to discuss *advantage* and not *deprivation*. He writes,

> Your ability to enjoy an uncrowded beach may depend on your knowing about that beach when others do not, so that the absolute advantage you will enjoy – being on an uncrowded beach – will depend on your *relative* position – knowing something that others do not. You want to have that information but this is not because you particularly want to do *relatively better than or as well as others,* but you want to *absolutely well,* and that in this case you must have some differential advantage in information. So your absolute achievement – not merely your relative success – may depend on your relative position in some other space.

There are two problems in the passage of Professor Sen's which do not appear to have been sorted out. It strikes me first as failing to distinguish between behaviour and motivation and trying to approach an explanation of social phenomena on the minor theme of individual motivation instead of the major theme of social organisation. It seems to me quite crucial to try to separate subjective (in both the individual and collective sense of that term) from objective aspects of deprivation in identifying and measuring poverty. People may be in poverty when they believe they are not, and vice versa. Or people may be in poverty and interested others – such as governments, or the public at large or even the economic and sociological professions – believe they are not, and vice versa. Perceptions which are filtered through, or fostered by, the value or belief systems of sectional groups, the state or whole communities can never be regarded as sufficiently representative of 'reality out there'. There have to be forms of 'objective' social observation, investigation and comparison against which they may be checked (even if those standards remain necessarily incomplete as well as necessarily creatures of socially produced modes of scientific thought).

The other problem in the passage quoted is that two substantive statements do not appear to have been disentangled and brought into the light of day. In so far as Professor Sen is trying to elucidate *objective* needs he appears to be saying that at diminished levels of resources people are unable to satisfy some needs at all rather than that they are only able to meet them to a reduced extent; and that even at the lowest level of resources some people remain better placed to meet at least some of their needs than are others (for example, they have information, access to transport, the kind of environment or family circumstances which allow resources to be stretched further or to be committed more economically). I do not disagree with these statements, though Professor Sen appears to think I do. But neither of them leads to the proposition that needs are absolute, which remains the point at issue.

Let me endeavour to make some comments which may help to clear up this fundamental confusion about the nature of poverty made by Professor Sen. It is not necessary to invoke 'absolute needs' in order to maintain a scientific distinction between poverty and inequality, as I have attempted to argue in putting forward a conceptualisation of poverty as 'relative deprivation'. I will provide an empirical description, necessarily over simplified. After allowing for size of family the correlation between level of income (or total *resources* – which is the conception, including the income equivalent of wealth and of income in kind, which I would wish to recommend) and extent and severity of deprivation in rich societies like Britain is by no means prefect, although it is highly significant. Some people are much less 'deprived' than others on the same income; some are much more 'deprived'. A lot will depend on local variations in social integration, association and exchange as well as local variations in prices, especially costs of housing, in relation to facilities gained, including locational facilities. But in any society and not only British society, the level of resources available to the local community, the family and individual (note that I do not refer just to the individual) seems in the end to govern whether or not individuals within that community can satisfy social obligation, expectations and customs and hence need. For as members of society (and hence of a network of sub-groups) people have needs which can only be defined by virtue of the obligations, associations and customs of such membership.

There seems to be not just a *continuum* of deprivation in accordance with ranked income (or total resources). Below an approximate threshold of income, deprivation seems to intensify, accelerate or multiply disproportionately. It is as if people strive to conform with what is expected of them when income shrinks (they economise in what they do but still undertake the same activities) but once it shrinks below a particular level they withdraw (or withdraw their children) from fulfilling certain social obligations or well-established customs or activities. They no longer meet friends, children are occasionally absent from school, heating is turned off, conventional diets are no longer regularly observed, visitors are no longer invited to the home, ill-health and disability become more common. It is not claimed that the existence of such a threshold has yet been systematically demonstrated. This would require conducting a survey with larger numbers than Professor Abel-Smith and I were able to mount with the help of the Joseph Rowntree Memorial Trust, in 1968-69, and perhaps in providing further clarification of the nature, and selecting more indicators, of deprivation. But some economists researching the same data (Desai, 1981, 1983) consider the conclusion highly arguable and some attempts have been made in other societies to apply similar methodology (e.g. Chow, 1982).

It may be that in making (or strictly, repeating, because the argument is set out at greater length elsewhere) these points Professor Sen will accept that if there is a threshold of low income below which there is evidence of disproportionately (that is, in relation to income or resources generally) severe or multiple deprivation, then this may be said to constitute a level of 'absolute' need in that society. Personally I think that in view of the history of the treatment of the term 'absolute' need it would breed misunderstanding to interpret 'absolute' as Professor Sen appears to want to interpret the term as variable, flexible and even in parts, relative. For one thing I don't think he goes very far down the road of relativity. For another he does not clarify exactly what he means by 'absolute'. There are passages where he appears to mean 'prioritised'. This is taken up in my next section.

Despite some qualifications Professor Sen links my advocacy of 'relative deprivation' with an advocacy of 'inequality'. Under the first section of his paper against 'relativism' he successfully criticises conceptions of poverty which do not attempt to distinguish between poverty and inequality. Thus he quotes a passage from Fiegehen, Lansley and Smith in which they say that poverty is likely to persist even in changing society '*since there will always be* certain sections of society that are badly off in the sense that they receive below-average incomes' (my emphasis). I do not consider there is much value in confusing inequality and poverty in this way and I would have been a lot happier if Professor Sen had attempted to distinguish rather more emphatically between these approaches 'to a relativist' view because I believe he would have represented both of them a lot more accurately than he does.[2] Poverty is much more than having relatively less than others.

The essence of the approach I am endeavouring to develop is that society, and especially the state, is creating or 'manufacturing' as well as reconstituting needs at the same time as it is determining the allocation of resources in the first place (and not just the redistribution of income) with which those needs can or will be met. Our understanding of changes in the extent of poverty depend fundamentally on scientific exposition of this dual process.

## *Absolute poverty*

This brings me to a more direct discussion of Professor Sen's grounds for retaining an 'absolute' core to the meaning of poverty. Professor Sen has made a big contribution to the recent discussion of poverty (see references set out in Sen, 1992, pp. 180-90). His expertise is rooted in Third World economies, especially that of India, and he has gradually extended his work to include comparisons with highly industrialised societies. In his major work *Poverty and Famines* he traces the analytical shift towards 'relative deprivation' as a driving concept in conceptions of poverty and yet resists abandonment of the idea of 'absolute' need or deprivation in the misguided belief that this is the only way of maintaining a central place for malnutrition in the conception of poverty. He writes:

> Poverty is, of course, a matter of deprivation. The recent shift in focus – especially in the sociological literature – from *absolute* to *relative* deprivation has provided a useful framework of analysis.... But relative deprivation is essentially incomplete as an approach to poverty, and supplements (but cannot supplant) the earlier approach of absolute dispossession. The much maligned biological approach, which deserves substantial reformulation but not rejection, relates to this irreducible core of absolute deprivation, keeping issues of starvation and hunger at the centre of the concept of poverty (Sen, 1981, p. 22).

Stung by different theoretical approaches developed in other work published at about the same time as his book he entered the fray more openly in his Geary Lecture, delivered in September 1982, published in a revised form in 1983. 'There is, I would argue, an irreducible absolutist core in the idea of poverty' (Sen, 1983, p. 159). He argues along very familiar lines 'If there is starvation and hunger, then – no matter what the *relative* picture looks like – there clearly is poverty.' What he calls the 'relative picture' (what to most of us would then be implied as other needs) have 'to take a back seat behind the possibly dominating absolutist consideration' (p. 159). I find this passage wholly unacceptable. He does not say anything about the scientific criteria by which we identify, or prioritise, human needs. In observations of behaviour in every society the drive to satisfy hunger sometimes takes second place to other drives, especially those which are conditioned by other people's expectations or because of an inculcated sense of obligation in the work place or at home, or through sheer coercion. I also find it a little significant that Professor Sen does not stick to 'starvation' but adds 'and hunger'. This opens the door to a great deal of ambiguity and discussion. The scientific literature demonstrates that exact criteria, and certainly clinical criteria, are not always easy to find for the condition of starvation' but 'hunger' is even more open to wide interpretation and is demonstrably a relative and social concept. On the evidence of reviews such as Evason (1980) in Northern Ireland and Burghes (1980) in England, there are many people in the United Kingdom – one-parent families, long-term unemployed, pensioners and the low paid – who feel the real pinch of hunger today.

The problem about this reiteration of the virtues of an 'absolutist core' to the meaning of poverty, is the underestimation of the importance of needs other than for food (and perhaps for other 'physical' goods and facilities) in the countries of the Third World like India and Pakistan and not just the rich countries of the First World like Britain. Without operational specification of the range of needs and resources required to satisfy those needs Professor Sen's argument carries the dangerous implication that meagre benefits for the poor in industrial societies are more than enough to meet their (absolute) needs and, depending on economic vicissitudes, might be cut. Thus in one passage Professor Sen actually argues that in Britain the level of supplementary benefits is determined by a variety of considerations *'going well beyond* reflecting the cut-off point of identified poverty' (p. 158, my emphasis). There have been 'other pressures, e.g. pulls and pushes of politically important groups, policy objectives *other than* poverty removal' which will have played a part in determining the rates. The same point can be made for the standards which are to be set in Third World development.

Professor Sen's 'minimalism' is worrying, therefore, not only because he appears to ignore or underestimate the importance of certain forms of social need, but because that indifference or underestimation carries an implicit recommendation for policy. It opens the door to a tough state interpretation of subsistence rations. What is theoretically naive is to fail to perceive that just as there may have been political 'pressures' in fixing benefit rates there may also have been such pressures in influencing professional, scientific, bureaucratic and public perceptions of poverty. There may be said to be a tendency of 'establishment' institutions, whether capitalist or state socialist, in the East European sense, to foster minimalist perceptions of the needs of the dependant poor and not only labour. In fact, as I have suggested already, Professor Sen does not appear to have clearly distinguished in principle between social (including state) and scientific or objective definitions of poverty. This is likely to arise if the historical roots of standards and methodologies are exposed. Social scientists must explain how ideas about minimum benefits and wages originate, how they come to be sponsored and justified by contending interest groups, and how the state tends to dodge or suppress efforts to reveal the shortcomings of standards adopted nationally. Fundamentally, such critical exercises depend on efforts to establish alternative standards – principally through the analysis of social structures and therefore of human behaviour – in response to the roles people are expected to perform, but also the roles they might perform in rearranged structures. At the risk of oversimplification, I mean that certain kinds or degrees of human need may not be perceived by any powerful group in a society – either because their own self-interest precludes it, or because fashions or customs are such that it does not seriously obtrude upon their attention. If this possibility is accepted and is to be treated seriously, then free and independent study to explore and demonstrate it must be encouraged. Independent of public, political and, yes, professional economic opinion, human needs must be subjected to that kind of scientific observation and measurement which will allow for unsuspected, as much as previously suppressed, findings to be revealed.

And this is the Achilles heel of Professor Sen's argument. He does not offer any serious criteria of poverty independent of income. I have argued that the subsistence concept is insufficient because criteria of 'physical' need (for food, shelter and clothing) are over-emphasised to the near exclusion of criteria of social need (in fulfilling the roles of citizen, parent, neighbour, friend, professional, client, etc.). I have attempted to provide an alternative definition and this has been discussed at length (Townsend, 1979, especially chapter 6). But the problem isn't merely to recognise social as well as physical needs, but to clarify the social determination and nature of physical needs and hence to comprehend the restrictive and unrealistic functions of an 'absolutist' conception of needs. On page 159 Professor Sen skips about from starvation and malnutrition to hunger. Which of these three concepts is to be regarded as important? What is their exact meaning? Doesn't the difference between the three hold enormous implications for the numbers in any population who are then categorised as being in poverty? This is by no means an inconsequential objection. Many observers of British society would probably agree that while few people at any time may be 'starving' the number who go hungry sometimes, or often, may run into millions.

On page 161 he suggests that there can be 'varying resource requirements of fulfilling the same absolute need' and yet admits that 'needs too can vary between one society and another'. There is some disposition, then, to accept elements of an alternative 'relative deprivation' analysis, without showing how these elements can be reconciled with his 'absolutist' perspective. Professor Sen's contributions to historical analysis show this. Thus he states (p. 154) that there was 'little real reason' for the Labour Government in 1950 'to be smug about eradication of poverty in Britain' despite the estimates of the fall in poverty produced by Seebohm Rowntree. But he does not offer any reinterpretation of what the change between 1936 and 1950 had actually been and therefore tries to ride both horses – namely that the eradication of poverty was not, after all, as substantial as it had seemed from Rowntree's work, but that we should still cling closely to the kind of subsistence conception of poverty (dominated by nutritional requirements) advocated by Rowntree. This seems to have it both ways.

## Capability

Having admitted some elements of relativism into his reasoning about 'absolute' poverty, Professor Sen feels obliged to give a different 'focus for assessing standard of living'. He argues that the right focus is neither commodities, nor characteristics, nor utility, but a person's capability. Having a bicycle, he goes on, by way of illustration, gives a person the ability to move about in a certain way that he may not be able to do without the bicycle. 'So the transportation *characteristic* of the bike gives the person the *capability* of moving in a certain way.' There is sequence from *commodity* (the bike) to characteristics (transportation) to capability to function (ability to move) to utility (pleasure from moving). This third category – of capability to function – 'comes closest to the notion of standard of living'. This notion of capability is basic to the conceptualisation of poverty. 'At the risk of oversimplification, I would like to say that poverty is an absolute notion in the space of capabilities but very often it will take a relative form in the space of commodities or characteristics' (p. 161). Thus, in one of Professor Sen's examples, Adam Smith had noted that the Greeks and Romans lived very comfortably, though they had no linen but 'in the present time, through the greater part of Europe, a creditable day-labourer would be ashamed to appear in public without a linen shirt'. And the necessities of life were 'not only the commodities which are indispensably necessary for the support of life, but whatever the custom of the country renders it indecent for creditable people, even of the lowest order, to be without.'[3]

Professor Sen reaches the point, then, of acknowledging that the *commodities* that people require are relative in the sense that they will be different for different generations and cultures. He states that there are 'varying commodity requirements of meeting the same absolute need' (p. 162). He even gives the example of television as a commodity requirement of the British child for his or her school education. But with certain qualifications he is arguing that capabilities are the same everywhere (see p. 162) and at all times (they are absolute – as emphasised on pp. 161 and 165), but the commodities required to service them are variable and depend on custom.

I happen to believe that Professor Sen has not yet begun to plumb the implications of this concession for the measurement of poverty comparatively in, say, Britain and India. Certainly he does not specify the implications for operational measurement and it cannot be said that his book *Poverty and Famines* reflects this new development in his thinking. Thus in his Geary Lecture he gives examples of 'the most basic capabilities'. These are: 'to meet nutritional requirements, to escape avoidable disease, to be sheltered; to be clothed, to be able to travel, to be educated... to live without shame, to participate in the activities of the community – and to have self-respect.' The possible structural interrelationships of these different notions are not explored. Astonishingly he suggests that the commodity requirements of all but the last three of these capability fulfillments 'are not tremendously variable between one community and another', although the variability is 'enormous' in the case of the last three (pp. 162–3).

But we must question more than the empirical implications and applicability of the thesis. We must ask how the capabilities are selected and in what senses they are 'absolute'. Are not nutritional requirements dependent upon the work roles exacted of people at different points in history and in different cultures, and dependent too upon the levels of extra work activities to which custom expects people to conform? What are the *requirements* for? Isn't the idea of 'avoidable disease' dependent on levels of medical technology and more basically, those conditions and symptoms which a country is prepared to identify as disease or as avoidable, and isn't disease (and its obverse) fundamentally linked with social behaviour? Isn't the idea of 'shelter' relative not just to climate and temperature but to what society makes of what shelter is for? The three little pigs had different ideas of the meaning of shelter. Shelter includes notions of privacy, space to cook and work and play and highly cultured notions of warmth, humidity and segregation of particular members of family and different function of sleep, cooking, washing and excretion. These are *social* notions and this is what I would want to insist upon. Types of need, even capabilities in the sense used by Professor Sen, are socially created and have to be identified and measured in that spirit. Human needs are essentially social, and any analysis or exposition of standards of living and poverty must begin with that fact.

I am therefore welcoming the few cautions steps which Professor Sen is taking in the direction of what he himself calls 'derived relativism' but I do not regard the outcome which he now recommends as analytically or theoretically consistent. Professor Sen's conceptualisation does not allow sufficiently for the social nature of people's lives and needs. He is continuously reverting to physical commodities (bikes, cars, refrigerators) for his examples and to individual states or wants (like his new concept of 'capabilities'). His is a sophisticated adaptation of the individualism which is rooted in neo-classical economics. That theoretical approach will never provide a coherent explanation of the social construction of need, and hence of the real potentialities which do exist of planning to meet need.

## Part 5: 'An econometric approach to the measurement of poverty' by Meghnad Desai and Anup Shah [1988] (Conclusion only)

We have in this paper provided a firmer conceptual basis for measuring deprivation than has hitherto been advanced in the literature. By defining relative deprivation as relative to the community norm and making the norm the modal behavior, we make the sociological view of poverty empirically measurable. The key here is to define consumption in terms of certain crucial events which are highly frequent and highly probable. We then proceed to define the modal value of frequency of consumption events and the difference between actual and modal value as a simple measure of deprivation for any particular event. By making a suitable econometric specification, we finesse the problem of tastes. In aggregating the differences between the actual and the modal value over the different events, we propose a procedure that weights events unequally but in a way that is robust against the inclusion of 'minority events'. This done, we explore the question as to whether our aggregate measure has any different information content from the income variable. We propose that one way to check this might be to use the canonical correlation approach. We implement a modified measure with Townsend's data.

Our empirical results show that it is possible to use Townsend's data in a sophisticated way to extract form them information that can locate who the deprived are. In terms of family size these are at either end of the distribution – single person households and large adult dominated households. The state of health matters as well. As far as income is concerned, there is a sharp decline in the deprivation index beyond the 160% of SB level. But income is far from being the only or even the most important variable.

Thus we hope to have shown that while Townsend's measure has been criticized, it is possible by a suitable formalization to meet most of the limitations. The notion of relative deprivation is more general than Townsend's particular measure of it and this notion is obviously worth formalising and measuring econometrically. Our approach produces a measure for each household and it captures the social, interpersonal aspects that are basic to the concept of relative deprivation.

Much further work remains to be done. The robustness of our measure could be tested by extending to more questions within the Townsend sample than the set used here. It could also be tried out on other samples. Ideally, of course, it should be tested by linking it to a questionnaire which allows the event-specific distance to be measured. This however remains for the future.

*Postscript: A reply by Amartya Sen to Townsend's rejoinder (Sen, 1985) was printed in the same issue of* Oxford Economic Papers. *This should be consulted for detailed counterarguments. Attempts to resolve the theoretical differences have been made for example by de Vos and Hagenaars (1988). Amartya Sen contributed further in later 1992 to the debate about poverty (Sen, 1992, especially chapter 7). Although his contributions to the debate always deserve close attention his theoretical position in his new book remains much the same as expressed in 1985. Thus, the central concern with 'commodities' and 'capabilities' is reiterated. For example, 'While the minimally acceptable capabilities to function may … vary from society to society, the variable commodity requirement for the same capabilities does not, in itself, require that we take a basically "relativist" approach to poverty, provided we see poverty as capability failure' (Sen, 1992, p. 116).*

### Notes

[1.] The conceptualisation of need, as of poverty, can be examined in terms of historical origins and the meanings given to the term or terms comparatively. I try to do both in chapter 1 and also the former in chapter 4 of *Poverty in the United Kingdom* (1979). I had become interested in the different meanings of the term used comparatively in *The concept of poverty* (1970). I still find the problem compulsive and have written a number of papers and articles in recent years to clarify the relative deprivation approach. This includes preliminary work in East Africa and ideas prompted by collaboration with colleagues attempting to coordinate research into poverty in Europe (Townsend, 1984a; 1984b; 1986 and see Chapters 8 and 9 below). The original formulation of the 'relative deprivation' approach is given at the beginning of my book *Poverty in the United Kingdom* (1979) (and also see Chapter 2, above, p. 36).

[2.] Others have wrongly supposed that 'relative deprivation' is just another version of the 'inequality' and have thereby erected a straw man to knock down. See, for example, Joseph and Sumption (1979). In fact I comment a number of times on the distinction between inequality and poverty, for example, in a passgae in Chapter 1 of *Poverty in the United Kingdom* which begins 'But poverty is not inequality...' (p 57).

[3.] Smith (1776), pp. 351–2.

## References

Burghes, L. (1980) *Living from hand to mouth*, London: Child Poverty Action Group and Family Service Units.

Chow, N.W.S. (1982) *Poverty in an affluent city: A report on a survey on low income families in Hong Kong*, Department of Social Work, Chinese University of Hong Kong.

de Vos, K. and Hagenaar, A. (1988) *A comparison between the Poverty Concepts of Sen and Townsend*, Erasmus, University of Rotterdam.

Desai, M.J. (1981) 'Is poverty a matter of taste? An econometric comment on the Piachaud–Townsend debate', London School of Economics.

Desai, M.J. (1983) 'On defining and measuring poverty', mimeograph, London School of Economics.

Desai, M.J. and Shah, A. (1988) 'An econometric approach to the measurement of poverty', *Oxford Economic Papers*, No 40, pp 505-22.

Evason, E. (1980) *Just me and the kids: A study of single parent families in Northern Ireland*, Belfast: Equal Opportunities Commission for Northern Ireland.

Fiegehen, G.C., Lansley, P.S. and Smith, A.D. (1977) *Poverty and progress in Britain 1953-73*, Cambridge: Cambridge University Press.

Joseph, K. and Sumption, J. (1979) *Equality*, London: John Murray.

Piachaud, D. (1981) 'Peter Townsend and the Holy Grail', *New Society*, September, p 421.

Piachaud, D. (1987) 'Problems and definitions in the measurement of poverty', *Journal of Social Policy*, vol 16, no 2, pp 144-64.

Sen, A.K. (1981) *Poverty and famines: An essay on entitlement and deprivation*, Oxford: Clarendon Press.

Sen, A.K. (1983) 'Poor, relatively speaking', *Oxford Economic Papers*, No 35, August.

Sen, A.K. (1985) 'A sociological approach to the measurement of poverty: a reply to Professor Peter Townsend', *Oxford Economic Papers*, No 37, November, pp 669-76

Sen, A.K. (1992) *Inequality re-examined*, Cambridge, MA: Harvard University Press.

Smith, A. (1776) *An inquiry into the nature and causes of the wealth of nations*, Everyman Edition, London: Home University Library.

Townsend, P. (1962) 'The meaning of poverty', *British Journal of Sociology*, vol 13, no 3, pp 210-27.

Townsend, P. (1970) *The concept of poverty: Working papers on methods of investigation and life-styles of the poor in different countries*, London: Heinemann.

Townsend, P. (1979) *Poverty in the United Kingdom: A survey of household resources and standards of living*, Harmondsworth: Penguin Books.

Townsend, P. (1981) 'Rejoinder to Piachaud', *New Society*.

Townsend, P. (1984a) 'Understanding poverty and inequality in Europe', in R. Walker, R. Lawson and P. Townsend (eds) *Responses to poverty: Lessons from Europe*, London: Heinemann.

Townsend, P. (1984b) 'The development of an anti-poverty strategy', in J. Brown (ed) *Anti-poverty policy in the European Community*, London: Policy Studies Institute.

Townsend, P. (1985) 'A sociological approach to the measurement of poverty – a rejoinder to Professor Amartya Sen', *Oxford Economic Papers*, vol 37, pp 659-68.

Townsend, P. (1986) 'Why are the many poor?', *International Journal of Health Services*, vol 16, no 1, pp 1-32.

Wedderburn, D. (1962) 'Poverty in Britain today – the evidence', *Sociological Review*, no 10.

# 19

# The construction of a measure of deprivation

[H]ealth does not exist in a social vacuum, for it is the manual working class, and within that class the poorer and more deprived sections of the population, those with fewest resources at their disposal, who generally experience the worst health (the Black Report, 1980). To provide a socio-economic framework within which to set our data on health, therefore, we have selected certain indicators derived from the 1981 Census which allow us to provide an operational definition of deprivation. Much of what we have said about the difficulty of encapsulating health through statistical indicators applies equally to 'deprivation', a concept which takes a variety of forms and has different meanings (Townsend, 1979; Brown and Madge, 1982). Some recent attempts to create an operational definition of deprivation have rested on confusing foundations and have led to confusing results (notably, Department of the Environment, 1983). Before we put into operation our own definition of deprivation, it is therefore all the more important that we clarify both the meanings of deprivation and the scope of indicators which are used to measure or reflect it.

In contrast with the limited number of available health indicators, there is at first sight no shortage of indicators of deprivation. The problem here is of a different kind – namely, the selection of a coherent set of indicators, or those which reflect a clear and preferably specific meaning of deprivation. The compilation of different measures of deprivation has been pursued energetically in recent years (e.g. Holterman, 1975; Department of the Environment, 1983; Jarman, 1983, 1984, 1985; Scott-Samuel, 1983, 1984; GLC, 1985; Thunhurst, 1985a, b). Yet too often there may have been a tendency to 'trawl' for possible measures without enough regard being paid to the overall sociological rationale for the selection. All recent examples pose problems and we will illustrate some of the problems from both official and independent measures. Two indices of deprivation have been put forward, for example, by the Department of the Environment and by Professor Jarman. Both studies combine indicators of conditions and people in a composite index. The Department of the Environment produces the

---

Extract (pp 34–8) from Townsend, P., Phillimore, P. and Beattie, A. (1988)
*Health and deprivation: Inequality and the North*, Beckenham: Croom Helm.

finding that the ten most deprived local authorities in England are all in London, with none from the Northern Region in the worst 20[1] (1983). In addition, Professor Jarman finds that seven of the ten most deprived health districts in England are in London, with none in the Northern Region (Jarman, 1985). However, Jarman uses the term 'underprivileged' rather than 'deprived' and carefully points out that his index is primarily 'an attempt to measure general practitioners' assessments of their workload or pressure on their services' (private communication; see also Jarman, 1984, p. 1592). Nonetheless, there are eight components of the index, which is the same number as in the Department of Environment index and six of these eight are also identical or nearly the same. The pattern of results produced by the two measures is not dissimilar.

What stands out from these measures is that the 'most deprived areas in England' do not include districts drawn from the Northern Region and this flies in the face of most observation and experience. In resolving this paradox, clearly a major issue is how deprivation has to be conceived, and how best that conception can be related to such official statistics as are available. Results such as those produced in the two studies mentioned here are only achieved by selecting certain indicators the relation of some of which to deprivation is either indirect or contentious.

The approach adopted in this study may be summarised as follows. Indicators of deprivation are sometimes direct and sometimes indirect, sometimes representing conditions or states and sometimes representing the victims of those conditions or states. From a sociological perspective it is important to distinguish between the measurement of deprivation in different areas and the kind of people experiencing that deprivation. Otherwise there is a danger of treating social categories like age, ethnicity and single parenthood as causes of the phenomenon under study. It is, we believe, mistaken to treat being black, old and alone, or a single parent, as part of the definition of deprivation. Even if many among these minorities are deprived, some are not, and the point is to find out how many *are* deprived rather than operate as if all were in that condition. It is the form which their deprivation takes and not their status which has to be measured. Yet it is precisely the indicators that merely reflect minorities at risk of deprivation to which the Department of the Environment and other studies give considerable weight. Three of the six measures combined in the Department of the Environment index (1983), and five of the eight combined in Jarman's index (1984, 1985) are of this kind. Moreover, this particular choice of indicators can be shown to determine the outcome; variables such as single parenthood, population loss and, above all, ethnicity each tend to produce high scores for a number of the inner London Boroughs, and relatively low scores for Northern districts. This will be clarified below. More generally, the selection and combination of deprivation indicators has major implications for the ranking of areas. Hitherto, these implications do not appear to have been given sufficient weight.

Our approach is also built upon the conceptual distinction between material and social forms of deprivation. Material deprivation entails the lack of the goods, services, resources, amenities and physical environment which are customary, or at least widely approved in the society under consideration. Social deprivation, on the other hand, is non-participation in the roles, relationships, customs, functions, rights and responsibilities implied by membership of a society and its sub-groups. People are socially isolated, withdrawn or excluded, for whatever reason. Such deprivation may be attributed to the effects of racism, sexism and ageism and other features of the social structures of modern economies, for example, and not only to what are taken to be the more 'natural' outcomes of ageing, or individual life processes like disablement and family bereavement. Both 'material' and 'social' deprivation can also be divided into different forms or sub-elements (see Townsend, 1987). In this study we concentrate on measures of material deprivation.

Four indicators from the 1981 Census have been selected to represent material deprivation. These have been combined in an Overall Deprivation Index, on the same lines as our Overall Health Index, with equal weights given to each measure. The four chosen variables are:

(1) *Unemployment*. The percentage of economically active residents aged 16–59/64 who are unemployed.
(2) *Car ownership*. The percentage of private households who do not possess a car.
(3) *Home ownership*. The percentage of private households not owner occupied.
(4) *Overcrowding*. The percentage of private households with more than one person per room.

Unemployment, at least at the present time, is to the assessment of material deprivation what mortality rates are to the measurement of health: an indicator which is acknowledged to be very wide in scope as well as reliable – for it reflects a great deal more than the lack of access to earned income and the facilities of employment, in that it carries implications for a general lack of material resources and the insecurity to which this gives rise. In short, unemployment is a harbinger of other misfortune.

The lack of a car is perhaps a more controversial choice, for it is not a clearcut and direct reflection of household or individual deprivation as such. However, a number of studies show that it is probably the best surrogate for current income. Not only does a family have to buy or replace a car to own one, but it also has to pay for licence, insurance and MOT, together with maintenance and repair. All this represents a substantial proportion of income. The indicator also pinpoints generally low income areas (in the absence of direct indicators of such data as children receiving free school meals and electricity disconnections, both of which were used in the Bristol study by Townsend *et al,* 1984).

Non-owner occupation reflects lack of wealth as well as income, and therefore the scope for choice in the crucial sector of the housing market. It is perhaps a more appropriate surrogate for income in a longer-term sense than car possession provides. Taken together these two criteria offer a fairly good reflection of income levels in different areas.

Finally, overcrowding gives a more general guide to living circumstances and housing conditions. An alternative indicator often used would be the proportion of households without exclusive use of basic amenities such as bath and indoor toilet. But this has been demonstrated to be no longer widely representative of poor housing. Many council estates with such basic amenities in every household have nonetheless often been shown to hold large numbers of flats or houses in poor structural condition or with poor facilities otherwise; accordingly its usefulness as one of the main indicators seemed to be small. As a priority indicator of poor housing the more broadly based yardstick of overcrowding seemed preferable. This overcrowding indicator also helps to balance that on housing tenure, bearing in mind that in the present day owner occupation by no means always represents substantial command of resources and may be partly determined by somewhat varying traditions of provision of public housing. Altogether, the index we have put together is not extensive, nor is it ideal, but we believe it is a clear and coherent index which makes good use of census variables.

As with the health indicators, the overall picture of deprivation will be presented first, going on to look briefly at each indicator separately. Other census measures of deprivation are not completely excluded from the analysis, and will be brought into the later presentation of evidence. However, the main emphasis will be on the four chosen criteria. One point deserves to be stressed: not all deprived people live in deprived wards, just as not everybody in a ward ranked as deprived themselves count as deprived.

Missing from this discussion to date has been any reference to social class – or more accurately, occupational class. The proportion of households with a head who is semi-skilled or unskilled (Classes IV and V), or the latter alone, is often included as an indicator of deprivation in census-based studies of area inequalities (Jarman, 1983, 1984, 1985; Thunhurst, 1985b). There is of course an important sense in which occupational class and deprivation are closely related and can almost be treated as different elements of the same phenomenon; and it is not hard to see why the proportion of unskilled is taken as a guide to deprivation. However, the same objection can be made to the inclusion of 'low' class as a measure of deprivation as to the inclusion of ethnicity, single parenthood or pensioner status. These are categories within the population which are especially prone to forms of deprivation, but should not be incorporated in the definition of deprivation as such. Moreover, if these categories of people are included in the definition, we are denied the opportunity of discovering how many of them are deprived in various ways. This is most feasible in the case of occupational class, where it is more important to see precisely how deprivation is distributed in relation to class than to treat one as an aspect of the other. Consequently, in this study data on occupational class will be handled separately from those on deprivation. This will allow different facets of the interrelationship between health, deprivation and class to be explored. [...]

**Endnote**

[1] This is the case in both the Department of Environment's 'Basic' or 'Economic' Z-scores.

**References**

Black, D., Morris, J.N., Smith, C. and Townsend, P. (1980) *Inequalities in health: report of a research working group, The Black Report*, London: Department of Health and Social Security.

Brown, M. and Madge, N. (1982) *Despite the welfare state*, London: Heinemann.

Department of the Environment (1983) *Urban deprivation, Inner Cities Directorate Information Note No 2*, London: Department of the Environment.

GLC (Greater London Council) (1985) *Inner city policy for London: A fresh approach*, London: GLC.

Holterman, S. (1975) 'Areas of deprivation in Great Britain: an analysis of 1971 Census data', *Social Trends*, No 6, pp 33-47.

Jarman, B. (1983) 'Identification of underprivileged areas', *British Medical Journal*, no 286, pp 1705-9.

Jarman, B. (1984) 'Underprivileged areas: validation and distribution of scores', *British Medical Journal*, no 289, pp 1587-92.

Jarman, B. (1985) 'Underprivileged areas', in *Medical Annual*, Bristol: John Wright.

Scott-Samuel, A. (1983) 'Identification of underprivileged areas', *British Medical Journal*, no 287, p 130.

Scott-Samuel, A. (1984) 'Need for primary health care: an objective indicator', *British Medical Journal*, no 288, pp 457-8.

Thunhurst, C.P. (1985a) *Poverty and health in the city of Sheffield*, Sheffield: Environmental Health Department, City of Sheffield, pp 93-116.

Thunhurst, C.P. (1985b) 'The analysis of small area statistics in planning for health', *The Statistician*, no 34, pp 93-106.

Townsend, P. (1979) *Poverty in the United Kingdom: A survey of household resources and standards of living*, Harmondsworth: Penguin.

Townsend, P. (1987) 'Deprivation', *Journal of Social Policy*, April.

Townsend, P., Simpson, D. and Tibbs, N. (1984) *Inequalities of health in the City of Bristol*, Department of Social Administration, University of Bristol.

# 20

# Child poverty in the developing world

Over one billion children – more than half the children in developing countries – suffer from severe deprivation of basic human need and over one third (674 million) suffer from absolute poverty (two or more severe deprivations).

- Over one third of children have to live in dwellings with more than five people per room or which have a mud flooring.
- Over half a billion children (31%) have no toilet facilities whatsoever.
- Almost half a billion children (25%) lack access to radio, television, telephone or newspapers at home.
- Over 20% of children (nearly 376 million) have more than a 15-minute walk to water or are using unsafe (open) water sources.
- Over 15% of children under-five years in the developing world are severely food deprived, over half of whom (91 million children) are in South Asia.
- 265 million children (15%) have not been immunised against any diseases or have had a recent illness involving diarrhoea and have not received any medical advice or treatment.
- 134 million children aged between 7 and 18 (13%) are severely educationally deprived in terms of lacking any school education whatsoever.
- There are differences both between and within regions that are masked by the overall average rates. For example, Sub-Saharan Africa has the highest rates of severe deprivation with respect to four of the seven indicators – severe shelter, water, educational and health deprivation. However, within the region, only 19% of Mali children live in severely water deprived conditions, compared to 90% of Rwandan children.
- Rural children are much more likely to be deprived than urban children in all seven areas of deprivation of basic human need and in all regions. This is particularly the case with respect to severe sanitation deprivation.

Extract (pp 25-31) from Gordon, D., Nandy, S., Pantazis, C., Pemberton, S. and Townsend, P. (2003) *Child poverty in the developing world*, Bristol: The Policy Press.

- At the global level, there are significant gender differences with girls more likely to be severely educationally deprived, particularly in the Middle East and North Africa, where they are three times more likely than boys to be without primary or secondary school education.

These findings are shocking given that severe deprivations of basic human need are those circumstances that are highly likely to have serious adverse consequences for the health, well-being and development of children. Severe deprivations harm children in both the short term and the long term. Many of the absolutely poor children surveyed in this research will have died or had their health profoundly damaged by the time this report is published, as a direct consequence of their appalling living conditions. Many others will have had their development so severely impaired that they may be unable to escape from a lifetime of grinding poverty.

The definitions used in this study to identify severe deprivation of children's basic human needs represent much worse living conditions than are usually reported by UN agencies. This research has measured absolute poverty using such severe criteria that any reasonable person would consider that these living conditions were unacceptable and damaging. No government or parent wants children to have to live like this. This final chapter looks at what lessons can be learnt from this research and what could be done to help eradicate absolute child poverty during the 21st century.

## The causes of absolute poverty

Absolute poverty has been measured within the internationally agreed framework of children's rights, using a definition of absolute poverty that has been agreed to by 117 governments as: "a condition characterised by severe deprivation of basic human needs, including food, safe drinking water, sanitation facilities, health, shelter, education and information. It depends not only on income but also on access to social services".

This research has shown that the severe deprivations that affect the greatest number of children are shelter, sanitation, information and water deprivation. Fewer children suffer from severe deprivation of food, health and education. This, in part, demonstrates the partial success of international agencies and donors that have focused on improving children's access to health and education services and preventing malnutrition.

However, lessons need to be drawn from the experiences of industrialised countries in combating poverty and improving children's health. During the 19th and first half of the 20th centuries, the most important improvements in standard of living and life expectancy of children in industrialised countries were as a result of significant public investment in housing, sewerage and water systems. Safe water, housing and sanitation facilities are prerequisites for good health and education. If children are made chronically sick as a result of unsafe water supplies or inadequate sanitation or overcrowded housing conditions, then they cannot go to school even if free high quality education is available. Similarly, good health facilities can help alleviate the symptoms of chronic sickness but they cannot tackle the underlying causes. Food aid will not be effective in reducing malnutrition if children suffer from chronic diarrhoea as a result of a lack of sanitation facilities and/or unsafe water.

The evidence presented in this report points to the conclusion that UN and other international agencies, governments and donors may need to give a higher priority to tackling the problems of severe shelter, sanitation and water deprivation than is presently the case.

There has been some recent debate within the international community about the need to tackle the problems of housing, water and sanitation deprivation. However, much of this debate has focused on facilitating the private sector to provide additional investment and infrastructure in urban areas. This research shows that far more children in rural areas suffer from severe deprivation than their urban peers[1]. Since the prime motivation of the private sector is the need to optimise profits, it is extremely unlikely that it will be able to provide water and sewerage infrastructure to all poor rural areas, as this would not be profitable. The only way to provide all absolutely poor rural children with adequate housing, sanitation and water facilities is by public investment to pay for these infrastructure facilities. International agencies could be more active in campaigning for greater shelter, sanitation and water infrastructure investment in rural areas of the developing world. Improvements to this rural infrastructure would be the most effective method of reducing absolute child poverty.

## Sanitation

Children are particularly affected by poor sanitation, since it is directly linked to the most serious of childhood illnesses – diarrhoea and malnutrition. Sanitation facilities provided for communities may often be unsuitable for children. If facilities are constructed for adults, they may be too large for young children and present obvious dangers (such as falling in); facilities lacking adequate lighting may intimidate young children wanting to use them at night; children wanting to use public facilities may be made to wait while adults use them first, and so on. The needs of adolescent girls and young women for sanitation and privacy also need to be a priority.

Sanitation facilities require effective drainage systems that carry sewage away from communities. Children use fields and open spaces to play, areas that are commonly used for defecation in the absence of public or private facilities. Organisations like UNICEF and the World Bank are already committed to improving children's access to sanitation and should support organisations that try to establish and maintain public sanitation facilities. Such organisations have started to provide child-friendly facilities, which children can use in safety, without fear or intimidation[2]. The provision of sanitation facilities in schools is also important and should be supported.

There has been some reluctance in the past to highlight the need to improve sanitation facilities as many people do not like to talk about human excreta disposal and donors have gained greater positive publicity for helping improve children's health and education facilities than for funding latrines. Organisations like UNICEF could play a lead role in both raising funds and highlighting the crucial importance of eradicating severe sanitation deprivation as a method of helping eradicate absolute child poverty. Toilet facilities are clearly a priority for children.

## Water

Severe water deprivation is an issue of both quality and quantity. Improving water quality is clearly important for the health of children. Children should not have to use unsafe (or unimproved) sources of water, such as lakes, ponds or streams, as these may become contaminated and dangerous. Communities need to have access to safe water (piped water, stand-pumps, covered wells and so on), through services that they can afford, run and maintain themselves. Such facilities will need to be located and provided near to where people live, to cut journey times for collection. Distance to the water source is of special significance to children since they often help collect and carry the water. Carrying water over long distances can result in injuries, especially to necks and backs, and the time spent collecting water can impact on school attendance.

The distance children need to go in order to get to their water supply is arguably of greater importance than water quality (Esrey, 1996). Water quantity is directly linked to distance to water supply, with less water used the further away the water source. The measure of severe water deprivation used in this report takes into account the issue of distance to water source – something the Joint Monitoring Programme (JMP) of UNICEF and WHO does not, that is, it focuses on water quality issues only. It is important that international organisations, governments and donors take steps to help increase both the quality and quantity of water available to poor children if absolute poverty is to be eradicated.

## Shelter

Overcrowded dwellings facilitate the transmission of disease (for example, respiratory infections, measles). They can also result in increased stress and mental health problems for both adults and children and lead to accidents and injuries. Poor quality shelter, constructed from inferior materials, does not protect against the elements. Successive UN conferences and conventions have sought to address the issue of poor housing and shelter deprivation in both developed and developing countries but progress on meeting children's basic shelter needs has been slow. Considerable international attention has focused on improving the housing conditions of urban slums, shanty towns and favelas. However, this research shows that severe shelter deprivation blights the lives of 42% of rural children in developing countries, compared with 15% of children in urban areas. Improving the housing conditions of families with children in rural areas needs to be given greater priority.

## Food

This research used severe anthropometric failure, that is, children more than −3 standard deviations below the international reference population median, as a measure of severe food deprivation. However, data on children's height and weights are only usually collected for children up to five years old. There is good scientific evidence that older children (particularly during puberty) may also be at risk of suffering from malnutrition. Anthropometric data on older children need to be collected, so that more accurate estimates of child malnutrition in the developing world can be made.

A technical innovation of this research has been the development and use of a Composite Index of Anthropometric Failure (CIAF), based on the work of Peter Svedberg (2000). It provides a more comprehensive indicator of malnutrition than existing measures, and thus may be more appropriate for use in target setting and resource allocation. UNICEF may want to consider development of this indicator and its potential use to monitor the international commitments to reduce child malnutrition by half by 2015. A number of countries, such as Thailand and Costa Rica, have managed to eradicate severe malnutrition and reduce mild–moderate malnutrition relatively quickly. Their success was based on clear political commitment to reducing malnutrition, the provision of food subsidies, the targeting of food supplements to children and mothers, health and nutrition education and regular growth monitoring and surveillance (ACC/SCN, 2002).

## Child and family benefit

Another lesson that can be drawn from the experiences of industrialised countries in reducing child poverty is that, after public infrastructure investment, the most effective anti-poverty policy for children is the establishment of a child or family social security benefit.

It has been argued elsewhere (Townsend and Gordon, 2002) that an international children's investment fund should be established under the auspices of the UN. Half its annual resources should be devoted to countries with extensive child poverty, where schemes of child benefit in cash or kind exist or where such schemes can be introduced. All countries with large numbers of children who are below an internationally recognised poverty line and also with comparatively low GDP should be entitled to participate. Such participation would require dependable information that the benefits are reaching children for whom they are intended. The remaining annual resources of the fund would be made available to countries for investment in housing, sanitation and water infrastructure, education, health and other schemes of direct benefit to children.

Programmes to gradually increase public expenditure so that categories of the extreme poor start to benefit offer a realistic, affordable and successful method for poverty alleviation. For example, in Brazil, the Zero Hunger Programme intends to provide regular and sufficient supplies of quality food to all Brazilians in conjunction with accelerated social security reform. The first includes food banks, popular restaurants, food cards, distribution of emergency food baskets, strengthening of family agriculture and a variety of other measures to fight malnutrition. The social security reform programme includes social assistance for low-income 15- to 17-year-olds, assistance for 7- to 14-year-olds who are enabled to go to school and avoid the exacting toll of the worst conditions of child labour, minimum income and food scholarships for pregnant and nursing mothers with incomes less than half the minimum wage or who are HIV positive, benefits for elderly disabled people with special needs and a range of other transfer programmes for the elderly, widowed, sick and industrially injured and unemployed that are being enlarged year by year (Suplicy, 2003: forthcoming).

The social security systems of developing countries present a diverse picture. Partial systems were introduced by colonial authorities in most of Asia, Africa and the Caribbean. They were extended in the first instance to civil servants and employees of large enterprises. There were benefits for relatively small groups that included healthcare, maternity leave, disability allowances and pensions (Midgeley, 1984; Ahmad et al, 1991). In India, there are differences among major states as well as a range of schemes for smallish categories of population (Ghai, 2001; Prabhu, 2001). In Latin America, some countries introduced schemes before the 1939-45 war and others followed suit after. Benefits tended to be limited in range and coverage. There were different systems for particular occupations and categories of workers and a multiplicity of institutions. Between 20 and 60% of the workforce were covered, compared with between 5 and 10% for most of Sub-Saharan Africa and 10 to 30% for most of Asia. "The greatest challenge facing the developing countries is to extend the benefits of social security to the excluded majority to enable them to cope with indigence and social contingencies" (Huber, 1996).

These recommendations are the key to a far better future for hundreds of millions of children. But how might social security systems now evolve to provide universal beneficial effects of more substantial redistribution? Human rights now play a central part in discussions of international social policy. This applies to civil and political rights, less so to social and economic rights. Articles 22 and 25 in the Declaration of Human Rights – dealing with the rights to an 'adequate' standard of living and social security – have been often overlooked in General Assembly and other reports from the UN. The fundamental right to social security is also spelt out in Article 26 of the Convention on the Rights of the Child and the related rights to an adequate standard of living in Article 27.

UNICEF and other international organisations (such as the International Labour Organization [ILO]) should campaign for a legal right to child benefit under Articles 25 and 27 of the Convention on the Rights of the Child.

## The needs of children in the 21st century

The needs of children in the 21st century are different from those of children in the 19th and 20th centuries and new policies will be required to meet these needs. For example, in the 21st century, severe information deprivation is an important constraint on the development of both individual children and societies as a whole – many consider that 'knowledge is power'. This study provides the first estimates of the extent of severe information deprivation among children. A quarter of children in the developing world are severely information deprived, with approximately 390 million living in rural areas and 60 million living in urban areas.

Reducing information deprivation will require action at a number of different levels, including getting children into school and increasing literacy rates for both children and adults. Without these basic essentials, the impact and provision of newspapers and other media (such as computers and the Internet) will be limited.

The most cost-effective intervention is through improvements to radio access. Radio is one of the main channels of information in developing countries. They are a cheap, effective means through which communities can be informed about the importance of education and health initiatives (for example, immunisation for young children, the benefits of hand washing, effective and cheap ways to treat diarrhoea, availability of food supplements for malnourished children, and so on). All countries have the means to make radio broadcasts. Governments could improve public information services and regularly broadcast programmes that inform communities about simple but effective changes they can make to their lives – for example, making simple water filters using locally available materials, constructing basic sanitation facilities at low cost, and so on. The development of cheap clockwork radios has meant the technology can be made widely available, at an affordable price.

There are many examples of community radio networks that have an important role in the provision of public information (for example, the Developing Countries Farm Radio Network[3], the World Community Radio Movement[4], Community Radios Worldwide[5]). Community organisations have campaigned for the installation of small, local transmitters that can provide information to local communities. They have also argued for the granting of broadcast licences to women's groups, local colleges and universities, cooperatives, and so on. However, commercialisation of the airwaves and the imposition of licence fees have begun to affect community radio stations, as they are pushed aside by commercial broadcasters.

Governments might consider allocating resources to the development of community media funds that would provide information over the airwaves on important issues such as health and education. UN organisations like the Food and Agriculture Organisation and the United Nations Educational, Scientific and Cultural Organization (UNESCO) have been committed to community media and radio networks for a number of years and support initiatives providing information to rural areas (Hughes, 2001; Ilboudo, 2001). As one UNESCO report stated:

> Community radio is low-cost, easy to operate, reaches all segments of the community through local languages and can offer information, education, entertainment, as well as a platform for debate and cultural expression. As a grass-roots channel of communication, it maximises the potential for development to be drawn from sharing the information, knowledge and skills already existing within the community. It can therefore act as a catalyst for community and individual empowerment. (Hughes, 2001)

UN agencies could help inform both governments and the public on the importance of information access for children and thereby raise the profile of this issue. They might also assist in the setting up of local radio networks, and help train communities in accessing and using information effectively.

## The poverty of girls

This study found that gender differences at the global level were greatest for severe education deprivation, with girls 60% more likely to be deprived. Significant regional and country disparities were revealed in the study, with girls in the Middle East and North Africa region three times more likely to be severely education deprived.

The reasons why children (and particularly girls) do not go to school vary and policies need to be targeted at the causes of non-attendance if they are to be effective. For example, children may not attend school because there is no school close enough or because it is too expensive or because the quality of the education is poor or because there is discrimination against girls going to school.

Abolishing primary school fees may encourage and enable poor parents to send their children – and particularly their daughters – to school. In some countries, there needs to be a concurrent effort made to change social attitudes about the value of education for girls. This applies to all levels of society including parents, politicians and schoolteachers. There are other practical interventions that can be pursued including the provision of incentives such as bursaries, free school meals and books, improved sanitation facilities and security. As part of the global Education For All campaign, UNESCO recently recommended a number of activities that governments should undertake to meet the goals of eliminating gender disparities in education by 2005 and achieving gender equality by 2015. These included:

- setting concrete targets and funding them adequately;
- educating mothers – the most crucial measure for the sustained education of girls;
- supporting gender-responsive schools and allowing pregnant girls and teenage mothers to continue their education;
- making educational content relevant to local cultural and economic contexts so that parents see that educating girls improves their quality of life;
- providing gender-sensitive curricula and textbooks;
- training more female teachers and make teacher training gender responsive;
- eliminating child labour. According to a recent ILO report, 352 million children between the ages of 5 and 17 are engaged in economic activities, of which 168 million are girls;
- including HIV/AIDS prevention in the curriculum;

- education is a powerful 'social vaccine' against the HIV/AIDS pandemic. Learning methods should address the fact that girls are heading households, caring for siblings and being forced to generate income;
- building schools closer to girls' homes to increase access, particularly for rural children;
- making schools safe for girls and equipping them with separate toilets.

## Regional and country-specific anti-poverty policies

This research has found that the major causes of absolute child poverty vary both between and within regions of the developing world. For the world as a whole, shelter combined with sanitation deprivation affects the greatest number of children. Whereas shelter combined with water deprivation is the biggest problem in Sub-Saharan Africa, in South Asia, almost 36% of households with children suffer from shelter and information deprivation. By contrast, in the Middle East and North African region, shelter combined with education deprivation affects the greatest number of poor children. It is clear that, in order to eradicate absolute poverty among children, policies will need to be targeted at the various problems they face. A single set of anti-poverty policies for the planet is not the most effective or efficient way to eradicate child poverty. Aid donors and international agencies need to be aware – and make the public aware – of the need for tailored anti-poverty strategies which deal with the 'real' problems faced by children in different countries. Investment in eradicating severe educational deprivation may be a very effective means of reducing absolute child poverty in some countries in North Africa and the Middle East but it would be much less effective in Latin America or South Asia where ending other severe child deprivations should be prioritised.

This report has shown – for the first time – the true extent of the scale and nature of absolute child poverty in the developing world. It has used internationally agreed definitions of poverty and applied a sound, scientific methodology that shows that over half a billion children in the developing world live in absolute poverty. However, due to the severity of the measures used, this is likely to be an underestimate. Research and reports from a number of international organisations (WHO, 2001; Vandemoortele, 2002; UNDP, 2003) suggest that the optimism shown at the end of the last millennium was either premature or misplaced. It is sadly the case that there is growing recognition of the fact that most of the Millennium Development Goals will not be met in time on current trends. Issues such as international debt, unequal trade and economic relations, declining donor commitment to international aid, and increasing political and economic instability continue to work together to undermine the efforts of governments, international and non-governmental organisations, communities and individuals. As things stand today (and as this report shows), the campaign to eradicate child poverty still has a long way to go.

**Endnotes**

[1] Approximately 530 million rural children suffer from severe shelter deprivation compared with 85 million urban children; 515 million rural children suffer from severe sanitation deprivation compared with 50 million urban children; 335 million rural children suffer from severe water deprivation compared with 40 million urban children – see Chapter 3 for details.

[2] One non-governmental organisation running such schemes is Gramalaya. Based in Tamil Nadu in India, the scheme came about after consultation with the local community. Facilities are constructed adjacent to community toilets. Water with soap is provided for hand washing after defecation. A caretaker from the community toilet teaches hand washing and its importance to the children and observes children's hygiene behaviours. Facilities are provided free to children (http://gramalaya.org/childtoilets.html).

[3] Developing Countries Farm Radio Network is a Canadian-based, not-for-profit organisation working in partnership with approximately 500 radio broadcasters in over 70 countries to fight poverty and food insecurity. It supports broadcasters in meeting the needs of local small-scale farmers and their families in rural communities and helps broadcasters build the skills to develop content that responds to local needs (www.farmradio.org).

[4] AMARC is an international NGO serving the community radio movement, with almost 3,000 members and associates in 106 countries. Its goal is to support and contribute to the development of community and participatory radio along the principles of solidarity and international cooperation (www.amarc.org/amarc/ang/).

[5] www.radiorobinhood.fi/communityradios/articles

**References**

ACC/SCN (2002) *Ending malnutrition by 2020: An agenda for change in the millennium*, Commission on the Nutrition Challenges of the 21st Century, ACC/SCN: Geneva.

Ahmad, E., Dreze, J., Hills, J. and Sen, A. (1991) *Social security in developing countries*, Oxford: Clarendon Press.

Esrey, S.A. (1996) 'No half measures – sustaining health from water and sanitation systems', *Waterlines*, vol 14, no 3, pp 24-7.

Ghai, D. (2001) 'Social security for all', *Technical Commissions*, Leo Wildmann Symposium, Stockholm, September, International Social Security Association, Geneva.

Huber, E. (1996) 'Options for social policy in Latin America: neo-liberal versus democratic models', in G. Esping-Andersen (ed) *Welfare states in transition*, Geneva and London: UNRISD and Sage Publications.

Hughes, S. (2001) Community multimedia centres: Integrating modern and traditional information and communication technologies for community development – A programme addressing the digital divide in some of the poorest communities of the developing world, Paris: UNESCO, available at www.fao. org/docrep/003/x6721e/x6721e17.htm

Ilboudo, J.P. (2001) FAO's experience in the area of rural radio, including information and communication technologies servicing rural radio: New contents, new partnerships, Rome: FAO, available at www.fao.org/docrep/003/x6721e/ x6721e38.htm#P5_1

Midgeley, J. (1984) *Social security, inequality and the third world,* New York, NY: Wiley.

Prabhu, K.S. (2001) *Socio-economic security in the context of pervasive poverty: A case study of India*, SES Papers, Geneva: ILO.

Suplicy, E.M. (2003) *President Lula's Zero Hunger Programme and the trend toward a citizen's basic income in Brazil,* London: London School of Economics and Political Science.

Svedberg, P. (2000) *Poverty and undernutrition: Theory, measurement and policy*, New Delhi: Oxford University Press.

Townsend, P. and Gordon, D. (eds) (2002) *World poverty: New policies to defeat an old enemy*, Bristol: The Policy Press.

UNDP (United Nations Development Programme) (2003) *Human Development Report 2003*, New York, NY: UNDP.

Vandemoortele, J. (2002) *Are the MDGs feasible?*, New York, NY: UN Development Programme Bureau for Development Policy.

WHO (World Health Organisation) (2001) *Macroeconomics and health: Investing in health for economic development*, Report of the Commission on Macroeconomics and Health, Geneva: WHO Publications.

# Section IV

# Inequality and social exclusion

*Edited by Ruth Levitas*

# Introduction

The selections in this section span a period of almost 50 years. They illustrate Peter Townsend's consistent political commitment to equality; his meticulous interrogation of data; his deeply sociological and holistic understanding of social processes relating to class, inequality and the generation of poverty and social exclusion; and his engagement with and development of new conceptual frameworks as well as responsiveness to changing social and political contexts.

The first piece (**Chapter 21**), 'The truce on inequality', originally appeared in the *New Statesman* in 1959. Much of its substance concerns the limited achievements of the welfare state, and the greater gains made by the middle classes relative to the working classes, let alone the poor. Insofar as there had been a reduction in inequality, and a commitment to some forms of universal social provision, these were largely the product of the war, rather than post-war policies. Townsend's core argument – that Labour had abandoned the principle of equality for that of an economic growth falsely assumed to benefit everyone – still rings true: it could have been written at any time in the following half-century, and most especially in relation to the New Labour governments after 1997. The arguments remain pertinent because the essential problems which Townsend perceived so acutely remain the same. And they remain, as he insists in this piece, ethical issues rather than merely technical ones.

The second article (**Chapter 22**) starts from that ethical question of the kind of society we want to create, but is essentially concerned with the related need for precise and accurate understanding of current conditions, in this case standards of living. It is a detailed critique, of the kind Townsend was to undertake repeatedly over the years, of official statistics and the partial – and sometimes quite erroneous – picture that they paint of trends in inequality. Here, in an article in *The Times* in 1971, he argues that contrary to much popular and political supposition, "in spite of social and incomes legislation, greater equality of real incomes was not achieved between the mid-1950s and 1970" (Townsend, 1971). Indeed, even taking into account the value of social services including health and education, if the regressive effects of indirect taxation, and especially the increasing value of fringe benefits to the most well-off are taken into account, the evidence points to a widening, rather than a narrowing, of inequalities. The third article (**Chapter 23**), from the *New Statesman* in 1976, has a similar theme, but is specifically concentrated on the methodology and conclusions of the Royal Commission on Income and Wealth. This critique is enormously important, as the findings of the Royal Commission (abolished in 1979 when Prime Minister Thatcher took office), are still widely regarded as a reliable account of trends in inequality over the 20th century. They show, incidentally, that 1976 was the year in which overall income inequality in Britain was at its lowest; there is no question that it has been widening ever since. Again, Townsend questions the view that top incomes have decreased in relative terms and inequalities narrowed: such a view ignores the fact that "in remunerating top executives, there has been a long-term, and continuing, substitution or supplementation of direct salary by indirect benefits in order to escape tax" (Townsend, 1976). Both evidence from the Family Expenditure Survey and evidence about fringe benefits presented to the Commission itself are used to cast doubt on the supposed fall in the share of real incomes taken by the most affluent.

By 1983, after four years of Thatcherite government, complete with de-industrialisation, soaring unemployment and poverty, and open redistribution in favour of the rich, there was less need to prove rising inequality – although throughout these years it was necessary to counter arguments that 'real' poverty no longer existed. Townsend argues in 'The pursuit of equality' (**Chapter 24**) that "in present conditions of extreme deprivation and mass poverty" the case for equality "deserves to be presented fully and more positively", and that one part of that "is to relate better the connected theories of poverty and of inequality". This involves accentuating the origin of needs in membership of society, and "the institutional processes by which social roles and customs are originated and maintained, and therefore the part played by the state, industry and the wealthy classes in 'manufacturing' poverty in the first place, rather than the part they might play in alleviating that condition once it is identified" (Townsend, 1983, p 13). Although Townsend does not use the term 'social exclusion' here, it reflects his sustained concern not simply with the social consequences of poverty, but with poverty as *social* deprivation. 'The truce on inequality' ended by affirming the need to improve the material circumstances of the poor in order to "enlarge [their] freedom to choose what kind of life [they will] lead" (Townsend, 1959, p 382). In *Poverty in the United Kingdom*, published in 1979, he argued that:

> Individuals, families and groups can be said to be in poverty when they lack the resources to obtain the types of diet, participate in the activities and have the living conditions and amenities which are customary, or at least widely encouraged and approved, in the societies to which they belong. Their resources are so seriously below those commanded by the average individual or family that they are, in effect, excluded from ordinary living patterns, customs and activities. (Townsend, 1979, p 32)

The crucial issue was always whether people had sufficient resources to participate in the customary life of society and to fulfil what was expected of them, and what they might reasonably expect, as members of it. In 'The pursuit of equality', the focus must shift from the poor to the rich, because:

> The obligations at work, in family and community and as citizens which we feel bound to fulfil, using such incomes as we can command, are moulded in predominant measure by the rich through state laws and the establishment of social norms. Therefore, we have to look at the influences exerted by the rich in defining and controlling the conditions, and setting the fashions, which are continually redefining and reconstituting the structures of need which citizens experience in their everyday lives. (Townsend, 1983, pp 13-14)

Again, in 'A matter of class', published in 1986 (**Chapter 25**), Townsend insists on the need to look beyond the failings of the welfare state to the "link to the policy institutions of the rich". Far more attention to structures and processes in society as a whole is necessary to explain the generation and growth of poverty.

These themes are taken up again in a detailed analysis of theories of social class, focusing on the social polarisation of the 1980s. The extracts from 'Underclass and overclass' reproduced here (**Chapter 26**) focus on two issues. The first is the development of an 'underclass'. The idea of an underclass was controversial, partly because it could be taken to mean many different things, especially in a US context. However, Townsend argued that there was evidence of class restructuring, not just as a result of rising unemployment, but through a series of state measures including "fiscal policy, cuts in public expenditure and state coercion" (Townsend, 1993, p 102). This was no accident: "If an underclass is being established on a substantial scale it is as a result of the exercise of new forms of power on behalf of vested interests" (Townsend, 1993, p 106). And so attention shifts to the rich and the super-rich – to the overclass. Again, the institutional mechanisms discussed here are changes in the financial markets, the internationalisation of the financial world, and the role of state in facilitating this. These excerpts omit several elements of the original article: a discussion of theories of class; the detailed evidence of widening inequality; and a discussion of the attitudes of the rich. For those interested in Townsend's overall sociology, a reading of the whole article is illuminating.

The following year, an editorial in the *British Medical Journal* (**Chapter 27**), castigates the "politics of vindictiveness and selfish complacency" (Townsend, 1994, p 1675) emerging from the attitudes of the rich to the poor – this too amid widening inequality, and the inflation of senior executive salaries and accompanying fringe benefits. It points out the new evidence that social inequality, rather than simply poverty, damages people's health, and calls for a 'responsibility' tax to curb excessive pay increases and "improve conditions for all".

The relationship between poverty, social exclusion and social polarisation is also the subject of a more detailed and more academic piece written in the opening years of the 21st century (**Chapter 28**). It opens with a reiteration of the problem identified in 1959: the assumption that poverty will be automatically diminished through economic growth. This, despite decades of accumulated evidence about rising inequality and social polarisation, remains the conventional wisdom. Here, Townsend points out that there is no agreed definition of either poverty or social exclusion, but that both address attention to only part of the problem: they focus on the groups at the bottom of society, and not on the system as a whole. If the state of inequality is the wider counterpart of the state of poverty, the process of social polarisation is the wider context of the process of social exclusion. Social polarisation remains key. The article documents the global process of social polarisation within and between nations, and the complicity of global economic institutions in this process. Again, "Far more attention has to be given to the entire hierarchical *system*, and especially rich institutions and rich individuals at the top" (Townsend, 2002, p 18). And since the institutions that are now involved in the production and reproduction of inequality and poverty are global, what is needed is nothing less than an international welfare state. To preserve the overall argument, it has been necessary to omit large sections of the article. They deal briefly with the debates about the concepts of poverty and of social exclusion and the needs for scientific agreement and validation of these. More importantly, they spell out in more detail the precise institutional processes involved in polarisation: defective structural adjustment policies, the concentration of hierarchical power, privatisation, the shortcomings of targeting and safety nets: the depth of Peter Townsend's analysis that leads to the call for new institutions is best conveyed by returning to the full text.

The last selection (**Chapter 29**) draws on the definitions of 'absolute' and 'overall' poverty agreed at Copenhagen in 1995, and deployed here in pursuit of internationally comparable measures of poverty. The argument embeds detailed evidence about perceptions of poverty taken from the Poverty and Social Exclusion Survey of 1999 – evidence which is not reproduced here for reasons of space. The definition of overall poverty, including as it does social discrimination and exclusion, as well as lack of social participation of many kinds, enfolds the idea of social exclusion, and encapsulates Townsend's longstanding insistence that our understanding of poverty needs to begin from the intrinsically social character of human existence. He reiterates "the importance of extending the meaning of poverty to include social as well as 'subsistence' needs", thus again raising the question "of the respective precise meanings of social exclusion and poverty" (Townsend, 2006, p 81).

What is remarkable about these writings over a period of nearly 50 years is how consistent, and persistent, they are. From the outset, Peter Townsend was committed to the objective of building economies to serve "human needs and aspirations" (United Nations, 1995, cited in Townsend, 2002). Many of these pieces do not simply document the evidence of how bad things are, although they do that stringently and analytically. They also point to what needs to change, the possibility of political and institutional change – the hope, always present, of a society based on equality, and free from poverty and social exclusion.

## References

Townsend, P. (1959) 'The truce on inequality', *New Statesman*, 26 September, pp 381-2.

Townsend, P. (1971) 'Poverty: has the welfare state failed?', *The Times*, 9 March.

Townsend, P. (1976) 'How the rich stay rich', *New Statesman*, 1 October, pp 441-3.

Townsend, P. (1979) *Poverty in the United Kingdom: A survey of household resources and standards of living*, Harmondsworth: Penguin.

Townsend, P. (1983) 'The pursuit of equality', *Poverty*, pp 11-15.

Townsend, P. (1986) 'A matter of class', *Poverty*, Winter, pp 12-14.

Townsend, P. (1993) 'Underclass and overclass: the widening gulf between social classes in Britain in the 1980s', in M. Cross and G. Payne (eds) *Sociology in action*, London: Macmillan, pp 91-118.

Townsend, P. (1994) 'The rich man in his castle', *British Medical Journal*, no 309, 24 December, pp 1674-5.

Townsend, P. (2002) 'Poverty, social exclusion and social polarisation: the need to construct an international welfare state', in P. Townsend and D. Gordon (eds) *World poverty: New policies to defeat an old enemy*, Bristol: The Policy Press, pp 3-24.

Townsend, P., Gordon, D. and Pantazis, C. (2006) 'The international measurement of 'absolute' and 'overall' poverty: applying the 1995 Copenhagen definitions to Britain', in C. Pantazis, D. Gordon and R. Levitas (eds) *Poverty and social exclusion in Britain: The Millennium Survey*, Bristol: The Policy Press, pp 71-85.

United Nations (1995) *Copenhagen Declaration and Programme of Action: World Summit for Social Development*, New York, NY: United Nations.

# 21

# The truce on inequality

Peter Townsend, who contributes this controversial assessment of the Labour Party's attitude towards social inequality, is a research sociologist by profession and a Socialist by conviction. The points he raises in this article will be discussed next week by the Rt. Hon. Harold Wilson, Labour's shadow Chancellor.

During the past ten years the general image of the Labour Party as presented to the public seems to have undergone a subtle but significant change. The party now seems to be characterised by a diminished attachment to moral and social principle and by a correspondingly greater concern with piecemeal reform, at least in social policy. Its leaders today rejoice in the impressions that they are honest, practical men of restraint dealing with the immediate realities of life. They are cautious about what they say they will do when they achieve power and are apt to be discouraged by the expert who tells them that a certain course of action will offend or produce too many technical difficulties. Their strength is their capacity for sustained practical activity; but, as Tawney has said more generally about the failings of the English, they are increasingly unwilling to test the quality of that activity by reference to principle. They seem to have become incurious about theory and therefore about their own destination.

Some such picture, with all the necessary qualifications, must emerge from any study of the recent history of the Labour Party and particularly of the policy documents that have been published since the defeat of 1951. A number of valuable plans and ideas have emerged from the work of various committees set up in the years of opposition; but there has been a strange reluctance either to integrate them into a coherent social philosophy, so that priorities can be decided, or indeed to pursue or spell out in any detail the more imaginative plans which call for hard work and resolution. The best has not been made even of the uncoordinated programme that now exists, and it is not therefore surprising to find so many people, even those, like myself, most attached to its cause, regarding the present version of British Socialism as intellectually tame and unadventurous.

---

Townsend, P. (1959) 'The truce on inequality', *New Statesman*, 26 September, pp 381–2.

Among the reasons for this shift in political character a future historian might well pick out for special attention the fading of interest in the subject of inequality. The main political parties and trade unions, together with economists and sociologists, appear to have called a truce over inequality. From time to time some efforts, it is true, have been made within the Labour movement to revive the subject, but more because of the nostalgic yearning for the fiery battles of the past than because the issues seem appropriate today. A policy pamphlet on the subject of inequality was indeed published two or three years ago, but it lacked any serious probing of hard fact and was therefore treated as rather inconsequential.

Why was the truce called? This, I think, is one of the fundamental questions about our post-war society. It hinges on the changing attitudes towards poverty in a society moving towards prosperity, if not affluence. There is first of all the prevalent belief that the Welfare State has lifted the poor out of poverty and, within rough limits, provided equal standards of treatment and income to all citizens. Secondly, there is the belief that incomes and riches have been much more evenly distributed and therefore the differences between the living standards of the working classes and those of the middle and upper classes have narrowed sharply. And thirdly, there is the belief that to step up production is the most important objective in our society, because everyone has shared in rising prosperity since the war and is bound to share in any future spoils. All these beliefs are widely held. They are held by Socialists as well as Tories, though some Socialists hold them in secret. Yet all three are highly questionable.

What precisely did the post-war social legislation bring about? Perhaps the essential feature of that legislation was the creation of an obligation, or contract, to provide all citizens with the basic needs of life in modern society – with certain standards of income security, medical care, housing and education. To a large extent the collective acceptance of this concept of universality was made possible by the war, by the sharing of privations and privileges, by the confrontation, in the armed services, through evacuation and the experiences of the blitz, of one half of society with the other, by the ideals and high levels of tolerance which the hardships of war aroused in the hearts of men. Rights were created by virtue simple of citizenship; no one was to be excluded because of his wealth, his religion, his colour or his parentage. People's needs were of like value.

But what preceded the acceptance of the concept of universality? What occupational groups were brought in for the first time? When measured in terms of increases in prices, population trends and proportions of the national income allocated to particular services, what did the changes in fact mean? Were the new standards generous or did they mean simply that people would not be allowed to starve?

As soon as we begin to look at such questions we begin to make the first assault on complacency. Improvements have been slow and uneven. Most of the poorest groups had been covered by national health and unemployment insurance before 1948. Their gains were not remarkable. Expressed as a proportion of average earnings, some of the insurance benefits even of 1959 compare very unfavourably with those of 1938. For the poorest sections of the community the crucial thing was the disappearance of the Poor Law test and the appearance of more humanity in administration. As Titmuss has said, "This is what universalism really meant to the working classes: some decline in discrimination".

Some better-off sections of the population did however gain in material benefits on extremely easy terms – especially pensions and sick pay. To achieve universalism in social security it was necessary in the first instance to favour these sections of society. Recent studies have demonstrated for some other social services that the right of free access has benefited the middle classes more than the working classes.

Without regard for the facts the various changes brought about by the post-war legislation have been called 'egalitarianism'. The essential thing here is not the confuse universality with egalitarianism. The National Insurance scheme is universal – subject to a test of contributions. Yet the benefits it confers are so low that the poorest are driven to seek help from the National Assistance Board and the richest regard them simply as convenient supplements to much more substantial benefits they may obtain from employers or from insurance companies.

Economists and sociologists have not allayed the misapprehensions which grew up about the achievements of the Welfare State. In the decade before the war there were more than a dozen published surveys of poverty – in London, Birmingham, York, Southampton and elsewhere. Poverty, or the threat of poverty, overshadowed the lives of a large proportion of the population – a vocal and active proportion. In the 13 years or so since the end of the war, there has been only one survey of poverty – and that a rather mismanaged one.

It is clear, of course, that poverty no longer threatens the majority of the most active and vocal sections of the population. The poor are a voiceless minority. Yet they comprise a large number of people. There are millions depending almost solely on inadequate social insurance and national assistance benefits – the old, the sick, the unemployed, the widows with young children; there are many hundreds of thousands of chronic sick, infirm and socially handicapped persons living in institutions and at home; and there are millions of people, especially those with large families, living on low wages. Although the figures are difficult to interpret the fraction of the population covered by these categories seems to be closer to one-fifth than one-tenth – ranging from five to ten millions. By tradition one of the chief functions of the Labour Party has been to speak for the underdog. But today it still seems inhibited from the outright criticisms necessary to fulfil that function: it is impelled to claim too much for the magic years after 1945.

Poverty is not only the subject to have attracted little attention in recent years. Before and during the war all the classical doctrines of the redistribution of income were at the political forefront of intellectual thought and political debate. Today these doctrines are often treated with amused indulgence by many intelligent people. They no longer appear to matter. Really, the arguments suggest, didn't we deal with all that old stuff during and after the war? Haven't we all but abolished poverty? Look at the results of 'punitive' taxation and of death duties.

To go quietly through what scraps of evidence there are is to make another assault on complacency. Whatever 'redistribution' may mean, it is plain that most of it occurred in the war. Since 1947, by a process which we may call 'piecemeal amelioration', the lot of the middle and upper-income groups has gradually improved. I am referring here not only to the more obvious steps taken to relieve surtax-payers in one of the latest budgets or to the general switch in emphasis from direct to indirect taxation, but to a series of big and small measures, from the removal of food subsidies to the tax relief granted to the parents of university students. The 1956 Finance Act, for example, allowed £50m a year in taxes to be lost to the Exchequer so that contributors to private superannuation might enjoy more generous tax concessions. That £50m was equivalent to the total sum being paid to old age pensioners by the National Assistance Board. The rich have gained most from the changes because they were affected most by taxation in the first place. The fiscal system is the biggest, if the most silent, social service we have.

The changes outside the tax system have been even more important. Comparisons between two persons' incomes tell us little about the real differences in their standards of living. All kinds of indirect subsidies are received by some people – meal vouchers, subsidised and free housing, salaries paid in full during sickness, free travel and so on. This is why some of the traditional statistics about the relative earnings of wage and salary earners have become uninformative. The last blue book on national income made a quiet change in one of its footnotes, to the effect that the proportion attributed to business expenses of the total spent on wines and spirits in the country had been raised from five to ten per cent.

In tracing the reasons for the current lack of interest in inequality we cannot be content with examining the exaggerated claims for the achievements of the Welfare State and of taxation in bringing about a more equitable distribution of income. We must look to the values of society. There is near unanimity between Tories and Socialists on the desirability of ever-increasing production. Why have a war of attrition between different sections of society about inequality and the redistribution of income when all can share in increasing wealth? Once those in poverty become, in Britain no less than in America, a voiceless minority, why bother with the classical doctrines of Socialism? In an advanced country increased production is an alternative to redistribution and is not associated with the same social tensions. Moreover, when the poor form a comparative minority why should they remain at the centre of a politician's interest? As Galbraith has said, "It becomes easy or at least convenient, to accept that use of the conventional wisdom which is that the rich ... are highly functional and also much persecuted members of society ... To comment on the wealth of the wealthy, and certainly to propose that it be reduced, has come to be considered bad taste. The individual whose own income is going up has no real reason to ... identify himself, even remotely, with soapbox orators, malcontents, agitators, Communists and other undesirables".

Yet look at the consequences. If public opinion, including the Left, puts expanding production first, then almost automatically there is a psychological obligation to subscribe to the importance of capital investment and of building so-called incentives into the tax system. In the policy documents of the Labour Party there is a noticeable shifting of feet whenever there is the slightest suggestion of using taxation as a weapon for social ends. Now we begin to understand part of the embarrassment of present-day Socialism.

The facts seem to be inescapable. It is not the changes in social insurance, not any radical redistribution of income, which has brought about the diminution of poverty in Britain. Full employment, and the increase in output of recent decades, have brought the increase in well-being of the average man. And subscription to the virtues of expanding output has sapped the moral fibres of the Left. Not only, it is thought, will wage-earners benefit, everyone will benefit, and there will be an end to poverty. Yet this, as much as the hoped-for diminution in equality, is not at all self-evident. On the contrary the evidence suggests both that a substantial minority of the population live in destitution or near destitution and that they have few prospects of improvement at a time when the wealth of some sections of the population is increasing rapidly.

This is the real challenge facing the next Labour government, which many of us earnestly hope will be taken up. Can it stomach the thought that the social legislation of its 1945 predecessor could be bettered and, what is more, should now be critically reviewed? Can it make sure that the evidence necessary to formulate policy on such subjects of national importance as poverty and living standards is being collected, either by a better financed research and information department of its own, or preferably, by some independent body? Can it disengage itself from the cloying attentions of those who think it better to invest in machinery rather than people? And can it end the truce over inequality? To do so, it must apply social principles which radically improve the income and living conditions if the poor and handicapped and – at the small cost of limiting the individual's ability to secure advantages outrageously in excess of those available to other citizens – enlarge his freedom to choose what kind of life he shall lead.

# 22

# Poverty: has the welfare state failed?

An overall view of the kind of society we want to create depends on understanding its present structure and the changes that have been taking place in recent years. Living standards comprise only one, but an important aspect of such structure. The standard of living depends on the price of goods and services that are available to different sections of the population and on cash incomes, assets, industrial 'fringe' or welfare benefits and free and subsidized public services. It is difficult to reach firm conclusions about trends in living standards while methods for measuring the distribution of cash incomes remain rudimentary. Analysis must depend to some extent on crude indicators and judgment.

There seem to have been two general phases in the recent history of living standards in Britain. First, the levelling of standards that took place in the Second World War, which were maintained by the Labour Government for at least the first few years after the war. Secondly, the partial reversion to former inequalities, slow at first, but probably quite fast by the end of the 1950s. In aggregate the country was becoming more prosperous but some minorities were losing ground and poverty was again growing. By the mid-1960s, there were signs that a new, third, phase may have begun, but there is, as yet, too little evidence to be sure.

The emphasis on economic growth, and on the value of certain professional, managerial and technological skills, together with the disproportionately large increase of dependents in the population may have set in motion a structural drift of growing inequality which may occupy a period of some years.

While there has been common agreement about the first phase (though not about its extent) there has been much controversy about the second. In the period immediately following the Second World War, the increase in employment of women as well as high levels of employment for men, the introduction of promised social reforms and continuing high levels of taxation led many people to believe that Britain had abolished poverty and created a much more equal society. The differences between rich and poor, it was widely supposed, had been sharply reduced.

Some interpretations of the statistics suggested that "levelling" was continuing into the 1950s. In a paper in the *Journal of the Royal Statistical Society* for 1959, Harold Lydall wrote: "A study of the period 1938–57 reveals

Townsend, P. (1971) 'Poverty: has the welfare state failed?', *The Times*, 9 March.

a continuous trend towards greater equality in the distribution of allocated personal income…. For the future, unless there is a catastrophic slump, the trend towards equality is likely to continue, though probably not as fast as in the past 20 years". He found that the tendency towards reduced inequality of pre-tax incomes seemed to have been accelerating.

In his book, *Income Distribution and Social Change*, Professor Richard Titmuss questioned the statistics on which such early analyses were based. Recipients of income were ill-defined, and included a heterogenous collection of individuals and income units. The proportionate increase of incomes in the middle range between 1938 and 1955 might be attributed to decreased unemployment and to more employment of married women rather than to any reduction of earnings differentials or more egalitarian effects of fiscal policies. The apparent levelling of pre-tax incomes might be attributed not just to a fall in incomes from investment and rent but the employment of tax-evasion techniques; for example, passing on wealth to members of the family to escape death duties, sometimes while they continued to live in the same household.

Because changes were taking place in the structure of the general and employed population, as well as in the kind and use during life of resources, it was difficult to pin down the changing dimensions of inequality. Even if postwar was more equal than pre-war society, the change was much less dramatic than had been asserted by some and the evidence for a continued trend after 1950 was very partial.

During the 1950s salaries advanced slightly faster than wages. The earnings of certain professional and managerial groups rose markedly. Property incomes from rents, dividends and interest increased between 1955 and 1965 by 139 per cent, compared with 84 per cent for earned incomes. Tax concessions in successive budgets and increases in certain tax allowances tended to favour the higher income groups, even if their effects were counterbalanced by the higher taxes paid on earnings which continued to rise during this period of inflation. A trend in the admittedly incomplete statistics of income distribution had come to a halt.

In a *Lloyds Bank Review* article in 1967, which he has subsequently brought up to date, R.J. Nicholson found that the proportion of income after tax received by the top 10 per cent of income recipients decreased at some stage between 1949 and 1957. But with minor fluctuations, the proportion remained about the same between 1957 and 1967. One per cent of the income recipients with the highest incomes continued to receive about 5 per cent and the next 9 per cent received 19 to 20 per cent of the aggregate of all personal incomes after tax. But the incomes of the 30 per cent with the lowest incomes continued to diminish during both periods: from nearly 15 per cent to about 12 per cent of aggregate income. Correspondingly, there had been little change, except at the lowest levels of income, in the general structure of pre-tax incomes. The reduction of inequality of personal incomes appeared to have come to an end by the mid-1950s.

By the late 1960s even those who had spoken of a "continuing" postwar trend towards equality of personal incomes were beginning to reverse their opinions. In an important book (*The Structure of Earnings*, 1968) Harold Lydall assessed a wide range of international evidence on employment incomes and concluded that in 10 of the 11 countries for which there was information, the distribution of pre-tax incomes had not merely remained stationary during the 1950s but had actually widened. They included France, Germany, Sweden, Australia, Canada, New Zealand and the United States as well as the United Kingdom.

This tendency to widen did not apply to the earnings distribution of male manual workers in some countries, but was particularly marked for the distributions of non-manual and female employees in most countries.

## Tax avoidance

These assessments do not tell the whole story, however. The statistics about personal incomes for the United Kingdom include no allowance for increased valuations of capital assets, differential movements in prices, or the effects of indirect taxation and free or subsidized social services. R.J. Nicholson, for example, accepted the possibility that if certain "tax avoidance" incomes and other claims on wealth outside personal income had increased in the late 1950s and early 1960s, "the distribution of incomes on some wider definition may have moved towards greater inequality".

The best source of information about changes in the real distribution of resources and one which could be further improved, is the Family Expenditure Survey. The non-response rate is disturbingly large and fluctuations attributable to sampling errors reduce the opportunities for reaching precise conclusions about trends from year to year. It is particularly difficult to generalize clearly about trends affecting the richest and poorest groups in the population. None the less, the accompanying table, based on a recent analysis of the survey in *Economic Trends*, shows, first, that except for the lagging of households with one child, the "final" incomes of different types of family have been rising at roughly similar rates since 1961. Second, the levels of income of most types of family remain in roughly the same relationship as they were in 1961: the family with three children, for example, having 150 per cent more income than the one-person household after paying all taxes and receiving all benefits, compared with 148 per cent eight years previously.

Finally, among the families within each type there has been no pronounced change in the dispersion of incomes, the poorest 20 per cent being in 1969 at about the same and, if anything, a little below the level of income

## Income after all taxes and social service benefits of different types of household

| Type of household | Income as per cent of: | | | | | | Per cent of the median income below which 20% of each category live | | |
| | Income in 1961 | | | Income received by one adult | | | | | |
| | 1961 | 1965 | 1969 | 1961 | 1965 | 1969 | 1961 | 1965 | 1969† |
|---|---|---|---|---|---|---|---|---|---|
| One adult (excl. pensioners) | 100 | 131 | 160 | 100 | 100 | 100 | 70 | 72 | 71 |
| Two adults (excl. pensioners) | 100 | 120 | 153 | 181 | 167 | 173 | 70 | 72 | 69 |
| Two adults, one child | 100 | 124 | 147 | 206 | 194 | 189 | 74 | 75 | 73 |
| Two adults, two children | 100 | 120 | 158 | 210 | 230 | 227 | 73 | 75 | 76 |
| Two adults, three children | 100 | 126 | 162 | 248 | 238 | 230 | 78 | 73 | 78 |
| Two adults, four children | 100 | 121 | 158 | 276 | 254 | 271 | 86 | 77 | 79 |
| Three adults | | | | | | | 74 | 75 | 73 |
| Three adults, one child | | | | | | | 80 | 76 | 79 |
| Three adults, two children | | | | | | | 80 | 76 | 77 |
| Four adults | | | | | | | 81 | 78 | 78 |
| All households | 100 | 123* | 156* | 208 | 192 | 196 | 56 | 55 | 54 |

* Estimated according to constant distribution by size of households
† Published figures increased at most by 1 per cent to maintain 1961 and 1965 definitions of income for 1969

they had reached in relation to the median income in 1961. There is no evidence of a trend towards equality at low levels of living but, if anything, a faint reverse trend. Compared with a slight relative improvement in the incomes of the poorest couples with two children, there has been a slight deterioration in the incomes of the poorest couples with one child and of couples with four or more children, as well as of households comprising three adults and children. The figures dip for seven out of 10 categories and although the fluctuations due to sampling must be remembered the trends were broadly the same in 1968.

These results allow for the effects of indirect as well as direct taxes. The Family Expenditure Survey data show that indirect taxes take a larger proportion of low than of high incomes and that among low-income families with children, indirect taxes have increased sharply as a proportion of income, particularly between 1965 and 1968. Recent increases in indirect taxes and national insurance contributions seem to have more than counter-balanced any progressive effects of income tax and surtax. The British tax system overall is very unprogressive.

But the results allow inadequately for the value to families of the social services. Actual cash benefits are allocated to personal incomes but only imputed average National Health Service and educational benefits. Because of higher rates of illness and disability, some low-income families may in fact obtain more value than average from the Health Service. On the other hand, when the children of high-income families attend grammar schools and universities they may benefit to a greater extent than average from the public subsidy. During the past 15 years, the middle-income groups have gained substantially from the disproportionate expansion of higher education. Some benefits that are received predominantly by middle and high-income groups, such as housing improvement grants, are not taken into account at all. Other benefits may be worth more than their face value. Between 1963-64 and 1969-70, the value of tax reliefs to private owner-occupiers increased from £90m to £215m. The average value per recipient, taking no account of capital appreciation, was about £48 in the latter year.

Industrial fringe benefits are now of considerable importance and, as Lydall remarks, may offset the equalizing effects of progressive income taxes in many countries. Recently they were estimated to add 20 per cent to managerial staff salaries of around £4,000 and over 30 per cent to salaries in excess of £7,000. Although the scope of such benefits has widened in recent years they are sharply regressive.

It is difficult to come to firm conclusions about trends in the distribution of wealth. Since the war there has been some decrease in the holdings of the richest 1 per cent, but this has been largely balanced by an increase in the holdings of the next 9 per cent, so that the concentration of wealth remains considerable. Indeed, wealth is distributed more unequally in Britain than in most other industrial countries. According to Board of Inland Revenue data the richest 10 per cent own nearly three-quarters of total personal wealth. Other studies show that the poorest 50 per cent have no liquid assets at all or very few.

Finally, price increases have affected the poor more than the rich. Since it was started the Retail Price Index for pensioners has kept slightly ahead of the general index. More generally, for the period 1955-66, D.G. Tipping has shown that at the lowest levels of income prices increased by 4.3 per cent more than they did for the highest levels of income – mainly because of the disproportionate rise in rents and the costs of fuel and light.

## Real incomes

The fact that differentials in pre-tax and post-tax incomes seem to have changed comparatively little in recent years is in some respects puzzling. Even Britain's slow rate of economic growth has been accompanied by a big change in the distribution of occupations. Between 1955 and 1969 the national salary bill increased by 198 per cent but the wages bill by only 106 per cent. As a proportion of all salaries and wages the former grew from 34 per cent to 42 per cent. But there is no evidence of depreciation of salaries relative to wages. The average salary has remained substantially larger than the average wage. How can this be explained? It would seem that some groups among wage-earners have not kept pace with the rise in real earnings and that the shift towards expensive salaried employment has been financed by the growth of inexpensive unemployment and retirement, including premature retirement.

It is therefore reasonably certain that, in spite of social and incomes legislation, greater equality of real incomes was not achieved between the mid-1950s and 1970. On the contrary, there seems to have been a shift in the reverse direction which is understated if attention is paid only to the conventional statistics of personal income distribution or even to the broader measures of the Family Expenditure Survey.

This conclusion contradicts a good deal of popular and political suppositions. The problem is not appreciated quite so keenly as that of inequalities between rich and poor nations. Unless properly documented and understood we may continue to fail to adapt our policies to bring about greater social justice and hence greater social cohesion and, it may be argued, economic prosperity.

# 23

# How the rich stay rich

A highly sophisticated struggle is going on for the soul of the Labour Party. There are those who believe that the rich, whether defined in terms of wealth or income, or both wealth and income, are getting substantially poorer (and therefore that socially redistributive policies no longer have to be pressed). Then there are those who believe that the rich, whether or not they are now getting poorer, have in the course of history become a relatively inconsequential element in the decisions that have to be made politically and economically. Thus, even if they were squeezed, it is supposed they could not provide more than a small fraction of the resources required to put major new policies into effect. Then, again, there are those who believe that the rich, whatever their wealth or power, have to be left alone either because of the risk of offending overseas creditors or because otherwise there would not be a sufficient system of inducements for the work force as well as management. Thus, any substantial shift from existing differentials and patterns of private consumption might be supposed to threaten the delicate balance of the whole economy and not just the livelihood of a small number of workers in particular industries. And finally, of course, there are those in whose interests it is to foster these illusions.

The volumes of evidence (particularly the third volume) submitted to the Royal Commission on the Distribution of Income and Wealth and just published[1] illustrate these benefits for socialists. They show how important it is to engage with, and to counter, the views accepting inequality which are so assiduously cultivated, and which have even infiltrated some of the principal conclusions of the Royal Commission itself. For example, major companies and financial organisations and their representative associations – like BP, Commercial Union Assurance, Dunlop, Esso Petroleum, IBM (UK), ICI, Rio Tinto-Zinc, Unilever, the CBI, the Brewers' Society, the British Bankers' Association, the National Westminster, the Institute of Directors – produced memorandum after memorandum to impress upon the Commission the onerous and responsible, and quite exceptional, job that senior executives perform, the low salaries and small value of non-monetary benefits which they receive, and the excessive taxes which they pay in relation to their peers in other countries, the threat to national prosperity if they were to emigrate, and, above all, the fall in their incomes in recent

Townsend, P. (1976) 'How the rich stay rich', *New Statesman*, 1 October, pp 441-3.

years relative to the average. The last sentence of ICI's evidence in 1975 summed it all up: "The company's case is not merely that there should be no further impositions on this group of employees but that action is needed to see that their relative position is restored" (p.207).

Support for some of these themes reiterated by representatives of the private sector of industry has come too from the nationalised industries and professional associations. The Central Electricity Generating Board, the National Coal Board, the National Gas Corporation and the British Railways Board, for example, made a plea for relatively higher salaries for top managers. British Rail argued that because the public sector could not compete with private industry in providing fringe benefits like profit bonuses, profit sharing, share options and company cars, its salaries should in fact be higher than in the private sector. And, while it did not mind unearned income being attacked, a joint committee representing top civil servants quietly urged the Commission not to 'subvert' the salary structures resulting from the work of Lord Boyle's Top Salaries Review Body, and the National Board for Prices and Incomes.

The TUC was a partial and the TGWU a more outspoken exception. But the TUC was depressingly evasive. While protesting at the non-disclosure of information about non-monetary as well as monetary rewards of senior executives and listing some of their perks, it did not proclaim an emphatic alternative policy: "£10,000 cannot be a practicable limit to earnings at the present time although there might be a case for saying that increases above that level should be the subject of particular restraint" (p.404). Or again: "The Royal Commission should first of all consider the incomes span which might be judged reasonable in terms of the various precepts by which the economic and social life of the country is carried on – such precepts as freedom and market forces on the one hand and social justice and the notion of the social contract on the other – and then proceed to consider the ways of handling the consequential difficulties of taking an upper figure (e.g. £20,000 before tax or £10,000 after tax) as a limit" (p.405). In oral evidence Len Murray, Lord Allen and Alan Fisher said the present range of incomes was too wide but "the TUC recognised the need for income differentials as a recognition of responsibility, training and scarce skills" (p.406). The first steps in legitimating very high employment incomes, even if not the top-most incomes, had been taken.

The problems for those within a Labour Government who are struggling to reduce inequality can begin to be seen. The Royal Commission had been established in 1974 to make a thorough and comprehensive inquiry into the existing distribution of income and wealth "to help secure a fairer distribution on income and wealth in the community". It was asked to prepare a preliminary general report within about 12 months and, almost before that task had been started, to prepare a second report on income from companies and its distribution, and a third on all forms of income over about £10,000 a year from employment and self-employment.

The three inquiries were conducted more or less simultaneously. Under its chairman, Lord Diamond, and with the help of its 40 staff, the Commission published three bulky reports on schedule in 1975-76. What now transpires from the evidence submitted as a basis for these reports is the almost inevitable impact upon the conclusions of a Royal Commission, if time has not been made or allowed for its own independent inquiries, of the cumulative weight of the conventional wisdom of the departments of state, industry and some of the principal professional associations – especially when its membership includes powerful advocates of such wisdom. Is it possible to check the 'fairness' of a system by depending upon its principal beneficiaries for information about it?

Much of the problem is in constructing a valid picture of the whole distribution of income and wealth, within which the position of the rich can be judged. The Commission valiantly reproduced the searching criticisms made of official statistics by some of the more independent-minded economists, like Tony Atkinson, Alan Harrison and Chris Trinder, as well as by the TUC and TGWU. Yet they shrank from asking whether inequality is as a consequence under-estimated and therefore whether existing data needed to be extensively reworked and new data collected, so that the nation might better be confronted with the realities of its own condition, and went on to draw conclusions from the very material which, on their own argument, were misleading.

## Defining income

For example, near the beginning of the first report they stated: "We began our inquiry without prejudging whether income and wealth might be susceptible of a single, all-embracing definition" (p.4). But the possibility of defining income as the sum of personal consumption and net capital formation was dismissed in four short paragraphs and the further possibility of expressing wealth as an annuity value, and, for purposes of giving necessarily crude measures of the distribution of 'real' living standards or total command over resources, adding such a value to income, was not even seriously discussed. Less ambitious alternatives too might have been tried – namely to estimate rental values for certain possessions (including owner-occupied housing) and add them to income, or to present analyses linking ranked levels of income with different amounts of wealth. A short section on the effect of including and excluding imputed rent was included in the report, but the experiment was vitiated by the use of official estimates admitted to be much too low.

The importance of this matter can be put quite simply. The distinction made between income as a 'flow' over a period of time and wealth as a 'stock' at a point in time, or between revenue and capital, has the effect in practice of concealing or underestimating inequalities in living standards or life styles. The ramifications culturally and politically of this distinction are profound. The distribution of wealth is more unequal than the distribution of income, and income is highly correlated with wealth. The connections and cumulations are insufficiently examined and presented. While conceding lamely the artificiality of the distinction the Royal Commission decided it was impracticable to do anything very different, and proceeded to develop separate analyses of income and wealth in their first report (pp.5-6).

This is not the only source of the underestimation of inequality. The definition and measurement of wealth is elusive and open to different interpretations. If the resources of the rich are held disproportionately by the extended family, and can be drawn upon through trusts and settlements at later stages of life, and depersonalised in part through the company share system, are spread among a large number of types of wealth, and have artificially low current market value, then the significance of restricted definitions of wealth becomes clear. By restricting the size of the social unit, the range of items to be counted, the currency of convertibility and the time in which measurement is to take place, inequality again may be understated. The relationship of wealth – and particularly of stocks and shares, pension rights and houses and flats – to top employment incomes can be critical.

The Royal Commission admitted in its first report that the official statistics on the distribution of income were 'deficient in many respects', largely because these were 'by-products of the administrative processes of government departments, particularly the Inland Revenue'. The Inland Revenue omits incomes below the effective tax exemption limit – the level at which a single person starts to pay tax if his income is wholly earned. It sometimes separates, and sometimes combines, the incomes of married couples. It excludes tax relief on mortgage interest, and the imputed rental value of owner-occupied housing, thus underestimating the share of income going to the top half of the distribution. It understates investment income, fringe benefits from employers and some other forms of income. These are among the commonly agreed weaknesses.

The top section of the table [overleaf] is an extract from Table 15 of the Commission's first report. It suggests a continuing fall since the war in the share of income after tax of top income recipients. The press seized on the Commission's conclusion to maintain the belief that the rich have become relatively poorer not just in post-war compared with pre-war years but in the 1970s compared with 1960.

The data collected in the annual Family Expenditure Survey, carried out regularly since 1957, are potentially more valuable than either the Inland Revenue data or the Central Statistical Office adaptations of those data. There are doubts about the representativeness of both extremes of the

## Distribution of Personal Income (United Kingdom)

| Quantile group | A: Percentage share of income after income tax (tax units; IR Survey of Personal Incomes supplemented by other data by the Central Statistical Office) | | | | | |
|---|---|---|---|---|---|---|
| | 1949 | 1959 | 1964 | 1967 | 1972/3 | |
| Top 1 per cent | 6.4 | 5.3 | 5.3 | 4.9 | 4.4 | |
| 2-5 per cent | 11.3 | 10.5 | 10.7 | 9.9 | 9.8 | |
| 6-10 per cent | 9.4 | 9.4 | 9.9 | 9.5 | 9.4 | |
| Top 10 per cent | 27.1 | 25.2 | 25.9 | 24.3 | 23.6 | |
| | B: Percentage share of net income (after direct taxes and cash benefits) (households; CSO, based on Family Expenditure Survey) | | | | | |
| | 1961 | 1965 | 1968 | 1971 | 1972 | 1973 |
| Top 1 per cent | 4.4 | 4.8 | 5.9 | 4.4 | 3.8 | 4.4 |
| 2-5 per cent | 9.9 | 9.5 | 9.7 | 9.9 | 9.6 | 10.0 |
| 6-10 per cent | 9.2 | 9.1 | 9.1 | 9.6 | 9.3 | 9.5 |
| Top 10 per cent | 23.5 | 23.4 | 24.7 | 23.9 | 22.7 | 23.9 |
| | C: Percentage share of final income (after all taxes and benefits in cash and kind) (households; CSO, based on Family Expenditure Survey) | | | | | |
| | 1961 | 1965 | 1968 | 1971 | 1972 | 1973 |
| Top 1 per cent | 4.6 | 4.5 | 4.2 | 4.2 | 3.8 | 4.2 |
| 2-5 per cent | 9.8 | 9.6 | 9.8 | 9.8 | 9.7 | 9.8 |
| 6-10 per cent | 9.3 | 9.2 | 9.4 | 9.4 | 9.5 | 9.4 |
| Top 10 per cent | 23.7 | 23.3 | 23.4 | 23.4 | 23.0 | 23.4 |

distribution, and, as the name implies, the survey is designed to obtain more comprehensive and reliable information about expenditure than about income. But the data apply to genuine household units, and also take into account the indirect as well as direct taxation, and a limited measure of fringe benefits. The Commission had produced data from the Inland Revenue, adjusted by the CSO, for the top 1 per cent, next 4 per cent and next 5 per cent, as shown in the table. Corresponding data which they took from the FES applied only to the top 10 per cent, and were included in an appendix to their first report.

In the lower part of the table, with the help of the Commission's staff, I have reproduced the corresponding estimates of percentage shares of net income and final income. Reservations have to be borne in mind. The figures for the top 10 per cent are more reliable than for the top 5 per cent, and the figures for the top 1 per cent are distinctly hazardous. Nonetheless the share of the top 5 per cent and top 10 per cent are consistent for a long span and tell a different story from the conclusions put forward by the Commission, based only on the Blue Book figures, that "there has been a continuing decline in the share of the top 5 per cent" (p.156). At the very least it should be said that there is no consistent evidence of a diminution in the last 15 years of the income share of the top 5 per cent and top 10 per cent. Indeed, if the fringe benefits and imputed rent for owner–occupation were properly reflected in the figures the trend might have been the *reverse* of that identified by the Commission.

One of the problems of interpreting trends is in allowing for changes in the proportions of households or income units of different size and composition. A recent study by Semple in *Economic Trends* (December 1975) reviewed the effect of changes in household composition between 1961 and 1973 on the distribution of income and found "relative stability in the degree of inequality in the distribution of final income".

Just as the FES data for a span of years may be used to cast doubt on the proposition in the first report that the percentage share of income of the top 5 per cent has diminished during the last 15 years, so material on fringe benefits and taxation in the third report (in chapter 4 and appendix H) and in the evidence submitted for that report casts doubt on the proposition that the values of the employment income of the top 0.01 per cent, the top 0.1 per cent and top 1.0 per cent of men have declined relative to the median and also in absolute purchasing power. Thus the top 0.01 per cent had net employment income estimated to be 1,140 per cent of the median in 1959-60 but 723 per cent in 1973-74 (Table 9, p.25). At constant 1959-60 prices this was stated to represent a decline from £6.952 to £5,903 (Table 11, p.30).

This finding, too, was widely reported in the press. But doubts about its reliability were raised by witnesses who should know. In their evidence the Inland Revenue Staff Federation states that "most directors might enjoy a higher standard of living than was revealed in the income tax statistics". "... Revenue control over non–monetary benefits might have declined ... while all benefits were taxable in practice, many were not." The Association of Her Majesty's Inspectors of Taxes suggested that income from self–employment was evaded more than in the past. It also agreed that because of tax avoidance on fringe benefits the number of employees earning over £10,000 per annum "looked smaller than might be expected". And the Central Statistical Office pointed out that only about one third of the total value of non–taxable benefits in kind could at present be allocated in their income distribution tables (in this case for 1972-73.) The Commission must be chastised for producing figures based on theoretical, rather than actual, taxation and for making no provision for a full definition of fringe benefits, and for their changing value.

## Fringe benefits

The Commission did give detailed evidence of types of fringe benefits and changes in coverage, though no attempt was made to relate these two trends in employment income. Thus between 1970 (or 1971) and 1975 companies offering pension coverage on a 'final salary' basis to their managerial staff grew from 84 per cent to 94 per cent, companies offering life insurance from 93 per cent to 98 per cent, medical insurance from 20 per cent to 53 per cent, and holiday entitlement of more than five weeks from 29 per cent to 43 per cent (p.91). The Commission admitted that share acquisition schemes and reduced interest or interest-free loans "can be of considerable financial advantage to their recipients" (p.89).

Fixed-term service contracts have now become a major factor in the remuneration of senior executives. They "might have been entered into with a view to providing employees with additional benefits" (p.93) and the first £5,000 of compensation is normally tax free. The Commission reported it had received no evidence on this point. But according to the Institute of Directors' evidence (p.228), the number of executive directors with a fixed contract, usually between three and five years, had increased from 35 per cent to 48 per cent between 1966 and 1974. Elsewhere McKinsey's had described these contracts as "handsome pay-offs for poor performance". This change alone might critically affect any representation of the share of the top 1 per cent and top 5 per cent of income recipients. Further, calculations of the value to managers of a company car, housing loans at reduced rates of interest, other loans and medical insurance all suggested substantial percentage additions to salary, and that "pension provisions have been growing as a proportion of salary for higher executives" (p.101).

Although I have not listed all the details, the thrust of my argument must be clear. In remunerating top executives there has been a long-term, and continuing, substitution or supplementation of direct salary by indirect benefits in order to escape tax in one form or another. The press and the Conservative Party made capital out of the alleged fall in top incomes, as in Tables 9 and 11 of the third report. No tabulations of trends should have been published without adjustments to take full account of the value of fringe benefits. And if, as the Commission stated, "it is not possible to allocate the value of fringe benefits by level of total employment income" without further work, that work should have been undertaken before publication. A few hastily concocted and politically misleading tables can wipe out the cumulative value of hundreds of pages which have been patiently compiled. Whether because of pressures of time or accumulated forces of established opinion the Commission appears so far to have nurtured myths convenient to the rich.

The TUC and the Labour Party have spent their time knocking the exceptionally wealthy instead of making a careful case against the affluent standards of income and property among the senior managers and professionals who comprise the bulk of the top 5 per cent. If there is to be hope for the 8 million in or on the margins of poverty that case must be made.

**Endnote**

[1] Royal Commission on the Distribution of Income and Wealth, Selected Evidence Submitted to the Royal Commission for Reports Nos. 1, 2 and 3, London, HMSO 1976.

# 24

# The pursuit of equality

All the concepts which are used to characterise social structure and social conditions, like 'inequality', but also 'family', 'community', 'class', 'solidarity', 'bureaucracy', 'poverty' and 'state', are highly debatable and are disputed even more keenly within the social sciences than they are politically. Such concepts remain controversial despite being central to theories, of social development and therefore to political practice. There are two reasons for this. One is that the key ideas which are passed on to people by parents, peers and educators, and which represent the living history of a culture, may not be necessarily valid or remain valid. The other is that the ideas we take over mentally to construct our images of society reflect, and usually reinforce, our position in society. This applies as much to professional people, including academic social scientists and those who speak on behalf of pressure groups, as to administrators, managers, the propertied rich and politicians holding office. Our perceptions of what inequality and injustice are depend in considerable measure on the position in society from which we look at the world.

These discoveries that culture may mislead and that perceptions as well as learned beliefs may be self-interested can be very unsettling. They may cause us to question some of the cherished beliefs which, as representatives of society and or the social classes in that society, we hold. But they may also lead to the search for a more objective or rational anchorage for our beliefs. Both discoveries can play their part in liberating us from unduly conservative and self-interested approaches to meaning and hence from subservience to the policy implications for social structures of conventional uses of language.

Abhorrence of inequality is part of a radical political tradition in Britain which has deep roots. The repeated protests of the nineteenth century were not just about differences of status, abstract notions of power, or even of enjoyment of life's comforts, but about thoroughly unjust, undeserved and unnecessary exploitation and misery, on the one hand, and thoroughly unjust, undeserved and unnecessary assertion of power and wealth, on the other. Rank and power are intertwined, so a concern with inequality reflects concern both about degrees of wealth and lack of rights. The structures and experiences of inequality give credence to both the social scientific and the political party preoccupation with inequality.

---

Townsend, P. (1983) 'The pursuit of equality', *Poverty*, pp 11–15.

The labour movement drew its inspiration from newly stated ideals of the substitution of equality for inequality. The objective adopted originally in 1890 by the Fabian Society, for example, reads: 'It ... aims at the reorganisation of society by the emancipation of land and industrial capital from individual and class ownership, and the vesting of them in the community for the general benefit. In this way only can the natural and acquired advantages of the country be equitably shared by the whole people.' The preoccupation with the cruel outcomes of inequality, from which logically followed policies to establish equality, became the bedrock of constitutional socialism, permeated the thought of socialists of successive generations like Robert Owen, William Morris, R.H. Tawney and, to give a modern example, E.P. Thompson, and came to dominate intellectual and policy debates about public ownership of industry, local government, education, housing and health.

The argument has proceeded at every level. It has become central to philosophical disquisition about the state, the rights of citizenship, and the relationship between equality and justice. How could particular policies to uphold or diminish inequality be legitimated? This is of lively concern to modern philosophers. In his *A Theory of Justice*, John Rawls has proposed that democratic societies require a fundamental principle of justice – called the 'difference' principle. 'Social and economic inequalities, for example inequalities of wealth and authority, are just only if they result in compensating benefits for everyone, and in particular for the least advantaged members of society.' Some of us would argue that this represents little more than a restatement of the traditional liberal-pluralist position, directing attention to the outcomes or consequences of inequalities rather than to their origins or maintenance, and that a more comprehensive criticism of the ideology and institutions which favour inequality is required. But even the degree of exposure of inequality to the principled analytic tests of people like Rawls has attracted a lot of criticism from conservative liberals in different strongholds of Weberian and functionalist sociology and political science, who uphold 'natural' or 'necessary' inequality. The neo-monetarists are currently dismissive of Rawls' attempts to reintroduce mild tests or criteria for the sanctioning of inequality. They are at the forefront of a philosophical, social scientific and political reaction against the principle of equality and the embodiment of these principles (albeit so weakly, we might comment) within the institutions of the welfare state and the militant agencies of the working class, particularly the trade unions. The values of the 'new' individualism are to be found not just in the thin prescriptions at the Institute for Economic Affairs and Sir Keith Joseph but in the professional economics of monetarism and its neo-Keynesian alternative. In his book *Testing Monetarism*, Meghnad Desai traces the resurgence of this ideology from the mid-1970s. More recently, Nick Bosanquet, Stuart Hall and Martin Jacques, and Ian Gough are among those who have written extensively in opposition to the case which is being made on behalf of inequality within the social sciences as well as by government ministers.

The arguments of those in favour of a more entrenched inequality need to be examined carefully and met. In this country Steven Rose has led the attack on those who have asserted natural inequalities between races, for example, and in the United States, Philip Green has published a review of what he calls the 'shabby historical record of inegalitarianism' in the first of a two-volume analysis. In *The Pursuit of Inequality* (Martin Robertson, 1981), he dissects the work of neo-conservative theoreticians who have sought to rationalise inequalities of race, class and sex, including Arthur Jensen, Richard Herrnstein and Steven Goldberg, and who have sought to justify the structural inequalities of the state, including Milton Friedman, Robert Nozick, Friedrich Hayek and Irving Kristol. As a result, he demonstrates the case for detailed exposition of the modern, and increasingly international, case for equality.

In present conditions of extreme deprivation and mass poverty that case deserves to be presented fully and more positively. One part of that case is to relate better the connected theories of poverty and of inequality. This implies making a change of scientific and political direction, to which a number of writers have lately contributed, including myself. Among other things, such a change means giving greater recognition to the fact that individual needs arise through membership of society and not only through bodily requirements for warmth, shelter, food and clothing. People are social beings and not just physical beings. Such recognition leads inevitably to interest in the institutional processes by which social roles and customs are originated and maintained, and therefore the part played by the state, industry and the wealthy classes in 'manufacturing' poverty in the first place, rather than the part they might play in alleviating that condition once it is identified. The obligations at work, in family and community and as citizens which we feel bound to fulfil, using such incomes as we can command, are moulded in predominant measure by the rich through state laws and the establishment of social norms. Therefore, we have to look at the influences exerted by the rich in defining and controlling the conditions, and setting the fashions, which are continually redefining and reconstituting the structures of need which citizens experience in their everyday lives.

This line of analysis has a number of consequences. It means that the poverty and deprivation experienced by large sections of the population are not simply experiences which have arisen by chance or by misfortune and which only have to be publicised to ensure that countervailing action will be compelled by a sympathetic and receptive public opinion, aided and abetted by liberal philosophers and politicians. They are experiences which flow directly and indirectly from the operations of industry, the banking system, the wage system and the property system generally, are condoned by the media, and can be met only by action to reorganise such institutions. The argument has to be shifted from redistribution to production and distribution. A shift also has to be made from individualistic to social values.

The connections between the production of wealth and the production of poverty have to be made, and therefore the philosophy and the strategies of prevention – through structural action – have to be given priority and carefully elaborated and discussed.

The preoccupation in debates about the welfare state with the 'casualties' of the economy or of the functioning of society, and with the use of the economic surplus for social services to aid such casualties, must be balanced by more assertive intellectual reasoning about the major beneficiaries of the system. On what principles ought power to be lodged in the productive organisations of the economy and the state? On what principles does the wage system come to be constructed, and on what principles should the receipt of high incomes but also inherited wealth be based? The creative forces of social structure and the economy deserve to be put under the spotlight.

A more comprehensive application of the principles of equality would therefore have the following implications for policy. The rewards of entrepreneurial and productive activity, as well as of rights to property, would have to be closely examined. The introduction of a maximum wage would be even more important, in bringing about greater equity, than the introduction of a minimum wage. Perhaps social control of wages and other incomes, via some kind of social dividend scheme (entirely different from oppressive schemes for negative income tax), would be substituted for income taxation as the primary instrument of fair distribution of disposable income. And society would play a more creative role in determining the nature of paid employment, as well as access to such employment. Social policy would be centrally about the social production and distribution of wealth, fair allocation of incomes and sponsorship of employment and access to employment – rather than largely about cash and services for dependent minorities. It would also be about equitable structures of relationships at work, in the community and at home and how they can be brought about and maintained.

The articles in this issue of *Poverty* explore some of the practical ways by which some aspects of inequalities, in particular in employment opportunities and in income distribution, may be reduced and equality strengthened. They make a small contribution to the need to revive the discussion on equality. Two pieces of evidence may be cited to demonstrate that the case for greater equality must not be regarded as a lost cause. In a recent national opinion poll carried out by MORI, three-quarters of the population said that the rich obtained more than their fair share of resources and large majorities gave their assent to other egalitarian sentiments. Secondly, the Treasury's statistics show that the wealthiest 20 per cent of the population would only need to lose about a fifth of their present disposable incomes to finance a doubling of the incomes of the poorest 20 per cent, and even then the richest 20 per cent would remain three or four times as well off. These are the grounds for a more comprehensive pursuit of equality in our national life.

# 25

# A matter of class

Poverty has returned to Britain on a mass scale, and in an increasing number of instances is taking an extreme form. What explains such a remarkable change within a single generation?

One explanation is to say simply that dependency has increased. The rise in the numbers of elderly, disabled and unemployed people, and one-parent families would then be described. But behind that rather superficial 'explanation' lies the fact that, irrespective of changes in the structure of the population, the deficiencies of the social security system and generally of the welfare state have remained largely uncorrected.

This opens up a more promising line of enquiry. Historically, redistribution never went as far in Britain as in some other countries. Intentions spoke louder than action. Whenever radical proposals threatened to be implemented, like national superannuation in 1964 or child benefit in 1975, the resolution of ministers weakened and expectations placed upon them were not maintained. Other proposals were watered down during the process of parliamentary legislation and administrative implementation.

What was wrong with the British welfare state in all these years? Benefits for the poor were low; anomalies abounded; revenue from progressive taxes remained small; and the middle classes gained quite a lot from fiscal welfare and employer welfare as well as from the public sector. During the last 20 years pressure groups and certain radical social scientists have put forward these themes in concocting an explanation for continuing, and now rapidly accelerating, poverty.

A single example will help to illustrate the argument. The OECD recently published an analysis of social expenditure in its 19 member countries. Between 1960 and 1981 Britain slumped from 9th to 12th in expenditure ranked according to gross domestic product (GDP). During the period 1960 to 1975 its rate of growth of social expenditure was second lowest of the 19 countries, and such rate of growth remained second lowest during the period 1975 to 1981.[1] In scale of development and level of benefits the British welfare state can be demonstrated to be one of the least impressive in Europe. Whether redistribution is also much less effective than in many other places is, of course, more difficult to demonstrate, though I believe likely.

---

Townsend, P. (1986) 'A matter of class', *Poverty*, Winter, pp 12-14.

The problem with this explanation is that it leads only to limited exposition of the failings of the welfare state, defensive statements about poor minorities, alternative policy scenarios which tend to be restricted to improvements in the system of benefits and, in the end, lame exhortations to radically disposed politicians to try harder. What is missing is the link to class and the link to the policy institutions of the rich. For though this approach to the growth of poverty, that is, the failure of welfare institutions, helps to explain why new as well as old forms of poverty are inadequately alleviated, it does not explain how poverty is being allowed to grow, nor what is generating it. A lot more has to be explained about structure, and about process.

## The manufacture of poverty

Britain is recognisably a more deeply etched class society than its neighbours. At one level, no one attempts to deny it. British residents even express a kind of masochistic self-satisfaction at the wonder displayed by overseas visitors at the variations in dress, accents, mannerisms and rituals which are everywhere to be encountered. We have plenty enough reminders of the foibles of the Royal Princes, Lords, Henley Regatta, Ascot and the private schools. The public are avidly interested, curious and indulgently amused by turns. But the icons of the rich in Britain provide more than a spectacle or a diversion. They condition attitudes to other relationships.

Currently the firm Nissan is sponsoring an advertisement which is taking the mickey out of the social distance from the shop floor which is a feature of British management. That carries the punch which my reference to the importance of class in Britain is intended to have. Enough work has been done to oblige analysts to concede that class has something to do with management's poor performance in the British economy. It also has a lot to do with the flight of investment and indifference to growing unemployment during this period of the internationalisation of the economy.

Class is as important to the explanation of growing poverty as it is to the explanation of flagging economic performance. Thus, despite many years of nearly full employment, and universal commitment to the principle of full employment, mass unemployment has been allowed to return in a very short span of years. Thirty years ago the late Tony Crosland wrote approvingly of the post-war agreement which existed between the major political parties about post-war social changes. 'Any government which tampered seriously with the basic structure of the full-employment welfare state would meet with a sharp reverse at the polls.'[2] By 1983 that assumption looked like ancient history.

With the benefits of hindsight we might argue that the fractions of class have defeated the contract of universal social rights constructed with difficulty in the war and early post-war years. It is not merely that unemployment has been allowed by public opinion to grow. The threat of unemployment was dormant in class attitudes, and was then used with growing confidence by employers and boards of management, who wished to restore a previous ascendancy, who undervalued sections of the labour force and who did not believe in any form of cohesion or identity with their fellow workers. They also assume they are not accountable for actions which have deep effects. A future generation will wonder how we could permit employers to make thousands immediately redundant and put communities at risk without extensive public cross-examination. All we can affirm is that those actions have arisen out of a system of class relationships and have been legitimated by the ideology of liberal-pluralism and, within that, monetarism.

The representatives of Labour have directly or indirectly subscribed to that change. They have preferred improvements in wages for a majority to the maintenance of jobs for that minority who have lost them. And despite the multiplication of insecure, dangerous and poorly paid jobs at the bottom end of the labour market, organised manual workers have continued to give high priority to the preservation of long-standing differentials and have not been committed to high or equal incomes for those among them who become ill, unemployed or redundant.

The importance of class can be shown in the manufacture of other forms of poverty. Examples are provided any week. This summer it was the turn of the 'medieval brigands' of Stonehenge. A relatively mild version of social non-conformity was treated with brutal savagery by the police, with the endorsement of Members of Parliament, the judiciary and the Home Secretary, as well as land-owners and farmers. The incidents provide a revealing cameo of class attitudes to poverty. These itinerants are modern gypsies, constructing a viable if hazardous life-style in reaction to a scarcity of jobs, housing, and even social security benefits. Their numbers have gained additional impetus from the government's policy of lodging allowances for young unemployed, which oblige many to keep on the move. How are people expected to respond to homelessness and very high rates of unemployment? What if councils refuse land for temporary structures and camps?

The National Farmers Union has consistently opposed every proposal for official caravan sites under the 1968 Caravan Sites Act. Some people who cannot price themselves into ordinary communities are creating their own. Must they be persecuted and hounded for a form of poverty not of their making? When several hundred police carried out a military-style operation to evict them from a relatively innocuous presence in the New Forest, they were deprived of their homes and transport. It was yet another painful glimpse in England of the tactics used by an increasingly authoritarian regime. It was reminiscent of the tactics used in South Africa against the fragile shelters of the squatter camps.

In the short run the British class system is not going to succumb to the blandishments of CPAG or anyone else in favour of more generous and civilised treatment of poor people. That system provides a fertile basis for current authoritarian versions of both state and market politics. The so-called hippies in Hampshire and Dorset, and the squatters evicted in Southwark, are only the latest groups to be drawn into the representation of the welfare state as the protective institution of the scrounger, the feckless poor and the workshy. That the evidence of fraud or abuse shows it to be tiny makes little impression on those whose class beliefs tell them otherwise. This is the populist folk-devil beloved of the British media but nurtured, both consciously and unconsciously, by powerful vested interests.

We must not make the mistake of supposing that the growth of poverty has been accidental, unintended and merely a by-product of economic or technological change. It is the logical, indeed inevitable, result of strategies of self-aggrandisement and cost or damage limitation followed by corporate enterprises and wealth-holders but also, to a lesser extent, by the professions and bureaucratic organisations which largely serve them. There is a danger in only blaming a distant state capitalism for the growth of poverty. Responsibility also resides in professions, unions and other administrative organisations for many actions which have furthered their own material prosperity and status at the indirect and sometimes direct expense of impoverished minorities. The gulf between relatively secure and certainly prosperous professionals and administrative staff and their poorest clients has widened sharply in the last few years. Dependency and deprivation have been created on a big scale in recent years.

## The need for collective values

This kind of analysis carries optimistic as well as pessimistic implications. Some will rightly interpret me as arguing that substantial improvements in the conditions experienced by particular minorities – for example, via improvements in levels of benefit pledged by the Labour Party – are very unlikely to come to pass without a pattern of change running through a long list of institutions – some of them appearing to have small relevance to the advance in question. I mean better conditions for clients in social security offices; staff selection, training and supervision to produce courteous and sympathetic treatment; and, more generally, reiteration of collective responsibility for personal and family adversity.

New financial, industrial and social institutions will need to be established, and others, in their rules and mode of operation, changed. All of this may be strategically planned or is implicit in popular action and reaction. Substantial improvements in the conditions experienced by Britain's poorest fifth will not result from the representation of minimum rights – only by restricting the exaggerated claims and predatory activities of the rich and by asserting general social and collective values.

It is difficult to construct examples without seeming over-fanciful. Limits could be set on inherited land or other property values and on increases in high pay. Indeed, I have long believed that a maximum wage would be more effective than a minimum wage in flattening wage differentials and so steering more resources into the lower levels of the wage system. In the short run, progressive taxation could be radically overhauled to generate substantial public resources. In the long run, publicly acceptable guidelines for wages and wage increases might be introduced. Certainly we could learn from the experience of the Swedish wage-earner funds, which were opposed root and branch by industry but which have made some, if slow, headway.[3]

In the meantime, organisations to trace the distribution of incomes and wealth among the rich and monitor developments need to be established as a priority so that the nature of the problem can be exposed in much starker detail than is currently possible. The Royal Commission on the Distribution of Income and Wealth, killed off in 1979 by Mrs Thatcher's government, did not do that job. I believe it to be one of the crucial potential developments in British politics. There is massive public support for the reduction of the gap between rich and poor and there are objective data about net disposable income from the Treasury which demonstrate that really meaningful redistribution is viable. But it will not happen until the connections between wealth and poverty are better, and more publicly, established.

## Change begins at home

Once some of the elements in a strategic programme to transform Britain's infrastructure fall into place, those of us in pressure groups and social services are apt to become overawed by the scale of the prospective task and inhibited therefore from committing our puny efforts to the cause. But the argument which suggests we aren't doing enough is also one which suggests that we can take immediate steps to set up groups, structures and activities. Structural change is not a top-down theory of change. It can begin at home, in the family, at the office, in the organisation, in the profession or in the community. There are a number of hopeful signs.

Feminism has succeeded in unsettling masculine power and attitudes of superiority and could yet become the driving force for more general social equalisation. The experiments led by the Greater London Council and other councils in promoting equal opportunities and confronting discrimination, giving priority to families with young children and demonstrating that previously oppressed minorities can take a valuable as well as valued place in society, have had a success from which party leaders in Parliament and many others should learn. Structural changes of a far-reaching kind can be achieved without massive additions to public expenditure.

The basis for a society free of poverty lies in the creation of local sets of relationships over which people can exert far more control than national measures. This does not mean there do not have to be agreed national principles in the allocation of resources and promotion of values. But social revolution begins at home and certainly not in the political establishment. Current examples of alternative life-styles as well as initiatives in local government and community, including decentralisation of district and area social services, provide examples of a nation prepared to march with its feet and not place all its hopes in the process of central election and representation.

### References

[1] *Social expenditure 1960-1990: problems of growth and control*, OECD 1985, p 21.
[2] C.A.R. Crosland, *The future of socialism*, London 1956, p 61.
[3] M. Linton, *The Swedish road to socialism*, London 1985, pp 26-9.

# 26

# Underclass and overclass

Conceptions of class, changes in class structure and changes in the rates of social mobility were all central themes of sociological work in the 1980s. But despite this, the measurement of trends in the number of identifiable classes, the distance between them in power, their command over resources or whatever, and the numbers of men, women and children allocated to those classes and moving between them, cannot be said to have been such a prominent focus of attention. Similarly, the role of policy and policy institutions in motivating the current and potential trends have been infrequently theorised and certainly not quantified.

[…]

Plainly, the theme of social polarisation is central to current as well as traditional preoccupations in sociology. What are the trends in social inequality? It cannot be seriously argued that living standards in Britain have not diverged in the last 20 and particularly in the last ten years. With variations for particular years the trends, on statistical data from government sources as well as from independent sources, are firmly established (for example, Walker and Walker, 1987; Townsend, Corrigan and Kowarzik, 1987). They are quite clearly attributable to a mixture of government policies, multinational developments in production, trade and finance, and demographic and cultural factors. The question is not *whether* divergence has taken place, but *how serious it is*, how it can be fully explained and what should be done about it – on strategic as well as moral grounds. Social layers in Britain have been partly reconstituted, more deeply etched and more widely spaced.

[…]

The measured annual reviews by the Central Statistical Office give emphatic testimony of income polarisation between 1975 and 1985, particularly between 1979 and 1985.

[…]

Not only has the gap between poor and rich widened. The real incomes of many groups of the poor have actually fallen, or remained about the same, since 1979.

[…]

---

Townsend, P. (1993) 'Underclass and overclass: the widening gulf between social classes in Britain in the 1980s', in M. Cross and G. Payne (eds) *Sociology in action*, London: Macmillan, pp 91–118.

## The underclass

Polarisation of course implies much more than the wider inequality of living standards or power. It implies restructuring as well as different patterns of consciousness at top and bottom of the social scale. Most attention has been concentrated on changes at the foot of the hierarchy. The emergence of an underclass has been proclaimed by a large number of sociologists, first in the United States and now in Britain. [...]

Unemployment grew quickly in the late 1970s, and not only in the aftermath of the 1979 election. It was accompanied, and in part, provoked, by a wider industrial and economic policy designed to restructure class in Britain. Laws were passed to restrict industrial action that could be taken by unions, cancel employment rights and strengthen the powers of employers. Wage-earners' rights of access to rented public housing were severely reduced. The skilled manual class was greatly weakened. At the same time the labour market was casualised.

[...] If the wider issues of fiscal policy, cuts in public expenditure and state coercion (Hillyard and Percy-Smith 1988) are carefully constructed as the appropriate context then we must bear witness to the simultaneous depreciation of the so-called traditional working class and the rapid establishment of a dependent and in part compliant underclass. [...]

The argument also needs to be freed from the preoccupation with the white, male, economically active population. [...] The participation rates of men and women in their late fifties and early sixties have been falling fast. For many of the people experiencing the phenomenon, 'retirement' conceals lifelong, and not just long-term, unemployment.

In the London survey in 1985-6 [...] we found a huge reservoir of untapped productive capacity among prematurely retired men and women, and also among younger women, who want to combine part-time employment with the care of children, and/or older people or people with disabilities. Another tranche of human waste is to be found among that group of, mainly middle-aged, women who no longer have dependent children or disabled relatives to care for and yet accept meagre roles as housewives which involve them in very few hours of activity each week. Many, certainly not all, comply with rather than are fulfilled by a situation which amounts to social subordination.

Retirement pensioners are doubly dependent. Retirement is an economic and social invention of twentieth-century society which most people have no option but to accept at an arbitrary age. With the institutionalisation of minimal pensions the status of retirement represents a structured dependency (Townsend, in Phillipson and Walker 1986). The social associations of retirement are not those of employment, nor are they so frequently connected with political institutions and activities. While it would be wrong to claim that retirement pensioners and the long-term unemployed comprise a single stratum or class in every respect there is little doubt that they are largely divorced from working-class organisation, status and influence; and they share social security status and minimal living standards. With dependents in the household they comprise a quarter of the population.

Two sets of evidence bear in particular upon the contention of class motivation to minimise redistribution through taxation, and to institutionalise, and therefore both legalise and legitimate dependency. One is the extrapolation of the effects of Government measures in 1979 to change the annual readjustment of state pensions from an earnings to a price basis and in 1985-6 to restrict the benefits of the State Earnings Related Pensions Scheme (SERPS). Even on modest assumptions about economic growth the 1985 green paper showed that the value of state pensions relative to earnings would be more than halved by the year 2033 (DHSS, 1985, vol. 3, p. 36). The second set of evidence involves more than 30 measures taken since 1979 with the overall effect of reducing the social security budget, and the level of employment benefit in particular. After a review of benefits for unemployed people, Atkinson and Micklewright concluded:

> Since 1979 ... there has been a major shift away from insurance benefit towards reliance on income-tested assistance for the unemployed. Without public debate, there has been a shift in principle underlying income support for the unemployed. The role of insurance benefits has been eroded by the tightening of the contribution conditions, the extension of the disqualification period, the restriction of benefits to students, the abolition of the lower rate benefits, and the abatement for occupational pensioners; their value has been reduced by the taxation of benefits; and the abandonment of statutory indexation has made the position of recipients insecure.... These measures add up to a substantial reduction in the amount of National Insurance benefit paid to the unemployed ... [and] the covert abandonment of the insurance principle. (Atkinson and Micklewright 1988: 31-2)

This amounts to much more than the eternal, if statistically variable, stigmatisation referred to by Runciman [1989] or the self-selecting life-style strategies adopted by individuals and sub-cultural minorities implied in much of the American literature on the underclass. It is a twentieth-century phenomenon of class reconstruction and the institutionalisation of a new stratum. It involves state control of livelihood and the social status of 'claimant' or 'pensioner', and not only 'worker' or 'wage-earner'. Women and blacks suffer disproportionately in this process and descriptive accounts of their experiences too often implicitly blame them for it.

[...]

## The rich and the super rich

The restructuring of class must not be assumed to apply only to the lower strata. That would be an absurd theoretical proposition, but it is one which seems to be implied in some of the literature. If an underclass is being established on a substantial scale it is as a result of the exercise of new forms of power on behalf of vested interests. I believe we have to examine the functions and effects of the growth of corporations and especially of multinational corporations, and the corresponding elongation of the wage hierarchy. We must also examine those financial centres and institutions and international agencies which have facilitated this critical change.

The restructuring of finance capital and the international role of the City (Murray 1985) are the dramatis personae in explaining changes in class structure at the top. As a number of analysts have argued, financial and commercial interests are not coincident with national industrial interests and, generally speaking, the British Government has maintained a closer rapport, through the Treasury and the Bank of England, with the City than with the representatives of industry. The international role of the City has always gained precedence in policy over the long-term development of British industry (see, for example, the discussion of the dynamics of class in Stanworth 1984 and Scott 1982). The re-emphasis by Government on the market, the free flow of capital, and the withdrawal from state intervention, regulation and public spending, has enhanced the power of those connected with the City to gain from developments in the international market, even at the expense of the national interest – as measured by current and prospective employment and rates of economic growth.

The City has a stake in having access to the world economy and the maintenance of an over-valued sterling and the free flow capital, commodities and commercial services. Decisions that have long-term implications for British industry are taken on the basis of short-term financial considerations adopted in the City (Minns 1982). The City is of course the most important centre of wealth creation for the rich in Britain, and is the main institutional location for the servicing of their wealth (Stanworth 1984; L'isle Williams 1981).

The rapid internationalisation of the economy is necessarily having its effects on the varying ranges of structural inequality within nation-states. For example, the social distance between owners or management and workforce is liable to be greater when corporations have multiple subsidiaries and multiple workforces in different countries. Certainly the difference in wage between the highest and lowest points in the hierarchy is much greater. State regulation is likely to become less effective in moderating low wages and poor working conditions, because national laws and governments, as agents of control over market operations, can more easily be ignored or sidetracked.

[...]

The 'internationalisation' of the economy is of course much more than the operation of similarly structured but larger companies in different countries. There has been a change in the rate of industrial accumulation: the decline in productivity growth and GDP growth in Europe and North America affects rich and poor economies alike and there is a trend away from the relative independence of operation of individual firms, plants and units towards a more integrated mode of operation. This is believed to be primarily social in character, which transforms the structure of the operation and style of management.

[...]

The 'big bang' of 1986 was a state-enforced attempt to prevent London from playing a reduced share in the internationalisation of capital formation. Too many in the City 'remained comfortably cosseted by the large earnings that could be earned in the restricted, fixed commission domestic securities market, and did not venture too far into the more competitive international arena'. Given growing international competition, profit levels could only be maintained by participation in larger deals. Outside financial institutions were allowed in. Capital was more centralised; the balkanisation of the market began to break up. Increased participation of outside companies is now resulting in the weak falling by the wayside. 'The viability of the city as a financial centre has been considerably enhanced. However, it has been at the cost of diminished national involvement in domestic financial transactions' (Thrift 1988: 24).

The London survey of 1985-6 produced evidence suggesting the emergence of 'pedestal' elites with immense power and wealth, having relatively little to do with working people in their native country, and sometimes taking contemptuous attitudes to large sections of the population, and especially the dependent underclass (Townsend with Corrigan and Kowarzik 1987: chapter 7). Long ago, Lundberg coined the name 'super-rich' for these individuals, but did not relate the phenomenon closely to the evolution of the international economy and did not ponder the changes in structure, social relations and classes (Lundberg 1969). Some of these socially remote rich people spend a small proportion of each year in their London homes, because of their roving roles as multinational managers, highly paid servants of international agencies and professional emissaries. Others have businesses which have profited from the growth of financial institutions servicing the internationalisation of the economy from London. This new 'overclass' is a counterpart of an 'underclass', some of whose members are impoverished partly as a consequence of the relocation of industry overseas and the more fanatical pursuit of monetarist policies at home.

## References

Atkinson, A.B. and Micklewright, J. (1988) 'Turning the screw: benefits for the unemployed 1979-1988', Discussion Paper No. TIDI/121, London: Suntory-Toyota International Centre for Economics and Related Disciplines, London School of Economics.

DHSS (Department of Health and Social Security) (1985) *Reform of Social Security,* vols 1-3, Cmnd 9517-9519, London: HMSO.

Hillyard, P. and Percy-Smith, J. (1988) *The coercive state*, London: Pan.

L'isle Williams, M. (1981) 'The social and economic significance of the British merchant banks', Paper presented to EGOS conference, York.

Lundberg, F. (1969) *The rich and the super-rich*, London: Nelson.

Minns, R. (1982) *Take over the city*, London: Pluto.

Murray, R. (1985) 'London and the Greater London Council: restructuring the capital of capital,' *IDS Bulletin 16, 1*, University of Sussex, Institute of Development Studies.

Phillipson, C. and Walker, A. (eds) (1986) *Ageing and social policy: A critical assessment,* London: Gower.

Runciman, W.G. (1989) *A treatise on social theory: vol II: Substantive social theory*, Cambridge: Cambridge University Press.

Scott, J. (1982) *The upper classes,* London: Macmillan.

Stanworth, P. (1984) 'Elites and privilege', in P. Abrams and R. Brown (eds) *UK society: Work, urbanism and inequality*, London: Weidenfeld and Nicolsen.

Thrift, N.J. (1988) 'The fixers: the urban geography of international commercial capital', in J. Henderson and M. Castells (eds) *Global restructuring and territorial development*, London: Sage.

Townsend, P. with Corrigan, P. and Kowarzik, U. (1987) *Poverty and labour in London*, London: Low Pay Unit.

Walker, A. and Walker, C. (1987) *The growing divide: A social audit 1979–87*, London: Child Poverty Action Group.

# 27

# The rich man in his castle

## In Britain inequality is spiralling out of control

At a time when there are vehement denunciations of its so called underclass Britain is in fact energetically restoring its overclass.[1, 2, 3] The trend characteristic of most of the 20th century – of a slowly shrinking share of aggregate wealth commanded by the richest 5% and 10% – is now in reverse.[1, 4, 5]

This year has seen recurring reports of the swelling salaries and breathtaking pronouncements of rich people. Early this month Iain Vallance, the chairman of British Telecom, described his salary – which, with additions, is now in excess of pounds sterling 750·000, as "modest." By comparison with what is going on at the top of Britain's hierarchy in the 75 largest nonfinancial companies perhaps he was right: average salaries of senior executives now range between pounds sterling 200,000 and pounds sterling 505,000, and each executive may receive average annual bonuses of 15% to 20% of salary, substantial share options, "top hat" pensions, and redundancy payments going into six and seven figures.[5]

The cultural and structural changes of the past 20 years are fostering attitudes to wealth and to the responsibilities it brings that evoke memories of the early days of the industrial revolution – before the Protestant ethic had taken hold and the welfare state had been established. In those days charity was supposed to begin at home but was too grudging, small scale, and sporadic to do anything for widespread destitution. The experience of poverty at the turn of the century and the depression of the 1930s provoked two waves of welfare legislation and adjustment in the views of the rich and powerful. Although Lloyd George and others laid the basis for welfare in the early years of this century, the shift towards public ownership and public services, which sustained full employment after the second world war, was decisive. Harold Macmillan declared on behalf of Conservatives in his autobiography, *Winds of Change*, that by the 1950s "we had to convince the great post-war electorate that we accepted the need for full employment and the Welfare State; that we accepted equally the need for central planning

---

Townsend, P. (1994) 'The rich man in his castle', *British Medical Journal*, no 309, 24 December, pp 1674-5.

and even, in times of scarcity, physical controls."[6] By and large, the values of "one nation" were embraced, or conceded, by rich and poor alike.

## U turn

The contrast with current pronouncements from government ministers could not be more stark. Deregulation, cuts in public spending, control of trade unions and local authorities, and privatisation have run a long and largely triumphal course. Zealots sustain the Thatcherite inheritance, paying obsequies to extreme forms of the enterprise culture and individualism. The powerless poor, and not the powerful rich, now bear the brunt of criticism. In 1992 Peter Lilley, now Britain's secretary of state for social security, promised to stop workshy "New Age" travellers, who were "spongers descending like locusts, demanding benefits with menaces." There were other frauds to tackle, such as "young ladies who get pregnant just to jump the housing list."

In 1993 he stated, "We have all too many home-grown scroungers," but now there was the abuse of "benefit tourism." It is, he said, "beyond the pale when foreigners come here expecting our handouts."[7] And in 1994 he widened the category of the undeserving poor to include "prisoners doing time inside [who] can get their rent paid for a year on their empty homes outside."[8]

## The quiet majority in the Post Office queue

Earlier this year Michael Portillo, now secretary of state for employment, spoke of the dismay of the "quiet majority" who found themselves "standing in the Post Office queue watching handouts going to people who seem capable of work; reading of yobbos sent on sailing cruises" and regretted that over the past 30 years "the safety net has become thicker, higher and wider. Help from government has become widely available with scant regard to whether the recipients have behaved reasonably or unreasonably, responsibly or irresponsibly."[9] Outside parliament such attitudes are staging a comeback: extreme monetarists, such as Patrick Minford, argue for the almost complete withdrawal of the welfare state.[10]

Among the rich in Britain there has always been a split between punitive and benevolent attitudes to the poor. A survey of all income groups in 1986 found very rich people who believed that there were "only isolated pockets of poverty" and who wanted "to control the way the poor spend their money."[11] Other rich people did not want any diminution of inequality but at the same time wanted the poor to have a "decent" standard of living. Some of them also recognised that their personal security and prosperity depended on their making concessions to collective welfare.

A third group gave the impression of shrugging their shoulders about their own relative affluence amid so much squalor and desperation. Some have prominent positions in big organisations and say that they are in the grip of events over which they have no influence or control. They represent themselves as small cogs in large machines, doing only what their professional skill and position allow them to do. Their self centred fatalism "compares unfavourably with the high moral commitment, if censorious condescension, of their Victorian predecessors and represents a kind of betrayal of their social position of power."[11]

The mix of punitive, benevolently superior, and fatalistic attitudes towards the poor shifts in response to signals, policies, and laws from the government. Casualisation and insecurity at one end of the workforce are matched by high rewards and the erection of "barricades" at the other. To the privileges of a wealthy home are added the privileges of increasingly segregated wealthy schools, clubs, and transport and health services and the discriminatory barriers to entry. When the punitive attitude is in the ascendant – as witnessed in Reagan's United States and Thatcher's Britain – the material divide between the rich and the poor and the numbers living in abject poverty both grow.

The impact on the population's health is substantial in both respects. New studies have confirmed that severely unequal societies[12] (and not just societies with high rates of poverty[13]) have worse health, quite apart from having a worse record of economic growth, than less unequal societies.[14] As the chief medical officer stated this month, scientific research must now be directed more emphatically to these questions.[15]

Widening inequality breeds social problems. Conspicuous consumption becomes more distasteful. The "culture of contentment" among the prosperous induces a politics of vindictiveness and selfish complacency.[16] No evidence exists that charitable, still less egalitarian, motives come to the fore. As Richard Tawney pointed out, in an acquisitive society excessive riches and excessive poverty have common roots in the insufficiently restrained exercise of economic power.[17]

In 1630 Charles I issued orders to regulate free trade in a time of dearth and scarcity. The better off were enjoined "charitably and bountifully to employ some good proportion towards the relief of those that shall be in penury and want."[18] In this year's Christmas message the Queen should explain that she regrets not having those powers but that John Major has; and instead of speaking generally and weakly about pay restraint at the top he should impose a swingeing "responsibility" tax – not only to cap excessive pay increases[19] but also to improve the conditions for all.

**References**

[1] Scott J. *Poverty and wealth: citizenship, deprivation and privilege*, London: Longmans, 1994.

[2] Townsend P. *The international analysis of poverty,* Hemel Hempstead: Harvester Wheatsheaf, 1993.

[3] Townsend P. Underclass and overclass: the widening gulf between social classes in Britain in the 1980s. In: Payne G, Cross M, eds. *Sociology in action*, London: Macmillan, 1993.

[4] Central Statistical Office, *Social Trends 24*, London: HMSO, 1994.

[5] Incomes Data Service, IDS management pay review 1994: 164.

[6] Macmillan H. *Winds of change,* Vol 2, London: Macmillan, 1969: 311.

[7] Lilley P. Conservative Party News 1993 Oct 6.

[8] Lilley P. Conservative Party News 1994 Oct 12.

[9] Wintour P. Portillo returns to fray, *Guardian* 1994, Apr 23.

[10] Minford P. State expenditure: a study in waste, *Economic Affairs*, 1984; 4 (3) (suppl): i–xx.

[11] Townsend P, Corrigan P, Kowarzik U. *Poverty and labour in London*, London: Low Pay Unit, 1987.

[12] Wilkinson R. The epidemiology transition: from marked material scarcity to social disadvantage. *Daedalus*, 1994; 123: 61–77.

[13] Phillimore P, Beattie A. *Health and inequality: the northern region: 1981-1991*, University of Newcastle: Department of Social Policy, 1994.

[14] Persson T, Tabellini G. Is inequality harmful for growth? *American Economic Review*, 1994, June: 600–21.

[15] Mihill C. Research into links between poverty and ill-health urged, *Guardian*, 1994, Dec 10: 9.

[16] Galbraith JK. *The culture of contentment*, London: Houghton Mifflin, 1992.

[17] Tawney RH. *The acquisitive society*, Brighton: Wheatsheaf Books, 1982.

[18] Orders appointed by his majestie to be straitly observed, for preventing and remedying of the dearth of graine and victual, London: R Barker, 1630.

[19] Wootton B. *Incomes policy: an inquest and a proposal*, London: Michael Joseph, 1970.

# 28

# Poverty, social exclusion and social polarisation

## Poverty

Poverty was at the top of the agenda of problems formulated by Robert MacNamara, Director of the World Bank, at the end of the 1960s. Despite the mixed story since then (development, indebted nations, multiplying barbarism, extreme inequalities in living standards in the aftermath of the collapse of the former Soviet Union, the East Asian economic crisis, and much more besides), it has again risen for the last decade to the top of the Bank's agenda. From 1990 onwards, reports on the subject from the international agencies have multiplied. The number of general, country-specific and methodological reports issued by the Bank that may be said to be poverty-related threatens to swamp us all. The Bank's eagerness is supported by the International Monetary Fund (IMF) and other international agencies, especially the United Nations Development Programme (UNDP), and by non-government organisations, especially Oxfam. [...] Poverty is a recognised evil but has lacked precise agreed definition and a scientifically constructed remedy[1] [...]

This is even more true of 'social exclusion'. Analysts such as Hilary Silver, Graham Room and Ruth Levitas, have in their own different ways written about the potentialities of the concept. It is, as Ruth Levitas shows in *The inclusive society* (1998), highly 'contested'. [...]

However, if we are to adopt practical policies to reduce the two problems of poverty and social exclusion, we need to be clear about how to distinguish them, as well as how they are to be applied cross-nationally, rather than erratically and variously in different cultures. [...]

[...]

One possible line of attack is to seek clarification, not just of the meanings of poverty and social exclusion, but of other, related ideas, such as deprivation. Another is to get better purchase on structural trends and upheavals.

---

Extracts (pp 3-5, 7-10, 17-19) from Townsend, P. (2002) 'Poverty, social exclusion and social polarisation: the need to construct an international welfare state', in P. Townsend and D. Gordon (eds) *World poverty: New policies to defeat an old enemy*, Bristol: The Policy Press, pp 3-24.

One virtue ascribed to many interpretations of social exclusion is that it signifies interest in process rather than state, and points to the need to scrutinise actions of governments. But if the problem with the concept of poverty is believed to be its calling attention only to a negative state or condition, then the problem of the concept of social exclusion is to call attention only to a negative process. Both concepts direct attention to only parts of the population. As a direct consequence, scientific investigation becomes distorted and priorities for policy hard to establish. By contrast, the concepts of inequality and social polarisation, which correspond with the ideas of state and process, are all-embracing. These two concepts are necessary, therefore, to the understanding of poverty and social exclusion, the other two concepts discussed so far.

Social polarisation – the third concept in this chapter's title – is therefore the key ingredient. Early in this century it is the correct focus for scientific accounts of development. It is a structural process creating reverberations the length and breadth of global, national and local society. And while there are other concepts and themes that have to be employed to describe and analyse world social problems, social polarisation is indispensable. Poverty and social exclusion are inevitable by-products. [...].

## A personal history of social polarisation

In the late 1980s, inequality in the UK became fast-growing. In a book entitled *Poverty and Labour in London*, reporting a survey of London households, the authors used the term 'social polarisation' to describe a trend, because it was far from being either small or temporary (Townsend et al, 1987). In its scale and change of direction, this trend was also unprecedented, certainly in the history of recorded measurement during the 18th and 19th centuries. Since the causes had to be unravelled, and because it would be strange if rapid polarisation were to happen in one country and not in another, I began to ask whether the process applied elsewhere.

Although the UK was exceptional, I found that inequality was growing in other European countries – including Belgium and Sweden (Townsend, 1991). During a research and teaching trip to the US in 1992, I found that inequality had widened as dramatically there during the 1980s as in the UK. In one respect the situation there was worse. Average earnings of the poorest 20% in the labour market had decreased significantly in real terms between 1979 and 1992.

An illustration can be given. The 1999 Human Development report from the UNDP shows that the industrialised countries with the greatest inequality (measured by comparing the richest and poorest 20% of each population) are Australia and the UK, with the US third (with a GDP per person ratio of 9.6:1, 9.6:1 and 8.9:1 respectively) (UNDP, 1999). These are also the countries with the largest proportions of the population with less than 50% of the median income (UNDP, 1999, p 149). Although polarisation is well testified for the UK and the US during the 1980s and 1990s, there is some doubt about Australia. In late 1999, I discovered that the international agencies' information about income inequality in Australia was hotly contested by organisations there, who argued it was misleading and outdated. Too little detail is said to be provided in the agencies' reports about methods of standardising comparisons of trends in income distribution across countries.

While there is no doubt of a predominant trend among industrialised countries of growing inequality, there exists wide variation in the extent of that inequality. There are, for example, industrialised countries such as the Czech Republic, Japan, Spain, the Netherlands and Sweden, where the richest 20% have only 3.9, 4.3, 4.4, 4.5 and 4.6 times, respectively, more income than the poorest 20% (UNDP, 1999, p 149).

Turning to developing countries, I have found over the last 15 years a similar growing divide (see, for example, Townsend, 1993, Chapter 1). There is a problem in a substantial number of countries about civil disorder and war, and the impossibility of giving information about collapse into poverty. For many of the other countries, qualifications have to be entered because of the scarcity of data in some of the poorest countries for different years, or because of doubts about reliability.

After the collapse of the Soviet Union at the end of the 1980s, there was an even bigger growth in inequality in the countries of the Commonwealth of Independent States than elsewhere. The economic transformation had dramatic social effects, including increases in the rates of mortality for different age groups in the 1990s (Nelson et al, 1997; Clarke, 1999; Cornia, 1999; Cornia and Pannicia, 1999; and see Ferge, 2000). In a visit to the Republic of Georgia in the former Soviet Union, on behalf of UNDP, I found severe impoverishment, especially among poor families, sick and disabled people and pensioners, not only because of the collapse of industry, but also the erosion of unemployment insurance benefits, pensions and other benefits to levels worth a few pence a week (Townsend, 1995, 1996).

## A global trend

How can the accumulating evidence of this unprecedented trend now be generalised? Reporting in mid-1999, UNDP found that income inequality had increased "in most OECD countries in the 1980s and early 1990s. Of 19 countries only one showed a slight improvement" (1999, p 37). Data on income inequality in Eastern Europe and the CIS "indicate that these changes were the fastest ever recorded. In less than a decade income inequality, as measured by the Gini coefficient, increased from an average of 0.25–0.28 to 0.35–0.38, surpassing OECD levels" (1999, p 39). In China "disparities are widening between the export-oriented regions of the coast and the interior: the human poverty index is just under 20 per cent in coastal provinces, but more than 50 per cent in inland Guizhou" (1999, p 3). Other East and South East Asian countries that had achieved high growth while improving income distribution and reducing poverty in earlier decades, like Indonesia and Thailand, were similarly experiencing more inequality (UNDP, 1999, p 36).

The gap *between* countries, as well as within them, has also widened. The latest studies show how the trend has accelerated: the average income of the world population's richest 20% was 30 times as large as the average income of the poorest 20% in 1960, but 74 times as large by 1997 (UNDP, 1999, p 36).

Of course, widening inequality has to be addressed at both ends of the spectrum. Executives' pay, and the disposable income and wealth of the richest people in the world, has been growing at an astonishing rate. For example, the UNDP points out that "the assets of the 200 richest people are more than the combined income of 41% of the world's people" (1999, p 38). The top three have more than the combined GNP of the 43 least developed countries.

A new report for the World Institute for Development Economic Research of the United Nations University confirms the trend. An econometric analysis of 77 countries (accounting for 82% of world population), found rising inequality in 45, slowing inequality in 4, no definite trend in 12, and falling inequality in only 12 (Cornia, 1999, pp vi and 7). "For most countries, the last two decades have brought about slow growth and rising inequality.… Growing polarisation among countries has been accompanied by a surge in inequality between countries.… Income concentration has risen in many nations of Latin America, Eastern Europe and the former Soviet Union, China, a few African and Southeast Asian economies and, since the early 1980s, almost two-thirds of the OECD countries" (Cornia, 1999, p 2).

> Since the early 1990s, the international community has made the eradication of poverty its foremost development objective. Yet, the decline of poverty in the years ahead depends also on trends in income inequality, a fact which still attracts little concern by the policymakers. Much of the recent rise in income inequality must thus be viewed with alarm, as it may well prove to be incompatible with poverty reduction objectives. (Cornia, 1999, p vi)

## Explaining polarisation

### Defective structural adjustment policies

What are the reasons for this structural change? There is an international analysis that has to be tied in with nationally circumscribed investigation. What has to be accepted is the increasing impact of international developments on national subgroups and local populations. I mean that exposition of familiar problems to do with gender, ageing, disabilities, and families with children, for example, now displays overriding international determinants. I mean also that local problems, such as conflict on inner city housing estates, drugs, closure of local factories, and unsatisfactory privatisation of local services, are generated or enlarged by global market and other international factors.

[...]

## The invention of the international welfare state

[...] The 1995 World Summit on Social Development in Copenhagen provides a good precedent of the model of theory, strategy and policy that we are seeking to develop (UN, 1995). [...] [D]espite its strengths, the Copenhagen Agreement and Programme of Action, failed to address, or illustrate, the key explanatory concept of social polarisation [...] in its necessary relationship with concerns about growing poverty and social exclusion.

What elements might the overall international strategy include? First, unless a scientific consensus is achieved in operationally defining, and measuring, international forms of poverty and social exclusion, the fact that the defeat of poverty worldwide has been put at the top of the international agencies' agenda will turn out to be empty rhetoric. Perhaps one hope is to build on the 1995 World Summit agreement to measure, and monitor, agreed definitions across countries of 'absolute' and 'overall' poverty (Gordon et al, 2000; Gordon and Townsend, 2000).

Second, unless, the *policy-related causes* of poverty and social exclusion are properly traced and publicised in relation to structural trends in all societies, we will find it difficult to discriminate effectively between what are the successful, unsuccessful and even counterproductive measures working towards, or against, the agreed objectives.

Third, since poverty and social exclusion can neither be traced nor explained except in the context of the structural changes embodied in social polarisation, it is this phenomenon that has to be explained.

The effect of policies that have been tried has to be clarified. The *stabilisation and structural adjustment programmes* of the 1980s and 1990s are alleged to have contributed to growing inequality. Policies contributing to the *institutionalisation of unequal power* are argued to deepen that process. Far more attention has to be given to the entire hierarchical *system*, and especially rich institutions and rich individuals at the top. The international agencies, regional associations and national governments must begin to analyse the extraordinary growth of transnational corporations, and ask what reasonable limits can be placed upon their powers. [...]

Policies representing the principles, or ideologies, of *targeting and safety nets* also deserve better assessment. There are grave doubts that they provide the right strategy to compensate for the inequalities and impoverishment induced by liberalisation and the enhanced power of markets. The international agencies are beginning to recognise that, as policy, means testing is neither easy to introduce nor successful. The advantages of modernised social insurance, for developing as well as industrialised countries, are beginning to earn renewed international interest. This is a sign of hope.

There are of course new policies that have to be found as well as existing policies that deserve to be abandoned or corrected if the damaging structural trend of social polarisation is first to be halted, and then turned round. There seem to be two stages. At the first stage the whole critique has to be pulled together and made more forceful. This includes the reformulation of the measurement of poverty, social exclusion and unemployment. It includes insistence on the monitoring and determined fulfilment of international agreements. And it includes the mobilisation of new coalitions or alliances across countries − of parties, unions, campaigning groups and voluntary agencies − to question the conventional wisdom and promote alternative strategies. At the second stage measures for international taxation, regulation of transnational corporations and international agencies, reform of representation at the UN, and new guarantees of human rights, including minimal standards of income, have to be introduced and legally enforced.

Recognition of social insurance as one of the best means of building an 'inclusive' society and preventing the slide into poverty, as well as contributing to social and economic stability, would represent one major step forward. [...]

**Endnote**

[1] This was the basis of our previous book *Breadline Europe: The measurement of poverty* (Gordon and Townsend, 2000). This book is concerned with remedies and policies, rather than definition.

## References

Clarke, S. (1999) *New forms of employment and household survival survival in Russia, Coventry and Moscow*, Coventry/Moscow: Centre for Comparative Labour Studies, University of Warwick/Institute for Comparative Labour Relations Research.

Cornia, G.A. (1999) *Liberalisation, globalisation and income distribution*, Working Paper no 157, Helsinki: UNU World Institute for Development Economic Research.

Cornia, G.A. and Pannicia, R. (eds) (1999) *The mortality crisis in transitional economies*, Oxford: Oxford University Press.

Deacon, B. with Hulse, M. and Stubbs, P. (1997) *Global social policy: International organisations and the future of welfare*, London: Sage Publications.

Ferge, Z. (2000) 'Poverty in Hungary and Central Eastern Europe', in D. Gordon and P. Townsend (eds) *Breadline Europe: The measurement of poverty*, Bristol: The Policy Press, pp 267-305.

Gordon, D. and Townsend, P. (eds) (2000) *Breadline Europe: The measurement of poverty*, Bristol: The Policy Press.

Gordon, D., Adelman, A., Ashworth, K., Bradshaw, J., Levitas, R., Middleton, S., Pantazis, C., Patsios, D., Payne, S., Townsend, P. and Williams, J. (2000) *Poverty and social exclusion in Britain*, York: Joseph Rowntree Foundation (www.bris.ac.uk/poverty/pse/).

Hoogvelt, A. (1997) *Globalisation and the postcolonial world: The new political economy of development*, Basingstoke, Hampshire and London: Macmillan.

ILO (International Labour Organization) (1989) *The ILO tripartite declaration of principles concerning multinational enterprises and social policy – Ten years after*, Geneva: ILO.

Levitas, R. (1998) *The inclusive society? Social exclusion and New Labour*, London: Macmillan.

Nelson, J.M., Tilly, C. and Walker, L. (1997) *Transforming post-communist political economies*, Task Force on Economies in Transition, National Research Council Commission on Behavioural and Social Sciences and Education, Washington, DC: National Academy Press.

Payer, C. (1982) *The World Bank: A critical analysis*, New York, NY: Monthly Review Press.

Payer, C. (1991) *Lent and lost: Foreign credit and Third World development*, London and New Jersey: Zed Books.

Townsend, P. (1991) 'Poverty and social polarisation', in *Eurocities, cities and social policies in Europe*, Barcelona: Ajuntament de Barcelona.

Townsend, P. (1993) *The international analysis of poverty*, Hemel Hempstead: Harvester Wheatsheaf.

Townsend, P. (1995) 'Poverty in Eastern Europe: the latest manifestation of global polarisation', in G. Rodgers and R. Van der Hoeven (eds) *The poverty agenda: Trends and policy options: New approaches to poverty analysis and policy – III*, Geneva: International Institute for Labour Studies, ILO.

Townsend, P. (1996) *A poor future: Can we counteract growing poverty in Britain and across the world?*, London: Lemos and Crane.

Townsend, P. with Corrigan, P. and Kowarzik, U. (1987) *Poverty and labour in London*, London: Low Pay Unit.

UN (United Nations) (1995) *The Copenhagen Declaration and Programme of Action: World Summit for Social Development*, New York, NY: UN.

UNDP (1999) *Human development report 1999*, New York and Oxford: Oxford University Press.

# 29

# The international measurement of 'absolute' and 'overall' poverty

## Introduction

Since the start of the 21st century, there has been increasing public concern about the failure to reduce – still less eradicate – world poverty. In the years from 1960 to the late 1990s, the share of world gross domestic product of the poorest 20% of population actually diminished and the numbers with incomes below the crude 'absolute' formula of $1 per day laid down by the World Bank increased (UNDP, 1997, 1998, 1999, 2000; UNICEF Innocenti Research Centre, 2000). This was during a period of substantial economic growth. In the early years of the new millennium, the same concern has been reiterated (Townsend and Gordon, 2002; Sachs, 2005).

The President of the World Bank had put poverty eradication at the top of the Bank's agenda in 1960. By 1990, the Bank had to admit that progress had been fitful – if not negative – and that a fresh commitment had to be made (for example, see World Bank, 1996). New strategies were duly announced but little evidence emerged of success at either global or national level – at least so far as the majority of countries were concerned. Other international agencies took up the theme strongly. However, although there were useful additions to the analysis, there was little significant departure from the Bank's prescriptions for action[1]. This has led to disbelief that the United Nations' (UN) expressed aim of halving world poverty by 2015 will be achieved or even approached[2]. Governments also find themselves with decreasing room for policy manoeuvre at a time when international agencies seem to be expecting them to do yet more to solve the problem.

To a growing number of European social scientists at least, the problem is not just policy prescription and conformity with Bank precepts or edicts. It is also a question of the definition of poverty, measurement of the trends in the problem and analysis of the causes of those trends. By means of

Extracts (pp 71–6, 80–2) from Townsend, P., Gordon, D. and Pantazis, C. (2006) 'The international measurement of "absolute" and "overall" poverty: applying the 1995 Copenhagen definitions to Britain', in C. Pantazis, D. Gordon and R. Levitas (eds) *Poverty and social exclusion in Britain: The Millennium Survey*, Bristol: The Policy Press, pp 71–85.

authoritative measurement of severe conditions, priorities in policy can be identified more precisely. Poverty has been the subject of intense scrutiny in some countries for decades and many reports on the phenomenon are very sophisticated.

These scientists are also aware that they must join in the struggle to extricate the concept of poverty from political ideology and simultaneously widen scientific perspectives from narrow concern with the physical and nutritional needs of human beings to include all their complex social needs. Part of the struggle has been to find reliable measures to compare conditions in different countries and, especially, conditions in rich *and* poor countries, so that priorities for change might be more securely established and agreed.

Therefore, an internationally comparable meaning of poverty has to be constructed so that a scientific – if not political – consensus might be sought for the threshold of income needed in different countries to escape multiple deprivation, incapacity and premature death. Societies are familiar with thresholds of risk derived from scientific work on radiation, pollution and global warming and 'poverty' can be treated similarly. Although some international organisations have contributed more than others to the sensitive handling of the investigation of poverty, the international community has failed to encourage the formulation of a scientific consensus around definition and measurement and, accordingly, identify precisely which policies have contributed to the worsening or the alleviation of poverty and by how much.

## The Copenhagen contribution

Some governments attempted to sidetrack the problem altogether. In 1989, John Moore, as Secretary of State for the Department of Social Security, stated that the problem of poverty did not apply to the UK (Moore, 1989). Only 10 years later, his successor, Alastair Darling, announced a programme to undertake a poverty audit "and so place the problem at the top of the nation's agenda"[3]. This illustrates the changes that can take place in political reactions to accumulating evidence of social problems. Substantial reduction of poverty in the UK became the declared objective of the Prime Minister and the Chancellor of the Exchequer.

Poverty is a recognised evil but has lacked precise international definition and a scientifically constructed remedy. For example, the USA has its own definition and measure, which the international agencies have not hitherto related to their priorities for development. Indeed, the amendments to measurement recommended by the National Academy of Sciences seems to have served the purpose of bolstering a US approach that is highly sophisticated but insular (Citro and Michael, 1995). Root and branch reform on an avowed scientific or international basis has not been considered.

However, the United Nations Children's Fund (UNICEF) has recently taken a novel step in reporting the extent of child poverty in rich nations. In comparing poverty rates across countries, the organisation used the familiar standard of 50% of the national median household income but also used a standard representing 'absolute' child poverty – as depicted by the official US poverty line (UNICEF Innocenti Research Centre, 2000, 2005). The latest report confirms startlingly high rates of child poverty for Mexico (28%), the USA (22%), New Zealand (16%), Portugal (16%) and the UK (15%). Denmark and Finland have the lowest poverty rates, at less than 3%. Rather worryingly, the proportion of children living in poverty has risen in 17 out of 24 OECD (Organization for Economic Cooperation and Development) countries during the 1990s, with increases of more than 4% for the Czech Republic, Luxembourg and Poland. The UK is one of only four countries (with Australia, Norway and the USA) where there have been significant reductions in child poverty rates (UNICEF Innocenti Research Centre, 2005).

The UNICEF initiative approaches the 1995 Copenhagen recommendation for a two-tier measure of poverty, though that is not yet applied to poor countries. It also reintroduces the problem of replacing – or supplementing – the US national standard with a more appropriate international standard of 'absolute' poverty.

The approach of the World Bank and other agencies has been concerned, above all, with the world's poorest. The social customs and relationships of the people in the poorest countries and, especially their social roles and obligations, attracted small interest. What mattered was the acquisition of the 'absolute necessities of life'. These were arbitrarily interpreted as minimal nutrition, warmth and shelter. It was along such lines of argument that the World Bank's $1 a day was originally justified.

Unfortunately, this led to a form of apartheid between the first and third worlds. The problem was defined differently in the two worlds and, as a consequence, comparisons relevant to the construction of priorities of policy were either avoided or were thoroughly confused. One absurd result of this has been the proliferation of different 'standards' for different regions – as in United Nations Development Reports – without any attempt to explore whether there might be, say, an international standard with the topping-up of variable standards conditioned by the particular circumstances of individual countries and regions.

The 1995 World Summit for Social Development was called because, among other things, many governments were becoming restive with the lack of progress in reducing the gap in living standards between rich and the poor countries during the 1980s and early 1990s and, despite the work of the international financial agencies, the persistence and growth of severe poverty (UN, 1995).

The report repeatedly emphasised that the gap between rich and poor *within* both developed and developing societies was widening, just as the gap *between* developed and developing societies was also widening. Calling world attention to this dual structural phenomenon is perhaps the most notable achievement of the summit – whatever might be said in criticism of the attempts in the text to please different governments and satisfy their conflicting objectives.

The intention was to try to promote sustained economic growth within the context of sustainable development and by "formulating or strengthening, preferably by 1996, and implementing national poverty eradication plans to address the structural causes of poverty, encompassing action on the local, national, subregional, and international levels. These plans should establish, within each national context, strategies and affordable, time-bound, goals and targets for the substantial reduction of overall poverty and the eradication of absolute poverty.... Each country should develop a precise definition and assessment of absolute poverty" (UN, 1995, pp 60-1).

After 1995, progress in following up the agreement was slow (Townsend, 1996). Ireland was one of the first Western countries to produce a follow-up report (Irish Government, 1996). Third world governments followed suit in later years, for example, Kenya in 1999 (Ministry of Planning and National Development, 1998a, 1998b). However, many reports seem to be addressed more to the agenda of the international financial agencies than to the 1995 agreement.

The two-level definition of poverty was designed to bridge first and third worlds and to afford a basis for cross-national measurement.

Absolute poverty is defined as "a condition characterised by severe deprivation of basic human needs, including food, safe drinking water, sanitation facilities, health, shelter, education and information. It depends not only on income but also on access to services" (UN, 1995, p 57).

Overall poverty takes various forms, including "lack of income and productive resources to ensure sustainable livelihoods; hunger and malnutrition; ill health; limited or lack of access to education and other basic services; increased morbidity and mortality from illness; homelessness and inadequate housing; unsafe environments and social discrimination and exclusion. It is also characterised by lack of participation in decision-making and in civil, social and cultural life. It occurs in all countries: as mass poverty in many developing countries, pockets of poverty amid wealth in developed countries, loss of livelihoods as a result of economic recession, sudden poverty as a result of disaster or conflict, the poverty of low-wage workers, and the utter destitution of people who fall outside family support systems, social institutions and safety nets" (UN, 1995, p 57).

By recommending a two-tier measure of 'absolute' and 'overall' poverty to be applied to every country, a means was found to bring all governments together in a common purpose. An opportunity was created to explore the severity of poverty according to standards that seemed to be acceptable everywhere. Even countries where it was assumed absolute poverty no longer existed found it easier to accept an international two-tier approach that self-evidently included their own conditions.

Accordingly, all governments were expected to prepare a national poverty eradication plan. In 1997, nearly a hundred European social scientists drew up a statement asking for an international approach to the measurement and explanation of poverty (Townsend et al, 1997, pp 34-5). This statement urged the use of the UN's two-level definition.

## Absolute and overall subjective poverty lines

The 1995 Copenhagen definitions of absolute and overall poverty were adapted to conditions in Britain in the Poverty and Social Exclusion (PSE) Survey. This used the MORI survey questions asked by Townsend and his colleagues (1997), which were subsequently modified by the results from focus-group research (Bradshaw et al, 1998). Survey respondents were invited to say what level of income was required by a household of their type to surmount 'absolute' – and what level, 'overall' – poverty and then they were asked to say whether the income, after taxes, of their household was *above* or *below* – or *a lot* above or below, the income given (see www.bristol.ac.uk/poverty/pse/welcome/htm).

In Britain, absolute poverty is perceived as being widespread. As many as 14% of the sample, including 'don't knows', representing over 7.5 million people, say they have less income than the level they identified as being enough to keep a household like theirs out of 'absolute' poverty. If the 'don't knows' are excluded, this figure rises to 17%.[...]

[...]

Significantly larger percentages in each case are found to place themselves in 'overall' poverty [...] Although, as expected, the additions applied to each family type, they are disproportionately high for families with children.

[...]

## Extending the measure in the first and third worlds

In establishing "economies to serve human needs and aspirations" – an ambitious objective built into the 1995 World Summit – the research in Britain shows, beyond reasonable doubt, that the scale of needs in some rich industrial societies are perceived by their populations to be much larger than generally allowed in national and international discourse. When taken with reports from poorer countries, where comparable methods have been piloted, this two-level measure deserves to be extended internationally. It can, of course, take the form of self-perceived poverty but also 'objective' poverty as revealed by sets of indicators of deprivation and low income.

Thus, a series of surveys of poverty and social exclusion sponsored by the International Institute for Labour Studies, affiliated to the International Labour Organization, included three that drew on methods of measuring poverty previously tried in London (Townsend and Gordon, 1989; Gordon and Pantazis, 1997). The three were reports on Tanzania, Yemen and Russia (Kaijage and Tibaijuka, 1996, p 7, pp 118-126, p 182; Hashem, 1996, p 86; Tchernina, 1996; see also Narayan, 1997 and the concluding report by Gore and Figueiredo (1996, p 18). Davies and Smith (1998) used a similar 'standard of living' methodology to measure poverty in Vietnam, also largely based on the categories adopted in Britain in the 1990s.

The World Summit in Copenhagen highlighted the problems in rich and poor countries of poverty and social exclusion. The report called for "the substantial reduction of overall poverty and the eradication of absolute poverty.... Each country should develop a precise definition and assessment of absolute poverty" (UN, 1995, pp 60-1).

In the process of developing comparisons between different countries, it is likely that a cross-national core of questions may be distinguished from country-specific or culture-specific ones. One possibility is to say to those interviewed that the World Bank estimated 'absolute' needs at approximately one dollar a day – though substituting the equivalent in national Purchasing Power Parity rate – and inviting their comments.

In most cases, the subjective method produces poverty lines at a relatively high level. Some European social scientists have argued that, in many cases, the poverty line is at such a level that it would be very difficult to maintain that all households below it are poor, in the sense of being socially excluded (Deeleck et al, 1992). The term 'insecurity of subsistence', meaning a situation in which households encounter financial difficulty in participating in the average or most widely shared lifestyle, would be more appropriate. However, this acknowledges the importance of extending the meaning of poverty to include social as well as 'subsistence' needs and begs the question of the respective precise meanings of social exclusion and poverty.

Empirical studies have shown that estimates of the subjective poverty line usually rise systematically with the actual income of the household/individual (Citro and Michael, 1995). Therefore, subjective poverty lines tend to fluctuate over time depending on changes in the social reference group (for example, due to an increase in the overall living standard of the elderly, they respond with a higher necessary minimum income) and on the period of reference (for example, in a period of crisis, aspirations might decline). Given the wide variations in economic and social circumstances between regions and countries, the subjective poverty lines are less suitable for comparative purposes across time and space.

The problem with subjective measures is that the elucidation of opinion takes precedence over the elucidation of behaviour. Although this is understandable, because of the limited resources made available for research, it does mean that there can be no easy check on the extent to which people's views about need correspond with the behaviour which may be said to be *revelatory* of need. The same point might be made about lists of needs drawn up by those conducting such research. Human priorities have to be ascertained in terms of observed actions and not only expressed views or preferences. People reveal their priorities as well as their needs in the way they act when short of cash as well as in expressions of their opinion. The investigation of individual opinion sits more easily with interpretations of them as consumers than as people obliged collectively and individually to meet, from their resources, obligations imposed by society and the general customs of their culture. The definition of conditions and the identification of the causes of those conditions may often lie outside the perceptions of individuals. The 'consensual judgement of society' may be said to be a necessary but insufficient criterion on which to build a poverty line and interpret conditions in a society.

Nonetheless, much research suggests that, while individuals in the same types of household will sometimes differ to an extreme extent in their opinions of their income needs, the majority are close to the mean. Moreover, for each principal type of household, people's perceptions of their income needs turn out to be quite close to objective measures of those needs. The perceptions therefore represent valuable indicators both of what people experience and how financial hardship can restrict their opportunities and activities.

[...]

### Endnotes

[1] For example, Ravi Kanbur, the prime mover of the World Bank's Development Report on Poverty in 2000, was reported to have resigned because he was "believed to have wanted to emphasise that economic growth alone will not be enough to reduce poverty and that it will also require equal emphasis on redistributive tax and spending policies" (M. Atkinson, *Guardian*, 15 June 2000).

[2] Thus, the Bank admits, "the number of poor people has risen worldwide, and in some regions the proportion of poor people has also increased" (World Bank, 1999). See also the statement of goals, including halving world poverty by 2015 (World Bank, 2000).

[3] The first report was published in late 1999 (see DSS, 1999).

**References**

Bradshaw, J., Middleton, S., Townsend, P. and Gordon, D. (1998) *Perceptions of poverty and social exclusion: Final report on preparatory stages of research*, York: Social Policy Research Unit, University of York.

Citro, C. and Michael, R. (1995) *Measuring poverty: A new approach*, Panel on Poverty, National Research Council, Washington DC: National Academy Press.

Davies, R. and Smith, W. (1998) *The Basic Necessities Survey: The experience of Action Aid Vietnam*, London: Action Aid.

Deeleck, H., van den Bosch, K. and de Lathouwer, L. (1992) *Poverty and the adequacy of social security in the EC: A comparative analysis*, Aldershot: Avebury.

DSS (Department of Social Security) (1999) *Opportunity for All: Tackling poverty and social exclusion*, Cm 4445, London: The Stationery Office.

Gordon, D. and Pantazis, C. (1997) *Breadline Britain in the 1990s*, Aldershot: Ashgate.

Gore, C. and Figueiredo, J. (1996) *Social exclusion and anti-poverty strategies*, Geneva: International Institute for Labour Studies.

Hashem, M. (1996) *Goals for social integration and realities of social exclusion in the Republic of Yemen*, Research Series No 105, Geneva: International Institute for Labour Studies.

Irish Government (1996) *Sharing in progress: National anti-poverty strategy*, Dublin: The Stationery Office.

Kaijage, F. and Tibaijuka, A. (1996) *Poverty and social exclusion in Tanzania*, Research Series No. 109, Geneva: International Institute for Labour Studies.

Ministry of Planning and National Development (1998a) *First report on poverty in Kenya, vol I: Incidence and depth of poverty*, Report presented by the Central Bureau of Statistics and the Human Resources and Social Services Department, Nairobi: Government of Kenya.

Ministry of Planning and National Development (1998b) *First report on poverty in Kenya, vol II: Poverty and social indicators*, Report presented by the Central Bureau of Statistics and the Human Resources and Social Services Department, Nairobi: Government of Kenya.

Moore, J. (1989) *The end of poverty*, London: Conservative Political Centre.

Narayan, D. (1997) *Voices of the poor: Poverty and social capital in Tanzania*, Environmentally and Socially Sustainable Development Studies and Monographs Series 20, Washington DC: World Bank.

Sachs, J. (2005) *The end of poverty: How we can make it happen in our lifetime*, London: Penguin.

Tchernina, N. (1996) *Economic transition and social exclusion in Russia*, Research Series No 108, Geneva: International Institute for Labour Studies.

Townsend, P. (1996) *A poor future: Can we counter growing poverty in Britain and across the world?*, London: Lemos and Crane.

Townsend, P. and Gordon, D. (1989) 'What is enough?', in House of Commons Social Services Committee, *Minimum Income*, House of Commons 579, London: HMSO.

Townsend, P. and Gordon, D. (2002) *World poverty: New policies to defeat an old enemy*, Bristol: The Policy Press.

Townsend et al (1997) 'An international approach to the measurement and explanation of poverty: statement by European social scientists', in P. Townsend, D. Gordon, J. Bradshaw and B. Gosschalk (1997) *Absolute and overall poverty in Britain in 1997: What the population themselves say*, Bristol: Bristol Statistical Monitoring Unit, University of Bristol.

UN (United Nations) (1995) *The Copenhagen Declaration and Programme of Action, World Summit for Social Development, 6-12 March 1995*. New York: United Nations.

UNICEF Innocenti Research Centre (2000) *A league table of child poverty in rich nations*, Innocenti Report Card No 1, Florence: UNICEF.

UNICEF Innocenti Research Centre (2005) *Child poverty in rich countries*, Innocenti Report Card No 5, Florence: UNICEF.

UNDP (United Nations Development Programme) (1997) *Human development report*, New York, NY and Oxford: UNDP.

UNDP (1998) *Human development report*, New York, NY and Oxford: UNDP.

UNDP (1999) *Human development report*, New York, NY and Oxford: UNDP.

UNDP (2000) *Human development report*, New York, NY and Oxford: UNDP.

World Bank (1996) *Poverty reduction and the World Bank: Progress and challenges in the 1990s*, Washington DC: World Bank.

# Section V
# Health inequalities and health policy

*Edited by Peter Phillimore*

# Introduction

There is probably no name in Europe as synonymous with efforts to research the extent of modern health inequalities, or to influence government policy to reduce these inequalities, as Peter Townsend's. His writing on health inequalities spans over a quarter of a century, starting in the mid-1970s; and probably more than any other social scientist in Europe he has insisted (a favourite Townsend word) on the responsibility not simply to describe and analyse inequalities but to advocate the policies which could reduce them. Peter Townsend's work on health inequalities started a few years before his major study of poverty in the UK was published, by which time he already had a substantial reputation in that field. His later attention to health developed directly from that work on poverty, both in the emphasis he placed on the health of the poorest in society, but also in the opportunity a sociological analysis of health patterns allowed to display the connections between the causes and consequences of poverty and wider social inequality. He reminded new generations not only how the poorest in society continued to experience disproportionate health burdens, but equally how greater wealth and status brought health advantages all the way up the class structure. Health inequalities became a vehicle for mapping the cumulative consequences of unequal living conditions and economic circumstances over time, illuminating the old adage that population health in the round revealed the 'downstream' outcome of all the social and economic inequality which had occurred 'upstream' over the life course.

The five extracts from Peter Townsend's writings presented in this section follow a chronological sequence, with one exception, for the first (**Chapter 30**) is taken from the Black Report on *Inequalities in health*. It would be hard to overstate the importance of this work. No other writing on health inequalities has had such an impact, immediately and over the long term. In 1977 the then Labour government had asked the Chief Scientist at the Department of Health, Sir Douglas Black, to chair a small working group to "initiate studies into the inequalities in health among the social classes" (Blume, 2002, p 107). Peter Townsend was one of its four members (alongside Jerry Morris and Cyril Smith). By the time that the group submitted their final report in April 1980, the Conservative Party was in power with Margaret Thatcher Prime Minister. Hostile both to the assumptions about inequality underpinning the report and to the principles and costs of its policy recommendations, the government kept publication deliberately low key, with a mere 260 copies produced over a public holiday. But the suspicion that government had sought to deflect attention from the Black Report backfired. News coverage was massive, both in Britain and abroad, and the government's indifference to the Black

Report guaranteed it special attention. At least ten summaries of the Black Report were produced, by NHS groups, trades unions and others, in part to compensate for the virtual unavailability of the original report. That was addressed in 1982 when Peter Townsend and a journalist, Nick Davidson, produced an edited version published by Penguin, from which the extract here is taken. Even the four authors of the Black Report could have had no inkling that their work would ignite such passionate debate then and for many years subsequently.

Health inequalities were not discovered – or even rediscovered – by the Black Report. Research on health inequalities has a long history in Britain, dating back to the writings of Farr, Chadwick, Engels, Mayhew and others in the 19th century. However, with the establishment of the welfare state after 1945 and the creation of a National Health Service in 1948, there had developed a tacit public and policy assumption that previous health inequalities in Britain would inevitably decline. The decision to set up the working group on health inequalities followed evidence emerging by the 1970s which pointed to the stubborn persistence of such inequalities. What the Black Report did was to marshal the available evidence from a vast array of disparate sources at a time of renewed awareness that health inequalities were not a thing of the past, covering different dimensions of health to illustrate that in relation to adult mortality, infant mortality, adult illness, and access to health services a consistent pattern emerged. The group weighed up the possible explanations for the patterns of health which were apparent, and proposed detailed policies to counter these inequalities. An editorial in the *British Medical Journal* concluded a few years after publication that, like the Bible, the Black Report was "much quoted, occasionally read and largely ignored when it comes to action" (*BMJ*, 1986, p 91). Yet in the longer term the Black Report triggered an unparalleled surge of research on these inequalities and their explanation, first in Britain and then in many other countries. If the value of research is reflected in the subsequent work it provokes, then the Black Report has few rivals. It also led directly to two successor reports which can be seen as direct heirs of Black, updating it in the light of the new evidence then emerging so rapidly: *The health divide* in 1987 (Whitehead, 1992), and the Acheson Report in 1998 (Acheson, 1998).

Few reports to government have attracted such interest afterwards in the internal dynamics of the working group, largely to try and identify lines of internal disagreement (Berridge, 2002). Invariably and revealingly, interest has focused on Peter Townsend's substantial influence, and how much his colleagues shared his sociological analysis and political judgements. Over the years the Black Report has also had no shortage of academic critics, with challenges to its emphasis on social class, the crude basis of the class indicators available for analysis, the comparability of class data over time, and the priority given to what the report called structural and material over behavioural explanations for health inequalities – to name only a few of the most important areas of contention. Yet, in retrospect, it is striking how well the Black Report has worn, its overall emphasis on the extent and persistence of health inequalities, across all measures of health, vindicated rather than undermined. Crucial here has been the more methodologically robust evidence from longitudinal studies, which was not available at the time (Fox et al, 1985; Power, 1991), and subsequent theorisation in terms of a life-course perspective on those influences which damage or enhance health (Kuh and Davey Smith, 1993; Davey Smith, 2003). Furthermore, the suggestion that inequalities may not simply be persisting, but may actually have widened, has been confirmed by later research. While there are undoubtedly ways in which the representation of patterns of health inequality is affected by both data availability and methodological approach, few would now argue that apparent health inequalities have been misleadingly inflated, an artefact of the measurement process. The extracts selected below illustrate both the evidence presented on inequalities in mortality and the explanation for these inequalities put forward by the Black Report (drawn from Chapters 2 and 6).

The second extract (**Chapter 31**) comes from a seminal article that Peter Townsend published in the *The Lancet* in 1974: 'Inequality and the health service'. Dedicated to the memory of Richard Titmuss, who had died the previous year, this paper provides the first sketch of themes which were developed much further in the Black Report. The argument addresses several audiences. He reminded politicians and policy makers of the dangers of complacency about public health a quarter of a century after the National Health Services was created; he reminded health professionals that health was a social matter, and medical institutions were social institutions; and he emphasised to sociologists that health and inequality was a prime sociological topic of investigation. The analysis summarises available measures of health, including evidence on trends over 20-30 years, before leading on to consider "inequalities in the development of services" (1974, p 1184). What is striking about this section particularly is the use of international comparisons, exemplifying his advocacy of a "systematic application of the comparative method" (1974, p 1180). I want to draw attention also to two themes which were to run as a leitmotif throughout Peter Townsend's work on health and inequality. The first is summarised in his rhetorical question, linking health services and policy to wider sources of inequality: "Can equality in medicine, like equality before the law, be practised on a kind of island remote from the cruel inequalities of the rest of social life?" (1974, p 1179). The second, germane to his emphasis on the role for social science in this field, highlighted how conceptions of need shift over time: definitions of need which may have been thought adequate when the NHS was created were no longer sufficient 25 years later, because needs, and the conceptions of ill-health associated with popular ideas about need, were social in character (1974, p 1180).

The third extract (**Chapter 32**) is the concluding chapter of a book written in the late 1980s. Peter Townsend, Alastair Beattie and I co-authored *Health and deprivation: Inequality and the north* (1988) towards the end of the long recession which marked the final decline of many of the old industries around which the towns and cities of the north had been built. Coming a few years after the Miners Strike and the subsequent wave of pit closures, unemployment in many areas had by the mid-1980s reached levels unseen since the Depression of the 1930s. If this provided the context for our analysis it was not the reason for it. That owed more to an interest in extending the lessons of the Black Report to produce a more fine-grained depiction of local inequalities, area by area. This allowed the full extent of health differentials to be highlighted, often showing contrasts within the same city which in extreme cases added up to more than a ten-year disparity in life expectancy between rich and poor neighbourhoods. It is interesting to note that this research had been funded by the Northern Regional Health Authority – not an easy commitment for a public body to make at a time when the very idea of documenting health inequalities was an anathema to the then government. The hostility of the government fuelled an oppositional appetite for such studies – demonstrated most clearly in *The health divide* (Whitehead, 1992 [1987]), published at the same time as *Health and deprivation*. This was, in fact, a time of considerable research effort in the health inequalities field, with fierce, often acrimonious debate. The study of England's Northern Region was the most ambitious and wide-ranging of several similar area-based projects which Peter Townsend directed at this time: starting with a study of inequalities in health in Bristol (Townsend et al, 1985), there also followed studies of London (Townsend et al, 1987; Townsend, 1990) and Manchester (Townsend, 1988). Methodologically, all these studies exploited new opportunities provided by the availability of small area statistics from the Census to map localised patterns of social inequality at the level of the electoral ward. Health data could then be mapped likewise to the same scale, allowing researchers to show patterns of health inequality down to neighbourhood level. For this purpose, and partly in response to criticisms of the Black Report for its over-reliance on the Registrar General's official definition of occupational classes, a new 'index of deprivation' was created out of four census variables to be used in both the Northern Region and London studies. It was not long before this became known as the 'Townsend index', to be widely adopted in numerous studies and reports across the UK. A supplement rather than a substitute for measures of class, it was intended to reflect more directly household living circumstances and resources (encompassing unemployment, car ownership, home ownership and overcrowding). In this way Peter Townsend harked back to his earlier research on poverty to refine the toolkit available for describing the extent of inequality in modern Britain.

The fourth extract (**Chapter 33**), published in 1990, is taken from 'Individual or social responsibility for premature death?'. This article reflects one of the controversies of the later 1980s, a controversy which was at once methodological, theoretical and political. Peter Townsend always challenged analyses of health differentials which placed explanatory weight primarily on the choices made by individuals – behavioural explanations, in other words. For him, structural factors always weighed more heavily: the material living conditions associated with housing quality and local infrastructure, or the economic determinants of class associated with income and employment. This article was a challenge to what he saw as the unacknowledged methodological individualism of proponents of 'lifestyle explanations' for health variations (a deliberate avoidance of the word 'inequalities' in favour of 'variations' was one detail in a bigger argument) within epidemiology, public health and among some social scientists. The argument Peter Townsend advanced here was also a challenge to the political climate of the time. The article can be read as a rejoinder to the denial of the social so memorably voiced in Margaret Thatcher's remark that 'there is no such thing as society'. There is something almost Durkheimian in Peter Townsend's reminder that patterns of premature death reveal social causation. For their part, his critics have seen him as over-deterministic, unwilling to give due weight to individual agency and behavioural choices – the battleground for this particular paper. This argument may have waned in intensity. But it has by no means gone away, and indeed shows signs of resurfacing amidst the current economic crisis.

The fifth extract (**Chapter 34**), written for the *British Medical Journal* in 1999, returns to government policy on health inequalities. 'Better benefits for health' was written by the four authors of the Black Report, returning to their theme for one last collective contribution. The occasion was the publication of the Acheson Report on inequalities in health (Acheson, 1998). This article, reproduced in full, was a reminder of the lineage of the Acheson Report, and more substantially a way of underlining its central argument about the persistence and accentuation of health inequalities over the previous two decades. But more than both of these aims, the article allowed the Black Report authors to provide their own commentary on the rather diffuse set of policy recommendations to come from the much shorter Acheson Inquiry, as well as the Labour Government's early policy responses to the issue (cf Davey Smith et al, 1998). The significance of the piece lay precisely in selecting the policy recommendations which Peter Townsend and his co-authors believed had special significance, and on which government still needed to act, drawing attention to the limitations of its tentative anti-poverty strategy. Two sections titled 'Adequacy of benefit' and 'Concerted radical action to improve health' focused attention on minimum income, tax and the benefits system in a manner that rehearsed some features of the earlier emphasis on structural and material factors. The ever-fashionable emphasis on personal lifestyle is conspicuous by its absence. In short, Acheson provided the ideal opportunity for his predecessors to update their own recommendations from nearly two decades earlier, but this time speaking to a Labour and not a Conservative government.

These five extracts concentrate on the subject of health inequalities and by no means exhaust Peter Townsend's interests in health and health policy. Notably, even before he turned to the analysis of health inequalities he had written a good deal on ill-health in older age, in *The family life of old people* (1957), extracts from which are included in Section VI of this volume, and in *Old people in three industrial societies* (Shanas et al, 1968). He also wrote about mental health on several occasions. Insights from this earlier work are evident in his *Lancet* paper (1974) discussed above. The breadth of his writing on health, as in the other fields in which he engaged, is striking. His own thoughts about this breadth of interest provide a fitting conclusion here. In an email written a few months before he died, Peter looked back on the way in which his work on health developed towards its later emphasis on inequality, emphasising particularly his collaboration with Brian Abel-Smith in that earlier period. He spoke of:

> the 'spread' of necessary work on health which I had in my head and tried to cover. I worked closely with Brian Abel-Smith and in the 1950s and 1960s we deliberately tried to complement each other at successive international conferences on health and especially geriatrics/ gerontology but also nursing, medicine, psychiatry and what is now called learning disabilities.... I believed that the 'acute sick' attracted disproportionate resources and that the longer-term myriad connections between acute and chronic were poorly understood. (personal communication 16 February 2009)

It is out of these concerns, coupled with his work on poverty, that a quarter of a century of research and writing on health inequalities emerged.

**Acknowledgements**
I am grateful to John Veit-Wilson and Linda McKie for helpful comments on an earlier version of this commentary.

## References

Acheson, D. (1998) *Independent inquiry into inequalities in health: Report*, Chaired by Sir Donald Acheson, London: The Stationery Office.

Berridge, V. (ed) (2002) 'The Black Report and the health divide: witness seminar', *Contemporary British History*, vol 16, no 3, pp 131-72.

Blume, S. (2002) 'The Black Committee on Health Inequalities (1977-80): a personal view of its work', *Contemporary British History*, vol 16, no 3, pp 107-19.

Davey Smith, G. (ed) (2003) *Health inequalities: Lifecourse approaches*, Bristol: The Policy Press.

Davey Smith, G., Morris, J.N. and Shaw, M. (1998) 'The independent inquiry into inequalities in health', Editorial, *BMJ*, no 317, pp 1465-6.

Fox, A.J., Goldblatt, P.A. and Jones, D.R. (1985) 'Social class mortality differentials: artefact, selection or life circumstances?', *Journal of Epidemiology & Community Health*, no 39, pp 1-8.

Kuh, D. and Davey Smith, G. (1993) 'When is mortality risk determined? Historical insights into a current debate', *Social History of Medicine*, vol 6, no 1, pp 101-23.

Power, C. (1991) 'Social and economic background and class inequalities in health among young adults', *Social Science & Medicine*, vol 32, no 4, pp 411-7.

Shanas, E., Townsend, P., Wedderburn, D., Friis, H., Milhoj, P. and Stehouwer, J. (1968) *Old people in three industrial societies*, London: RKP.

Townsend, P. (1957) *The family life of old people*, London: RKP.

Townsend, P. (1988) *Inner city deprivation and premature death in Greater Manchester*, Ashton Under Lyne: Tameside MBC.

Townsend, P. (1990) 'Living standards and health in the inner cities', in S. MacGregor and B. Pimlott (eds) *Tackling the inner cities*, Oxford: Oxford University Press, pp 93-126.

Townsend, P., Corrigan, P. and Kowarzik, U. (1987) *Poverty and labour in London: Survey of Londoners' living standards*, Report No 1, London: Low Pay Unit.

Townsend, P., Simpson, D. and Tibbs, N. (1985) 'Inequalities in health in the city of Bristol: a preliminary review of statistical evidence', *International Journal of Health Services*, vol 15, no 2, pp 637-63.

Whitehead, M. (1992) 'The health divide', in *Inequalities in health: The Black Report and the health divide*, Harmondsworth: Penguin (original publication 1987).

# 30

# The Black Report

## The pattern of present health inequalities

Inequalities in health take a number of distinctive forms in Britain today. This chapter examines the pattern of inequalities according to a number of criteria: the relationships between gender and mortality, race and mortality, regional background and mortality, plus a range of measures of ill-health. But undoubtedly the clearest and most unequivocal – if only because there is more evidence to go on – is the relationship between occupational class and mortality. […]

### Occupational class and mortality

Every death in Britain is a registered and certified event in which both the cause and the occupation of the deceased or his or her next of kin are recorded. By taking the actual incidence of death among members of the Registrar General's occupational classes and dividing this by the total in each occupational class it is possible to derive an estimate of class differences in mortality. This shows that on the basis of figures drawn from the early 1970s, when the most recent decennial survey was conducted, men and women in occupational class V had a two-and-a-half times greater chance of dying before reaching retirement age than their professional counterparts in occupational class I (Table 1). Even when allowance is made for the fact that there are more older people in unskilled than professional work, the probability of death before retirement is still double.

What lies behind this gross statistic? Where do we begin to look for an explanation? If we break it down by age we find that class differences in mortality are a constant feature of the entire human life-span (see Fig. 1). They are found at birth, during the first year of life, in childhood, adolescence and adult life. At *any* age people in occupational class V have a higher rate of death than their better-off counterparts. This is not to say that the differences are uniform; in general they are more marked at the start of life and, less obviously, in early adulthood.

---

Extracts (pp 43-9, 104-14, 125-6) from Townsend, P., Davidson, N. (eds) and Whitehead, M. (1992) *Inequalities in health: The Black Report and the health divide*, 2nd edn, Harmondsworth: Penguin.

**Table 1:** Death rates by sex and social (occupational) class (15-64 years) (rates per 1,000 population, England and Wales, 1971)

| Social (occupational) class | Males | Females* | Ratio M/F |
|---|---|---|---|
| I (Professional) | 3.98 | 2.15 | 1.85 |
| II (Intermediate) | 5.54 | 2.85 | 1.94 |
| III N (Skilled non-manual) | 5.80 | 2.76 | 1.96 |
| III M (Skilled manual) | 6.08 | 3.41 | 1.78 |
| IV (Partly skilled) | 7.96 | 4.27 | 1.87 |
| V (Unskilled) | 9.88 | 5.31 | 1.86 |
| Ratio V/I | 2.5 | 2.5 | |

\* In this table women with husbands have been classified by their husband's occupation, women of other marital statuses are attributed to their *own* occupational class.
*Source: Occupational Mortality 1970-72* (microfiches and HMSO, 1978, p. 37)

**Figure 1:** Mortality by occupational class and age

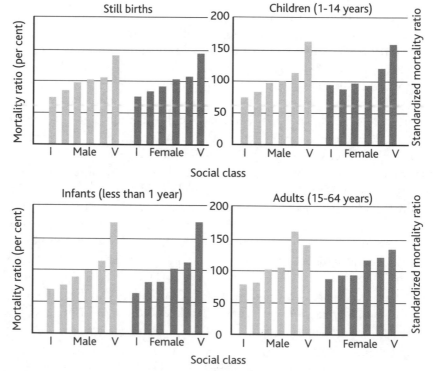

Relative mortality (%) is the ratio of rates for the occupational class to the rate for all males (or females).
*Source: Occupational Mortality 1970-72* (HMSO, 1978, p. 196)

At birth and during the first month of life the risk of death in families of unskilled workers is double that of professional families. Children of skilled manual fathers (occupational class IIIM) run a 1.5 times greater risk.

For the next eleven months of a child's life this ratio widens still further. For the death of every one male infant of professional parents, we can expect almost two among children of skilled manual workers and three among children of unskilled manual workers. Among females the ratios are even greater.

If we measure this against different causes of death – Fig. 2 – we find that the most marked class gradients are for deaths from accidents and respiratory disease, two causes which we will show later to be closely related to the socio-economic environment. Other causes, associated with birth itself and with congenital disabilities, have significantly less steep class gradients.

**Figure 2:** Infant mortality by sex, occupational class and cause of death

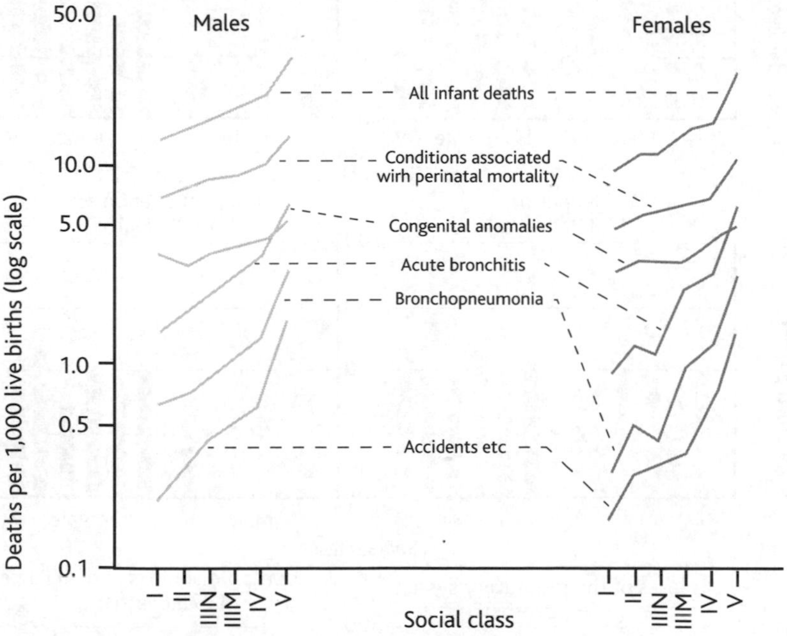

Source: Occupational Mortality 1970-72 (HMSO, 1978, p. 158)

Between the ages of 1 and 14 relative class death rates narrow, but are still clearly visible. Among boys the ratio of mortality in occupational class V as compared with I is of the order of 2 to 1, while among girls it varies between 1.5 and 1.9 to 1.

Once again the causes of these differences can be traced largely to environmental factors. Accidents, which are by far the biggest single cause of childhood deaths (30 per cent of the total), continue to show the sharpest class gradient. Boys in class V have a ten times greater chance of dying from fire, falls or drowning than those in class I. The corresponding ratio of deaths caused to youthful pedestrians by motor vehicles is more than 7 to 1. Trailing somewhere behind this, but also with a marked class gradient, are infectious and parasitic diseases, responsible for 5 per cent of all childhood deaths, and pneumonia, responsible for 8 per cent of the total. Most other causes of death show less clear evidence of class disadvantage (Fig. 3).

**Figure 3:** Class and mortality in childhood (males and females 0-14)

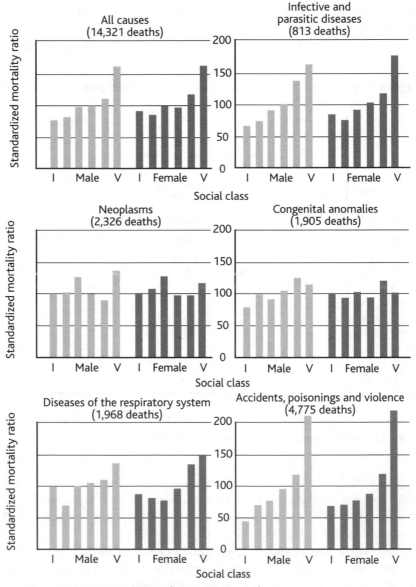

Source: *Occupational Mortality 1970-72* (HMSO, 1978, p. 160)

Among adults, taken in this context to be people aged between 15 and 64, class differences appear to narrow further, but the overall statistic conceals a large difference for those in their twenties and thirties and a relatively small one for adults nearer pension age.

As in childhood the rates of death from accidents and infectious disease show steep class gradients, but equally an extraordinary variety of non-infectious diseases like cancer, heart and respiratory disease also show marked class differences (Fig. 4). This will be discussed further in the next chapter when we come to describe *trends* in the pattern of death rates.

Finally, as pension age is reached, class differences in mortality diminish still further, but by this age classification by occupational class becomes less meaningful. Information about occupation and cause of death recorded on death certificates for people over 75 is sometimes imprecise or inaccurate, particularly in the case of widows who, dying in their seventies or later, may still be classified according to the last occupation of husbands who may have died many years earlier. Again, there is some movement late in working life from skilled to unskilled occupations which is not reflected in the occupation reported at death. A minority of men, dying in their sixties, are recorded with the skilled occupation held for most of their working life rather than the unskilled occupation they may have had in the last five or ten years of that life.

Occupational class may therefore be a weak indicator of life-style and life chances over lengthy periods. Bearing this in mind, data about the mortality of men aged 65 to 74 in 1970/72 showed that there were very large differences between some groups of manual and non-manual workers. For example, the mortality ratio for former miners and quarrymen was 149, gas, coke and chemical makers 150, and furnace, forge, foundry and rolling mill workers 162, compared with administrators and managers with a ratio of 88 and professional, technical workers and artists with a ratio of 89 (OPCS, 1978, p. 107).

Now let us look at some other criteria for dividing the population which have a bearing on any attempt to describe the 'structure' of health among the population.

## Sex differences in mortality

The gap in life expectancy between men and women is one of the most distinctive features of human health in the advanced societies. As Table 1 indicates, the risk of death for men in each occupational class is almost twice that of women, the cumulative product of health inequalities between the sexes during the whole lifetime. It suggests that gender and class exert highly significant but different influences on the quality and duration of life in modern society.

**Figure 4:** Occupational class and mortality in adult life (men and married women 15-64), by husband's occupation

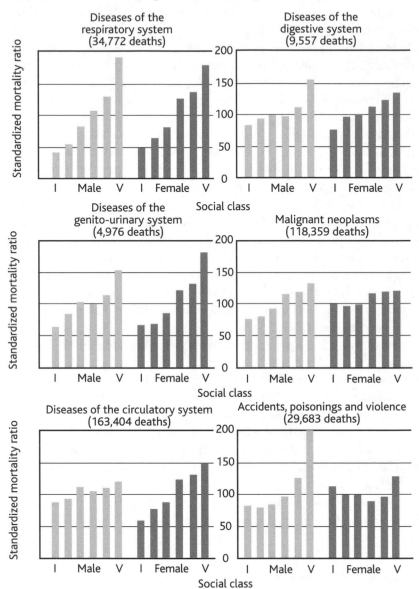

Source: Occupational Mortality 1970-72 (HMSO, 1978)

It is also a gap in life expectancy which carries important implications for all spheres of social policy, but especially health, since old age is a time when demand for health care is at its greatest and the dominant pattern of premature male mortality adds the exacerbating problem of isolation for many women.

Although attempts have been made to explain the differences between the sexes, comparatively little systematic work exists on the aetiology of the mortality and morbidity differences between men and women and much remains to be disentangled. Women suffer uniquely from some disease and it would be wrong, for example, to assume too readily that all wives share the same living conditions or even standards as their husbands. Some men have the advantage, for instance, not only of a preferential diet at home but subsidized meals at work. Where both husband and wife are in paid employment, the meals they get in the day, as well as working conditions and the nature of the work, may be radically different. There is a great deal more research to be undertaken to sort out these various influences.

[...]

## Towards an explanation of health inequalities

Death rates in present-day Europe have reached what appear to be their lowest points in the history of human society. The twentieth century has witnessed a dramatic decline in the rate of infectious disease, as well as the introduction of powerful therapies for its treatment. Common causes of death like TB and diphtheria, often linked with poverty and material deprivation, have greatly diminished, though they have been replaced by new diseases, some of which have been linked in particular studies with affluence and material abundance. On that account inequalities in health might have been expected to diminish. But the evidence which we have presented ... suggests that this has not been the case. In this chapter we ask why occupational class continues to exert so significant an influence on health in Britain.

There are a number of approaches to an explanation, though none in our view provides a wholly satisfactory answer. Indeed, the variable of occupational class is in itself multifaceted, and its influence probably varies according to age or stage in the life-cycle and according to the natural history of disease.

### Theoretical approaches

Theoretical explanations of the relationship between health and inequality might be roughly divided into four categories:

1. Artefact explanations.
2. Theories of natural or social selection.
3. Materialist or structuralist explanations.
4. Cultural/behavioural explanations.

In some respect each one of these approaches sheds light on the observed relationships between class and health in present-day Britain. We shall first describe and discuss in general terms the four approaches and then go on, by reference to the problems of different age groups, to show that any satisfactory explanation must build essentially on the ideas of the cumulative dispositions and experience of the lifetime, and of multiple causation.

### The artefact explanation

This approach suggests that both health and class are artificial variables thrown up by attempts to measure social phenomena and that the relationship between them may itself be an artefact of little causal significance. Accordingly, the failure of health inequalities to diminish in recent decades is believed to be explained to a greater or lesser extent by the reduction in the proportion of the population in the poorest occupational classes. It is believed that the failure to reduce the gap *between* classes has been counterbalanced by the shrinkage in the relative size of the poorer classes themselves. The implication is that the upwardly mobile are found to have better health than those who remain, or that their health subsequently improves relative to the health of those they join. We would make two comments. One is that informed examination of successive census reports shows that the poorer occupational classes have contracted less sharply than often supposed.... The other is that indicators of relatively poor progress in health apply to much larger sections of the manual occupational classes than just those who are 'unskilled'....

### Natural and social selection

Occupational class is here relegated to the state of dependent variable and health acquires the greater degree of causal significance. The occupational class structure is seen as a filter or sorter of human beings and one of the major bases of selection is health, that is, physical strength, vigour or agility. It is inferred that the Registrar General's class I has the lowest rate of premature mortality because it is made up of the strongest and most robust men and women in the population. Class V by contrast contains the weakest and most frail people. Put another way, this explanation suggests that physical weakness or poor health carries low social worth as well as low economic reward, but that these factors play no causal role in the event of high mortality. Their relationship is strictly reflective. Those men and women who by virtue of innate physical characteristics are destined to live the shortest lives also reap the most meagre rewards. This type of explanation has been invoked to explain the preponderance of individuals with severe mental disorders in social class V (a thesis which was reviewed critically in, for example, Goldberg and Morrison, 1963). It is postulated that affected people *drift* to the bottom rung of the Registrar General's occupational scale. Similar selective processes are thought to occur with other forms of disease even though the extent of drift may not be so great and there is little actual evidence of it.

## Materialist or structuralist explanations

The third type of explanation emphasizes the role of economic and associated socio-structural factors in the distribution of health and well-being, and, because it is frequently misunderstood, requires fuller exposition. There are several separate strands of reasoning within it which can be ordered more or less according to the extent to which the primary causal significance is assigned directly or indirectly to the role of economic deprivation. Amongst explanations which focus on the *direct* influence of poverty or economic deprivation in the production of variation in rates of mortality is the radical Marxian critique. With the benefit of a century's hindsight the validity of much of this nineteenth-century theory of the relationship between health and material inequality has been accepted today, especially for the earlier phase of competitive industrial capitalism (Stedman-Jones, 1971; Thompson, 1976). Exploitation, poverty and disease have virtually become synonymous for describing conditions of life in the urban slums of Victorian and Edwardian cities, as they are today for the shanty towns of the underdeveloped world.

But can it be so readily applied to contemporary health experience? Can the premature mortality of the working class still be directly attributed to subsistence poverty and exploitation? It is true that a relationship between material deprivation and certain causes of disease and death is now well established, but then so is the capacity of the capitalist mode of production to expand the level of human productivity and to raise the living standards of working people. Economic growth of the kind most readily associated with the European style of industrialization has in itself been credited with the decline in mortality from infectious disease during the nineteenth and twentieth centuries (cf. McKeown, 1976; Powles, 1975). Today death rates for all age groups in Britain are a fraction of what they were a century ago and many of the virulent infectious diseases have largely disappeared (cf. Morris, 1975; OPCS, 1978), and the 'killer' diseases of modern society – accidents, cancer and heart disease – seem less obviously linked to poverty. Against this background, the language of economic exploitation no longer seems to provide the appropriate epithet for describing 'Life and Labour' in the last two decades of the twentieth century. Through trade-union organization and wages council machinery it is now argued that labour is paid its price and, since health tends to be conceptualized in optimum terms as a fixed condition of material welfare which, if anything, is put at risk by affluent living standards, it is assumed by many that economic class on its own is no longer the powerful determinant of health that it once was.

The flaw in this line of reasoning is the assumption that material subsistence needs can be uniquely and unambiguously defined in terms independent of the overall level of economic development in a society. People may still have too little for their basic *physiological* as well as social needs. Poverty is also a relative concept, and those who are unable to share the amenities or facilities provided within a rich society, or who are unable to fulfill the social and occupational obligations placed upon them by virtue of their limited resources, can properly be regarded as poor. They may also be relatively disadvantaged in relation to the risks of illness or accident or the factors positively promoting health.

It is worth illustrating how this can happen. New types of industrial process can introduce entirely new risks for the workforce or the population in the area. Certain forms of building or construction or town planning can introduce new hazards for adults as well as children. Changes in distances from work, type of participation in the local community and in leisure can alter the balance for many people in their access to health services as well as their knowledge about health. People living alone who have a fall, or people who have a heart attack, face different problems in different communities. Warnings about undesirable food and other products (inflammable clothing and furniture, for instance), as well as the latest information about the means of obtaining a healthy diet, may or may not be communicated, depending on their social circumstances. Many other examples of how new problems of health arise in a changing society might be given. The material deprivation of some sections of the population can paradoxically grow even when their income increases, relative to changing structures and amenities.

How far might differences in access to resources help to explain this? How unequal is the distribution of wealth in Britain? Historically the structure of living standards has been slow to change. Personal wealth is still concentrated in the hands of a small minority of the population, as reports of the Royal Commission on the Distribution of Income and Wealth have shown.

The question whether the richest men and women in Britain have maintained their economic position at the expense of less well-endowed citizens eludes a categorical answer. The Royal Commission has referred to the 'remarkable' stability of the unequal distribution of income over the past two decades.... Moreover there is no doubt that the proportion as well as number of the population dependent on a subsistence or near-subsistence income from the state has grown. For some groups, and especially manual groups, relative lifetime resources will have been reduced. Earlier retirement, unemployment and redundancies, single-parent status and disablement, as well as the proportionate increase in the elderly population, all play some part in this development. For recent years Table 32 shows the tendency for those at the lowest relative income standards to increase in number and proportion.

**Table 32:** Numbers of persons in poverty and on the margins of poverty (Family Expenditure Survey)

| Income relative to supplementary benefit | Britain (000s) | | | |
|---|---|---|---|---|
| | 1960* | 1975 | 1976 | 1977 |
| Under supplementary benefit standard | 1,260 | 1,840 | 2,280 | 2,020 |
| Receiving supplementary benefit | 2,670 | 3,710† | 4,090† | 4,160 |
| At or not more than 40 per cent above standard | 3,510 | 6,990 | 8,500 | 7,840 |
| Total | 7,740 | 12,540 | 14,870 | 14,020 |
| Per cent of population | 14.2 | 23.7 | 28.1 | 26.6 |

* From Abel-Smith and Townsend, 1965, pp. 40 and 44. The data are for the UK and are on a household rather than an income unit basis. It should be noted that this column is based on national assistance scales, not supplementary benefit scales.

† Drawn separately from a supplementary benefit sample inquiry with people drawing benefit for less than three months excluded. In the FES, such people are categorized according to their normal income and employment.

*Sources:* For 1960, Abel-Smith and Townsend, 1965, pp 40 and 44. For 1975-7, DHSS (SR3), Analyses of the FES.

There is therefore a paradox: while we would not wish to assert that the evidence is consistent and complete, the proportion of the population with relatively low lifetime incomes (in the widest sense of 'income') seems to have increased in recent decades, just as the proportion assigned to classes IV and V seems to have decreased, though the latter continue to comprise more than a quarter of the population. While economic growth has improved the access of both groups to income and other resources, other groups have gained in proportion, and since neither facilities nor knowledge is a finite commodity, those with relatively low incomes (in increasing numbers) have remained relatively disadvantaged.

So it has been with health. Occupational classes IV and V may in time catch up with the contemporary levels achieved by I and II but by that time the latter groups will have forged even further ahead. There is nothing fixed about levels of physical well-being. They have improved in the past and there is every likelihood that they will improve in the future. But class inequalities persist in the distribution of health as in the distribution of income or wealth, and they persist as a form of relative deprivation.

Unfortunately the opportunity for examining the association between income and health is restricted by lack of information and the role played by material factors in creating the pattern of health and ill-health which can be found in the population is complex. Occupational class is multi-faceted in 'advanced' societies, and apart from the variables most readily associated with socio-economic position – income, savings, property and housing – there are many other dimensions which can be expected to exert an active causal influence on health. People at work, for instance, encounter different material conditions and amenities, levels of danger and risk, degree of security and stability, association with other workers, levels of self-fulfillment and job satisfaction and physical or mental strain. These dimensions of material inequality are also closely articulated with another determinant of health – education.

[...]

### Cultural/behavioural explanations

A fourth approach is that of cultural or behavioural explanations of the distribution of health in modern industrial societies. These are recognizable by the independent and autonomous causal role which they assign to ideas and behaviour in the onset of disease and the event of death. Such explanations, when applied to modern industrial societies, often focus on the individual as a unit of analysis emphasizing unthinking, reckless or irresponsible behaviour or incautious life-style as the moving determinant of poor health status (cf. Fuchs, 1974). What is implied is that people harm themselves or their children by the excessive consumption of harmful commodities, refined foods, tobacco and alcohol, or by lack of exercise, or by their under-utilization of preventive health care, vaccination, ante-natal surveillance or contraception. Some would argue that such systematic behaviour within certain social groups is a consequence only of lack of education, or individual waywardness or thoughtlessness. Explanation takes an individual form. What is critical, it is implied, are the personal characteristics of individuals, whether innate or acquired – their basic intelligence, their skills obtained through education and training, their physical and mental qualities, and their personal styles and dispositions. Others see behaviour which is conducive to good or bad health as embedded more within social structures – as illustrative of socially distinguishable styles of life, associated with, and reinforced by, class.

Tables 33, 34 and 35 provide the kind of data sometimes used to illustrate a cultural/behavioural type of explanation. Certain styles of living, like a diet strong in carbohydrates, cigarette-smoking and lack of participation in sporting activities, are known to cut across class. It is implied that there are individual or, at most, sub-cultural life-styles, rooted in personal characteristics and level of education, which govern behaviour and which are therefore open to change through changes in personal activities or educational inputs. However, data of the kind illustrated in these tables are not easy to interpret. For one thing, the observations are themselves only indicators which are subject to qualification if their meaning is to be put into context.

**Table 33:** Household food consumption by income group (oz./person/ week) (Great Britain, 1979)

| Income group | Food | | | | |
|---|---|---|---|---|---|
| | White bread | Brown, including wholemeal bread | Sugar and preserves | Potatoes | Fresh fruit |
| A | 17 | 5.3 | 11 | 39 | 25 |
| B | 22 | 4.5 | 12 | 40 | 20 |
| C | 26 | 4.3 | 13 | 48 | 16 |
| D | 29 | 4.3 | 15 | 48 | 15 |

Gross weekly income of head of household: A = £145+; D = less than £56 per week.
*Source:* Adapted from *Household Food Consumption and Expenditure*, HMSO (see Morris, 1979).

**Table 34:** Cigarette-smoking by socio-economic group (males and females aged 16+) (1980)

| Socio-economic group | Current smokers % | |
|---|---|---|
| | Men | Women |
| Professional | 21 | 21 |
| Managerial | 35 | 33 |
| Intermediate non-manual | 35 | 34 |
| Intermediate manual | 48 | 43 |
| Semi-skilled manual | 49 | 39 |
| Unskilled manual | 57 | 41 |
| All | 42 | 37 |

*Source: General Household Survey:* OPCS Monitor, 28 July 1981.

Thus, a balanced diet, or balanced physical activity, to promote health is easy neither to define nor measure. People who eat one type of food to excess may make up for that disadvantage in some other respect. And manual workers who are spectators rather than active sportsmen include those who have to exert physical strength and agility in their everyday jobs.

Again, the data can be interpreted in other ways than in relation to level of knowledge or education, or personal responsibility. Commercial advertisements are planned to 'educate' tastes, and the education provided in schools is not always calculated to prepare young people to ward off

**Table 35:** Active leisure pursuits by males: ratio of participation rates, non-manual to manual workers, by age (males aged 16 or over engaging in each activity in the four weeks before interview) (Great Britain, 1977)

| | Age group | | |
|---|---|---|---|
| | 16-29 | 30-59 | 60+ |
| Squash/fives | 4.4 | 6.9 | * |
| Athletics (incl. jogging) | 3.3 | 3.3 | * |
| Rugby | 2.9 | * | * |
| Golf | 2.8 | 3.2 | 4.9 |
| Badminton | 2.8 | 2.8 | * |
| Cricket | 2.4 | 1.7 | * |
| Tennis | 2.4 | 4.1 | * |
| Table-tennis | 1.7 | 3.1 | * |
| Swimming outdoors | 1.6 | 2.1 | * |
| Walking (more than 2 miles) | 1.6 | 1.8 | 1.7 |
| Bowls (indoor) | 1.4 | 1.3 | 1.1 |
| Bowls (outdoor) | 1.4 | 1.4 | 1.6 |
| Playing football | 1.1 | 1.6 | * |
| Swimming (indoor) | 1.1 | 2.2 | * |
| Dancing | 0.9 | 1.1 | 1.2 |
| Gymnastics/yoga/keep fit | 0.9 | 2.1 | * |

* Ten or fewer participants in either manual or non-manual group.
*Source:* General Household Survey, 1977.

influences upon their consumption and behaviour which may be undesirable for health. Moreover, access to good food and sports facilities depends also on the area in which people live and the resources they can command, and not only their personal characteristics or behaviour, or education. But, in emphasizing these reservations we must also call attention to the *cumulative* importance of those contributions to personal behaviour made by genetic endowment of attributes, the influence of family upbringing and practices and the evolution of modes of self-management which contribute to wide differences in health achieved by different members of the same occupational or socio-economic class.

The interpretation of level of personal knowledge or education as a causal factor in health illustrates our theoretical problem. It is on the basis of success or the lack of it at school that children are selected for manual and non-manual work and, as we have seen, this occupational distinction plays an important part in measured health status differentials. But we can go further. Bernstein has argued that distinctive patterns of child rearing and socialization, such as those which tended to differentiate between working-class and middle-class families, produce quite different linguistic capacities which are in turn correlated with quite different intellectual approaches to the social world (Bernstein, 1971). The working-class child is rendered at a particular disadvantage on account of these differences because of the *fit* which exists between middle-class norms of socialization and the dominant structure of the educational system. The outcome of this is that children from middle-class homes enter the school system already equipped with the appropriate mode of communication and, as a result, they have more successful educational careers and leave school with a greater facility to manipulate their social and economic environment (which of course includes health services) to personal advantage. These ideas carry the variable of education far beyond the simple idea of the transmission of knowledge and skills. They imply that the educational system tends to be substantially developed and maintained in conformity with the class system or with that pattern of differential material advantages or disadvantages, and social opportunities or obstacles, which govern both the place taken in the system by the individual child and the chances of that child having a successful career within the system. On this reasoning, level of education becomes difficult to treat as intrinsically independent of class.

More theoretically developed as the basis for cultural/behavioural explanations is the 'culture of poverty' thesis – which has much in common with the idea of 'transmitted deprivation'. As originally proposed by Oscar Lewis, an anthropologist who studied poor communities in Central America and, later, migrant groups in New York, the 'culture of poverty' was intended to apply only to market-organized social structures with poorly developed public systems of health, welfare and income maintenance (cf. Lewis, 1967). Starting from a distinct cultural anthropological perspective, Lewis argued that human existence in any given environment involves a process of biological and social adaptation which gives rise to the elaboration of a structure of norms, ideas and behaviours. This culture over time acquires an integrity and a stability because of the supportive role it plays in helping individuals to understand and cope with their environment but, through its influence on socialization practices and the like, it also comes to have an important autonomous influence in the social consciousness of individuals. The integrity of the culture ensures its autonomous survival even when the material base from which it emerged has changed or been modified. It is for this reason that people cling on to outmoded ideas or old-fashioned practices which do not seem to accord with the changed material realities of modern existence. The 'culture of poverty' thesis has been widely criticized by British social scientists (Holman, 1978, Chapter 3; Rutter and Madge, 1976; Townsend, 1979, pp. 65-71).

[...]

355

## Conclusions

Several conclusions can be drawn from this look at different stages in the human life-cycle. First, while cultural and genetic explanations have some relevance – the latter is particularly important in early childhood – more of the evidence is explained by what we call 'materialist' or 'structural' explanations than by any other.

Secondly, some of the evidence on class inequalities in health can be understood in terms of specific features of the socio-economic environment: features such as accidents at work, overcrowding and smoking, which are strongly class-related in Britain. Since such features are recognized objectives of various areas of social policy we feel it sensible to offer them as contributory factors, to be dealt with in their own right, and not to discuss their incidence further in social-structural terms. The same is true of other aspects of the evidence which we feel show the importance of health services themselves. Ante-natal care, for example, is important in preventing perinatal death, and the international evidence presented in Chapter 5 [of *Inequalities in health*] suggests that much can be done through improvement of ante-natal care and of its uptake. The international evidence also suggests the importance of preventive health within health policy, despite studies, to which we alluded earlier, which suggest that few of the differences in mortality either between nations, or between British regions, can be explained in terms of health care provision. But beyond this there is undoubtedly much which cannot be understood in terms of the impact of such specific factors. Much, we feel, can only be understood in terms of the more diffuse consequences of the class structure: poverty, work conditions (and what we termed the social division of labour) and deprivation in its various forms in the home and immediate environment, at work, in education and the upbringing of children and more generally in family and social life.

It is this acknowledgement of the complex nature of the explanation of health inequalities – involving access to and use of the health services; specific issues in other areas of social policy; and more general features of class, material inequality and deprivation – which informs and structures the recommendations we make....

### References

Abel-Smith, B. and Townsend, P. (1965) *The poor and the poorest*, London: Bell.

Bernstein, B. (1971) *Class, codes and control*, London: Routledge.

Fuchs, V. (1974) *Who shall live? Health, economics, and social choice*, New York, NY: Basic Books.

Goldberg, E.M. and Morrison, S.L. (1963) 'Schizophrenia and social class', *British Journal of Psychiatry*, no 109, pp 785-00

Holman, R.T. (1978) *Poverty: Explanations of social deprivation*, Oxford: Robertson.

Lewis, O. (1967) *The children of Sanchez*, New York, NY: Random House.

McKeown, T. (1976) *The modern use of population*, London: Arnold.

Morris, J.N. (1975) *Uses of epidemiology*, 3rd edn, London: Churchill Livingstone.

Morris, J.N. (1979) 'Social inequalities undiminished', *Lancet*, 13 January, p 87.

OPCS (1978) *Occupational mortality 1970-72*, London: HMSO.

Powles, J. (1975) 'Health and industrialization in Britain', Proceedings First World Congress on Environmental Medicine and Biology, Paris.

Rutter, M. and Madge, N. (1976) *Cycles of disadvantage*, London: Heinemann.

Stedman-Jones, G. (1971) *Outcast London*, Oxford: Clarendon Press.

Thompson, P. (1976) *The Edwardians*, London: Paladin.

Townsend, P. (1979) *Poverty in the United Kingdom*, London: Penguin Books.

# 31

# Inequality and the health service

Many histories of the evolution of health services are based on the naïve assumption of continuous progress. Sometimes progress is assumed to be steady and sometimes, after a dramatic discovery in medical science, the introduction of a new method of treating disease or the introduction of a legislative and administrative reform, is assumed to be rapid. The establishment of the National Health Service in England and Wales, and of the parallel services in Scotland and Northern Ireland, tends to be regarded as a glorious achievement which will endure forever. But the truth is more complex, the achievement less certain and the future less optimistic. If achievement means just the pieces of paper which are approved by Parliament it must logically be final. If it means a living reality serving certain principles of care and distribution of resources better and better as the years pass on, it is more contentious.

## Social institutions of health

Health services are social institutions, and as such they can change relatively to their own past, to other institutions, and, most important of all, to the health needs of the community. This must include the possibility of retrogression as well as progression. Sociology is only beginning to trace the implications for medicine, nursing, and public policy of a thorough social analysis of the provision of health services in these three distinct senses. That is partly because sociologists are only slowly becoming aware of the close relationship that exists between the form of the health services, definitions of the need for such services or even definitions of health, and social structure and values. That same awareness has also been slow to take root in medicine. Despite the distinguished history of epidemiology[1] the proportion of resources devoted to research and teaching in that subject remains miserably small. To take one small example, there were the whole-time equivalent of only 7 specialists in social medicine among 8500 consultants attached to hospitals in England in 1972.[2]

Until very recently sociological work, notably in the United States, has taken the restricted forms of study of professional and patients' roles; of particular conceptions of illness, such as mental illness; and of particular

Townsend, P. (1974) 'Inequality and the health service', *The Lancet*, vol 303, issue 7868, 15 June, pp 1179–90.

organisations such as general hospitals for the acutely ill and mentally ill. Now the need to study the entire system of health care and its internal structure as well as its external relationship to other systems, like the economy and the polity, and particularly its relationship to national and international systems of social stratification is better recognised as providing the right framework for specialist study. This means, first, study of the structure of public and private health services through the various tiers of central Government, regional and area health authorities and local government, and hospitals, health centres, and general practice; industrial, voluntary, and private agencies and services; the structure and distribution of professions, their training, and recruitment; the social and other characteristics of the different occupational groups concerned with the health of the individual and of local communities; the allocation and control of resources; and the experiences, attitudes and conditions of patients. But, second, this 'internal' system cannot be separated from its national, cultural, economic and social setting. How far are health-care values and practices shaped by the general structure of inequality in society? Or, to put this type of question the other way round, how far has the development of the medical and other professions within the structure of health services positively contributed to the conceptions of status and rewards generally held in society? Does the system of health services help to shape the structure and values of society in general, or is the direction of influence the other way? Can one, indeed, be disentangled from the other? Can equality in medicine, like equality before the law, be practised on a kind of island remote from the cruel inequalities of the rest of social life?

The development of health services takes place not only, of course, within a national but also, third, a world setting. Through social means knowledge about scientific discoveries, methods of curing, preventing and controlling illness, and new types of health services is diffused. But we tend to dwell on the promotional and apparently constructive features of international relations between health systems instead of their exploitative and destructive features. Some uncomfortable facts about inequalities between nations are, it is true, revealed. Thus the statistical yearbooks of the United Nations and the World Health Organisation have called our attention to the fact that while there are between 120 and 200 doctors per 100,000 population in Britain, the United States and much of Europe, there are only 32 in Taiwan, 22 in India, 19 in Pakistan, 4 in Indonesia and Tanzania, 2 in Malawi and Nepal, and 1 in Ethiopia.[3] Too often such information is presented without any attempt to explain that some of the privileges of the rich countries are gained at the expense of the poor countries. A large proportion of Britain's hospital medical staff has been drawn from the Commonwealth. In the 12 months ending October, 1969, 164 of 169 new general practitioners moving into underdoctored areas came from overseas.[4] Foreign doctors account for 20% of annual addition to the American profession, and it has been calculated that the United States gains more in dollar value of medical aid from the rest of the world than it provides in aid to foreign countries, publicly, and privately.[5] The third world is also disadvantaged in some respects by attempts to introduce inappropriate Western concepts of medicine and treatment and by the profit-seeking operation of the drug companies. The international profit-and-loss account in relations between health-service systems requires searching scrutiny, not just because systems in the third world remain deprived but because inequalities in care in Western systems may be reinforced and because Western conceptions of health care may be culturally insular if not smug. There may be instructive lessons to be drawn from health services in developing countries.

This analytic framework, although very sketchily drawn, has implications for any evaluation of change. I have spoken of conceptions of illness or health, the structure of the health-care system, and the pattern of health needs in society. Any one, or all, of these three may change significantly over time. If our definition of what constitutes illness and states of health is greatly extended and complicated, our expectations of the health services and the standards by which we judge them change correspondingly. By this test the health services may fall further short of expectations. Even if our definition remains roughly constant we may find that the reduction in the prevalence of some diseases has to be weighed against the growth in prevalence of others. The reasons for disappointing as well as encouraging trends have to be sought in the structure and operation as much of the health-care system as in society generally. I am alluding not simply to changes, for example, in the number, distribution, and quality of health personnel, compared with the past, but also their responsiveness to present patterns of need.

The development of health services, therefore, has to be measured in relation to changing conceptions of illness or health and to patterns of need. Conceptions are constantly being amended or revised. There are substantial cultural differences between developing and market or planned societies, and also among the latter. Revisions are made not just in response to the recognition and communication of social discovery and innovation, or to professional judgements of objective needs and of the status of different diseases and treatments, but also in response to the pressure of vested interests, and the level and type of public anxiety and demand. Pain, discomfort, debility, and different forms of incapacity may come to play, in relation to prospective sudden death or physiological malfunctioning, a more prominent part in social and medical conceptions. Types of human behaviour may be shifted into the territory labelled 'illness' and controversies about the demarcation of the boundaries may be settled. The boundary is continually being redrawn and disputed. This could be illustrated from the history of so-called 'fringe' medicine, the history of the treatment of madness, and the diverse history in different countries of the treatment of severe mental handicap. Fundamentally, all societies distinguish between those abnormal conditions and actions requiring sympathetic indulgence and expert aid, and those conditions and actions regarded as deviant and requiring reprobation and correction. Inevitably medicine is drawn into the argument by virtue of its responsibility for definitions of illness and disability. In this debate, we may observe, medicine is by no means necessarily on the side of humanitarian or radical values. While some types of criminals have been reclassified as sick and have as a consequence received rehabilitative rather the custodial or punitive forms of treatment, some types of healthy people, who happen to have been critical of Government or an embarrassment to the community, have been classified as sick and removed from view.

Just as the scope of the conception may change, elements within it may be accorded different weight or priority. Views are reached about the seriousness of certain states of health. The construction and priorities of the health services follow suit. The relative scale and importance of different services tend to get distorted whether, for example, as a result of willingness on the part of consultants and general practitioners to accede to requests for certain forms of treatment and surgery (cosmetic surgery is a case in point) or as a result of the disproportionate esteem in which certain types of specialist roles are held within the medical profession (as in the unequal value accorded to acute as compared with chronic sickness, physical as compared with mental illness or handicap, surgery as compared with preventative health). Health personnel, patients, and organisations come to be divided up more for purposes of status differentiation than mere convenience or efficiency. Once institutionalised, an unbalanced structure affects the behaviour of participants. It affects priorities, for example, by influencing the number and urgency of referrals and distorts professional as well as public judgements of medical need, and hence what is believed in society to be the nature of illness itself. In short, conceptions of illness or disability and therefore also of severity of condition are shaped socially. They are institutionalised in medical practice and the organisation, subdivision, and administration of services.

That is why, under the ægis of the medical and social sciences, there has to be an unremitting search for independent, detached, or objective standards of measurement and evaluation. As I have suggested, this can be done to a large extent by systematic application of the comparative method: conceptions of health, standards of care and investment of resources can be compared cross-culturally, resources and quality of service can be compared regionally and locally, between short-stay and long-stay patients, between services in institutions and those in the community, between rich and poor, people of different age, the employed and the non-employed, and people with different types of disease or disability. Like the scientist's use of the randomised control trial,[6] this approach represents one of the social scientist's methods of attempting to escape subjectivity and convention and so to comprehend the subtle operations of prejudice and privilege in our midst.

## The National Health Service

Some of these ideas can be applied to the NHS. Its creation has deeper roots than is often supposed. The vast majority of hospital patients, for example, were treated free long before 1948. Paying patients had never accounted for more than a small fraction, perhaps 5%, of all hospital patients.[7] As elsewhere in Europe there was a long history of the sponsorship and control by consumers of prepayment methods of meeting medical costs. In 1804, long before the British Medical Association was founded, there were about a million members of friendly societies in Britain and, in 1900, seven million.[8] Between 1918 and 1939, beginning with the Dawson Report in 1920, a succession of studies and reports recommending a comprehensive health service were issued by a wide range of different organisations, including the British Medical Association. The Emergency Medical Service and the extension of national health insurance in the 1939-45 war preceded the declaration of principle in the Beveridge Report and the Coalition Government's white papers. A Conservative Government would have been obliged in 1945 to sustain the momentum.

[…]

## Measures of health

Estimates of the effect or value of the Health Service depend of course on the kind as well as availability of information used to measure such effect or value. There are measures of health, as such, which depend on conceptions of health, and there are measures of utilisation and provision of services, each of which is needed to assist explanations of trends in health, and of social differences in mortality and morbidity.

Measures of the health of populations can take many different forms. Among the most familiar are mortality-rates, prevalence or incidence morbidity-rates, sickness-absence rates, and restricted-activity rates. Each is limited as an indicator of health and involves problems of measurement. If we were to concentrate too much attention on mortality we would imply that health services can adopt the goals of death in life or medicated survival, and if on medically identifiable morbidity that some conditions of listlessness, depression, sleeplessness, and anxiety can be discounted or at least treated relatively lightly. It was to bring wider conceptions of states of health into the picture that the World Health Organisation adopted the sweeping goal of positive physical, mental, and social wellbeing rather than the absence of disease. This posed problems not only of measurement in research and the collection of statistical data but of the practical use of such measures in preventive and curative health policies. Attempts are indeed being made to construct more sophisticated health indicators. Thus, one "state of health" indicator combines the two dimensions of pain and restricted activity.[9] The problem here is that the pursuit of novel methods can lead to an arrogant disregard of the valuable lessons that can be drawn by continuing to apply the simpler methods used in pioneering studies, like Titmuss' *Poverty and Population*.

Let me give a few examples. By the test of trends in mortality-rates, critical questions have to be posed about the performance of Britain's health services. The test can be made in different ways. First, reduction in mortality-rates has been slower in Britain than in some other advanced industrial societies. A Scottish study pointed out that despite a continuing reduction of infant mortality over the past 20 years England and Wales slipped from 5th to 8th place, and Scotland from 8th to 12th in the ranking of countries.[10] Table I gives illustrations of the differential rates of improvement, including remarkable improvements in the Netherlands, Belgium, France, and, especially, Japan.

**Table I – Infant mortality: rate per 1000 live births**

| Country | 1950 | 1960 | 1970 | 1971 |
|---|---|---|---|---|
| Netherlands | 25.2 | 17.9 | 12.7 | 11.1 |
| USA | 29.2 | 26.0 | 19.8 | 19.2 |
| United Kingdom | 31.4 | 22.5 | 18.4 | 17.9 |
| Canada | 41.3 | 27.3 | 18.8 | 17.6 |
| France | 52.0 | 27.4 | 15.1 | 14.4 |
| Belgium | 53.4 | 31.2 | 20.5 | 19.8 |
| USSR | .. | 35.0 | 24.4 | 22.6 |
| Germany (Fed Rep) | 55.5 | 33.8 | 23.6 | 23.2 |
| Japan | 60.1 | 30.7 | 13.1 | 12.4 |
| Italy | 63.8 | 43.9 | 29.2 | 28.3 |

*Source:* UN Statistical Yearbook 1972

The same trends can be followed, though less reliably, at later ages. Even a cursory scrutiny of the United Nations *Statistical Yearbook* shows, for example for men, that while the expectation of life at birth has lengthened in England and Wales by 2 or 3% in 20 years, it has lengthened more dramatically in other industrial nations, some of which have now surpassed, and others almost attained, our figure.

The explanation of the figures can be pursued by examining inequalities between the sexes, age–groups, classes, areas, types of disease, and disability. Over a period of 20 years the ratio of female to male expectation of life in England and Wales has increased at all ages. While female expectation of life has lengthened at all ages male expectation has increased to only a modest extent among those in their 20s and 30s, has barely increased among men aged 45, and has decreased marginally among older men (table II).

**Table II** – Expectation of Life, England and Wales (yr)

| Age | Males | | Females | |
| --- | --- | --- | --- | --- |
| | 1948-50 | 1968-70 | 1948-50 | 1968-70 |
| 0 | 66.3 | 68.6 | 71.0 | 74.9 |
| 5 | 64.2 | 65.3 | 68.4 | 71.3 |
| 25 | 45.3 | 46.0 | 49.4 | 51.7 |
| 45 | 27.0 | 27.1 | 30.9 | 32.6 |
| 55 | 18.8 | 18.7 | 22.4 | 23.8 |
| 65 | 12.2 | 11.9 | 14.6 | 15.8 |

*Source:* DHSS[33]: table 1.6

The trends are different for people of different class, and, in terms of probing constructively the operation of the Health Service, are perhaps the most important of all to examine. Between 1949-53 and 1959-63 inequality between social classes in mortality experience appears, from data published by the Registrar General, to have widened. Indeed, "the social class gradient increases with successive censuses so that in 1959-63 the Standardised Mortality Ratio for social class I is only about half that of social class V."[11] The trouble is that the figures do not represent the real trends very accurately, because of changes introduced in 1960 in the classification of occupations, possible changes in the number and extent of discrepancies between the recording of occupations on death certificates and on census schedules, and the fact that occupations in the Census of 1961 were based on a 10% sample.

Statisticians and social scientists have therefore been slow to utilise the data, dismayed perhaps by the Registrar General's statement that "It is impossible to disentangle real differential changes in mortality in this context from apparent differences due to changes in classification."[11] But the Registrar General must bear responsibility for failing to disentangle these elements, for example by working out the SMRS for each class in 1959-63 according to the 1950 Census of Occupations and not only for social class V, which he did as a kind of partial addendum. Specialist analysis and anxiety, and public comment, have been inhibited.

Yet the data are of immense significance. Further examination suggests that even if its exact extent remains debatable the trend of growing inequality is securely established. For example, the Registrar General points out that among the closed professions the data are "substantially free from the effect of classification changes, and errors due to mis-statement of occupation or change of occupation must be few" and between 1951 and 1961 the mortality-rates for middle-aged lawyers, teachers and clergymen fell more sharply than those for all men. So "not all the improvement in social classes I and II is due to differences in classification". Moreover, he finds that "the most disturbing feature of the present results when compared with earlier analyses is the apparent deterioration in social class V … whilst the mortality of all men fell at all ages except 70-74, that for social class V men … rose at all ages except 25-34. *Even when the rates are adjusted to the 1950 classification*, it is clear that class V men fared much worse than average" (my emphasis). [11] An adjusted figure for class V as a whole is not given, but the adjusted figures for particular age groups (table D6) suggest that if the old classification had been used the figure in table III of 143 for social class V would still be around 128, representing a clear deterioration between 1949-53 and 1959-63.

[…]

## Table III – Standardised mortality ratios by social class

| Social class | Men (15-64) | | | Married women (15-64) | Single women (15-64) |
|---|---|---|---|---|---|
| | 1930-32 | 1949-53 | 1959-63 | 1959-63 | 1959-63 |
| I. Professional | 90 | 86 | 76 | 77 | 83 |
| II. Managerial | 94 | 92 | 81 | 83 | 88 |
| III. Skilled manual and non-manual | 97 | 101 | 100 | 102 | 90 |
| IV. Partly skilled | 102 | 104 | 103 | 105 | 108 |
| V. Unskilled | 111 | 118 | 143 | 141 | 121 |

(1) Information about occupations in the 1961 Census, with which information from death certificates for 1959-63 was compared, was based on a 10% sample.

(2) Occupations in 1961 were reclassified on a new basis with the result that approximately 24% would have been allocated to a different class if the 1950 basis of classification had been used. However, the vast majority of these (92%) were reclassified to the next ascending or descending class in rank order.

(3) The SMRS for 1949-53 in column 2 have been adjusted by the Registrar General from the figures first published to correct certain errors.

*Source:* Registrar General's Decennial Supplement[11]; tables D4 and 4.

Taking all adults of both sexes between the ages of 15 and 64 the disadvantages during the 5 years 1959-63 can be summarised. If the mortality experience of social class I had applied to social class V only just over half of them would have died; 40,000 lives would have been spared.

This disturbing trend has to be judged in the context of a wide variety of other data. Although maternal mortality among married women has continued to fall, the differences between the social classes have widened.[11] Trends in infant mortality are harder to establish. As Morris and others have shown, the differential between the classes narrowed between 1930 and 1950 but this was during a period when the differential was greater than it was in the case of adult mortality.[12] By 1959-63 the differential seems to have come to correspond more closely with that for adults (see table V), but separate data for each social class and for different occupations for the three Census periods have not been published.[13] This is a serious gap in medical and social knowledge, as Hart has eloquently argued.[14]

In the early 1960s the Department of Health became concerned about the slow decrease in the death-rate for infants at ages between 1 month and 1 year and undertook a study in three areas to try to identify avoidable factors contributing to deaths. Two pædiatric assessors estimated that there were avoidable factors in 28% of cases, in about a third of which social factors, another third parental factors and a quarter of which general-practitioner or hospital factors were believed to be responsible. The GP factors included a diagnostic delay or failure, slowness in reference to hospital, failure to realise severity of the situation, and delay in visiting. The hospital-service factors involved diagnostic failures or delay, hospital-acquired infection, and faulty management.[15] This was a pilot inquiry and it is likely that more rigorous research on a comparative basis would come better to grips with all the factors involved and demonstrate inadequacies not only of income, environment, and education but of health services too.

A good start has been made in parallel work in hospitals. A number of research studies have demonstrated sharp differences among hospitals in the outcome of treatment for specific conditions, some types of hospital, for example, having much higher rates of fatality.[16] This type of work begins to call attention to inequalities in the distribution of resources, and quality of care, in the hospital service.

To what extent are the patterns produced by analyses of mortality a misleading representation of patterns of illness? One source of information is sickness-absence rates. While pointing out the unusual degree of care that has to be exercised in interpreting sickness-absence statistics, some studies show, for example, high correlations between mortality and inception rates of sickness, and between mortality and days of sickness.[17] Various reservations have to be made about particular types of diseases and causes of mortality. Thus, diseases of the respiratory system "cause a considerably larger proportion of sickness than of mortality, but the average length of such spells of sickness is comparatively short. On the other hand, arteriosclerotic and degenerative heart disease cause over a quarter of male deaths in the age range 15-64, but only a very small part of the total sickness is recorded against them, but where such sickness does occur, it is of long duration."[17] But in compiling mortality and sickness absence ratios both for specific occupations and for social classes, such factors tend to balance out, and there are high correlations between the two, especially between mortality and days of sickness. Table VI compares mortality with sickness–absence ratios by social class. The sickness–absence ratios were derived from claims for sickness benefit in Britain for the period June 5, 1961, to June 2, 1962, as analysed in a Government report.[18] Spells of notified sickness lasting less than 4 days were excluded, since very few such spells are reported. Some long-term sickness was excluded because those who had been ill for a long time were less likely to be on an employer's payroll.

**Table VI** – Comparative ratios for mortality (1959-63) and sickness absence (1961-62) for males by social class

| Social class | All males 15-64 | Employed males 15-64 sickness | |
| --- | --- | --- | --- |
| | | Comparative inception figure | Comparative duration figure |
| I and II | 80 | 64 | 50 |
| III | 100 | 100 | 93 |
| IV | 103 | 109 | 117 |
| V | 143 | 124 | 154 |

*Source:* Daw[17].

A second measure of morbidity has been developed recently. For 1972 the General Household Survey found that in England and Wales nearly three times as many unskilled as professional men and more than three times as many females suffered, by their own account, from "limiting long-standing illness, disability or infirmity"[19] (Table VII). For 1971, according to the same source, nearly 2½ times as many unskilled as professional men reported absence from work due to illness or injury during a two-week period and they lost an average of 4½ times as many days from work in the year.[20] Like mortality ratios, both sickness–absence ratios and measures of "limiting long-standing illness" demonstrate the disadvantage of the partly skilled and unskilled occupational classes.

Another, indirect, measure of state of health is of physique. Careful measures of differences in height and weight in a population can be valuable indicators of trends in health. In the mid-1960s data from the National Child

Development Study for 7-year-olds showed that there had been "little if any change in Social Class differences" since 1953. The actual figures derived from the two studies show a slight widening of the gap – though this could be attributable to sampling and slight differences in method. An average difference of 3.3 cm between children from social class I or II and those from social class V in height was found, compared with 2.8 cm between "upper middle class" and "lower working class" children in 1953.[21, 22]

## Inequalities in the development of services

I am painfully aware that these measures of health are incomplete and that a more comprehensive picture might be built up patiently from the rich literature which we possess, even if, in the end, the aim to develop in precise terms a balanced index of the health needs of the population remained unfulfilled. But the measurement of inequalities in need by class or income is, I believe, central to that task and to the evaluation of the Health Service.

The role of the Health Service is by no means the only or even the crucial factor in determining social differences in mortality and morbidity. Explanations for inequalities in health have complex ætiologies. The quality and distribution of different health services could improve relative to other social institutions as well as the past and yet, because of a relative growth in other forms of inequality of incomes or wealth, work conditions and physical arduousness, home, family and social conditions and life styles, the effects of such improvement on trends in mortality, morbidity, and states of health could be cancelled out. But trends in the organisation and utilisation of the health services must themselves be summarised and understood.

We must proceed from the general to the particular. Britain devotes a smaller proportion of its total resources to the health services than several other advanced industrial societies, and this proportion is growing less swiftly (Table VIII). Earlier studies for WHO[23, 24] and by the Canadian Royal Commission on Health Services[25] had shown that Britain's percentage of gross national product devoted to health had remained fairly static in the first years after the establishment of the National Health Service in 1948, while that of other countries had been growing. The latest comparative study shows that although Britain's figure grew in the 1960s, it grew relatively slowly: "Three countries, France, Canada, and Sweden, have the most rapid adjusted rate of growth in health expenditures, ranging from 8.7 to 9.0 per cent. In contrast, Germany and the United Kingdom show the slowest growth rate, 4.7 and 5.1 per cent, respectively".[26] The rate of growth was approximately the same under the Labour Administration of 1964-70 as under the Conservative Administration of 1959-63, and was distinctly smaller than the rate for other social services (eg, education).[27, 28] According to the latest public-expenditure programme for the years up to

1977-78, this pattern is unlikely to change – indeed, proposed expenditure on health for the next 5 years has been cut back from what was envisaged in the previous white-paper.[29]

**Table VIII** – Total expenditures for health services as % of GNP and average percentage rate of increase, seven countries 1961-69

| Country | Early 1960s | | 1969 | Average annual rate of increase in real terms (%)† |
|---|---|---|---|---|
| | Year | % of GNP | % of GNP | |
| Canada | 1961 | 6.0 | 7.3 | 7.7 |
| United States | 1961-62 | 5.8 | 6.8 | 9.0 |
| Sweden | 1962 | 5.4 | 6.7 | 8.7 |
| Netherlands | 1963 | 4.8 | 5.9 | 8.7 |
| Germany (Fed. Rep.) | 1961 | 4.5* | 5.7 | 4.7 |
| France | 1963 | 4.4 | 5.7 | 6.5 |
| United Kingdom | 1961-62 | 4.2 | 4.8 | 5.1 |

* Estimate made by the US Social Security Administration.
† Health expenditures adjusted by the US Social Security Administration according to average consumer price index and wage index changes.
*Source:* Simanis[26] and Abel-Smith[24].

Although Britain spends relatively less than, say, the United States, this is partly because its health services are less expensive and partly because its rates of admission to hospital and rates of surgery are lower.[30] There is evidence too that, from a smaller cost base, services are in some respects more equally distributed. Thus, utilisation of medical services by different status groups, by the acute and chronic sick or mentally ill and handicapped, and by adults below and above pensionable age, is more unequal in the United States than in Britain.[31, 32] On the other hand, services in some European countries, such as Czechoslovakia and Sweden, are less equally distributed in some respects than in Britain, for example, between the acute sick and the chronic sick, mentally ill or handicapped in hospital.[23, 24]

The hospitals have more than maintained their share (more than half) of total expenditure on health services. Against a slightly lower total number of inpatient beds (though with much higher admission and discharge rates) has to be set a doubling of both hospital medical and nursing staff between 1949 and 1971. But the number of general medical practitioners has not changed substantially. In 1959 there were 38% more general practitioners than hospital medical staff in England and Wales: in 1971 there were 8% less. This suggests the power or predominance of the hospital in the British system, the increasing location of clinical expertise outside local communities, and the evolution of a better-developed status hierarchy in medical practice, consultants obtaining enhanced power.

[…]

I am arguing that measures of utilisation have to be related to measures of need. This principle has been applied imaginatively in Britain by some writers lately[34, 35] but no opportunity seems to have been taken to apply it as systematically as in some other societies. For example, a Finnish study published in 1968 showed that the average number of consultations per 100 days with a physician was higher in the lowest than in the highest income group, but when consultations were standardised in respect of days of sickness, the trend was reversed. Moreover, the advantage of the relatively rich was shown for both the acute and chronic sick. "The lower the income, the higher the morbidity and the lower the utilisation of medical services in relation to morbidity." Incidentally, and this has important implications for the development in Britain of group practice, health centres, and district general hospitals of substantial size, the use of a physician's services was found to decrease with increasing distance to physician for all groups.[36]

In building up a picture of utilisation of different health services it must not be supposed, because some services are heavily utilised by the poorer working classes, that this is necessarily contributory evidence of equitable provision of health services as a whole. Like other major institutional systems of society the health system is organised in a hierarchy of value and status. No one today would argue that the heavy utilisation of secondary-modern schools by the working classes constitutes evidence of equality of educational provision. Despite the scarcity of data the point can be made for health institutions. In a national study of the elderly in institutions in the mid-1960s I found that more of those from non-manual than unskilled or partly skilled manual backgrounds were in geriatric hospitals than in psychiatric hospitals, even when some attempt was made to standardise among patients by type of incapacity, confusion, and lucidity, and were also in the better endowed hospitals within these sectors – defined by furnishings and shared spaces as well as staffing ratios. The same applied to the populations of private, voluntary, and newly built local-authority residential homes, when compared with the populations of older local-authority homes.[37-39] At least to some extent, clinical and administrative decisions seem to be influenced both by the status of institutions and the social class of patients. More too of the poorer working classes may stay longer in certain health and residential institutions for social reasons, either because there is no easy alternative mode of life for them in the community (they cannot find homes, have no capital and little income) or because the institutions in which they live develop a functional need for their labour, their lack of demand upon a hard-pressed medical and nursing staff or their value for teaching.

[…]

## The problems of professionalism, managerial control, and privileged access to knowledge

I have pursued the twin themes of inequality in health conditions or needs and of provision of services. The evidence invites searching reappraisal of the whole development of our health system. There are problems of identifying performance, understanding the interconnections within the health system of different branches of service and defining its boundaries, and explaining why policies designed to lead to more equitable distribution of services have been frustrated. A deeper analysis of the persistence and even the widening of inequality may be required.

Of course, however widely the health system is conceived and drawn, its potentiality is restricted. The system is not the only determinant of mortality or morbidity. States of health depend on peace or war, nutrition, living standards, education, and the working environment. One illustration might be given. Whereas staffing ratios for health visitors, consultants, obstetricians, pædiatricians, and general practitioners are all slightly higher in Scotland than in England and Wales, the infant-mortality rate in Scotland remains relatively high. Scotland has a legacy of poor housing, especially in the major cities, and a Scottish Health Service study found, for example, that the infant-mortality rate was directly proportional to the degree of overcrowding.[40]

The interdependence of services within the system also deserves to be better understood. Measures of adequacy and efficiency must be developed not just for particular services, because that implies they are isolated from one another, and isolated in their effects. They must be designed to represent that interdependence. General practice complements and is interconnected with hospital and specialist medicine on the one hand and with public health and welfare or personal social services on the other. The relative scale, balance, and working functions of each part of the system have to be identified for local communities as well as for the nation as a whole.

[...]

The right of the sick to free access to health care, irrespective of class or income, remains to be firmly established. The treatment in particular of many of the aged, chronic sick and disabled, mentally ill and mentally handicapped, remains scandalously poor and can in the long run be dramatically improved only be a redefinition of health and health needs, and by a reconstruction of professional values and organisation, the education and involvement of the patient, and the establishment of social equality.

### References
[1] Morris, J.N. *Uses of Epidemiology*, London, 1964.
[2] DHSS *Health and Personal Social Services Statistics for England 1973*; p 39. HM Stationery Office, 1973.

[3] United Nations Statistical Yearbook for 1971.

[4] DHSS *Annual Report for 1969*, HM Stationery Office, 1970.

[5] Titmuss, R.M. *Commitment to Welfare*; p 126. London, 1969.

[6] Cochrane, A.L. *Effectiveness and Efficiency;* chaps 4 and 6. London, 1972.

[7] Abel-Smith, B. *The Hospitals, 1800-1948*, London, 1964; Hart, J.T. *Int. J. Hlth Serv.* 1972, **2**, 349.

[8] Abel-Smith, B. *Bull. of N.Y. Acad. Med.* 1964, **40**, 545.

[9] Culyer, A.J., Lavers, R.J., Williams, A. in *Social Indicators and Social Policy* (edited by A. Shonfield and S. Shaw), London, 1972.

[10] Scottish Home and Health Department. Joint Working Party on the Integration of Medical Work. *Towards an Integrated Child Health Service*; p. 8. Edinburgh, 1973.

[11] Registrar General's Decennial Supplement, England and Wales, 1961: occupational mortality tables. HM Stationery Office, 1971.

[12] Morris, J.N. *Lancet*, 1959, i, 303.

[13] Spicer, C.C., Lipworth, L. *Stud. Med. Popul. Subj.* no. 19. London, 1966.

[14] Hart, J.T. *Lancet*, 1972, i, 192.

[15] *Rep. publ. Hlth med. Subj.* 1970, no. 125, p. 18.

[16] Ashley, J.S.A., Howlett, A., Morris, J.N. *Lancet*, 1971, ii, 1308.

[17] Daw, R.H. *J. Inst. Actuaries*, 1971, **97**, 17.

[18] Ministry of Pensions and National Insurance. Report on an Enquiry into the Incidence of Incapacity for Work: part II, incidence of incapacity for work in different areas and occupations. HM Stationery Office, 1965.

[19] *Social Trends* no. 4, table 69.

[20] Office of Population Censuses and Surveys Social Survey Division. The General Household Survey; p. 304. HM Stationery Office, 1973.

[21] Goldstein, H. *Hum. Biol.* 1971, **43**, 92.

[22] Douglas, J.W.B., Simpson, H. *Millbank Meml Fnd Q.* 1964, **42**, 20.

[23] Abel-Smith, B. *Paying for Health Services: a Study of the Costs and Sources of Finance in Six Countries*. Geneva, 1963.

[24] Abel-Smith, B. *An International Study of Health Expenditure*. Geneva, 1967.

[25] Report of the Royal Commission on Health Services; vol. I, p. 482. Ottawa, 1964.

[26] Simanis, J.G. *Soc. Sec. Bull.* March, 1973, p. 41.

[27] Townsend, P. *Times*, March 11, 1971.

[28] Townsend, P. *Social Policy*. London, 1974.

[29] Public Expenditure to 1977-78; pp. 6, 96. Cmnd. 5519. HM Stationery Office, 1973.

[30] Mechanic, D. *J. Hlth soc. Behav.* 1971, **12**, 18.

[31] Mechanic, D. *Medical Sociology: a Selective View*; p. 266. New York, 1968.

[32] Townsend, P. in *Old People in Three Industrial Societies* (edited by E. Shanas, P. Townsend, D. Wedderburn, H. Friis, P. Milhøj and J. Stehouwer); p 97. London, 1968.

[33] DHSS Health and Personal Social Services Statistics for England (with Summary tables for Great Britain); HM Stationery Office, 1973.

[34] Morris, J.N. in *The NHS: Three Views*. Fabian Research Series no. 287. London, 1970.

[35] Morris, J.N. *Proc. R. soc. Med.* 1973, **66**, 225.

[36] Purola, T., Kalimo, E., Sievers, K., Nyman, K. *The Utilisation of the Medical Services and its Relationship to Morbidity, Health Resources and Social Factors*; p. 144. Research Institute for Social Security, Helsinki, 1968.

[37] Townsend, P. in *Needs of the Elderly for Health and Welfare Services* (by R. W. Canvin and N. G. Pearson). University of Exeter, 1973.

[38] Townsend, P. *The Last Refuge*; p. 580, London, 1962.

[39] Carstairs, V., Morrison, M. *Scott. Hlth Serv. Stud.* 1972, no 19, p. 40.

[40] Richards, I.D.G. Scott. *Hlth Serv. Stud.* 1971, no. 16.

# 32

# Health and deprivation

## The widening mortality gap

This book aims to contribute to the scientific understanding and explanation of inequalities in health in Britain, partly by reviewing recent national evidence about mortality but mainly by examining detailed statistical evidence for small areas covering a major region of the country. For the populations of 678 wards throughout the Northern Region of England the book explores the meaning and practicable measures of 'material deprivation' and 'poor health' and demonstrates a consistent and very strong association between the two.

The publication of the Black Report in 1980 provided emphatic confirmation that the years since the establishment of the National Health Service had not seen a decline in social inequalities in health in Britain. Indeed, it produced evidence of widening inequalities and not just vivid statistical illustrations of big differences in health experience. Perhaps partly fuelled by the Government's dismissive response to that report, and faced with the implications for health posed by the deepest economic recession since the 1930s, public and scientific interest in health inequalities has continued to grow during the 1980s. The swelling number of papers on the problems of resource allocation for health care and area studies of health are just two relevant examples. The present study epitomises this recent development, and provides, perhaps for the first time, an analysis of the health of small areas across an entire region of the country.

The Northern Region is not a microcosm or reflection of the country as a whole, either in health or social and economic terms: rather, it is one of its most deprived constituent parts. The areas of biggest mortality and morbidity in Britain are overwhelmingly to be found in the North and North-West, in Scotland and in Wales; they are almost entirely absent in Southern England, except for one or two areas of inner London. These are also areas where the recession and its human dimension of unemployment and reduced living standards have been felt most severely. An analysis of inequality in health in the North is, therefore, biased towards the worse end of the health spectrum in Britain, as we showed in the early part of this book.

Townsend, P., Phillimore, P. and Beattie, A. (1988) 'Conclusions' in *Health and deprivation: Inequality and the North*, Beckenham: Croom Helm, pp 151-9.

## Aims and concepts

The study has had two principal aims: firstly, to find ways of depicting the severity and distribution of both poor health and material deprivation – particularly across hundreds of areas within a single region; and secondly, to help to account for the unequal distribution of health by studying its association with material deprivation in particular but also with occupational class.

The first step has been to clarify the key concepts and to select practicable measures for study and analysis. Poor health must be understood as more than a risk of premature death and as more than the prevalence of clinically ascertainable disease. However, in dealing with other features of poor health, it has to be admitted that there is a lack of practical measures of reduced vitality or activity, discomfort or pain, debility or low morale among the population – to give different examples. At this stage of the analysis of health, it nonetheless seems important to symbolise the principle that scientists must deal with more than mortality experience, even when they include mortality as a necessary datum. Three measures were chosen in this report as examples of this broader approach to the meaning of poor health, namely:

(1) *Mortality*. SMRs for persons (i.e. both sexes together) aged under 65 years, based on deaths over a three-year period, 1981-3.
(2) *Disablement*. The proportion of all residents in private households aged 16 and over who classed themselves as permanently sick or disabled at the 1981 Census.
(3) *Delayed Development*. The proportion of live births below 2,800 gm, based on births over three years, 1982-4.

These three measures have been described separately and in combination, in the form of an 'Overall Health Index'. Analysis of poor health has focused both on the separate and the combined measures.

A coherent conceptualisation of deprivation is equally important. Material deprivation needs to be separated in principle from social deprivation and then represented, so far as possible, by a sufficient 'spread' of sub-elements or measures which do not simply reproduce or overlap each other and hence misrepresent the reality being measured. A distinction must also be drawn in favour of direct experience of deprivation and not just membership of a sub-group or minority at risk of that deprivation. The incompatibility, duplication and poor coverage of indicators appears to be a problem with much of the scientific study of deprivation at the present time. In this research the following variables were each drawn from the 1981 Census. As discussed in the text, each was independently validated in regression analyses, and in combination provided a much more powerful explanatory variable than any separate component.

(1) *Unemployment.* The percentage of economically active residents aged 16-59/64 who were unemployed.
(2) *Non-ownership of a car.* The percentage of private households not possessing a car.
(3) *Non-ownership of a home.* The percentage of private households renting rather than owning or buying a home.
(4) *Overcrowding.* The percentage of private households containing more than one person per room.

The four separate measures of deprivation were combined to form an 'Overall Deprivation Index'.

## Findings

What were our principal findings? Firstly, the differences in health between local populations are very wide and perhaps more consistently wide than presumed in recent scientific discussion. Different examples can be given. According to the chosen indicators the ward with the poorest overall health was Wheatley Hill in Easington. With a population of 3754 the ward had 52 deaths of persons under 65 and 23 low-weight births in three recent years, and there were 145 people reported as permanently sick or disabled in 1981. At the other extreme, with a roughly comparable population of 4,014, the ward of Hutton in Langbaurgh had 11 deaths and 9 low-weight births and there were only 18 reported as permanently sick or disabled in 1981. Standardised Mortality Ratios (SMRs) and rates worked out on the appropriate population basis are shown for all 678 wards in Appendix 6. The ward with poorest health (Wheatley Hill) had three times as many people unemployed, more than ten times as many households without a car, more than fifteen times as many overcrowded households and twelve times as many households not owning their homes as in the ward of comparable size with best health, namely Hutton.

Although there are pockets of ill-health to be found in every district in the North, there are certain major concentrations of poor health to compare with more dispersed areas of good health. Thus, for example, very high rates of premature mortality were found across a large number of adjoining wards on the south side of the Tees in Middlesbrough and Langbaurgh and in a smaller area straddling the Tyne in Newcastle and Gateshead. The severity of poor health in Easington and Hartlepool is also particularly striking: no less than six of Easington's wards feature among the 25 wards out of the total of 678 with the worst overall health in the Region. Another method of demonstrating inequalities is to compare wards divided into ten or five bands or groups on different criteria. When all 678 wards were divided into ten groups ranked according to SMRs, the 10 per cent with worst mortality had an SMR of 165, compared with an SMR of 58 for the 10 per cent with the lightest mortality (Table 6.5). The ratio between the two is 2.8:1.

The wards were also divided into five groups according to their overall health. The fifth (136 wards) with poorest health had an SMR for persons aged 0-64 of 143 compared with 80 for the fifth with best health. There were 18 per cent of low-weight births in the worst fifth, compared with 10 per cent in the best fifth, and nearly three times as many residents aged 16 and over who were permanently sick and disabled in that fifth of wards with worst overall health. Moreover, through all five ranked bands of wards there was a clear step-wise gradient. This was also true for the available indicators of deprivation.

One graphic illustration of inequalities in health is provided by the two groups of 136 wards each at the top and bottom of the ranking by overall health. In the group of 136 wards with the best health (with a population of 376,000) the SMR is 80, the proportion of people permanently sick is 1.3 per cent and the proportion of low-weight births is only 10.1 per cent. On this basis we can then calculate the 'excess' mortality and morbidity in the 20 per cent of wards with worst health. If the low rates of ill-health had been experienced by the population of 788,000 who live in the 136 wards with the poorest health, then there would have been 1,356 fewer deaths of people under 65 each year; there would have been 13,823 fewer people permanently sick or disabled; and there would have been 890 fewer low-weight live births each year. Such statements can be used to formulate and clarify national and regional health objectives. They can be converted into definitions of attainable objectives in the development of future national health policies.

The second principal finding was that across the spectrum of wards in the Region, variations in health tended to correspond closely with variations in material deprivation or affluence. In other words, whilst the contrast between the extremes of the regional distribution of health and deprivation illustrates most dramatically the argument that a strong association exists between the two, even in the middle ranges of the regional distribution it is apparent that slight variations in social and economic well-being have parallels in slight variations in health. The association between poor health and material deprivation is statistically highly significant, with a correlation of 82 per cent between the Overall Health Index and the Overall Deprivation Index, and is relatively consistent. The different measures of health are also highly inter-correlated (though the measures of mortality and permanent sickness more so than of either of these two when matched with low birthweight). The different measures of deprivation are also highly intercorrelated, and that association is explored in various stages of the analysis above [see Figure 8.1].

**Figure 8.1:** The relationship between health and deprivation in the Northern Region

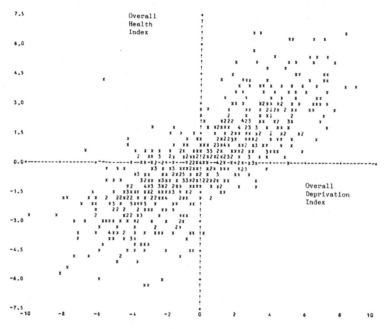

*Note:* Each 'X' represents one of the 678 wards; a number instead of an X indicates that more than one ward is situated at that point.

One part of the analysis centres on the concept of class, as made operational in the Registrar General's occupational classification.... Having presented evidence for occupational class gradients in mortality and low birthweight in wards at either end of the health spectrum, an attempt is made to explain how actual patterns of mortality differ from those which might be predicted on the basis of the occupational class composition of the populations of local areas, and how much of the high mortality in the two predominantly urban counties of the Region may be explicable solely in terms of the class structure of those areas. In practice it was unfortunately impossible to standardise for age and class simultaneously; nevertheless, the indications are that in areas of high mortality a large number, but by no means all, of the additional or 'excess' deaths may be attributed to the occupational class structure. There are also significant variations between one area and another. Most of Sunderland's raised mortality would seem explicable in terms of occupational class composition. In contrast, North Tyneside's high mortality is only to a small degree explained by occupational class composition alone.

These examples help to show that occupational class alone does not uniformly reflect the distribution of mortality: either there are factors independent of occupational class which contribute in substantial measure to any further explanation of excess deaths; or occupational class includes systematic variations in the experience of material deprivation which need to be revealed if a further large number of the observed excess deaths are to be explained. Another way of expressing this point is that occupational class is an imperfect representation of social class. If that is true then a substantial number of individuals will have been in effect misallocated to the wrong 'social' class. This leads to a second stage of our further analysis, in which the deprivation variables are reintroduced into the discussion, and are examined to discover how much of the variation in health they severally and in combination 'explain'.

What were already strong associations between individual measures of poor health and deprivation were found to become stronger when they were replaced by the combined measures – that is, the Overall Health and Overall Deprivation Indices. The strongest of the associations obtained was that between permanent sickness or disability and material deprivation. As is inevitable among a large number of local populations, there were interesting paradoxes. Areas with similar levels of severe deprivation sometimes differed significantly in health. Middlesbrough and Sunderland provide the most clearcut illustration of this, both districts containing large numbers of extremely deprived wards: but whilst in Middlesbrough these highly deprived wards for the most part experience ill-health which places them amongst the very worst in the region, in Sunderland the most deprived wards consistently experienced significantly less bad – though certainly by no means good – health. Regression analysis has been used to assess how much of the variation in health in certain groups of wards can be explained in statistical terms.

All four of the components of the Overall Deprivation Index make a significant contribution to explaining the variation in overall health. However, when individual counties are compared, different patterns emerge. The forms of deprivation with greatest explanatory value, and the extent to which they can explain the variance in health, are by no means identical in the five counties and the patterns are discussed in some detail in the text. Among the four deprivation indicators, only car ownership, the one which seems best to reflect relative material affluence, stands out in the regression equations for all five counties [see Table 8.3].

In each county the four deprivation indicators explain more of the variation in health than any of the indicators based on occupational class. Perhaps that is because they are closer to reflecting material economic standing in the

**Table 8.3:** Regression of Overall Health Index separately on deprivation and class indicators for each Northern Region county: proportion of variance in overall health explained by each regression

| County | Combination of some or all of the four main deprivation indicators chosen by stepwise regression | Percentage of households with head in manual class | Percentage of households with head in Class IV or V |
|---|---|---|---|
| Region | % Households with no car — 65% | 48 | 32 |
| | % Unemployed | | |
| | % Households overcrowded | | |
| | % Households not owner occupied | | |
| Tyne and Wear | % Households with no car — 78% | 60 | 76 |
| | % Households overcrowded | | |
| | % Households not owner occupied | | |
| Cleveland | % Unemployed — 81% | 60 | 64 |
| | % Households with no car | | |
| Cumbria | % Unemployed — 49% | 33 | 27 |
| | % Households with no car | | |
| | % Households overcrowded | | |
| Durham | % Households with no car — 56% | 49 | 34 |
| | % Households not owner occupied | | |
| | % Households overcrowded | | |
| Northumberland | % Households with no car — 52% | 33 | 3 |
| | % Households overcrowded | | |

*For* example, across the region as a whole (ie 678 wards) it is possible to explain 65% of the variance in overall health by a combination of the four main deprivation indicators, whereas only 48% and 32% respectively can be explained by two class variables.

community. Even when occupational class is incorporated into an extended set of deprivation measures, any improvement in accounting for variations in health is at best marginal. In other words, the explanatory power of the four deprivation variables is shown to be considerable – thereby justifying their initial choice.

In a final analysis, concentrating on mortality in Cleveland and Tyne and Wear, the regression technique is used to show how far actual mortality differs from that predicted on the basis of the experience of deprivation in each area. Mortality was higher in South Tees and especially central Tyneside than knowledge of the deprivation experienced in these areas would seem to imply. In contrast, mortality was relatively lower in North and West Sunderland.

Pollution has not figured in our operational measures of material deprivation. This problem needs to be remedied in future research, and depends upon producing measures which can be applied to small areas. It seems likely that the particular industrial configuration of the Teesside basin, and of factors operating in areas along the Tyne, and associated consequences of long-term exposure to various forms of environmental pollution, may be an important additional influence contributing to the high mortality in these areas. Given the limited sources of data available, the possibility can be no more than raised. We hope it will be followed up rigorously.

At the end of July 1986, the long-heralded OPCS report on occupational mortality was published. That report is equivocal about the value of analyses by social class but incorporates ... mortality data which demonstrate both the relatively worse mortality of the Northern Region and the widening national health gap between sections of the population ranked high and low on the social scale. In a special analysis of the microfiche tables issued with the OPCS report in July 1985, we compared trends in rates of mortality for occupational Classes I and II (now 27 per cent of the population) with those for Classes IV and V (now 29 per cent of the population). The change since the late 1940s is unmistakable. Relative to the poorer classes the mortality rates of the richer classes have substantially diminished since 1949. For men and women aged 25-34, the rates of Classes I and II in the early 1980s were less than half what they were in 1949-53. Rates of Classes IV and V have also diminished at the younger adult ages, but not as quickly. In middle age, however, there is now a striking difference. In 1979-83 the male mortality rate in England and Wales for those aged 45-54 in Classes IV and V was only 7 per cent lower, and for those aged 55-64 only 3 per cent lower than in 1949-53, whereas the rates in the richest classes had diminished by 37 per cent and 33 per cent respectively. The trends among women were similar, though the differences were a little less sharp.

At the beginning of Chapter 2 we referred to the work in the 1930s by M'Gonigle and Kirby (1936). This documented the social inequalities in health existing within Stockton-on-Tees and within Newcastle upon Tyne. Such inequalities persist today – between North and South, between the professional and managerial classes and the semi-skilled and unskilled classes, and between wards within each of the towns and cities in the North. This last point needs emphasising: the differences in levels of deprivation or privilege between wards in each town and city in the North are generally mirrored by differences in the health of their populations. Fifty years after M'Gonigle and Kirby were writing, the situation they described still exists.

In September 1984 the British Government joined all other European member countries in endorsing a World Health Organization Regional Office for Europe strategy. The primary aim was a reduction in inequalities in health by 25 per cent by the year 2000. The present study has documented just how great are the present inequalities in health within one severely deprived region of Britain.

## Reference

M'Gonigle, G.E.N. and Kirby, J. (1936) *Poverty and public health*, London: Gollancz.

# 33

# Individual or social responsibility for premature death?

[...]

A more developed sociological theory of trends in inequalities in health is badly needed. There is enormous, and growing, scientific and public interest in such inequalities. Some of the sources of that interest are easily recognised. Thus, the current program of the European Office of the World Health Organisation dealing very largely with that theme has stimulated a lot of research and debate (1), and even before that program began, reports and books had been published calling attention to the disconcerting trends in some of the advanced industrial societies, such as Britain, France, and Hungary, where there was evidence of a widening of inequalities (2, especially Chap. 3; 3). But there have also been indirect and even paradoxical reasons for the growth of interest, such as renewed concern with industrial hazards, the differential and unanticipated impact of some forms of environmental pollution, and the ramifying effects in first and third world countries alike of the internationalization of capital, production, and power.

In recent years a lot more work has been done on tracing and measuring inequalities in different countries. In one study, for example, inequality in mortality appeared to be greatest in France, somewhat less marked in England and Wales, Hungary, and Finland, and smallest in Denmark, Norway, and Sweden (4, 5). In the Nordic countries the gradients had remained constant, rather than increased (4; 5, Chap. 5; 6). On the other hand, those who had refused to accept the findings (7-13) were shown to have concentrated attention only upon a small part of the evidence and had confused the meaning of social inequalities (14-17; see also 18, pp. 13-16). Wide-ranging statistical studies showed that inequalities had in fact grown in England and Wales not just in the 1970s but, for both sexes and for nearly all age-groups, since the early 1950s (19-21; see also 2, pp. 63, 68). (For a longer historical view see 22-27.)

The relatively atheoretical absorption with statistical trends in different social or occupational classes and in different geographical areas, regions, and countries has been matched by a growing absorption on the part of

Extracts (pp 373-6, 380-3) from Townsend, P. (1990) 'Individual or social responsibility for premature death? Current controversies in the British debate about health', *International Journal of Health Services*, vol 20, no 3, pp 373-92.

social scientists in the 1980s with the problem of constructing better theory to account for the distribution of deaths, diseases, and disabilities. Let me give a few examples of the reasons for this newfound concern, each of which could be discussed at considerable length. First, the health care and preventive health policies of major countries are increasingly seen not to be connecting with the evidence of inequalities in the distribution of ill-health and premature death; in a real sense, and usually for quite clearly identifiable political and professional reasons, priorities in the construction of health policies are far from being influenced by science. This has been found to be very unsettling, partly because of the huge, and rising, costs of national health services. Second, there have been increasingly sharp social reactions against the casualty-oriented and individualized preoccupations of medicine. Third, sociologists and other social scientists have begun to ask insistently whether a sufficient balance for the 'social' or the 'institutional' is being provided in research, teaching, and the ideologies behind the organization of service by means of the traditional deployment of epidemiology and social medicine alongside medicine. Fourth, there has been growing pressure, especially within major European cities, and communicated politically as well as academically, to reopen the 19th century debate about public health. And, finally, there have been, and continue to be, widespread misgivings about the somewhat separate threats to population health of industrial pollution, trends in commercial food products, and the unpredicted hazards of many pharmaceutical products.

In this article I urge the value of what might be called a 'structural' approach – of recognising more consciously the innovating implications for population health of changes in economic and social institutions, and therefore of the interconnections and ultimate importance of general economic and social policies. My theme is the individual and the social, in the history of medicine and public health; ideas or concepts of health; contemporary economic management; the designation of responsibility for premature death and disease; and the construction of life-style.

## History of medicine and public health

Early medicine was not monolithic in its ideology. This is true of pre-scientific medicine. Hippocratic medicine was broad, because it drew on the ideas of experimental science, was patient-centred but doctor-directed, took a guild approach to practice and knowledge, and reflected, through the Hippocratic 'oath,' symbolic gods: Aesculapius (practicing on the basis of self-help), Hygeia (the goddess of cleanliness and a kind of forerunner to public health), Panacea (the forerunner of modern alternative medicine), and Apollo (the physician or god of medicine). Such medicine was concerned with knowledge gained at the bedside, but it was consciously understood to be shared knowledge, that is, knowledge confined to a closed circle under Pythagorean teaching about the community of property, including intellectual property. Some of the elements of Hippocratic medicine have continued to dominate medicine – confidentiality, personalized teaching, personal observation and examination, strict sexual mores, self-dependent authority, and an element of mysticism – many of which were designed to gain absolute control of professional practice. By isolating the individual for treatment, the politics of what transpired could be freed from the supervision or close involvement of others.

Foucault shows (28) that at the end of the 18th century the professional ideal became more complex. An aesthetic came to be defined which prescribed the norms of an art. The doctor was conditioned to look at the disease and not at the patient. The patient's admission depended on the prospective advantage to the clinician and his students. In a chapter entitled "Material for Teaching and Research," Brian Abel-Smith traces for England and Wales the change, as well as the accelerated development, of hospital practice (29, pp. 16–17):

> Before the founding of the hospital medical schools, medical teaching had been conducted by a combination of theoretical instruction and somewhat casual apprenticeship... There was a rush of students to the hospitals in the second decade of the nineteenth century... More hospitals acquired associated medical schools: more hospital surgeons took on teaching responsibilities and more hospitals were founded: the supply responded to the demand. While in the eighteenth century hospitals had been founded by laymen to meet to needs of the sick poor, in the first half of the nineteenth century many hospitals were founded to serve the needs of medical students and their teachers.

The patient's body and the recent context of his or her personal life and situation were not so much subjected to close and comprehensive examination as that his or her symptoms were deciphered. An order was imposed on the scrutiny of objects by the circle of doctor, students, and nurses at the bedside so that they would be better remembered and tested by experience. "Theory falls silent or almost always vanishes at the patient's bedside" (30, p. 174; as cited in 31). Instead of science determining organization, it was organization, or the development of the clinic, that conditioned and controlled the emergence of medical ideas.

From around the middle of the 19th century the scientific mode of medicine gained rapidly in influence. It reflects the Cartesian duality of the body and mind, and professes to be concerned with the body only as a machine, affected by its chemistry as well as its physics. This is the modern-day engineering model of medicine, with the doctor becoming a kind of biotechnician. The engineering approach to health is addressed essentially to the cure of diseases in individuals. Medicine is 'structured' in terms of cure rather than prevention, the identification and control of disease rather than the promotion of health and welfare, and the examination and treatment of the individual rather than of populations, groups, and families. Sociologically this can be demonstrated through observation and measurement in a variety of ways. Particular tests are the allocation of resources, particularly the neglect of the quantification of effect in the allocation of resources to research, and the scope of subject matter treated in medical journals, conferences, and syllabi.

It is important to recognize the sophisticated way in which the organization and practice of medicine confirm what is central in its conception and make more difficult the conception of an alternative 'social' model. As the Black Report (2) affirmed, medicine takes account of chronic diseases and long-term disabilities, and there are medical departments and preventive practices associated with the 'social' but they are not given priority or highest status. In the colleges, and in teaching, it is surgery and the treatment of the acutely ill that attracts the best-qualified personnel, and the highest rewards.

Nonetheless, a powerful critique of the medical model has developed in recent years. The dehumanizing effects of medical practice when carried to extremes, as in some forms of chemotherapy, surgery, and obstetrics, have been widely publicised. Illich (32), for example, argued that medicine was a threat to health through clinical, social, and cultural 'iatrogenesis.' Many other writers have followed, describing the unnecessary medicalization of wide areas of human experience [as in Ann Oakley's account of childbirth (33)] and the documentation of dangerous side effects, misplaced surgery, and addiction to drugs that had been prescribed by doctors. Marxist analysts have agreed with the 'medicalization' theme but have chosen a rather different path of criticism, because they consider Illich to have placed emphasis on industrialism rather than capitalism as the prime causal culprit. In the words of one of the most penetrating exponents, "By displacing social problems to the realm of individual behaviour management, medicine presumably frees itself and capital to pursue narrow economic interests through the manipulation of social goods and resources" (34; but see also 35–38). There were also broadly based scientific as well as moral arguments for a more socially grounded understanding of development (39–41).

Throughout the debate about medicine, there has been a constant attempt the make sense of the social statistics of ill-health. Traditionally, studies of the health of populations living in regions and small areas, together with studies of the relationship between health and social class, have had a powerful influence on Government policy in Britain. These two traditions of research were respected internationally as well as nationally. With hindsight it is possible to pick out the influence of the work of Farr (22), Chadwick (42), and others on the public health movement of the 19th century. Another example is the influence in the 1930s of Boyd Orr (43), Titmuss (23), M'Gonigle and Kirby (44), and many others. This tradition of population analysis had a big effect on the adoption of public health policies and, paradoxically, on the campaign in Britain for a national health service, but causal origins were not pursued to the point of demanding some reconciliation with the theoretical basis of medical practice. Public health remained an unconceptualized element of social policy and was kept at arm's length from medicine, which was allowed a momentum that came to dominate in the 20th century.

The force of the tradition of population health inquiries was, however, maintained. Statistical evidence of the gulf in health between rich and poor, and between populations living in prosperous and those in depressed areas, filtered remorselessly into the consciousness of all those playing a part in public life. This proved to be particularly important in the 1939-45 war. A Coalition Government acted to ensure minimum living standards for all and access to health care without regard to means. Both were articles of faith of successive Labour and Conservative administrations. And again, at the start of the 1990s, that tradition is bearing fruit once more.

[...]

## Individualism and theories of health and the economy

There is an international as well as economic dimension in our analysis of the structural determinants of inequalities of health. We are living in a world in which the internationalization of the economy is having effects that governments are increasingly powerless to countermand. The concerns of health cannot be divorced from wider economic and social developments. National welfare states are finding it increasingly difficult to maintain balanced internal development at a time when the power of international agencies and corporations has been growing so fast.

The distribution of health in the population has to be related to a theory of economic and social development. There are three broadly different theoretical approaches to the development of modern economics and their effects on health: neo-monetarist, Keynesian, and productionist. Those favoring the neo-monetarist approach perceive the decline of manufacturing employment and decentralisation as a natural process. But this is to accept market forces as prior and unalterable. Competition from alternative land uses such as warehousing and offices is believed to be squeezing old industry out at the same time as the advantages to manufacturing industry of being located in the center of cities have begun to evaporate. Large-scale public investment is regarded as a burden on the rest of the economy. European governments'

387

duty is to remove hindrances to market forces and to remove bureaucratic controls. The trouble with this approach, as Keynesians have pointed out, is the social and economic costs in the long run as well as the short run may be larger than the benefits gained, and that society may be thought to have some obligation to meet the needs as well as the structures that have been created over many years by previous policies within communities that cannot be expected to move bodily to new locations, or at the very least, not without a lot of special help. In recognizing the force of these objections, neo-monetarists sometimes accept the temporary need to stem the process of decline by grants and subsidies, and to provide some financial incentives to industry and the application of new technology in the replacement of former patterns of subsidy through regional employment policies.

Regional employment subsidies, which played a big part in the early 1970s, have been greatly reduced in real terms to enhance market rules of competition (as set out for members of the European Economic Community under the Rome Treaty), and at the same time very little has been done to enlarge the Social Fund and begin to establish European social services, or even controls on multinational enterprises at a time when the nation state is increasingly powerless to protect vulnerable sections of the labor market as well as the elderly and younger dependent poor. In conspiring with the unfettered development of an international market, governments have been prepared to accept industrial wastelands, dereliction, and widespread hardship – or they have found them inescapable. The European Social Charter is not much stronger than a paper house reconstructed to withstand a gale.

Neo-monetarist management is a combination of different features. Adherents point to uncompetitive high wages, poor productivity, and the need to reduce trades union influence and various legal restrictions on employees, eliminate artificial regulators of the labor market, such as Wages Councils and allegedly inflated unemployment benefits, and promote individual enterprise, as for example by helping those who cannot otherwise find work to start up in business themselves. All of this turns on a discriminatory view of the abilities and qualities of different sections of the population. While business elites are lauded, the poor are regarded with disparagement and even contempt. Much unemployment is presumed to depend on the characteristics and motivations of the unemployed themselves.

Britain in the 1990s presents an object lesson for any understanding of neo-monetarist edicts and their likely effects on population health. There has been a steady squeeze on low wages and social security benefits alike, the disparagement of public service as well as public expenditure, and taxation windfalls for the already rich. There is strong evidence, even before the 1988 budget and the start in April of a social security system condemned by expert groups representing all shades of political opinion (with the exception only of the Monday Club and the Conservative Centre for Policy Studies), of the substantial growth in inequality of living standards. This derives from official and not merely independent sources. Thus, reports of the Department of Employment's Family Expenditure Survey show that the real disposable incomes of the poorest quartile of the population actually fell between 1979 and 1985 (45). Other reports have traced the growing divide in terms of earnings, employment facilities, housing, and health (e.g., 46). This division has a geographical dimension too. The growth of unemployment after 1979 was sharper in inner city than in outlying city areas, and other features of deprivation have been shown to have grown disproportionately in the inner city. (For a study of mortality variations in Greater Manchester see 47.)

What has to be grasped is not just the deepening plight of the poorest third of the population, but the swelling prosperity of the most prosperous third. Because of the fall in family size, together with cuts in taxes and rising salaries in business, especially international business, and booming property values in sought-after locations, there are many couples in middle life whose joint real disposable income is more than £50,000 in 1990 prices. A third of the population is extremely prosperous and owes a lot to the selective social policies of monetarism. This is a feature of changing political power with which Britain, and perhaps other countries too, will have to come to terms – to develop rational health policies no less than rational social policies.

The best-known theoretical alternative to monetarism or neo-monetarism is the Keynesian approach, which dominated British politics from the war years until the early 1970s. Keynes held that government regulation of the market was a necessary element for economic and social development. The government had to intervene to influence aggregate levels of consumption and investment, and to set interest and exchange rates. Recession could be softened by stimulating demand, as by increasing unemployment benefits and indirectly creating jobs.

Government was the instrument for redistributing public resources to depressed areas and improving the terms under which firms would be prepared to operate in those areas. And just as there had to be national action to revitalize the economy and ensure the fiscal and institutional conditions in which it could operate smoothly, so it was necessary to buttress this with a social 'floor' of rights for citizens. Minimum conditions of employment and income had to be guaranteed, and a variety of measures were required for those outside as well as inside the labour market – through better universal education, retraining, extension of health and safety legislation, equal opportunities legislation, and so on. But the Keynesian approach, which did so much to reconcile labor with capital, conducted too little analysis of the developing pattern of different industries, especially in relation to overseas parallels, and therefore few prescriptions were worked out for the modernization and restructuring of specific industrial sectors. Too little concern was shown with the state of local economies and their products, technology, and organization. Planning was insufficiently comprehensive and also unspecific. There was too much repair and mend and too little direction and creation in this approach. It also represented a 'casualty' approach to the interpretation of the Welfare State. It both drew on the medical model and further institutionalized that model at the centre of the Welfare State.

A third, and in some respects embryonic, approach has been designated as 'productionist' (e.g., 48). This puts as much weight on the need to analyse changes taking place in production, and therefore in the processes of industrial reorganization, redundancy, and the rest, as on examining trends in external economic conditions. External, and especially international, factors of a dynamic and implicitly 'restructuring' kind had to be combined with internal characteristics of the firms and industries concerned but also with the sets of social relationships, including working relationships, in the relevant locations if an adequate explanation of economic development was to be given.

Under the productionist approach, therefore, much more attention is given to the analysis of productive forces and the actions of management in explaining unemployment and poverty. The productive potentialities of the nonemployed are viewed more optimistically. Less discriminatory and more integrative social policies can be pursued: productive occupations for women, the elderly, and certain minorities are necessarily given higher priority. The extension of employment rights, the introduction of new forms of employment, and the improvement generally in conditions and kinds of work available in the inner city are all pursued more vigorously. This approach also allows a much more substantial role in development for local authorities and other bodies. However, sufficient support for a productionist approach to our economic and social problems looks to be many years away. It is neo-monetarist social as well as economic management that holds sway in Britain, and a more even-handed combination of Keynesian and monetarist approaches in many continental European countries.

## Choice and lifestyle

In focusing in this article on the association between material deprivation and ill-health it is implicitly assumed that an exhaustive explanation for present health inequalities cannot be given. The nature of the available evidence does not allow that to be attempted. One small, technical reason is that the analysis of deprivation depends primarily on what can be extracted from official statistics. Inevitably, therefore, any assessment of the importance of the material conditions of life (as well as of the criteria of health that lie at the disposal of the research scientist) is incomplete. A more important reason is that health is determined by so many different influences, interacting in complex and still only partially understood ways, that we would not wish for a moment to deny that factors other than those that have been selected in this article are bound to play a part in shaping the health of the population. However, although patterns of health in the community cannot be reduced to patterns of deprivation, as if the two were synonymous, it remains certain that variations in health cannot be understood without overriding emphasis being given to material conditions of life.

One very crude illustration is to be found in a report on variation in health in Northern England. In a study of 678 wards, three measures of health – standardized mortality, percentage of disablement in the population, and percentage of babies with low birth weight – were combined into a single index. Four indicators of material deprivation were found to explain as much as 65 per cent of the variance in health across the region (49, p. 118). A study of the borough of Sefton on Merseyside, using identical methods, found that 68 per cent of the variance among the wards of the borough could also be explained by these four indicators (50).

In the current debate a sharp distinction is often made between social or environmental factors influencing health and those over which the individual has some control or choice: diet, exercise, and smoking are the obvious instances. Two observations need to be made about the impact of life-style upon health. The first is that proponents of the individualistic approach consistently overlook the fact that smoking and eating habits, as well as the amount of exercise taken by people, are far from being activities determined solely by individual choice. Diet is profoundly influenced by cultural or local social customs, informal and formal education, the availability as well as the price of goods in local markets, advertising, recipes and fashions recommended by the media, and decisions taken by farmers and the manufacturers of food products as well as by government. Similar considerations apply to other behaviour such as physical exercise, smoking, and drinking. In other words, what is attributed to individual choice is in fact substantially shaped by powerful economic and social forces, the goods and facilities that are immediately available, and level of income (among recent discussions of this theme, see 51 in particular).

The second observation is that, contrary to some stereotypes of the way low-income families handle their money, there is evidence that they obtain necessary nutrients more efficiently at less cost than do richer families (52). Even so, such families do not have incomes large enough to buy the kind of diet recommended for health. So the adequacy or otherwise of household diet, which is supposed to epitomize the way in which the individual can crucially determine his or her own health prospects, depends substantially on the income available to the family and other facets of material deprivation.

The problem of disentangling the causal chain that is necessarily involved in behaviour which we refer to as "choice" implicates, among other institutions, the state. [...]

## References

1.  World Health Organization (1985) *Targets for health for all – 2000*, Copenhagen: WHO Regional Office.
2.  Black Research Working Group (1980) *Inequalities in health* (The Black Report), London: Department of Health and Social Security.
3.  Preston, S., Haines, M. and Pamuk, E. (1981) 'Effects of industrialisation on mortality in developed countries', in *Solicited Papers, Vol 2*, International Union for the Scientific Study of Population, 19th Population Conference, Manilla: Liegi Imprimerce Derouaux, pp 233-54.
4.  Valkonen, T. (1981) *Social inequality in the face of death*, European Population Conference, Helsinki: Central Statistical Office of Finland.
5.  Whitehead, M. (1987) *The health divide: Inequalities in health in the 1980s*, London: Health Education Council.
6.  Fox, A.J. (ed) (1989) *Inequalities in health in Europe*, London: Gower.
7.  Klein, R. (1988) 'Acceptable inequalities', in D. Green (ed) *Acceptable inequalities? Essays on the pursuit of equality in health care*, London: Institute for Economic Affairs.
8.  LeGrand, J. and Rabin, M. (1986) 'Trends in British health inequality, 1931–83', in A.J. Culyer and B. Jonsson (eds) *Public and private health service*, Oxford: Basil Blackwell.
9.  Illsley, R. (1986) 'Occupational class, selection and the production of inequalities in health', *Quarterly Journal of Social Affairs*, vol 2, no 2, pp 151-61.
10. Illsley, R. (1987) 'Occupational class, selection and the production of inequalities in health – a rejoinder to Richard Wilkinson's reply', *Quarterly Journal of Social Affairs*, vol 3, no 3, pp 213-23.
11. Illsley, R. (1987) 'The health divide: bad welfare or bad statistics?', *Poverty*, no 67, pp 16-17.
12. Illsley, R. and LeGrand, J. (1987) 'The measurement of inequality in health', in A. Williams (ed) *Economics and Health*, London: Macmillan.
13. LeGrand, J. (1987) 'An international comparison of inequalities in health', *European Economic Review*, no 31, pp 182-91.
14. Wilkinson, R.G. (ed) (1986) *Class and health: Research and longitudinal data*, London: Tavistock.
15. Wilkinson, R.G. (1986) 'Occupational class, selection and the production of inequalities in health: a reply to Raymond Illsley', *Quarterly Journal of Social Affairs*, vol 2, no 4, pp 415-22.
16. Wilkinson, R.G. (1987) 'A rejoinder', *Quarterly Journal of Social Affairs*, vol 3, no 3, pp 225-8.
17. Wilkinson, R.G. (1989) 'Class differentials and trends in poverty, 1921-81', *Journal of Social Policy*, vol 18, no 3, pp 307-35.
18. Townsend, P., Davidson, N. and Whitehead, M. (eds) (1988) *Inequalities in health: The Black Report and the health divide*, 2nd edn, Harmondsworth: Penguin.

19. Koskinen, S. (1985) 'Time-trends in cause-specific mortality by social class in England and Wales', Paper presented at the International Union for the Scientific Study of Population Conference, Florence, June.

20. Pamuk, E.R. (1985) 'Social class inequality in mortality from 1921-72 in England and Wales', *Population Studies*, no 39, pp 17-31.

21. Marmot, M.G. and McDowall, M.E. (1986) 'Mortality decline and widening social inequalities', *The Lancet*, vol 328, no 8501, pp 274-6.

22. Farr, W. (1860) 'On the construction of life tables', *Journal of the Institute of Actuaries*, IX.

23. Titmuss, R.M (1938) *Poverty and population*, London: Macmillan.

24. Titmuss, R.M (1950) *Problems of social policy*, London: Her Majesty's Stationery Office.

25. McKeown, T. (1965) *Medicine in modern society*, London: Routledge & Kegan Paul.

26. McKeown, T. (1976) *The role of medicine: Dream, mirage or nemesis?*, [2nd edn, 1980], Oxford: Blackwell.

27. Winter, J.M. (1982) in T. Barker and M. Drake (eds) *Population and society in Britain 1850-1950*, London: Batsford.

28. Foucault, M. (1973) *The birth of the clinic: An archaeology of medical perception*, trans. A.M. Sheridan, London: Tavistock.

29. Abel-Smith, B. (1964) *The hospitals? 1800-1948*, London: Heinemann.

30. Corvisart, J.-N. (1808) Preface to L. Auenbrugger, *Nouvelle méthode pour reconnaitre les maladies internes de la poitrine par le percussion de cette cavité*, Paris: l'Imprimerie de Migneret.

31. Jacob, J.M. (1988) *Doctors and rules: A sociology of professional values*, London: Routledge.

32. Illich, I. (1977) *Limits to medicine, medical nemesis: The expropriation of health*, Harmondsworth: Penguin.

33. Oakley, A. (1980) *A woman confused*, Oxford: Martin Robertson.

34. Stark. E. (1982) 'Doctors in spite of themselves: the limits of radical health criticism', *International Journal of Health Services*, vol 12, no 3, pp 419-58.

35. Powles, J. (1973) 'On the limitations of modern medicine', *Sci Med Man*, 1, pp 1-30.

36. Navarro, V. (1986) *Crisis, health and medicine: A social critique*, London: Tavsitock.

37. Eyer, J. and Sterling, P. (1977) 'Stress-related mortality and social organisation', *Review of Radical Political Economy*, vol 9, no 1.

38. Ehrenreich, J. (ed) (1978) *The cultural crisis of modern medicine*, New York, NY: Monthly Review Press.

39. Virchow, R. (1958) *Disease, life and men*, Stanford, CA: Stanford University Press.

40. Dubos, R. (1968) *Man, medicine and environment*, London: Pall Mall.

41. Szasz, T. (1979) *The theology of medicine: The political-philosophical foundations of medical ethics*, Oxford: Oxford University Press.

42. Chadwick, E. (1842) *Report on the sanitary condition of the labouring population*, London.

43. Orr, J.B. (1936) *Food, health and income*, London.

44. M'Gonigle, G.E.N. and Kirby, J. (1936) *Poverty and public health*, London: Gollancz.

45. Townsend, P., with Corrigan, P. and Kowarzik, U. (1987) *Poverty and labour in London*, London: Low Pay Unit.

46. Walker, A. and Walker, C. (1987) *The growing divide: A social audit, 1979-87*, London: Child Poverty Action Group.

47. Townsend, P. (1988) *Inner city deprivation and premature death in Greater Manchester*, Ashton Under Lyne: Tameside Metropolitan Borough Council.

48. Wannop, U.A. and Turok, I. (1987) *Targeting urban employment initiatives*, Glasgow: Universities of Strathclyde and Glasgow.

49. Townsend, P., Phillimore, P. and Beattie, A. (1987) *Health and deprivation: Inequality and the North*, London: Croom Helm.

50. Marssden, J. (1989) *Health and deprivation: Inequalities in Sefton*, Liverpool: Department of Geography, University of Liverpool.

51. Hart, N. (1986) 'Inequalities in health: the individual versus the environment', *Journal of the Royal Statistical Society*, Series A, no 149, pp 228-46.

52. Cole-Hamilton, I. and Lang, T. (1986) *Tightening belts: A report for a Working Party on Food and Low Income*, London: London Food Commission.

# 34

# Better benefits for health

## Call for a plan to implement the message of the Acheson report

As authors of the Black report, we welcome the report of the independent inquiry into inequalities in health by the scientific advisory group under the chairmanship of Sir Donald Acheson.[1,2] In particular, we welcome the attention given in the report to the increasing problems caused since the late 1970s by the rapidly widening gap in living standards. We also welcome recommendation number 3 (among the 39 principal recommendations) which specifies the need for policies to "reduce income inequalities and improve the living standards of households in receipt of social security benefits."[1] The report specifies that benefits in cash or in kind must be increased to reduce "poverty in women of childbearing age, expectant mothers, young children and older people." Nine other recommendations (numbers 8, 13, 20, 21, 22, 27, 31, 35, 36) were explicitly linked to recommendation 3, reinforcing the call for integrated action to alleviate unemployment and the deprived condition of many ethnic minority groups, elderly and disabled people, and families with children; and increase benefit levels and real living standards. Another 10 recommendations are concerned with meeting material needs in schools, housing, the environment, transport, and diet.

## Summary points

The 1998 Acheson report echoes the findings of the 1980 Black report that the gap in inequalities in health has been steadily increasing and that differences in material deprivation are a major cause of the increase

The likely effects on inequalities in health of the chief policies implemented in the 1980s and 1990s still need to be estimated so that strategies to improve health can be improved

The level of benefit that is minimally sufficient to maintain health and effective working and social capacity among different types of families needs to be defined and related to a programme to improve benefits

A staged programme of the action needing to be taken by different government departments needs to be specified by the government

Black, D., Morris, J.N., Smith, C. and Townsend, P. (1999) 'Better benefits for health: plan to implement the central recommendation of the Acheson report', *British Medical Journal*, no 318, 13 March, pp 724-7.

These priorities reflect those expressed in our 1980 report. We said then: "We have tried to confine ourselves to matters which are practicable now, in political, economic and administrative terms, and which will, nonetheless, properly maintained, exert a long-term structural effect.... We have continued to feel it right to give priority to young children and mothers, disabled people and measures concerned with prevention.... Above all, the abolition of child poverty should be adopted as a national goal."[2]

Although the cost of implementing our recommendations was not as high as was claimed by Patrick Jenkin, who was secretary of state at the time, affordability was a key issue then as now. History shows that governments can introduce radical changes but, when they occur, they are ordinarily built on precedents and are divided into a succession of steps. To be influential, scientific advice has to be pitched in a practicable and manageable, as well as desirable, form. What matters most in 1999 is that the government changes the direction of trends that increase poverty and inequality. This change depends on mobilising popular support for a number of principal measures and on introducing new institutions at the same time as strengthening existing ones. There exists overwhelming evidence of support from national opinion surveys for the kind of measures presented in table 1.[3]

## Affordable reduction of inequalities of health

We believe that it is possible and desirable, following the publication during the past two decades of the evidence reviewed by Acheson and his colleagues, to reach a scientific and popular consensus about the necessary combination of measures required to tackle this problem. The Acheson group, unlike ourselves, was expected to keep "within the broad framework of the government's overall financial strategy."[1] This included the chancellor's strict limits on public expenditure. Accordingly, policies to improve benefits were not specified and costed. However, the group expressed the same priorities as we did in 1980. In table 1 we have reproduced the principal recommendations made in our report with estimates of cost made at the time by Margaret Thatcher's government,[4] and we have updated these estimates to the late 1990s with information supplied by the Department of Health in a written answer to a parliamentary question in late 1998.[5] Although an exact estimate of current costs would depend on allowing for different sources of potential revenue as well as changes in the population affected, these estimated costs may provide a useful basis for agreement on how the measures required to implement the Acheson report might be reached.

In 1980 there were, in theory, many alternative options available to help solve the United Kingdom's divisive problem of the widening gap in living standards. The Black working group recommended a combination of measures, most of which could have been introduced through existing legislation, which had a great deal of public support, and which would have made a substantial and measurable initial difference in meeting what was then, and is even more so now, a huge national problem.

**Table 1.** Annual estimated cost of meeting the principal recommendations of the Black report on inequalities in health

| Recommendation | 1982[4] (£m) | 1982 costs in 1996 prices[5] (£m) |
|---|---|---|
| 10 Free milk for children under 5 | 300 | 700 |
| 12 Expansion of day care for children under 5 | 550* | 1250 |
| 23 Special programmes in 10 areas with highest mortality | 65 | 150 |
| 24 Child benefit increased to 5.5% of average gross male earnings | 950† | 2200 |
| 25 Age related child benefit | 1275‡ | 2900 |
| 26 Maternity grant increased to £100 | 60 | 140 |
| 27 Infant care allowance | 440§ | 1000 |
| 28 Free school meals for all children (net extra cost) | 640¶ | 1460 |
| 29 Comprehensive disablement allowance | 1175** | 2700 |
| Total annual cost | 5455 | 12,500 |
| Total cost (as % of gross domestic product) | 2.2 | 1.7†† |
| Total cost (as % of social security budget) | 13 | 11.7†† |

* An initial capital cost of about £300-£400m would also be required.
† Cost of raising child benefit to £7.57/week.
‡ Assuming average increase of £3/week for children aged 5-15.
§ The cost of a benefit of £5.85/week if half of the 2.9 million women at home looking after children had a child under age 5.
¶ Assuming 70% uptake.
** As estimated by the Disability Alliance in 1981.
†† As percentage of 1996 figure.

We believe that policy recommendations should routinely be costed. This was done in the Black report. As table 1 shows, in relation to national measures of gross domestic product, or even the current cost of social security, the extra resources needed were not unachievable. In today's terms important advances could be made for less than 2% of the gross domestic product or about one tenth of the expenditure on social security. The total amount is of an order illustrated by the chancellor's decisions in 1997-8 to introduce the windfall tax (which should generate £5bn ($8bn) between 1997 and 2002) and to change tax allowances and National Insurance contributions. Another indicator is the £2.5bn surplus of contributions overpayments in the National Insurance Fund in 1997-8, which will rise to £7bn in 2000-1.

## Policies causing standards of living to diverge

The task ahead is daunting but must be accepted. One problem, which has not been examined by successive governments during the past two decades, is the effect of specific policies on trends in the inequalities of living standards and, hence, health. The biggest influences on structural trends need to be identified and explained. In the United Kingdom these influences include the abolition of the link between social security benefits and earnings, restraints on the value of child benefit, abolition of lone parent allowances, abolition of the earnings related addition to incapacity benefit (which enabled people who were disabled before reaching pensionable age to draw early on their entitlement to the State Earnings Related Pension Scheme), and the substitution of means tested benefits for universal social insurance and non-contributory benefits for particular population categories such as disabled people.

We estimate conservatively that but for changes in entitlement to social security benefits the poorest 20% of the population would today have about £5bn (20%) more in aggregate disposable income, that the ratio between the richest and poorest 20% would be reduced, and that poverty by European standards would be reduced by more than one third.

The problem of poverty is larger than is often represented.[6-12] Even narrowly drawn government statistics, for example the annual Department of Social Security reports on households with below average income, reveal a serious divergence of living standards in the 1980s and 1990s.[13] Thus, in the 1990s the number of adults and children with incomes below the low income standards set for 1979 has remained as high as, or even higher than, in 1979 (table 2). This represents an "absolute" standstill or deterioration in their living standards. The latest report shows that in 1979 1.2 million children were living in households with incomes below half of the national income after housing costs but, despite a big increase in living standards nationally and among wealthy people in the intervening 17 years, there were 1.3 million children below that standard in 1996-7.[13] If instead we look at

**Table 2.** Number of people (children, when data available) in millions living below given standards of income, excluding people who are self employed.[13] Data adjusted according to the retail price index

| Standard | 1979 | 1993-4 | 1994-5 | 1995-6 |
|---|---|---|---|---|
| Below lowest tenth of 1979 median income | 2.8 | 3.0 | 2.9 | 3.0 |
| Below half of 1979 average household income | 4.5 (1.2) | 4.35 | 4.25 | 4.4 (1.3) |
| Below half of contemporary average household income | 4.5 (1.2) | 11.6 | 12.1 | 12.2 (3.9) |

the "relative" situation and take average household income as it was in both 1979 and 1996-7 then the number of children in households earning less than half that average grew from 1.2 million to 3.9 million.

Denying even half of the average household living standards to so many children is bound to impair both health and access to education, gravely diminishing the stock of national skills. The widening gap has recreated and worsened the problem of two nations: we must do whatever is required to banish it.

The problem is growing. The latest national survey data show that the poorest 20% of households (more than 11 million people), who depend for 80% of their income on benefits, had an average disposable weekly income of only £86 a week (at 1997-8 prices) in the financial year 1994-5 and, three years later, £87.[14] The richest 20% of households had an average of £707 in disposable weekly income in 1994-5, and this increased to £753 a week in 1997-8. Table 8.3 of these data shows that the richest 20% had 8.2 times the income of the poorest 20% in 1994-5 and 8.6 times their income in 1997-8.[14] Late into the 1990s the gap in disposable income continues to widen.

The part played by successive policies in redirecting income trends has not been examined in reports on public health, almost as if there were no connection between government measures and changes in the structure of society. These links must be shown. The Acheson report has made a start, pointing out that while average household income has grown by 40% in real terms during the past two decades it has grown much faster among the richest in the population. "For the poorest tenth, average income increased by only 10 per cent (before housing costs) or fell by 8 per cent (after them)."[1] However, this statement is not precise; it needs clarification and an account of the exact contributions made to the trend in different years by policy changes. Indeed, a brief paragraph on income distribution early in the report which is intended to set the socioeconomic scene seems to contradict this statement. This paragraph describes increases in "median real household disposable income before housing costs," and shows that "the bottom decile point rose by 62 per cent from £74 per week to £119 per week."[1] But this covers the years 1961 to 1994. This was a time when, as the report later states, there was a movement towards greater equality – in the 1960s and 1970s – followed by a "reversal" of this trend.

These two periods of recent British history, roughly dividing the 1980s and 1990s from the 1960s and 1970s, must be distinguished. A computerised simulation of the national distribution of income, whereby the effect of different recent and prospective policies can be more exactly described and conclusions drawn, could be sponsored by the government and undertaken by the Office for National Statistics.

## Adequacy of benefit

The second problem to be neglected by successive governments is the adequacy of benefit. Defining a poverty line has become increasingly important both internationally and scientifically. A breakthrough occurred in 1995 with the agreement to issue a declaration and programme of action after the world summit on social development, which had been convened by the United Nations. The declaration was signed by 117 countries, and individual nation states committed themselves to the preparation of national plans to eradicate poverty by applying two standardised measures of "absolute" and "overall" poverty.[15] In the United Kingdom, a national opinion poll carried out in late 1997 found that 20% of the population perceived themselves as living in "absolute" poverty.[16] The people surveyed gave estimates of income need which, when aligned with the composition of their households, showed that they considered that income support levels were generally from 25% to 50% too low. Expert statistical and scientific work on household income needs, some of it recent, broadly confirms this scale of shortfall.[7-12, 17] The combination of scientific investigation and democratically representative opinion polling provides forceful evidence of the severity of this national crisis.

## Concerted radical action to improve health

In the 1998 budget the chancellor announced a welcome increase in the rate of child benefit together with improvements in income support rates for children, to take effect from April 1999. However, the increase in child benefit applies only to the eldest or only child in the family and, since the real value of the benefit had fallen, it primarily represents a catching up exercise. If the chancellor decides to tax the benefit, a move that has been suggested but for which there is little support,[18,19] the benefit may be withdrawn from higher income households later and converted into a means tested benefit. In 1999 the government will also replace the family credit with the working families tax credit, which is designed to increase the level of benefit as well as the numbers entitled to it. This credit is also means tested and is intended to increase by about half a million the number of low income families receiving such a credit. On the basis of written answers to parliamentary questions, investigations into the minimum necessary family income, and after protracted research some observers have concluded that the new credit "will not provide Low Cost Allowance level incomes to two-parent families."[17] On all the available evidence, means tested benefits are poor in coverage, costly to administer, do not encourage savings, and are generally inadequate in meeting needs, as well as being unpopular.

The Acheson group argues for policies that "increase the income of the poorest," and shows how important it is to raise benefit levels, restore the earnings link to national insurance and other non–means tested benefits, and introduce more progressive taxation.[1] These general recommendations have to be turned into exact operational elements of a bold and integrated national plan.

## Social exclusion and poverty

How might an effective antipoverty programme be related to the government's strategy to reduce social exclusion? In its third report to the prime minister in September 1998 the Social Exclusion Unit proposed a broad programme for "tackling poor neighbourhoods."[20] A "new deal for communities" will begin in 17 districts, with more areas able to join the programme later. There will be funds to develop and implement community based plans covering everything from jobs and crime to health and housing. Ten government departments will be involved. Their assignments are to get more people into work; improve the social management of neighbourhoods and housing; reduce antisocial behaviour; develop schools and youth facilities; improve access to shops, financial services, and information technology; and make the government work better.

The strategy is imaginative and undoubtedly obliges different departments and specialists to work together. However, some observers believe that the strategy is tilted too far towards the long term and that more urgent structural action needs to be taken to begin to remedy some of the worst problems of poverty. These problems need to be dealt with immediately.

The work of the unit is distinct from that concerned with poverty. The unit's approach is interdepartmental, pump priming, and experimental. The department is preoccupied with antisocial behaviour and access to services, jobs, and other opportunities rather than with the scope and adequacy of benefits and other influences on the distribution of income.

A single paragraph in the command paper discusses social security. "Problems with the benefit system are being addressed by welfare reform, the Working Families Tax Credit, and the minimum wage …. The relationship between housing policy and housing benefit is being reviewed." Poor pensioners are to be helped by "boosting income support levels to provide a guaranteed minimum income," getting more pensioners to apply for benefit, and by making annual payments towards their winter fuel bills.[20] The Acheson report confirms that a more ambitious programme is necessary. Alternative strategies to reduce poverty, especially those not involving additions to means tested programmes, have not yet been discussed.

## Conclusion

We have argued for public recognition of the central message of both the 1998 Acheson report and the 1980 Black report on inequalities in health – that is, the need to increase benefits for poor people, especially families with children. In conjunction with other recent reviews of income and health,[21-25] – including those formally sponsored by the royal colleges of general practitioners, nursing, and physicians; the Faculty of Public Health Medicine; Action in International Medicine; and the *BMJ*,[26] – we call for acknowledgment of the harmful effects on the distribution of income and, therefore, on health of particular policies (such as the abandonment of the link between earnings and benefits, cuts or reductions in benefits for some vulnerable groups, and the inadequate level of child benefit). We also recommend that:

- Future policy proposals that affect income should be accompanied by estimates of their effects on the structural distribution of income and their likely general effects on health, and
- Priority should be given by the government to the annual determination of what are "adequate" levels of benefit (this could be incorporated into the poverty audit announced on 17 February 1999 by the secretary of state for social security).

We propose that a government report should be prepared that defines the minimum income and benefit needs for differently constituted families as the basis of a phased programme designed to increase benefits accordingly. This should be the government's top priority. This would represent a necessary step towards implementing the recommendations of the Black and Acheson groups; making improvements in child benefit, lone parent benefit, incapacity and disability living allowance benefits; and improving the basic state retirement pension.

### References
[1] Acheson D. *Independent inquiry into inequalities in health*. London: Stationery Office, 1998 (Acheson report).
[2] Black D, Morris JN, Smith C, Townsend P. *Inequalities in health: report of a research working group*. London: Department of Health and Social Security, 1980 (Black report).
[3] Jowell R, ed. *British social attitudes*. Aldershot: Ashgate 1991-1998 (8th to 15th reports).
[4] Clarke K. Inequalities in health: reply to Gwynneth Dunwoody MP. *House of Commons official report (Hansard)* 1982 Dec 16: cols 242-3.

[5] Jowell T. Written answer to a parliamentary question by Jean Corston MP. *House of Commons official report (Hansard)* 1998 Nov 25 (column numbers not available at time of writing).

[6] Bradshaw J, Chen J-R. Poverty in the UK: a comparison with nineteen other countries. *Benefits* 1997; 18: 13-17.

[7] Bradshaw J. *Budget standards for the United Kingdom.* Aldershot: Avebury, 1996.

[8] Cohen R, Coxall J, Craig G, Sadiq-Sangster AS. *Hardship in Britain: being poor in the 1990s.* London: Child Poverty Action Group, 1992.

[9] Gordon D, Pantazis C, eds. *Breadline Britain in the 1990s.* Aldershot: Ashgate, 1997.

[10] Kempson E. *Life on a low income.* York: Joseph Rowntree Foundation, 1996.

[11] National Children's Home Action for Children. *Factfile '95.* Rochester: NCH Action for Children, 1995.

[12] National Children's Home Action for Children. *Factfile '99.* Rochester: NCH Action for Children, 1998.

[13] Department of Social Services. *Households below average income.* London: Stationery Office, 1994-8.

[14] Office for National Statistics. *Family spending: report of the family expenditure survey.* In: London: Stationery Office, 1998.

[15] United Nations. *The Copenhagen declaration and programme of action: world summit for social development, 6-12 March 1995.* New York: United Nations Department of Publications, 1995.

[16] Townsend P, Gordon D, Bradshaw J, Gosschalk B. *Absolute and overall poverty in the UK in 1997: what the population themselves say.* Bristol: Bristol Statistical Monitoring Unit, 1997 (Bristol poverty line survey: report of the second MORI survey.)

[17] Parker H, ed. *Low cost but acceptable. A minimum income standard for the UK: families with young children.* Bristol: Policy Press, 1998.

[18] Dilnot A. *Evidence to Social Security Committee.* London: The Staionery Office, 1998 (16 December 1998).

[19] Clark T, McCrae J. *Taxing child benefit.* London: Institute for Fiscal Studies, 1998 (Commentary 74).

[20] *Bringing Britain together: a national strategy for neighbourhood renewal.* London: Stationery Office, 1998 (Report by the Social Exclusion Unit) (Cm 4045).

[21] Hills J. *Income and wealth: the latest evidence.* York: Joseph Rowntree Foundation, 1998.

[22] Davey Smith G, Hart C, Blane D, Gillis C, Hawthorne V. Lifetime socioeconomic position and mortality: prospective observational study. *BMJ* 1997; 314: 547-52.

[23] Wilkinson RG. *Unfair shares: the effects of widening income differences on the welfare of the young.* Ilford: Barnardo's, 1994.

[24] Davey Smith G, Morris JN, Shaw M. The independent inquiry into inequalities in health. *BMJ* 1998; 317: 1465-6.

[25] Davey Smith G, Dorling D, Gordon D, Shaw M. *The widening health gap – what are the solutions?* Bristol: Townsend Centre for International Poverty Research, 1998.

[26] Haines A, Smith R. Working together to reduce poverty's damage: doctors fought nuclear weapons, now they can fight poverty. *BMJ* 1997; 314: 529-30.

# Older people

*Edited by Chris Phillipson*

# Introduction

Peter Townsend created a remarkable body of research on older people, stretching over a period of some 50 years. In respect of the UK, he can be regarded as the founder of the 'sociology of old age', establishing the basis for this approach in numerous books and articles published in the 1950s and early 1960s. The context informing Peter Townsend's initial research into ageing is important to establish. The late 1940s and 1950s saw an upsurge of research in the different disciplines comprising gerontology. This work reflected the influence of two main factors: first, greater awareness about the significance of long-term population trends (highlighted in the 1949 report from the Royal Commission on Population); second, economic pressures arising from the impact of the Second World War, these leading to concerns about the potential costs associated with population ageing. As Townsend and Wedderburn observed, in their introduction to *The aged in the welfare state* (1965, p 10), "Suddenly, in the late forties and fifties ... the problems of old age were discovered". A growth in research was an important part of this process, led by work on the social medicine of old age (cf Sheldon, 1948), problems of psychological adjustment (cf Welford, 1958), the biology of ageing (cf Comfort, 1954), older people in the workplace (cf Clark and Dunne, 1954), and Townsend's (1957) own investigation into family and social relationships in later life.

Placing Peter Townsend's own work in this wider context clarifies the originality of his contribution to research and public policy. He was first and foremost, as indicated above, concerned with using insights from sociology to advance knowledge and understanding about the lives of older people. In doing this, Townsend combined two strands of sociological and social anthropological research: first, survey methodology developed through the work of Booth, Mayhew and Seebohm Rowntree; second, the tradition of personal investigation of particular communities, developed in British social anthropology through the research of Radcliffe-Brown and Malinowski (Bulmer, 1985). Both these traditions are applied to powerful effect in books such as the *Family life of old people* and *The last refuge*, with survey evidence combined with intimate individual portraits of older people.

At the same time, Townsend was insistent that sociology brought a particular set of concerns to the study of gerontology. Sociological perspectives focus attention on the role of social structures and social institutions in the organisation of daily life – in contexts such as urban neighbourhoods and residential homes. The sociologist is especially interested in asking questions about how these settings are changing and the forces behind such change. For Townsend, population ageing was itself a major source of social change, raising concerns about the social integration of older people, financial support and social care. All this required attention to social theory, and Peter Townsend was influential in stressing the importance of theory and the testing of hypotheses as an essential element in the development of research. He was, for example, one of the early critics of the theory of 'disengagement' as advanced by the American sociologists Cumming and Henry (1961), this theory suggesting that normal ageing was characterised by a process of 'mutual withdrawal' by the older individual and society. In fact, from empirical evidence collected in *Older people in three industrial societies* (Shanas et al, 1968) he was able to challenge this approach, demonstrating that processes resulting in 'reintegration' were also at work, these compensating for the losses associated with events such as retirement and bereavement.

But the development of theory and the collection of facts about older people comprised, for Townsend, just one aspect of research in gerontology. Researchers were also required to attend to the broader implications of their activities. Townsend and Wedderburn (1965, p 11) expressed this point forcibly in *The aged in the welfare state*, suggesting that "... no one who is active in social gerontology can feel comfortable in dealing with theoretical questions alone. Questions of policy arise insistently." And Townsend emphasised this point in *The last refuge* (1962, p 436) in which he stressed that the range of policy proposals identified in the study: "... simply represent an attempt to derive practical recommendations for public policy from sociological evidence". The integration of theory, empirical data and policy remains a striking feature of Peter Townsend's work, elements which are brought out in different ways in the illustrations below of his writing and research about older people.

The extracts selected here cover work published over the period from the mid-1950s to the mid-2000s. The first (**Chapter 35**) draws upon *The family life of old people,* one of Peter Townsend's most influential books. First published in 1957, it was part of a series published by the Institute of Community Studies, of which Townsend, along with Peter Marris, Peter Willmott and Michael Young, had been a founder member. The Institute, located in the London Borough of Bethnal Green (now part of Tower Hamlets) had set itself two main aims: first, to examine issues facing working-class people and the effectiveness of social policies directed at their needs; second, to develop a more intelligible social science, one free of unnecessary jargon (Willmott, 1995). An initial concern of the Institute was to examine the extent to which family and community ties had altered as a consequence of changes associated with the development of the welfare state and more specifically housing policies associated with slum clearance in inner-city areas.

Reflecting the aims of the Institute, *The family life of old people* set itself the task of examining the extent to which older people were isolated from ties with their family and community, taking the working-class district of Bethnal

Green as a case study. Townsend himself carried out most of the interviews, with respondents visited on at least two occasions. The result was a powerful account of the strength of family ties, one which also demonstrated, as J.H. Sheldon noted in his foreword to the book, "genuine affection for the older people interview[ed]". The findings demonstrated clearly the continued importance of family life in old age, with Townsend (1957, p 210) concluding that: "To the old person as much as the young [the family] seems to be the supreme comfort and support … it continues to provide a natural … means of self-fulfilment and expression, as the individual moves from the first to the third generation…." The book was to have a major influence on studies of ageing. For those researchers coming into social gerontology in the 1970s – a period of steady growth in PhDs specialising in ageing – *Family life of old people* was a huge source of inspiration. Many of its findings became staple topics for further research: the importance of the reciprocal role played by older people in the provision of support; the importance of daughters in providing care; the significance of grand-parenting; and the centrality of the couple relationship. These and many other observations were to be become central features of the sociology of the family in old age over the decades following the book's publication.

The second extract (**Chapter 36**), devoted to the issue of retirement, is derived from interviews from the Bethnal Green study, some of which can also be found in the *Family life of old people*. However, Townsend (1955) presented preliminary findings from the research as part of a talk delivered to the Association of Industrial Medical Officers, subsequently published under the title 'The anxieties of retirement'. The paper reflects worries in the early 1950s about the impact of retirement on older men, an issue also being explored by those working in the field of social medicine (for example, Anderson and Cowan, 1956). The opening section of the paper illustrates Townsend's rejection of alarmist views about the 'burden of old age', an issue he returned to on numerous occasions throughout his career. But the article goes on to make the point that while the broader economic impact of retirement may have been exaggerated its effect on the individual was important to acknowledge. Townsend argued that his interviews suggested that "Most men view approach retirement with uneas[e] and ill-concealed fear … usually the individual has to face up to a fundamental change in the pattern of his daily activities and relationships" (1955, pp 21, 22). Bringing a sociological perspective to the issue, Townsend highlighted the ambiguity of the retirement role for the retired male, and the crisis resulting from his detachment from long-established associations within the workplace. This concern with the social impact of retirement was to have long-lasting influence, notably in initiatives around securing employment for older workers, and the development of initiatives around preparation for retirement (Heron, 1962).

The third extract (**Chapter 37**) is taken from *The last refuge*, research on residential institutions and homes for older people, intended to complement the community-based *Family life of old people*. There is a good case to be made for viewing *The last refuge* as one of the finest pieces of British sociology to emerge over the past 50 years. There have been few equals in respect of the integration of quantitative and what is now termed 'qualitative research', and few equals either which make such an effective link between the sociological evidence and policy recommendations. First published in 1962 (with an abridged version in 1964), the book retains its power through the importance of the empirical findings, the depth of observation (enhanced by Townsend himself working as an attendant in one of the old workhouses); the haunting photographs – plate 24 'Day-room with no floor covering in a former workhouse' – lingering long in the memory; and of course the quality of the writing itself – restoring a measure of humanity to a group pushed to the margins of society. Its findings were also of immense importance, not least that the majority of older people in institutions were not so infirm that they could not be supported in their own homes with appropriate domiciliary support. Townsend's summary conclusion was to provide a powerful rationale for the expansion of community care: "A large number enter Homes for reasons of poverty, lack of housing, social isolation, and absence of secondary sources of support among relatives and friends, and they do so unwillingly ... rarely are they offered practicable alternatives" (1962, p 434).

The fourth extract (**Chapter 38**) is taken from Peter Townsend's contribution to the first issue of the journal *Ageing & Society*, based on a talk given to the Canadian Association on Gerontology in 1980. 'The structured dependency of the elderly' explored in greater theoretical detail many of the issues raised in his earlier work, providing a new analytical framework to the sociology of ageing. The publication of the paper – in 1981 – proved to be a watershed in critical thinking about old age. Prior to this time, most writing about older people had focused, according to Townsend, on "individualistic instead of societal forms of explanation" (1981, p 6) or "acquiescent functionalism" as he referred to it. Townsend, however, challenged this approach, arguing that it was social processes which created "...the framework of institutions and rules within which the general problems of the elderly emerge and, indeed, are manufactured" (p 9). For Townsend, in common with a number of other emerging writers on ageing at the time (cf Walker, 1980), the marginalisation and dependency of older people could more properly be viewed as 'socially created', a product of forced exclusion from work, poverty, institutionalisation and passive forms of community care. 'Structured dependency' proved to be a fruitful concept for sociologists and others to explore, contributing as well to the development of a 'critical gerontology' which emphasised the roles of the state, social class, gender and ethnicity in the construction of inequalities in old age (Baars et al, 2006; Bernard and Scharf, 2007).

The fifth extract (**Chapter 35**) is taken from *New pensions for old: The key to welfare reform,* published in 1999 and a response to a Labour Government Green Paper *A new contract for welfare: Partnership in pensions* (DSS, 1998). Pension provision was a key area of concern for Townsend and he spent much of his life defending the basic state pension, urging improvements, and arguing for help for the most vulnerable – especially for women, the widowed and those who were single. Future historians of social policy will certainly speculate why the advice of someone who had engaged with the pensions debate for over 50 years might not have been drawn on by Labour administrations in the period after 1997. The 1998 Green Paper outlined three measures to improve the pensions system: the Minimum Income Guarantee (MIG), a State Second Pension (SSP) for low earners, and a money-purchase Stakeholder Pension. *New pensions for old* provided a major critique of the proposed approach, highlighting the need for diminishing rather than increasing means-testing (as with the MIG), questioning the viability of money-purchase schemes, and doubting the impact of the SSP.

In fact, nearly a decade was to pass before legislation emerged – in 2007 and 2008 – combining modifications to the Basic State Pension (BSP) with attempts to encourage new forms of pension savings. The former included indexing the BSP to average earnings, and reducing the number of years required to work for receipt of a full BSP. The latter included introducing a new pension saving scheme of portable individualised savings accounts (from 2012), automatic enrolment into a qualifying workplace pension, and a national minimum contribution from employers. None of these approaches are likely to resolve Townsend's concerns about growing inequalities among pensioners and the problems facing the low paid. In the UK, the reforms introduced in 2007 will mean that even an individual on median earnings retiring in 2055 can expect to achieve a replacement rate of just 32 per cent from the BSP. Large groups of workers will struggle to achieve a decent standard of living if reliant on the public pension alone. Townsend's insistence on the importance of 'collective provision', as outlined in *New pensions for old*, one that fully compensates for periods of care and for low wages, remains still a fundamental goal for an equitable social policy.

The sixth extract (**Chapter 40**) is from a paper first presented at the 2005 annual meeting of the British Society of Gerontology, subsequently appearing in *Ageing & Society* in celebration of 25 years of publication of the journal. 'Policies for the aged in the 21st century: more "structured dependency" or the realisation of human rights' returned, as the title suggests, to many of the issues raised in the 1981 paper 'The structured dependency of the elderly'. However, the themes also hark back to issues about choice, rights and dignity, first elaborated in *The last refuge*. Again, the paper takes a highly original stance, combining approaches to welfare with those linked to issues about human rights. From a historical perspective on the development of human rights legislation, the paper examines the ways in which the European Convention on Human Rights and the European Social Charter can be used to analyse some of the conditions experienced by older people. Townsend explores the violation of rights in residential settings, highlighting the potential use of instruments such as the 1998 Human Rights Act. Again, though, returning to earlier themes, he emphasises the importance of financial resources and effective domiciliary care as bulwarks against the abuse of older people – whether in the community or in residential homes.

'Policies for the aged in the 21st century' concludes with a powerful articulation of a human rights perspective which offers: "a framework of rigorous analysis and anti-discriminatory work". Townsend went on to conclude that "Success depends on good operational measurement – to produce reliable evidence of violations and monitoring progress – and the incorporation nationally and internationally of institutions and policies that reflect those rights" (Townsend, 2006, p 177). The words here provide an effective summary of Peter Townsend's approach to the issue of old age and his work in the field of social policy more generally: collection of data, rigorous analysis, monitoring of progress and results; but also passionate advocacy for those under study: the connection between all of these areas – from hypothesis building to social action – comprising the building blocks for the development of social policy.

## References

Anderson, W.F. and Cowan, N. (1956) 'Work and retirement: influences on the health of older men'. *The Lancet*, December 29, pp 1344-7.

Baars, J., Dannefer, D., Phillipson, C. and Walker, A. (eds) (2006) *Ageing, globalization and inequality*, Amityville, NY: Baywood Books.

Bernard, M. and Scharf, T. (eds) (2007) *Critical perspectives on ageing societies*, Bristol: The Policy Press.

Bulmer, M. (1985) 'The development of sociology and of empirical social research in Britain', in M. Bulmer (ed) *Essays on the history of British sociological research*, Cambridge: Cambridge University Press, pp 3-38.

Clark, L.G. and Dunne, A.C. (1954) *Ageing in industry*, London: The Nuffield Foundation.

Comfort, A. (1954) *The biology of senescence*, London: Routledge & Kegan Paul.

Cumming, E. and Henry, W.E. (1961) *Growing old: The process of disengagement*, London: Basic Books.

DSS (Department of Social Security) (1988) *A new contract for welfare: Partnership in pensions*, Cm 4179, London: The Stationery Office.

Heron, A. (1962) 'Preparation for retirement: a new phase in occupational development', *Occupational Psychology*, nos 1-2, pp 1-9.

Shanas, E., Townsend, P., Wedderburn, D., Friis, H., Milhoi, P. and Stehouwer, J. (1968) *Old people in three industrial societies*, London: Routledge & Kegan Paul.

Sheldon, J.H. (1948) *The social medicine of old age*, Oxford: Oxford University Press.

Townsend, P. (1955) 'The anxieties of retirement', *Occupational Medicine*, vol 5, no 1, pp 19-24.

Townsend, P. (1957) *The family life of old people: An inquiry in East London*, London: Routledge & Kegan Paul.

Townsend, P. (1962) *The last refuge: A survey of residential institutions and homes for the aged in England and Wales*, London: Routledge & Kegan Paul.

Townsend, P. (1981) 'The structured dependency of the elderly: a creation of social policy in the twentieth century', *Ageing & Society*, vol 1, no 1, pp 5-28.

Townsend, P. (1999) *New pensions for old: The key to welfare reform*, Bristol/London: Townsend Centre for International Poverty Research, University of Bristol/Tribune Publications.

Townsend, P. (2006) 'Policies for the aged in the 21st century: more "structured dependency" or the realisation of human rights', *Ageing & Society*, vol 26, no 2, pp 161-79.

Townsend, P. and Wedderburn, D. (1965) *The aged in the welfare state: The interim report of a survey of persons aged 65 and over in Britain, 1962 and 1963*, London: Bell.

Walker, A. (1980) 'The social creation of poverty and dependence in old age', *Journal of Social Policy*, vol 9, no 1, pp 45-75.

Welford, A.T. (1958) *Ageing and human skill*, Oxford: Oxford University Press.

Willmott, P. (1995) 'Resolving the dilemma of bigness', in G. Dench, T., Flower and K. Gavron, (eds) *Young at eighty: The prolific public life of Michael Young*, Manchester: Carcanet Press.

# 35

# The family system of care

The proximity of relatives greatly affects the way the domestic affairs of old people are managed and how they are looked after in illness and infirmity. As old people may be members of a home containing one, two or three generations of relatives the first step in describing the pattern of care is to see whether we can distinguish between these three types of home in their functioning.

Of the 203 [older people in our study], 29 or 14% lived in homes containing relatives of three generations. With one exception – a bachelor living with his sister's daughter and her children – they all lived under the same roof with their children and grandchildren. To say they were living together does not necessarily mean that they formed part of the same household for all purposes. Married couples in their sixties usually ate separately from their children and grandchildren and pursued some evening interests independently. Almost invariably they had separate kitchens. But the wives often joined forces in the day when the men were absent from the home. The latter were sometimes unaware of the extent of this.

> Mrs Belliers said she did most of her own shopping, cooking, cleaning and washing, although her married daughter living in the house 'mucks in with lots of things, especially the washing.' The two couples ate meals separately, 'unless we're invited upstairs' (usually meaning week-ends). But there was much coming and going. While I was there the son-in- law came in and immediately had his habitual evening cup of tea with his parents-in-law. She said, 'My grandson is more down here than upstairs. We don't know whether he's their son or ours.' Later her husband expressed surprise when she said she often had her midday meal upstairs with her daughter and grandson and sat with them afterwards.

The pattern was not the same for widows. They shared much more with their children. Fewer of them maintained separate kitchens and more sat down to eat all meals with their children. The difference in home arrangements once a person was widowed rather than married was shown most clearly in one

---

Townsend, P. (1957) 'The family system of care', Chapter V in *The family life of old people: An Inquiry in East London*, London: Routledge & Kegan Paul.

home, where the grandfather had died only a year previously. The married daughter, who shared the cooking and housework with her mother, 'never interfered with Mum while Dad was alive. We each had our own kitchen and got on with ourselves.'

> Mrs Lyons, a widow of 68, lived with her married daughter, son-in-law and four grandchildren. She did the cooking, bathed the baby and the next youngest child, and looked after the baby when her daughter went to collect two other children from school. Her daughter said, 'It helps me really, having her. She keeps an eye on the children for me.' And she added, as if her mother had a proper and rightful share in the children's world, 'My husband likes messing about in the garden…. I don't like leaving her on her own.' The daughter did all the shopping, managed the household and, in partnership with her mother, attended to the children, besides working four hours a day as a machinist.

Married sons and their wives, when living in the home, maintained more of a separate establishment than married daughters. One widow, for example, usually took her meals separately from her son, daughter-in-law and grandchildren. 'We don't make a habit of it.' And the widow had less to do with the twin grandchildren. I don't look after them. "You've done enough," my son said. She takes the babies round to her sister.' But she did not lose sight of them altogether. 'Sometimes she brings the twins in here to give them their supper. That's when it's a bit cold to take them upstairs.'

## The two-generation home

There were 68 people, or over a third of the sample, living in two-generation homes. Fifteen lived with married or widowed children, 44 with unmarried children and 9 with other relatives, including nephews, nieces and grandchildren. Illustrations will be taken from the first two of these three groups.

When married children were at home but not grandchildren, the two generations were on the whole less dependent on each other and their relationships were more strained, particularly when the married child was a son. It seemed less easy for old people to reciprocate a service such as shopping or cleaning performed by their children when there were no small grandchildren to be watched, dressed and fed. They had fewer natural interests to share, and so spent more time on their own.

> Mrs King was a widow of 75 living with a recently married son in a small council flat. Her daughter-in-law paid the rent and

most bills. 'I turned everything over to her when she moved in. It's only right. The wife has to do it.' The daughter-in-law did the shopping and the cooking at weekends. Mrs King did the washing and prepared tea during the week for the young couple when they returned from work. 'They have theirs in their own room and I have mine in my room.' At one point, in answer to a question as to her evening activities, she said, 'I don't enjoy myself. I keep to my room and listen to the wireless.' She was anxious not to disturb the first few months of marital bliss and so prejudice her own delicate position in the household.

Such examples of widows sharing a home with married sons, although comparatively rare, suggested that the mother's authority was delegated to the younger woman and her role sometimes became that of a subordinate housekeeper. She tended to be divested of domestic power and her responsibilities were much more consciously (and narrowly) defined. Only in this way was harmony preserved and the rights and responsibilities of a wife honoured. This shows some of the difficulties to be contemplated by some old people not able to live alone.

We can see that married children living in both two- and three- generation homes had varying degrees of independence in their home activities.[1] They were more independent if both mother and father were present in the home and not only a mother. They were more independent if the parents were active rather than infirm and if no grandchildren were in the home. And they were more independent if the parents in the home were parents of the husband and not the wife.

When unmarried children lived with old people the situation was much simpler. The right of the old mother to have a controlling say in the home was never in doubt. Even so, the distribution of responsibilities varied according to state of health, whether the husband was alive, and whether the children were sons or daughters. An active woman in her sixties, for example, often did most of the housework.

Mrs Tout, an active woman of 65, allowed her husband and son to do little in the home. She prepared the meals, cleaned the flat, did the shopping and washing and many of the odd jobs. Talking of her husband she said, 'He's tired when he gets back and he makes a fuss if I ask him to. He's never been used to it. If I'm not well, of course, they do it. That's the top and bottom of it.'

When the old people were infirm or ill the unmarried children took a greater responsibility.

Mr Anchor suffered from chronic bronchitis and became breathless at the slightest exertion. His wife was infirm and had not left the house for some months. Mrs Anchor did most of the cooking, but her single daughter at home did it at weekends. This daughter also did most of the cleaning. 'Last night she scrubbed all the place through, and tonight when she comes home she'll say that perhaps she wants to do the other room.' Mrs Anchor and her daughter did most of the washing between them, but 'the heavy is sent out.' As for shopping, a married daughter living about ten minutes' walk away did that every day.

Some widows living with unmarried children treated them like they had treated their husbands. The unmarried son, or indeed, daughter, having taken the place of the husband as wage-earner, was not expected to do much in the home.

Mrs Wiles cooked during the week but 'my girl does the cooking on Sunday. She says, "I'll make it, Mum." We work together.' She admitted her daughter did some cleaning and washing, but she tried to do most of it. 'I do the dirty. Her hands have to be kept for dressmaking. They have to be just so. So I always do the dirty.' She was very much aware that her daughter was the breadwinner. 'You've got to put yourself out for the one who gets the wages. They've got a right to a bit of peace and quiet in the evening. It's a hard job and the girl gets tired.'

## The one-generation home

Just over half the old people lived in homes containing no relatives of any other generation: 43 were alone, 46 in married pairs, 14 with other relatives, mostly brothers or sisters, and the remaining three boarded with non-relatives. For the great majority of these people the management of their domestic affairs could not solely be understood by reference to their own capacities and their activities at home. Few of them were obliged to be self-sufficient. In the previous chapter we found that most people living alone in fact saw relatives frequently. Now, we find that most received much help from them, not only in times of illness, but every day.

Mrs Tilbury, 69, lived in a small cottage with her husband. She managed most of her own household affairs but not all. 'My daughter does some. She's a bit rough and ready like me. She wanted to stop off work. She said she wanted to turn her job up so that she could look after me. But I didn't want to stand in her light.' The daughter worked as a waitress in the City from 10 till 3.30 p.m. and lived nearby. 'She comes over here before she goes and cooks me a bit of dinner. My two granddaughters come from school and have it with me.' Mrs Tilbury fetched the youngest granddaughter from school. Indeed on one call she came in with the youngest granddaughter and the elder one followed later. Once a week when her daughter went out with her son-in-law to the cinema she had the two granddaughters to stay with her. She said, 'I like to make things for my grandchildren. Everything they've got on is what I made.' If she were ill, her daughter would look after her. 'When she comes in here she says, "I'm going to scrub up", and nothing you can do will stop her.'

Mrs Rilk, an infirm widow in her early sixties, lived alone. A married daughter living nearby regularly did her cleaning and gave her meals on Sundays. The shopping was done by a 13-year-old grandson. 'He comes every morning before school.' As for washing, another grandson 'calls in when he's on his milk round on Sunday and collects it. My daughter gets it done on a Monday and Charlie [the grandson] brings it back.' Her grandchildren chopped firewood for her, exercised her dog and took her to the cinema or to the bus-stop. Her daughter collected the pension. But Mrs Rilk prepared a meal for her daughter and grandchildren six days of the week, often entertained her relatives in the evenings and once or twice a week she took a meal to an old lady in the same block of flats.

Most people living alone considered themselves part of a family circle spread over neighbouring streets in Bethnal Green, or sometimes over greater distances.

Mrs Hopkins, a widow in her early sixties, lived alone in a new council flat. She did most of her own shopping, cooking, cleaning and washing, although she had some help with the errands from one of her daughters-in-law, a grandson and one of her two sons, all of whom lived in an adjoining borough. In the day she looked after a grandson, aged six, and at midday her son came to a meal and so did her other son's wife. She charged them 2s. each for a meal. 'I wouldn't trouble to cook for myself. That's why I like them coming.' She spent her week-ends with one or other of her sons.

Some of the people living alone or only in married pairs did not have children, but where they had sisters or nieces living near they produced similar evidence of domestic co-operation between related households. Childless people were not necessarily handicapped.

> Mr and Mrs Marshall had no children and they lived alone. The last time Mrs Marshall was ill in bed one of her married nieces nearby looked after her, and she said she could depend in future on any one of at least four nieces in Bethnal Green. A large number of relatives lived nearby and they were seen throughout the week and at week-ends. The previous Saturday they had had eleven to tea. Mr Marshall said proudly of his wife, 'She's always helping one or another of them out. She's always going to one or another when they're ill. There's her brother who was living round the corner and is now in hospital, she always used to do his washing and give him meals every day before he went in hospital. Now she goes round and cleans out his place. We've always helped one another in the family. That's how it should be.'

Those with no available relatives were in the worst position. They were acutely conscious of what they considered to be a misfortune. In describing their own feelings they gave perhaps the strongest, if most indirect, testimony to the dependence of old people on available relatives of other generations.

> Miss Kabel, aged 77 and very infirm, lived with a single brother aged 80 and a single sister aged 71. Their parents died when they were in their teens and they had no relatives in England. The brother had looked after his two sisters and he and one of the sisters used to go to work while the other sister looked after the home. The pattern of their lives had not altered until Miss Kabel and her brother retired. Her younger sister managed the household and they paid a cleaner 4s. for a weekly visit. They looked after each other in illness and had no help from friends or neighbours. 'Single folks, they don't bother with you. They'll ask how you're getting on. One even visited me in hospital.... But that's all.' They talked at great length of their lack of relatives and many remarks were of the kind, 'How can you feel happy with no family behind you?'

> Mrs Frazier, an infirm widow of 75, lived alone in one room. Her husband died three years previously. They had no children and none of their brothers and sisters were alive. Her parents had died when she was a child and she had no knowledge of any aunts or uncles or cousins. 'I can't help myself.' She envied other women who had surviving children. 'If I'd had a couple of daughters they'd

have been a help to me. If you've got children at the back of you you're all right.'

Evidence of the way people's lives were bound up with those of close relatives was so often forthcoming in the interviews that one is forced to reconsider what is meant by old people 'living alone'. The concept had little value in Bethnal Green when applied only to the dwelling. It was wrong to consider the domestic affairs of the elderly in terms of the bricks and mortar of a structurally separate home, as much as for those living alone as for those living with relatives of two or three generations. This became clearer upon detailed analysis of the help received and given by people in their own homes, regularly and in emergencies.

## Regular help in the home

[...]

As women got older and more infirm their relatives took over first the shopping, then the heavy cleaning and washing, and only in the last resort the cooking and the payment of rent and other regular outgoings. One service for infirm people was the collection of the pension from the Post Office. In the sample 163 people had a pension or other State benefit and 26 of them, or 16%, had this collected by relatives. More than half those helping with home tasks were daughters, and most of the remainder were daughters-in-law, sisters and nieces. A number of neighbours, friends or employees of the Home Help service gave substantial help.

Some people had help only with their shopping and others only with their cleaning. Table 11 shows the percentage being helped with each separate item. When the items are combined we gain a rough idea of the total proportion dependent upon their relatives. Altogether, 68% regularly

**Table 11:** Main charge of household jobs

| Person doing job | Shopping | Cooking | Cleaning | Washing |
|---|---|---|---|---|
| | % | % | % | % |
| Self or spouse only | 41 | 74 | 43 | 60 |
| Self or spouse *and* relatives | 23 | 13 | 13 | 7 |
| Self or spouse *and* others | 2 | 0 | 4 | 1 |
| Daughter | 21 | 6 | 22 | 20 |
| Other relative | 8 | 4 | 8 | 6 |
| Neighbour or other | 5 | 2 | 10 | 5 |
| Total | 100 | 100 | 100 | 100 |
| Number | 203 | 203 | 203 | 203 |

had help in the management of their homes from relatives living with them or elsewhere; 21% had occasional help and 11% none.

## Regular help for others

Why did so many get help? The essential answer is that they were members of a tightly-knit family group and as such they received help because they also gave or had given help in the comparatively recent past.

In previous surveys the fact that old people perform services for others has had less attention than the fact that others perform services for them. What seems to be an essential principle of the daily renewal of an intimate bond between adult relatives is the reciprocation of services between them. Children, for example, shop for their old parents; the latter give them meals or look after the grandchildren. It was suggested earlier that relations in three-generation homes were easier than in two. Old people with no grandchildren may find it difficult to justify themselves to a married child at home. In the same way people seeing a lot of grandchildren in the locality may, on that account, attract more help from their children.

What services do old people in fact perform for others? There are those for other people at home. Excepting individuals living entirely alone, 91% of the women, and 60% of the men, performed at least one service every day or every week for others. Most women did a great deal; a few, who were very infirm, could do no more than share in the preparation of meals.

Then there are services for people living outside the home, ranging from daily shopping and preparation of meals to such things as fetching a pension once a week for a blind sister. Altogether 40% of the women in the sample, and 14% of the men, performed at least one regular service for relatives not living with them. Regular services for neighbours or friends were undertaken by 8% of women and 2% of men. Besides those performed regularly there were many occasional tasks, such as shopping for a sick neighbour, looking after a relative's child for a time after the death of one of the parents, or taking a relative to hospital.

The care of grandchildren was one of the most important tasks of all. As many as 105 women and 50 men had grandchildren. Of the women, 66, or 63%, performed some or many regular services for at least one of their grandchildren, such as fetching them from school, giving them meals, looking after them while their parents were at work, or sitting in during the evenings. This is perhaps one of the most significant findings of the whole inquiry. Of the old men, 20% shared in the care of grandchildren, baby-sitting, fetching them from school or accompanying them on regular expeditions to the park. They usually did much less than grandmothers.

Few old people took no part in helping others, only one in eight of the women and two in five of the men undertaking no regular domestic or personal services. Some of these in fact made an indirect contribution to the welfare of others through their work, as Table 12 shows.

While it is hard to find a criterion which allows exact measurement and comparison it is clear that in general there were almost as many old people helping others as were themselves being helped during the weekly round. This evidence compels us to look more critically into the assumed 'burden' of old age. We may be attaching too little weight to the contribution to society made by the aged and too much to their claims on it.

[...]

**Table 12:** Old people performing services for others

|  | Men | Women |
|---|---|---|
|  | % | % |
| Performing regular domestic or personal services* for others (including those also at work) | 59 | 87 |
| Not performing regular domestic or personal services |  |  |
| (i) At work | 17 | 1 |
| (ii) Not at work | 23 | 12 |
| Total | 100 | 100 |
| Number | 64 | 139 |

* Such as shopping, cleaning and preparing meals; washing the windows, chopping firewood; minding a grandchild, or fetching him from school; collecting a pension. Some men performed only one small service. By 'regular' is understood at least once a week.

## The old woman's place

The pattern of care was greatly influenced by the structure and geographical scatter of the family. If daughters were available, particularly the youngest, they were the ones to help. If they were not, then the duty passed to daughters-in-law, sisters and nieces. If a close female relative was not available or was herself infirm (or if there was a rift with the only available relative, such as a daughter-in-law) then the duty tended to fall on a husband, if he was still active.

While some men performed valuable domestic and personal services for their families, this was usually when female relatives were not available. Men, young as well as old, rarely occupied a vital role in family care. The system was chiefly organised around female relatives. At its focal point stood the old woman. As we have seen, she usually retained important functions as housewife, mother and grandmother. In her social and occupational life she had experienced much less change than had the man. These differences between man and woman corresponded with the sharp differences in health and physical capacities already described. The man experienced more violent and unsettling changes. These were largely connected with his retirement from work, which we will discuss later.

By contrast the woman was eased more gradually into an awareness of her age. Final retirement from *her* job in life rarely occurred. When it did, it was usually after the relinquishment of one small job after another, by easy stages, over many years, until she was bedridden. Usually she managed the home, be it with increasing assistance from her daughters and other relatives. Of the 42 infirm women in the sample, although most received help with household tasks from relatives, nearly two-thirds of them retained complete control of the cooking and nearly half of them the washing. Two-thirds performed some services for others. It is hardly possible to over-emphasise the way in which old women, even when infirm, continued to occupy an important place in the family.

Mrs Plum, a widow in her mid-sixties, was almost stone deaf. She complained of headaches, severe arthritis in her legs and incontinence, and one of her feet had to he bound with bandages each day. A married daughter living with her said, 'She's not been out for more than a month. She's frightened of going out on her own. And she doesn't like it because if people speak to her she doesn't understand what they say. She gets embarrassed about it. She went out last Easter Sunday and that's when her leg first gave way. She was up all night with the pain. I had to get a taxi Monday morning and take her round to the hospital [for treatment]'. Yet the widow did nearly all the cooking for the household, a lot of the washing and she often looked after the three grandchildren. One was a baby granddaughter. When the widow and daughter were asked who bathed the baby, the widow indicated herself and rocked with laughter. Her daughter said 'She bathes the baby, nine times out of ten. The other night I took the child up to sleep and she wouldn't go to sleep. I had to bring her downstairs and *she* took her up. I suppose she's used to her putting her to bed.'

Mrs Blenkinsop was in her early sixties. She said she contracted pneumonia one winter a few years previously and the doctor was dumbfounded when she did not die. A year later she was found to have TB. 'They took half one lung away and then they had to take the rest. I came out of the hospital and then I had a relapse and vomited blood and had to go back.' She was very thin, suffered from arthritis and giddiness and could not sleep. She also said her husband was 'not fit to go to work. He has to be up at 5.30 and has to use that pump for his asthma and take tablets, to get himself right for the day.' Her married daughters came in to help with the shopping and cleaning and her grandchildren ran errands. But she looked after her husband during a recent illness and she provided a midday meal for two of her children and usually two or three of the grandchildren. On two later calls I found five and possibly seven grandchildren in her home. They were so much on the move it was not easy to make a count.

Some older and more infirm women had not been able to withstand such a pace. To them their children were a comfort. A woman who was crippled and had not left her house for ten years delighted in the daily visits of her son and daughter-in-law living locally. A widow in her eighties had had a long spell of illness. One of her daughters said that six or seven of the children then called every day. Between them they got her shopping and gave her meals. 'Mary stopped there and nursed her. And Annie and Rose were always over there helping. She had a bottle of brandy every three days. We all clubbed together to get it. She still likes a nip, and says that's what pulled her through. I have to go there, because I can't rest.' Another woman in her eighties was housebound and had just spent months in hospital. She was glad to be out. 'The nurses have not got the feeling of your own.' Her daughter looked after her. 'She used to lift me so that I could go to bed but that got too much for her and (pointing at an armchair) I sleep here.'

Among the oldest infirm people those without children were worst off, particularly if they were confined to the home.

A married man explained that his wife, in her mid-seventies, depended on an elderly niece for help and company while he went to work. 'I don't know what I'd do without her. I could not go to work if she wasn't here. The old girl has a lot to bear and I don't know what she thinks stuck up here every day. (They lived on the fourth floor of a tenement block and his wife had rarely left the flat in the previous four years.) Sometimes I come home and there she is sitting in the corner of the room and she doesn't say a word. She just looks at me. She goes on looking at me as I go about getting the tea and I say, "What's the matter? Are you thinking how it was years ago?" And then sometimes she will burst into tears. I don't know how she stands it. It fair breaks your heart to see her hobbling about. Mind you, if I didn't have her here I'd pack up and go. There'd be nothing left for me, would there?'

Such people were in a small minority. For the majority of women increasing age was a gradual unwinding of the springs of life, They gave up part-time occupations, visits to the cinema, shopping, cleaning and washing, services for neighbours and associations with them, friendships outside the family, holidays and week-ends with relatives, the care of grandchildren, the provision of meals for children, and finally their own cooking and budgeting, one by one as their faculties grew dim and age took its toll. Their last refuge was their family. They did not want to escape from their homes, to a cottage in the country any more than to an institution. They wanted to spend their last months in their homes and among their families, where possessions and faces were familiar and where an unsteady foot was most secure.

Their activities became adjusted to a limited routine. They went out little and slept longer. They bemoaned their frailty but even when wholly incapacitated they kept, because they were women and not men it was said, 'a closer touch on things'. They knew what was happening to their relatives, had a finger on the details of family history, and were respected and admired for their canniness and insight into what went on. 'She's a marvel, really', said more than one daughter, 'she's got such spirit and she can still have a laugh.'

## The limits of care in illness

The shortcomings of this system of care must not be overlooked. Much depends on whether or not there is a family and, if there is, whether help is readily available. Nearly a fifth of the old people in Bethnal Green were, after all, single or childless and several of the others had relatives unable to help. If there were only one or two female relatives living at home or nearby and if they themselves had young children or were at work the care of the old could not always be properly undertaken or could be undertaken only at the cost of severe strain. 'I wouldn't expect her to. She's had TB.' 'My daughter's got her own worries. She's got three kiddies and her husband's been off work for three weeks.' 'It's such a long way for her and she can't afford the fares.' 'My daughter's husband has got artificial legs. She's got enough to do looking after him.' 'He's got his job and he couldn't give that up. They've got to study the work.' These remarks each referred to an only child.

Two other limits to the care available to the aged are less obvious and arise more from the nature of family relationships than from family size, structure and circumstances. As we have seen, part of the strength of family relationships comes from individuals receiving *and* returning services. Some old people can no longer reciprocate the services performed for them and this seems to make them less willing to accept help and their relatives sometimes less willing to give it. Among infirm people in the sample it was noticeable that a few getting least help were not in a position to give anything in exchange. For example, a man and wife in their late seventies who were both infirm had little help from a married son and daughter-in-law living in the same house. The wife had a wheel-chair and the younger couple rarely volunteered to take her out. Son and daughter-in-law were at work in the day and their only child, a son, was on National Service. The old couple's other married children and grandchildren no longer lived in the borough although some were seen fairly often. The old woman said she was happiest when she had her grandchildren around her but 'that wasn't so often now'. The cause of the separation between the generations was, it seemed, not so much the infirmity of the old couple as the absence of common interests and responsibilities.

The second limit concerned the union between man and wife. A number of people who were ill or infirm were in need of bodily care, such as dressing a wound, providing and emptying bed-pans and washing soiled linen. Some old people refused to allow anyone except a spouse to do such things. This was particularly true of men. The care of a man's body was felt to be the prerogative of his wife and it was thought to be a break with propriety,[2] if not vaguely incestuous, for a female relative, even a daughter, to undertake such an intimate task. She could do the shopping and fetch prescriptions; rarely, if ever, was she allowed to wash his body or make his bed. Some married women also preferred an infirm husband, rather than a daughter, to look after their personal toilet. Old widows were less reserved, perforce, and were often grateful for the personal services of a devoted daughter. The inhibitions of men who were more reluctant than women to accept care from daughters may be one explanation why more old widowers and bachelors enter hospital in England and Wales than widows and spinsters, though fewer married old men than women.[3] In sickness married men are mostly looked after by wives and when they do not have them it may be hard to find a substitute among female relatives.

Except for the widowed, what the children could do often stopped short of bodily care. This was why old people often experienced enormous strain in caring for a spouse in a final illness.

> A widower in his mid-seventies explained that before his wife died two years previously she had been bedridden. Although his children came every day and helped with all the household chores he had attended to most of her personal needs, 'I had to sit with her for months. The last two or three months, her motion was coming away from her all the time and it was terrible, I can tell you. She wouldn't go away to hospital although the doctor tried to get her to.'

> I visited one man three times during his final illness. His single daughter living at home and his married children who visited him frequently took over nearly all the shopping and cleaning from his infirm wife. But his wife washed him and did all the 'messy' jobs.

He bled continuously from the chest, He said, 'Mum changes the dressing at least twice a day and we wouldn't want our daughter to do it. You couldn't expect it.' And his wife added, 'it even turns my stomach sometimes seeing poor Dad's chest. It's like a bit of raw meat.' She washed bloodstained sheets every day, lifted him on to bedpans, washed him and dressed his wounds, despite her own frailty.

An infirm widow gave a long account of her husband's death, in which she said, 'It happened all of a sudden. Jack had been strong and healthy all his life and he suddenly went to nothing. For over three months I never had any rest.' She sat with him, washed him and gave him his meals, though her daughter prepared them. 'He kept talking about the pain in his chest in the night. One day he came in here and lay down on the bed with his coat on. He said, "I'm done, Nan." I said, "Come on Jack, don't get depressed." But we were crying our eyes out before the ambulance came. He wouldn't get into the chair for them to take him to the ambulance. He said, "I can walk." I was as ill as I could be but I told him, "Don't walk, Jack", and of course I was breaking my heart, but he said while he had legs he was going to use them. He was in hospital three weeks. Bad as I was I tried to get along to see him...'

When the husband or wife was dead one relative rather than several tended to assume responsibility for the survivor. Often this seemed to be understandable because no other suitable relative was available. The old person had one child only or one daughter only; other members of the family did not live nearby or were themselves sick or disabled; and other members of the families had young children of their own or husbands with disabilities to look after. In particular it seemed wholly natural for the remaining unmarried child at home to take on the care of a parent. When all this is said it still seems to be true that one person in the family was singled out to carry more than a fair share of the burden of care simply because the old person found a need to replace a spouse with someone in almost the same intimate standing. A particular child sometimes undertook tasks of a personal character which no other child was expected to undertake and which were previously borne by the husband or wife. All these reasons perhaps explain why the care of the old seems too often to be unequally distributed among their children.[4]

[...]

We started this chapter by examining the three types of family home, three, two and one generation, as a first step in finding how domestic affairs and illness were managed in old age. We found that one person in one dwelling was rarely living alone in any real sense. The domestic unit was generally spread over two or more households in proximity. We found old people getting a great deal of help, regularly and in emergencies, from their female relatives, particularly their daughters, living nearby. The remarkable thing was how often this help was reciprocated – through the provision of meals, the care of grandchildren and in other ways. The traffic was not all one way. This exchange of services seemed to be an essential feature of the relationship between the generations; this is one of the main conclusions of the book. The family system of care was mainly organised around female relatives, with an old grandmother at its centre. To find that there were limits to what it could do for old people, that it sometimes produced strain and that a minority of people fell outside its scope, simply because they had few or no surviving relatives, modifies, but does not alter, this conclusion.

**Endnotes**

[1] In a survey of London life between the wars it was said of old people, 'It is remarkable that whereas many share their rooms and their meals with some unmarried relative, those who live with married couples almost invariably have separate rooms and run their establishments independently – an arrangement which they consider tends to preserve friendly relations.' (Smith, Sir H.L., 'Old age and poverty', *The New Survey of London Life and Labour,* vol. 3, 1932, p. 210)

[2] 'Some have a high sense of decorum and of what is, and is not, proper. An old-age pensioner, e.g., should not be expected to nurse his still older mother-in-law; it would not be decent.' (Jephcott, P., and Carter, M. P., *The Social Background of Delinquency*, 1954)

[3] In 1951, 6.6% of bachelors aged 65-74 and 8.5% aged 75 and over were in hospital in England and Wales, compared with 3.8% and 5.9% of spinsters. Of widowers 1.8% of those aged 65-74 and 3.2% of those aged 75 and over were in hospital, compared with 1.4% and 2.9% of widows. For married men, on the other hand, the relative percentages were lower, being 1.0 and 1.5 respectively, compared with 1.2 and 2.4. (Abel-Smith, B., and Titmuss, R.M., *The Cost of the National Health Service in England and Wales,* 1956, p. 140)

[4] Sheldon, J. H., *op. cit.,* p. 159

# 36

# The anxieties of retirement

We in this country have done our best in recent years to fill old people with a profound sense of guilt. Instead of congratulating ourselves on our success in reducing the amount of premature death we have talked of the "crippling burden of old age" and have eyed with dismay the future prospects of a society composed of elderly dotards. It has been assumed that the weight of Methuselah will rest on the backs of a working population no larger than it is now, and all kinds of hasty inferences have been drawn, some of them in high places, about the difficulties of providing adequate pensions and about the need for postponing retirement. To put the matter sharply, the act of retiring and drawing a State pension is now to some extent regarded, even if unconsciously, as a piece of anti-social behaviour.

What is the evidence on which this pessimism is founded? There is all too little. An uninformed crusade to make more people stay on at work in old age may have the wrong effect on those who are no longer fit to work or who feel they have earned their retirement. The fear of being an unwanted burden on society must not be added to the other economic, social and emotional problems of readjustment a person faces when he gives up work. I believe that in most of the recent discussions far too much prominence has been given to the dubious economics of hypothetical population changes and far too little prominence to the social problems of retirement. My view is that if there is to be a policy encouraging older people to remain at work it must rest mainly on social or psychological grounds. [...]

The first observation that might be made is that in terms of population trends the problem is now believed to be less severe than when the Beveridge Report was written or when the National Insurance Act was passed. The number of people of pensionable age in Great Britain is now about seven million. During and after the war the number was expected to reach 10½ million by 1979, but the Government Actuary now expects the number to be 9½ million in that year. Even this estimate may be too high, for it is based on the assumption that the average decline in the death rates of older people in the last half century will be maintained. Recent evidence does not support that assumption. In the last ten or twenty years there is little evidence of more than a slight increase in the expectation of life of a

---

Townsend, P. (1955) 'The anxieties of retirement', *Occupational Medicine*, vol 5, no 1, pp 19-24.

woman of 65 and virtually none at all for a man of that age. If death rates at the advanced ages remained constant over the next twenty-five years, the population of pensionable age would be just over 8¾ million, not 9½ million. Even should the Government Actuary be right, a calculation of the ratio of people of active age to those of dependent age in twenty-five years' time is very little different from the present ratio. The conclusion emerging from the official estimates is that, other things being equal, the proportion of the population at work is unlikely to change at all. Although there may be four old people not at work in twenty-five years time for every three now, there are likely to be fewer children and more people at work between the ages of 15 and 65.

Viewed in terms of the demographic changes that have taken place in various decades of the last century, the prospects are by no means grim. In the last fifteen years, for example, the number of children and old people increased by over 2½ million, although the numbers of people between fifteen and the pensionable ages remained the same. The changes most likely to take place in the future will occur at a slower rate than those experienced in the years during and immediately following the war. It should perhaps be remembered that we are not suddenly entering a phase of rapid demographic change. So far as the proportion of old people in the population is concerned, we are three parts of the way through it.

There are two other encouraging trends I should like to refer to because they are often overlooked in present discussions. First, more women in middle-age are going out to work. In 1931, out of 6.2 million women aged 35-54, only 1.4 million were gainfully occupied; in 1951, out of 7.3 million women in the same age group, 2.5 million were gainfully occupied. Over 1 million more women of these ages entered the labour force, raising the proportion at work from 23 to 34 per cent. The increase was almost entirely confined to married women. It could be argued that part of this increase may be passed on to the older age groups, if many of these women remain in employment, in their late fifties and early sixties.

Secondly, the tendency in the years before the war to retire earlier now appears to have been arrested and perhaps reversed. Estimates made by the Ministry of Labour and National Service show an increase in the years 1950-53 of 21 and 10 per cent respectively in the number of female and male employees of pensionable age.

So far my purpose has been to indicate rather than exhaust the reasons why it seems particularly important not to regard the population changes that are taking place as either new or alarming and not to assume that the national economic problems of an increasing number of old people are in any way excessive. No one, it is true, has yet fully explored the economic and financial consequences of the extremely rapid growth of occupational pension schemes, but even if these are greater than we are inclined to suppose at the moment we must not forget the probability of substantial future increases in the real national income. Present population trends and patterns of work give no grounds for arguing that more old people must work because within the next twenty-five years there are otherwise likely to be fewer workers doing more work to maintain more dependants in the population. The case for encouraging more old people to stay at work must rest chiefly on social or psychological grounds or on grounds of making faster improvements in national living standards. The question is not so much, how can we reduce the burden of old age but rather, what can be done to understand and to improve the social, occupational and financial circumstances of old people at a time when their numbers are steadily increasing? It is to these problems that we should devote more attention.

Although much has been written about old age since the war, there is singularly little information about the social and financial circumstances of elderly people. The Phillips Committee, in its recent report on old age (1954), emphasised that there has been no systematic analysis of the income and expenditure of households in which older people live. In the same way, there has been no systematic analysis of the social and financial changes experienced with retirement. There is in addition the fact that we still know too little about the causes of retirement.

My aim now is to indicate the ways in which these gaps in our knowledge might be filled, by illustrations from the preliminary results, of a small scale inquiry, financed by the Nuffield Foundation, now in progress in the borough of Bethnal Green, in the East End of London. It is primarily a study of the social, particularly the family, life of older people and the problems they have experienced and are experiencing. The method of the inquiry was to draw a random sample of the names and addresses of 200 people of pensionable age from doctors' lists. Over one hundred of these people have now been interviewed. Each interview lasts about two hours and most people are visited a second, and some a third time. In interpreting this work it should be remembered that the inquiry is on a small though intensive scale and is confined to a mainly working-class urban district.

Of over-riding importance to older people is the family. By this I mean not simply the husband or wife and the children at home but the children and grandchildren, brothers and sisters and nephews and nieces, living in households both near and far. Three in four of the old people so far interviewed in Bethnal Green are members of effectively functioning three-generation family groups in one, two or more households in close proximity. By "effectively functioning" family, I mean that reciprocal services are performed and activities shared. This family group provides its own home-helps, baby-sitters, nurses, advice bureaux, holiday organizers and case workers. Here is one example of a fairly typical family.

A widow in her sixties lives alone except for a dog and a budgerigar. She is infirm and rarely goes out. A married daughter lives two minutes' walk away with her five children. One grandson does her shopping, another collects and returns the washing which is done by another married daughter living ten minutes' walk away. A young grandson often stays a night with his grandmother. The widow cooks lunch for one of her daughters and two of her grandchildren, and all four sit down together for the meal. The grandchildren do all kinds of odd jobs; they fetch her papers, chop firewood and take the dog out. The second daughter collects the pension every Friday and her mother spends every Sunday in her home. One son keeps a stall in the market, brings vegetables every morning and gives his mother 10s. a week. He lives five minutes' walk away with his wife and child. A second married son lives in Norwich and that is where the widow spends a fortnight's holiday every summer. One sister lives in the next street and a niece comes over from a housing estate twelve miles away every Thursday afternoon. Fifteen relatives are seen at least once a week, several of them every day.

Family life of such intensity is a characteristic feature of the area and must be true of many other areas throughout the country. Although the borough has lost half its population in the last twenty or thirty years, analysis of the results of the first 100 interviews shows that of 300 living children (born to 84 of the 100 informants), nearly 60 (of these 300) live in the same household as the elderly informant, about 50 within 5 minutes' walk and a further 50 within a mile. All but 18 of the remaining 140 live in other London or outer London areas. Half the old people with children alive have at least one married or unmarried child living with them and most of the remainder have at least one child living within a mile. As for the frequency with which these children are seen, more than a third of the 300 children are seen every day or nearly every day and another third between once and three times a week. Fewer than 10 per cent are seen less often than once a month and only three of the 300 children were said not to have been seen at all in the last year.

It would be out of place to give here an analysis of the quality of family life that these figures imply or to go on to describe the role of brothers and sisters, nephews and nieces and other relatives in the lives of older people. The point I want to make is that, by comparison with the family life of older people and the constant renewal of the bonds of kinship, clubs, community centres and various welfare services, important as they undoubtedly are, pale into comparative insignificance. What is the bearing of all this on retirement? I believe it is a very close one.

For convenience I have divided the men interviewed or the husbands of women who have been interviewed into three groups: those who are still at work, those who retired at some point in the previous four years and those who retired more than four years previously. The numbers involved are as yet small: 26 in the first group, 15 in the second group and 21 in the third.

There are marked differences between the sexes in their household and family roles with the onset of old age, and old age means much more to the man than to the women. This cannot be stressed too strongly. First, I want to consider those still at work. The man remaining at work spends the bulk of his time away from the home. If he is earning £7 or £8 a week, he normally hands over something between £3 10s. and £5 to his wife at the end of the week, a sum which is usually intended to cover rent, insurances, food and everything else. The wife rarely knows what her husband earns, and the husband rarely knows what his grown-up children give his wife. The belief that "what he does with his money is his affair," "what she does with her money is her affair," runs deep. In some homes the man seems to have the privileges of a hotel guest. Occasionally a husband will pay an electricity bill or, when presented with a united front of wife daughters and perhaps grand-daughters, he will buy a new strip of oil-cloth or some new curtains for the home. The man rarely has much to do with domestic affairs. "I'm finished when I come home from work." "He just sits down and reads the papers. He puts his feet up on the sofa. I don't ask him to do anything." "My husband don't even clean the windows. He only did that in the first year of our marriage." And so forth. Such remarks are common.

Of course, it would be wrong to convey the impression that the older man is completely idle in the home, for he does indeed perform minor household tasks when necessary, such as shopping or repairs and interior decoration, but his general participation in the running of the household is insignificant. It also appears to be true that he plays a relatively small part in wider family contacts. His wife sees a lot of the children, grandchildren and other relatives when he is at work, and in the evenings and at the week-ends, it is she who makes most visits to members of the family. More is usually seen of the wife's siblings than the husband's and, significantly, even the visits of married children to the home are sometimes described by the men in such terms as "they come up every Saturday and Sunday to see their mother".

Most of the activities and interests of this group of older men who are still at work (in contrast to those of their wives) are shared with workmates and acquaintances in the locality. A joke can be shared over a glass of beer in a pub, friends treat and can be treated, and the relative merits of workplaces, football teams and political parties can be thrashed out among those who have much in common. The workplace, the trade union, the local pub and the football ground are all, in a sense, home from home. A man takes pride in his membership of one or another of the groups and he often takes pride in his own strength, skill and know-how as a member with a contribution to make.

Most men view approaching retirement with uneasiness and ill-concealed fear. One man, in his seventies, and still working as a labourer said, "I'd sooner be at work but if they retire me I suppose I will have to, and then I will have to grin and bear it. I don't want to stand at the corner and watch the other people do it, but I suppose it will come to that." Another said, "I want to go on working till I'm a hundred. How can you retire when you've been working all your life? Work fills a gap when you get older. There was a time when I was waiting for the time I could get away, but now I'm glad to work, it fills a gap." Not only the men, but also their wives. One said, "there's nothing for them to do when they stop work in places like these. It's not as if there's a garden. As soon as they're down they're gone (she meant men break up and die soon after retirement) … I don't want him here."

Those soon to retire often notice a falling off in their physical capacity and their speed of work. This can often be masked for a long time through experience of the minimum effort required to perform certain tasks satisfactorily, and also by reliability and regularity of performance. In the different groups to which they belong, authority and experience acquired over the years act, although not indefinitely, as substitutes for the loss of physical capacity and drive. Approaching retirement, to many men, spells the end or virtually the end of many of the long-standing associations of adult life. In their eyes too, it often seems to serve as a mark of their failing strength and skill and as a mark of the end of their period of usefulness to others. Often a man will prefer to step down into a job of inferior status rather than take the bigger step outside into retirement. Several of the men interviewed have full or part-time jobs as lavatory attendants, door-keepers or labourers which they have taken on in recent years. A much higher proportion of all the older men interviewed than of the population at large are in or have recently been in occupations which are classifiable in Social Class V.

It is worth pausing to consider this. First, the man's wage may fall in the last years before retirement. It is impossible to give a useful average figure for the fall in income because the figures obtained refer to different periods within a general period of inflation but two illustrations may be given. In 1954 one man was forced to accept a job of inferior grade on the railway because of infirmity and his earnings fell from £7 15s. to £6. Another man who had been earning £6 as a railway porter recently accepted a job as lavatory cleaner at £4 10s.

Second, the man's position in the home and family becomes less secure. While the mother is continually renewing her bonds with her children through seeing them frequently, advising and helping in the rearing of their babies and receiving, in her turn, help with the household chores, the father relies mainly on his traditional authority in the home, and on the authority deriving from his experiences in his occupation and in his outside sporting and social activities. This authority and prestige has been weakened by some of the deep-seated social changes of our time. It is the father's, and especially the old father's, role in the family which, over the years, has been affected most by the new educational opportunities of advancement, the raising of standards of living, the improvement in work techniques and organization. His sons are often in occupations of higher skill and status. His words of advice or of authority begin to sound hollow. "But, Dad, things have changed since you were young." He begins to take refuge in spine-chilling accounts of the cruelty and harshness of the past to gain sympathy and respect when he can no longer command obedience.

Disability or sickness is a means or reconciling some men to the fact of retirement but usually the individual has to face up to a fundamental change in the pattern of his daily activities and his social relationships. What is the nature of this fundamental change? I should like now to draw briefly from the evidence relating to the second and third groups of men I enumerated earlier, those who retired less than four years ago and those who retired more than four years ago.

Those who have retired recently provide the most vivid information. One said, "I tell you straight I don't like sitting here now. I'd sooner be working. I wish this leg would allow me to go out to work again." Again, "I'm about getting fed up with it. I've nothing to occupy my mind. I don't do much in the house. Mum runs the house. If I do a job it's never done satisfactory and they (his wife and daughter) do it again … Thirty-two and six. It's a lousy sum to give her." A wife complained, "It's different with him at home. Because he's at home he wonders what you're doing. Before that he wasn't here and you could get on with things. Now he's asking what you're doing this for and what you're doing that for." One man had had several spells off work before his retirement at 63. "I kept losing time. It was on account of my health. The work was too heavy. I went to my doctor and he said that I'd never be able to do any work again. The next week I got the sack." His wife added, "that was a day, that was. There was him crying and the children up here crying too. They thought he'd done too much." The man continued, "I had the hump. I didn't know what to do. It was like being stuck in the Army in a detention camp. All I could see were these four walls. I used to go out and see the boys on Saturday evenings. I'd meet my sons-in-law and we'd go out to a pub. Now I can't do it. It's like being a pauper. I had to turn away from that because I didn't have a pound in my pocket any longer. I couldn't stand anybody anything. I couldn't do my share … Life's hardly worth living when you retire."

Upon retirement the individual man is thrown back more and more on his family. He finds, with regret and often bitterness, that old friendships cannot be maintained. He no longer provides the daily bread for the household, with all that this implies for his status within the family. His wife draws her pension of 21s. 6d. and sometimes she draws her husband's at the same time.

His 32s. 6d. goes, as it is said, "on the table" and he is usually dependent on his wife or on his children for pocket money. (Several wives said they allowed their husbands between two and four shillings a week). This means he has less opportunity of providing drinks to his friends at the local and he feels a blow has been struck at his prestige and standing in both locality and family. He finds his wife the household cashier and manager and she is the effective if not the nominal or judicial head of the family. She has the closest ties with their children and has more to share with them. He is drawn closer to her for in old age they seem to depend more on each other, but he cannot match the range or quality of her ties with the immediate and extended family, particularly with the daughters. If his wife is not infirm and thus has little need of his help he has the problem of filling in his time. He potters about in the home doing odd jobs, he goes for a stroll to meet a few old acquaintances in the park or stand with them at a street corner. In time he is more likely to reconcile himself to the reality of being an old age pensioner and is more likely to join an old people's club. He has, all too often, a feeling of purposelessness and of shame, and although family relationships and activities now become all important they cannot give him back the skills, experiences and associations of youth and middle age.

It is against a general background of this kind that it becomes easier to understand the causes of and attitudes to retirement and the financial changes experienced with it. In a recent survey by the Ministry of Pensions of the reasons given for retiring or continuing at work, conducted by means of a questionnaire, 28 per cent of the men retiring at 65 gave ill health or heaviness or strain of their work as the chief cause of retirement. A further 25 per cent had retired because of chronic illness, having experienced spells of not less than six months illness before minimum pension age. Another twenty-eight per cent, said they were retired by their employers and the remainder said they gave up work because they wanted a rest or because of other reasons. It is difficult to know how reliable such figures are because a great deal of knowledge about the health and social background of older people is needed before the answers to questions about retirement can be fully assessed. For example, although the group of men giving ill-health as the cause of retirement in the Ministry of Pensions inquiry had in general more incapacitating illness in the years before retirement than men giving other reasons, three in every ten of them had practically no record of such illness. Again, many of those retired by their employers may in fact have proved capable no longer of performing their work adequately, through ill health, infirmity or other reasons.

It would therefore be wrong to generalise too readily about the causes of retirement or the ways in which it might be delayed. More searching inquiries into the causes of retirement are required in different areas, industries and social groups. Among the small group of men interviewed in Bethnal Green the real reasons for leaving work were often found to be other than those first stated. This is particularly true of those saying they had been laid off by their employers. In one of several similar cases a man had two long spells off work followed by a medical examination and a resumption of work. After a third occasion the industrial doctor found the man was not fit to continue work and he received three months notice. In other cases it was difficult to separate the employer's dismissal from ill-health or strain as the cause of retirement. When the reasons for retirement were checked with evidence relating to health and to financial and social circumstances it appears that two thirds of all the men no longer at work had retired because of ill-health, disability or strain, about one in five partly because of an employer's action though mainly because of ill-health, less than one in ten because they were dismissed by an employer and less than one in 20 because they felt they deserved a rest. The average age of retirement was 67½. This conceals wide differences in the individual age at retirement, some retiring before the age of 60 and some over the age of 75. Over a third of the men were still at work and the average age of these men was 68½. The inquiry points to the outstanding importance of the social and psychological motives for remaining at work.

Retirement certainly produces sharp financial changes. In the sample the average earnings of the men still at work were approximately £7 10s. Most of these men were still in their sixties and often their wives were in full or part-time employment and they may have had one or more single children still living at home and contributing to the upkeep of the household. The prospect of a flat-rate retirement pension of anything from just over a quarter to about a third of this sum, according to marital status, did not arouse intense feelings of pleasure. Although nearly a third of the men now retired have occupational pensions or gratuities from their previous employers of between £1 and £3 a week and although many others obtain supplementary national assistance in addition to retirement pensions, the average income of those not at work, excluding savings and income from relatives, was about 75s. per week. Many receive much less than this sum and the abruptness of the fall in income experienced upon retirement, a fall of anything up to three-quarters of previous earnings, makes it imperative to consider again the whole question of minimum flat-rate State pensions in relationship to occupational pension schemes, based as they are on different principles and the latter covering only part of the working population. Most men in superannuable employment think it reasonable upon retirement to expect a cut in income of about a third. Their expenses and their needs are likely to be less and their social activities and their previous standard of living can be broadly maintained. Is it fair to expect men covered only by the State Insurance Scheme and by national assistance (if indeed they are willing to accept it) to face a much more drastic reduction?

The account I have given of some of the social problems of retirement refers only to a limited inquiry in a mainly working-class area. No attempt has been made to describe the material in detail. While this account must be treated with caution I believe it shows the urgency of making a reappraisal of the social context within which retirement takes place. I have tried to show, in social terms, what it means to the individual to give up work. It has a much more drastic effect on him than on his wife. An appreciation of this is perhaps fundamental to an understanding of mental and physical deterioration with age. It may go some way towards explaining Dr. Sheldon's finding, in his Wolverhampton study, that whereas old men tend to be in either very poor or very good health a much higher proportion of women tend to be subnormal in health but have a more tenacious hold on life.

The evidence from Bethnal Green suggests ill-health may be the real cause of retirement in more cases than we have hitherto supposed. But it suggests too that a proportion of reasonably fit men are retired against their will and some cannot find alternative employment. As retirement seems to be a social disaster to so many working-class men, we have a tremendous obligation to avoid decisions leading to early retirement. Decisions to prolong employment cannot be imposed on grounds of national economic need, because those grounds are virtually non-existent. But they can be taken on social or psychological grounds. The choice should, wherever possible, be left to the individual and he should not be made or advised to retire unless his unfitness is certain. I have stressed this point because this seems to be the implication of a study of the older man in the setting of home and family. What I cannot describe is the position of the older man at his work. We know extremely little about the problems of retirement on the other side of the factory gates – who takes the decision to retire employees in different industries, how far medical advice is sought or given and how far age-limits do or do not represent the limits of the period of usefulness or working capacity.

I have been urging that without a deeper understanding of the social, particularly the family, pressures on older men to stay at work and without an appreciation of the social or financial consequences of retirement we are unlikely to develop wise policies for employment in later life or for genuine security in old age.

**Reference**

*Report of the Committee on the Economic and Financial Problems of the Provision for Old Age* (1954) Cmd 9333, London: HMSO.

# 37

# Some effects upon old people of living in residential homes

What are the effects upon old people of living in one of these institutions or homes? This is not an easy question to answer. Those living in residential homes are extraordinarily diverse in physical and mental capacity, personality, social background and experience, and the homes themselves vary widely in their management and facilities. But first, have there been any other studies of the effects upon individuals, whatever their age, of living in institutions, which will help us to put the findings from this inquiry into perspective and judge their importance?

There have been a number of research studies ranging from the systematic to the largely discursive which have in fact shown that many people living in institutions have unsuspected potentialities and capacities and that the environment may have harmful effects upon them, particularly when they have been exposed to it for some months or years.

This research mainly refers to mental hospitals and institutions for children and handicapped adults, but documentary accounts of general hospitals, approved schools, prisons and even camps for refugees and prisoners of war suggest that the conclusions to be gathered about the effects on individuals of different types of institutions may often be similar. The general picture might be summed up as follows.

## The meaning of living in institutions

In the institution people live communally with a minimum of privacy, and yet their relationships with each other are slender. Many subsist in a kind of defensive shell of isolation. Their social experiences are limited, they lack creative occupation and cannot exercise much self-determination, and they are deprived of intimate family relationships. The individual has too little opportunity to develop the talents he possesses and they atrophy through disuse. He may become resigned and depressed and may display no interest in the future or in things not immediately personal. He sometimes

---

Extracts (pp 171–2, 176–82, 188–90) from Townsend, P. (1964) 'Some effects upon old people of living in residential Homes', Chapter 10 in *The last refuge: A survey of residential institutions and homes for the aged in England and Wales*, London: Routledge & Kegan Paul.

becomes apathetic, talks little and lacks initiative. His personal habits and toilet may deteriorate. Occasionally he seems to withdraw into a private world of fantasy. In some of the smaller and more humanely administered institutions these various characteristics seem to be less frequently found but they are still present.

This rather crude summary is derived from many different sources. Clinical studies of children in the first months of life show the effects of institutional life. Compared with those outside the institution, H. Bawkin, for example found that babies are less vocal; they smile less; they show diminished interest and reactivity, and more develop psychiatric disturbances.[1] Several studies, such as that of K.M. Simonsen, develop the picture for the second and later years of life, drawing attention to backwardness in speech and in mental development. Even in institutions with high staffing standards and liberal routines the children still seem to be significantly different from others living in their own or in foster homes. Similar effects have been noted by J. Tizard, B.H. Kirman and others for mentally retarded children and adults, comparing those living at home with those in institutions.

[…]

## Loss of occupation

How far do the data from the present inquiry fit into this general picture from research in institutions? The rest of this chapter will be devoted mainly to evidence about the elderly residents who had been admitted within the four months previous to our visits and whom we interviewed. Of these only 11.9 per cent of the men, and 17.5 per cent of the women, had a regular task connected with the management of the home. The proportions were highest in the voluntary and post-war local authority homes. Two-fifths of them helped with the washing-up, a fifth laid tables and served meals, and the others made beds, cleaned rooms, prepared vegetables and did some gardening. Very few received any form of payment. None did any cooking although 49 per cent had prepared their own meals when at home just before their admission.

Of all the elderly residents who were interviewed nearly half the men and a third of women were not performing any regular task and were also active or comparatively active. Many expressed a willingness to help. When asked whether there was any job which they would like to do or help with 29 per cent of all the new residents said there was, irrespective of payment or reward (in addition, of course, to the 15 per cent who actually had a job). A further 9 per cent said there was, providing there was adequate payment.

The old people were also asked whether they followed any pastime or hobby. Fifty-three per cent named some occupation, two-fifths mentioning knitting, sewing or embroidery and the others football pools, racehorse betting, reading fiction, playing cards, writing letters and, an isolated few, handicrafts such as gardening and woodwork. Half of the remaining 47 per cent said that they only listened to the radio, watched television or looked at newspapers, and the others that they did nothing at all. A substantial number of active or fairly active persons are included among the latter.

Attitudes towards occupation were affected by experiences in the homes. Many persons found that they were not expected to do any work or that there was no opportunity of having satisfying occupations. Some persons poured scorn on those among them who worked many hours for little or nothing.

> A number of residents said that Mr Oakley was a fool for doing the work he did, and he confessed that their sneers sometimes drove him to the solitude of a bathroom, where he sat on a chair. He is a bachelor in his late sixties, very shy and unassuming in manner. 'I help the bath attendant, see to the laundry, clean the door-knobs, floors, basins and baths. I start at about 8 o'clock in the morning and I'm on till 4 in the afternoon.' He gets a reward of 5s. a week. He said he was not happy in the home but had enough to occupy his time.

Most active people did no work of such a nature. Some went out in the day, played cards and chatted with other residents, or sat reading; many said they were bored. 'I get terribly bored. I would like to do something rather than waste my time day after day.' 'I've done nothing here. I get fed up. In my own place I'd be doing things.' 'After getting washed and dressed and having breakfast there's nothing to do but sit down. We sit and look at one another until it's time for dinner.' These remarks were made by people living in homes opened since the war.

Infirm old people were often more plaintive than others.

> Mrs Binderton is a widow of 84 who is blind, deaf and requires two sticks to walk. 'I can't read, I can't sew, I just sit and sit and I've never done that in my life. I don't do anything at all. I'm just a dummy. I have my meals and I sit and that's my life....They bath me once a week so they're doing their duty.'

Some people suggested that they were given no opportunity of doing certain things of which they were still capable, even if they were slow or not particularly efficient. 'In hospital I used to make my bed with one hand and wash up with one hand, but they don't let me do that here.' A blind, very deaf and diabetic woman said, 'I'd like to wash up or peel potatoes or anything.' When two bedfast persons were asked how they occupied their time one said, 'Reading and counting the panes on the windows,' and the other laid her hands perfectly still on the counterpane in a symbolic gesture, 'just like that'.

Altogether 42.4 per cent of the men and 36.7 per cent of the women said they did not have enough to keep themselves occupied. Another 5.8 per cent and 5.9 per cent respectively were uncertain. Relatively more infirm than active people are included in these figures. There were no significant differences in attitude between middle- and working-class residents.

## Isolation from family, friends and community

Talking to visitors was one means of passing the day. Two-thirds of the men, and nearly four-fifths of the women had been visited by relatives since entering the home and smaller numbers by friends, but only 18 per cent of the men and 22 per cent of the women had been visited more than once a week. The pattern of visiting did not differ strikingly as between residents of different types of homes. Rather more middle- than working-class people were visited, but not more frequently.

These figures might lead one to take a poor view of the relatives and friends. Here were old people, many of them infirm, who had been in institutions and homes for only brief periods. Many were likely to have a number of relatives and friends who could visit them. Yet only about a fifth of them were being visited more than once a week. The facts are, however, rather complex and need to be examined critically. Significantly more of those with than without children had been visited at least once a week. But a substantial proportion of the residents had neither surviving children nor brothers and sisters. They relied on cousins, sisters-in-law and nieces and nephews to visit them. Often they had few relatives. Even those who had children had sometimes lost contact with them years previously. One man said, for example, 'My children didn't like me marrying again. Who is going to make them come?'

Some close relatives, particularly the brothers and sisters of unmarried people, were themselves ill, infirm or disabled, and often lived rather far away. Frequently we were told of journeys of ten and twenty miles. One woman said that a brother and two nieces came fifty miles every Sunday to see her. The number of residents visited was found to be closely related to the siting of the homes. This is, of course, an important fact in planning the opening of new homes.

In many homes there was little privacy and few facilities for visitors. Old people and their relatives often had to sit in a crowded lounge. There was no opportunity to have tea together nor for the relatives to feel of some constructive use, by washing underclothes, preparing meals or dusting furniture. Some elderly residents recognized their loss of status and independence and were embarrassed if relatives or friends visited them. 'If my son comes it brings to mind too much why I've come here.' 'I wouldn't dream of asking any of my neighbours or friends to come. I wouldn't like them to see me like this.'

Some of the more active old people preferred to go out to their relatives' homes. 'I'd rather go to their homes. You see a little bit of home life.' A few men met their brothers or sons in a local pub. Other old people went to relatives for a day at week-ends. Altogether 21 per cent of the new residents had made such visits since their admission – nearly half of them once a week or more. Most who paid visits also received them once a week or more.

Significantly more of the infirm than of the active residents were visited fairly frequently by relatives. This suggests that the relatives more often made an effort to visit old people when they were infirm. Much the same was true of friends, although fewer old people, whether infirm or active, had been visited by them.

When asked whether their relatives should visit them more often, only 21 per cent of the men, and 28 per cent of the women, said they should. The volume of complaints was roughly the same whether the residents were middle- or working-class and whether they possessed surviving children or not. Old people with several close relatives often felt neglected by some but not by others. One woman said her relatives should visit her more but it transpired that she was referring only to her eldest son. Other children visited her several times a week. Many people felt they were visited as often as they could reasonably expect and did not express any resentment, whether explicit or implicit. Perhaps some of them were too loyal to criticize those they loved. Nonetheless it would be true to say that the majority keenly missed the family life they had enjoyed at home.

Those who had no relatives or had not been visited by them also had little contact with friends. Only 28 per cent had been visited by friends and few of these as often as once a week. Some of those who were visited neither by relatives nor friends were active enough to go out, but did not do so. Altogether 18 per cent of the men and 24 per cent of the women who were judged to be fully mobile had not left the precincts of the home since their admission.

It is clear that many of the residents had maintained some contacts with the outside world. But it is also clear that such contacts had declined markedly both in frequency and quality. However one studies the complex relationships between these old people and persons living outside the home, three facts have to be remembered: 44 per cent had not left the precincts of the home since their admission; 22 per cent had not been visited by anyone, and another 31 per cent did not have as much as one visit a week from either relatives or friends.

## Tenuousness of new relationships

Once introduced to their new life elderly people had more opportunities for establishing social relationships with others of their own age than individuals living in private households outside. We attempted to obtain some idea of the quality of these relationships.

Twenty-one per cent of the men and 17 per cent of the women said they helped someone else, regularly or fairly often, and another 10 per cent of the men and 14 per cent of the women said that someone else helped them with such things as dressing and walking outside in the grounds. But despite this evidence of mutual aid among the residents, less than a third of those with unlimited mobility gave help and less than a third of those unable to walk outside the building received help.

Slightly more of the men than of the women claimed to have a friend among the other residents – 19.4 per cent compared with 17.2 per cent. More of the residents living in the post-war local authority and the voluntary homes had formed friendships than in the former workhouses and private homes. Fewer of the infirm than of the active old people had made friends.

Sometimes there was the chance renewal of former relationships. One woman said, 'When I came here I found I had worked with one woman when I was 17. It was almost like a welcome.' Another found a former neighbour with whom she had been friendly. 'We saw each other's children grow up.' Most other friendships had developed because two persons had come from a particular neighbourhood or because one had the opportunity of directly assisting the other. Fewer friendships were formed between persons sleeping in one room than between persons sleeping in single rooms. There were occasional attachments between old people of the opposite sex.

But most replies to questions about friends revealed reserve, suspicion and even hostility. 'I've been here over three months. I don't make friends. I don't like any of them.' 'They're all fairly decent. But they're not my style or class. They're just all sorts.' 'If you're among old people you don't want to talk much. It's better to have a still tongue. You're better thought of ... We're not allowed to help each other…Nobody here makes friends. We all lead more or less isolated lives.' 'I can't get on with these old people. I want atmosphere. I've never been used to this sort of thing.'

Close associations with members of the staff were also few. Matrons and attendants were often conscious of the difficulties of showing affection for a particular individual. They are very jealous,' said one matron, 'and if I give one of them more attention than the others, even in illness, there is trouble.' Few old people spoke of members of the staff as they would of friends. 'They're all right. I never answer them back. I do what's right.' This lady [the matron] seems to have too much on her mind. She never has time

to discuss things. She's very nice when she does *have* to speak to you…'
Nothing emerged from our interviews with new residents to contradict the
evidence described in earlier chapters: that comparatively few close personal
relationships were formed between different residents, or between residents
and members of the staff.

## Loneliness

Nineteen per cent said they were often and 27 per cent sometimes lonely.
These proportions are much larger than those found in local surveys of
old people living at home. In J. H. Sheldon's survey in Wolverhampton,
for example, there were 8 per cent and 14 per cent respectively. Fewer
unmarried than married or widowed persons said they were often lonely
but the differences between those who had surviving children and those
who had not were small.

Loneliness often arose as the result of the loss of a husband or wife,
brother or sister or child -- which a large number of the new residents had
experienced. The old people would have been lonely, perhaps, wherever they
lived, but the loss of home, separation from relatives and growing infirmity, as
well as the shortcomings of institutional life, often reinforced such feelings.
'Christ, yes, I'm lonely! It's the worst thing in the world to bear. You can
be lonely and surrounded by people.' 'It seems like a dozen years instead
of a month. I'm broken-hearted all the time. I see all these strangers and
all I want are my own.' There were only a few people making comments
which suggested they were *less* lonely because they now had company.
These examples suggest how important it is to distinguish between social
isolation and loneliness in old age. People who were unmarried and had
led an isolated life tended not to complain about loneliness unless they had
lost contact with a close friend. Those who had lost or been separated from
someone they loved often felt lonely even when they had lived with other
people. In fact the majority seemed to feel their loss more keenly, because
there were fewer opportunities of losing themselves in household activities
and relationships with other members of their families and friends.

## Loss of privacy and identity

Much has been said already of old people's yearning for any acknowledgment
of their individuality. There were times when they preferred solitude and
privacy, and they sought any opportunity to keep and look after personal
possessions and furniture. One good indication of their feelings was their
attitude towards sleeping in a room with others. We asked whether they
slept in a single room and, if not, whether they would prefer to do so.
Although many of them were living in institutions which had no single

rooms and therefore found the question unreal, only 26 per cent of those sharing a room wanted to go on doing so (though another 8 per cent were uncertain). Sixty-six per cent of the men and 65 per cent of the women said they would prefer to have a single room. If those who already had a single room are included the respective figures both become 72 per cent. There was comparatively little difference in attitude between people of different social class, or between residents living in different types of homes.

Who were the persons who preferred to share a bedroom? Our anticipation was that they would be predominantly infirm and predominantly those who had had long experience of institutional life. The information we obtained supported this assumption, but only to a very slight extent. For example, only 30 per cent of the most incapacitated residents sharing rooms in the sample wanted to go on doing so, compared with 25 per cent of the most active.

Motives for sharing rooms were diverse. Some had lost a husband or wife and liked the company, some needed help in dressing and some were used to life in hostels and lodging houses. Some, however, seemed merely to be frightened of any further change. They had been moved around so much that they disliked the thought of yet another upheaval. Nearly all these people preferred to share a room with one other person rather than with two or more.

The great majority of the residents were emphatic in their desire for a single room. 'That's the most natural thing in the world. I've had my own room ever since I was a girl.' 'When my relatives come there's nowhere to talk. No privacy.' 'I'd give anything for a room of my own. I miss that most of all.' 'There's three in my room. One of them goes to bed early and one doesn't. One wants the light on and one doesn't. One sings and one coughs. I like the window open at night but the others like it closed. I scarcely have any sleep at all.' In the sample there were eighty-seven who already had a single room. It is perhaps significant that none of them wanted to change.

[...]

## Length of stay and the preservation of individuality

Most of the evidence in this chapter has referred to old people who had lived for four months or less in the sample of homes which were visited. It may well be argued that they were therefore unrepresentative of all the residents in many different ways, because they had not yet had time to settle down to make friends. Are the other residents different? We carried out a number of elaborate checks on our information about the persons we interviewed, taking account of length of stay and in particular studying the reactions of those among them who had had prior experience of institutions. In their attitudes towards homes the longer-stay residents did not differ strikingly from the short-stay residents. To take just one small but useful example, we found that there were thirty-eight individuals in the sample who had not lived in a private household for at least five years, some of them not for more than ten years. Twenty-two of these thirty-eight did not want to stay in a home and twenty-nine said they preferred to have a single room (including nine who already had one).

We also studied some limited evidence about *all* the 7,689 elderly residents living in the homes in our sample which showed, first, that the number of long-stay was much smaller than the number of short-stay residents who were visited frequently and, second, that there was little change with length of stay in the number of active residents who did in fact go outside the homes fairly often.

So far as we can judge from our interviews it seemed that while the old people who had recently entered a residential home for the first time were still suffering in some degree from the shock of being parted from their homes, families and friends, some of them still wanted to believe they had taken the right step or were anxious, at the least, to give the staff and others the benefit of any doubts they had. The newness of residential life itself gave a few of them a mild sense of adventure and they had not yet felt any disillusionment.

On the other hand, despite their familiarity with residential life, and their diminishing contact with the world outside, many of the longer-stay residents hung on grimly to their desire for a home of their own and greater recognition of their individuality. The lapse of time had intensified rather than diminished these feelings, even though they did not appear to increase their relationships with other residents. Our information revealed no hint of greater apathy among them. However, we did not obtain very much evidence about residents who had lived in homes for long periods and much more research is needed before emphatic conclusions can be drawn.

Studies in children's homes, hospitals, prisons and homes for the handicapped of the effects of living in institutions have tended to give credence to the hypothesis that those who live for considerable periods in institutions become apathetic, lack initiative and otherwise increasingly become physically and emotionally debilitated (so much so that they fear any proposal to remove them from this protective environment). Our inquiry, does not, so far as it goes, lend support to this hypothesis, or, at the least, suggests that it is a gross over-simplification.

We would suggest that the chief changes in an individual's psychology and behaviour occur during the first days or weeks after his admission to a communal institution. In other words there are likely to be much bigger psychological and social differences between persons living in private households and those living in institutions than between short and long-stay residents of institutions. The individual seems to receive an initial shock which causes him to adjust quickly to a new level of behaviour and to adopt certain new attitudes towards his environment and himself. This behaviour and these attitudes seem to 'set' in a pattern which, for many people though not all, does not change drastically thereafter. The resident may *appear* in time to become more resigned, apathetic or contented, but this probably means only that, as his familiarity with the institutional régime grows, he conforms to the rules of the game to obtain certain limited ends, whether to be left in peace by the staff, or given an extra cup of tea or piece of cake because he is a 'model' resident. He presents an amiable, submissive self to the outside world. Yet despite outward appearances and long experience of a communal life many individuals appear to cling tenaciously to their individual identity and ideals. If this is so, then the task of rehabilitation may be easier than is often supposed.

Many qualifications and exceptions of the kind described earlier in this book need to be made to this general account but it may help to explain the extraordinary resilience of some individuals whom we met and interviewed, which was to us a source of wonder. Some individuals seemed to have survived almost every form of personal humiliation and public supervision. One dignified man of 74 had just entered an old workhouse after spending thirty-nine years in mental hospitals. According to his case-record an eventual review had cast doubt on whether certification should have been re-imposed, as it was, in each of the previous twenty years. The staff of the workhouse told us that there had been no sign of any mental infirmity or abnormality and certainly he spoke intelligently and quietly during the interview. In reply to the question, 'Now that you are here, do you want to stay permanently?', he said, 'It's easier here and more comfortable. I don't want to complain. They do what they can. But all my life I have wanted just two things, a job of my own and a home of my own.' Despite nearly forty years' continuous experience of living in institutions, the flame still burned.

## A fundamental dilemma

As society has begun in recent years to recognize the psychological and social needs of sick and handicapped individuals – partly by transforming the institution and its management and partly by experimenting with alternative methods of care – a fundamental dilemma has been posed for us. While rejecting the social philosophy of the nineteenth century we have yet to find a coherent philosophy to put in its place. We are torn between the desire to segregate persons for therapy according to their physical and social condition and the desire to give them the advantages of living in a 'normal' community. It is difficult if not impossible to do both through the medium of the 'custodial' or long-stay institution and perhaps the most logical resolution of our dilemma would be gradually to abandon this institution as an instrument of social policy.

## Endnote

[1] Bawkin, H., 'Emotional Deprivation in Infants', *Journal of Pediatrics*, Oct. 1949. For a summary of the results of many different studies of infants and young children see Bowlby, J., *Maternal Care and Mental Health*, Geneva, World Health Organization, 1952.

# 38

# The structured dependency
# of the elderly

## Introduction

For many years after the Second World War scientific research into old age was extraordinarily restricted, and only latterly has fundamental enquiry begun to assume a critical and wide-ranging and hence more constructive cohesion. The physical, mental, and social features of ageing were seen as natural, or as largely inevitable. Instead of asking what brought about the modern phenomenon of retirement and accentuated social dependency and the chances of isolation and extreme deprivation in old age, or what explained the mainly custodial and impersonal forms of institutional care for the elderly and the large-scale use to which they were put, many scientists, scholars and practitioners have asked only how can people *adjust* to retirement, or how can the burden for relatives or the state be lightened, or how can the administration of institutional care be made more efficient? The inexorable process by which the status of older people has been lowered, or rather, defined at a lowly level in the course of the development of the industrial societies, has been largely ignored. The evolution of the economy, the state and social inequality has been taken for granted, and the implications of the trends for people as they become older neglected. Rather than ask how and why is society restricting life chances and opportunities at older ages, most scientists have directed their attention to the problems of elucidating adjustment so as to soften the impact of that adjustment but, indirectly, legitimise its operation.

This might be illustrated copiously from the literature on ageing, particularly compendia published in the United States between the 1950s and 1970s, such as the *Handbook of Social Gerontology*[1] and *The Sociology of Ageing: Selected Readings.*[2] More recent examples are *Old Age in European Society* and *The Economics of Individual and Population Ageing.*[3]

Townsend, P. (1981) 'The structured dependency of the elderly: a creation of social policy in the twentieth century', *Ageing & Society*, vol 1, no 1, pp 5-28.

## The individualistic approach to ageing and the origins of an alternative approach

This emphasis on trying to explain individual ageing within a structure, and especially class structure, which was accepted without question, rather than trying to explain that structure, its interrelationships and its development, as a necessary precondition in the exposition of a theory about ageing and the aged, was shared by most social gerontologists. It was derived from neo-classical economic theory and the associated thinking of those working within the tradition of functionalism in sociology, as well as the more descriptive and empirical traditions of social work and social administration. The bias was towards individualistic instead of societal forms of explanation. Elsewhere I have characterized this as 'acquiescent functionalism', or the kind of theory of ageing which attributes the causation of problems to the difficulties *of* individual adjustment to ageing, retirement or physical decrescence, while acquiescing in the development of the state, the economy and inequality.[4] Perhaps the single most important influence during this period in reflecting an individualistic interpretation was the work of the 'disengagement' theorists, in particular, Cumming and Henry.[5,6] From the beginning there were those like the Israeli, Yonina Talmon, who challenged this interpretation[7-9] and the normative assumptions of this theoretical approach came increasingly under close scrutiny.[10] There were those who challenged in detail the evidence of occupational and social but also psychological disengagement.[11] Alternative modes of explanation, whether of a radical structural or class-oriented, or even broadly Marxist kind, have been slow in developing.

[...]

## The tasks ahead

Two levels of analysis therefore become necessary. One is to explain how the general position, status and functions of the elderly within existing society have been determined or established. The other is to examine and explain the kind of relationship within different structures which elderly people have, the roles they play and experience, concurrently and sequentially. The second is much more common in the literature but of not much help to understanding without explicit formulation in relation to the first. Let me discuss these in turn. We are too inclined to accept the existence of contemporary economic and social institutions as inevitable and necessary. Only by reminding ourselves repeatedly of the emergence and decline of certain kinds of institution in different countries in the span of less than a hundred years, and of the transformation of their functions, composition, systems of authority and independence can we achieve that degree of detachment necessary to a scientific perspective. The changes which are taking place in the external community and the whole system of institutions, and in the central value system and economic and political value systems of society, ramify and infuse the particular relationships between old people and others in the family, the community, and the social services. The full implications of this process need to be thoroughly understood. A good example is the history of the workhouse. This became a necessary ingredient of emerging capitalism. It was brought about by enclosure and new definitions of the private rights to property, and not just the need to establish a compliant workforce. There were bound to be victims of the operation of the new rules as well as a need in principle for examples of what would happen if the rules were broken. An Assistant Commissioner of the Poor Law wrote, 'Our object is to … establish therein a discipline so severe and repulsive as to make them a terror to the poor and prevent them from entering.'[12] The intention was to enforce the willingness to work and, at the same time, inhibit recourse to public relief. A growing number of elderly people were submitted to a style of life intended centrally for the able-bodied poor. For most of the 19th century, admission to the workhouse (later to become public assistance institutions) was seen more in relation to the individual's accommodation to society than society's creation of a system of control. As one commentator put it recently, admission

> 'continued to be seen as a sign of individual moral decay and bad management among the working classes rather than as a consequence of social change and the economic order. In this way older people were seen to have caused 'a problem' for the payers of the poor rate and for those in authority. The situation was perceived as a social problem, the cause of which was the irresponsibility and imprudence of the inflated population of work-house inhabitants.'[13]

In some respects the problem was therefore a direct creation of the system. Victorian morality was also strait-laced, as well as being deeply influenced by the work ethic, and in both respects there were consequences for the elderly in residential institutions. This affected access to relatives and the outside world and resulted in the segregation of the sexes internally, for example. One historian has lately shown that the consequences for the elderly were not only harsh in the decades following 1834 but were deliberately punitive in the 1870s and 1880s, when efforts were redoubled to implement the principles of the new Poor Law.[14] In many countries it is arguable that evidence of this suffering can still be found, and is attributable to the inheritance, too little modified, of those self-same values. There are tendencies to withhold commitment of medical and occupational resources, depreciate individuality and foster passivity and dependence. Our task then is to properly trace and identify those forces and values which govern not just the arrangements made for older people in residential institutions, but the ideas with which we interpret those arrangements.

I am arguing, then, that society creates the framework of institutions and rules within which the general problems of the elderly emerge and, indeed, are manufactured. Decisions are being taken every day, in the management of the economy and in the maintenance and development of social institutions, which govern the position which the elderly occupy in national life, and these also contribute powerfully to the public consciousness of different meanings of ageing and old age. There are decisions familiar to all of us about the commitment of public expenditure which directly govern the services and benefits of older people. Then there are decisions about employment, wages and taxation, transport, urban planning and housing which have a powerful indirect effect on the situation and standard of living of the elderly. And the question is not just one of the flow of resources to the elderly population and the determination of their material amenities, but the scope for action and self-help on the part of the elderly which becomes feasible, and therefore the interpretation that they, and not only others, place upon their status and functions.

## The effects of retirement in promoting increased dependency

Let me review the more crucial factors. Retirement has become a social phenomenon of vast importance in the short span of the last fifty years. According to statistics published by the International Labour Office, between 40 per cent and 70 per cent of men 65 and over in all industrial countries were still economically active in the 1930s. But by the mid-1960s, with the exception of Japan, where the percentage had declined only slightly, the proportion had shrunk dramatically to between 10 per cent and 40 per cent with the mean about 20 per cent. The reduction has continued during the 1970s, though not so rapidly. This change cannot be attributed to changes in the risk of ill-health or disability, or the masking of disability in periods before substitute pensions were available. It is attributable to changes in the organization of work and in the kinds of people wanted for work. [...]

Closer historical examination of retirement as a social institution shows that its adoption has also been associated with pressures to shed moral if not contractual obligations to loyal workers and to exclude certain groups of workers from the bargaining process. The public are encouraged to accept the lessened value to the economy of workers past certain ages. Changing technology and the successive adoption of forms of training and educational qualifications have encouraged over-valuation of the productive capacity of younger workers and under-valuation of the productive capacity of older workers. This has affected other priorities. Less consideration tends to be given in sickness and disability at older than at younger ages and, indeed, retirement is cavalierly associated with failing health and capacity. Thus the combined effects of industrial, economic and educational re-organization are leading to a more rigid stratification of the population by age. [...]

## The effects of pensions in promoting dependency

While the institutionalization of retirement as a major social phenomenon in the very recent history of society has played a big part in fostering the material and psychological dependence of older people, the institutionalization of pensions and services has also played a major part. The propensity to poverty in old age could be said to be a function of low levels of resources, and restricted access to resources, relative to younger people. Secondly it is due to restricted access to the new styles and modes of living being promoted in the community. In Britain there is official evidence for the last 15 years of about 10 per cent being in poverty, as defined by the state, and another 30 per cent or 40 per cent being on the margins in the sense that they are living at the state's standard or within 40 per cent of that standard.[15,16] Independent measures suggest the first of these figures (10 per cent in poverty) is underestimated because of methodological shortcoming.[17] Restriction of resources is determined by different causal factors. State pensions and other cash benefits administered centrally comprise the most important source of income for the elderly in most advanced industrial societies and the initial rate of state pensions after retirement, and the amount of substitute or supplementary benefits which are paid, after the pensionable age or upon retirement, tend to be low relative to the earnings of younger adults. [...]

There is a sharp contrast between the low status in which old people are held publicly and the regard in which they are held privately in their families. In the family age is of secondary importance. People are grandparents, parents, brothers or sisters and friends or neighbours first and foremost. Retirement from familial roles is a much more flexible contingency, dependent primarily upon health or disablement. In some respects the family also provides escape from the psychological and social bruises which can be inflicted externally, and up to a point provides meaningful activity and genuine respect. The positive contribution to the welfare of grandchildren and children of many elderly women is greatly underestimated just as their labour specifically on behalf of their husbands and in general on behalf of the economy throughout adult working life goes largely unrecognized. Capital and state separately or in combination, may have fostered the dependency of women within the family but, paradoxically, has created an independent system of interdependence, occupation, mutual respect and loyalty. The defensive and restorative mechanisms of the family temper the dependency created by the state.[18]

## The effects of residential care in creating dependency

Rich societies have still to come to terms with the engineering of retirement and mass poverty among the elderly in the twentieth century. These two are of course linked and they have been pre-eminent in creating the social dependency of the elderly. But their connection with the development of residential and community care is *too* frequently overlooked. When we turn to examine the part played by these two trends in fostering dependency it is important to understand how the assumptions of all the participants are already greatly affected by the facts of retirement and poverty. Not only do they materially restrict life chances. They govern the attitudes and not only the actions of professional staff, on the one hand, and elderly clients or residents, on the other.

[…]

## Social rather than physical and mental dependence

Evidence of the imposition of dependency upon inmates can be divided into at least two categories – physical or mental evidence about individual capacities which shows that people need not be there and evidence of social restriction. The relevant legislation places a duty on local authorities to provide residential Homes for those 'in need of care and attention'. Tests of mental, physical and social capacity can in principle be applied to the different inmate populations to find how far formal conditions for inmate status are in fact met. Tests of mental capacity are less common than of physical capacity but have been attempted. In a 1963 national survey, for example, 42 per cent of elderly psychiatric patients were said by staff to be severely mentally impaired. Fifty-five per cent were said to have no incapacity or only slight or moderate incapacity. In short, independent checks or assessments of mental conditions can be made to explore need in relation to organizational function.[19]

During the last three decades extensive evidence about capacities for self-care on the part of residents has been published. There are of course different options in converting conceptualization into measurement.[20] In a 1958-59 survey of England and Wales, 74 per cent of new residents of Homes were found to have only slight or no incapacity and a survey in 1963 of all residents produced a roughly comparable figure of 58 per cent.[21] A 1969 survey of Scotland showed that 67 per cent of residents of local authority homes were able to wash, dress and use toilets on their own initiative, and 45 per cent were defined as 'fit', that is, having complete capacity for self-care. The authors concluded that 54 per cent could have lived in sheltered housing.[22] A DHSS census in 1970 showed that as many as 45 per cent in local authority homes were 'minimally dependent' in the sense that they were 'mobile without assistance, continent, able to feed themselves and mentally alert'.[23] While this kind of evidence can be quoted from a wide range of reports it should not be forgotten that at the other extreme there is evidence of a substantial minority of residents who are extremely frail. In the Scottish survey, for example, 14 per cent were classified as requiring hospital care.[24]

During the 1970s a succession of further studies has produced substantially more evidence. Despite a tendency for the average age of residents of homes to rise and representations on the part of staff understandably to be made about the increasing numbers of very frail residents, evidence continues to be published from different parts of the country testifying to the non-frailty of a substantial proportion of the residents.[25-36] Let me illustrate from a report published in 1980. Booth arranged for detailed questions to be put about ability for self-care, continence and social integration, of the residents of one local authority.

> 'Over one-fifth (22.1 per cent) of all residents in homes in Sheffield were assessed as requiring care and support of a degree which rendered them substantially dependent on residential staff. On the other hand, the census also shows that a much larger proportion of residents (37.3 per cent of the total) were rated as largely independent in their personal functioning within the home; and bearing in mind the possibility that the method of assessment may have tended to over-predict the extent of dependency, then the estimate is likely to under-represent the time ratio of active and able residents in the homes.'[36]

The concept of dependency includes more than is implied by this extract[37] but Booth brings out something which is not acknowledged in many of the studies – that staff must not be treated as disinterested or unbiased witnesses of residents' capacities. Because of organizational constraints and the formal expectations placed upon them in fulfilling their roles staff are liable to take an unduly pessimistic view of residents' capacities. There is a double problem. On the one hand there are very disabled residents. Staff are acutely conscious of the difficulties of managing severely disabled residents. Medical, psychiatric and nursing skills in residential institutions are generally sparse. In previous decades many of these elderly residents would have been cared for in hospital, but there has been a reduction in the proportion and even the absolute number of patients in geriatric wards of hospitals and in psychiatric hospitals at the same time as the elderly population has increased.

On the other hand, the expression of this problem and the organization of appropriate forms of care must not be allowed to overshadow the needs of non-disabled residents at the other end of the disability scale. A large proportion of residents are quite active and alert and could happily live in a less constrained and regulated environment in sheltered or special housing. The tasks of meeting their needs as well as those of the severely disabled residents are incompatible.[38-45]

## Forms of social dependence in residential care

The evidence about capacity is important but arguably inconclusive in analysing the functions of Homes and the potentialities of residents. Obviously there can be anxious debates about the appropriateness of applying relatively crude measures of capacity and whether such measures can be used for fluctuating levels of capacity over short spans of time. For this reason among others we need also to consider a second set of evidence. If a high proportion of inmates do not satisfy the formal physical or clinical criteria for residence then there must be some key social determinants to be unravelled, whether to do with the social origins (or characteristics) of inmates or of the institutions in which they live. (This is not to say that social determinants are not also important in explaining the presence of incapacitated inmates.)

Let us consider the social evidence. Far from being a representative cross section of the elderly the inmates of institutions are very unrepresentative. Thus there is a consistent relationship between the 'closeness' of someone's familial network and his chances of being in an institution in old age. According to the census of 1971 relatively four times as many bachelors as married men and three times as many spinsters as married women of 90 years of age or over in Britain were in different types of institution. As many as 37 per cent of bachelors and 44 per cent of spinsters of this age were living in institutions.[46, 47] But marital status is a crude indicator of family status, and it is the familial situation which is the vital matter for study and measurement. [...]

The evidence therefore suggests that in part institutions emulate, or deputize for, families in providing care for certain elderly people whose family resources are meagre. In this sense they complement the family. But while this helps to explain the presence of sick, disabled or infirm people who lack, or have become isolated from, close relatives it does not explain the presence of relatively active or independent people. We then have to draw on various studies which show the scale of homelessness among single people – not only as a consequence of loss of job, failure to pay rent, or eviction from housing provided by an employer or a husband's employer, but dispossession of property during stays in hospital. This might be summarized as the loss of rights to housing in the community.

There are other external determinants of inmate status which can be understood most easily in terms of social deviance. There are elderly people who are labelled as 'confused' or 'wandering', 'forgetful', 'a danger to themselves', 'dirty', 'undernourished', 'restless' and 'aimless' and who are urged to move into a hospital or Home. The reason for their admission is more one of social disquiet, embarrassment or intolerance than that such people meet strict criteria of dependency or of the need for treatment or confinement.

Once we try to account for the continued residence of relatively active long-stay inmates our attention shifts from external to internal factors. Some people who are frail or malnourished when first admitted become stronger after a period of care. A Home or a hospital is an on-going social system. It may or may not enjoy strong relationships with external society. The number of visitors or inmates who have social contacts or relationships outside the precincts of the institution may be relatively small or large and in other ways it can be socially marooned or integrated. Goffman has helped us to comprehend the relative imperviousness of some institutions to external social change and the total, and sometimes frightening, authority exercised by some staff over inmates.[48] Access to income is extraordinarily restricted and financial deprivation, as a source of extreme dependence, is rarely measured and analysed. In Britain, as in some other countries, there have been a series of revelations about abuses occurring in long-stay institutions. Since the late 1960s, in particular, there have been a stream of reports on individual mental illness, mental handicap and geriatric hospitals and residential Homes which have revealed conditions and staff practices which are socially unacceptable.[49-51] Many of these reports have emanated from official inquiries – in particular those of the Hospital Advisory Committee. It is important to appreciate that problems arise not only in the forbidding environment of the largest long-stay hospitals but also in both small private Homes and brand-new local authority Homes. Let me give two examples. The authority of the matron in a small private Home for six or ten residents can often be close to total and society has failed either to properly investigate or prevent abuses. Secondly, fear of being transferred to an old institution has operated as a sanction to control the behaviour of residents and even elderly residents in many local areas. Many councils have been slow to close these old buildings, and some are still used. But as their numbers have diminished new forms of control are being developed. For example, separate wings or units of some newly built Homes have been reserved for the elderly mentally infirm.[52] An early report on such arrangements, which is certainly the finest post-war study of the subject, severely criticized them.[53] Unhappily social deviants or miscreants and not only those categorized as mentally infirm tend to be allocated to such units and although there has been some discussion[54-56] the case against these units needs to be discussed much more openly, and anxiously, than it is.

Socially, then, institutions are structured to serve purposes of controlling inmates. The type and level of staffing, amenities and resources have been developed not only in relation to the characteristics, including the perceived capacities, of inmates but also the roles staff expect inmates to play. Staff tend to resist any increase in the number or proportion of inmates requiring a great deal of attention. They become conscious of the value of inmates who perform large and small tasks in the organization and tend to give excuses rather than rational grounds for the presence in the institution of these inmates. On the other hand, the roles are distinguished from those played by staff by their subordinate and even menial status and the derisory forms of payment which accompany them. Occupational roles are clearly distinguished partly to maintain the lower status and presumed dependency of inmates. The majority of residents in Homes are placed in a category of enforced dependence. The routine of residential Homes, made necessary by small staffs and economical administration, and committed to an ideology of 'care and attention' rather than the encouragement of self-help and self-management, seems to deprive many residents of the opportunity if not the incentive to occupy themselves and even of the means of communication. These statements are based on a large number of citations.[57-75]

[...]

The maintenance and even increase of the share of resources going to hospitals and to residential institutions has been something of a paradox. Despite the powerful movements in favour of community care the emergence of that sector cannot be said to have properly materialized. This is not easy to explain. The failure to achieve a shift in priorities has to be explained partly, as I have implied, in relation to the powerful vested interests of certain branches of the professions, unions of hospital staffs and certain sections of the administration. The brute fact is that the majority of medical staff and the vast majority of nursing staff work in hospital, and the majority of local authority care staff work in residential Homes. The failure to shift the balance of health and welfare policy towards community care also has to be explained in relation to the function of institutions to regulate and confirm inequality in society, and indeed to regulate deviation from the central social values of self-help, domestic independence, personal thrift, willingness to work, productive effort and family care. Institutions serve subtle functions in reflecting the positive structural and cultural changes taking place in society.

The numbers of bedfast, severely incapacitated and infirm old people living in the community dwarfs the number in institutions and there are real dangers in the present situation of committing available resources for the care of a few at the expense of the much larger number living in the community who require only modest forms of support to live independently with their families.[76-80] Our object must be a renewed attempt to replace institutional care by increased and new forms of support in the home. While the costs of care in residential institutions are not always easy to compare with the costs of providing alternative services when old people are living at home (depending on levels of disablement as well as the types of benefit or service included in the measurement), most of the studies that have been carried out have concluded that the costs of care at home are smaller.[81-83]

However, so much energy has been invested by radical analysts in arguing for community care as an alternative mode of support for the elderly that some of the less happy practices incorporated within the conventional administration of community care services have attracted little scrutiny. Thus, day centres are sometimes organized on the same lines as residential Homes, but without residence at night. Meals and perhaps physiotherapy are laid on but little scope allowed for various forms of occupation and self-management. The duties of home helps and community nurses are also heavily circumscribed. The elderly are usually viewed as the grateful and passive recipients of services administered by an enlightened public authority. This can but reinforce their dependency both in their own eyes and that of the public. The possibility of organizing collaborative services with elderly clients and non-clients would be regarded in most areas as entirely alien or utopian.

## Summary

I have tried to argue that the concepts of retirement, pensionable status, institutional residence and rather passive forms of community care have been developed in both capitalist and state socialist countries in ways which have created and reinforced the social dependency of the elderly. Such 'structured' dependency is a consequence of twentieth-century thought and action, and especially of the management of modern economies and the distribution of power and status in such economies. The severity and extent of that dependency cannot be justified by appeal to certain major types of evidence. Empirical studies of capacity and desire for productive occupation, reciprocation of services, and familial and social relationships, as well as self-care, challenge the assumptions which prevail. There is clearly room for an alternative interpretation of the roles to be played by the elderly whereby many more of them continue in paid employment, find alternative forms of substantial and productive occupation, have rights to much larger incomes, and have a much greater control over the place and type of accommodation where they live, and the kinds of community services to which they contribute as well as have access.

## Endnotes

[1] Tibbitts, C., *Handbook of Social Gerontology,* Chicago, University of Chicago Press, 1960.

[2] Atchley, R., and Seltzer, M., *The Sociology of Ageing: Selected Readings,* Belmont, California, Wadworth, 1976.

[3] And see also Stearns, P. N., *Old Age in European Society,* London, Croom Helm, 1977; and Clark, R.L., and Spengler, J.J., *The Economics of Individual and Population Ageing,* Cambridge, Cambridge University Press, 1980.

[4] Townsend, P., 'The care of the elderly in Britain and Japan: the relative effectiveness of community care and residential services for the elderly', paper given to the Japanese National Committee of the International Council on Social Welfare, April, 1978, published in Japanese, Tokyo, 1979 (English version in mimeograph).

[5] Cumming, E. and Henry, W.E., *Growing Old,* New York, Basic Books, 1961.

[6] Cumming, E., 'Further thoughts on the theory of disengagement', *International Social Science Journal,* XV, 3, 1963.

[7] Talmon, Y., 'Dimensions of disengagement. Ageing in collective settlements', paper given at research seminar on social gerontology, Markaryd, Sweden, 1963.

[8] Talmon, Y., 'Ageing in Israel: a planned society', *American Journal of Sociology,* LXVII, 3, 1961.

[9] Talmon, Y., *Family and Community in the Kibbutz,* Cambridge, Mass., Harvard University Press, 1972.

[10] See, for example, Hendricks, J., and Hendricks, C.D., *Aging in Mass Society,* Cambridge, Mass., Winthrop, 1977.

[11] Shanas, E., *et al., Old People in Three Industrial Societies,* London, Routledge, 1968.

[12] Thompson, E.P., *The Making of the English Working Class,* London, Victor Gollancz, 1963, p. 295.

[13] Johnson, M.L., 'Relations and relationships', Block I, Unit 4 of the Post-experience Courses Unit, Course: *An Ageing Population,* Milton Keynes, The Open University Press, 1979.

[14] Thomson, D., *Provision for the Elderly in England 1830-1908,* University of Cambridge, Ph.D., 1981.

[15] Ministry of Pensions and National Insurance, *The Financial and Other Circumstances of Retirement Pensioners,* London, HMSO, 1966.

[16] DHSS, 'The DHSS Perspective', in Barnes, J. and Connelly, N., *Social Care Research,* London, Bedford Square Press, 1978.

[17] Townsend, P., *Poverty in the United Kingdom,* Harmondsworth, Penguin, 1979, Chapter 7.

[18] Shanas, E. *et al, op. cit.*, Chapters 5 and 14.

[19] Townsend, P., 'The needs of the elderly, and the planning of hospitals', in Canvin, R.W. and Pearson, N.G. (eds) *Needs of the Elderly for Health and Welfare Services,* University of Exeter, 1972, pp. 53-4.

[20] Bebbington, A.C., 'The elderly at home survey: changes in the provision of domiciliary social services to the elderly over fourteen years' (mimeo), University of Kent, 1978. Bebbington, A.C., 'Scaling indices of disablement', *British Journal of Preventive and Social Medicine,* 31, 1977. Munnichs, J.M.A. and van den Heuval, W.J.A., *Dependency and Interdependency in Old Age,* The Hague, Martinus Nijhof, 1976. Harris, A.I., with Cox, E. and Smith, C.R.W., *Handicapped and Impaired in Great Britain,* OPCS, London, HMSO, 1971.

[21] Townsend, P., *The Last Refuge,* London, Routledge, 1962. See also Townsend, P., 'The needs of the elderly and the planning of hospitals', *op. cit.*, p. 54.

[22] Carstairs, V. and Morrison, M., *The Elderly in Residential Care*, Scottish Health Service Studies, No. 19, 1971, p. 74.

[23] DHSS (Department of Health and Social Security), *The Census of Residential Accommodation, 1970. Volume I: Residential Accommodation for the Elderly and the Younger Physically Handicapped,* London, HMSO, 1975, p. 44.

[24] Carstairs, V. and Morrison, M., *op. cit.*

[25] Shreeve, M., 'A survey of people admitted to old people's homes and on the waiting list over a three-month period', internal report, Warwickshire Social Services Department, 1973.

[26] Kimbell, A. and Townsend, J., *Residents in Elderly Persons Homes,* Cheshire County Council Social Services Department, April 1974. Townsend, J. and Kimbell, A., 'Caring regimes in elderly persons' homes', *Health and Social Service Journal,* 11 October 1975.

[27] East Sussex County Council Social Services Department, *Key Issue 1: The Elderly: Main Report on the Findings,* 1975.

[28] Smith, R.G. and Lowther, C.P., 'Follow-up study of two hundred admissions to a residential home', *Age and Ageing,* 5, 3, 1976.

[29] Whitfield, J. and Symonds, J., *Alternatives to Residential Provision for the Elderly,* Essex County Council Social Services Department, 1976.

[30] Townsend, P., *The Failure to House Britain's Aged,* London, Help the Aged, 1976.

[31] Hare, E.J., *Three Score Years and Then? A Study of Practical Alternatives to Residential Care,* Norfolk County Council, 1977.

[32] Plank, D., 'Caring for the elderly: report of a study of various means of caring for dependent elderly people in eight London boroughs', research memorandum, Greater London Council, 1978.

[33] Oldfield, J.J. and Whitbread, A.W., *At Home or in a Home?* Warwickshire Social Services Department, April 1978.

[34] DHSS, Social Work Service, London Region, *Residential Care for the Elderly in London,* January 1979.

[35] Clarke, M., Hughes, A.D., Dodd, K.J., Palmer, R.I., Brondon, S., Holden, A.M. and Pearce, D., 'The elderly in residential care: patterns of disability', *Health Trends,* Vol. II, 1979.

[36] Booth, T., 'Measuring dependency', *Community Care,* 31 January 1980, pp. 15–18.

[37] Bond, J., 'Dependency and the elderly: problems of conceptualisation and measurement', in Munnichs, J.M. A. and Van den Heuvel, W.J.A., *Dependency or Interdependency in Old Age,* The Hague, Nijhoff, 1976.

[38] Bosanquet, N., *A Future for Old Age,* London, Temple Smith, 1978.

[39] Brearley, C.P., *Residential Work with the Elderly,* Routledge, 1977.

[40] Brocklehurst, J.C. and Shergold, M., 'What happens when geriatric patients leave hospital?', *The Lancet,* 23 November 1968.

[41] Exton-Smith, A. and Grimley Evans, J., *Care of the Elderly: Meeting Challenges of Dependency,* London, Academic Press, 1977.

[42] Harris, A.I., *Social Welfare for the Elderly,* Government Social Survey, Vol. I, London, HMSO, 1968.

[43] Isaacs, B., Livingstone, M. and Neville, Y., *Survival of the Unfittest: A Study of Geriatric Patients in Glasgow,* London, Routledge, 1972.

[44] McLauchlin, S., 'Report of a survey of dependency levels in elderly people in residential homes and hospital accommodation on Tameside', Unpublished, 1979.

[45] Sumner, T.G. and Smith, R., *Planning Local Authority Services for the Elderly,* London, Allen and Unwin, 1969.

[46] Census, 1971, *Non-Private Households,* London, HMSO, 1975, p. 124.

[47] Johnson, M.L., *op. cit.*

[48] Goffman, E., *Asylums: Essays on the Social Situation of Mental Patients and Other Inmates,* Garden City, N.Y., Doubleday Anchor, 1961.

[49] *Reports of the Committee of Inquiry into Allegations of Ill-Treatment of Patients and other Irregularities at the Ely Hospital, Cardiff,* Cmnd. 3975, London, HMSO, 1969.

[50] Robb, B., *Sans Everything: A Case to Answer,* London, Nelson, 1968.

[51] *Findings and Recommendations Following Enquiries into Allegations Concerning the Care of Elderly Patients in Certain Hospitals,* Cmnd. 3687, London, HMSO, 1968.

[52] DHSS, *The Census of Residential Accommodation,* 1970, *op. cit.,* p. 93.

[53] Meacher, M., *Taken for a Ride,* London, Longmans, 1972.

[54] Pasker, P., Thomas, J.P.R. and Ashley, J.S.A., 'The elderly mentally ill – whose responsibility?', *British Medical Journal,* 3, 1976.

[55] Peterson, M., *Confusion More Confounded: A Study of Separatism in a Home for the Elderly,* Department of Sociology, University of Essex, 1976.

[56] Wilkin, D. and Jolley, D.J., 'Mental and physical impairment in the elderly in hospital and residential care', *Nursing Times,* 74, 29 and 30, 1978.

[57] Burrage, M. and Phillips, D. (eds) *Nine Old People's Homes in a London Borough,* London School of Economics, 1973.

[58] Clarke, M. *et al.,* 'The elderly in residential care: patterns of disability', *Health Trends,* II, 1, February 1979.

[59] Davies, B.P. and Knapp, M.R.J., *Old People's Homes and the Production of Welfare,* London, Routledge & Kegan Paul, 1980.

[60] Fiske Lowenthal, M., *Lives in Distress,* New York, Basic Books, 1964.

[61] Fiske Lowenthal, M., 'Social isolation and mental illness in old age', *American Sociological Review,* 1963.

[62] Isaacs, B. *et al., Studies of Illness and Death in the Elderly in Glasgow,* Scottish Health Service Studies No. 17, Scottish Home and Health Department, Edinburgh, 1971.

[63] Jelf, P., 'A survey of the population of the social services' department's homes for the elderly as at 9 March 1976', Clearing House for Local Authority Social Services Research No. 6, 1976.

[64] King, R.D., Raynes, N.V. and Tizard, J., *Patterns of Residential Care,* London, Routledge & Kegan Paul, 1971.

[65] Lipman, A. R. and Slater, R., 'Homes for old people – towards a positive environment', *Gerontologist,* 17, 1977.

[66] Lowther, C. P. and MacLeod, H. M., 'Admissions to welfare home', *Health Bulletin,* 32, 1, 1974.

[67] Ministry of Health, *Residential Accommodation for Elderly People,* London, HMSO, 1966.

[68] Peace, S.M., Hall, J.F. and Hamblin, G.R., 'The quality of life of the elderly in residential care', mimeo, Survey Research Unit, The Polytechnic of North London, 1979.

[69] Personal Social Services Council, *Residential Care Reviewed,* London, 1977.

[70] Rees, A. M., *Old People and the Social Services: A Study in Sunderland,* Department of Social Administration, University of Southampton, 1972.

[71] Shiphorst, B., 'Some aspects of residential care', *Social Work Service,* 10, July 1976.

[72] Spasoff, R.A., Kraus, A.S., Beattie, E.J., Holden, D.E.W., Lawson, J.S., Rosenburg, M. and Woodcock, G.M., 'A longitudinal study of elderly residents of long-stay institutions', *Gerontologist,* 18, 1978.

[73] Townsend, P., *The Last Refuge, op. cit.*

[74] Meacher, M., *op. cit.*

[75] Peterson, M., *op. cit.*

[76] Abrams, M., *Beyond Three Score and Ten.* Age Concern, London, 1st report, 1978, 2nd report, 1980.

[77] Booth, T., 'Finding alternatives to residential care: the problem of innovation in the personal social services', *Local Government Studies,* July 1978.

[78] Hunt, A., *The Elderly at Home. A Study of People aged 65 and over Living in the Community in England in 1976,* Office of Population Censuses and Surveys, Social Survey Division, London, HMSO, 1978.

[79] Davies, B. and Knapp, M., 'Hotel and dependency costs of residents in old people's homes', *Journal of Social Policy,* January 1978.

[80] Economist Intelligence Unit, *Care with Dignity,* National Fund for Research into Crippling Diseases, 1973.

[81] Wager, R., *Care of the Elderly,* London, Institute of Municipal Treasurers and Accountants, 1972.

[82] Moroney, R.M., *The Family and the State,* London, Longmans, 1976.

[83] More complex conclusions were reached in work supervised by L.J. Opit. See, for example, Opit, L.J. and Shaw, S.M., 'Care of the elderly sick at home: whose responsibility is it?' *The Lancet,* 20 November 1976; and Opit, L.J., 'Domiciliary care for the elderly sick', *British Medical Journal,* 1 January 1977.

# 39

# New pensions for old

## Introduction

In 1996, when in opposition, Labour set out its ideas about future policies on pensions. It sought to make a break with past policies and introduce a new package – including a minimum pension "guarantee" and a cheaper and better regulated form of private pension schemes – called "stakeholder" pensions.

In December 1998, the Labour Government issued a Green Paper setting out these ideas in greater, but not complete, detail (Cm 4179; and see also the critical reviews offered by the Government's own Pension Provision Group, the Ross Reports, 1998 and 1999; and by Barbara Castle and others, 1998). The fact that the proposals were only in a Green Paper meant they were not set in stone. Time was allowed for consultation and comment until 31 March 1999.

Why write another pamphlet? The Government has received a lot of advice already. My point in writing is to argue that, unless certain changes are made, the Government's own stated objectives are not going to be fulfilled. "Security for all" will not materialise. The "guarantee" will be a chimera. Inequality among pensioners will go on increasing. Poverty among pensioners, in a real sense, will grow. The proposals are fraught with problems for future generations.

The alternative is not necessarily the spectre of Old Labour policies conjured up by some New Labour extremists. It is more in the nature of being a last ditch compromise between extremes to get things right. This compromise also involves addressing the future needs of the UK as judged in the year 2000. They are quite different from the year 1900 because of the rapid growth of the global market. Although the Government, and its advisers, have become more aware of this fact than many of its critics, they have been slow to work through to the full implications and the necessity for different kinds of collective provision.

*Within* the framework laid down by the Government, it would be possible to provide a better minimum pension for those with below average earnings,

---

Extract (pp 1-2, 17-22) from Townsend, P. (1999) *New pensions for old: The key to welfare reform*, Bristol/London: Townsend Centre for International Poverty Research, University of Bristol/Tribune Publications.

which could be guaranteed to lift future pensioners out of poverty *and* which is as affordable as the scheme broadly described in the Green Paper. So long as the public sector plays a sufficiently strong part, genuine *security* is within the nation's grasp.

What is required is a defined "adequate" pension, matched by regular "working investments" (paid and/or unpaid) from individuals, employers and sponsoring organisations drawing on paid or unpaid services. What is also required for the "partnership in pensions" that the Government properly seeks is a 60:40, or even 50:50, mix of public and private sectors in the development of the strategy rather than the 40:60 mix set out in the Green Paper. The public side of the equation has to be stronger or there will be divisions and disarray and not just greater inequality and poverty.

Some such amendment to the Government's strategy would ensure a minimally adequate rate of pension for all pensioners. It would be simpler than the scheme put forward saving administrative waste in labour and money. On the basis of precedent, it would obtain popular consent.

[...]

## Conclusion

[...] The test of this pamphlet is whether readers accept its argument that the Labour Government should reduce both means-testing and privatisation in its proposed strategy laid out in the Green Paper (Cm 4179) and ensure that a first tier of adequate income in retirement, say 40% of previous earnings, is provided collectively. Let me summarise this argument.

First, **means-testing**. When in opposition Labour vigorously opposed Tory substitution of means-tested benefits for benefits earned as of right through contributions from earnings. As a percentage of the costs of social security, means-tested benefits increased under Tory Governments between 1979 and 1997 from 17 to 34%. By adding the means-tested Working Families Tax Credit and Minimum Income Guarantee schemes and limiting annual increases in disability and National Insurance benefits to annual increases in prices, not earnings, the Labour Government will continue the trend. But all the reasons given formerly for *diminishing* and not *increasing* means-tests still apply.

A minimum income guarantee to replace discredited means-tested national assistance had been proposed long ago by the Wilson Government of the 1960s. This proved to be a failure. In those years this means-tested scheme was found to have been disguised as a "guarantee". A lion turned into a mouse. All that ensued was that so-called "Supplementary Benefits" took the place of "National Assistance". Only a small additional number of pensioners not then drawing means-tested national assistance – to which they were entitled – were drawn into means-tested supplementary benefits in 1967 (Atkinson, 1998; Parker *et al*, 1970). No convincing reasons have been given by the Government that the minimum income guarantee for pensioners will work better and be more effective this time.

Second, **privatisation**. Something like the "stakeholder" scheme now proposed – the "approved society" schemes of the 1930s – were judged in 1941 by Beveridge to have been a failure and he sought to replace them by simpler, and fairer, public provision (see Whiteside, 1997). Pensions misselling after the Tory subsidies for contracting out of the State Earnings Related Pensions Scheme after 1987 has been shown to be widespread, and the present Government's intention to expand similar types of private pensions is difficult to understand or justify.

Caution is also justified from international experience and commentary. The World Bank and the IMF have strongly advocated the privatisation of pensions in the past two decades. This has led to huge problems not only in Eastern Europe but in other countries, and some in these organisations have now begun to argue differently. Although some observers argue that the change is more apparent than real (Ferge, 1999) there is no doubt that, compared with the 1980s and early 1990s, the international agencies are beginning to recognise the historical and contemporary strengths of public sector schemes. They are also being obliged to admit that the economic arguments are by no means as favourable to private pension schemes as many economists have believed and still believe. There are signs of accepting substantial public first tier pension schemes which still allow considerable private "topping up" (see, for example, UNCTAD 1995).

Clearly, the level and types of pensions in any country are relevant to the question of competitiveness in the global economy. Some countries are strongly competitive and yet invest heavily in collective social insurance. A variety of issues are involved in the debate about pensions and economic competitiveness. These include the labour market, the special interests of the financial agencies, the major economic strategy of privatisation, cuts in public spending, "reining-in" the power of labour, structural adjustment and liberalisation. However, economists have pointed out there is no evidence that countries with "weak" pension provision are more competitive, or grow faster, than those with "heavy" pension provision (Atkinson, 1995, 1998).

Countries with substantial public sector schemes are often also those making the heaviest personal savings in the economy. Money-purchase schemes can be much less secure than pay-as-you-go contributory schemes. For example, periods of deflation can seriously reduce the likely benefits of money-purchase schemes. The fashion in the 1980s and 1990s of switching to pre-funded or private money-purchase schemes has been found to be ill-conceived in a large number of countries.

As one economist wrote of experience under the previous Government "the switch from state to private pensions may negatively affect the rate of capital formation, reversing the conclusion that is conventionally drawn" (Atkinson, 1995).

In this pamphlet, I have argued for the state or public sector to play a much larger role than the Government has so far suggested in pensions policy. One positive argument for stronger **collective provision** lies in the evidence from public opinion. There is continuing massive public support for National Insurance benefits and especially the old age pension, as testified in a range of regular surveys (for example, Jowell, 1991-98; see also the Fabian Society, 1998). There are also submissions reviewing the evidence from social scientists, and clearly formulated reactions from campaigning groups, especially the National Pensioners Convention, the Coalition Against Poverty, Barbara Castle's influential Security in Retirement for Everyone, Age Concern, Help the Aged and the Disability Alliance, as well as representations from the principal churches and even some of the financial and insurance companies – some of which believe a division of labour between public and private sector bodies is desirable as well as efficient. This range of evidence was not discussed in the Green Paper.

The evidence also comes, for example, from a quarter which the Government is likely to find embarrassing. In late 1997, the Department of Social Security commissioned 16 group discussions (focus groups) with members of the public. Among the principal findings was the following: "Most people feel the state should provide a 'bread-and-butter' pension. This would be higher than the current basic pension which is generally felt inadequate. Most people thought the single person's pension should be between £80 and £120.... Working people were usually willing to pay enough extra National Insurance to fund another £10 a week ... and probably to add £20-£30.... Most people are strongly opposed to means-testing the basic state pension. Everyone who pays in should be able to draw out as of right" (Hedges, 1998, p.1).

Under its existing proposals, the Government is restricting public provision of an eventual as well as the existing state pension to an unnecessarily low flat-rate amount, on test of means and mainly for the low paid. The Government does not envisage that the combined value of the basic state retirement pension and the proposed State Second Pension will reach more than 21-26% of average earnings by the middle of the next century.

Many thousands in the population will not obtain even this measure of "security". They will have to depend on the means-tested Minimum Income Guarantee – or Income Support as it is presently known. Such means-tested schemes are notorious for missing hundreds of thousands of pensioners.

For the middle and high paid the Government offers a mixture of untried, expensive and unpredictably variable money-purchase private schemes. These measures will not enable the great majority of retired people to escape poverty or means-tested Income Support and will introduce greater insecurity into retirement. On the evidence of past experience, three new measures – the proposed Minimum Income Guarantee, the State Second Pension and the Stakeholder Pensions – will not work or combine well together to achieve the Government's stated objectives.

## Recommendations

What practical recommendations therefore arise from these arguments to reduce the elements of both means-testing and privatisation in the Government's proposed strategy? There are five:

(i) **The pension scheme should consist of two tiers – with the lower tier being a defined minimum but *adequate* income, financed by collective provision through weekly individual "working investments" as a percentage of earnings**. A realistic, affordable and economical partnership between public and private schemes can be constructed – with the former making up the lower tier, upon which all in the population can depend, and the latter the higher tier, of pensionable income. This change, together with supporting proposals made below, is necessary to the achievement of the principles and objectives declared in the Government's Green Paper (Cm 4179) – namely to retire "on a decent income" and in "security" with pensioner poverty greatly reduced.

The definition of a minimally adequate pension would arise in part from the Government's new "poverty audit" and from DSS and other evidence about the income required to meet "absolute" needs as set out by 117 countries in the 1995 Copenhagen World Summit (UN, 1995). In Britain, an opinion poll conducted by MORI in 1997 found that single pensioners estimated that the weekly income required to meet the absolute necessities of life was £118 (Townsend *et al*, 1997). A DSS research report concluded, in the same year, that the basic pension should be between £80 and £120 (Hedges, 1998).

Affordability depends on only minor modifications to contributions and taxes. Between 1979 and 1997, the Tory Government had already substantially reduced prospective and current pension benefits as a percentage of GDP (Eurostat, 1998; Brazier *et al*, 1999; Cm 4199, 1999). Relative to GDP, the UK raises less revenue than average in Europe by social insurance contributions and different taxes. Moreover, revenue raised through social insurance contributions from employers is especially low (Eurostat, 1998).

The Chancellor has shown that the National Insurance Fund is buoyant and that a surplus of magnitude (approximately £2bn a year) has been derived from the first two years of Labour Government. Everything is therefore in place for a moderate increase in the basic state retirement pension and reconstruction of contributions to the state earnings–related element, as the **Contributory Additional Pension 2000**.

(ii) **Entitlement to the basic state retirement pension should be widened and its link with earnings restored.** For the low paid the proposed State Second Pension is intended to roughly replace the additions they would otherwise have expected to get if the earnings link with the basic retirement pension were to be restored for everyone. In a flexible global and national labour market, the aim is unlikely to be achieved. People will have complex problems maintaining entitlement to a "decent income in retirement" during variable paid and unpaid work experience and of transferring from one pension scheme to another. This additional scheme is unnecessary. Extension of entitlement through social insurance and renewal of the earnings link would be simpler, administratively less costly, more effective and still easily affordable. If considered necessary, steps could be taken to tax back pension increases to the rich.

(iii) Because coverage of those on middle and low incomes by the proposed Stakeholder Pension scheme is likely to be poor, certainly in the first 10 to 20 years, **an option to join a new scheme, the Contributory Additional Pension 2000, based on the former SERPS, should be built into new legislation, to reinforce and enlarge the lower tier of pensionable income.** This would reflect some of the aims of the SSP and the Stakeholder Pension but would ensure better coverage of the different groups of working age, especially women, and would ensure a level of pension of at least 40% of previous lifetime earnings, so removing for most people the need to seek a means-tested addition. There would be a smoother transition from the existing to a future scheme.

(iv) As a consequence, **the Stakeholder Pension should be a major or even the primary element of the second tier of pensionable income** – enabling everyone covered by the basic state retirement pension and SERPS or a good occupational scheme to bring their retirement income up from at least 40% to a level closer to their previous average earnings. This would be a second tier of what might be described as "quality" income. Employers, insurance companies and other organisations would then have opportunities to introduce schemes to match the provisions of the Stakeholder Pension.

(v) **Means-testing could then be diminished by treating the basic retirement pension as the Government's "minimum income guarantee" and raising it in value first to catch up a little of what has been lost in the previous 20 years, and second to ensure an**

**annual share in national economic growth.** At present, the "guarantee" is intended to be means-tested and, like Income Support, will therefore not reach a million of the poorest elderly. Means tests are poor in coverage as well as socially divisive. They deter people from saving and taking paid work. Action to modernise social insurance for the elderly, through the basic state retirement pension and SERPS, is the only practicable and effective way of meeting poverty among those not being reached by means-tested schemes.

If the Government could accept these recommendations, the problems of saving for pensions in a flexible labour market would be a lot easier for individuals and families to surmount, and understand. Two additional elements of an already complex package for future pensions – the State Second Pension and the Minimum Income Guarantee – would become unnecessary (and major savings made). Poverty, and social inequality, would be more effectively reduced and welfare reform in its most positive sense would be back on track.

## References

Atkinson A.B. (1995) *Incomes and the welfare state: Essays on Britain and Europe*, Cambridge: Cambridge University Press.

Atkinson A.B. (1998) *Poverty in Europe*, Oxford: Blackwell.

Brazier A., Greener K., Jarvis T., Roll J. and Wilson W. (1999) *Welfare Reform and Pensions Bill*, Research Paper 99/19, Westminster: House of Commons Library.

Castle B. *et al.* (1998) *Pensions as of right for all*, London: Security in Retirement for Everyone.

Castle B., Townsend P., Davies B., Lynes T., Land H. and MacIntyre K. (1998) *Fair shares for pensioners*, London: Security in Retirement for Everyone.

Cm 4179 (1998) *A new contract for welfare: Partnership in pensions*, London: The Stationery Office.

Cm 4199 (1999), *Uprating orders*, Government Actuary, London: The Stationery Office.

Eurostat (1998) *Structures of the taxation systems in the European Union 1970-1996*, Luxembourg: Office for Official Publications of the European Communities.

Fabian Society (1998) *Public attitudes on the future of welfare: Research findings*, London: Fabian Society.

Ferge, Z. (1999) 'The politics of the Hungarian pension reform', in K. Müller, A. Ryll and H.-J. Wagener (eds) *Transformation of social security: Pensions in central–eastern Europe*. Heidelberg, Physica.

Hedges, A. (1998) *Pensions and retirement planning*, DSS Research Report No 83, London: Department of Social Security.

Jowell, R. (ed) (1991-98) *British Social Attitudes, 8th–15th Reports*, Aldershot: Ashgate.

Parker, R., Land, H. and Webb, A. (1970) *Change, choice and conflict in social policy*, London: Allen and Unwin.

Ross Report (1998) *We all need pensions: The prospects for pension provision*, Pension Provision Group (Chair Tom Ross), London: The Stationery Office.

Ross Report (1999) Pension Provision Group, *Response to the Government's Green Paper*, London: The Stationery Office.

Townsend, P., Gordon, D., Bradshaw, J. and Gosschalk, B. (1997) *Absolute and overall poverty in Britain in 1997: What the population themselves say: British Poverty Line Survey*, Report of the Second MORI Survey, Bristol: Statistical Monitoring Unit, University of Bristol.

UN (United Nations) (1995) *The World Summit for Social Development: The Copenhagen Declaration and Programme of Action*, New York, NY: UN.

UNCTAD (1995) *Comparative experiences with privatisation: Policy insights and lessons learned*, New York/Geneva: UNCTAD.

Whiteside, N. (1997) 'Private agencies for public purposes', *The Whitehall Programme*, Swindon: Economic and Social Research Council.

# 40

# Policies for the aged in the 21st century

By the late 20th century, the plight of millions of older people in many developed countries was regarded as serious and was acknowledged to require concerted cross-national remedial action. Sociologists and social gerontologists only then were beginning to put together explanations rooted in the evolution of social policy and its corresponding institutions. One thesis that attracted support was that the dependency of the aged had been 'structured' by long-term economic and social policies. During the final decades of the 20th century, older people were perceived and treated, according to accumulating research evidence, as more dependent than they really were or needed to be. This had been fostered by the emerging institutions of retirement, income maintenance, and residential and domiciliary care. This development had been the responsibility primarily of the State, which tried to deliver welfare but also to accommodate the market. Forms of discrimination against older people had become, or continued to be, as deep as forms of discrimination against women and ethnic minorities. Such 'institutionalised ageism' had to be countered. Hopes were invested in antidiscriminatory policies that reflected good reciprocal relationships between the generations in many families and the rights of individuals of any age to human dignity and opportunities to practise their skills. The globalisation of the market and affiliation to neo-liberal policies, together with the simultaneous passage of various instruments of human rights, have changed the nature of the problem, and therefore the debate, during the early 21st century. This paper argues that the release and implementation during and after the Second World War of collective liberal egalitarian values, expressed in many countries in international statements on human rights, as will be shown, had a big impact on the design of public services, including those for older people. If the claims for the elderly in the welfare states of 50 years ago were exaggerated, as we can now safely conclude, the claims for older people today are even more exaggerated – at a time of heightened emphasis on individual rights and individual market powers. The

Townsend, P. (2006) 'Policies for the aged in the 21st century: more "structured dependency" or the realisation of human rights?', *Ageing & Society*, vol 26, no 2, pp 161–79.

various problems of 'structured' dependency persist, and seem set to grow in many parts of the world. Human rights offer a framework of rigorous analysis and anti-discriminatory work. Success depends on good operational measurement, and the incorporation of international and national institutions and policies that reflect those rights.

[...]

## Human rights and welfare

In this paper, I draw together the long-established institutions of welfare and the developing and potential institutions of human rights (Steiner and Alston 2002). Because this bridging is historical, international and scientific, it contains the core of the paper's argument, but first some general points. The language of human rights has particular virtues of moral obligation. Each of the rights is 'universal', non-fulfilment is a 'violation', and rights are 'human', not only civil or political, and multiple and inter-dependent. Corrective anti-discriminatory measures have to be directed not at the separate existence of racial, religious, gender, disability or ageist discrimination, but rather in a comprehensive, connected and proportionate manner against all forms of discrimination.

The *methodology* of human rights is in its infancy. The operational definition of rights (and therefore their violations) demands imaginative and sustained quantitative and qualitative methods of investigation (Steiner and Alston 2002). The violations are not those only that end life or involve extreme abuse, the scale of which is assembled in statistical handbooks, but also those that affront human dignity and identity, which are unrecorded. Research into the quality of life of older people carried out by several of the United Kingdom Economic and Social Research Council Growing Older programme projects offer rich contributions to this objective (Walker 1996, 2004; Walker and Hennessy 2004). In operationalising definitions of rights, there has been a tendency to reproduce the familiar, single indicators that are over-generalised representations of complex conditions or entitlement (including health, economic growth, education and human development), rather than to elaborate new requirements for survey data that reliably identify the extreme conditions that demand unremitting scrutiny.

The 'indivisibility' of human rights seems to have deterred some social scientists (including lawyers) from developing *multiple* indices of certain general conditions or priorities. And the seeming inflexibility in defining the thresholds or criteria for the satisfaction and non-satisfaction of each nominated right, *viz.* the individual either has a right or has not, creeps into the use of single indicators to test whether that right has or has not been fulfilled (because multiple indicators raise many questions about the multiple criteria for a threshold, when in reality different individuals in a population are at different points on the scale, from extreme non-fulfilment to generous fulfilment). Only very recently have serious efforts been made to organise operational definitions that allow the multiple non-realisation of rights to be measured reliably and unambiguously. Later I will suggest how energetic use of the international *Demographic Health Surveys* (DHS) and the *Multiple Indicator Cluster Surveys* (MICS) of cross-national panel survey data for world regions on material and social deprivation among older people, and of similar data about limiting long-standing illness or disability, might be adapted for research into violations of rights in later age in Europe and more widely in the developing world.

One must also understand the *politics of rights*. This is crucial in the choice of methodology, investigative priorities, and for the persuasive assessment of needs and policies. As many as 191 nations have ratified the Convention on the Rights of the Child, far more signatories than for the original Universal Declaration of Human Rights, and impressively high when compared with approval of other human rights instruments. Access to rights plays a crucial role in public discussion about economic and social developments, for example in responses to conflict, anti-terrorism measures and different types of discrimination. Acknowledgment of the influential role of human rights has spread rapidly among campaigning organisations, departments of state and international organisations of every kind. To base both research and action on human rights instruments is to apply the leverage of accepted authority and democracy. To the long-established positive national arguments for promoting welfare, we can therefore now add the perceptions as well as revelations of cross-national agreed rules of a quasi-legal kind – a growing number of which have been incorporated into domestic laws. Knowledge of that process can now enthuse those concerned with the abiding domestic policy disputes that concern older people; one consequence will be to inflame those like Hayek [1944] and his successors who have been attached to an older and more discriminatory ideology.

## British and European perspectives on human rights

The UK Human Rights Act 1998 specified rights based on the European Convention on Human Rights (ECHR), and that are not guaranteed against repeal or amendment by Parliament. The emphasis is on civil and political rights, not economic, social and cultural rights. The rights to life, not to be subjected to torture, inhuman or degrading treatment or forced labour, to an effective remedy and to non-discrimination, all raise questions of social protection and reconstruction, and therefore stray into the range of possible social and economic rights, but these cannot be pressed strongly in law. Although the courts cannot strike down primary legislation that is incompatible with its provisions, following precedents elsewhere, expressed rights are nonetheless beginning to have a substantial impact on the law, and on the activities and thinking of administrators, lawyers and politicians. To give one example, the number of solicitors who profess expertise in human rights has been transformed during the last 10 years (Chambers 1998; Feldman 2002: 1088).

Lack of the guarantee of rights is not proving to be as serious a weakness as feared, partly because of the manner in which the ECHR is being observed in Europe. There is also the fact that justiciable and constitutionally-entrenched Acts do not provide a complete answer to the demands of individuals and groups – as shown by the work of the European Court of Justice and the United States Supreme Court, and by public reactions to their decisions. Public officials, rights-activists, politicians and individual citizens have to share responsibility for the acceptance and the institutionalisation of rights. One of the finest examples of what must and can be done is a report for the British Institute of Human Rights by Jenny Watson (2002), which makes clear that the problem is how simultaneously to disestablish and redistribute entrenched powers. The trickle-down and trickle-up challenges can be better organised and pursued. My argument is that a new analytical framework has evolved very rapidly, with which social scientists of every persuasion and department must engage. A particularly valuable contribution is David Feldman's (2002) *Civil Liberties and Human Rights in England and Wales*, which draws from his experience, until late 2003, as the legal adviser to the UK Parliament's Joint Committee on Human Rights.

The reports of this committee testify to both the influence of the Act and the way in which certain objectives of the new British legislation can be framed in accordance with human rights and implemented quickly and effectively without provoking political storms.[1] The Committee came to see and comment routinely on drafts of *all* parliamentary bills, which assisted the task of implementing human rights with Parliament's agreement. The Committee also developed a special programme of work to implement features of the principal Act. It argued successfully for a strategic, rights-based Commissioner for Children and Young People, and for an integrated Equalities Human Rights Commission, to work in a more concerted way than the extant disparate bodies that worked against discrimination in all its forms.[2] It is now being set up as the Commission for Equalities and Human Rights, and non-discrimination by age will become legally enforceable in 2006.

## The European Convention and the European Social Charter

A counterpart of the ECHR is the European Social Charter (ESC) (Council of Europe 2002; Samuel 2002; Directorate General of Human Rights,

Council of Europe 2005). Member states of the Council of Europe signed the ESC in 1961 and it came into force in 1966. By 2001, 30 member states had signed and ratified the document. It includes rights to special protection for women, children and young people in employment, rights to provision for health care, social security, welfare services and care for disabled persons. Unlike the ECHR, there is no mechanism of enforcement, but instead biennial reports on progress in relation to rights have to be submitted to the Secretary General of the Council of Europe. These reports are then examined by a Committee of Experts appointed by a Committee of Ministers, and reviewed by the Council's Governmental Social Committee. Until recently this procedure had not been very influential with the British and other member-state governments. Like the various International Labour Organization conventions, the ESC imposes obligations on states which take effect in international law, but does not confer enforceable rights on individuals. Representative or campaigning organisations, and individuals, do not have rights of participation in, or access to, this process.

Matters 'changed dramatically' with the collapse of the Soviet Union at the end of the 1980s (Feldman 2002: 119). The ESC was suddenly perceived as an invaluable instrument for evaluating the performance of the new Republics in protecting and enhancing social and economic rights. The Director General of the Council of Europe shifted responsibility for the operation of the Charter to the Council's Directorate of Human Rights, thus greatly increasing the responsibilities of the ECHR. New proposals to streamline supervision and accountability were introduced. The UK signed the relevant Protocol, and in 1997 signed the revised version of the Charter, though ratification of these agreements is awaited.

At the same time, the Social Chapter of the evolving European Treaty gained importance, because at the Maastricht summit in 1991 it was agreed by 11 of the then 12 member states (excluding the UK), and in 1992 became part of the Treaty on European Union, which came into force in 1993.[3] During the immediately following years, the UK was alone among the 15 member states in objecting to the Charter on the grounds that it invaded domestic sovereignty and would make industry less competitive, but in 1997 the Labour government reversed this policy and accepted the Social Chapter, so that at the summit that year, it was incorporated into the Treaty of Amsterdam 1997 that consolidated the European Community.[4] Since that Treaty came into force in 1999, the revised Charter, reflecting the Treaty, has become an integral part of the structure of the European Community. Many of its Articles reflect European agreement on the European Social Model, and several are relevant to the social and welfare conditions for older people. In particular, Article 4 of the Additional Protocol of 1988 spelt out, as here reproduced, *the right of elderly persons to social protection*:

Contracting parties undertake directly or through private or public organisations, to take measures:

1. to enable elderly persons to remain full members of society for as long as possible by means of: (a) adequate resources enabling them to lead a decent life and play an active part in public, social and cultural life; and (b) provision of information about services and facilities available for elderly persons and their opportunities to make use of them;
2. to enable elderly persons to choose their lifestyle freely and to lead independent lives in their familiar surroundings for as long as they wish and are able, by means of: (a) provision of housing suited to their needs and their state of health or of adequate support for adapting their housing; and (b) the health care and the services necessitated by their state;
3. to guarantee elderly persons living in institutions appropriate support, while respecting their privacy, and participation in decisions concerning living conditions in the institution.

The EU Social Chapter was therefore a significant step towards converting the aspirations of the ESC into 'hard law' applicable in national courts. In particular, the scope of European anti-discrimination law – affecting ageism as well as other forms of discrimination – was, as a result, enlarged. The EU continues to extend access to economic and social rights and integrate these with other, better institutionalised civil and political rights (e.g. the proclamation of the EU Chapter of Fundamental Rights in 2000).

## Violations of the rights of older people in 2005

Both the ESC and the ECHR can be widely used in the analysis of the conditions experienced by older people and in necessary alternative policies. For example, Help the Aged and Age Concern England have given worrying contemporary evidence of the lack of rights. Help the Aged noted in 2003 that, 'older people whose human rights are violated are often not in a position – or do not choose – to take action themselves.… Few staff, and few members of the public were yet informed about the 1998 Act' (Joint Committee on Human Rights 2003: II, Evidence 310). Elderly people subjected to abuse rarely complained. The Dignity on the Ward campaign by Help the Aged in 1999–2001 produced 1,300 complaints, generally from relatives after a death of an old person. 'It was very common for the older person not only to remain silent, but to plead with relatives "not to make a fuss", while relatives themselves often felt that complaining would only put the person concerned at even greater risk' (Joint Committee on

Human Rights 2003: Ev. 314). The collected evidence about allegations of abuse had five forms: physical, psychological, financial, sexual and neglect. About one-quarter of the total were allegations about institutional settings, such as hospitals, nursing homes or residential homes – a disproportionately large fraction in relation to the number of older people who live in them (Joint Committee on Human Rights 2003: Ev. 314).

Among the confirmed instances is that of an inquest at Eastbourne, Sussex, in October 2002 of an elderly woman with Alzheimer's disease who was dying of dehydration a week after admission to a care home. No one appeared to have understood that she needed help with eating and drinking. Another instance was of a man in North London with mild dementia who was taken off medication despite his wife's detailed instructions. He deteriorated rapidly and died within a few weeks because, instead of his customary prescription for a heart condition, he was given one for insomnia. Moreover, no inquest was held (Joint Committee on Human Rights 2003: Ev. 311). These instances are pale in relation to others collected by the British Institute of Human Rights:

> A man aged in his eighties in a nursing home required use of a catheter and assistance in dressing. He was made to sit naked in a room with five male and female staff while one washed him, another changed his catheter bag, and a third changed his medication. The door into a busy corridor was left wide open. No one spoke to him. In the end he messed himself and was then rolled over onto his side, whilst they proceeded to put a towel underneath him, and then wash him, on the bed, still with no attempt made to protect his dignity.

> A care-worker entering a residential home was instructed to get the residents up for breakfast and to seat them on commodes. When she began to help them off, to finish dressing for breakfast, she was stopped. 'The routine of the home was that residents ate their breakfast while sitting on the commode and the ordinary men and women who worked there had come to accept this as normal.'

> A resident was prescribed morphine as part of her palliative care. 'The home did not supply the medication and she died in pain, crying. No resident has their medical needs noted and many residents are not receiving the correct medication' (Watson 2002).

Of course, abuses of rights also occur at home and in families. In the example below, it did not occur to the staff and to social workers that they could use the Human Rights Act, which might have helped to engineer a rapprochement between family and social services and have protected the older woman from five years of abuse:

> A woman aged 85 years was living with her daughter. For five years social services had been trying to work to remedy a disastrous situation. The elderly woman 'was regularly found in her home in just a t-shirt, in a house without soap, flannels or towels. Her daughter would take her out of day services after an hour to make her take money from a bank's cash machine. She would be taken out of respite care by her daughter in the middle of the night. She had medication withheld by her daughter. ... The police were called to shouting and slapping incidents in the street when her daughter abused her. ... Eventually she went happily into residential care, but her daughter turned up at the home with her husband, and was found by staff to be inspecting her mother's backside by flashlight, saying that she was not clean. ... Eventually she was banned from the home because of her disruptive behaviour, after she tried to take other residents to the toilet (Watson 2002).

Unconscious and conscious discriminatory assumptions or beliefs are held by professionals, including doctors (Jacobs 1999), and by families of older people, including sons and daughters. The British Institute of Human Rights thus found that 'DNR' – do not resuscitate – a clear violation now of human rights, was written on some case-notes. Again, the daughter of a woman placed in a residential home in Bristol said the doctor had advised her to sell her mother's house because it was 'safer' for her to be in the residential home; one is inclined to ask, 'safer for whom?' When an outsider subsequently visited the elderly resident and looked into her eyes, it was evident that she had decided to die, and so it proved within a few weeks. As Jenny Watson concluded her review, 'Access to benefits, access to transport, and access to good domiciliary care services are all necessary in order to allow older people to make the same kind of choices about their lives that the rest of us simply take for granted' (2002: 45).

[...]

## The required research

How can the scale and severity of the abuses be represented effectively? The question is the same as it might have been 25 years ago. Then, as now, multiple material and social deprivation must be acknowledged and investigated by identifying and then counting different types of deprivation or abuse. One type of horror, and the identification of horror in one location, must be placed in a context that is national and international, multi-generational, and applicable to both public and private sectors. I have believed for many years that specialised research can only carry force if there is also generic research, and vice-versa. The best national work is also international or cross-national. Of course it is never easy to ride two horses, and improvisations and shortcomings will exist, but that is the first necessity. The effort remains crucial and will allow what is truly international and objectively scientific to emerge. It is vital in authenticating priority, in analysis as well as treatment. It is a value that can be lived and rehearsed at every level.

Let me give two examples of the methodology. One is an old-style multiplication of material and social deprivation. Table 1 is drawn from the Poverty and Social Exclusion Survey of 2000 sponsored by the Joseph Rowntree Foundation. After setting aside certain overlapping indices, there remained 31 items that represented the commonly agreed necessities of life. As many as 37 per cent of people of pensionable age were deprived of at least one necessity, and nine per cent were deprived of five or more – of these, one-third were deprived of 10 or more necessities. The nine per cent amounted to more than one million people, but did not include the half-a-million older people in hospitals, nursing homes and residential care. Severe multiple deprivation is therefore a common experience, and one that raises acute questions about human rights.

The second example is an indexation of human rights that derives from recent work on children in which I have participated. A research team based in the University of Bristol found that certain articles of the Convention

**Table 1:** Levels of material and social deprivation among older people, Great Britain 2000

| Number of the necessities of life from which deprived | Male pensioners (aged 65+ years) | Female pensioners (aged 60+ years) | All pensioners (aged 60+/65+ years) |
|---|---|---|---|
| Percentages | | | |
| 0 | 66 | 61 | 63 |
| 1 | 18 | 12 | 14 |
| 2 | 5 | 5 | 5 |
| 3 | 2 | 7 | 5 |
| 4 | 3 | 5 | 4 |
| 5-9 | 4 | 7 | 6 |
| 10+ | 3 | 3 | 3 |
| All | 100 | 100 | 100 |
| Sample sizes | (157) | (249) | (406) |

*Note on sources*: Derived from the Poverty and Social Exclusion Survey 2000 (Gordon *et al.*, 2003), and secondary analysis by Demi Patsios.

on the Rights of the Child lent themselves to measurement, as grades of violation of material and social deprivation from 'extreme' through 'severe', 'moderate' and 'slight' to 'non existent'. Eight articles of the Convention could be categorised in this way, including levels of malnutrition and of access to adequate shelter, good drinking water, sanitation and forms of information (Gordon *et al.* 2003: 8, 35–6, *passim*). The results proved more reliable, and certainly less disputable, than the crude estimates of dollar-a-day poverty estimated by the World Bank. The next stage has been to apply articles of human rights to the measurement of multiple deprivation among adults.

For older people, we can move in successive stages from the ECHR, through the ESC, to the United Nations' International Covenant on Economic, Social and Cultural Rights.[5] The stages of such research can be proposed, the first being to develop the ways in which the ECHR can be represented, as exemplified in Table 2. Additional use could be made of other Articles, like the right to marry (Article 12), and of some of the Protocols, such as Article 5 of Protocol 7, on equality between spouses, and Article 1, on safeguards in the expulsion of aliens. The next step is to do the same for the European Social Charter, which opens the way to more sophisticated measurements. A preliminary outline is given in the lower part of Table 2. A third step – prompted partly by the slow influence of the ESC on the UK government in anticipating the growing acknowledgement of economic and social rights – is to examine the International Covenant on Economic, Social and Cultural Rights.

To identify policy priorities in developing countries, one recent approach that has accelerated progress with the measurement of multiple violations of human rights is to focus on violations of different aspects of material and social deprivation (Gordon *et al.* 2003). Another is to focus on the twin rights to social security and an adequate standard of living (Articles 22 and 25 of the Universal Declaration, Articles 9 and 11 of the International Covenant on Economic, Social and Cultural Rights, and Articles 26 and 27 of the Convention on the Rights of the Child ). The advantages of building afresh on these two rights are especially promising.

[...]

**Table 2:** Types of violations of human rights and possible indicators

| Source document and human right | Indicator |
|---|---|
| **A. European Convention on Human Rights** | |
| Right to life (Article 2) | Premature death, by location, age and gender |
| Prohibition of torture or 'inhuman or degrading treatment or punishment' (Article 3) | Degrading care practices in residential and home care |
| Right to respect for private and family life (Article 8) | Wish in disability to stay in own home; access to surrounding possessions of a familiar kind |
| Prohibition of discrimination 'on any ground such as sex, race, colour, language, religion, political or other opinion, national or social origin, association with a national minority, property, birth or other status' (Article 14) | Acceptance for care services, standardised for disability, by minority or gender status |
| **B. European Social Charter** | |
| Resources adequate for full and active life | Annual subjective/objective survey assessment of amount required to escape poverty/multiple deprivation |
| Facilities and information to lead an active, participating life | Access to range of public and private services, and facilities providing information |
| Opportunity to lead a life in a home of their choosing | Type of accommodation by degree of disability and preference |
| Access to appropriate health care | Frequency and speed of utilisation in relation to degree of disability, degree of material and social deprivation and whether and when need for health care identified |
| Freedom of action and quality of living conditions in residential institutions | Subjective expression of opportunities to act freely; objective assessment of living conditions in relation to measured degree of disability |

## Conclusions

During the last 50 years, the world has seen only mixed success for the declared objective of reducing violations of human rights, including the different forms of severe deprivation noted earlier in the paper, which prompts re-examination of the links between 'universalism' or human 'rights' and both comprehensive public social services and social security.

'Targeting' as a strategy to reduce poverty in developing countries has become highly controversial and its forms are increasingly criticised. Reports of persistent poverty and deepening inequality in many countries outweigh the modest results that, at best, reflect the structural adjustment programmes and their successors, including the social funds that have been introduced. In developing countries, the Programme of Action to Mitigate the Social Cost of Adjustment, which was set up during the late 1980s to correct the excesses of structural adjustment programmes, has been criticised for being under-funded and lacking direction (Donkor 2002). The success of the programmes intended both to restrict public expenditure and to relieve extreme poverty by targeting resources has been elusive.

The idea of 'structured dependency' helps to explain the box into which many older people are placed and which itself contrives to evolve (Catalyst Forum Working Group 2002). Unintentionally, or for reasons of economy and convenience, their dependency has been created in market, residential and hospital care practices and in free-market and public social-care policies. Dependency is also assumed or excused by many elderly people themselves. The various problems of 'structured' dependency persist and seem set to grow in many parts of the world (Fennell, Phillipson and Evers 1988; Guillemard 1983). Human rights offer a framework of rigorous analysis and anti-discriminatory work. Success depends on good operational measurement – to produce reliable evidence of violations and monitoring progress – and the incorporation nationally and internationally of institutions and policies that reflect those rights. Human rights instruments offer the hope of breaking down blanket discrimination and of using resources more appropriately and generously, according to the severity of need. But investment in human rights is not only a moral and quasi-legal salvation from things that are still going depressingly wrong. Used best, human rights offer a framework of thought and planning that will enable society to take a fresh and more hopeful direction.

**Endnotes**

[1] In the first four years of the Joint Committee's existence, 87 reports were published, not including subsidiary reports and collections of written evidence (see Joint Committee on Human Rights 2005).

[2] 'The decision to reorganise the institutional arrangements for the promotion of equality has made it an urgent necessity to consider the institutional arrangements for the promotion and protection of human rights more generally. The government's decision in principle to establish a new Equality Commission, which will have to consider human rights issues in the context of its own work, makes it necessary for the Government now to resolve the question of a human rights commission. …There is still a long way to go in establishing the culture of respect for human

rights, and the momentum from the Human Rights Act is ebbing. If it is not revived, the loss will detract from or adversely affect the conduct and performance of public services, and consequently the wellbeing of those who use them.... We believe an independent commission would be the most effective way of achieving the shared aim of bringing about a culture of respect for human rights. ' (Joint Committee on Human Rights 2003: 86–7).

[3] The Treaty on European Union, which was signed in Maastricht on 7 February 1992, entered into force on 1 November 1993. The Maastricht Treaty changed the name of the European Economic Community to simply the European Community. It also introduced new forms of co-operation between the member-state governments, for example on defence and in the area of justice and home affairs. By adding this inter-governmental co-operation to the existing 'Community' system, the Maastricht Treaty created a new structure with three 'pillars' which is political as well economic. This is the European Union (EU) (from http://www. europa.eu.int/abc/treaties_en.htm).

[4] The Treaty of Amsterdam, signed on 2 October 1997, entered into force on 1 May 1999: it amended and renumbered the EU and EC treaties. Consolidated versions of the EU and EC treaties are attached to it (see http://www.europa.eu.int/abc/treaties_en. htm).

[5] For details, visit http://www2.ohchr.org/english/law/cescr.htm

## References

Catalyst Forum Working Group (2002) *The challenge of longer life: Economic burden or social opportunity?*, Catalyst Paper 7, London: Catalyst Forum.

Chambers, G. (1998) *Practising human rights: UK lawyers and the European Convention on Human Rights*, The Law Society and Policy Planning Unit Research Study 28, London: Law Society.

Council of Europe (2002) *European Social Charter: Collected texts*, 3rd edn, Strasbourg: Council of Europe.

Directorate General of Human Rights, Council of Europe (2005) *The European Social Charter*. Strasbourg: Council of Europe.

Donkor, K. (2002) 'Structural adjustment and mass poverty in Ghana', in P. Townsend and D. Gordon (eds) *World Poverty: New policies to defeat an old enemy*, Bristol: The Policy Press, pp 226–8.

Feldman, D. (2002) *Civil liberties and human rights in England and Wales*, 2nd edn, Oxford: Oxford University Press.

Fennell, G., Phillipson, C. and Evers, H. (1988) *The sociology of old age*, Buckingham: Open University Press.

Gordon, D., Nandy, S., Pantazis, C., Pemberton, S. and Townsend, P. (2003) *Child poverty in the developing world*, Bristol: The Policy Press.

Guillemard, A.-M. (ed) (1983) *Old age and the welfare state*, Beverly Hills, CA: Sage.

Hayek, F. A. (1944) *The road to serfdom*, Chicago, IL: University of Chicago Press.

Jacob, J. (1999) *Doctors and rules: A sociology of professional values* (expanded 2nd edn), New Brunswick, NJ/London: Transaction.

Joint Committee on Human Rights (2003) *The case for a Human Rights Commission*, Sixth Report of Session 2002–3, vols I and II, HC 489-I and II, London: Stationery Office.

Joint Committee on Human Rights (2005) *The work of the Committee in the 2001-2005 Parliament*, Nineteenth Report of Session 2004–5, HC 552, London: Stationery Office.

Samuel, L. (2002) *Fundamental social rights: Case law of the European Social Charter*, Second edn, Strasbourg: Council of Europe Publishing.

Steiner, H. J. and Alston, P. (2002) *International human rights in context*, 2nd edn, Oxford: Oxford University Press.

Walker, A. (ed) (1996) *The new generational contract: Intergenerational relations, old age and welfare*, London: UCL Press.

Walker, A. (ed) (2004) 'Quality of life in old age', *Ageing & Society*, vol 24, no 5 (special issue), pp 657–813.

Walker, A. and Hennessy, C. H. (eds) (2004) *Growing older: Quality of life in old age*, Maidenhead: Open University Press.

Watson, J. (2002) *Something for everyone: The impact of the Human Rights Act and the need for a Human Rights Commission*, London: British Institute of Human Rights.

# Section VII

# Disability

*Edited by Alan Walker*

# Introduction

Disability was a long-term scientific and policy interest of Peter Townsend's stretching back to the early 1960s and, in the 1970s, it became a passionate campaigning one. He made major contributions to this field across a broad front although, sadly, these are not always consistently recognised in the recently created discipline of disability studies. For the purposes of this selection five key aspects of his work on disability are highlighted. As with the other sections, the choice of extracts is to some extent arbitrary because he wrote many thousands of compelling words on this topic, but I have been guided by his own editorial suggestions, confirmed by the chance discovery of a hand-written list while sifting through the piles of papers in his study.

First of all he made early, landmark, contributions to the sociological understanding of disability and, in particular, to the formation of what later became known as the social model of disability (Hunt, 1966; Oliver 1983, 1990). In the division between the sociology of disability and medical sociology he was always in the former camp (Barnes and Mercer, 1996). That is, for him, disability is a social construction. Although he never adopted social oppression terminology (see below) he nonetheless saw discrimination against disabled people (disablism) in exactly the same light as ageism, homophobia, racism and sexism. It was definitely not a matter of social deviance as argued by the structural-functionalists (Thomas, 2007). During the latter part of his career he witnessed the emergence of the discipline of disability studies, with disabled people firmly in the vanguard, and his work was undoubtedly a part of the foundations of this new paradigm focussed on the social model of disability. As we will see he also played an active, if unwitting, role in this formative process. Unusually for academics working in the disability field Peter's work focused on both physical and mental disability and he made theoretical and policy-oriented contributions to both areas.

Second, he persistently and painstakingly dissected official statistics and criticised governments concerning the inadequacy of evidence on both the numbers and needs of disabled people. For him there was a fundamental issue of human rights as well as social policy: there has to be an accurate quantification of both numbers and needs in order to prepare appropriate policy responses. Failure to do so systematically leads ultimately to a denial of rights: first the right to be known and then, potentially, the right to compensation. This strand of his work started with a critique of national statistics and ended with our joint research for the Department of Health on new approaches to the assessment of functional capacity. Unfortunately the latter was never published and cannot be represented here. It did, however, point to the official and public neglect of the fact that the majority of disabled people are over pension age. Inevitably the issue of measurement raised questions of definition and his favoured functional approach led to accusations, from disabled people, about the element of control over their lives that such expert assessments entail (UPIAS and DA, 1976).

Third, much of Peter's research and writing in this field centred on the segregational effects of social structure and social policy on disabled people. The most prominent aspect of this corpus was his analyses of the impact of poverty and deprivation. This research formed part of his major life's work on poverty, because disabled people are one of those groups that are consistently found among the poor. In addition, he highlighted on many occasions the special needs of this group that create additional expenses which, if uncompensated, lead to or deepen poverty. Another element of this body of work on the social exclusion of disabled people was his research and campaigning on their lack of access to employment and the failure of social policy to protect them from the effects of discrimination in the labour market.

The fourth strand of Peter's writing on disability highlighted here concerned the inadequacy of institutional care regimes for disabled people, which echoed his damning critique of residential care for older people (Townsend, 1962). In this case his focus was primarily on long-stay institutions for people with learning disabilities, although at the time of his writing the term in common usage was 'mental handicap'.

The fifth aspect, a logical progression from his research on disability and poverty, was the campaign-oriented case for a comprehensive disability income. The twin aims here were, on the one hand, to replace the inadequate hotchpotch of existing social security provision, with its many invidious gaps and exclusions and, on the other, to ensure the inclusion of those who received no official recognition of their disabilities, such as people over pension age, or those with caring responsibilities for disabled relatives. The main vehicle to advance this case was the Disability Alliance, an umbrella organisation, which we co-founded in 1974. I must declare a personal interest here as we worked closely together, for more than 20 years, on this campaign and the related endeavour to promote disability rights.

These five key aspects of his work on the sociology and social policy of disability, including his campaigning contribution, are not in chronological order because they overlapped at different points of Peter's career. There is a single red thread running through them, however, and that is his affront at the injustices suffered by disabled people, in various institutionalised ways, and his passionate commitment to righting these wrongs. The extracts in this section are selected to give a flavour of his contribution in each of the five areas. Although he had earmarked for inclusion our joint critique of common law compensation for disability (Walker and Townsend, 1980) because of the limited space available, I decided not to do so. His equally important work on the social determinants of ill-health and disability are dealt with elsewhere in this volume.

## The sociology of disability

The two extracts in this thematic area illustrate different aspects of Peter's contribution to the sociology of disability. The first, **Chapter 41**, is drawn from 'The disabled in society' (1976), which was based largely on Sally Sainsbury's survey conducted for the Greater London Association for the Disabled. It is an early expression of the social model of disability or the social construction of disability by processes of social exclusion and segregation. By distinguishing between different definitions of disability he helped to open the path for subsequent disability theorists to cross the Rubicon by severing the link entirely between impairment and disability: the former being a physical characteristic and the latter the result of oppression.

The second extract **(Chapter 42)** comes from the Foreword to Pauline Morris's book *Put away* (1969) and focuses on learning disability (mental handicap). The extract follows critiques of social constructions of learning disability in terms of subnormal intelligence and personal incapacity and highlights the social construction of deviance. As in many instances of his writing in this field, Peter tries to draw the connection between those labelled as disabled and common humanity in terms of a continuum of capacities and incapacities.

## Counting and measuring disability

Peter devoted much time and effort to the painstaking task of trying to produce reliable estimates of the disabled population. A great deal of his critical attention was directed at the official estimates produced by the then Office of Population Censuses and Surveys and, in various places, he demonstrated their inadequacy. A concise summary of this theme in his research can be found in *Poverty in the United Kingdom* (1979) pp 695-705. The three extracts in this section built on that basic critique. The first (**Chapter 43**) follows directly on from Chapter 41 and sets out the case that he made repeatedly for the definition and measurement of disability in functional terms, so that the effects of disability or the capabilities of disabled people come to the fore rather than the cause of the disability. For Peter this was a matter of social justice – people with equally severe disabilities should be treated the same by social policy whereas, in practice, those injured in the armed forces or at work receive superior disability benefits to those disabled at birth or as a result of accidents.

The fourth extract **(Chapter 44)** comes from *Disability in Britain* (1981) and addresses the key point that disability is highly correlated with age. In this extract Peter summarises the reasons why disability in old age is neglected by social policy. Evidence on the extent of such disability can be found in *Poverty in the United Kingdom*, pp 705-7. The fifth extract **(Chapter 45)** focuses on the opposite end of the age spectrum and sets out the case for policy to recognise the special needs of all disabled children. It was written in response to the Conservative Government's decision, in January 1973, to establish a trust fund to help severely congenitally disabled children following the Thalidomide scandal.

## Poverty and social exclusion

This theme represents a major part of Peter Townsend's research legacy in the disability field and, as noted, it was linked closely to his life's work on poverty. The first of the extracts in this section **(Chapter 46)** is a general statement on the disabling effects of society: an early expression of the social model of disability. It was written in 1966 as the Foreword to Paul Hunt's book *Stigma: The experience of disability*. Paul was a founder member of the Union of the Physically Impaired Against Segregation (UPIAS) with which, less than a decade later, Peter found himself in, sometimes disconcerting, dialogue (see below).

**Chapter 47** comes from *Poverty in the United Kingdom* and sets out the evidence from the poverty survey on the extent of poverty among disabled people. **Chapter 48** concerns the exclusion of disabled people from paid employment. It represents Peter's work on both documenting this exclusion and his role in opposing the perennial official endeavours to scrap the 1944 Quota Scheme. (Observant readers will spot the subtle change in terminology, from disabled people to people with disabilities, which was briefly the in vogue terminology in the early 1980s, until, that is, disabled people asserted their own preference.)

## Critique of institutional care

This theme of Peter's work is represented by **Chapter 49**. Although written nearly 40 years ago and inevitably dated in terms of its political context, it still provides a timeless analysis of both the need for radical change in policy towards people with learning disabilities and the barriers to such change. His comments on the dangers of institutional regimes being transported into community homes are as highly relevant today as they were then.

## Campaigning for a comprehensive disability income

As will be clear from the previous extracts in this section the political campaign for social justice with regard to disabled people went hand in hand with the sociological analysis in Peter's work. As in other elements of his massive corpus they were inseparable. The focal point of his campaigning, although by no means the beginning and end of it, was the goal of a comprehensive income scheme for all disabled people, regardless of how and where the disability originated. The key issues were social justice and human rights. The fairest approach, he believed, was to assess disability in functional terms (that is, what people can or cannot do with regard to everyday activities) and allocate income according to severity.

**Chapter 50**, dating from 1967, provides a clear expression of his social policy perspective – from measurement, to assessment, to income provision – that he adhered to, more or less, until his death. The extract includes a powerful injunction against means-testing.

Following Peter's involvement in the formation of the Disablement Income Group in 1965, the main pressure group campaigning on incomes for disabled people, in the early 1970s his attention switched to the creation of a new type of pressure group based on the combined efforts of a wide range of different disability organisations most of whom were not specialised in the income or benefits field. The impetus for action was the Thalidomide scandal in the late 1960s and early 1970s, in which the Distillers Company, which manufactured the 'wonder drug' that caused severe birth defects, tried to conceal evidence of these 'side-effects'. The parents of the Thalidomide children pursued the company in the courts and won settlements in 1968 and 1973. As noted in the introduction to Chapter 41, the government of the day decided, in 1973, to establish a trust fund for severely congenitally disabled children, which left the majority unprovided for. This prompted a round-robin letter to the Prime Minister calling for a more comprehensive approach which was signed by many disability organisations and a selection of the great and the good (picked mainly from Peter's address book). The response from Prime Minister Heath provided a remarkable, never to be repeated, admission that the government was not doing enough on this front! The following year the White Paper *Social security provision for chronically sick and disabled people* was a damp squib, promising only £23 million per annum in additional benefits (averaging out to around 34p per disabled person). This galvanised action and, that year, a protest meeting was called at which the Disability Alliance was formed to campaign for a comprehensive disability income. **Chapter 51** is taken from a key Alliance policy document which sets out the case for a comprehensive disability income (Peter and I were its main authors).

Peter's campaigning commitment to the Disability Alliance remained resolutely strong until his death. *The disability rights handbook*, of which he was the original primary author in 1975, has been revised and updated annually ever since, has a print run of 30,000 and is now in its 34th edition. Although the Disability Alliance is today well established as the leading campaigning organisation in the disability income field, its early passage was by no means smooth. Apart from the struggle to raise and sustain funding, there were formidable political challenges in trying to maintain a broad coalition of disability organisations. One of the most difficult and bruising encounters in the early days was with the UPIAS and it is mentioned here because of its apparent significance in the history of disability studies (Thomas, 2007). Although a group of us were involved from the Disability Alliance side there was no doubt that Peter was regarded, on both sides, as the main spokesperson. The discussions were initiated in an attempt to persuade the leaders of this new grassroots disability movement to join the Alliance, an approach that was eventually rebuffed. Published accounts of this episode do not do justice to the political sociology of the encounter (Campbell and Oliver, 1996; Thomas, 2007). In particular there was, on the one side, the delicate nature of the newly formed coalition represented by the Alliance, which had struggled to persuade the Disablement Income Group to join it, and on the other, the fundamentalist line adopted by the UPIAS. In the face of the latter it was impossible to simply endorse the UPIAS's Fundamental Principles (as our moral and political instincts favoured) because this would have wrecked the broad coalition.

This was a painful outcome for those of us involved from the Alliance side, none more so than Peter, because we were deeply committed to the social model espoused by the UPIAS. Equally strong, however, was the conviction that the grave injustices of disability discrimination could be, at least, ameliorated by social policy. This, of course, is the classic dilemma facing the social reformer. History will pass judgement on which organisation has had the most beneficial impact on the lives of disabled people in general. This is undoubtedly the most important legacy of Peter Townsend's labours in the disability field. He has benefited millions of disabled people by his passionate and, in some cases, such as in his campaign for the Attendance Allowance, successfully persuasive arguments for improved social security provision.

Also he led the campaign to establish disability rights as a legitimate focus for both social policy and grassroots action (another contribution that is given insufficient attention within disability studies). Sadly, however, very few of the beneficiaries of this legacy will have ever heard of him.

## References

Barnes, C. and Mercer, G. (eds) (1996) *Exploring the divide: Illness and disability*, Leeds: The Disability Press.

Campbell, J. and Oliver, M. (1996) *Disability politics: Understanding our past, changing our future*, London: Routledge.

Hunt, P. (ed) (1966) *Stigma: The experience of disability*, London: Chapman.

Oliver, M. (1983) *Social work and disabled people*, Houndmills: Macmillan.

Oliver, M. (1990) *The politics of disablement*, Houndmills: Macmillan.

Thomas, C. (2007) *Sociologies of disability and illness*, Houndmills: Palgrave.

Townsend, P. (1962) *The last refuge*, London: Routledge.

UPIAS (Union of the Physically Impaired Against Segregation) and DA (the Disability Alliance) (1976) *Fundamental principles of disability*, London: UPIAS.

Walker, A. and Townsend, P. (1980) 'Compensation for disability: the wrong course', in M. Brown and S. Baldwin (eds) *The year book of social policy in Britain 1978*, London: Routledge, pp 57-80.

# 41

# The disabled in society

In Britain about 1½ million people, or 3 per cent of the population, are found in groups *officially* described as disabled or handicapped[1]. Over a million live at home. The Ministry of Labour lists 654,000 persons on the Disabled Persons Register[2]. There are approximately 450,000 disablement pensioners from the two world wars and nearly 200,000 industrial injury disablement pensioners[3]. The local authorities' registers contain the names of 110,000 blind, 30,000 partially sighted and 205,000 other disabled and handicapped persons, the great majority of whom live at home[4]. There are many persons with long-term mental or physical handicaps, probably about 200,000 who reside in hospitals, particularly those for the chronic sick and mentally ill, or in residential homes and hostels[5]. They include 65,000 subnormal and severely subnormal and another 71,000 mentally ill or psychopathic persons living at home have mental health services provided by local health authorities[6]. The Supplementary Benefits Commission (formerly the National Assistance Board) pays allowances to 138,000 incapacitated persons living at home who are not receiving sickness or other insurance benefits[7]. There are 76,000 handicapped children of whom about 32,000 are physically handicapped in special schools or units[8]. Other administratively defined categories might be added. There is considerable duplication in these figures. Their very fragmentation and the confessed inability of the Ministry of Health to give 'comprehensive national statistics'[9] forces us to ask whether we are doing all we should to develop our understanding of handicap and disability and whether services to meet the needs of disabled people are adequate.

In this paper I shall describe the results of a survey carried out between 1964 and 1966 from the University of Essex. This was carried out in London, Essex and Middlesex by Sally Sainsbury, a research officer at the university, under my guidance. [...]

The chief conclusion of this study is that there is an imbalance between the impulses of the disabled towards integration into ordinary social and occupational life and the segregative practices of society. One wants what the other largely fails either to recognise or translate into real opportunity.

---

From a lecture given at the Royal College of Surgeons on 5 May 1967, later published as Chapter 7 in:

Townsend, P. (1973) *The social minority*, London: Allen Lane, pp 109-12.

Although a majority of the people registered with the local authorities are severely incapacitated and a majority middle-aged or elderly, most emphasise physical and economic independence and integration in work and society. They are usually realistic about their limitations but believe that they could obtain more help with physical aids, housing, transport and employment. In general, they regard special clubs or residential homes and special workshops as second-best, like other symbols of separate disability status. By contrast, society tends to give weak support to the principles of economic independence and social integration or participation and fairly strong support, some of it unwitting, to the enforced dependence and social segregation of the disabled.

This conclusion naturally requires qualification, for the supporting arguments are by no means entirely consistent. It depends on a wide variety of evidence about the actual situation of the disabled – their environment, work and income and their relationships with family and social services. There is lamentably little factual knowledge. I shall endeavour to present some of the more important strands of evidence in this lecture. A necessary first step is to discuss the underlying concept of disability and explain why new definitions and measures are essential for both knowledge and policy.

## The meaning of disability

What do we mean when we say someone is disabled? First, there is anatomical, physiological or psychological abnormality or loss. Thus we think of the disabled as people who have lost a limb or part of the nervous system through surgery or an accident, become blind or deaf or paralysed, or are physically damaged or abnormal in some particular, usually observable, respect.

Secondly, there is chronic clinical condition altering or interrupting normal physiological or psychological processes, such as bronchitis, arthritis, tuberculosis, epilepsy, schizophrenia and manic depression. These two concepts of loss or abnormality and of chronic disease tend in fact to merge, for although a loss may be sustained without disease, disease long-continued usually has some physiological or anatomical effect[11]. Among the people whom we interviewed a wide range of conditions were represented. About 31 per cent specified rheumatoid arthritis, osteo-arthritis or just arthritis and between 4 per cent and 13 per cent in each instance specified the after effects of poliomyelitis, disseminated sclerosis, bronchitis, epilepsy, coronary thrombosis, or were amputees or hemiplegics. For both meanings of disability the clinical reference-object is the normal human body, of like sex and age.

A third meaning is functional limitation of ordinary activity, whether that activity is carried out alone or with others. The simplest example is incapacity for self-care and management, in the sense of being unable or finding it difficult to walk about, negotiate stairs, wash and dress, for example[12]. But this principle of limitation can be applied to other aspects of ordinary life. By reference to the average person of the same sex an estimate can be made of the individual's relative incapacity for household management and performance of both general social roles as husband, father or mother, neighbour or church member, say, and of specific occupational roles.

A fourth meaning is a pattern of behaviour which has particular elements of a socially deviant kind[13]. This pattern of behaviour is in part directly attributable to an impairment of pathological condition – such as regular physical tremor or limp, or an irregularly occurring fit. But it is also attributable to the individual's perception of his condition and his response to others' expectations of him. Thus, activity may not only be limited, but different. And it may be different as much depending on how it is perceived by the individual and others as on its physiological determination. Two people with identical physical impairment may differ greatly in their behaviour, one acting up to the limit of his capacities and the other refraining from actions of which he is capable. Alternatively a man with little or no impairment may play the disabled role. Sociologists have recently paid increasing attention to the concepts of the sick role and of illness behaviour[14]. Society expects the blind or the deaf or the physically handicapped to behave in certain approved or stereotyped ways. We all know of instances of people assuming deafness or handicap. They may adopt whole patterns of behaviour. Individuals can be motivated towards such behaviour when their physical or neurological condition does not compel it. A family or sub-culture can condition it. There are cultural differences in disability behaviour. People of different nationality or ethnic group vary in their stoicism in the face of pain and handicap[15]. All this can be a fascinating focus for inquiry.

Finally, disability means a socially defined position or status. The actor does not just act differently. He occupies a status which attracts a mixture of deference, condescension, consideration and indifference. Irrespective of a disabled individual's *specific* behaviour or condition he attracts certain kinds of attention from the rest of the population by virtue of the 'position' that the disabled, when recognised as such, occupy in that particular society. There are countries and populations which do not recognise or identify mild forms of subnormality, schizophrenia or infirmity for example. In working-class British society euphemisms for certain handicaps are used. Someone has 'nerves' or is 'hard of hearing' or is 'a bit simple'. So far this would mean that deviance simply is not recognised or clearly distinguished. But the technical, conclusive and stigmatising labels are avoided. A place is not taken in a rank or a hierarchy. This can, or course, have its advantages. Some people can continue to be treated as ordinary members of the community. To identify or register them as disabled may entitle them to certain special benefits or professional treatment but it may also separate them from society and encourage people to look on them if not as a race apart, like lepers, then with aloof condescension. Disability can imply inferior as well as different status[16]. The extent to which an individual belongs to special groups or clubs, has special sets of relationships with doctors and nurses and social workers, relies on particular forms of income and sheltered forms of occupation and is patronised by voluntary organisations will all determine his particular position and status or the extent to which he is integrated into the social fabric. Of much of this doctors, social workers and administrative personnel may be unaware. While the sociologist would not pretend to be able to advance medical knowledge, casework and administration as such, it is his responsibility to develop this aspect of knowledge.

**Endnotes**

[1] The figure is a conservative estimate which allows for double – or multiple – counting of the same persons in some of the categories listed in the rest of this paragraph. Judging from research in other countries, for example, Denmark and Sweden, a figure of 6 per cent of all adults aged 21-64 is likely to be reached when disability is defined broadly. Allowing for a smaller proportion of children but a much larger proportion of the elderly the figure for the whole population would probably be higher. See, for example, Andersen, B.R., *Fysisk Handicappede i Danmark*, Socialforskningsinstittutets Publikationer 16, Copenhagen, 1964, pp. 55-6. [On the basis of a major survey carried out by the Government in 1969, 1.1 million in Britain aged sixteen and over were estimated to be very seriously, severely or appreciably handicapped, and a further 1.9 million were impaired but needed little or no support for normal everyday living activities. Harris, A., *Handicapped and Impaired in Great Britain*, H.M.S.O., 1971.]

[2] *Ministry of Labour Gazette*, April 1967, p. 308.

[3] *Report of the Ministry of Pensions and National Insurance for the Year 1965*, Cmnd. 3046, H.M.S.O., 1966.

[4] For England and Wales, *Report of the Ministry of Health for 1965*, Cmnd. 3039, H.M.S.O., 1966, pp. 127-30. Figures for Scotland obtained from Home and Health Department and added.

[5] About 48,000 of those living in council or supported voluntary Homes in England and Wales are described as 'handicapped'. See *Report of the Ministry of Health for 1965*, p. 119.

[6] England and Wales, *Report of the Ministry of Health for 1965*, p. 119.

[7] In March 1967 the total had reached 144,000 (private communication, Ministry of Social Security). Most of them 'are persons incapacitated since birth or early childhood and living with their parents'. *Report of the National Assistance Board for the Year ended 31 December 1965*, Cmnd. 3042, H.M.S.O., 1966, p. 13.

[8] *Education in 1966 – Report of the Department of Education and Science*, Cmnd. 3226, H.M.S.O., 1967, p. 44.

[9] *Health and Welfare: the Development of Community Care*, Cmnd. 1973, H.M.S.O., 1963, p. 31.

[10] Many of those receiving retirement pensions and unemployment or sickness benefits were also receiving supplementary national assistance. People receiving personal disablement benefits (war or industrial injury) were also eligible to receive national insurance benefits.

[11] See also the analysis by Nagi, S.Z., 'Some Conceptual Issues in Disability and Rehabilitation', in Sussman, M.B. (ed.), *Sociology and Rehabilitation*, Washington, D.C., American Sociological Association, 1966, particularly pp. 100–103.

[12] An attempt to develop a measure of this was made in 'Measuring Incapacity for Self-Care', in Townsend, P., *The Last Refuge*, Routledge, 1962, pp 464–76.

[13] Goffman, E., *Stigma: Notes on the Management of Spoiled Identity*, Englewood Cliffs, N.J., Spectrum Books, 1963; Friedson, E., 'Disability as Social Deviance' in Sussman, M.B. (ed.), *Sociology and Rehabilitation*, Washington, D.C., American Sociological Association, 1966. More generally see Becker, H.S., *Outsiders: Studies in the Sociology of Deviance*, New York, The Free Press, 1963, particularly Chapters 1 and 2.

[14] See, for example, Mechanic, D., 'The Concept of Illness Behaviour', *Journal of Chronic Diseases*, vol. 15, 1962; Mechanic, D., 'Response Factors in Illness: The Study of Illness Behaviour', *Social Psychiatry*, vol 1, August 1966.

[15] See, for example, Zborowski, M., 'Cultural Components in Responses to Pain', *Journal of Social Issues*, vol. 8, 1952; Jaco, E.G. (ed.), *Patients, Physicians and Illness*, New York, The Free Press, 1958.

[16] The 'dependent and segregated status [of the disabled] is not an index merely of their physical condition; to an extent only beginning to be recognized it is the product of cultural definition – an assumptive framework of myths, stereotypes, aversive responses, and outright prejudices, together with more rational and scientific evidence'. Ten Broek, J., and Matson, F.W., 'The Disabled and the Law of Welfare', *California Law Review*, vol 54, no. 2, May 1966, p. 814.

# 42

# Social planning for the mentally handicapped

[...]

There is a tendency for society to separate people into strictly distinct categories of deviant and non-deviant, incapacitated and non-incapacitated, subnormal and normal, irrespective of the graded differences of degree revealed in any objective study of behaviour. In one psychiatric study a research team found that although a majority of people in a community could accept a proposition that mental illness could be cured they found it hard to stomach a proposition that abnormality and normality were not distinct but shaded into one another[1].

It seems that people are prepared to ignore mental illness as far as possible and tolerate a wide range of behaviour. But once this tolerance is exhausted and illness recognised people at once wish a patient to be segregated and sent off to hospital. A potential danger to the community is removed, and a sick person is symbolically identified as different, going through all kinds of 'stripping' or 'degradation' procedures, and being deprived of common rights and resources. If people admit that abnormality is just one end of a continuum then they might have to admit that a sick or handicapped person might not be different from themselves, and segregation might not be the obvious solution. We have to be aware that different beliefs are linked in a system of belief.

## Explaining variations in the prevalence of mental handicap

There are a number of implications of this approach for the study of mental handicap. One is that society may go through a cycle of identifying relatively large and relatively small numbers of mentally handicapped persons, even though the prevalence of handicap, when measured according to objective criteria of subnormal intelligence, personal incapacity and behavioural deviance, may remain constant. Or again, its mode of treating them may depend on the relative weight attached socially to each of these three criteria. The development in the late nineteenth century of a national

---

Townsend, P. (1969) 'Foreword: Social planning for the mentally handicapped', in P. Morris, *Put away: A sociological study of institutions for the mentally retarded*, London: Routledge and Kegan Paul.

school system brought to light those who could not be accommodated, or accommodated only with difficulty, in that system. So occurred an expansion in the proportion in society who were identified as mentally handicapped and this was enforced by the rigid and punitive trends in the moral code of society during the Victorian period. Custodial values were extolled by eugenicists who claimed that the subnormal would reproduce their kind disproportionately and contribute to a decline in national intelligence[2].

Although from the fourteenth century a legal distinction was drawn between 'lunatics' and 'idiots' most persons with mental disorders were in practice housed indiscriminately in workhouses and, later, asylums. It was only in the middle of the nineteenth century that the first 'idiot asylum' was opened by a voluntary society, and later still before such asylums added the term 'institutions for the feeble-minded' to their title[3]. I am therefore arguing that as time went on the demands of the educational system, together with the imposition of a stricter moral code, increased the proportion of persons with mildly subnormal intelligence or mildly deviant behaviour who were institutionalised. It was the incursion of many 'feeble-minded' persons without personal incapacity but with supposedly fixed low intelligence which cause institutions independent of asylums to be set up. The system of mental deficiency hospitals evolved. More recently there has been a tendency for the rates to diminish, partly because intelligence is now seen to be more complicated and adaptable than formerly supposed, and partly because punitive control of individual departures from moral conformity is thought to be less necessary.

It is within some such framework that the prevalence of mental handicap in different societies, and the division between institutionalised and community care, has to be explained. In appreciating what the imprecise criteria of subnormal intelligence, personal incapacity and deviance contribute to our concept of mental handicap we can perhaps see the need to revise our standards of humanity and justice. For the significance of this analysis is much more than semantic. It implies that there may be persons who are deprived of full civic rights and responsibilities and even in some cases of their personal freedom because their ability to read and write has not yet been perceived, their relatively inadequate intelligence has not been measured (or not measured efficiently), their behaviour is found to be morally distasteful or they are an embarrassment in school. It also implies that *any* physical segregation, even of people of extreme handicap, may be improper.

## Endnotes

[1] Cumming, J., and Cumming, E., 'Mental Health Education in a Canadian Community', in Paul, B., *Health Culture and Community*, New York, 1955.

[2] These claims were confounded by measures over time in the distribution of national intelligence and by studies of the handicapped. Penrose, for example, found that over 90 per cent of the mildly subnormal in his hospital survey had parents of normal or dull average intelligence. Penrose, L.S., *A Clinical and Genetic Study of 1280 Cases of Mental Defect*, HMSO, 1938.

[3] *Report of the Royal Commission on the Law Relating to Mental Illness and Mental Deficiency, 1954-57*, Cmnd. 169, London, HMSO, 1957.

# 43

# Operational measures of disability as a guide to action

It would be impossible to assemble a large number of data on each of these interpretations of disability. All of them have implications both for our understanding of disability as well as the means with which to offer help and service. Clinical particularisations are essential if pathology is to be investigated or arrested but there can be unfortunate social and administrative consequences. The proliferation of specialist consultants for particular diseases or disabilities and of statutory and voluntary organisations gives emphasis on the separateness rather than the similarity of many disabled conditions with consequential confusion, fragmentation of effort and injustice. Some conditions receive favourable publicity and attention. Others, with worse effects, are neglected. The thalidomide children have attracted vastly more public sympathy than children suffering from subnormality or congenital syphilis. The Spastics Society has an income of around £2 million but the National Society for Handicapped Children only £40,000[1].

One consequence is inconsistency of assessment. How do we assess *degree* of disability so as to determine level of provision or of other needs? The McCorquodale Committee on the Assessment of Disablement repeatedly referred in its report to the principle that assessment should be determined by 'means of a comparison between the condition of the disabled person and that of a normal healthy person of the same age'[2], but took no steps to apply that principle empirically. The committee did not obtain information systematically about disabled persons and healthy persons of equivalent age. Nor did the committee try to examine the rationale of the current medical assessment. They largely confined their attentions to amputations and loss of limb or eye and did not, even for these minority disabilities, seek empirical justification for percentage assessments. For example, they accepted the loss of four fingers and of a leg below the knee (leaving a stump of between 3½ and 5 inches) each as equivalent to 50 per cent disability. We might question the logic of both rate and equivalence. The loss of three fingers, the amputation of 'one foot resulting in end-bearing stump', the amputation 'through one foot proximal to the metatarsophalangeal joint' and the loss

---

Extract (pp 112–14) from Townsend, P. (1973) 'The disabled in society', in *The social minority*, London: Allen Lane.

of vision in one eye were all regarded as equivalent to 30 per cent disability. In refraining from exploring the functional, psychological and social effects even of different kinds of limb amputation they failed to take advantage of the growing body of knowledge and research methods developed by the social sciences in the last twenty years. The same kind of criticisms might be made of the more general and rather different definitions of disability currently used by the Ministries of Social Security, Labour and Health[3]. Britain is still largely governed in its conduct towards the disabled by the *source* rather than the *effect* of disability. Too little effort has been made to develop *functional* indices, based on questions about individual capacities. Such indices are difficult to develop and have to be treated with caution. But they are implicit in nearly all official definitions and have been partly but unsystematically used in some medical and administrative procedures. For example, the information supplied by doctors on a form used by the Ministry of Labour includes the kinds of conditions which doctors believe the disabled person should *avoid* in his employment. The information does not adequately reflect either the general or specific capacities of the disabled person although some 'functional' information is given[4]. Britain is not alone in having failed to size up to this problem[5]. If we did apply functional measures it is likely that we would identify between 3 per cent and 6 per cent of adults under pensionable age as physically or mentally handicapped. A recent Danish survey established that around 6 per cent of adults were physically handicapped. There was little difference between the rates for men and the rates for women but both rates increased sharply in the fifties. About 3 per cent in the twenties and thirties were disabled and 7 per cent in the forties, but by the late fifties the figure reached 17 per cent, topping 20 per cent in the early sixties[6]. In Sweden disability pensions reach 2½ per cent of the adult population. The rate also rises sharply in the fifties and early sixties. But some of the less disabled may not qualify for such pensions.

We developed a crude index of incapacity to manage personal and household activities which involved assessing twenty-three tasks and activities[7]. Each activity was scored two if it could not be done at all and one if it could be done only with difficulty. Altogether as many as 17 per cent of the disabled in the three counties were very severely incapacitated (scoring 23 and over). Another 36 per cent were severely incapacitated (scoring 15-22), making 53 per cent altogether. Only 11 per cent were slightly incapacitated (scoring 6 or less). Incapacity tended to increase with age. Only a third of those younger than 45 were severely or very severely incapacitated in our sense, compared with nearly half those aged 45-64 and nearly two thirds of those aged 65 and over.

This kind of approach allows us to compare persons with multiple disabilities. Nearly half the sample had at least two. It also allows us to begin comparing the effects of different disabilities and the ways in which the extent of incapacity changes over time. Very little work has been done on this. Nearly 20 per cent had disabilities which were quickly progressive and another 40 per cent slowly progressive. Many were prone to depression and feared increasing dependence on others. Some people found that their capacities fluctuated according to the nature of their condition and changes in the weather. Even those whose disabilities were quickly progressive found there were periods of recovery or restoration of capacity. In all this I am stressing the relativity of disability, like the relativity of intelligence. There are times, for example in illness or after accidents, when most of us cannot walk or cannot dress or cannot speak. Many of us have a 'permanent' limitation of some kind. It is appropriate therefore to ask to what degree the disabled are more incapacitated than ourselves as a way of asserting a common involvement and preparing the ground for a rational examination of their occupational and social opportunities.

**Endnotes**

[1] According to the Charity Commissioners the Spastics Society received £1.8 million in 1962, and the National Society for Mentally Handicapped Children £39,000 in 1964.

[2] *Report of the Committee on the Assessment of Disablement* (the McCorquodale Report), Cmnd. 2847, H.M.S.O., December 1965.

[3] In awarding war pensions and industrial injuries disablement pensions the Ministry of Pensions bases assessments on comparison between 'the condition of a disabled person and that of a normal health person of the same age. Assessment on this basis measures the general handicap imposed by loss of faculty. Loss of faculty may be defined as loss of physical or mental capacity to lead a normally occupied life and does not depend on the way in which the disablement affects the particular circumstances of the individual. A normally occupied life includes work as well as household and social activities and leisure pursuits.' *Report of the Committee on the Assessment of Disablement*, p. 4. To be admitted to the Ministry of Labour's Register for Disabled Persons an applicant must (1) 'be substantially handicapped on account of injury, disease (including a physical or mental condition arising from imperfect development of any organ) or congenital deformity, in obtaining or keeping employment or work on his own account otherwise suited to his age, qualification and experience; the disablement being likely to last for twelve months or more; (2) desire to engage in some form of remunerative employment or work … and have a reasonable prospect of obtaining and keeping such employment or work…' Finally, local authorities are empowered by Section 29 of the National Assistance Act, 1948, to promote the welfare of persons who are blind, deaf or dumb, and others' who are substantially and permanently handicapped by illness, injury or congenital deformity or such other disabilities as may prescribed by the Minister'. Registers are compiled on this basis from a variety of sources.

[4] The Medical Report form includes a section which allows the doctor to indicate whether an individual can use upper limbs (shoulders, arms, hands, fingers and touch) and lower limbs (walking, standing, sitting only, hurrying, balancing, climbing stairs, climbing ladders), and can kneel, stoop, push and pull, and lift and carry. The extent of hearing and vision also can be noted. The need for better functional assessment was recognized by a Working Party of the British Council for Rehabilitation of the Disabled reporting in 1964: *The Handicapped School-Leaver*, British Council for the Rehabilitation of the Disabled.

[5] See, for example, Hess, A.E., 'Old Age, Survivors and Disability Insurance: Early Problems and Operations of the Disability Provisions', *Social Security Bulletin*, U.S. Department of Health, Education and Welfare, December 1957.

[6] Andersen, B.R., *Fysisk Handicappede i Danmark, Bind II*, Socialforskningsinstittutets Publikationer 16, Copenhagen, 1964, pp. 55-6.

[7] Including going up and down stairs, getting about the house, washing and bathing, dressing and putting on shoes, cutting toe nails, brushing and combing hair, going to the toilet on own, cleaning floors, cooking a hot meal, seeing, speaking and hearing, and organizing thoughts and lucid speech.

# 44

# Elderly people with disabilities

## The failure to acknowledge disablement among the elderly

The failure fully to acknowledge disablement among the elderly takes at least three forms. Firstly, there is a failure to appreciate that *poverty is greater among disabled than non-disabled elderly people*. DHSS analyses show that the proportion of elderly people living at or below the state's poverty line is very much higher than of young people (See Table 2.2). According to the recently abolished Supplementary Benefits Commission, there were at least 600,000 old people entitled to supplementary benefit but not claiming benefit in each of the years of the mid-1970s (SBC, 1977, p 136). What has to be faced is that a disproportionately high proportion of these were severely disabled. What is the evidence for this? An OPCS survey showed that the disabled have incomes and other resources which are relatively low when compared to the non-disabled, even when standardised by age (Harris et al, 1972, pp 8, 13). (The survey also found a correlation between greater handicap and lower income.) An independent national survey of poverty found that a much higher percentage of elderly people with appreciable or severe incapacity (73 per cent) than with none (48 per cent) had incomes below or on the margins of the state's standard of poverty. Moreover the correlation remained significant after standardising for age *and* household composition (Townsend, 1979, pp 712, 816). Again, a DHSS survey of prolonged sickness found that the risk of poverty is closely connected with the length of sickness. Though this study was of people of working age, it demonstrated the impoverishing effects of chronic illness, including the effects experienced by those reaching pensionable age (Martin and Morgan, 1976). The material and social deprivation of long-stay hospital patients and residents of Homes should also be remembered. If we apply similar criteria of income needs therefore, we can conclude both that more elderly than other people are poor and that more disabled than non-disabled elderly are poor. (Table 2.2 illustrates these statements.)

Extract (pp 97-101) from Townsend, P. (1973) 'Elderly people with disabilities',
in A. Walker and P. Townsend (eds) (1981) *Disability in Britain*,
Oxford: Martin Robertson, pp xxi-xxiii.

**Table 2.2:** Numbers and percentage of total and disabled population living in poverty or on the margins of poverty, 1977

| Level of income | Total population | | | Disabled over pensionable age (000s) | Sick and disabled under pensionable age (000s) | Disabled of all ages ages (000s) |
| --- | --- | --- | --- | --- | --- | --- |
| | Over pensionable age (000s) | Under pensionable age (000s) | All ages (000s) | | | |
| Below supplementary benefit level | 760 | 1,270 | 2,020 | 250 | 70 | 320 |
| Receiving supplementary benefit | 2,000 | 2,160 | 4,160 | 790 | 240 | 1,030 |
| At or up to 40 per cent above supplementary benefit level | 3,010 | 4,830 | 7,840 | 860 | 400 | 1,260 |
| More than 40 per cent above supplementary benefit level | 2,750 | 35,960 | 38,720 | 690 | 1,380 | 2,070 |
| Total | 8,520 | 44,220 | 52,740 | 2,590 | 2,090 | 4,680 |
| Below supplementary benefit level (%) | 8.9 | 2.9 | 3.8 | 9.7 | 3.3 | 6.8 |
| Receiving supplementary benefit (%) | 23.5 | 4.9 | 7.9 | 30.5 | 11.5 | 22.0 |
| At or up to 40 per cent above supplementary benefit level (%) | 35.3 | 10.9 | 14.9 | 33.2 | 19.1 | 26.9 |
| More than 40 per cent above supplementary benefit level (%) | 32.3 | 81.3 | 73.4 | 26.6 | 66.0 | 44.2 |
| Total (%) | 100 | 100 | 100 | 100 | 100 | 100 |

*Note:* The estimate of sick and disabled persons under pension age applies to those sick or disabled for three months or more and includes dependants in the income unit.
*Source:* DHSS (SR3) Analysis of FES 1977 for columns 1, 2, 3 and 5. The distribution of column 4 is based on evidence about those of pensionable age who were 'appreciably or severley incapacitated' in P. Townsend (1979, p 712) (and survey printout).

Secondly, there is the failure to recognise that *disabled people require higher incomes than non-disabled people*. It is not simply that certain specific expenses are incurred for certain disabilities (Harris et al, 1972, p 8). There are of course direct costs, as for drugs, emollients, hearing aids, spectacles, sticks, callipers, surgical belts, wheelchairs, hoists, special diets, forms of transport, slip-on clothing, incontinence pads, specifically designed implements for eating, purpose-built shoes or boots, books or newspapers in braille or in large print, breathing apparatus, non-slip mats and handrails. Some of these items are required only once, others occasionally or frequently. It would be wrong to assume that all of them can be or are paid for or made available without personal charge under existing health and welfare legislation. NHS prescriptions for the elderly are free, but some goods required or felt to be required have to be purchased from chemists or from shops selling mechanical aids.

But there are also many indirect costs of disablement to which attention should be drawn. Some old people suffer conditions such as diabetes or heart disease for which a particular diet is prescribed. But there are many others who are in practice restricted to a range of foods which are difficult or costly to obtain. People with limited mobility may have to depend on nearby shops rather than on cut-price stores and supermarkets. They cannot afford to buy in bulk and do not often have freezers. Because of their disability they are likely to be in the home longer than non-disabled people, and hence have larger heating costs. Because of poor circulation they may need extra heating, or cushions, hot-water bottles and electric blankets to offset pain or discomfort. Those who are unable to drive or to use public transport may have to depend on paying privately to get about, or at least feel obliged to offer a gift in exchange for unpaid services. Much the same applies to activities like cleaning, cooking and housekeeping, going on holiday, or going to a cinema or football match.

Some people argue that the additional costs of disability in old age are balanced in part by a more limited range of social activities which produces savings in cost, including the costs of food. One objection to this argument, however, is that poverty forces people to restrict the range of their activities, and many disabled people are less active because they cannot afford the goods and services to compensate them for the restrictions of disability upon ordinary activities. So there is a problem of confusing the effect with the cause. A key question here is whether disabled elderly people with high incomes in fact lead contained lives upon modest budgets. A small number were traceable in the sample interviewed for the national poverty survey. They appeared to spend well and had little deprivation. Most of them undertook activities enjoyed by younger non-disabled people, such as going on summer holidays, staying with relatives and friends, having friends and relatives to stay, having an evening out and so on (Townsend, 1979, p 818).

Thirdly, disability among older people is not fully acknowledged because it is parcelled up into categories. *The tendency within medicine as well as within voluntary agencies to identify and try to serve the needs of people with particular conditions or types of disability diverts attention from those needs which such people share with other disabled people and has the effect of minimising a problem of huge proportions.* It would be wrong of course to suggest that people suffering from a particular type of disability do not have unique problems, but it would be even more wrong to suggest that all their problems are unique. There are young people who suffer from two or more disability conditions and many examples of people suffering from both physical and mental handicap. But it is in old age that the absurdity of treating disablement in terms of specific symptomatology becomes evident. During this period of life, a large proportion of people have physical and mental limitations which are generalised and tend to merge with the limitations associated with particular conditions. The extent to which people are prevented from leading activities common for those of their age (*or common for adults of any age*), is what becomes important. The degree of restriction, and the means of making it up or compensating for it through alternative activities or through the compensating acts of others, becomes crucial. While this is necessarily an expression of value it is also a question of fact. Whether or not the problems of different disabled people are similar, and how far they are similar deserves more attention today than the fragmentation of disability into a thousand and one specialities. Fortunately, developments in definition and measurement are beginning to redress an historical tendency to compartmentalise disability categories. An example is provided in the report in the OPCS national survey, where causes of impairment (such as neoplasms, diseases of the respiratory system, diseases of the central nervous system, congenital malformations, blindness, amputations, 'senility' and many others) are classified in relation to degree and category of handicap (Harris [et al], 1971, pp 224-225).

## References

Harris, A.I., Cox, E. and Smith, C.R.W. (1971) *Handicapped and impaired in Great Britain*, Part 1, London: HMSO.

Harris, A.I., Smith, C.R.W. and Head, E. (1972) *Income and entitlement to supplementary benefit of impaired people in Great Britain*, London: HMSO.

Martin, J. and Morgan, M. (1976) *Prolonged sickness and the return to work*, London: HMSO.

Supplementary Benefits Commission [SBC] (1977) *Annual Report 1976*, London: HMSO.

Townsend, P. (1979) *Poverty in the United Kingdom*, London: Allen Lane.

# 45

# An aid scale for disabled children

The announcement by Sir Keith Joseph, in the wake of the campaign by *The Sunday Times* and MPs, including Mr Jack Ashley, that £3m would be given to the Joseph Rowntree Memorial Trust to help severely congenitally disabled children, including the thalidomide children, seems to be wrong on all counts: many severely handicapped children are excluded; benefit should take the form of weekly or monthly payments rather than a lump sum; the total of £3m is therefore much too small: and the task of administration would be best undertaken by a statutory body.

Which families should qualify for Government help? Sir Keith has rightly decided that children other than thalidomide children should be included but has referred only to children with "very severe" disabilities "found to be present at birth or immediately after". But some major disabilities are not in practice identified in early infancy and only come to light, or develop, much later.

Muscular dystrophy, for example, may not become apparent until a child begins to walk and severe mental handicap may not be diagnosed among children under five, or even under 10. The reported incidence is only 0.5 per 1,000 under five years of age, compared with 3.5 per 1,000 at 15-19. As the Tunbridge Committee stated in its recent authoritative report on Rehabilitation: "Disability in children is rarely easy to analyze in the early years. The early identification of disability is best achieved by a periodic developmental assessment for all children."

Can assessments after infancy, therefore, and reassessments to take account of changes in severity of disability, be included in the proposed scheme? Should financial aid be withheld from parents of children disabled, say, after a road accident or a long illness? Unless questions such as these are answered from the start by the Government itself an arbitrary and inequitable system is bound to result.

The scale of the problem is still largely guesswork. In spite of a variety of studies of handicap in recent years, information about handicapped children is inadequate. The lack of reliable estimates of the number of disabled caused the Government to commission a survey in 1968-69. The third report on that survey, making an implicit case for a disability pension and showing that about 70,000 disabled adults are not drawing but are entitled

Townsend, P. and Walker, A. (1973) 'An aid scale for disabled children', *The Times*, 23 January.

to supplementary benefit, has just been published. Handicapped children under 16 were excluded from the survey, and estimates of their numbers are uncertain. The table below sums up the figures that can be gleaned or estimated from different Government reports. There is an overlap between some of the estimates, for example, between those in the care of local authority mental health services and those awaiting admission to special schools and a few small groups such as the physically handicapped in ordinary schools and in hospitals, have not been included. Altogether there are over 150,000 handicapped children known to different services. This is in fact the minimum figure officially assumed by the DHSS but many handicapped children are not known to any service, and the rate varies between areas. Greater efforts have been made in Scotland than in England to locate the handicapped and, though the Scottish Home and Health Department admits there is still some way to go, far more physically handicapped children have been registered than in the whole of England, despite the much smaller population. According to Scottish experience there should be 80,000 to 100,000 handicapped children who are mentally handicapped, deaf, blind or partially sighted, on the English local registers. In fact there are fewer than 6,000.

### Estimated numbers of handicapped children in the United Kingdom

| | |
|---|---|
| Number mentally handicapped children in hospital | 7,100 |
| Registered blind | 2,300 |
| Registered partially sighted | 3,300 |
| Registered deaf and partially deaf | 6,300 |
| Handicapped (general classes) on local authority registers | 15,700 |
| Number physically handicapped and delicate children in special schools | 19,500 |
| Number of educationally subnormal children in special schools | 59,000 |
| Additional number attending special schools, formerly training centres | 21,400 |
| Number educationally subnormal children awaiting admission to special schools, and those receiving education in their own homes | (a)10,400 |
| Number in care of local authority mental health services | 31,100 |

(a) England and Wales only.

According to functional criteria the total numbers of children with every kind of handicap in the population are likely to lie between 300,000 and 500,000. Our estimate is 400,000. This figure is based on information from areas where special efforts have been made to register the handicapped, research surveys of children, and rates per 1,000 population of certain types of handicap among people between the ages 15 and 19. For example, in the comprehensive National Child Development Study, which included medical examinations, but did not establish functional effects, 2.6 per cent of seven-year-olds were found to have various congenital disorders of a serious kind, and another 1.6 per cent were in need of special educational treatment, were injured after accidents or had progressively disabling illnesses or were severely or partially deaf. Applied to all children under 15 the combined total of 4.2 per cent represents over 550,000 children.

The pattern of handicap is changing. During the past 50 years cerebral palsy and spina bifida have begun to replace poliomyelitis and heart disease as principal causes of handicap. The change is, of course, based largely on the development of new drugs and methods of surgery but also on the acceptance by more of the medical profession and of the public of malformation, at least among children. The numbers of handicapped children who survive the critical weeks after birth is likely to increase steadily.

Little is known about numbers with different degrees of handicap. Some children may be only mildly handicapped and require little more parental supervision and maintenance than children who are not handicapped. Others place severe psychological, physical and financial demands on their parents. Some need special aids, frequent replacements of shoes and clothing, a special diet, a specially designed home environment, or regular subsidies for transport.

What form should financial aid take? The attendance allowance can be paid to the parents of severely handicapped children of two years of age and over, but by April 1972 only 11,600 awards had been made for children under 10 in Britain and the allowance is one for attendance and not other special needs. The provision of aids by social service departments, which would reduce financial needs, is also still on a tiny scale. Finally, the Royal Commission on civil liability and compensation for personal injury and death, which was set up under Lord Pearson by the Prime Minister just before Christmas, [1972] cannot fill the gap in policy. The terms of reference are sadly restricted.

While forms of compensation might be preserved in law for liabilities which can be traced, such a system is plainly unsatisfactory as a method of providing financial support for all those in need and according to degrees of need. Liability cannot be traced in most instances, it is not related uniformly to need, courts vary in their decisions and inflation quickly reduces the value of any award. Instead, a strong argument can be made for an allowance which can be paid at a special rate, and which could be varied according to degree of handicap. The advantage over lump sum compensation of a special allowance for handicapped children, which could be paid like a supplementary family allowance, is that it can be changed from time to time to allow for any changes in the condition of the child, the economy or society's perception of need.

The administration of grants or allowances for handicapped children must be based on a wide range of expertise and be accountable directly to the public. Any voluntary association concerned with the handicapped would find it impossible to assess even all congenitally disabled children. The Government is being unfair in asking the Rowntree Trust to attempt the task. Elaborate enquiries will have to be made in all parts of the country and information collected. The needs of children and their parents will have to be carefully weighed, with full opportunity for appeal and public discussion of the principles upon which payments are made. The closest contacts with health, welfare and social security services will be necessary.

The allocation of £3m is significant because Sir Keith tacitly acknowledges that under the present law a fair outcome of the dispute between the Distiller's Company and the parents of the thalidomide children cannot be guaranteed – or cannot be achieved without special Government measures. There are difficulties in finding an equitable solution for the future as well as the present needs of these children. But for each one of them there are another 1,000 handicapped children, some of whom deserve as much, or even more, financial aid. The Government should therefore announce a comprehensive policy to replace what is little more than an ineffectual gesture. It should appoint an advisory committee, perhaps linking with the committee advising on the attendance allowance, to supervise its introduction. The Rowntree Trust's administration of the first £3m could be treated as an integral part of the first phase of that work. But no one should be under any illusion that less than the expenditure of 30 times this figure should be committed annually if families are to receive adequate financial support for handicapped children.

# 46

# Stigma: the experience of disability

This is an uncomfortable book. Firstly, it is uncomfortable because it reveals how inadequate are the existing services for the disabled in Britain. Pensions are not paid to many persons, particularly to housewives, who need them. The amounts that are paid are generally too small and they vary unfairly according to whether the disability was incurred in war, industry or civil life. Payments for dependent children are poor when compared, for example, with those by local authorities for foster children. Information about aids to disability, specially designed housing and household gadgets is hard to obtain. Voluntary and statutory organisations concentrate too much on publicity 'shows' – like parties and Christmas visits, parcels and pantomimes – instead of continuing care – such as home help, physiotherapy, hydrotherapy and supporting help for relatives at holidays and other times. The Disabled Persons Employment Act has proved of small value to those other than the less seriously disabled. Many persons have little help either from employers or Disablement Resettlement Officers.

Secondly, the book is uncomfortable because it shows that these inadequacies are not just unwitting gaps in the outer fabric of the Welfare State which would be filled if called to public attention. They reflect a much deeper problem of a distortion of the structure and of the value-system of society itself. Achievement, productivity, vigour, health and youth are admired to an extreme. Incapacity, unproductiveness, slowness and old age are implicitly if not explicitly deplored. Such a system of values moulds and reinforces an elaborate social hierarchy. The disabled are as much the inevitable victims of this system as the young professional and managerial groups are its inevitable beneficiaries. The question that is therefore raised is not a straightforward one. It is complicated and immense. Is it possible to secure real gains for those who are disabled without calling for a reconstruction of society and schooling new attitudes in the entire population?

Several of the writers of the following essays [in *Stigma*] dwell on this problem. Although they describe the miserable lack of facilities and services this is not what worries them most. They keep coming back to the quality of the human relationships which lie behind. They are concerned not only about relations with husbands, wives, children and friends but with workmates, neighbours and the rest of the community. They realize how

---

Townsend, P. (1966) 'Foreword', in P. Hunt (ed) *Stigma: The experience of a disability*, London: Chapman.

widespread are feelings of protectiveness, superiority, aloofness and even revulsion towards them. Ordinary people often expect them to become passive and compliant independents, an isolated category of the pitied who are thrust out of sight at home or in institutions no wonder they write of the bitterness and frustration involved in playing the role of invalid.

Many struggle instinctively against this stigmatization. They refuse to reconcile themselves to a separate life and status. 'Our longing to have a real place in society ... indicates that we are not meant to live as isolated beings.' 'The partially disabled person ... needs to become part of "normal" society and not isolated among his own kind.' And again, 'Society has to realize that first and foremost we are people equally with the non-disabled. Our social needs and aspirations are identical with theirs.' These extracts from three of the essays show how powerful is the desire for integration with ordinary social groups. The disabled tend to dislike self-conscious togetherness as much as ostrich-like security. If only special types of housing were available in ordinary neighbourhoods and steps could be taken to fit them into ordinary forms of employment, clubs and societies instead of segregated workshops and institutions, their view is that the social stigma from which they suffer would gradually be removed.

This does not mean they want to be treated as if their disabilities did not exist. On the contrary, many feel that their difference from other people has to be acknowledged realistically by both themselves and by others. They feel they will gain nothing by disguising their limitations. If they are to adjust successfully to disability they have to accept less than full membership of society. And, equally, if the non-disabled are to adjust to them then some diminution of privilege has to be accepted. Social justice involves some people's loss as well as others' gain.

One remarkable feature of these essays is the insight given into the nature of the individual's relationships with society. The authors continually reach beyond the immediate problems of persons who happen to suffer from muscular dystrophy, rheumatoid arthritis or the effects of poliomyelitis. They show that adjusting to disability is simply a special version of the universal problem of adjusting to personal shortcomings and loneliness. Those who are disabled experience in an extreme form the self-consciousness, inadequacy and pain which touches at certain times and in varying degree all mankind. As Paul Hunt writes, 'Our "tragedy" may be only the tragedy of all sickness, pain and suffering.' To some readers this may seem to be a forlorn, if brave, message of hope, but it seems to me to be fundamentally correct. Disability, like intelligence, is more a matter of degree than of kind. It is more a relative than an absolute condition. If this is correct then our conception of human diversity has merely to be extended beyond the customary limits. And the conclusion that has to be drawn is that fewer of the disabled should be sheltered from the mainstreams of life and more of them integrated with society. This would benefit not only the disabled. Many in the population would be encouraged to overcome their fear and shock of disability and would be helped thereby to come to terms with their own shortcomings and see more clearly their own relationships with the community.

Another feature of these essays is the authors' assertion of the need for a fresh interpretation of social equality. They disentangle themselves from conventional expressions of gratitude for services rendered and propose introducing new patterns of rights into a situation which has traditionally been dominated by condescension and patronage on the one hand and inferiority or deference on the other. By insisting on these rights they are saving many from a benevolent but indifferent superiority and laying the basis for a general pattern of more equal and less discriminatory social relationships. Some new but important steps have been taken to establish a common humanity.

# 47

# Disabled people and the long-term sick

## Poverty

Not only do disabled people have lower social status. They also have lower incomes and fewer assets. Moreover, they tend to be poorer even when their social status is the same as the non–disabled. This will now be demonstrated. Table 20.10 shows the distribution of cash incomes in relation to the state's standard of poverty. With increasing incapacity, proportionately more people lived in households with incomes below, or only marginally above, that standard. Fewer lived in households with relatively high incomes. More than half those with appreciable or severe incapacity were in households in or on the margins of poverty, compared with only a fifth of those with no incapacity.

**Table 20.10:** Percentages of people with different degrees of disability living below and above the state's standard of poverty

Net disposable household income last year as % of supplementary benefit scales plus housing cost

| | Degree of incapacity (score) | | | | | |
|---|---|---|---|---|---|---|
| | None (0) | Minor (1-2) | Some (3-4) | Some (5-6) | Appreciable (7-10) | Severe (11+) |
| Under 100 | 5 | 11 | 12 | 11 | 11 | 12 |
| 100-39 | 19 | 25 | 29 | 36 | 39 | 46 |
| 140-99 | 36 | 27 | 26 | 24 | 23 | 24 |
| 200+ | 41 | 37 | 33 | 29 | 27 | 18 |
| Total | 100 | 100 | 100 | 100 | 100 | 100 |
| Number | 4,026 | 453 | 189 | 185 | 197 | 109 |

Extract (pp 711–13) from Townsend, P. (1979) 'Disabled people and the long-term sick', in *Poverty in the United Kingdom*, London: Allen Lane.

More of the incapacitated than of the non–incapacitated are aged 65 and over, and it might be supposed that the correlation shown in the table is explained more by the low incomes associated with advancing age than disability as such. But while changing age distribution underlies the correlation, poverty is still associated with increased incapacity, even when age is held constant. Indeed, when attention is paid to the incomes of the income unit rather than of the household as a whole, and to household stocks, and assets, the association between poverty and disability is more marked. Nearly three times as many people aged 40 and under pensionable age who were appreciably or severely incapacitated as of those who were not incapacitated were in units with incomes close to or under the poverty line. The increase in risk of poverty with increase in incapacity was marked even among those of pensionable age (Table 20.11). Another method of examining the effects of disability is to examine income according to the level of disability of the most disabled member of the income unit....There is a marked inverse relationship between increasing income and disability.

**Table 20.11:** Percentages of people of different age with different degrees of incapacity who were living in income units with incomes in previous year below or on the margins of the state's standard of poverty

| Age | Degree of incapacity (score) | | | |
| --- | --- | --- | --- | --- |
| | None (0) | Minor (1-2) | Some (3-6) | Appreciable or severe (7+) |
| 15-39 | 25 | (30) | (54) | a |
| 40-pensionable age | 15 | 22 | 30 | 49 |
| Pensionable age and over | 48 | 62 | 65 | 73 |
| All ages 15 and over | 23 | 41 | 52 | 68 |
| Number all ages | 2,802 | 464 | 389 | 311 |

Note: a Equals number below 20.

More of the incapacitated than of the non–incapacitated, for each major age group, were in debt or had no assets or had less than £100. Fewer had assets over £5,000. Fewer of the disabled were owner-occupiers, held a personal bank account, owned a car or had personal possessions other than furniture or clothing (such as jewellery, silver and antiques) worth £25 or more.

The next table is perhaps the most compact illustration that the survey can offer of the deleterious effects upon living standards of disability. In this the annuity values of assets owned by the incapacitated and non–incapacitated are added to their net disposable incomes for the previous twelve months, and the resulting 'income net worth' is expressed as a percentage of the state's standard of poverty, that is, the supplementary benefit rates which were in force at the time of the survey, plus housing cost (Table 20.12). A significantly higher proportion of the incapacitated than of the non-incapacitated, within each major group, had an income net worth of below, or only just marginally above, the state's standard of poverty. The incapacitated were at a disadvantage throughout the income scale. For example, for those in their fifties, only 20 per cent of those with appreciable or severe incapacity, compared with 31 per cent of those with some incapacity and 56 per cent of those with no incapacity had an income net worth of more than 250 per cent of the supplementary benefit standard.

**Table 20.12:** Percentages of people of different age with different degrees of incapacity in units whose income net worth[a] was below or only marginally above the state's standard of poverty[b]

| Age | Degree of incapacity (score) | | | |
| --- | --- | --- | --- | --- |
| | None (0) | Minor (1-2) | Some (3-6) | Appreciable or severe (7+) |
| 15-39 | 21 | (31) | (44) | c |
| 40-pensionable age | 9 | 13 | 27 | 43 |
| Pensionable age and over | 28 | 36 | 35 | 52 |
| All ages 15 and over | 17 | 25 | 33 | 50 |
| Number all ages | 2,434 | 416 | 342 | 266 |

*Notes:* [a] Annuity value of assets plus net disposable income in previous year (less any income from savings and property) for income units.
[b] Supplementary benefit scales for income units of different size and composition plus actual cost of housing.
[c] Number below 20.

# 48

# Employment and disability

## Unemployment and deprivation in employment

Even if an agreed basis of information about the availability of, and eligibility for, employment among people with disabilities eludes us, the same cannot be said of their disadvantages compared with the non-disabled. In relation to employment there are four specific disadvantages which can be documented and which help to explain why people with disabilities are more likely than others to be in poverty: (i) fewer are employed; (ii) fewer have high earnings and more have low earnings; (iii) more hours tend to be worked to secure the same earnings; and (iv) slightly fewer have good conditions of work. These will be considered briefly in turn.

More people with than without disabilities are unemployed. In 1981, 16 per cent of the registered disabled, compared with 8 per cent of the workforce as a whole, were unemployed. Moreover, nearly three-fifths of the former, compared with a quarter of the latter, had been unemployed for more than a year. There were 72,000 unemployed registered disabled, and there were a further 102,000 unregistered disabled people registered as unemployed – making a total of 174,000. Of this huge total nearly half were under 45 (House of Commons, 1981). But these are official figures which depend on registration for unemployment, and there is research evidence that there are many more people with disabilities who would like to be employed and are capable of at least light or sheltered employment but who do not register for work. Thus, on the basis of a national survey, it was estimated that there were some 1,220,000 men and 1,870,000 women under 65 with some, appreciable or severe incapacity. The latter figure becomes 1,245,000 if women aged 60-64 are excluded. Those unemployed comprised 28 per cent of men, and 56 per cent of women. Table 3.2 gives these estimates in more detail (they are subject to large sampling errors but are derived from a sample of the entire population, and broadly correspond with the General Household Survey figures on 'limiting long-standing illness'). Two important conclusions may be drawn from this evidence: fewer than half the employed disabled were registered; and the rate of unemployment among people with

Extract (pp 57-63) from Townsend, P. (1981) 'Employment and disability', in A. Walker and P. Townsend (eds) *Disability in Britain*, Oxford: Martin Robertson.

disabilities was much higher, even before the rapid rise in unemployment in the late 1970s, than among the rest of the population of working age.

In the national study described in these pages, the earnings of the disabled worker were significantly lower than of the non-disabled (for supporting evidence see also Harris et al, 1972; Royal Commission on the Distribution of Income and Wealth, 1978; Layard et al, 1978). According to alternative definitions of disablement, more of the disabled than non-disabled had relatively low earnings, and fewer had relatively high earnings for the year as a whole. The degree of disablement was also related to the level of earnings. More of the severely than of the less severely incapacitated had low earnings. There was little suggestion that lower earnings were a function of fewer working hours. Slightly more of the incapacitated than of the non-incapacitated worked under 30 hours a week. The great majority worked as many hours as the rest of the working population, and as many as a quarter of the men worked more than 50 hours. When earnings were related to hours both disabled men and disabled women were found to have a lower rate of earnings. For people working indoors, conditions of work could also be compared. Ten features of work were listed: (i) sufficient heating; (ii) availability of tea and coffee; (iii) indoor flush w.c.; (iv) facilities for washing or changing; (v) place to buy lunch or eat sandwiches; (vi) place to keep coat and other articles; (vii) safe place to keep personal items; (viii) availability of first aid; (ix) availability of phone; (x) raise or lower lighting over work. Fewer incapacitated than non-incapacitated people enjoyed all or nearly all of these facilities.

This preliminary exploration of the work situation of people with disabilities needs to be greatly extended. There is growing interest in access for physically disabled people but little hard information about the difficulties under which so many people labour, and the modifications – to premises, machinery and working routines – which could be made at little or no cost.

## The specialised problems of employment

People with certain forms of disability have especially severe problems in obtaining, and keeping, employment. This is true, for example, of the blind and partially sighted (Reid, 1975), the deaf and hard of hearing (Loach, 1976), and people with epilepsy and multiple sclerosis (Davoud and Kettle, 1981). But it applies with particular force to people with mental handicap or with mental illness (see, for example, Shearer, 1981; Hughes, 1978; McCowen and Wilder, 1975). To be effective, an overall employment policy would have to be addressed to different categories of the disabled population.

The need to build special components into any general policy becomes evident when the problems experienced at particular stages in the development of disability or illness, or stages in the life cycle are examined. Thus youthful disabilities interrupt or restrict education and make the acquisition of skills and qualifications difficult (Buckle, 1971; Blaxter, 1976). There are major problems of adjustment in cases where short-term disease turns into long-term disability, or where disease is progressively disabling (Martin and Morgan, 1976). There is the question of relating degree of disablement to 'intensity' or level of employment – usually expressed in the terminology of 'open' employment, sheltered workshops, home work and occupational therapy or pastimes. There is the particularly acute question of what opportunities for rehabilitation exist for those recovering from damaging disease or injury. Ex-hospital patients, especially if they have been psychiatric patients, have major obstacles to surmount, and there is clear evidence of the difficulties of re-establishment in employment and community. Attention has been called, for example, to the problem of the single and homeless living in lodging-house areas of the major cities (McCowan and Wilder, 1975).

What stands out from the evidence is the need for accompanying measures – basic cash allowances, accommodation, perhaps certain services, and continuing social support, sometimes by means of support for the family – if ex-patients are to be re-established in employment. What also stands out is the simultaneous need to reduce derogatory labelling of people with disabilities and enhance their prospects of moving from protected to less protected forms of employment as they recover or learn to accommodate disability in employment. Research workers have called attention to the stigmatising effects sometimes of working in sheltered workshops, so that the opportunity to move on to 'open' employment rarely arises (Blaxter, 1976, pp 175-180). These problems seem to apply alike to employment rehabilitation centres, blind workshops, local authority workshops and training centres, and Remploy (for further discussion see Jordan, 1979).

Many of these problems apply acutely to women. Only recently have the occupational and employment problems of women with disabilities begun to be taken seriously. Indeed, if the Tomlinson, Piercy and Tunbridge Reports in the period 1943-72 and the Department of Employment and MSC reviews during 1973-81 are studied, there are barely any references at all to their problems. Yet, as Tables 3.1 and 3.2 show, the number of women with disabilities of economically active age and the levels of unemployment among them are much higher than among men. Since the mid-1970s the growing activities of the women's movement, and the concern expressed about disabled married women in particular, have begun to awaken public interest in this major feature of the employment problem (Loach, 1977; Loach and Lister, 1978; Glendinning, 1980 and 1981; Campling, 1981).

**Table 3.1:** Estimated number of people of economically active age (in private households) with disabilities in the UK (1969) (thousands)

| Sex | Age | With appreciable or severe disability[a] | With some, appreciable or severe disability[b] | With one or more disablement conditions which limit activities[c] |
|---|---|---|---|---|
| Males | 15-40 | 75 | 240 | 450 |
| | 40-49 | 80 | 250 | 265 |
| | 50-59 | 200 | 460 | 570 |
| | 60-64 | 120 | 320 | 320 |
| | All adults under 65 | 475 | 1,270 | 1,605 |
| Females | 15-40 | 90 | 295 | 755 |
| | 40-49 | 70 | 330 | 490 |
| | 50-59 | 220 | 630 | 670 |
| | 60-64 | 285 | 600 | 455 |
| | All adults under 65 | 665 | 1,855 | 2,370 |
| Males and females | 15-40 | 165 | 535 | 1,205 |
| | 40-49 | 150 | 580 | 755 |
| | 50-59 | 420 | 1,090 | 1,240 |
| | 60-64 | 405 | 920 | 775 |
| | All adults under 65 | 1,140 | 3,125 | 3,975 |

[a] On the basis of nine criteria on self-care and household care.
[b] Note that the estimates in the first column are included in this wider category.
[c] Based on questions about handicapping conditions, together with check list.
*Source:* Townsend (1979), pp. 1049 and 1050.

**Table 3.2:** Estimated numbers of men and women with some, appreciable or severe incapacity who are employed and not employed, UK (1969) (thousands)

| Age | Men | | Women | | Men and Women | |
|---|---|---|---|---|---|---|
| | Employed | Not employed | Employed | Not employed | Employed | Not employed |
| 15-29 | 80 | 40 | 75 | 85 | 155 | 125 |
| 30-39 | 65 | 25 | 80 | 35 | 145 | 60 |
| 40-49 | 200 | 45 | 175 | 155 | 375 | 200 |
| 50-59 | 310 | 135 | 220 | 420 | 430 | 555 |
| 60-64 | 220 | 100 | 110 | 515 | 330 | 615 |
| | 875 | 345 | 660 | 1,210 | 1,535 | 1,555 |

*Source:* Townsend (1979), p 1055.

## The difference of view between people with disabilities and the bureaucracy

The problem of unemployment among people with disabilities is therefore larger, and more complex, in relation to communities and workforces, than is acknowledged in government discussions and statements of policy. This needs to be fully understood and absorbed if an effective alternative policy is ever to be developed. For the truth is that a narrow, uninformed, and indeed unsympathetic bureaucratic view about employment for people with disabilities has evolved, regrettably, during the 1970s and early 1980s. This centres on government management of the quota scheme and the discussion of possible alternatives, and will be briefly explained. It is of course a specific example of theories of the development of the 'corporate state' and of the 'bureau-professional' (see, for example, Cockburn, 1978; Parry *et al*, 1979).

In the early 1970s, the Department of Employment decided to review its services for disabled people and in 1973 published a consultative document on the quota scheme (Department of Employment, 1973a). This concluded that the scheme was now 'less relevant' than it had been, was 'a considerable administrative burden both for the employer and the Department', used resources which 'might perhaps be better employed on behalf of disabled people in other ways' and meant that the Department was both 'salesman and policeman'. In any event, disabled people were losing faith in the scheme; fewer were registering and there was 'no positive evidence' that the scheme exerted 'a significant effect on the prospects of individual disabled people'.

> Finally, it can be argued that compulsion in this field is no longer relevant, desirable or practicable and that the quota scheme should therefore be abolished and resources concentrated on improving the employment and training services available to disabled people; both by ensuring that they share the benefits that will accrue from the modernisation of the general employment service and the expansion of general training facilities; and by improving the specialised employment and training facilities provided for disabled people. This would avoid the need to continue labelling disabled people as such; improve the relationship between the Department and employers in this field; make it easier to develop their goodwill; and give the DROs and BPROs more time to devote to their clients, to visit employers and to liaise with hospitals. [Department of Employment, 1973b, pp 30–32]

Although the document included a subsequent reference to the possibility that the quota might nonetheless exert some influence on employers to engage and retain people with disabilities, there is little doubt that the Department of Employment was pressing for the abolition of the scheme. However, its document was not welcomed by many organisations and, after due deliberation, the Minister announced in 1975 that the scheme would be retained. In 1976 this decision was upheld by an authoritative working party, chaired by Lord Snowdon, which has set up a sub-committee to produce a report on employment – ' We believe that a statutory framework along the present lines is vital if the employment of the disabled is to be kept to the fore as a specific objective of employment policy'. The Working Party sub-committee went on to propose the introduction of a levy/grant system and various financial incentives to make the quota scheme work (Snowdon Working Party, 1976, pp 21-29).

But in the late 1970s the civil servants returned to their dislike in principle of the quota scheme. In 1979 the Manpower Services Commission published a discussion document, very much in the spirit of the 1973 review, inviting submissions from interested parties (MSC, 1979). Again, this document attracted considerable criticism from a variety of bodies representing people with disabilities (see, for example, the letter from the General Secretary of the Royal British Legion, *The Times*, 8 September 1980; and the Disability Alliance, 1980). Despite this criticism, the Manpower Services Commission stuck to their guns and in July 1981 formally recommended the substitution of the statutory quota scheme by a 'statutory general duty on employers requiring them to "take reasonable steps to promote equality of opportunity in employment for disabled people"', together with a code of practice and a continuation of educational and other measures designed to persuade employers to improve opportunities for disabled people (MSC, 1981).

**References**

Blaxter, M. (1976) *The meaning of disability*, London: Heinemann.

Buckle, J.R. (1971) *Work and housing of impaired persons in Great Britain*, London: HMSO.

Campling, J. (1981) *Images of ourselves*, London: Routledge.

Cockburn, C. (1978) *The local state*, London: Pluto Press.

Davoud, N. and Kettle, M. (1981) *Multiple Sclerosis and its effects upon employment*, London: Multiple Sclerosis Society.

Department of Employment (1973a) *The quota scheme for disabled people*, London: DE.

Department of Employment (1973b) *Sheltered employment for disabled people*, London: DE.

Disability Alliance (1980) *Comments on the MSC's discussion document: The quota scheme for the employment of disabled people*, London: Disability Alliance.

Glendinning, C. (1980) *After working all these years*, London: Disability Alliance.

Glendinning, C. (1981) 'Married women and disability: the long campaign for equal treatment', *Poverty*, No 48.

Harris, A.I., Smith, C.R.W. and Head, E. (1972) *Income and entitlement to supplementary benefit of impaired people in Great Britain*, London: HMSO.

House of Commons (1981) *Hansard*, 5 August.

Hughes, D. (1978) *How psychiatric patients manage out of hospital*, London: Disability Alliance.

Jordan, D. (1979) *A new employment programme wanted for disabled people*, London: Disability Alliance and Low Pay Unit.

Layard, R., Piachaud, D. and Stewart, M. (1978) *The causes of poverty*, London: HMSO.

Loach, I. (1976) *The price of deafness*, London: Disability Alliance.

Loach, I. and Lister, R. (1978) *Second class disabled*, London: Disability Alliance.

McCowen, P. and Wilder, J. (1975) *Lifestyle of 100 psychiatric patients*, London: Psychiatric Rehabilitation Association.

Martin, J. and Morgan, M. (1976) *Prolonged sickness and the return to work*, London: HMSO.

MSC (1979) *The quota scheme for the employment of disabled people – A discussion document*, London: MSC.

MSC (1981) *Report of a Review of the Quota Scheme for the Employment of Disabled People*, London, MSC.

Parry, N. *et al* (1979) *Social work, welfare and the state*, London: Hodder Arnold.

Reid, F. (1975) *The incomes of the blind*, London: Disability Alliance.

Royal Commission on the Distribution of Income and Wealth (1978) *Report No 6: Lower incomes*, Cmnd 7175, London: HMSO.

Shearer, A. (1981) *Disability: Whose handicap?*, Oxford: Basil Blackwell.

Snowdon Working Party (1976) *Integrating the disabled*, London: National Fund for Research into Crippling Diseases.

Townsend, P. (1979) *Poverty in the United Kingdom*, London: Allen Lane.

# 49

# The political sociology of mental handicap

It is commonly agreed that there is a crisis in Britain in the services for the mentally handicapped. Instances of bad treatment of patients in hospital, poor conditions, and understaffing in many wards have been revealed and have attracted wide publicity. Different solutions to the problems have been canvassed. None has yet been put into effect. This may be surprising to some people in view of the seriousness of the problems, the concern of the public and of medical, nursing and other staff, and the avowed intentions of Ministers in successive governments to put things right. How can our failure to do more in the last two years and to adopt and unambiguously specific policy be explained? My purpose is to analyse some of the structural and political factors standing in the way of a swift improvement of services and of the quality of life enjoyed by the handicapped. Political sociology has come to be differentiated from political science principally because of the sociologist's emphasis on the social aspects, both informal and formal, of political behaviour and political institutions. Political acts are those which determine the fate of men other than the actors. They are sanctioned not only by law but by custom and structural situation. The fate of the mentally handicapped is determined not just by Parliament, Ministers of State and local councils, but by the powers entrusted in or assumed by all those caring for them. The sociologist's interest in 'bureaucracy' and 'organization' leads him to investigate special problems like those of rough treatment in hospitals. But he tends to review social control in terms both of internal structure and external relationships.

The problem of understanding the gap between aims and performance is not, of course, peculiar to Britain. The deprivation which many of the handicapped experience, relative to the living standards in the societies to which they belong, is an international phenomenon. This continues to be so, even when powerful lobbies gradually arise to press for improvements. At the same time it is important to understand that conditions may not be uniformly bad. There is considerable variation in quality in many different systems, whether of firms, schools or hospitals. There are new hospitals as at Northgate in England as well as those 50 or 100 years old. Similarly, there

---

Townsend, P. (1973) 'The political sociology of mental handicap: a case-study of failure in policy', in *The social minority*, London: Allen Lane, pp 196–207.

are new hospitals in Denmark, such as Vangede and Lillemosegard, with high standards of material provision, but other hospitals like Ebborogard, in North Zeeland, which are 75 years old[1]. In any national system there are elements which tend to become showpieces for international display or placatory gestures to the best elements among the professional staff, rather than models which can be and are designed to become standard practice within a very short span of time. Variation in conditions is perhaps wider in Britain than in some countries. For instance, more buildings seem to have been adapted from other uses and embellished with annexes and architects' follies. This gives the sub-communities who live in them a certain distinctiveness from the rest of the hospital population. I have been in hospitals and other institutions in the United States and on the Continent with worse living quarters and stricter custodial regimes than any I have seen in Britain.

## Ministerial initiative to deal with a scandal

Britain's experience in the last two years, then, is an instructive example to study in order to understand why the problems of the mentally handicapped are so difficult to solve in any society. For it was two years ago this month that the report of an independent committee of inquiry into allegations of ill-treatment of patients in a Welsh hospital was published, and provoked immediate public anxiety[2]. Official inquiries are conducted from time to time but rarely made public. After allegations had been published in a Sunday newspaper in 1967 a committee was set up under Sir Geoffrey Howe, Q.C. (now Solicitor General in the Conservative Government) towards the end of that year. The committee completed its hearing in early 1968[3]. While there it must clearly have become the subject of acute controversy. To his credit, Mr R.H.S. Crossman, the Secretary of State for Social Services, who became responsible for the amalgamated Department of Health and Social Security in the late summer of 1968, decided that the report should be published. It appeared in March 1969. The nature of the report should be clearly understood. It did not just find certain members of staff at fault in their treatment of patients but traced responsibility through the senior nursing staff to the chief male nurse, the physician superintendent, the Hospital Management Committee and its officers, the Regional Hospital Board and, finally, the administrative structure of the National Health Service itself, including the authority exercised by the Minister. Junior staff were to some extent the victims of an inadequate system and of inadequate resources provided by the Government, the Boards and local authorities to that system.

> The present tripartite administrative structure of the National Health Service has failed, so far as Ely is concerned, to produce a

sufficiently integrated service and pattern of care for the mentally subnormal. The concept of community care has been insufficiently developed.[4]

The Secretary of State then began to develop this theme with great energy. Recently I have studied afresh many of the press reports for 1969, 1970 and 1971. I would be surprised if there is any period in the history of Britain or any other country, even in the United States during President Kennedy's patronage of the issue, when the needs of the mentally handicapped have attracted greater public attention and sympathy. Having established a public bridgehead why was this advance not then consolidated?

It would, of course, be possible to give a narrative history at length. Mr Crossman visited hospitals, gave speeches and held press conferences throughout the country. He was applauded in Parliament for demonstrating in detail what he called the 'underprivilege' of the mentally handicapped inside and outside hospitals[5]. In April 1969 he set up a working party to advise him on policy. By coincidence, soon afterwards Dr Pauline Morris's national survey of hospitals, which had been financed by the National Society for Mentally Handicapped Children, was published. It reinforced with a wealth of factual evidence the case for reorganization of services[6]. Valuable information was becoming available also from Professor Tizard's and Dr Kushlick's research studies[7]. Instances of ill-treatment at other hospitals came to light and were the subject of court cases. It will, of course, be many years before the full history of this period can be written. The Official Secrets Act prevents part of the story from being given. However, it is evident that the momentum was not sustained. A detailed statement of policy was delayed, first during the final six months of the Labour Government and then for the first nine months (so far) of the new Tory Government[8].

## Early contradiction in policy

In retrospect I think it can be shown that under both Governments, and very early in the crisis, a fundamental contradiction in policy emerged. Both Mr Crossman and Sir Keith Joseph have pursued simultaneously two policies, on the one hand diminishing and on the other increasing the already large role played by hospitals in the total system of services for the handicapped. On 18 June 1969, for example, Mr Crossman said, 'My own top priority in the hospital service at present is to divert more resources to the long-stay hospitals which, I fear, have in the past often been a deprived sector of the hospital service'[9]. However, on 25 September 1969, for example, he said, 'The basic policy will have to be that never again do we pile up human rejects behind these high walls'[10], and on other occasions added that there were thousands of the 60,000 long-stay patients who could live outside if there were places for them[11]. Although no doubt Mr Crossman, Sir Keith Joseph and others would argue that it is possible to reconcile both objectives I do not believe they have insisted on spelling out the implications in full. Had they done so the contradiction would have become more apparent.

This contradiction has its roots in the structural contradictions of the management of the health and welfare services and in society itself. We have to draw on both political sociology and the sociology of communities for aid in constructing explanations. There are formal limitations on the powers of the Secretary of State which can largely obstruct him from putting into effect certain policies. To these can be added informal limitations as well − in terms of personnel, procedures and communications. There is a long chain of command down through the Regional Boards, Hospital Management Committees and hospitals, buttressed by Exchequer control of finance. The length of the chain and the weaknesses in some of its links make difficult the adoption and implementation in hospitals of new policies. The management committees badly need strengthening. Resolute policies can evaporate halfway down the hierarchy[12]. Moreover, a country which sets considerable store in the principles of local democracy and family self-determination is bound to find it difficult to accommodate a hierarchical system of this kind.

Secondly, control over the local authorities is indirect. Ministers can enforce statutory regulations, inspect, exhort and tempt in a variety of ways. But their powers are emasculated in part by the lack of authority over staff, by lack of forms of specific grant and subsidy (especially since the percentage grant system was withdrawn) and by the cultural convention that local councils are supposed to have a very large measure of independence. Moreover, when all or nearly all local services can be shown to be starved of resources a Minister is likely to be inhibited from pressing his own particular claim too strongly. It would not have been surprising if Mr Crossman had been forced to conclude that the most important part of any new policy needing to be developed was ruled out because he was powerless to put it into execution. Even exhortation may have seemed impossible. During the campaign Mr Crossman was reported to have called all the Regional Hospital Board chairmen to meetings. To call together the representatives of nearly 200 local authorities in England and Wales must have seemed much less manageable. In any analysis of the distribution of power to determine the fate of men the cumulative effect of leaving out a key element at many stages of discussion and policy-making has to be remembered. Throughout 1969 and 1970 neither of the successive Secretaries of State could have been fully appraised of the importance of the community care services in any strategy. Even in the Department of Health itself the Secretary of State cannot be said to have an administrative staff which includes powerful representation in numbers and expertise of their interests. The same might be said of research. Those conducting research for the Hospital Boards are bound to have a different orientation to the mentally handicapped than if they had been working for the local authorities.

Thirdly, any proposed change of policy which appears to threaten the interests of bodies holding considerable power is likely to be resisted and to be diverted to those interests. The Secretary of State was indicating changes which might weaken the far-ranging authority of the nursing and medical professions, particularly those branches of the professions concerned with the long-stay hospitals for the mentally handicapped. Politicians and others called attention to the social and occupational needs of patients and therefore to the appointment of far more specialist staff, such as social workers, and occupational therapists, the introduction of volunteers from the community and the encouragement of patients to visit and work in the outside community. The call to reduce hospital numbers came not only from the Government benches but also from the Opposition[13]. There was a classical reaction on the part of nursing staff and medical superintendents. They closed ranks. All that was required, they said, was better resources and an end to the hurtful smears which sapped morale and endangered staff recruitment. Far from being run down the hospitals should be re-created and developed as centres of excellence, upon which the services for the community as well as the inmates could be based. Because so few staff work for the handicapped outside hospital and are also poorly organized, and because the nursing and medical staffs are dominant inside these hospitals and can bring pressure to bear on the Department of Health through a range of committees, it is not surprising that they were so successful in opposing the announcement of a new kind of policy.

Fourthly, the act of isolating mentally handicapped people, usually in large institutions, is also a political act. It confers greater power than perhaps we suspect on certain people but also certain ideas and values. The staff determine every detail of life of patients to an extent which is unrivalled in, say, the most paternalistic firm. This creates special problems for staff as well as patients. But this conferment of power has other effects. Physically we create populations which are fundamentally different from any local community. In structure they do not consist of three or four generations, with very small family units, and complex social and occupational networks, which are in personal contact with a wide range of different public services. It would be misleading to suggest that they are 'communities' in any ordinary sense of that term. Scientifically they do not satisfy certain conditions which might be laid down for rural and urban communities[14]. As a consequence the system of political authority is much more oppressive for the patients. Compared with members of rural or urban communities they have fewer alternative groups to which to escape if the one in which they spend most of their time makes them feel unwanted or uncomfortable. There are fewer alternative channels of complaint, fewer alternative political agents to proselytize their interests and fewer possessions and less space in which to manoeuvre to show personal authority and independence. The individual patient is politically weak and vulnerable. It is important for us to understand that the very existence of the long-stay hospital shapes our concepts of mental handicap itself, our values, our fears and even our willingness to assume that the problem is one primarily for medicine and nursing[15].

## The structural factors obstructing reform

These four structural factors in the distribution of power over the fates of the mentally handicapped – the despotic but also fragile chain of command from Government and Secretary of State to individual hospital and ward; the restricted power of the central Government over the local authority; the concentration of real power over the handicapped upon hospital medical and nursing staffs, and the separation in space of ghettos for the mentally handicapped – seem to me to be the crucial factors in explaining the failure of policy to match needs. For nothing effective to alter them was introduced during 1969-70. They are the fundamental political obstacles to improvement of services. These four factors in the political sociology of mental handicap help to explain why the radical policy which might have emerged in 1969 shows even less signs of emerging now. A more subtle and powerfully planned strategy to overcome each obstacle would be required. Instead, they were reinforced. At the end of 1969, for example, the Government announced certain stop-gap measures to spend money on food and furnishings in hospitals and build pre-fabricated units. The sums committed were not large by national standards[16] and do not seem to have resulted in other than minor improvements[17]. The statement unfortunately weakened the demand for major measures to meet the crisis, and the pre-fabricated units have clearly been a mixed blessing. The need to reduce the hospital service in scale by rapidly building up local authority services and change its nature, by developing occupational and social therapy and introducing a new system of staffing, was quietly forgotten or at least postponed. As a consequence, policy was distorted into something almost the opposite of what was intended and radical reforms became much harder to introduce. This was a strategic mistake of the first order.

Nor should we ignore the impact that these changes might have wrought on the images of mental handicap held by first the medical and associated professions and secondly by other key groups in society – politicians, senior civil servants in the Department of Health and Social Security and organizations representing the interests of the mentally handicapped. By excluding mental handicap from having any substantial part in the medical curriculum the teaching hospitals have done notable disservice to the interest of the handicapped. The lack of adequate study and research has helped to perpetuate images of the mentally handicapped as incomplete persons and hence exposed them to custodial and authoritarian attitudes. All this can only gradually be undermined and replaced. Action on the four structural factors can accelerate the process.

## Three solutions

Various attempts to rationalize the crisis are still being made. I shall refer briefly to three – the fake 'normalization' solution, the Central Board solution and the hostel solution. In Britain, as in other countries, great emphasis has been placed in recent years on policies which allow the mentally handicapped to lead a normal life. Thus 'normalization' has been defined as 'making available to the mentally retarded patterns and conditions of everyday life which are as close as possible to the norms and patterns of the mainstream of society'. This would allow them to sleep in a private bedroom, mix easily with people of both sexes, eat breakfast in a small group, have considerable choice in clothing and leisure-time pursuits and leave home each day for a place of work where they earned wages[18]. The Government has broadly supported this thesis[19]. But much depends on how it is interpreted and worked out. It can, of course, be distorted.

Dr H.C. Gunzberg and others have seized on the concept of 'normalization' and invested it with a peculiar meaning partly, it would seem, to justify power being left with the hospitals. The term is, of course, a dreadful piece of jargon used to express an idea almost as old as man himself, namely that he should lead as normal a life as possible. But the elaboration of the concept seems to bear little relationship to our knowledge of human relationships. For example, no attempt is made to discuss the kinds of group within which individuals learn and practice the ordinary skills of living and whether the hospital can even in principle create the conditions necessary to offer the same opportunities. The family and the private household are, after all, very intimate units in social and emotional terms and their complex qualities are not easy to reproduce. If we were to attempt to investigate how to do so we would have to draw extensively upon social psychology and sociology. But the huge literature on family relationships, community behaviour and the socialization of the child is almost ignored by latter-day adherents of the view that the hospital is omnipotent. Dr Gunzberg argues that the hospital 'should be recognized to become a preparatory stage before placement in normal conditions'. He asserts that it can 'normalize' people although he admits that it is 'not normal in itself'[20]. This seems to me to be a very damaging admission. It is rather like suggesting that if you want to teach a child what it is to follow a normal family life you cannot do better than to commit him to the care of parents who are far from being normal. One wonders why it is necessary in the first place to remove many handicapped people from the family and the community if hospital would find it so difficult to reproduce their benefits. Dr Gunzberg does not pursue the implications of introducing more training, employment and social education for a 'hospital', its staffing and staff training, nor does he analyse numbers of patients involved in the different activities. This is especially important since he admits that there will continue to be many patients who will have to be protected from 'the mainstream of society'. Throughout history the rehabilitation ward, the therapeutic community, and similar experiments have in part served as distractions from the fact that most long-stay institutions have essentially negative functions. The study by Julius Roth and Elizabeth Eddy of the myth of rehabilitation in the institution on Welfare Island in New York stands as a warning to all those who suppose that a form of institutional service fulfils a laudable function when in reality the function applies to a tiny minority of patients and amounts to an elaborate deceit not properly grasped by the public or even by all the staff. Unless words are to be drained of all meaning, 'normalization' can only mean the gradual abandonment of the hospital as the principal agent of caring for the handicapped. This is in fact the central idea of some experts overseas whose conception of 'normalization' is very different from that discussed by Dr Gunzberg[21].

A Central Board for the mentally handicapped on the model of those in Denmark and Sweden is currently regarded by some people in Britain as offering an alternative solution to all problems. They believe it would help to release much bigger resources for the mentally handicapped. But similar administrative forms play different functions in different countries. There are arguments from principle against such a change – for example that this would almost automatically give too much reliance to institutions in the overall system of care, make more difficult the sharing of responsibility with parents and the community, strengthen the already considerable powers of the professions, and reduce efficiency by hiving off certain kinds of services which are needed as much for the physically handicapped and elderly as the mentally handicapped. Some problems would therefore be solved at the expense of creating others. There are also arguments from history. Britain had a Central Board of Control which was wound up by stages in 1948 and 1959 – although with the benefit of hindsight it might have been preferable to place the service, like residential and welfare services for old people and the disabled, under the entire jurisdiction of local authorities. Moreover, the Kilbrandon and Seebohm Reports have led to acts of Parliament integrating the local personal social services. No country would easily contemplate the dismantling of legislation so soon after enacting it.

The argument for hostels as a substitute for hospitals has to be developed carefully and questioned critically at each stage. If hostels are remote from urban centres, unintegrated with any local community and managed in an authoritarian way they can suffer from most of the disadvantages of existing hospitals together with other disadvantages as well. It is social structure and organization that is important. Private households, sheltered housing, local authority hostels, hospital hostels and large hospitals form a continuum of domestic and social organization. Measures of intelligence and other abilities among the mentally handicapped show that the majority do not fall far short of the mean in the normal distribution. My implication is that the domestic unit in which they live should also be close to a private household. The development of small children's Homes, with six or seven children and houseparents, is a model which comes close to the ordinary family household. It is this which Dr Grunwald has in mind for the mentally handicapped[22]. In British cultural terms this would be an extension to the mental handicap series of practice not only in large parts of the children's service but the services for old people and the disabled. In recent years local authorities have rapidly developed sheltered housing for small groups of elderly and disabled people. They can be placed in localities with which they are familiar and within easy distance of family and friends. Adapted or new flatlets or converted houses could be developed on the same model for mentally handicapped adults. The danger of the hostel of say 25 or 50 places, from a strictly sociological point of view, is that it is not a household, a hospital, a family or a community.

This is not the place to elaborate alternative policy. If we were to confront the major obstacles which I have tried to identify we would need to adopt a programme of reducing overcrowding in hospitals, rapidly increasing sheltered housing, day centres and workshops in the community, by introducing a new percentage grant, or a five-year centrally financed community care programme to balance the reduction of the subnormality hospitals' share of the total costs of the National Health Service. Many other strategies would have to be pursued – such as the association of parents and local representatives with management of staff of hospitals and hostels, and the training of new types of community work staff to support and advise the family. This amounts to a complicated redistribution of power. I have argued that the forces accounting for the present impasse lie deep. But the Government is now exhibiting moral cowardice. Only by putting its considerable weight unambiguously behind this central policy can the nation begin to resolve the crisis of the last two years.

**Endnotes**

[1] See Shearer, A., *The Quality of Care. Report of A Study Tour in Denmark*, National Society for Mentally Handicapped Children, 1971. Whether there are similar variations in, say, the U.S.S.R., is problematical. Certainly there are first-hand international accounts of very good standards of treatment and staffing in 'children's houses' for the severely subnormal. See Boom, A.B., 'Children's House No. 15 for

Severely Subnormal Children', in Segal, S.S., *Backward Children in the U.S.S.R.*, Leeds, Arnold, 1966.

[2] *Report of the Committee of Inquiry into Allegations of Ill-Treatment of Patients and Other Irregularities at the Ely Hospital, Cardiff,* Cmnd. 3957, H.M.S.O., March 1969.

[3] The proceedings were clearly treated as a matter of urgency and evidence was last heard on 23 February 1968 (Report, p. 8). Reference is made (Report, p. 105) to the fact that 'the recommendations of a Special Sub-Committee have been adopted (*to come* into effect on 1 April 1968)' [my italics], which suggests that the report was completed in the spring. I also understand that the Department of Health requested the committee more than once to shorten its report.

[4] *Report of the Committee of Inquiry into Allegations of Ill-Treatment of Patients and Other Irregularities at the Ely Hospital, Cardiff,* Cmnd. 3957, H.M.S.O., March 1969.

[5] For example, on 11 February 1970: 'In 1968 43 per cent of patients in hospitals for the mentally handicapped were in wards of more than 50 beds and 58 per cent had less than 58 square feet of bedspace. Thirty-one percent had no lockers ... The minimum standard is far below the minimum standard we set ourselves way before I was Minister...' . The difference in costs for acute and mentally handicapped patients was 'inexplicable except on the grounds of underprivilege'. *The Times*, 12 February 1970.

[6] Morris, P. *Put Away*, Routledge and Kegan Paul, 1969.

[7] Tizard, J., *Community Services for the Mentally Handicapped*, Oxford University Press, 1964; Tizard, J., King, R.D., Raynes, N.V., and Yule, W., 'The Care and Treatment of Subnormal Children in Residential Institutions', *Proceedings Association for Special Education*, 1966; Kushlick, A. and Cox, G., 'The Ascertained Prevalence of Mental Subnormality in the Wessex Region on 1 July 1963', *Proceedings of the First Congress of the International Association for the Scientific Study of Mental Deficiency*, Montpelier, September 1967.

[8] [A Government White Paper was published in June 1971...]

[9] In a speech (in the event read for him) to the Annual Conference of the Association of Hospital Management Committees at Weston-super-Mare.

[10] The *Guardian*, 25 September 1969.

[11] ibid., 16 April 1970.

[12] The Ely Report gives instances of the local H.M.C. failing even to see major Government circulars about policy, op. cit. p. 106.

[13] For example, Lord Balniel, the Opposition spokesman on health and social security, stated in Parliament on 11 February 1970 that 'At least half of the 60,000 patients in subnormality hospitals are not in need of constant nursing care at all although they need some kind of residential care. The emphasis should be on development of domiciliary services.'

[14] See the review of meanings of 'community' by Stacey, M., 'The Myth of Community Studies', *British Journal of Sociology*, June 1969.

[15] The point has not escaped research workers. For example, 'Treating the institution as if it were primarily a hospital introduces at the outset an obstacle to thinking about how it may best be used to serve the inmates', Roth, J.A., and Eddy, E.M., *Rehabilitation for the Unwanted*, New York, Atherton, 1967, p. 205.

[16] In the financial year 1969-70 Regional Hospital Boards were believed to have been persuaded to re-allocate £2 million to long-stay hospitals from other uses. For the financial year 1970-71 the Government announced a further £3 million for these hospitals (or 7.3 per cent) but more than half of this would have been allocated in any case, since health service expenditure increases regularly each year, and current expenditure on all kinds of hospitals was planned to increase by 3.7 per cent at 1969 prices anyway. See Serota, Baroness, in *Subnormality in the Seventies, The Road to Community Care*, National Society for Mentally Handicapped Children, 1970, p. 5; and also *Public Expenditure 1968-9 to 1973-4*, Cmnd. 4234, H.M.S.O., December 1969, p. 52.

[17] For example, press reports on the first pre-fabricated units to relieve over-crowding have called attention to the relatively ungenerous space and facilities. See also the reservation by Kushlick, A., 'Residential Care for the Mentally Subnormal', *Royal Society of Health Journal*, September/October 1970, pp. 260-61.

[18] Nirje, B., 'Normalization', *The Journal of Mental Subnormality*, December 1970, p. 62, and Nirje, B., 'The Normalization Principle and its Human Management Implications', in Kuegel, R., and Wolfersberger, W., *Changing Patterns in Residential Services for the Mentally Retarded*, Presidential Commission on Mental Retardation, Washington, 1969.

[19] Most recently in the White Paper, *Better Services for the Mentally Handicapped*, Cmnd. 4683, H.M.S.O., 1971. For example, the White Paper asks for help and understanding to give the mentally handicapped person 'as nearly a normal life as his handicap or handicaps permit' as one of the principles on which services should be based (para. 40).

[20] Gunzberg, H.C., 'The Hospital as a Normalizing Training Environment', *The Journal of Mental Subnormality*, December 1970, pp. 71-2.

[21] See, for example, the work of Dr Grunewald from Sweden. In particular, he stresses the small group home for an average of seven people. Grunewald, K., 'The Guiding Environment: The Dynamic of Residential Living', Conference on *Action for the Retarded*, 28 March 1971 (publication forthcoming).

[22] Conditions in Sweden are in any case much more favourable to the handicapped than in Britain. For example, only 11 per cent of those in any form of residential care are in hospitals. Practically half of the mentally handicapped sleep in single rooms and altogether 97 per cent are in bedrooms with four beds or fewer.

# 50

# The disabled need help

It is now two years since the Disablement Income Group presented a memorandum to the cabinet minister then responsible for co-ordinating the social services, Douglas Houghton, arguing strongly for the introduction in Britain of a disability pension of the kind operating in Sweden, where about 2 per cent of the adult population aged 16 to 65 receive such pensions.

It seemed then that the government was including the disabled in its much-vaunted long-term review of social security. Certainly references were made in ministerial speeches to the disabled, and indeed it is difficult to understand how any reform of social security, incorporating a national superannuation scheme, can make sense unless it provides for those who are obliged to retire early, many of whom are of course disabled.

Yet the Prime Minister himself wrote recently to the Disablement Income Group to say that the government could hold out no hopes of introducing fundamental changes to social security for the disabled in the near future but that the Ministry of Social Security was "considering the possibility" of undertaking research on the subject. This was dismal news, because it meant that although the government had become aware of the public's growing interest in the issue, it had made little or no progress in preparing, still less introducing, a reform.

No one should suppose, however, that the right solutions are conveniently at hand. Our state of ignorance is far greater even than with many other domestic political issues, and it would be wrong to build up expectations of early and decisive reform. First, there are no comprehensive national statistics about disability. Secondly, no country in the world has, so far as I am aware, yet devised an objective, consistent and practical method of linking degree of disability with amount of benefit. Thirdly, existing methods of integrating the disabled into society through employment and housing policies and community services have still to be properly assessed. Finally, there is the long job of schooling the right attitudes in the general public towards disability and so laying the final basis for genuine reform.

First, the lack of comprehensive national statistics about disability. Research studies now being undertaken by the Universities of Essex and London will produce some national figures, but much depends on whether certain kinds of mental handicap, as well as all forms of unrecognised and minor handicap, can be identified and counted without clinical examination, and it will be some time before the studies are completed. In the meantime all we can

Townsend, P. (1967) 'The disabled need help', *New Society*, 28 September.

reasonably conclude from scattered batches of statistics kept by government departments is that the total number in touch with official departments and services – allowing for duplication – is unlikely to be less than 1½ million, or 3 per cent of the population.

The different groups include around 650,000 on the Ministry of Labour's disabled persons register, 330,000 on the local authorities' registers for the handicapped, 160,000 subnormal and mentally ill persons living at home and another 200,000 chronically sick as well as subnormal and mentally ill in hospital, 76,000 handicapped children in special schools, 144,000 incapacitated persons at home who receive allowances from the Supplementary Benefits Commission and around 650,000 receiving industrial injury or war pensions.

What the total would be if we include disabled people who are not in touch with any of these services we can only guess. Research studies in Scandinavia suggest a rate of 6 per cent of adults under 65. In his letter to the Disablement Income Group the Prime Minister referred only to a possible inquiry about the number of the *physically* handicapped, and not to the chronically sick and mentally handicapped. It would be tragic if a narrow view were taken of disability in any official inquiry. Half the pensions paid in Sweden are for various forms of mental handicap.

Secondly, there is the problem of linking degree of disability with amount of benefit. Britain awards some benefits according to the place and circumstances where disability was first incurred, some according to contribution record, some according to present individual circumstances and some on test of means. The disablement pension under the war pension scheme for a major-general at the 100 per cent rate is £12 13s per week and for a private £6 15s. For some war disabled there are in addition unemployability supplements, constant attendance allowances, exceptionally severe disablement allowances, comforts allowances, allowances for lowered standard of occupation and age and clothing allowances.

The disablement pension under the industrial scheme is also £6 15s at the 100 per cent rate, and there are supplementary allowances too, though not quite as many as under the war pensions scheme. Men can draw full disablement pension while in full-time paid work, and can obtain sickness benefit in addition to the pension. But if a man who gained his disability, in effect, at work does not meet the conditions of eligibility for pension, he may receive nothing but sickness benefit, although paradoxically he is more severely incapacitated. And a man who is disabled outside his workplace gets no pension and has to depend on a basic rate of sickness benefit (currently £4, plus £2 10s for dependent wife).

A housewife may not even qualify for sickness benefit and may depend wholly on supplementary benefit on test of means. If her husband is in full-time work she may not be entitled to any benefit whatsoever. The new earnings-related benefits for the first six months of sickness and the new automatic supplement of 9s for those who have been receiving sickness benefits for two years have further complicated the problem of equity. And the list of anomalies does not end here. So far as the disabled are concerned Britain has an irrational patchwork and not a system of social security.

On what principles should a reformed system be built? Much has lately been heard of the means test – that it is no longer the scourge of the poor, that it can be applied in a still more civilised manner, and that it is the only method we can afford to help the poor. Last month the Minister of Labour, Ray Gunter, asked if emotional memories were "really relevant to what is a different world." Some cabinet ministers forget that historically the means test has played, and it continues to play, a crucial function in helping to maintain Britain's elaborate social hierarchy. Official methods of procedure in dealing with applications for assistance have certainly improved in recent years, particularly for old people, and this improvement is due more than many realise to the work behind the scenes of leading civil servants in the former National Assistance Board (now the Supplementary Benefits Commission). Nevertheless, it is doubtful whether the improvements have been greater than in most branches of consumer service.

At the present time, so far as the disabled and other groups are concerned, it can be argued that an extension of the means test would be wrong in principle, inefficient and impractical. What do ministers like Gunter mean? That the major-general's disablement pension should be reduced in line with his income? That the disablement pensioner who manages to secure paid employment should have his pension reduced, while another pensioner who stays at home continues to get the full rate? And if politically we hesitate to tamper with state benefits such as these, dare we use the word "principle" to explain our actions?

Applying the means test to the disabled is not in principle the right way of concentrating resources where they are most needed. For the important thing is not the measurement of their income as such, but their degree of disability, need of mechanical aids and transport, need of domestic and personal help and loss of earning power. Moreover, on the basis of all existing evidence, a means test would be inefficient because large numbers of people would not apply for allowances, and administrative assessments of means are very costly.

The computerised income test is still a pipe dream and what is critical to its future viability is not the throughput and output but source of information. *Who* is going to tell the computer the characteristics of the persons who live in the household and when their changes in circumstances occur, from week to week and month to month, as earnings fluctuate and children leave school and husbands become sick? Ultimately the flow of information about household income depends on the level of education, knowledge and motivation of members of the household.

Finally, the means test has little relevance to the disabled because the great majority of them have very low incomes. The basic need is for a general advance in their incomes. Sally Sainsbury's survey of persons on the registers of the local authorities in London, Middlesex and Essex showed that, in 1964-65, 60 per cent had a total income of less than £10 per week and 86 per cent altogether less than £20. A third of the households contained three or more persons. Three quarters had less than £50 savings.

As an alternative we should establish a right to benefit according to degree of disability and a right to supplementary benefits according to individual circumstances, not means. This would be a two-tiered system. The fundamental question is that of defining degree of disability. Many countries, including the United States, the Soviet Union and Sweden, base their systems on the principle of earning capacity or limitation of earning power. In Britain this principle only operates for supplementary allowances – the special hardship allowance in the case of the industrial injuries scheme, and the allowance for lowered standard of occupation in the case of the war pensions scheme. Sometimes, the principle seems to make good sense. It seems to be applicable to a man who is injured at work and after a period of recovery is obliged to accept a less well-paid job in the same factory. But it is difficult to decide what is a man's earning capacity or his loss of earning power if there has been a change from manual to non-manual work, or vice versa. And when disability develops over a long period it may be difficult to judge what the earnings were before the onset of disability. How we estimate the earning capacity of a man who has been disabled from birth, or of a housewife of 40 who may have worked since the age of 20, becomes all the more baffling.

Judgements of earning capacity are in fact very subjective and are often left to doctors who have little idea of technological change and process and little idea of the varied conditions of industry and of the possibilities within industry of sheltered employment for the disabled. If we were to accept the principle of earning capacity or of limitation of earning power as a basis for disablement pension we would, unwittingly perhaps, restrict a future system to certain categories of employed persons.

We might instead base a new system on the principle of limitation of capacity to undertake ordinary human activities. Then it would be feasible to establish the range of activities of an average person of a given age, and measure how many of these activities a disabled person is able to undertake or undertake only with difficulty. I mean activities such as walking, running, climbing stairs, stooping, shopping, washing and dressing. The award of pension would be based on this assessment and would be paid irrespective of subsequent earnings.

This method would be extremely difficult to work out and apply in detail, but would be no more difficult and probably easier than any other method. By reconstituting the medical boards on disablement, and taking advantage of the long experience of these boards and the various appeal tribunals, an effective method of assessment, together with safeguards, can be developed. The 100 per cent pension should be related to average earnings and then could be increased automatically from year to year instead of requiring special legislation every year or two. A reasonable level at present would be 30 per cent of average industrial earnings, amounting to over £6 a week, plus allowance for dependants. This system could be planned gradually to supersede the existing war pensions and industrial injury schemes.

There would then be a second tier-system of supplementary benefits as of right, such as constant-attendance and special-hardship allowances. The Ministry of Social Security already has long experience of making these allowances. The great need is to extend them consistently to other categories of disabled and review whether there ought to be special allowances and grants for transport, mechanical aids, furnishings and adaptations.

What steps should now be taken? First, the government should declare in unambiguous terms that it intends to introduce new pensions for all disabled persons according to degree of disability, without discrimination between those disabled in war, industry or civil life. It should immediately sponsor or launch a national research study to establish the numbers of disabled in the population, including the mentally handicapped, and appoint an expert committee to work out a modern method of assessment and review the social services for the disabled. In the early 1950s the Piercy committee did not uncover much evidence about the disabled and the whole situation has now changed.

Finally, the government should introduce two interim measures to ease the poverty of many disabled persons. It should extend some of the supplementary allowances now paid to war and industrial pensioners, such as constant attendance and clothing allowances, to other disabled. And it should reimburse employers with the full amount of selective employment tax for each disabled employee.

There are a number of other steps that can be taken by other ministries. Sally Sainsbury's study revealed the deplorable housing in which many disabled persons live. More important than adaptations is the method by which the disabled secure ordinary modern housing with good amenities. The Ministry of Housing should immediately invite local authorities to report what steps they take in allocating housing to the disabled and in reviewing whether those living in council housing who become disabled have good facilities available to them, and should approve a new procedure for allowing housing and perhaps centralise methods of modernisation and adaptation.

Linked with this is the need for the Ministry of Health to become really tough with local authorities which make little or no effort to register names and addresses of the disabled, check on their housing and other problems, and develop services. Several authorities have registered from six to ten times as many disabled as other authorities. Among the most backward are Kent, Staffordshire, Leicester, the North Riding, Portsmouth, Oxford, Southport, Northampton, Hampshire and Liverpool.

The whole problem is bigger than most people suppose. Disability underlies a great deal of long-term unemployment, premature retirement and loss of skilled employment. It accounts for much isolation and loneliness throughout society. We need constantly to be searching for new evidence and making sure it is discussed in press and television.

The new pressure groups, like the Disablement Income Group and the Child Poverty Action Group, are unconscious agencies of popular education. They sometimes try to measure their success by reference to statements of government policy and even legislation and pull long faces at the results. But their concern, and their active interest in disseminating knowledge about their subjects influences public values and behaviour beyond measure. They are at the same time helping to shape the sense of commitment to their profession of doctors, nurses and social workers. In the long run, public education may be their most important contribution to reform, for it is the way in which people behave to each other that establishes the quality of a society.

# 51

# Poverty and disability

## Preface

The Disability Alliance was set up in 1974 to campaign for a **comprehensive disability income scheme** for all people with disabilities. The Disability Alliance is a federation of organisations of and for people with disabilities, and since 1974 the number of its member organisations has grown from 30 to over 90. Despite commitments by all the major political parties to the introduction of a comprehensive disability income scheme, little progress has been made in practice.

Current social security provision for people with disabilities is both inadequate and discriminatory. Even taking account of the available benefits, people with disabilities are still more likely to suffer from poverty than are non-disabled people. Also, people who are equally severely disabled can receive widely differing amounts of money according to the cause or origin of their disability, their national insurance contribution record, their age, or their marital status.

It is a fundamental principle that people with disabilities should have equal rights to participation in customarily accepted activities, roles and relationships within society. There are many areas in which changes need to be made to the way that society is organised, in order to ensure that these rights can be fully exercised. Access to adequate levels of income, although not sufficient alone, is one essential element.

The Disability Alliance believes that society should pay an income as of right to all people with disabilities. This income should be paid, regardless of the cause, type or origin of disablement, and regardless of the age, sex, marital status or national insurance record of the person concerned. Instead, it should be based on the severity of disablement.

Such an income – along with benefits for disabled people who are retired, unemployed, or unable to work because of their disability – would form part of the process of transforming the position and status of disabled people in society. It would aim to eliminate poverty and financial hardship among people with disabilities. The Disability Alliance also believes that

Townsend, P. (1987) 'Preface' and 'Introduction', in Disability Alliance, *Poverty and disability*, London: Disability Alliance, pp 1-7.

adequate financial provision must be made for people caring for someone with a disability.

A Comprehensive Disability Income Scheme would consist of:

- **A Disablement Allowance**, payable solely on the basis of the severity of disability. This would be measured in terms of the degree of restriction that the disability places on a person's activities. The disablement allowance alone would not be sufficient to live on, but would go towards meeting the extra costs of disability, and therefore towards equalising the standards of living for people with and without disabilities.
- **A Disablement Pension**, payable to everyone who is unable to work because of long term illness or disability. Provision would also be made for people who, through illness or disability, have a restricted capacity for work.

In addition, there should be adequate **provision for carers**, both to maintain the incomes of the carers who are unable to undertake paid employment and to recognise the costs and restrictions involved in caring.

**It is time for the political commitments of the past 20 years to be put into practice. The relationship between disability and poverty is well established and the case for a comprehensive disability income scheme widely accepted. The country can afford such a scheme, and people with disabilities cannot afford to wait any longer for its implementation.**

## Introduction

The Disability Alliance was set up in 1974 in response to the disappointing proposals put forward by the Government in the White Paper 'Social Security Provision for Chronically Sick and Disabled People'[1]. The White Paper came after a decade of pressure – following the formation of the Disablement Income Group[2] in 1965 – for a comprehensive disability income scheme designed to meet the problems of poverty and inadequate incomes faced by many people with disabilities in the UK.

Despite commitments by successive governments to improve social security provision for people with disabilities, the 1974 White Paper announced a package of measures costing only £23m a year. This was equivalent to just 34p per disabled person per week. Although these measures represented improvements on previous provision, organisations of and for people with disabilities were 'united in fury' at the poverty of this package.

In 1975, the Disability Alliance set out the case for a comprehensive disability income scheme for people with disabilities[3]. It identified the three principal financial problems faced by people with disabilities as poverty, lower incomes and assets than non-disabled people, and the inequity in the levels of provision by the State to different groups of disabled people. Three long term policy objectives were therefore stated for a comprehensive disability income scheme:

- to eliminate poverty amongst people with disabilities.
- to bring average incomes of people with disabilities up to the levels of the non-disabled, and to provide for the extra costs of disability.
- to distribute resources among people with disabilities so that people with equally severe disablement are entitled to the same allowances and pensions, irrespective of the cause or place of disablement.

Underlying these three objectives were three fundamental principles of equity:

- **Equity between people with disabilities and non-disabled people** – through measures to raise the living standards of people with disabilities at least up to those of non-disabled people; to meet the additional expense of disablement; and to provide special protection against living standards being eroded at times of inflation.
- **Equity among people with disabilities** – so that people with different types of disability shall have a right to income on equal terms. This should apply to all kinds of disability, whether mental or physical; from birth or acquired; contracted in the home, at work, or at war.
- **Equity between degrees of disability** – by assessing the severity of the disability, so that benefit shall vary according to the degree, and not the type of disability.

## Commitments in principle...

All the major political parties have now accepted the case for the introduction of a comprehensive disability income scheme:

> "Much has been done in recent years to help the disabled, but there is a long way to go. Our aim is to provide a coherent system of cash benefits to meet the costs of disability, so that disabled people can support themselves and live normal lives. We shall work towards this as swiftly as the strength of the economy allows." (Conservative Party Manifesto, 1979)

"We shall give priority to ... the introduction of a disablement allowance to help offset the costs of disablement." (Liberal Party Manifesto, 1983)

"In principle there is a strong case for supporting the introduction of a general disability income scheme payable irrespective of cause of disability." (Social Democratic Party Green Paper No. 11, 1982)

"Labour is committed to introducing a new and comprehensive disability income scheme with two separate non-contributory elements: an allowance to compensate for the additional indirect (as well as direct) costs of disablement, payable according to the severity of disablement; and a more streamlined income maintenance benefit." (Labour Party policy document, 'Social Security and Taxation', 1986)

### ... but little progress in practice

Despite these expressed commitments, no substantial progress has been made towards the introduction of a comprehensive disability income scheme. The past decade has instead seen a series of piecemeal changes which, although sometimes useful, have failed to correct the longstanding anomalies in social security provision for people with disabilities. Furthermore, in a number of vital areas, benefits have been cut and new anomalies created.

Cuts have taken place in a whole range of benefits. Long term benefits – such as retirement and invalidity pensions – are now increased in line with the rise in prices only, rather than using the increase in average earnings when this is greater. Unemployment, sickness, invalidity and maternity benefits were cut by 5% in 1980. Unemployment benefit and supplementary benefit for unemployed people have been made taxable, and the earnings related supplements to unemployment and sickness benefit abolished. Cuts have also been made in child dependency additions and in support for housing benefit[4]. In total, the level of social security spending is now over £11 billion lower than it would have been but for the cuts which have been made since 1979[5].

Although a number of new benefits for disabled people were introduced in the late 1970s, people with disabilities have not been protected from these cuts. Nor, according to the 1979 Conservative Government, could they expect to be exempted:

"There were simply not the available resources for major improvements in benefits and services for disabled people. Nor could disabled people be entirely shielded from the effects of high unemployment." (Hugh Rossi, Minister for the Disabled, 'IYDP and After – the UK Response', DHSS, July 1982)

Many people with disabilities rely on retirement pensions, housing benefit and employment benefit, which have all been cut. In addition, as mentioned, the value of certain specific disability benefits, such as invalidity benefit and sickness benefit, has been reduced.

There has also been the tightening of the linking rule for sickness and invalidity benefits; the introduction and extension of statutory sick pay, with losses for many claimants[6]; the abolition of injury benefit and the recent cuts in industrial disablement benefit; further cuts to invalidity benefit in 1985; and the provisions in the Social Security Act 1986 to abolish supplementary benefit additional requirements and replace them with flat rate disability premiums[7].

In addition to these cuts in social security benefits, people with disabilities have also been hit by the massive increase in NHS prescription charges, and cuts in Local Authority services[8].

In many ways, despite the commitments of the political parties, the prospect of a comprehensive disability income scheme seems less immediate now than it did in the late 1960s and early 1970s. One reason for this is the increasing use of the argument that the country cannot afford a decent and dignified social security system for people with disabilities. The 1979 Government made clear their view that any major reform must await an upturn in the economy:

> "We have made it clear that our first priority is to strengthen the economy. I regret that until that has been achieved, no progress can be made towards our objective of a coherent system of benefits for disabled people, which will cost thousands of millions of pounds."
> (Hugh Rossi, Minister for the Disabled, July 13 1982)

Although ... the Disability Alliance has never accepted that there is any validity in this argument, it has undoubtedly had a crucial influence on policy making.

A second reason for the apparent remoteness of a comprehensive disability income scheme is the effect on public debate of the continual attacks on social security provision since 1979. These have shifted the attention of the public and of pressure groups away from improvements in social security, and into a fight against the further erosion of existing rights. The necessity for this 'defensive' battle was intensified by the setting up of the 'Fowler Reviews' into social security in 1984.

## The way forward

For a number of years it has been argued that sweeping changes in the system of benefits for people with disabilities could not be made because the Government lacked up to date information on the size of the disabled population. Although, in reality, it has been the lack of political will which has been the main barrier to change, the excuse of inadequate information will soon be redundant. In 1984 the Government announced the setting up of a new survey to investigate the number of people with disabilities, their incomes and needs[9]. This survey – covering Great Britain but excluding Northern Ireland – is currently being carried out by the Office of Population Censuses and Surveys (OPCS), and the results are expected to be available by 1988. The recent White Paper on the 'Reform of Social Security'[10] announced that there will be a full review of disability benefits in the light of the results of the OPCS survey.

**The intention of this pamphlet is to put forward a case for positive action on incomes and to ensure that people with disabilities do not experience poverty and are able to participate fully in society. Provision of adequate incomes as of right for all people with disabilities is not, of course, sufficient on its own to enable full participation. There are many other aspects of the way that society is organised which place restrictions on the lives of people with disabilities. It is crucial that provision of adequate incomes does not lead to any reduction in the level of services designed to help people with disabilities maintain independent lives in their own homes and communities. Nevertheless, adequate incomes as of right are a necessary part of participation in modern society, and the lack of such an income is a major cause of exclusion, isolation, and material deprivation.**

### Endnotes

[1] Department of Health and Social Security (DHSS), *Social Security Provision for Chronically Sick and Disabled People*, HC 276, London, HMSO, 1984.

[2] The Disablement Income Group has recently republished its own proposals for social security benefits for people with disabilities: *DIG's National Disability Income*, London, DIG, 1987.

[3] Disability Alliance, *Poverty and Disability*, London, Disability Alliance, 1975.

[4] Franey, R., *Hard Times: The Tories and Disability*, London, Disability Alliance, 1983.

[5] House of Commons Library Research Division, *Research Note No. 262 addendum 2 October 1986*, London, House of Commons, 1986.

[6.] Baloo S., McMaster I. and Sutton, K., *SSP: The Failure of Privatisation in Social Security*, London, Disability Alliance ERA, Leicester Rights Centre, and Leicester City Council Low Pay Campaign, 1986.

[7.] As note 4, and Disability Alliance, *Social Security White Paper: Summary and Comments*, London, Disability Alliance, 1985.

[8.] As note 4, and Walker A., *The Care Gap*, London, Local Government Information Unit, 1985.

[9.] The survey of disablement in Great Britain is being carried out for the DHSS by the Office of Population Censuses and Surveys (OPCS). This survey was announced by the Secretary of State for Social Services, Norman Fowler, on 2 April 1984, and is the first national survey since 1968-9. The survey is in three parts: adults in private households, children in private households, and adults in institutions. The survey work began in 1985 and is now complete. The full results are not expected until 1988, although a preliminary report is due in the autumn of 1987.

[10.] DHSS, *Reform of Social Security: Programme for Action*, Cmnd 9691, London, HMSO, 1985.

# Section VIII

# Social justice and human rights

*Edited by Margot E. Salomon*

# Introduction

In his work of the past 15 years Peter Townsend laid claim to the potential of human rights. In his own words: "To base both research and action on human rights instruments is to apply the leverage of accepted authority and democracy" (Townsend, 2007a, p 33). By introducing the language and aims of human rights into his research Peter was free to assert the existence of national and international consensus for strategies and outcomes that had long informed his intellectual programme (Townsend, 2008a). Through the lens of human rights he reinterpreted issues that had for decades been at the heart of his writing, teaching and advocacy – poverty, inequality, social security and welfare, the well-being of children, the disabled, older people, and the negative social impacts of the shift to neoliberalism in the UK and internationally.

International human rights instruments – the Universal Declaration of Human Rights, the International Covenant on Civil and Political Rights, the International Covenant on Economic, Social and Cultural Rights, the Convention on the Rights of the Child, the Disabilities Convention – offered Peter inspiration in his determined pursuit of the ideas of social justice they articulated. To Peter, the codification of human rights standards represented an invitation to social scientists: it summoned their expertise to assist in giving effect to noble objectives, just as it brought the demands of international law into the realm of social policy. As he saw it, nothing short of a multidisciplinary enterprise was required to advance these common ideals.

Peter recognised and readily embraced perhaps the best of what human rights had to offer: normative guidance on the direction in which any humane society would want to go, a blueprint for how to get there, and a built-in system for addressing any failures of best efforts in securing the universally established standards. Notions of international responsibility and of accountability that inform the legal project resonated with Peter too, speaking to the 'rights' of the most disenfranchised, that is, to their unimpeachable claims to minimum standards of dignity.

## Realising the right to social security

> Of course these proposals will cost money. But poorer people in society should be helped to obtain what is their right. (Townsend, 1969, p 9)

In his 1969 article for the Child Poverty Action Group (**Chapter 52**) Peter argues for legal aid to be extended to social services tribunals so that poor people can seek proper redress in disputes over benefits and allowances. Besides presenting trenchant and well-researched arguments for his case along with specific recommendations for government action, this paper represents an early foray into what are readily framed as human rights procedures and claims today. His unease with the number of social security appeals in which the appellant is not legally represented thus resulting in unfair outcomes is recognised in this work as an "injustice" (Townsend, 1969, p 2); interruptions during hearings give rise to questions of "fair hearing" (p 2); the inability of the poor to afford representation results in the "the rights of the poor individual and of the poor family [being] grossly restricted" (p 3).

While an explicit human rights–based analysis is not used in this early piece, the social justice failures it highlights are clearly understood by the author as synonymous with government failures at guaranteeing the rights of the poor (p 4). Today, the need for "greater participation in decisions which vitally affect [the poor]" (p 5) is recognised as a fundamental principle of international human rights law and central to the legitimacy of government policies and programmes. Peter was acutely conscious of another foundational human rights principle – the need not merely for formal equality but also for substantive equality, remarking that "in the long run equality in law may be ensured only by developing legal aid as a universal free public service" (p 6).

There are other areas that the article identifies as important that are today linked to giving meaningful effect to a range of human rights issues: access to information (for example, "the need to publicize the new scheme" pp 6-7); gender equality ("[advice] centres are rarely open at hours which suit housebound mothers or working husbands": pp 7-8); neglect of poor and or rural areas ("solicitors ... are more likely to be found in prosperous parts of the country and larger conurbations": p 8); monitoring and evaluation (p 9); appropriate training of officials (p 10); and representative membership on tribunals (p 10).

A decade after the publication of the article, the European Court of Human Rights issued a landmark judgment in the case of *Airey v Ireland* substantiating an argument at the heart of Peter's concern with access to justice for the poor (*Airey v Ireland*, 1979). In concluding that the unavailability of legal aid meant that Joanna Airey, a woman of humble means, could not secure adequate representation (in this case in seeking a decree of judicial separation from her husband on the grounds of his alleged cruelty to her and her children), the Court applied the principle of effectiveness. The European Court rejected the argument that there was no bar to Mrs Airey conducting her own case before the Irish Courts, the view advanced by the Irish Government. In finding a violation of the right to a fair trial under the European Convention of Human Rights at Article 6(1), the Court made clear that human rights must be "practical and effective" as distinct from "theoretical and illusory" (*Airey v Ireland*, 1979, para 24). It was around that same time that the United Nations International Covenant on Economic, Social and Cultural Rights entered into force,[1] enshrining in a binding international human rights instrument the right of everyone to social security;[2] a right articulated in the aspirational Universal Declaration of Human Rights almost three decades earlier.[3] Social justice issues that Peter held dear were receiving the human rights imprimatur.

A more general case for social security (and social services), including comprehensive social insurance, is methodically laid out in a recent report Peter produced for the International Labour Organization (ILO) (Townsend, 2007b)[4] (**Chapter 53**). Pared down to its core messages, this rich and rigorous piece of research argues that redistribution – in whatever form or at whatever level – contributes to poverty reduction, with higher levels of spending resulting in lower poverty and inequality (p viii).[5] It establishes that industrialised countries relied on social security when they were developing, just as they do today: most countries of the Organization for Economic Cooperation and Development (OECD) currently commit more than 20% of their GDP to public social services and social security[6] (p viii) as compared to less than 5% of GDP in total to public social services and benefits in low-income countries, with some spending less than 1% or 2% GDP (p 9).[7] The average for all OECD countries today is 13.5% of GDP (**Chapter 54**). The third key message of the ILO report is that the policies that served the then emerging OECD economies and the poor within those countries well are simply not available to low-income countries nowadays, not least of all as a result of the influence of international donor agencies.

The role of external agents in shaping social policy to the detriment of the poor in developing countries is a central concern of Peter's and in the ILO report he focuses on the World Bank. He also argues for a greater degree of responsibility for foreign governments and transnational corporations (TNCs) in advancing and contributing to social security in low-income countries from which they benefit through trade and investment (see Section II of this volume). In the case of TNCs, the extent of the resources of the 500 largest global corporations requires that we look afresh at where resources come from[8] including through employer contributions (Townsend, 2008b).[9] What in fact Peter was addressing when he turned his attention beyond the state acting nationally are obligations of 'international cooperation', understood within international human rights law to reflect a critical element in the realisation of socio-economic rights in developing countries.[10] The *right* of *everyone* to social security and social insurance and the *right* of *everyone* to an adequate standard of living[11] signify that economic and social development can no longer be divorced from human rights, just as the principles, standards and obligations that define human rights offer a basis for re-casting development policies (Townsend, 2007b, pp 1, 4-5).[12]

Peter clearly found human rights to offer a schema allied to his own preoccupations. Fundamental issues that he had long sought to highlight – the need to define, measure and address poverty in terms of both social and material need, and confronting the responsibilities of international actors implicated in poverty in low-income countries – find expression also within the human rights project, bringing a legal framework to bear on claims and strategies to reduce poverty.[13]

There are few more incisive elucidations on policies of the Left than that which Peter provides in his critique of Labour's 1995 Report of its Commission on Social Justice (The Borrie Report) (Townsend, 1995). Reproduced here almost in its entirety (**Chapter 55**), his assessment allows for no political duplicity, no state complicity with the powerful, no individual in need unaccounted for, and a catalogue of national and international policy recommendations that leaves no excuse for inaction. Peter rigorously defends his position that tackling poverty and inequality and instituting a sustainable economic agenda require both 'enabling strategies' (social protection and a move towards principles of distribution and welfare) and 'structural strategies' ("legal and democratic control of international financial and market forces") (Townsend, 1995, p 145). The language of rights is at times explicit in his article, but consistently implicit, with demands of inclusion, voice, fairness, access, and of course, accountability, woven through this concise manifesto. Written perhaps for a domestic audience, the insights and lessons he offers resonate widely after three decades of global neoliberalism, and apply as much in 2009 in the wake of the financial and economic crisis as they did when they were written.

His profound concern with both the social impacts of the neoliberal agenda and the rights of older people converge in a recent work on 'Using human rights to defeat ageism' (**Chapter 56**). Here Peter criticises the body of thought among various social scientific disciplines in the latter half of the 20th century that yielded to the dominant economic agenda and in so doing accepted as givens the changing structural inequalities of a competitive market that reinforced individualistic rather than social values (Townsend, 2007a, p 30). He characterised their work as 'acquiescent functionalism' for attributing the problems associated with old age to the natural consequences of physical and mental deterioration or the failures of adjusting to ageing and retirement, "instead of the continuing as well as new exertions of state economic and social policy partly to serve and partly to moderate the play of market forces" (Townsend, 2007a, p 30).

## Of patronage and power

> It is this network that is determining the social conditions and destinies of nation-states. (Townsend, 1994, p 18)

In his work on social justice, social development and human rights, Peter's most trenchant criticisms are reserved for what Upendra Baxi refers to as "active networks of global patronage and power" (Baxi, 2007, p 153). The 'hollow sham' of global monetarism (Townsend, 1994, p 18) enriching the rich, increasing inequality within rich and poor countries alike, reducing the access of poor countries to global resources while facilitating the growing affluence of the richest countries demanded, then as now, not capitulation to the neoliberal order and arguments of 'golden straightjackets'[14], but rather an imperative placed upon the UK government and others to "fill the international leadership vacuum" (Townsend, 1994, p 18). As the *New Statesman* article of 1994 reflects (reproduced here in full as **Chapter 57**), Peter was never short of practical ideas as to how this could be achieved.

In the wake of the financial crisis Peter rejects a lead role for the World Bank and instead suggests that reconstruction of the banking system must include the World Bank. For Peter, the Bank retains no moral authority, having helped to implant

> neo-liberal ideology among governments, corporations and consumers, weaken the state and reinforce economic inequality and destitution. ... The Bank advocates disastrous policies, like its meager and superficial anti-poverty policies, lends with antisocial discriminatory conditions, and has little experience or resources to invest grants directly in jobs, services and people. (Townsend, 2009b)

In his 2002 piece on human rights, TNCs and the World Bank he effectively charges the international financial institutions with collusion having "played an increasing role in developing social policies favourable to TNCs" (Townsend, 2002, p 355) with the privatisation of social security and health services among the policies highlighted (**Chapter 58**). We've taken our eye off the ball in focusing on Bank conditionality to the near exclusion of the 40,000 World Bank contracts issued to private firms (p 355).

To bring human rights into the picture is to place people at the centre of development policy – not markets, not the expansion of capital, not trade for their own sakes. Peter's work had long sought to demonstrate that those driving the institutional economic and financial order were serving the wrong master if social justice, in any form, was going to be part of the equation. The international human rights instruments offered a singularly important weapon in Peter's arsenal. He advocated for close monitoring of trends in access to rights, including through indicators of their non-fulfillment, for improved measurement and policies related to the right to an adequate standard of living ("right to an adequate income") and for (international) child benefits consistent with the Convention on the Rights of the Child (pp 367-9).[15] His call for an international financial transaction tax implicit in Keynes' approach to Bretton Woods, resurrected in 1972 by James Tobin, revived in the 1990s and raised at the 2002 Monterrey international conference on financing for developing (p 369), is once again part of political imaginings in the post-crisis world of 2009 (see Persaud, 2009;[16] Benoit, 2009).

As this chapter reveals, Peter's work reflects an acute awareness of the structures that sustain the poverty he has spent his professional life attempting to dismantle. He knew that great poverty and great wealth could only be understood when considered together, as part of a single arrangement. In 1979 he wrote:

> A theory of riches depends not only on theories of acquisition …[i]t depends also on theories of denial of access to wealth… . The law and the values and norms of society have to be examined, and also the part played by different agencies distributing wealth or controlling access to wealth. … If we are to understand how wealth arises and is unequally distributed, we have to explain their constitution, rules of operation and membership (Townsend, 1979, p 365).

The human rights model takes us part of the way there, and may well possess unfulfilled potential in the fight against poverty and other grave ills of contemporary society. But it has further to go in order to implement meaningfully these core ideas of rights and obligations, in attributing responsibility, and in ensuring a system of accountability under conditions of globalisation (see Salomon, 2007).

## Conclusion

Although published 15 years ago Peter could have been penning these words in 2009 when he wrote "of capitalism over-reaching itself to the brink of self-destruction" (1994, p 18) or a year later when he spoke of the dream of deregulators being ruled out as "theirs is a future of extremes" (1995, p 143). Peter saw the place human rights could claim among his causes, but he was no idealist. He recognised "the paradox of global hope" reflected in the widening allegiance to human rights treaties alongside the grim facts about inequality and poverty globally (2008b). His contribution has been enormous, and he has harnessed every tool he can, not least his own energy, commitment, intellect and passion. Among the poor and disenfranchised, women, children, older people, the disabled, rural dwellers, ethnic minorities, and the places where these multiple characterisations intersect, is where we will find Peter's voice.

Importantly though, his was also a call to arms, and he led by example. I close with Peter's own words in what has become a small tribute to his manifold contribution, not only to the lives of those he sought to support, but to the emerging field of human rights itself. Here, in a piece he wrote in 2007, he calls on each and every one of us to carry on the struggle. We would honour his life and his memory to do nothing less.

> Most of us are assaulted by the day-to-day pressures of finding our way, and we look down at our desks or our feet rather than over the rooftops and fields or at our immediate and far away social surroundings. We come to learn that the here and now is a fragment in an awesome sweep of life before our birth and after our death. We can be lucky to capture some sense of what shapes social and not just individual life; and convey, even if only to a few, and to them for only a few weeks or years, a reasoned account of predestination, so that they may join in the difficult and usually unsuccessful task of putting continuing and emerging wrongs right. (2007a, p 28)

**Endnotes**

[1] International Covenant on Economic, Social and Cultural Rights, GA res 2200A (XXI), 16 December 1966, entered into force on 3 January 1976 (ICESCR).

[2] ICESCR Article 9: "The States Parties to the present Covenant recognize the right of everyone to social security, including social insurance". See also, the Convention on the Rights of the Child, GA res 44/25 of 20 November 1989, entered into force on 2 September 1990, Article 26(1).

[3] Universal Declaration of Human Rights, General Assembly res 217A (III), 10 December 1948, UN GAOR, 3rd Session Resolutions, pt 1 at 71, UN Doc A/810 (1948), Articles 22 and 25(1). For a list of affirmations of the right to social security in international instruments see, UN Committee on Economic, Social and Cultural Rights (CESCR), General Comment No 19, *The right to social security* (Article 9), (39th session, 2007) UN Doc E/C.12/GC/19, para 6. See also, ILO Convention No 102 on Social Security (Minimum Standards) (1952).

[4] A slightly abbreviated version of the Discussion Paper is found in Townsend, 2009a.

[5] Moreover, findings that lower spending on social services and social security promotes higher growth are not conclusive, with evidence from the countries of

the Organization for Economic Cooperation and Development indicating that substantial social security spending is often consistent with above average economic growth (Townsend, 2007b, p viii).

[6] These figures exclude education.

[7] "For the low-income countries, including India and China, the percentage of GDP [in total public social security expenditure] is around 1-3% [of GDP]" (Townsend, 2008b).

[8] An oral comment from Peter Townsend at the Seminar on the UN Draft Guiding Principles on Extreme Poverty and Human Rights, Geneva, January 2009 (notes on file with author).

[9] "If a small percentage of the resources of global corporations was committed to social security, a minimum wage and the right to improved employment conditions in low-income countries, they could share the kind of stability across the world that companies and European governments achieved domestically centuries ago. … The global corporations should add one or two per cent of wage costs, for example towards a universal child benefit to help banish malnutrition, poverty and premature child death, and encourage more schooling and access to healthcare. Employer contributions towards domestic social insurance schemes in the OECD countries could be applied to employer operations in low-income countries" (Townsend, 2009b).

[10] See, *inter alia,* ICESCR Article 2(1): "Each State Party to the present Covenant undertakes to take steps, individually and through international assistance and co-operation, especially economic and technical, to the maximum of its available resources, with a view to achieving progressively the full realization of the rights recognized in the present Covenant by all appropriate means, including particularly the adoption of legislative measures". Convention on the Rights of the Child: Article 4: "States Parties shall undertake all appropriate legislative, administrative, and other measures for the implementation of the rights recognized in the present Convention. With regard to economic, social and cultural rights, States Parties shall undertake such measures to the maximum extent of their available resources and, where needed, within the framework of international co-operation".

[11] UDHR Article 25; ICESCR Article 11; CRC Article 27.

[12] Peter was acutely aware of the particular needs of, for example, children, the severely disabled and the elderly, strongly recommending in his remarks on the draft General Comment on the Right to Social Security that the Committee on Economic, Social and Cultural Rights distinguish and prioritise the rights of these vulnerable groups in the staged introduction of a universal right to social security (notes on file with author). Given his commitment to overcoming gendered elements of social security schemes, elsewhere Peter advocated for the years spent raising a family to be counted as a contribution towards receipt of social security (oral comment, Seminar on the UN Draft Guiding Principles on Extreme Poverty and Human Rights, Geneva, January 2009; notes on file with author).

[13] On the multidimensional definition of poverty see CESCR, 2001, para 8:"In light of the International Bill of Rights, poverty may be defined as a human condition characterized by sustained or chronic deprivation of the resources, capabilities, choices, security and power necessary for the enjoyment of an adequate standard of living and other civil, cultural, economic, political and social rights. While acknowledging that there is no universally accepted definition, the Committee endorses this multi-dimensional understanding of poverty, which reflects the indivisible and interdependent nature of all human rights". For a consideration of the responsibilities of international actors see, CESCR, 2008, paras 52-8.

[14] Chapter 6 in T. Friedman (2000) *The Lexus and the olive tree: Understanding globalization*, New York, NY: Random House:"Globalization has only the Golden Straightjacket. If your country has not been fitted for one, it will be soon".

[15] For Peter human rights also offered a framework for strong anti-discrimination work, for more appropriate and generous use of resources according to severity of need, and through its commitment to the principle of indivisibility, to the advance of multiple indices of the non-realisation of rights (see Townsend, 2007a, pp 32, 43). For a summary of the United Nations work on human rights indicators see, *Report on Indicators for Promoting and Monitoring the Implementation of Human Rights,* UN Doc. HRI/MC/2008/3, 6 June 2008, available at: www.ohchr.org

[16] Persaud is current Chair of the Warwick Commission. Referring to the call for a Tobin Tax by the Chairman of the UK Financial Services Authority he explains that financial taxes are commonplace and not difficult to enforce. In 2001 Peter writes:"There is a groundswell of support for the Tobin Tax – a small tax of, say, 0.1 or 0.5% on international financial transactions to raise substantial resources for the poorest countries. But the proposal has remained vague, and because it is vague it has attracted opposition from the banks. Its exact use needs to be defined. … The priority for such a tax must be a child benefit in cash or kind – for social development as well as to end poverty and malnutrition" (Townsend, 2001); in 2009 he writes: "if a small percentage of the resources of global corporations was committed to social security, a minimum wage and the right to improved employment conditions in low-income countries, they could share the kind of stability across the world that companies and European governments achieved domestically a century ago. … [M]ore effective international taxation would be a necessary component" (Townsend, 2009b).

## References

*Airey v Ireland* (1979) Judgment of 9 October, Series A, No 32 (1979-80), 2 EHHR 305.

Baxi, U. (2007) *Human rights in a posthuman world: Critical essays*, Oxford: Oxford University Press.

Benoit, B. (2009) 'Steinbrück calls for global finance tax', *Financial Times,* 12-13 September.

CESCR (UN Committee on Economic, Social and Cultural Rights) (2001) *Statement on poverty and the international covenant on economic, social and cultural rights,* (25th session, 2001), UN Doc E/C12/2001/10, Geneva: CESCR.

CESCR (2008) *The right to social security*, General Comment No 19, Geneva: CESCR.

Persaud, A. (2009) 'Time to put sand in the wheels of the market', *Financial Times*, 28 August.

Salomon, M.E. (2007) *Global responsibility for human rights: World poverty and the development of international law*, Oxford: Oxford University Press.

Townsend, P. (1969) *A policy to establish the legal rights of low-income families*, London: Child Action Poverty Group.

Townsend, P. (1979) *Poverty in the United Kingdom: A survey of household resources and standards of living*, London: Penguin.

Townsend, P. (1994) 'We have got a fair way to go', *New Statesman & Society*, 25 March, pp 18-19.

Townsend, P. (1995) 'Persuasion and conformity: an assessment of the Borrie Report on social justice', *New Left Review*, no 213, Sep/Oct, pp 137-50.

Townsend, P. (2001) 'Humanitarian coalition must start with children', *The Guardian*, 2 June.

Townsend, P. (2002) 'Human rights, transnational corporations and the World Bank', in P. Townsend and D. Gordon (eds) *World poverty: New policies to defeat an old enemy*, Bristol: The Policy Press, pp 351-76.

Townsend, P. (2007a) 'Using human rights to defeat ageism: dealing with policy-induced "structural dependency"', in M. Bernard and T. Scharf (eds) *Critical perspectives on aging societies*, Bristol: The Policy Press, pp 27-44.

Townsend, P. (2007b) *The right to social security and national development: Lessons from OECD experience for low-income countries*, Discussion Paper 18, Geneva: International Labour Organization.

Townsend, P. (2008a) 'Reflections', Peter Townsend's work: Looking back and looking forward, Presentation, 11 November, London School of Economics and Political Science.

Townsend, P. (2008b) 'Using human rights to reduce inequalities in economic and social development', paper presented to the Egmont Institute conference, 'World inequality: a challenge to globalisation', Brussels, 17-18 March.

Townsend, P. (2009a) 'Social security and human rights', in P. Townsend (ed) *Building decent societies: Rethinking the role of social security in development*, Basingstoke/Geneva: Palgrave/International Labour Organization, pp 29-59.

Townsend, P. (2009b) 'The World Bank has also failed', *The Guardian*, 19 June.

# 52

# A policy to establish the legal rights of low income families

## Introduction

In most instances social service tribunals are more important to the poor in redressing their grievances than the established legal system. Disputed decisions concerning unemployment benefit, supplementary benefit, sickness benefit, special hardship allowances, industrial injury benefit, family allowances and rents are crucial to their family income and wellbeing. These disputes are not settled in the courts. And legal aid has not been extended to tribunals, although legal *advice* can in theory be obtained.

The powers of the social security tribunals are considerable. The Franks Committee stated in its report of 1957 that a number of tribunals "have a status equal to that of the county courts and involve greater legal cost".(1) But it did not discover how people who use the existing social security tribunals fare in obtaining help and assistance with their appeals. The whole question of the constitution and procedure of tribunals in relation to legal aid and advice needs to be looked at afresh – especially since other aspects of civil rights have been given considerable attention in recent years (thus three major reports, the Evershed, Streatfield and Beeching Reports on the civil and criminal courts, have been published since 1950).

The Beeching Committee has recently pointed out that "the excellence of the judiciary and the thoroughness and impartiality of legal procedure are of little avail to those who cannot get their cases into court".(2)

The Child Poverty Action Group considers that the Beeching statement applies especially to those whose education and status in life ill-equips them to take their own appeal cases to tribunals.

## 1. Grounds for concern

Four aspects of this judicial system, which mainly affects poorer people, are causing particular concern to the Child Poverty Action Group.

Child Poverty Action Group (Brooke, R., Field, F. and Townsend, P.) (1969) *A policy to establish the legal rights of low income families: Legal aid and advice*, Poverty Pamphlet 1, London: Child Poverty Action Group.

### (a) Possible injustice

We are concerned about the number of social security appeals in which the appellant is not legally represented, when there is good reason for believing that if he were represented the outcome would be different. [...]

### (b) Tribunal procedure

At present the representative of the Supplementary Benefits Commission is invariably well-briefed and may refer to regulations to which the appellant does not have access. He is usually allowed to develop his argument uninterrupted by the appellant or Tribunal members. The appellant, however, is by no means always allowed to present his (or her) case without considerable interruptions. Consequently, there is real doubt as to whether the appellant gets a fair hearing. Most people on supplementary benefit are sick, elderly, disabled or are young mothers often with small children who require looking after while they attend the hearings. In general, they have been denied the kind of education which would help them to cope with Tribunal procedure, and they need representation even more than most people.

### (c) The need for both legal aid and advice

[...] Although they can be represented at a Tribunal, only a few, it would appear, ask a friend to accompany them and none can afford to employ a lawyer at the usual rates. Legal aid is not available before these Tribunals. As a consequence, the rights of the poor individual and of the poor family are grossly restricted.

### (d) Tribunal composition

Rarely do Supplementary Benefits Tribunals have any member who is a lawyer; they do not have lawyer chairmen, unlike tribunals for sickness or industrial injuries. Although little research has yet been done on the composition of such tribunals, our investigations suggest that tribunal members are generally of late middle-age or retired. In terms of legal expertise and representativeness of the population they leave something to be desired.

## 2. Official recommendations for a more comprehensive legal aid and advice scheme

Previous committees of enquiry have reported in favour of more comprehensive legal aid and advice.

### (a) The Rushcliffe Committee

In 1945 the Rushcliffe Committee on Legal Aid and Legal Advice in England and Wales stressed the "need for a new approach to the whole question of legal assistance".(3) The Committee recommended that legal aid should be available in "all courts and in such matters as will enable persons in need to have access to the professional help they require". Further, they specifically recommended that legal aid should be available for "any tribunal where audience is normally granted to barristers and solicitors". This recommendation was made, the Committee concluded, because "the total of all the existing free facilities is inadequate to meet the demand ... a service which was at best somewhat patchy has become totally inadequate if all members of the community are to secure the legal assistance they require, barristers and solicitors cannot be expected in future to provide that assistance to a considerable section as a voluntary service". In order to achieve this aim of improved legal services, the Committee went on to recommend that legal aid "should not be limited to those who are normally classed as poor but should include a wider income group". They recommended that the scheme should be free to those who could afford nothing, and that the cost of the scheme should be borne by the state. But these proposals of the Rushcliffe Committee were not heeded when the Legal Aid and Advice Scheme was set up.

### (b) The Franks Committee

The Franks Committee of 1957 reinforced the Rushcliffe Committee's argument. It pointed out, moreover, that the "continuing extension of governmental activity has greatly multiplied the occasions on which an individual may be at issue with the administration or with another citizen or body, as to his rights, and the post-war years have seen a substantial growth in the importance and activities of tribunals".(4) The Franks Report stressed the need for citizens to know about the right of appeal, to understand the procedure at the hearing, to obtain legal advice, and to know in advance the case he would have to meet. The Committee accordingly recommended that legal aid should be made available for tribunals.

## 3. A deteriorating situation

These two reports show that the case we are presenting is not new. But the case needs to be reiterated forcefully at the present time because the scale of the problem of poverty as well as the difficulties of guaranteeing the rights of those in poverty are now recognized to be much greater than at the time these committees were sitting. A lower proportion of the population is eligible to receive legal advice than in 1960. The income level of the present means test for legal advice has not been raised since April 1960, despite the rise in cost of living (partly because of devaluation), the rise in real wages, and the raising of supplementary benefit and other social security benefits.

## 4. Need to extend legal advice and legal aid

[...]

### (a) Gap between legal advice and legal aid

The necessity for going to court or tribunal might be avoided if a poor person could obtain legal help beforehand. [...]

### (b) Confused priorities

The Advisory Committee on Legal Aid recommended recently that legal aid should be made available in the Lands Tribunals.(5) Yet, if this recommendation were implemented, it would begin at the wrong end of the income scale. Poorer people and their families, whose income and welfare is at stake, are much more likely to need legal aid for Social Security and Rent Tribunals than for disputes over land.

### (c) The general principle

We regard the current demands by individuals and groups for increased government accountability and their greater participation in decisions which vitally affect them as a thoroughly healthy development. The area of welfare law covered by this memorandum is of primary interest to a large percentage of the population and in particular the most disadvantaged. People should be encouraged to use fully the existing tribunal appeals system. More than any other single action, this would convince the public that the whole judicial system is open, accountable and fair, and that justice can still be obtained when a wrong administrative decision has been made.

As a first recommendation therefore the Child Poverty Action Group proposes that legal aid should be extended to all tribunals, in particular Supplementary Benefit Tribunals. This recommendation has a further advantage; solicitors would have greater incentives to learn about these areas of law and so would be better prepared to advise clients under the legal advice scheme.

## 5. Payment for legal aid and advice

The existing system of legal aid to persons with low incomes (which does not extend to tribunals) is available only on test of means. A great deal of evidence shows that substantial numbers of people eligible to benefit from services which are subject to a means test are deterred from using them, and in the long run equality in law may be ensured only by developing legal aid as a universal free public service. Until this becomes widely recognized there is a powerful case in the short run for making existing means tests much more liberal. […]

Our second recommendation is therefore that the upper income and capital limits for legal advice should be raised to a level higher than the existing Supplementary Benefit level.

## 6. Need to publicize the new scheme

The members of the Rushcliffe Committee were fully aware of the need to publicize the Legal Aid Scheme so that "those whom it is intended to benefit may have no difficulty in ascertaining the advantages open to them under the scheme".

We consider that the case for adequate publicity has in no way diminished. […] It is not enough that the law should be just. The poorest in the community must know that they can use it and must be shown to be able to use it.

The Child Poverty Action Group's third recommendation is therefore that more effective publicity should be given to the legal aid and advice scheme, using local newspapers, television and posters.

## 7. Need for experiment in and expansion of advisory services

### (a) Information services

Any extension of legal aid and advice requires a supporting development of information services. The Child Poverty Action Group, in evidence to the Seebohm Committee, pointed out that "many families who qualify for rate rebates and free welfare foods … are perfectly capable of managing their own affairs, given the material resources to which they are entitled", and urged the Committee to set up information centres.

At present there is no systematic information available on a national scale about information services. There are 490 citizens' advice bureaux in the United Kingdom. But how many information centres are run by local authorities, and how many family advice centres are there? There is no national information about the number, the hours and days of opening of such centres. In our experience, centres are rarely open at hours which suit housebound mothers or working husbands. Nothing is known about the number and qualifications of secretaries and supporting staff who purport to advise, and how they are trained. Nor is the information available about the siting and quality of the office accommodation.

A full review needs to be made of these centres and their actual as well as stated functions. [...]

From the research evidence available ... it would appear there is an urgent need for a better national network of information offices to buttress the work of welfare lawyers. [...]

### (b) Distribution of solicitors

The distribution of solicitors is most uneven over the country. They are more likely to be found in prosperous parts of the country and larger conurbations. [...]

We recommend the government to develop a two-stage programme, first financing more experimental schemes on the lines of the American neighbourhood law firms, the Law Society Liaison Advisory Service, and the provision of lawyers in Citizens' Advice Bureaux, and second, establishing a national network of legal aid and information centres within five years. The experimental schemes set up in the first two or three years should be adequately evaluated. [...]

We also recommend that an incentive scheme should be developed to encourage the better distribution of lawyers and persuade more to work in poor areas. It would be helpful if specialisation could be encouraged, so that lawyers expert in landlord and tenant law, consumer protection, hire purchase, insurance and social security, could service several bureaux or centres. Not all lawyers need be employed on a full-time contract. A scheme whereby some contract to work a number of half-days a week, like the present consultant scheme in the National Health Service, would be practicable. When lawyers are attached to Citizens' Advice Bureaux the bureaux should receive a grant from central funds to enable them to meet legal salaries. A national service is needed and it should be nationally financed.

We recommend that a National Civil Rights Council should be established with members appointed by the Crown on the advice of the Lord Chancellor.(6) The members would include nominees of such bodies as the Bar Council, the Law Society, the National Council of Social Service, the National Council of Civil Liberties and representatives of the populations of poor areas. The Council would be responsible for developing and financing a network of centres and for introducing training programmes for lawyers, social workers and information officers.

Of course these proposals will cost money. But poorer people in society should be helped to obtain what is their right. Lawyers could be of great assistance to poorer people in tribunals and these proposals would help those altruistic and idealistic solicitors (probably not many) who at present advise on the matters covered by this memorandum without adequate remuneration. Those solicitors with lucrative commercial and conveyancing practices are unlikely to take up this work. In one sense, these proposals will put money into lawyers' pockets, but probably only a few. The results of doing so will be to put more money into the pockets of the poorer members of society.

### (c) Training of social workers and lawyers

Lawyers and social workers, whom we regard as the prime potential helpers, are inadequately trained and equipped to advise on rights under the Rent Act and social security legislation. [...]

We recommend that legal and social work education should cover topics which are of crucial importance to poorer people, amongst whom social workers at least are most likely to work.

### (d) Composition of tribunals

We believe it is important for democratic institutions to be representative of those people over whom they have jurisdiction. In particular, it is important that some members of a tribunal should have a sympathetic and firsthand experience of the kind of people who appear before them.

We therefore recommend that tribunal membership should be made more representative and should include members with greater competence in the process of adjudicating. If necessary sufficient payment would have to be made in order to achieve a high level of competence in this work.

## References

[1] Report of the Committee on Administrative Tribunals, HMSO 1957, Cmnd 218.

[2] Report of the Royal Commission on Assizes and Quarter Sessions, HMSO 1969, Cmnd 4153.

[3] Report of the Committee on Legal Aid and Legal Advice in England and Wales, HMSO 1945, Cmd 6641.

[4] Report of the committee on Administrative Tribunals, HMSO 1957, Cmnd 218.

[5] Report of the Lord Chancellor's Advisory Committee in the Seventeenth Report if the Law Society on Legal Aid and Advice, HMSO 1968.

[6] A similar suggestion is made in B. Abel-Smith and R. Stevens, *In Search of Justice*, London, Allen Lane, 1968.

# 53

# The right to social security and national development

## Executive summary

Mounting acceptance throughout the world of human rights puts pressure on all countries to re-cast development policies and eliminate poverty. Human rights have come to play a central part in discussions about economic and social development, and the great majority of governments in the world have ratified the various instruments. This report traces the divergent historical experience in "developed" and "developing" countries of putting into practice the fundamental rights to social security, including social insurance, and an "adequate" standard of living. The rights are enshrined in Articles 22 and 25 of the Universal Declaration of Human Rights; 9 and 11 of the International Covenant on Economic, Social and Cultural Rights; and 26 and 27 of the Convention on the Rights of the Child.

The impact of social security systems in the OECD countries over more than a hundred years best illustrates the gathering importance of these rights.

The two rights to social security and an adequate standard of living that are specified in various Conventions and Charters have not been routinely investigated during a long period of intensifying world concern about the persistence of large-scale extreme poverty. Thus, they were not regarded as a necessary element of the discussions of structural adjustment policies and then the Social Fund in the 1980s and 1990s, in the fraught regions of Sub-Saharan Africa, Latin America, South Asia and Eastern Europe, nor later at the time of the introduction by the UN of the Millennium Development Goals. The international financial agencies focused attention on targeting and short-term means-tested benefits at least expense rather than also, or instead of, minimal living standards for all. This mistake was compounded by an over-generalised, ambiguous and undirected international antipovertystrategy

Extracts (pp vii-x, 1-5, 7-11, 14-17, 19, 32-38) from Townsend, P. (2007) *The right to social security and national development: Lessons from OECD experience for low-income countries*, Issues in Social Protection Discussion Paper 18, Geneva: Social Security Department, International Labour Office.

– concerned in the broadest and most indirect terms with economic growth, overseas aid, debt relief and fairer trade. Whether there was "trickle down" or even proportionate benefits derived by the poorest sections of population was not precisely investigated and monitored.

In more than three decades economic development policies advocated by the international financial agencies and leading governments have not incorporated sufficient information and direction about the course of corresponding, not to say consequential, social development. Policies designed to establish and invigorate universal public social services and social security payments came to be treated as aberrations of the past rather than as institutions as necessary to the future as to the past. Attempts to restrain and roll back social security were made with too little understanding of the accumulating historical impetus in all OECD countries of its elaborate institutions and multiple functions. This report reviews that history.

Since 2000 the strengths of comprehensive or universal public social services and social protection or security payments have begun to be recognised, partly at the instigation of international organisations such as the ILO and UNICEF. Recognition of the strengths in particular of (i) contributory social insurance and (ii) tax-financed group benefits on behalf of children, disabled people and the elderly, may follow. These two types of benefit – long-established in OECD countries – are "universalistic" measures; they are not "selective" or discriminatory on test of means. Once these two can be recognised cross-nationally the urgent re-formulation of development policies to reduce poverty may be welcomed – and bring tangible success.

The strength of a universalistic, human rights, approach to social security, is in turning to future advantage what, after extraordinary struggle, proved to be a highly successful strategy in the past. Working people responded to extreme individual need by combining in collective interest to contribute creatively to economic development and the alleviation of the poverty of others in their midst, and contributory social insurance and group benefit schemes turned out to be favoured instruments. Collective protest and action led to the social good – often by the extension of the ideas of representative democracy and citizen participation.

Human rights to social security and an adequate standard of living have today put these ideas on the international stage. Poverty can be reduced more emphatically by universalistic measures that also improve social relationships. For example, social security systems help coalitions to be built between groups in society of a more varied kind, say, than those representing familiar ethnic or religious divisions. Again, social security systems have created and continue to create cross-cutting and three generational social identities and have moderated multiple forms of discrimination and social inequality.

Nationalism re-interpreted as universalism re-enforces good multi-cultural and multi-generational values that promote stability.

The lessons of the review of social security in OECD countries in this report can be summarised here for the convenience of readers:

- In aiming to reduce poverty, establish basic social services and meet individual adversity, OECD countries have come to spend an average of one eighth (12.6 per cent) of their GDP on public social security cash benefits, and altogether more than a fifth (20.9 per cent) on public social services and social security, excluding education. This has been, and remains, an emphatic endorsement of redistribution of national income in the social good;
- All member countries of the OECD have substantially lower rates of poverty as a consequence, whatever type of system or level of redistribution individual governments, including the US and the UK, have introduced;
- Member countries with higher levels of spending have lower rates of poverty and inequality than those with lower levels of spending;
- Some member countries industrialised first and, during their "development" to their present conditions of prosperity, they steadily increased the percentage of national income invested annually in universal social services and social security;
- With fluctuations their economies have continued to grow;
- Evidence that lower spending by OECD governments on social services and social security promotes higher economic growth is not conclusive. For selected groups of high- and low-spending member countries, and for selected recent historical periods of ten years or more, the reverse can be demonstrated;
- The evidence from the OECD countries shows that substantial social security spending, i.e., more than a sixth of GDP, is often consistent with above-average economic growth;
- Despite pressures to reduce social spending and fluctuations among certain members the proportion of national income, that is per cent of GDP, devoted to public social expenditure, and social protection or social security in particular has continued to increase in the OECD as a whole in recent years, though more slowly;
- Such historically constructed investments in redistribution dwarf the percentages of national income committed by the developing countries to the public social services and to social security and pose critical questions about discrimination between countries as well as within countries. The international agencies and the richest governments are today part of the cause of mass poverty in the world – as surely as they also possess the means of providing most of the answer;

- Every country has exceptional features. Nonetheless there is support on grounds of economic and social performance for a classification into three models, represented in this report by Norway ("Nordic" or "Social Democratic"); Germany ("Corporatist") and the United States and the United Kingdom ("Liberal" or "Residual");
- Poverty and inequality rates are smallest in the first of these three models and largest in the third. The evidence about economic performance is less conclusive. In all three models comprehensive social insurance and tax-financed group schemes covering everyone in certain population categories (such as elderly, disabled, children) account for much more than half the expenditure, and means-tested social assistance for the smaller part of expenditure in nearly all OECD countries;
- Comprehensive social insurance and tax-financed benefit schemes for entire social groups account for between three-fifths and two-thirds of the costs of schemes in the OECD to redistribute income to reduce poverty. And for the three principal social groups who benefit – children, disabled and elderly – these can therefore be regarded as the "bedrock" measures in social security systems everywhere;
- Means-tested social assistance and tax credit schemes account for around one-third of OECD social security costs and have well-testified social and administrative disadvantages. Social scientists have shown that the more conditional and even punitive forms of selective social assistance are counter-productive for social cohesion, well-being and productivity;
- Therefore social security schemes involving entire populations and categories of the population like young children and disabled people in developing countries, i.e. social insurance and tax-financed "universal" group schemes, deserve priority, even if for reasons of limited resources they have to be phased in by stages;
- Developing countries experience conditions very different from those that applied in the 19th and 20th centuries to the original OECD members. Countries like Germany, England and the United States were not subject to the domination of much more powerful external governments, agencies and corporations. International taxation and not just national taxation to finance social security in developing countries is therefore at issue;
- If developing countries are to adopt a contribution-based or group tax-based system of social security two new facts have to be recognised: (1) that because of population movements and interchanges the systems will have to be brought step by step into greater conformity with systems in the industrialised countries, and this includes social insurance, tax-financed benefits and social assistance; (2) that the current influence of the TNCs and big powers over local economies and populations in the global market has to be matched by international tax-revenue and employer contributions raised for particular groups in those countries. Sources of

international revenue will have to augment the meagre resources from national revenues available to the governments of developing countries in today's global market. International social security is coming to stay.

The main recommendations of the report are:

(1) Turning research into action: [For] cross-national research to identify social insurance and group tax-financed schemes in the OECD countries that have worked best in relation to their economic and social development. This can show how their key principles and mechanisms might be applied by stages to the emerging institutions of developing countries, with tax contributions from industrialised countries, to reduce poverty quickly. Also research is needed with the developing countries themselves to review how their own schemes for social protection can be most quickly extended;

(2) Universal coverage: To extend agreements by governments to give greatest weight to "universal" contributory social insurance and tax-financed group benefits in constructing social security systems to defeat poverty. Contribution-based social insurance depends on revenue willingly provided from wages by employers and employees to earn entitlement to individual and family benefits in adversity, including unemployment, sickness, disability, bereavement and retirement benefits. Tax-financed group schemes will be crucial for some groups unable to work, such as children, the severely disabled and the elderly of advanced age. Transnational companies should play their part on behalf of sub-contracted labour in countries with which they trade. Similarly, Governments trading extensively with low-income countries must accept greater responsibility for the establishment and growth of social security in those countries. The need for a catching-up exercise and for more coherent international development has become urgent.

## Introduction

The introduction and confirmation of successive United Nations Charters and Conventions in the last half-century demonstrates the increasing acceptance of human rights as a basis for re-casting development policies. Human Rights have come to play a central part in discussions about economic and social development, and have been ratified by the great majority of governments in the world. This report traces events of recent decades in relation to the fundamental rights to social security, including social insurance, and an "adequate" standard of living (Articles 22 and 25 of the Universal Declaration of Human Rights; 9 and 11 of the International

Covenant on Economic, Social and Cultural Rights; and 26 and 27 of the Convention on the Rights of the Child).

These rights have not been widely invoked during a long period of intensifying concern about the persistence of large-scale extreme poverty in the world and the formulation of the Millennium Development Goals. Thus, they were not regarded as a necessary element of the discussions around the structural adjustment policies and then the Social Fund in the 1980s and 1990s, in the fraught regions of Sub-Saharan Africa, Latin America, South Asia and Eastern Europe[1]. Attention was focused by the international financial agencies on targeting and short-term means-tested benefits at least expense rather than also, or instead of, minimal living standards for all. This mistake was compounded by an over-generalised, ambiguous and undirected international anti-poverty strategy – concerned in the broadest and most indirect terms with economic growth, overseas aid, debt relief and fairer trade. Whether there was "trickle down" or even proportionate benefits derived by the poorest sections of population was not precisely investigated and monitored.

In their reports of the late 1990s and early 2000s the international agencies have begun to recognise the strengths of comprehensive or universal public social services and benefits, partly at the instigation of international organisations such as the ILO and UNICEF. Recognition of the strengths of social security for all, including social insurance, may follow. The urgent re-formulation of development policies to reduce poverty may then be welcomed – and may bring tangible success.

Attempts to restrain and roll back social security in the last three decades have been made with too little understanding of the accumulating historical impetus in all OECD countries of its elaborate institutions and multiple functions. This report has sought to review that history because of the critical contemporary need to establish an economic and social as well as political consensus about strategy. It is part of the answer to a wider question, expressed sharply by one writer: "How did the rich countries *really* become rich?" (Chang, 2003, p. 2). In looking back at the policies and institutions created and used it may be that egg shells have to be broken in this process.

The task is not just to re-introduce a successful historical model. It is to re-shape that model to meet new problems as well as problems that have been familiar for generations. The strength of a universalistic approach in social security, coincident with human rights, is in building coalitions between groups in society of a more varied kind, say, than those representing familiar ethnic or religious divisions. Social security systems have created cross-cutting and three generational social identities and have moderated multiple forms of discrimination. Shrewdly interpreted, universalism can encompass rights by gender, race, ethnicity, age and disability and give nationalism a stronger edge both in negotiating with outside powers and withstanding international shocks.

Although the case for rolling back social security is far weaker than believed by many mainstream contemporary economists, the promotion of their case for cuts, particularly in contributory social insurance, has faltered, largely because of persisting severe world poverty and growing social inequalities; and disturbing evidence of the inconclusive, at best, and negative, at worst, outcomes of the current international anti-poverty policies. The restoration of the social contract is becoming urgent. That contract must take a new form, but one that invokes the institutions that have served many countries so well in the past. Plans for the future of social security have to be compatible with cost controls and economic efficiency in a multi-national world. The human rights and social identity of social security has to be extended at the same time.

The momentum of international agencies, transnational corporations and the global market compels modernisation and a realistic extension of social security, including social insurance. Movement of labour and population between countries, delegating work from a headquarters country to sub-contracted labour in 50 or 100 countries, brokering new social relations and healing divisions, demands corresponding flexibility in those institutions that embody universal values of non-discriminatory support and security.

It is now widely accepted that the MDGs adopted with world acclaim in 2000 have small likelihood of being fulfilled by the intended year 2015. At current rates of progress, some of the goals are not going to be met for more than 100, or 150, years (Brown and Wolfensohn, 2004). Table 1 provides one, conventional, illustration of trends, drawing on World Bank data. According to these figures there has been progress in reducing poverty, though better proportionately than in reducing absolute population numbers. In the 14 years to 2001 numbers in "dollar-a-day" poverty declined by less than 100 million. On previously published data from the World Bank absolute numbers, excluding China, had increased by more than 100 million between 1987 and 1998 (Townsend and Gordon, 2002, p. 363).

However, World Bank data showing progress are no longer acceptable. There has been swelling criticism of the Bank's measurement of poverty, casting doubt on the estimates reproduced in Table 1 (Pogge and Reddy, 2003; Reddy and Pogge, 2001; Wade, 2004; Townsend and Gordon, 2002).

There are two major scientific issues in reaching a conclusion about trends. One is the technical issue of updating the poverty line from year to year, *and* translating that poverty line into the equivalent purchasing power (or cost of consumable goods and services) in the currency of each particular country. A new research study on the updating of the poverty line has brought a number of the cogent criticisms of the last two decades into sharp focus, arguing that the World Bank's poverty line was lowered

**Table 1:** Population living below $1.08 per day at 1993 PPP (World Bank)

| Region | Percentage of population in households consuming less than the poverty line | | Number of poor (in millions) | |
|---|---|---|---|---|
| | 1987 | 2001 | 1987 | 2001 |
| East Asia | 26.6 | 14.9 | 418 | 271 |
| Eastern Europe and Central Asia | 0.2 | 3.5 | 1 | 16 |
| Latin America and Caribbean | 15.3 | 10.0 | 64 | 52 |
| Middle East and North Africa | 4.3 | 2.4 | 9 | 7 |
| South Asia | 44.9 | 31.9 | 474 | 439 |
| Sub-Saharan Africa | 46.6 | 46.4 | 217 | 312 |
| Total | 28.3 | 21.3 | 1,183 | 1,098 |

*Source:* For 1987, Townsend and Gordon, 2002, p. 363, drawing on Chen and Ravallion, 2001, Table 2; and for 2001, Kakwani and Son, 2006, Table 2.

from 1993, when the former roughly devised 1985 poverty line of $1.00 per person per day was pitched questionably at $1.08 per person per day, instead of a more representative and much higher figure, estimated at UNDP's International Poverty Centre recently to be $1.50 (Kakwani and Son, 2006). For 2001 Table 2 shows what a big increase there is in world poverty when $1.50 rather than $1.08 is treated as the correct baseline for 1993 and subsequent years[2]. Absolute poverty in the world becomes 36%

**Table 2:** Population living below $1.08 per day and $1.50 per day at 1993 PPP in 2001

| Regions | Percentage of poor | | Number of poor (millions) | |
|---|---|---|---|---|
| | World Bank ($1.08) | IPC ($1.50) | World Bank ($1.08) | IPC ($1.50) |
| East Asia | 14.9 | 28.5 | 271 | 520 |
| Eastern Europe and Central Asia | 3.5 | 8.6 | 16 | 41 |
| Latin America and Caribbean | 10.0 | 15.7 | 52 | 82 |
| Middle East and North Africa | 2.4 | 9.0 | 7 | 27 |
| South Asia | 31.9 | 56.6 | 439 | 779 |
| Sub-Saharan Africa | 46.4 | 61.8 | 312 | 417 |
| Total | 21.3 | 36.1 | 1,098 | 1,865 |

*Source:* Kakwani and Son, 2006, Table 2. They reproduced World Bank estimates based on $1.08 per person per day, and then calculated estimates based on a poverty line of $1.50 per person per day, i.e. the median of the poverty lines of 19 low-income countries in Africa and Asia in the 1990s.

and not 21% in 2001 – raising the population numbers by 800 millions to little short of 2 billions.

The second scientific issue is the practice since 1985 of limiting the measure of a "poverty line" to material needs and not also to social needs – and adjusting that line in subsequent years not for changing needs but only by applying a cost-of-living index to a historically fixed list of consumables and services. In the 1990s the World Bank stated that two elements – material and social needs – had to be combined in the operational definition and measurement of poverty (See the discussion in Townsend and Gordon, 2002, pp. 358–367). Research to establish social needs was promised but not fulfilled (World Bank, 1990, p.26; and see also World Bank, 1993a, 1993b, 1996, 1997, 2000, and 2001). Subsequent measures were based only on fixed basic material needs. Therefore, according to the World Bank's own carefully chosen definition, the scale of world poverty must be under-estimated. By re-pricing only the cost of meeting the defined material needs of a base year rather than also calculating the changes in those needs, the trend from year to year in such scale of poverty must also be under-estimated. Were orthodox measures of household and individual needs to be periodically up-dated to reflect changes in the customary norms of consumption and the roles and obligations being laid on citizens, workers and members of families, the scale of world poverty would be recognisably much more serious.

However, whether allegiance is paid to the orthodox World Bank estimates of the scale of poverty, or to the different, more dismaying, estimates based upon the material and social needs of populations swept along by contemporary market and other powerful social, economic and political forces, the slow progress in reducing the vast extent of poverty, and dealing with the remorseless increase in levels of world inequality, is now generally agreed to be unacceptable. The anti-poverty policies of the 1980s and 1990s have been unsuccessful. New national and international anti-poverty policies have to be substituted, or added, as a matter of urgency.

The biggest and most practicable contribution to a solution rests in social security. Social security developments in the context of growing commitments to human rights in the last 50 years deserve examination. Has the process of introduction and consolidation of systems of social security continued, among other effects, to substantially reduce poverty nationally? The public argument for and about social security has existed for many years but has been virtually dormant since 1980. The right to social security was expressly included in formal declarations of human rights by the great majority of countries from 1948 onwards. It formed part of the Universal Declaration of Human Rights in 1948. It was included in the International Covenant on Economic, Social and Cultural Rights in 1966 and the Convention on the Rights of the Child in 1989, coming into force respectively in 1976 and 1990. It became the documented spur for early statistical handbooks on development (e.g. Russett et al., 1964). It has also formed a basis of more enlightened appeals for action to reduce poverty.

Three steps in formulating a new approach might therefore be proposed: to (i) explain how human rights, and especially the right to social security, have been re-iterated and expanded in legal and quasi-legal form in the last 50 or 60 years; (ii) show broadly how social security systems of considerable scope and scale were established by the OECD countries and whether the history and structure of those systems, especially in relation to economic growth, hold any lessons for current development policies; and (iii) describe in what respects early attempts in the developing countries to institutionalise social security do or do not, and perhaps cannot, resemble the pathways to the reduction of poverty through the establishment of systems of social security taken in the history of the OECD countries.

## The fundamental right to social security

International human rights instruments provide a legal framework for strategies to reduce poverty:

> "A rights-based approach allows links to be made between otherwise disparate issues and gives legal weight and content to many of the concepts that are traditionally seen and analysed in terms of development, management and welfare. It thus moves away from the instrumentalist and utilitarian language of development economists to that of the entitlements and obligations enshrined within the formal legal system, while retaining the moral authority which other approaches lack" (Chinkin, 2002, p. 564).

One corollary of this argument about entitlement and obligation is to move away from state-oriented international law to international law concerned equally with the rights of individuals and with "the responsibility of states and other international actors" (Chinkin, ibid, p. 564).

Social security systems were established in all OECD countries and the history of the process of establishing human rights has much to offer the framing of current and prospective anti-poverty policies in the developing countries. The rights were expressed first in the Universal Declaration of Human Rights but later repeated, with particular reference to social insurance as part of social security, in later instruments, such as the International Covenant on Economic, Social and Cultural Rights and the Convention on the Rights of the Child (see Figure 1). In the last two decades public discussion of world poverty has been increasingly related to violations of, and future fulfilment of, human rights (see for example, UN,

**Figure 1:** The rights to social security and an adequate standard of living

| Authority | Social security | Adequate living standard |
|---|---|---|
| Universal Declaration of Human Rights (1948) | **Article 22** – Everyone, as a member of society, has the right to social security and is entitled to realisation, through national effort and international co-operation and in accordance with the organisation and resources of each state, of the economic, social and cultural rights indispensable for their dignity and the free development of their personality. | **Article 25(1)** – Everyone has the right to a standard of living adequate for the health and well-being of their family, including food, clothing, housing and medical care and necessary social services, and the right to security in the event of unemployment, sickness, disability, widowhood, old age or other lack of livelihood in circumstances beyond their control. |
| International Covenant on Economic, Social and Cultural Rights (1966-came into force 1976) | **Article 9** – The States Parties to the present Covenant recognise the right of everyone to social security, **including social insurance**. | **Article 11 (1)** – The States Parties to the present Covenant recognise the right of everyone to an adequate standard of living for himself and his family, including adequate food, clothing and housing, and to the continuous improvement of living conditions. |
| Convention on the Rights of the Child (1989) | **Article 26(I)** – States parties shall recognise for every child the right to benefit from social security, **including social insurance**, and shall take the necessary measures to achieve the full realisation of this right in accordance with their national law. | **Article 27 (I)** – States parties recognise the right of every child to a standard of living adequate for the child's physical, mental, spiritual, moral and social development. **Article 27 (3)** – ... and shall in case of need provide material assistance and support programmes, particularly with regard to nutrition, clothing and housing. |

1995 and 1997; UNDP, 1998a; 1998b, 2000, 2004; UNICEF, 2004; CHRI, 2001, Townsend, 2004).

The apparent correlation between a lack of progress on the MDGs and levels of spending on social security in the developing countries that have remained very low may not be coincidental. Substantial ongoing social security investments in the OECD countries contrast vividly with slow or non-existent progress in creating social security in poor countries. Eighty per cent of people worldwide still do not have access to adequate social security yet a small percentage of GDP (say 5–10 per cent for each population) would be sufficient in development programmes to provide everyone with a minimum standard of social security. Thus the right to social security was taken for granted in early formulations of development programmes (e.g. in modernisation theories of the 1950s and 1960s).

From the 1980s to the 2000s the objectives of the international financial agencies were to advise cuts in public expenditure and encourage privatisation, using low-cost targeted welfare sparingly in substitution of basic social security and services for all. In the middle of the first decade of the millennium there have been, as noted earlier, signs of change. The latest positive sign of a change of mood is the circulation of advanced drafts by the Committee on Economic, Social and Cultural Rights of its proposed General Comment No. 20 *The Right to Social Security (article 9)*, 16 February 2006. Among the listed obligations of States Parties to fulfil the right to social security are steps to legislate and adopt a social security strategy that include, for example, "establishing a contribution-based social security system or a legislative framework that will permit the incorporation of the informal sector" (CESCR, 2006, para. 37). This re-enforces the value for development in the low-income countries of the earlier history of the establishment of social security systems in the industrialised countries.

## Social insurance as a key component of social security

[…]

In general, social security in most if not all OECD countries began as fragmented, grudging means-tested social assistance and evolved, because of discriminatory selection of beneficiaries, meagre level of benefits and poor coverage of those theoretically entitled to assistance, into a predominantly social insurance based system. This provided protection to the unemployed, sick, disabled and elderly, and their dependants, and constituted a springboard back into paid employment. The reason for social insurance overtaking social assistance was mass protest against social assistance, and the fact that the working-class were taking initiatives to fill the holes. There were growing demands for more extended and sufficient coverage of benefits for those experiencing severe adversity beyond their control.

[…]

The problem is that the OECD countries established social security institutions early in industrial history, and developing countries are much worse placed to do the same today. Some are at the bottom of the global heap. But inch by inch some of them can begin to build on the right to social security, "including social insurance," by introducing laws and expecting international companies to bear a reasonable share of the costs of minimal benefits in adversity (as well as a minimum wage) – ensuring that this applies to subcontracted labour forces. This would begin to reduce the problems posed by the informal economy – by providing incentives to both employees and employers to abide by the terms of contractual social insurance – and hence extend the range of the formal economy. It would be a mistake to assume that only tax-financed benefits have a part to play in new social security measures in developing countries. International organisations, and institutions, also have to make a necessary contribution.

In identifying the components of social security in history readers will find that the individual, the employer and the government each made a formal contribution to social insurance. In today's conditions each of these three are differently placed. The individual is increasingly interested in his or her entitlement in another country (professional readjustment, migrant labour, remittances, asylum seeker, refugee, re-settlement, transfer of pension, family members in different country locations). The employer is increasingly a transnational company, with costs and responsibilities extending to many countries, and involving indirect, informal or sub-contracted labour. And the Government is increasingly dependent on international laws and agreements, including those affecting national tax revenue, and has an interest in harmonising taxation in different countries, and affording access to benefits and services cross-nationally and nationally. Later in this report the implications for the re-design of social security in both developing and industrialised countries will be assessed. In a global society there may have to be greater standardisation of social security and services, as well as a more prominent role in funding and designing national and regional schemes for the most powerful industrialised countries.

## The history of systems of social security

How were the human rights to social security and an adequate standard of living in practice introduced in the OECD countries? In fact all member countries put in place the right to social security over many years – going back long before the 1939-45 war. As the reader will see, many of them were successful in achieving long-term sustainable economic growth at the same time as they substantially reduced poverty. Whether as cause or effect of economic growth all countries evolved extensive systems of social security. [...]

First, [Table 3] compares total public social expenditure with its largest component, social security, as per cent of GDP, in OECD countries for the year 2001. As can be seen, with the exceptions of Mexico and Korea, between 8% and 19% of GDP was committed in that year to social security cash benefits. Most OECD countries are committing more than 20% of GDP to public services and cash benefits. Crucially, more than half of this is committed to cash benefits. This contrasts dramatically with the meagre levels of GDP committed both to services and to benefits in the developing countries.

**Table 3:** Total Public Social Expenditure, and Total Public Social Security Expenditure (included), as percentage of GDP (countries ranked highest–lowest for 2001)

| Country | Total public social expenditure as % GDP (2001) | Total public social security expenditure (cash benefits) as % GDP (2001) | Total public social security expenditure (cash benefits) as % GDP (2001) (new OECD series) | | | | |
|---|---|---|---|---|---|---|---|
| | | | 2001 | 2002 | 2003 | 2004 | 2005 |
| Sweden | 29.8 | 14.4 | 17.2 | 17.3 | 18.1 | 17.8 | 17.4 |
| Denmark | 29.2 | 15.2 | 16.3 | 16.4 | 17.0 | 16.8 | 16.2 |
| France | 28.5 | 17.9 | 17.1 | 17.3 | 17.5 | 17.6 | 17.9 |
| Germany | 27.4 | 15.6 | 18.6 | 19.5 | 19.8 | 19.4 | 19.2 |
| Switzerland | 26.4 | 18.2 | 11.0 | 11.4 | 12.1 | .. | .. |
| Austria | 26.0 | 18.9 | 18.6 | 19.0 | 19.2 | 18.8 | 18.6 |
| Finland | 24.8 | 15.4 | 15.9 | 16.3 | 16.7 | 16.8 | 16.4 |
| Belgium | 24.7 | 16.2 | 15.4 | 15.8 | 16.1 | 16.0 | 16.0 |
| Italy | 24.4 | 17.1 | 16.2 | 16.5 | 16.8 | 16.9 | 17.1 |
| Greece | 24.3 | 16.5 | 16.9 | 16.9 | 17.6 | 17.1 | 16.7 |
| Norway | 23.9 | 11.6 | 13.7 | 14.8 | 15.6 | 14.8 | .. |
| Poland | 23.0 | 17.9 | 17.4 | 17.6 | 17.5 | 16.8 | .. |
| UK | 21.8 | 14.2 | 13.7 | 13.2 | 13.3 | 13.3 | 13.4 |
| Netherlands | 21.4 | 13.3 | 11.1 | 11.2 | 11.5 | 11.5 | 11.1 |
| Portugal | 21.1 | 13.2 | 12.0 | 12.6 | 13.8 | 14.1 | 14.9 |
| Luxembourg | 20.8 | 14.5 | 13.9 | 14.6 | 15.0 | 15.0 | 14.7 |
| Czech Republic | 20.1 | 12.4 | 12.7 | 12.5 | 12.3 | 11.9 | .. |
| Hungary | 20.1 | 13.0 | 12.8 | 13.5 | 14.0 | 14.1 | 14.8 |
| Iceland | 19.8 | 8.4 | 7.0 | 8.0 | 9.4 | 8.9 | 9.1 |
| Spain | 19.6 | 12.8 | 11.7 | 11.8 | 11.7 | 11.7 | 11.6 |
| New Zealand | 18.5 | 11.6 | 10.9 | 10.5 | .. | .. | .. |
| Australia | 18.0 | 9.9 | 8.5 | 8.2 | 8.6 | 8.4 | .. |
| Slovak Republic | 17.9 | 11.9 | 12.0 | 11.8 | 10.9 | 10.4 | .. |
| Canada | 17.8 | 8.0 | 10.8 | 10.7 | 10.5 | 10.2 | .. |
| Japan | 16.9 | 9.1 | 10.5 | 11.1 | 11.2 | 11.3 | .. |
| USA | 14.7 | 7.9 | 11.4 | 12.0 | 12.1 | 12.0 | 12.0 |
| Ireland | 13.8 | 7.5 | 8.3 | 8.7 | 9.0 | 9.0 | .. |
| Turkey | 13.2 | .. | .. | .. | .. | .. | .. |
| Korea | 6.1 | 2.3 | 2.0 | 1.9 | 2.3 | 2.5 | .. |
| Mexico | 5.1 | 1.3 | 1.8 | 1.6 | .. | .. | .. |
| OECD 23 | 22.0 | 13.6 | | | | | |
| OECD 25 | — | — | 13.2 | 13.5 | 13.8 | 13.7 | (13.6) |
| OECD 30 | 20.9 | 12.6 | | | | | |

*Source:* OECD (2004), Social expenditure database, SOCX via www.oecd.org/els/social/expenditure series 2001, 2nd and 3rd columns, and new National Accounts series,4th-8th columns – showing total public social expenditure and total public social security/cash expenditure for 2001-2005.

Second, the table shows no marked fall in expenditure in the last 5 years. On the contrary, in 2005, 10 of the 17 countries for which expenditure on social security could be tracked up to and including 2005, including the US, increased expenditure as a percentage of GDP. In five countries such expenditure, expressed as per cent of GDP, was reduced and in the remaining two countries expenditure in the two years remained approximately the same.

Most low-income countries commit less than 5 per cent of GDP in total to public social services and benefits, some of them less than 1 or 2 per cent of GDP. Table 4 draws a few examples from high- and middle-spending OECD countries to compare with data for developing countries compiled by the ILO (ILO, 2001). The table shows the gap in spending between countries such as France, Germany and the UK and developing countries like China, Mexico, India, Kenya, Ghana and Indonesia. In high-spending countries total public social security expenditure is between 14 per cent and 18 per cent of annual GDP. In low-spending countries it can be a fraction of 1 per cent to 4 or 5 per cent.

The key role of social security becomes striking when the distribution of income in "developed" countries before and after taxes and social transfers is considered. Table 5 gives a summary of the effects on the extent of poverty – by current definitions of poverty in European (and OECD) member countries. Some OECD countries reduce domestic poverty more than others but everywhere the combined effects on existing institutions of social security are very substantial. In the table it can be seen that there is strong evidence in support of the division of countries by theorists into different types of welfare state, especially in relation to social security, that were established in the 20th century.

Table 5 illustrates vividly the extent of redistribution through

**Table 4:** Total public social security expenditure as percentage of GDP in selected high-, middle- and low-spending countries

| Countries | Total |
|---|---|
| *High-spending* | |
| France | 17.9 |
| Germany | 15.6 |
| UK | 14.2 |
| *Medium-spending* | |
| Australia | 9.9 |
| Japan | 9.1 |
| Chile | 8.2 |
| United States | 7.9 |
| *Low-spending* | |
| Ghana | 2.1 |
| China | 1.5 |
| India | 1.5 |
| Indonesia | 1.1 |
| Mexico | 1.1 |
| Kenya | 0.3 |
| Zambia | 0.3 |

*Source:* High- and middle-spending countries – see Table 3 above. Low-spending countries – data adapted from ILO (2001) Statistical Annex. The data for the low-income countries apply to 1996 (1995, China) and exclude health care (then counted in "social security expenditure").

social transfers in OECD countries (total public expenditure, including public social security).

**Table 5:** Percentage of population no longer in poverty – post-social compared with pre-social transfers, by country and welfare regime (1999)

| Welfare regime/country | Per cent of total population no longer in poverty | Per cent of total population in poverty after transfers | Mean per cent in poverty (grouped by regime) |
|---|---|---|---|
| *Social Democratic/ Nordic* | | | 11.4 |
| Denmark | 30.3 | 10.8 | |
| Sweden | 35,5 | 10.2 | |
| Finland | 33.1 | 13.3 | |
| Netherlands | 31.2 | 11.4 | |
| *Corporatist* | | | 13.8 |
| Austria | 35.6 | 14.2 | |
| Germany | 29.6 | 11.8 | |
| France | 32.8 | 15.9 | |
| Belgium | 32.0 | 13.9 | |
| Luxembourg | 31.8 | 13.3 | |
| *Liberal/residual* | | | 18.3 |
| United Kingdom | 25.0 | 18.7 | |
| Ireland | 23.4 | 17.9 | |
| *South European* | | | 19.6 |
| Italy | 27.5 | 18.5 | |
| Spain | 28.9 | 17.3 | |
| Greece | 25.5 | 21.9 | |
| Portugal | 25.9 | 20.6 | |
| EE12 | 28.6 | 16.5 | |
| EE15 | 29.8 | 15.5 | |

*Source:* Derived from Papatheodorou and Petmesidou, 2004.

The correlation between high social transfer rates and low poverty rates prompts specific questions about cause and effect. One test is to investigate examples of unusual advances in social spending attributable to new or greatly extended schemes introduced by government. Traditionally these have not been closely tracked and the impact on poverty rates of different elements of multiple policies apportioned. But some exceptions of this kind have been documented. Thus, there was a marked decline in 1968, compared with the immediately preceding years of 1966 and 1967 and with years after 1968, of elderly poor in the United States. The direct cause was a 13 per cent increase in social security (Old Age and Survivors Insurance) effective from February 1968 – which was the only across-the-board social security benefit increase enacted between 1965 and late 1969 (Fisher, 1976, p. 59). The research covered the period 1959-1974 and showed that variations in the level of social security benefit, as well as access to benefit, largely accounted for variations in the proportion of aged persons in poverty. A linear least squares regression was run for 1959 and all years in the period 1966-74.

Support for the key role of social security for the elderly, as well as for other groups, in all OECD countries, is found in a number of the statistical surveys of the Luxembourg Income Study. Thus "without social security income, a large proportion of the older population would live in poverty in all developed countries" (Wu K., 2005).

[...]

[T]wo of the common features of the various OECD systems must be specified. One is that despite periodic levelling off, and sometimes reduction, of the annual sums included in the national budgets, relative investment by OECD countries in social security has, on average, continued to grow.

**Table 6:** Social Security Transfers as per cent of GDP

| Year | United States | Japan | Germany | France | United Kingdom | Italy | OECD |
|------|---------------|-------|---------|--------|----------------|-------|------|
| 1960 | 5.0 | 3.8 | 12.0 | 13.5 | 6.8 | 9.8 | 7.0 |
| 1970 | 7.6 | 4.6 | 12.7 | 14.8 | 8.8 | 12.4 | 8.8 |
| 1974 | 9.5 | 6.2 | 14.6 | 15.5 | 9.7 | 13.7 | 10.5 |
| 1990 | 11.1 | 7.4 | 15.2 | 16.9 | 11.8 | 15.5 | 12.2 |
| 2000 | ... | 10.0 | 18.8 | 18.0 | 13.2 | 16.7 | 12.6* |
| 2005 | 12.0 | 11.3 | 19.2 | 17.9 | 13.4 | 17.1 | 13.6* |

*Source:* 1960 – OECD (1992), *Historical Statistics 1960-1990,* Paris, OECD, p.67; 1970-2000 – OECD (2001a) *Historical Statistics 1970-2000,* and *2004* – OECD (2005), *National Accounts of OECD Countries,* Paris, OECD. The data for 2005 are provisional and also drawn from a new OECD series on cash benefits. In comparison with earlier decades, the admission of new members has slightly lowered average spending.

Table 6 illustrates the rising cost of social security in six of the highest-profile countries, some of which have a history of reluctance on the part of government to tax substantially or extend the welfare state.

During the last half-century the percentage of GDP devoted to social security transfers on average by OECD countries has continued to grow, albeit more slowly in the last decade. [...]

A feature of social security in nearly all countries is the greater investment in social insurance and non-selective group benefits than in means-tested social assistance. This structural feature suggests that a similar balance will work best for developing countries. Schemes that apply to all members of a population or group might predominate over schemes dependent on selecting those with the lowest incomes. This bears on the fact that social security, *including social insurance* (author's emphasis), is one fundamental right that is included in several of the human rights instruments, to be routinely noted by States Parties. But this could also serve as a structural feature or model for international "pump-priming" and hold lessons for new or additional forms of international aid to eradicate poverty.

[...]

## Economic growth and social security

Do large-scale social transfers handicap economic growth? What came first, growth or social security? National histories of both social security and economic growth, and of their interrelationships, are of course chequered. Here only a start can be made in identifying cause and effect. However, a sufficient statistical account allows the provisional conclusion to be reached that the institutionalisation of social security and economic growth has been mutually interdependent and is a major factor accounting for the relative prosperity and low poverty rates of OECD compared with developing countries.

[...]

Low-spending countries tend to have a more unequal distribution of gross or original incomes, before as well as after social transfers, and higher rates of poverty by EU and OECD standards. [...]

A generation of research has failed to demonstrate a clear relationship between economic growth and trends in the incomes of poor people. One of the most incisive reports was that of Newman and Thomson (1989) who assembled economic data from a large number of countries and cast doubt on "trickle down" to such effect that the reverse seemed to be the more correct interpretation (see also Foster and Székely, 2001). World Bank analysts continued to argue for "trickle-down". Thus Dollar and Kray purported to show that "incomes of the poor rise one-for-one with overall growth", namely that for every 1% increase in GDP the incomes of the poorest 20 per cent also increase by 1%. They concluded that public spending on health and education is of little benefit to the poor (Dollar and Kray, 2000). However, their findings turned out to be a statistical artefact from a flawed methodology. When applied to random numbers (instead of real data) their method produced the same result (Vandemoortele, 2002, especially pp. 385 and 394–5).

Following study of the concept of "pro-poor" economic growth and its application to particular countries at UNDP's International Poverty Centre (see for example Son and Kakwani, 2004, Kakwani et al, 2004; Vandemoortele,

2004), a cross-country analysis of 80 countries was completed. In these countries a total of 237 spells of economic growth were examined. In 106 the average real per capita income actually declined. In 131, pro–poor growth, i.e. proportionately more of the average increase in income going to the poorest deciles, could be reliably confirmed for only 55 – or 23% of the total – while less of the average increase in income went to the poorest deciles in the remaining 76 countries (32% of the total). Growth in these countries was "anti-poor" (Son and Kakwani, 2006).

The influential idea of the last 30 years, therefore, that high investment in public social services and social security deters growth, and that economic growth alone will automatically lead to a reduction in poverty, has not attracted convincing supporting research evidence. There is more support for the alternative idea, that high public social expenditure has positive effects on growth. For example one research team completed an analysis of economic and social data accumulated from panel data over 10 years for the United States, Germany and the Netherlands, representing the Neo-Liberal, Corporatist and Social Democratic (including Nordic) welfare regimes that came to be separately identified by social scientists in the 20th century. The welfare regimes of the three countries were compared in terms of their success in promoting efficiency (economic growth and prosperity), reducing poverty, and promoting equality, integration, stability and autonomy. The US did not turn out to be more efficient than the other two. Overall, the statistical data collected over time suggested that on both economic and social criteria the Social Democratic regime had advantages over the Corporatist, and both had advantages over the Neo-Liberal welfare regimes[3]. Altogether, there has been a large range of research studies refuting the argument that social security has had a negative impact on economic development (good examples are Koskela and Viren, 1983; Atkinson, 1995; Singh, 1996; Gramlich 1997; and the general review in Hall and Midgeley, 2004, Chapter 8).

[...]

## The growth and diversification of social protection

[...]

In the mid-20th century the member states of Europe came to insure the majority of their populations against the social risks of sickness, disability, old age and unemployment and of welfare deficiencies related to childhood, motherhood, housing and education. They shared a common historical legacy. [...]

[S]ocial insurance contributions rather than taxes came to play the majority role in funding expansion. This was put in place by member countries of the EU. Rarely has this agreement across countries been identified as the key

feature of the development of strategies to defeat poverty and simultaneously secure citizens against some of the worst risks to life and livelihood.
[...]

## Social security in developing countries

The history of social security in the OECD countries holds particular implications for antipoverty action and social and economic stability in the developing countries. Before drawing these together one prior question requires an answer. How does the historical and current account of systems in the OECD countries in this report relate to the policies currently being followed in the developing countries?

One implication of the historical analysis above is the value to governments of using "direct" measures to reduce poverty. For example, contributory social insurance schemes for those of working age who may become sick, disabled, unemployed or bereaved, and non-contributory tax-based benefit schemes, especially for children, disabled people and the elderly, have been shown to have an early but also lasting impact.

Existing social security schemes in developing countries are desperately under-resourced, as Table 4 graphically illustrates. The schemes present a diverse picture (see, for example, ILO reports cited for 2001 and 2003). A semblance of a system had been introduced by colonial authorities in most of Asia, Africa and the Caribbean 100 or more years ago. They were extended in the first instance to civil servants and employees of large enterprises. There were benefits for relatively small percentages of population that included health care, maternity leave, disability allowances and pensions. In general they neglected the poor, and especially rural poor.

In the last decades there has been mounting concern about slow progress in developing social security in the poorest countries. In 2005 the ILO reported a modelling exercise – applying three models of very basic social protection packages. Costs turned out to be "within reasonable affordable limits" if countries were committed to reducing poverty (Pal et al, 2005, p i). But the "mobilisation of international resources will be needed in order to make this an achievable target" (ibid, p. xii). In an early page of this report (p. 13) the extent of the gap in percentage of GDP redistribution that needs to be closed is illustrated.

Today there are a number of examples of new as well as previous initiatives taken in developing countries themselves to establish social protection schemes. For example, in India there are schemes in different states intended for large numbers as well as a range of schemes for small categories of population such as middle- and high-ranking civil servants. Cash allowance schemes for children, disabled and elderly are however few and far between. Allowances for children seem likely to develop only as a by-product of other social protection schemes. In 1995 the Government of India introduced an all-India social protection scheme – the National Social Assistance Programme (NSAP). Social assistance benefits are intended to become gradually available to poor households in the case of old age, death of the breadwinner and maternity. Thus there are three types of benefit: the National Old Age Pension Scheme, the National Family Benefit Scheme and the National Maternity Benefit Scheme. Along with expenditure on education, health, public health, labour welfare and family welfare, total "social security" expenditure per person grew very slowly at constant 1980–81 prices from 128 rupees in 1973 to 142 rupees in 1999, or by 11 per cent. "Although this increase is not large, it is nonetheless likely to have contributed towards the sharp decrease of poverty in India in recent years" (Justino, 2003, p. 16).

One current national initiative, also relevant to children, is the National Rural Employment Guarantee Act of 2005 (NEGRA), launched by the Prime Minister Manmohan Singh in February 2006. The Act seeks to guarantee employment for 100 days a year at the minimum wage to one person from every poor household to improve rural infrastructure – roads, school buildings and village water supply and to regenerate the land while reducing soil erosion (Mehrota, 2006, p. 13). A major problem in developing a social security system for those who cannot be employed, or are unlikely to be employed in the foreseeable future, and especially in considering child allowances, is that the Government collects only 8-9% of GDP in taxes, compared with 22% (2003) in China and 14% generally in low-income countries (1990–2001). And tax revenues from the richest sections of the population have actually fallen in the last two decades (ibid, p. 13).

In Latin America some countries introduced social insurance and other schemes before the 1939 war, and other countries followed suit after the war. In that continent there is already more of an established system of social security on which to build. However, benefits tend to be limited in range and coverage. In earlier decades they were not administered by one central government agency. There were multiple schemes for different occupational groups (Hall and Midgeley, 2004, p. 241). Social insurance had to be greatly extended. And in the informal sector of the economy non-contributory schemes, or schemes with minimal contributions were needed.

A good start has been made by individual governments in the 21st century, including Brazil, especially in schemes for children, for example, the *Bolsa Escola* programme. Relatively local "Conditional Cash Transfer" (CTT) schemes preceded this programme, which was launched in 2001. In less than a year 5 million households with children between 6 and 15 were receiving a cash benefit. Transfers were limited to US$ 15 a month per family, conditional on school attendance. In 2003 the programme was absorbed with other federal CCTs into *Bolsa Familia* (Britto, 2006a, p.

15). Early research showed positive effects on schooling and nutrition but longer-term effects on rates of poverty and child labour remained unclear (ibid, pp. 15-16) 19. The enlarged Bolsa Familia programme now reaches 11 million households. Mexico was in fact the first country in Latin America to introduce a nation-wide CCT programme – *Progresa*, in 1997. This was expanded and re-named Oportunidades in 2002. This confers cash or in-kind allowances to the household (up to US$ 60 a month) on condition the children attend school and health check-ups are arranged for all members of the household (ibid, p. 15).

Less publicised than the Bolsa Familia programme in Brazil has been the "Continuous Cash Benefit Programme," or "Beneficio de Prestacao Continuada" in Portuguese (BPC). Since 1993 people aged 65 and over and people with a severe disability whose household per capita income is less than a quarter of the minimum wage (approximately US$ 1 a day in March 2006) are eligible for a transfer equivalent to the monthly minimum wage (approximately US$ 4 a month). In December 1996, after its first year of operation, as many as 346,000 benefited. At the end of 2005 2.1 million benefited, just over half being disabled and under 65 (Medeiros et al, 2006, p. 15). There are other cash transfer mechanisms, including one of invalid pensions, which is a contributory scheme for workers in the formal market and benefited 2.6 million in 2005.

This illustration shows that programmes to gradually increase public expenditure so that categories of the extreme poor start to benefit offer a realistic, affordable and successful alternative. Under President Lula da Silva, the Brazilian Government's Zero Hunger Programme was planned to provide quantity, quality and regularity of food to all Brazilians in conjunction with accelerated Social Security reform (Suplicy, 2003). The Zero Hunger Programme includes food banks, popular restaurants, food cards, distribution of emergency food baskets, strengthening of family agriculture and a variety of other measures to fight malnutrition. The Social Security reform programme includes social assistance for low-income 15-17 year-olds; assistance for 7-14 year-olds who are enabled to go to school and avoid the exacting toll of the worst conditions of child labour; minimum income and food scholarships for pregnant and nursing mothers with incomes less than half the minimum wage or who are HIV positive; benefits for elderly disabled with special needs; and a range of other transfer programmes for the elderly, widowed, sick and industrially injured and unemployed that are being enlarged year by year (Suplicy, 2003).

The social security programmes being developed in Mexico, Chile, Costa Rica and especially Brazil are useful models for poorer countries in Africa and South Asia. They provide a parallel set of evidence to that for social security in the OECD countries, and can help governments and international financial agencies from making mistakes in their plans to reduce poverty and improve social and economic wellbeing.

Africa presents a more varied picture of measures taken to counter poverty than often appreciated. In some countries new social insurance schemes have been introduced – for example a maternity and sickness scheme in Namibia. Mauritius and the Seychelles have universal benefit programmes (and relatively low poverty rates). Means-tested cash benefits are found in Botswana and Mozambique. Zambia has successfully piloted a social cash transfer scheme targeted to the poorest tenth of households (Gassmann and Behrendt, 2006). But social security expenditure in countries like Burundi, Cameroon, Ethiopia, Ghana, Kenya, Madagascar, Mauritania, Nigeria, has declined or remains at a tiny level compared with GDP (ILO, 2002).

South Africa has high rates of poverty, labour migration and unemployment, and the problem of HIV/AIDS has become acute. Nonetheless, since the fall of apartheid in 1994 strong attempts have been made to begin to introduce a comprehensive social security system. In 1998 a Child Support Grant was started, worth R100 for each child below the age of 7 whose carer had an income of less than R800–R1100, depending on composition of family and other factors. The 1998 figure of R100 has been increased regularly in line with inflation, reaching R180 in 2006. By early 2003 there were 2.5 million beneficiaries. By late 2005 the age limit had been increased gradually to 13, and the number of beneficiaries reached over 6 million (and the number of adults 4 million). There are criticisms of coverage. While there is good evidence that the grant reaches some of the poorest of children (Case et al, 2003) the increasingly large numbers of orphans, street children and child-headed households, in many cases the consequence of the spread of HIV/AIDS, remain largely ineligible (Barrientos and DeJong, 2004, and see the initiatives in measuring child poverty by Noble et al, 2005). Despite the difficulties many South Africans regard the development as the "road to universality" and give the example of the Child Support Grant when illustrating the significance of the incorporation by South Africa of the principle of the "progressive realisation" of economic and social human rights into their common law jurisdiction. The idea of a staged programme towards comprehensive coverage was a feature of a major commissioned report (Committee of Inquiry into a Comprehensive System of Social Security for South Africa, 2002).

There is a new cash grant in South Africa. But everywhere wider non-contributory schemes for children are urgently needed, preferably schemes that are categorical and not means-tested.

China has the largest population in the world (though India is rapidly catching up). Information about social security is improving rapidly and social surveys in particular are providing data about poverty and policy measures – particularly for urban areas – that were previously inaccessible. For example, one survey draws on 1998 urban household survey data covering 17,000 households in 31 provinces, conducted by the National Statistics Bureau (see Hussain, 2002). The research team, made up of experts from China and from other countries, including the UK, decided to distinguish between a "food poverty line" – defined by the average cost in different provinces for people among the poorest 20% of just buying enough food to provide the minimum necessary average of 2,100 calories per person per day – and a (higher) poverty line. The cost of meeting the poverty line was the cost of meeting the "food poverty line" plus the cost of meeting other basic non-food needs. These were worked out using a regression exercise on the urban data and, just as food needs were calculated on the basis of an average of 2,100 calories per person, non-food needs were calibrated for different households in accordance with basic non-food expenditure of households just satisfying the criterion of spending on food to ensure a minimum of 2,100 calories.

The national average food poverty line of 1,392 yuan per month was estimated to be 32 per cent lower in the province of Qinghai, at one extreme among the 31 provinces, and 69 per cent higher in the province of Shanghai, at the other extreme. The general poverty line is lower than the purchasing power parity equivalent of the World Bank's poverty standard of $1 per day. It produces an estimate for the whole of China of 4.7 per cent, or 15 million in poverty, when income is the standard, and 11.9 per cent, or 37 million in poverty, when expenditure is the standard. Where the exact poverty line is drawn matters in China because a large proportion of population have very low incomes. Thus, if the poverty line were drawn 50 per cent higher than the very stringent threshold in fact adopted, the figure of 4.7 per cent in poverty becomes 20% or nearly 90 million in urban areas. It would be even higher if it measured the costs of subsistence, like that undertaken by the Institute of Forecasting of the Chinese Academy of Sciences and even by the National Statistics Bureau and the Ministry of Civil Affairs.

The key policies for the urban poor in China are the Minimum Living Standard Scheme (MLSS), a recent addition, and a longer-established social security package that includes social insurance. The MLSS began as a local initiative that was gradually extended to regions and then all urban areas. With the disappearance of the living allowance for laid-off employees by the end of 2003, the MLSS and unemployment insurance will be the "two last lines of defence against urban poverty." By the end of the 1990s 3.3 million registered unemployed, or 55 per cent were receiving unemployment benefit; and 3 million of the 460 million urban population were recipients of the MLSS. Eligibility is restricted and special investigation of particular cities found that only about a quarter of those in poverty were receiving assistance.

For China to make improvements in anti-poverty policies many authorities seem to agree that publicly provided social assistance and social insurance need to be extended and benefits raised; the administrative infrastructure greatly strengthened; poverty monitored more successfully, and the methods of financing benefits overhauled. Certainly different models of social security in both rich and poor countries are being scrutinised closely.

According to the ILO "One of the key problems facing social security today is the fact that more than half of the world's population are excluded from any type of statutory social security protection" (van Ginneken, 2003, p. 1; see also van Ginneken, 1999; Cichon and Scholz et al, 2004; Kulke et al, 2006; Midgeley, 1984; ILO, 1984; Rodgers, 1995; Reynaud, 2001). In South Asia and Sub-Saharan Africa approximately 90 per cent and in middle-income countries between 20 and 60 per cent lack such protection. "Social security has become more necessary than ever due to globalisation and structural adjustment policies. ... The challenge for governments, social partners and civil societies is to create such conditions that the large majority of the population contributes to basic social insurance schemes" (ibid, p. 66).

The ILO Social Security (Minimum Standards) Convention (No. 102) 1952 laid down minimum income requirements per child, of either 3 per cent of the ordinary manual labourer's wage, for the economically active, or 1.5 per cent of that wage for all other families. In families with four children the benefit would amount to 12 per cent (or 6 per cent in the case of those not in work). The ILO Convention was signed by 40 countries – including Niger, Senegal and Mauritius. It became part of the European Code of Social Security and the blueprint for such instruments as the European Social Charter, the Treaty of Amsterdam of the European Union and regional agreements in Africa and Latin America (Kulke et al., 2006, p. 4). If the World Bank had sought policies to enforce this Convention rather than extend its neo-liberal anti-poverty strategy there would have been a dramatic fall in world poverty.

A serious obstacle to the extension of social security schemes in developing countries to reduce poverty has been the difficulty of reaching agreements on trade (see, for example Watkins 2002; Offenheiser and Holcombe, 2003; Held 1995; Kanbur, 2000) and therefore the exact needs and rights to income of people to be employed directly and indirectly by transnational corporations. Discussions about the nature, still less the legal enforceability, of "corporate social responsibility" (see ILO 1998; OECD 2001b) have not been resolved – in particular the question of employing TNCs making contributions to the extension of social security in developing countries in which they have a substantial interest and where many workers are employed on their behalf. Another serious obstacle has been the difficulty of re-building and/ or strengthening tax administration. Taxation and contributory insurance systems can be introduced or strengthened to raise national revenue to match international tax or aid revenues both for the protection of children and families, but also to be fully answerable to representatives of national electorates as well as participating overseas governments, with independent powers to monitor policies and outcomes.

Because of mounting criticism of the insufficient powers and therefore the policies of nation states to resolve poverty in the global economy of the 21st century joint funding of social security between countries is likely to evolve (see, for example Townsend, 2004 for an illustration of joint funding of child benefit). Demands for joint action, including action to build and enforce tax and contribution revenues, will necessarily lead to the introduction of new forms of international taxation and accompanying independent international inspectorates.

## Conclusion: Bringing social security into the 21st century: the lessons of the OECD models

The results of the study of the different OECD models hold special lessons for the governments of developing countries. But the latter have taken particular social security initiatives themselves, despite being relatively small in scale, from which lessons may also be derived by the governments of the OECD countries – for internal reflection and action applied to their own systems as well as for external collaborative support.

The rapid evolution of the global market compels bridging operations between systems of social security rather than increasing a risk of outright collision. The OECD countries are bound to be caught up in anxious internal reviews of their future international anti-poverty strategy. This will be explained. In sheer scale the commonalities of need, interest and practices at equivalent stages of wealth dwarf the differences noted in the pages above among "welfare" regimes or among individual countries in the prosperous North.

The principal anti-poverty strategy for developing countries advised by the North will have to be changed. Using various techniques and combinations of social groups the early-industrialised countries introduced social security systems of substantial scale in relation to GDP to alleviate the major part of poverty in their midst. But the instructive history of OECD countries' programmes to overcome their own domestic poverty in the late 19th and early 20th centuries has not been generally explored, even in rough terms, as a model to be followed by and for the poorest countries. The dominant Washington consensus has been to argue for a reduction in the size of the state – reducing public expenditure, extending private ownership and management and de-regulating rules about business, trade and labour conditions. This was to apply to rich and not only poor countries. But the starting-points have been poles apart, and have been getting wider.

It was assumed that social security, except in the form of safety nets or means-tested selective measures for the extreme poor, was neither affordable in very poor countries nor desirable. Social security, in any extensive form, many economists argued, was an albatross. As we have seen, this flies in the face of current as well as historical practice in the OECD countries – including, it must be emphasised, the United States[5]. But many of the policies recommended for developing countries in the last 30 years are becoming increasingly doubtful as bringing about lower rates of poverty and enhanced social, political and economic stability. Affordability seems to be the wrong criterion in the 21st century when set against *both* the current developments in low-income and middle-income countries, *and* the history of the high-income countries.

What are the principal recommendations, therefore, that emerge from our analysis? The conclusions of this investigation of early and late 20th century social security in OECD countries stand, in their context, as implied strategic recommendations or principles for all governments – whether developing or industrialised:

(1) Social security came to be accepted by *all* OECD member countries as one of the major paths to modernisation and sustainable growth as well as the principal means to reduce domestic poverty. That path continues to be actively pursued, by and on behalf of the new member states of both the OECD and the EU.

(2) The path to social security for low-income countries today will necessarily be different, because of the existence and operation of a global economy, including powerful transnational corporations, and modern international communications, but cannot be rejected.

(3) In all OECD countries a mix of universal (that is, social insurance and tax-financed group schemes) and selective measures (that is, benefits conditional on test of means) came to be developed. The range was from selectively coercive schemes with paltry resources to universally protective low-benefit schemes, and finally to universally positive development schemes, designed to achieve minimally adequate standards of living and social participation and minimally creative collective enterprise.

(4) Generally the greatest weight came to be placed on "universal" contributory social insurance and then tax-financed group benefits. When breaking social security into its three key components it becomes clear that if they are to be considered for adoption in the developing countries they have to be modernised along the following lines:

(a) contribution-based social insurance depends on revenue willingly provided from wages by employers and employees to earn entitlement to individual and family benefits in adversity, including unemployment, sickness, disability, bereavement and retirement benefits. As employers of huge numbers in their international labour forces transnational companies will be required to make contributions on behalf of subcontracted labour in countries with which they trade. Individuals will need to be contractually and not informally employed – with beneficial results for the reduction of extensive violations of human rights – especially child labour and other labour violations. Individuals will also require rights when moving to, and/or employed in, other countries. Correspondingly, companies will acquire easier relationships with governments in whose countries they seek to establish production and services;

(b) Tax-financed group schemes will be crucial for some groups unable to work, such as children, the severely disabled and the elderly, say over 75. Children have had no opportunity to qualify for benefit through contributory social insurance. Very old people were in paid employment long before social security systems were established. The tax base can no longer be applied only to one country – because of the mobility of labour and the multi-country practices of employers;

(c) And, to be effective, selective social assistance will also depend on revenue from companies, and all, but especially rich, countries, employing relevant labour and making cross-national profit. In a supplementary report to follow this publication methods of finding the global revenue to meet social security rights, and bring current practices up-to-date are set out in some detail. The principal illustration is of a new application of the 1972 Tobin Tax, a Currency Transfer Tax, to raise quickly a sum much larger than current levels of overseas aid and debt relief for a UN Child Investment Fund to develop a system of child benefit in cash and kind in the poorest countries.

(5) The path to social security of similar scale and importance for developing countries as for already industrialised countries has effectively been obstructed or not actively supported, at the same time as social security in the industrialised countries has continued to grow, or has remained at a high level, proportionate to GDP. This has fostered a remorseless growth of inequalities between rich and poor countries, and of inequalities within low-income and middle-income countries, especially those of considerable size and growing economic importance globally, such as Brazil, India and China. The

need for a catching-up exercise and for more coherent international development of social security systems has become urgent.

**Endnotes**

[1] See the extended discussion in Townsend and Gordon, 2002, chapters 1 and 17 but especially 8 and 9. "The structural adjustment policies pursued in most developing countries have often contributed to a decline in the small percentage of the working population in the formal sector. The successive waves of structural adjustment programmes have also led to wage cuts in the public and private sectors, thereby eroding the financial base of statutory social insurance schemes. ... [The programmes have] often resulted in severe cuts in social budgets" (ILO, 2001, p. 34).

[2] The choice of $1.08 reflected the median of the 10 *lowest* poverty lines among a sample of 33 countries. In 2006, independent examination of the national poverty lines of 19 low-income countries (15 in Sub-Saharan Africa and 4 in Asia, including India) constructed in the mid-and late-1990s, produced a different median figure of $1.50 (Kakwani and Son, 2006, p. 6).

[3] "... It turns out that the social democratic welfare regime is 'the best of all possible worlds.' [Of the three alternative regimes it] turns out to be the best choice, regardless of what you want it to do. [It] is clearly best on its home ground of minimising inequality. But it also turns out to be better at reducing poverty than the liberal welfare regime, which targets its welfare policy on that to the exclusion of all else. The social democratic welfare regime is also at least as good in promoting stability (and arguably at least as good at promoting social integration) as is the corporatist welfare regime, which ostensibly attached most importance to those goals. The social democratic welfare regime is also best at promoting autonomy, something valued by all regimes if not necessarily prioritised by any. Thus, no matter which of those goals you set for your welfare regime, the social democratic model is at least as good as (and typically better than) any other for attaining it" (Goodin et al., 1999, p. 260).

[4] "Initial evaluations have shown positive effects of CCTs on schooling and nutrition. The evidence regarding the impact on child labour is not conclusive, since school attendance can be frequently combined with work and requires broader interventions. The impact on poverty is still not so clear ... In the long run, the translation of higher educational attainment into higher earnings cannot be taken for granted. It depends on the quality of education, rates of employment, absorption of skilled labour in the economy and general rates of return to education" (Britto, 2006a, pp. 15-16; see also Britto, 2006b).

[5] After a long review of developments in the US after 1935 two analysts concluded in 1997: "Universal eligibility for Social Security remains sound policy and an essential feature of a public pension programme designed to provide widespread protection, especially to low- and moderate-income populations" (Kingson and Schulz, 1997, p. 59).

## References

Atkinson, A.B. (1995) 'Is the welfare state necessarily an obstacle to economic growth?', *European Economic Review*, 39, pp 46-96.

Barrientos, A. and DeJong, J. (2004) *Child poverty and cash transfers*, Childhood Poverty Research and Policy Centre CHIP, Working Paper 2, available from the Institute for Development Policy and Management, University of Manchester.

Britto, T. (2006a) 'Conditional cash transfers in Latin America', in UNDP, *Social protection: The role of cash transfers, Poverty in Focus,* International Poverty Centre, Brasilia.

Britto, T. (2006b) 'Recent trends in the development agenda of Latin America: an analysis of conditional cash transfers' (see www.eldis.org).

Brown, G. and Wolfensohn, J. (2004) 'A new deal for the world's poor', *The Guardian*, 16 February.

Case, A., Hosegood, V. and Lund, F. (2003) *The reach of the South African child support grant: Evidence from KwaZulu-Natal*, Working Paper 38, Centre for Social and Development Studies, University of Natal, Durban.

Chang, H.-J. (2003) *Kicking away the ladder: Development strategy in historical perspective*, London: Anthem Press.

Chen, S. and Ravallion, M. (2001) 'How did the world's poorest fare in the 1990s?', Development Research Group, World Bank, *Review of Income and Wealth*, pp 1-33.

Chinkin, C. (2002) 'The United Nation Decade for the Elimination of Poverty: what role for international law?', *Current Legal Problems 2001*, Oxford: Oxford University Press.

Cichon, M. and Scholz, W. et al (2004) *Financing social protection*, Geneva: ILO.

CESCR (Committee on Economic, Social and Cultural Rights) (2006) *General Comment No. 20, The right to social security Article 9*, Geneva: CESCR.

CHRI (Commonwealth Human Rights Initiative) (2001) *Human rights and poverty eradication*, New Delhi: CHRI.

Committee of Inquiry into a Comprehensive System of Social Security for South Africa (2002) *Transforming the present, protecting the future*, Draft consolidated report, Pretoria: Committee of Inquiry into a Comprehensive System of Social Security for South Africa.

Dollar, D. and Kray, A. (2000) 'Growth *is* good for the poor', www.worldbank. org/research.

Fisher, G.M. (1976) 'Poverty among the aged and social security benefits', in F.E. Waddell (ed) *The elderly consumer*, Columbia, MD: The Human Ecology Center, Antioch College, pp 54-64.

Foster, J. and Székely, M. (2001) 'Is economic growth good for the poor?', Paper presented at the WIDER Development Conference on Growth and Poverty, Helsinki, 25-26 May.

Gassmann, F. and Behrendt, C. (2006) *Cash benefits in low-income countries: Simulating the effect on poverty reduction for Tanzania and Senegal*, Issues in Social Protection Discussion Paper 15, Geneva: ILO.

Goodin, R.E, Heady, B., Muffels, R. and Dirvan, H.-J. (1999) *The real worlds of welfare capitalism*, Cambridge: Cambridge University Press.

Gramlich, E.M. (1997) 'How does social security affect the economy?', in E.R. Kingston and J.H. Schulz (eds) *Social security in the 21st century*, New York: Oxford University Press, pp 147-55.

Hall, A. and Midgeley, J. (2004) *Social policy for development*, London: Sage.

Held, D. (1995) *Democracy and the global order: From the modern state to cosmopolitan governance*, Cambridge: Polity Press, pp 297-323.

Hussain, A. (2002) 'Urban poverty in China: incidence and policy response', in P. Townsend and D. Gordon (eds) *World poverty: New policies to defeat an old enemy*, Bristol: The Policy Press.

ILO (International Labour Office) (1984) *Into the twenty-first century: The development of social security*, Geneva: ILO.

ILO (1998) *The ILO Tripartite Declaration of Principles Concerning Multinational Enterprises and Social Policy – Ten years after*, Geneva: ILO.

ILO (2001) *Social security: A new consensus*, Geneva: ILO.

Justino, P. (2003) *Social security in developing countries: Myth or necessity? Evidence from India*, Poverty Research Unit at Sussex, Working Paper No 20, Brighton: University of Sussex.

Kakwani, N., Khandker, S. and Son, H.H. (2004) *Pro-poor growth: Concepts and measurement with country case studies*, Working Paper No 1, Brasilia: UNDP, International Poverty Centre.

Kakwani, N. and Son, H.H. (2006) *New global poverty counts*, Working Paper Number 20, Brasilia: UNDP, International Poverty Centre.

Kanbur, R. (2000) 'Economic policy, distribution and poverty: the nature of disagreements', for the Swedish Parliamentary Commission on Global Development, 22 September.

Kingson, E.R. and Schulz, J.H. (eds) (1997) *Social security in the 21st century*, New York: Oxford University Press.

Koskela, E. and Viren, M. (1983) 'Social security and household savings in an international cross section', *American Economic Review*, vol 73, no 1, pp 212-17.

Kulke, U., Cichon, M. and Pal, K. (2006) 'Changing tides: a revival of a rights-based approach to social security' (draft), Geneva: Social Security Department, ILO.

Medeiros, M., Diniz, D. and Squinca, F. (2006) 'Cash benefits to disabled persons in Brazil: an analysis of the BPC – Continuous Cash Benefit Programme,' Working Paper 16, Brasilia: UNDP, International Poverty Centre.

Midgeley, J. (1984) *Social security, inequality and the third world*, New York, NY: Wiley.

Newman, B. and Thomson, R.J. (1989) 'Economic growth and social development: a longitudinal analysis of causal priority', *World Development*, vol 17, no 4, pp 461-71.

Noble, M., Wright, G. and Cluver, L. (2005) *Conceptualizing, defining and measuring child poverty in South Africa: An argument for a multi-dimensional approach*, Oxford: Centre for the Analysis of South African Social Policy, University of Oxford.

OECD (Organization for Economic Cooperation and Development) (1992) *Historical statistics 1960-1990*, Paris: OECD.

OECD (2001a) *Historical statistics: 1970-2000*, Paris: OECD.

OECD (2001b) *The OECD guidelines for multinational enterprises: Focus: Global instruments for corporate responsibility*, Paris: OECD.

OECD (2004) *Social expenditure database*, SOCX, www.oecd.org/els/social/expenditure.

Offenheiser, R.C. and Holcombe, S.H. (2003) 'Challenges and opportunities in implementing a rights-based approach to development: an Oxfam America prospect', *Nonprofit and Voluntary Sector Quarterly*, vol 32, no 2, pp 268-306.

Pal, K., Behrendt, C., Leger, F., Cichon, M., Hagemayer, K. (2005) *Can low-income countries afford basic social protection? First results of a modelling exercise*, Geneva: Social Security Department, ILO.

Papatheodorou, C. and Petmesidou, M. (2004) 'Inequality, poverty and redistribution through social transfers in Greece in comparative perspective', in M. Petmesidou and C. Papatheodorou (eds) *Poverty and social exclusion*, Athens: Exandas (in Greek).

Pogge, T. and Reddy, S. (2003) *Unknown: The extent, distribution and trend of global income poverty*, www.socialanalysis.org.

Reddy, S.G. and Pogge, T.W. (2001) *How not to count the poor*, New York, NY: Departments of Economics and Philosophy, University of Columbia.

Reynaud, E. (2001) *The extension of social security coverage: The approach of the ILO*, ESS Paper No 3, Geneva, ILO.

Rodgers, G. (ed) (1995) *The poverty agenda and the ILO: Issues for research and action*, Geneva: International Institute for Labour Studies.

Russett, B.M., Alker, H.R., Deutsch, K.W. and Lasswell, H.D. (1964) *World handbook of political and social indicators*, New Haven, CT: Yale University Press.

Singh, A. (1996) 'Pension reform, the stock market, capital formation, and economic growth: a critical commentary on the World Bank's proposals', *International Social Security Review*, vol 49, no 1, pp 21-44.

Son, H.H. and Kakwani, N. (2004) *Economic growth and poverty reduction: Initial conditions matter*, Working Paper 2, Brasilia: UNDP, International Poverty Centre.

Son, H.H. and Kakwani, N. (2006) *Global estimates of pro-poor growth*, Brasilia: UNDP, International Poverty Centre.

Suplicy, E.M. (2003) 'President Lula's zero hunger programme and the trend toward a citizen's basic income in Brazil', London: London School of Economics and Political Science.

Townsend, P. and Gordon, D. (eds) (2002) *World poverty: New policies to defeat an old enemy*, Bristol: The Policy Press.

Townsend, P. (2004) 'Direct policies to fight child poverty', *In Focus*, Rio de Janeiro: UNDP, International Poverty Centre.

UN (1995) *The Copenhagen Declaration and programme of action: The World Summit for Social Development 6-12 March 1995*, New York, NY: United Nations Department of Publications.

UN (1997) *Sustaining social security*, New York, NY: Department for Economic and Social Information and Analysis, UN.

UNDP (1998a) *Overcoming human poverty*, UNDP Poverty Report 1998, New York, NY: UNDP.

UNDP (1998b) *Poverty in transition? Regional Bureau for Europe and the CIS*, New York, NY: UNDP.

UNDP (2000) *Overcoming human poverty: UNDP Poverty Report 2000*, New York, NY: UNDP.

UNDP (2004) *Children and poverty*, *In Focus*, Newsletter of the International Poverty Centre, Rio de Janeiro: UNDP.

UNICEF (2004) *The state of the world's children 2005*, New York, NY: UNICEF.

Vandemoortele, J. (2002) 'Are we really reducing global poverty?', in P. Townsend and D. Gordon (eds) *World poverty: New policies to defeat an old enemy*, Bristol: The Policy Press, pp 377-400.

Vandemoortele, J. (2004) *The MDGs and pro-poor policies: Related but not synonymous*, Working Paper No 3, Brasilia: UNDP, International Poverty Centre.

van Ginneken, W. (1999) *Social security for the excluded majority: Case studies of developing countries*, Geneva: ILO.

van Ginneken, W. (2003) *Extending social security: Policies for developing countries*, ESS Papers No 13, Geneva: ILO.

Wade, R.H. (2004) 'Is globalisation reducing poverty and inequality?', *International Journal of Health Services*, vol 34, no 3, pp 381-414.

Watkins, K. (2002) *Rigged rules and double standards: Trade, globalisation and the fight against poverty*, New York, NY: Oxfam International.

World Bank (1990) *World Development Report 1990: Poverty*, Washington, DC: World Bank.

World Bank (1993a) *Implementing the World Bank's strategy to reduce poverty: Progress and challenges*, Washington, DC: World Bank.

World Bank (1993b) *World Development Report 1993: Investing in health*, New York, NY: Oxford University Press for the World Bank.

World Bank (1996) *Poverty reduction and the World Bank: Progress and challenges in the 1990s*, Washington DC: World Bank.

World Bank (1997) *Poverty reduction and the World Bank: Progress in fiscal 1996 and 1997*, Washington, DC: World Bank.

World Bank (2000) *Balancing protection and opportunity: A strategy for social protection in the transition economies*, Washington, DC: World Bank.

World Bank (2001) *World Development Report 2000/2001: Attacking poverty*, Washington, DC: World Bank.

World Bank (2006) *World Development Report 2006*, Washington, DC: World Bank.

Wu, K. (2005) *How social security keeps older persons out of poverty across developed countries*, LIS Working Paper No 410, Luxembourg: LIS.

# 54

# Using human rights to reduce inequalities in economic and social development

Better measurement and more effective strategy are critical if we are to resolve our crisis of social development. The two are equally important and both have to be bridged. It is vital to deal with both inequality and poverty.

On the one hand, the world is faced with conclusive evidence of the growth of inequalities within and between countries. This trend carries great dangers for our future – as we can understand because of conflicts in which 43 countries are presently involved, the huge scale of HIV/AIDS, the disastrous prospects of climate change, young children engaged in bonded labour, the hundreds of millions still existing in extreme poverty and, at the other end of the spectrum, the relatively few but growing number of dollar billionaires.

On the other hand, there is widening allegiance to human rights. Most countries of the world have continued to put their signatures to the continuing stream of treaties about human rights. Despite grim trends in the facts about inequality and poverty, there exists the paradox of global hope. Discouraging evidence about developing economic and social divisions coexists with encouraging news about the willingness to agree the beliefs and values shared by more and more countries.

There has been a very rapid historic evolution of human rights treaties since 1948. The latest treaty to be signed was the Convention on Disabilities in March 2007. The need to establish equality with other people is felt more and more keenly, but at the same time this equality is disintegrating before our eyes. This is my starting idea.

Human rights instruments provide a framework for the analysis of development as well as for the eradication of multiple violations of rights that occur every day. The operational scientific definition and measurement of a meaningful poverty threshold, in contrast to the dollar-a-day pretence, demands professional time and attention and early international agreement. My focus today, however, is on the link between reiterated agreement on the

Townsend, P. (2008) 'Using human rights to reduce inequalities in economic and social development', Paper presented to the Egmont Institute conference, 'World inequality: a challenge to globalisation', Brussels, 17-18 March.

fundamental rights to social security and an adequate standard of living and the development of quite substantial social security systems in proportion to GDP in all the OECD countries. This is a key method of dealing with poverty in low-income countries and simultaneously addressing the extreme problems being created by the structural forces behind increasing global inequalities. This option is overlooked in the discussion about overseas and humanitarian aid.

To illustrate: the Universal Declaration of Human Rights of 1948 included Article 22 on the right to social security and Article 25 (1) on the right to an adequate standard of living. The United States, paradoxically, originally helped to initiate those particular rights, and they were repeated in the International Covenant on Social, Economic and Cultural Rights (adopted in 1966 and coming into force in 1976) and the Convention on the Rights of the Child in 1989.

Professor Decoster's presentation shows how necessary it is for scientists to reject the dollar-per-day thesis as a reasonable and dependable measure of poverty in the world. One reason is that the World Bank does not measure the true effects of inflation, as demonstrated by a number of experts, for example Kakwani and Son of the International Poverty Centre of UNDP. The World Bank estimated that between 1985 and 1993 inflation amounted to no more that 8% – compared with a figure of 50% estimated by Kakwani and Son. The numbers in poverty in the 1990s and early 2000s were clearly under-estimated. The IPC authors constructed a conservative estimate of the inflation pressures and they showed that the number of extreme poor in the world actually grew. The international financial agencies should have the grace to admit their mistake and accept more independent scientific evidence.

The second element of criticism for the dollar-a-day thesis is that the successive reports of the early 1990s stated that two elements should be sustained in a measure: the first to do with the minimum costs of nutrition and other basic needs and the second with the costs of participation in society or playing the necessary roles of membership of society.

Everyone has roles, as parents, as children, as neighbours, as citizens, all of which require resources. According to the World Bank this was a necessary element of the definition but it has not been scientifically followed through and calculated with care. After nearly 20 years, the reasons for that neglect demand attention.

There are many examples of inequality lying behind high rates of malnutrition and premature death, even in countries with mass poverty. In 2007 the WHO was able for the first time to distinguish between the wealthiest and poorest 20% in many countries, using an approximate indicator of asset ownership. The results showed, for example, that widespread stunting of children under 5 years of age applied in India and Sub-Saharan Africa to families above the poverty line. The problem applied to more poor families in India than in Sub-Saharan Africa. Other scientific studies have been demonstrating the value of measuring multiple deprivation rather than single forms of deprivation in low-income countries.

The World Bank, by providing us with a very rough figure about a dollar-per-day poverty, is taking a leading role in influencing international social policy about inequality and poverty. It is important to look more closely to the EU policies and to the social policies of the transnational corporations (TNCs) and international financial agencies. Their financial and legal powers are far greater than those of low-income countries. The World Bank lending reached $22 billion in 2005, but that represents a very tiny percentage (five hundredths of one per cent of world total GDP). The figure compares unfavourably even with the social security spending in the rich states like the UK currently spending a total of $210 billion on public social security (for the elderly, children, disabled unemployed and sick). The OECD (30 countries) total public expenditures on "social protection" in 2005-06 was $4,150 billion. Such figures dwarf the spending on the non-working poor in low-income countries and suggest what change of strategy is required.

In social security, we see very high levels of commitment of the Northern countries to their social security system. One illustrative table of statistics shows the total public social security expenditure as % GDP in selected high-, middle- and low-spending countries. France, UK, Germany are spending around 14 to 16% of GDP, a very considerable fraction is redistributed through social security. The average for all OECD countries is 13.5% of GDP.

For the low-income countries, including India and China, the percentage of GDP in these forms of redistribution is around 1-3% and that is a huge difference. Applying the OECD history to the low-income countries, they need to be allowed some chance of developing similar systems. Because of their place at the foot of the income pile globally, the conditions that are imposed on loans made to them and their dependence in trade they are not in a position tax wise to do much about that. We can do a lot through collaborative arrangements to establish the infrastructure they require but also to join in providing the percentage resources through necessary social insurance and employer (i.e. TNC) contributions. New forms of international taxation will also be needed. The Tobin tax or a currency transfer tax could easily be introduced regionally or by the UN. Experts have estimated that a currency transfer tax could easily raise $400-500 billion per year and the UN could use half or more of these proceeds as an investment fund for children. These ideas have been developed in the recent past, and can be put forward in a lot more detail. Perhaps they might capture the attention of the kind of leadership that is represented here today.

# 55

# Persuasion and conformity: an assessment of the Borrie Report on social justice

The Labour Party is recasting its policies on the welfare state and one substantial contribution to its thinking is the report of its Commission on Social Justice.[1] What informed the Commission's approach? Without saying as much, they appear to have been governed by the belief that to win the next election the Labour Party must bow to the pressures of the international market, reduce long-standing aspirations to social equality and withdraw from the most costly commitments to the welfare state. This led them to neglect what might be done about globalization, to discount stark national evidence about current economic trends and to ignore the implications of that evidence for social policies.

The Commission's Report attempts to bring off a fine balancing act – but on several counts does not succeed. Modernization is conceived as a problem of maintaining the allegiance of traditional Labour supporters while persuading them that it is no longer necessary or possible to aim for social equality and community through structural change. In the process, it is supposed, Labour will placate business interests or even harness them to its cause, and appeal to middle-of-the-road voters. New Labour will 'transform the welfare state from a safety net in times of trouble to a springboard for economic opportunity' with measures which enhance employability by investment in training and adult education, establish a minimum hourly wage and other legal rights, and possibly shift taxation from earnings to environmental pollution and resource use, including the use of roads.

If this characterization is correct, Labour's domestic policies on health, education, housing, community care, social security, personal taxation and employment will now be altogether different from those it pursued after the Second World War. The policies seem to depend on vacating the 'social' place in Europe and the world associated with Labour's construction of a welfare state. This conclusion, if not the exact policies which flow from it, appear to be endorsed by Tony Blair – for example in his speech on the fiftieth anniversary of Labour's victory of 1945.[2]

Townsend, P. (1995) 'Persuasion and conformity: an assessment of the Borrie Report on social justice', *New Left Review*, no 213, Sep/Oct, pp 137-50.

## What is the alternative?

There is an alternative approach, which the Commission did not seriously consider. It starts from the recognition that problems of impoverishment, social polarization and political instability have reached dramatic, and indeed threatening, proportions because powerful forces within the international market are operating in conditions of diminishing democratic restraint. The evidence for these disturbing trends is overwhelming.[3] As a consequence poverty and inequality are deepening at an alarming rate.[4] In these circumstances, a major national plan for social reconstruction, put forward in common cause with partners in Europe and elsewhere, is urgently needed to slow down, halt and even reverse these disastrous social trends. Given this background, the tasks for domestic policy then fall into place: complicity with international market forces will not do the trick. Only resolute dependence on collective interests and their expression through principles of public organization, control, and service will work. The formulation of such an approach in the UK might also reinvigorate a disillusioned electorate – as well as disillusioned democratic socialists. One point in particular appears repeatedly to have been ignored by the Commission: the basis of any partnership between public and private sectors depends on a strong public sector. Yet of course the public sector has been, and continues to be, undermined.

Serious proposals have to be put in place to restore and enhance its viability as an institutional force.

## The welfare state in different forms

This alternative approach can be considered at various different levels. If we consider different models of the welfare state, then we must ask whether Britain should, following the United States, take the path of the 'gradual erosion'[5] of what is already close to becoming a 'residual' welfare state; or whether it should instead emulate the greater resistance to such institutional dismantlement displayed by some of the central European and Scandinavian countries; or even attempt to reinstate welfare in conformity with a new European model involving better integrated social and economic development.[6] Of course, a more forthright case for measures to establish a radically more democratic and equal society, with necessarily a much larger public sector and system of public service, should be argued. But we can start by registering the decline from past standards. Social scientists attempt to classify the policy systems of different countries – sometimes in relation to measured fulfilment of declared objectives like social equality or equality of opportunity or sometimes just in relation to expenditure on certain arbitrarily defined public (and private) services. [...]

In the past some social scientists and historians saw the British welfare state largely as an accommodation to capitalism, and as perpetuating, rather than seriously modifying, class inequalities.[7] Such criticism did not register the extent of concessions and actual gains it represented. Likewise little effort was made to account for significant variations between states, whether classified by welfare or political criteria. This led to complaints that 'neo-Marxist grand theorists have largely rested content with abstract conceptual elaborations tied to illustrative case materials for one nation at a time.'[8] In recent years there have been changes. There are more attempts to compare developments empirically across countries, with the delineation of three worlds of welfare capitalism: the socialist – Denmark and the Netherlands, as well as Sweden; the conservative-corporatist – France and Germany; and the liberal – the United States.[9] Hitherto analysts have been inclined to distinguish the UK from the conservative–corporatist sub-category, but now the link with the US is more often made – mainly because of the extent of privatization, deregulation and means-testing since 1979. Another important theoretical development has been to look at particular welfare-state institutions and services – like pensions or housing – in depth, and across countries, in relation to the type of welfare state, as a basis for explaining social trends. Thus Michael Harloe has studied developments in public housing in relation to social policy theory.[10] Such research helps focus attention on social and economic policies as the prime agents of social change – whether progressive or regressive, whether tending towards or away from social disaster. Civil instability, and the collapse of civil rights, including welfare rights, are now properly regarded as part of the record to be studied. In theoretical reviews of the recent past and future of the welfare state the need to combine structural and political perspectives is recognized.[11] They also bring to the forefront the need, analytically, to understand the *linkages* between different sets of policies. Against this background the Commission for Social Justice was given the task of producing a reasoned theoretical basis for systematizing social planning.

The Borrie Commission's formal assignment was therefore potentially path-breaking. Its work was bound to reflect the preoccupations of its members. The Commission was set up in December 1992 and its report was published in November 1994. Its chairman was Sir Gordon Borrie, formerly the Director-General of Fair Trading. Among the fifteen other members of the Commission were some who were not members of the Labour Party and one, David Marquand, who had been a member of the Steering Committee of the Social Democratic Party from 1981 to 1988. Trades union and public service representation was very thin. The chairman declined to reassure Labour supporters that their historic commitments would be respected. Indeed, his press comments often gave the Conservatives a stick with which to beat the Labour Party. For example, an article in the *Observer* on 20 June

1993 indicated that the welfare state was at risk. It became increasingly clear that key principles of universality – particularly those affecting basic state pensions, child benefit and disablement benefit – were not inviolate. It is one thing to modernize policies, but surely another to repudiate the achievements and aspirations of generations of socialists.

## Indifference to public opinion

From an early date the Commission also discounted the substantial popular support for higher universal state benefits. Despite the blandishments of Thatcherite ideology, deregulation and privatization, and the continuous cuts made in the structure of benefits, repeated opinion polls in the eighties and nineties have shown big majorities in favour of improvements in basic benefits. […] Yet popular opinion about the direction of policy plays no part in the Commission's report: that was a miscalculation of the first magnitude.

## 'To live free from want'

Aside from the curious decision to ignore widespread public support for the welfare state, another of the Commission's mistakes was to sidestep key features of its terms of reference – terms which had been carefully agreed with the former Labour Party leader, John Smith. Thus, the last half of the terms of reference reads:

> To analyse public policies, particularly in the fields of employment, taxation and social welfare, which could enable every individual to live free from want and to enjoy the fullest possible social and economic opportunities;
>     And to examine the contribution which such policies could make to the creation of a fairer and more just society.

These terms have not been met. The whole emphasis of the report is on *strategy*, as in the title, not *policies*. The job set to the Commission by John Smith was clearly to examine the connections between policies and 'freedom from want'. This required careful assessment of past Labour policies – like earnings-related pensions – and of their overall and specific social effects. It also required a willingness to consider whether alternative policies should now be devised to meet the objective as, or more, effectively. Any alternative policy options would have to be accompanied by appropriate costings. But such a review was not undertaken. There is no pretence that the current report represents a detailed plan or set of policies which an incoming government could accept and implement, or modify in relation to defined priorities. The crucial instruction to find policies which would enable 'every' individual to 'live free from want' was disregarded. That word 'every' made unambiguous the injunction to discard means-tested solutions – which have never reached 'every' individual – and to choose measures which were inclusive or integrative, and not socially exclusive, which tend to build support for welfare, and not those which undermine it. All along, the Labour leadership kept its distance from the Commission's work, and therefore was not committed to accepting its principal recommendations, especially if alternative options were set out in detail. [...]

Thus, while the Commission was expected to produce a 'plan' of linked policies, the result was rather different. It was supposed to analyse present conditions, together with the policies which had brought them about, and show what had to be changed, and how, judiciously weighing short-term and long-term considerations. As it turns out, the Commission is surprisingly reticent about desirable policies either for the short or long term. Figures are hard to come by, and serious questions about scale, balance, priority, finance, likely public support, the relationship between public and private sectors, and conformity with European policies are left unexplored and unresolved. It is difficult to attach any figures to the Commission's proposals or to apply to them tests of 'fairness' by gender, age or economic status, either in relation to the individual or the family.

I am particularly concerned about the proposed economies. Nowhere does the Commission list the cuts, work out the savings gained by them, and go on to argue what should – and what could not, or should not – be restored from the destruction of the institutional apparatus built up with difficulty by Labour governments of the 1960s and 1970s. This applies most of all to pensions, child benefit, disability benefits and unemployment benefits, but also to the health and education services. The peremptory dismissal of the welfare inheritance, the achievement of post-war Labour governments, is shameful and shocking.

A review of the Commission's Report should mention the supporting papers. [...] [T]he second interim report of the Commission produced ten propositions on social justice.[12] [...] The first proposition read: 'Social Justice is about more than poverty – it concerns everyone. The best way to help the minority who are poor is to advance social justice for all.' The poor are of course only a section, sometimes a large section, of the population of a country. But 'poverty' is a condition brought about by distorted institutional control of the allocation and distribution of resources. There was no acknowledgment of that systematic control, through capital ownership and an institutionalized hierarchy of inequality, either in this early paper or in the subsequent series. Proposition 5 canvassed a 'widening access to wealth' but only in terms of individual home ownership and personal pensions. Proposition 9 referred to 'welfare state rights' but only in the context of 'heightened responsibilities'.

The supplementary texts do nothing to remedy the deficiency of the Report.

## A new philosophy?

To the first failure, not addressing public opinion, and the second, not fulfilling key features of the terms of reference, was added a third: namely, of not expressing, or even indicating, a coherent body of principle or theory to inform the proposed strategy. To modernize is to bring up to date, but presumably to do so without jettisoning worthwhile gains from the past, without alienating the most committed of one's supporters and without shirking an analysis of the nation's problems which may carry uncomfortable lessons for its leaders. Surprisingly, the Commission on Social Justice neglects key principles which have been held to define 'socialist' policies, including equality, solidarity, minimum sufficiency, public service, public ownership, progressive taxation, redistribution, service-affordability and internationalism. These principles can, it is true, be abstracted from operational detail, just as operational detail – in the form of the small print of contracts, regulations and policies – can be set out without clarifying the general principles which govern them. Logically, one can be inferred from the other. Yet something important is lost if principles are not clearly proclaimed. There is no doubt that the linked exposition of both the general philosophy and the particular proposals can be invaluable to party adherents and the public alike, focusing hopes and arousing enthusiasm, as the Beveridge Report, and perhaps a few other post-war reports, illustrated very well.

The nearest the Report comes to a formulation of principle or philosophy can be found in its early pages. After an account of the state of the nation in a changing world the Commission suggests there are three rival strategies or possible futures for policy (Chapter 3). We could become 'deregulators', 'levellers' or 'investors'. These categories are, of course, debatable and cannot be said to cover all shades of opinion.

One of the three options is ruled out. Deregulators 'dream of a future in which dynamic entrepreneurs, unshackled by employment laws or social responsibilities, create new businesses and open up new markets; in which there is no limit to how high earnings at the top will rise – and no limit to how low wages at the bottom will fall.... Theirs is a future of extremes.' It depends upon 'the unceasing drive for competitiveness through ever-cheaper production of what we already produce; socially ... upon the reduction of public service and public spending; politically ... on a logic of centralization and exclusivity, destroying publicly accountable institutions that stand between law-making government and individual decision-making in the market place.'[13]

The second is also ruled out, though less convincingly than the first. Levellers, it is claimed, are 'pessimists who do not see how we can turn the economy round, and in any case argue that economic renewal should not be the concern of a Commission on Social Justice. They say our job is [only] to protect the poor from economic decay. They believe we should try to achieve social justice primarily though the tax and benefits systems.'[14] This is a straw man. The authors of the report assert, 'The Levellers are concerned with the distribution of wealth to the neglect of its production; they develop policies for social justice independent of the economy.'[15] Many on the Left would not recognize this characterization of 'levellers', a title transparently intended to refer to their alternative strategy. They see redistribution and universal benefits as the right basis for policies of economic growth, and not just as an adjunct of employment rights, alongside a minimum wage and planning for the enlargement of public services, and not just their greater efficiency and responsibility. They would also see certain desirable forms of 'levelling' – namely social rights in employment and national insurance – as part of 'turning the economy round'. The description of Levellers in the report is a grotesque caricature of responsible thinking on the Left.

The third alternative, of course, is what the Report would have us endorse. Investors 'combine the ethics of community with the dynamics of a market economy. Investment in people by means of the extension of economic opportunity will provide the basis for prosperity as well as social justice.' The trouble is that this alternative is fitfully argued and poorly illustrated. There is some useful discussion of investment in child care and of measures to promote employment. Indeed, much of the analysis of the condition of the self-employed, of part-time work, the poverty trap and the threshold of entitlement to social insurance is helpful. But it is more than counterbalanced by omissions of a structural kind, and by various nods to Thatcherism. Thus, 'A higher social security budget is a sign of economic failure, not social success', and 'Restraints on top incomes, coupled with high tax rates, would send some – perhaps a large number – of the top earners and businesses abroad.'[16]

There is a fundamental problem with the Report's notion of an 'Investors' Britain'. The principle of *adequacy* both for earnings and benefits that it is expected to deliver is not spelt out nor argued for. Consequently the balance of different policies – their financing and their likely combined effect – are not presented or explained even as alternative options. To put the problem in the kind of language adopted by the Commission, the true division of strategy on the Left is that between 'Labour pretenders' and 'Labour realists'. The 'pretenders' believe that greater inequality is inescapable, and has to be dressed up in New Labour language; they are committed to market-compliant policies which at best may slow the slide down the slippery slope but not challenge the logic of polarization. The 'realists', by contrast, make a pessimistic diagnosis of current trends and see that the only way to defend people on average and low incomes, whether employed or not – and to halt and perhaps reverse impoverishment, growing inequality and instability – is to undertake structural reforms which reinforce social protection and move toward socialist principles of distribution and welfare, and to advocate legal and democratic control of international financial and market forces. The first is an 'enabling' and the second a 'structural' strategy.

## Gaps in the report

I have respect for the work of several members of the Commission and hoped for the best from the Report when I went along on 24 October 1994 to attend the launch. But like many other observers I had already become uneasy because of the chairman's articles and the Commission's procedures for dealing with evidence. The Report does furnish evidence for the growth of social inequality but does not spell out how serious it has become – for example, for pensioners, children and the disabled in the poorest fifth of the population – nor how far recent trends can be, and should be, reversed. Paradoxically the emphasis is all on equality of opportunity rather than equality as such, and nowhere is there any discussion of the deepening institutional hierarchies of power nor of how the rich and powerful might be held to better account. What is the point of all this stress on improving opportunities when the occupational and class positions to which these opportunities supposedly give access are being inexorably driven further apart? There is little point in enhancing people's opportunities to climb ladders if the ladders grow ever longer, the gap between rungs wider, and the chances of falling greater.

Principles of social justice must involve applying standards of comparison not just at one moment of time but over a period to establish trends, and therefore invite explanations and remedies for what has gone wrong. Between 1979 and the early 1990s the richest 20 per cent improved their share of disposable income from 36 per cent to 43 per cent. The poorest 20 per cent experienced a fall in their share from 10 per cent to 6 per cent.[17] Had the percentages stayed the same the richest 20 per cent would be £35 billion or £6,000 per household worse off than they now are. The poorest 20 per cent would be £17 billion or £3,000 per household better off than they now are. The Commission does not attempt to examine the causes, apportion blame, or explain how the slide can be halted or reversed. This is the biggest single recent change in British society, and it has many ramifications: it has to be given priority in political discussion.

Another defect of the Report is its failure to deal with disability. Affecting more than six million people at any one time, and many more over the course of their lifetimes, disability is given short shrift. There is a fleeting reference on one page to the campaign, which has been running for nearly 30 years, for a comprehensive disability income yet the Report asserts that 'further debate is needed' about how best to implement this measure. Such a treatment of this issue is dismissive, and unacceptable. [...]

## Full employment

Elements of the strategy proposed on jobs, education and training are welcome and would have a positive effect. These include a re-employment service, better training and education, child care facilities for lone parents, 'family-friendly' employment for men and women, reduction in working hours and vigorous promotion of equal opportunities. [...]

The problem remains that the Report contains no serious analysis of what Britain must do to contribute to a European and international strategy to halt and reverse the rising trend of mass long-term unemployment, nor to identify how more jobs can be created, particularly in the public sector. Despite friendly reference to a Delors plan to increase the share of GDP devoted to investment (p. 164) and the use of wage subsidies to boost employment, the different elements of a workable strategy are not thought through in an integrated and coherent fashion. In OECD countries the long-term rate of unemployment has doubled between the 1970s and the 1990s and the OECD has now resigned itself to continuing high rates of joblessness. World Bank policies on deregulation, privatization and cuts in public expenditure – especially in public social services – will not be changed without collaborative international pressure and tough national policies. [...]

What is required is a clear exposition of the structural causes of unemployment – especially those resulting from unnecessary lay-offs and transfers of plants and employment overseas – and a positive statement about the new role of public utilities and public services, especially the social services, in any up-turn in employment. Doing this convincingly will necessarily involve an accompanying statement about the principles and the extent of public ownership and public investment. A future Labour government cannot afford to neglect the unanswerable case for greatly enlarged public-sector employment. The case must also be made to the multinationals that the benefits of such a policy would be in their long-term interests and are even a condition of their continued stable operation. Without positive promotion of the public sector, Labour's attempt to appeal to the private sector is bound to take on the features of appeasement.

## Universal benefits

The Borrie Commission Report issues contradictory messages on universalism – giving emphatic support to the principle of universal benefits but recommending contrary practice. It refers to the need for a tax and benefit system that provides incentives, not disincentives, for employment, and one of the ways of achieving this is said to be 'a reduction in reliance on means-tested benefits' (p. 156). [...] The most important departure from these stated objectives involves the proposed minimum pension guarantee. [...] The Commission tries to disguise the fact that its proposed pensions guarantee will be means-tested. [...] The proposal for a minimum pensions guarantee has not been thought through. Similar proposals in the past have died a quick death. [...] It would have been a great help if the Borrie Commission had been sufficiently independent to set out the attractions of a properly organized, and democratic, insurance-based state pension scheme. Rest assured, the European Union is far from being in any position to establish an acceptable federal scheme. [...]

## 'Compulsory' private pensions

New schemes have been proposed to deal with the pensions problem. In addition to the minimum pensions guarantee recommended by the Borrie Report, there has been a proposal for compulsory private pensions put forward by Frank Field.[18] He has argued that 'changes for the poor will only come about if the self-interest of the majority is mobilized in a way which also promotes the common good', and that those who argue for redistribution of wealth to the poor are 'a public menace distracting from the real task'.[19] He proposes a new National Insurance Corporation of employers, employees and government representatives with power to determine rates of benefits and contributions. The government itself would retain only the power of veto. Secondly, there would be a Private Pensions Corporation to 'universalize' private pension provision 'within a framework of compulsory contributions by employees and employers'.[20] This proposal suffers from misconceptions about the nature of the private sector and about equal rights in representative democracy. A programme by which means-tested benefits might be reduced and 'as of right' benefits extended has to be set out step-by-step, costed, and shown to be controllable. Privatization and the relinquishing of elected power to a quango are not the measures which will establish a balance of power between low-paid wage-earners and high-paid elites, but rather a surrender of power to the primary forces in the private sector. Furthermore, the idea of 'compulsory' personal pensions is a contradiction in terms.

## An alternative strategy

What would an alternative strategy to that of the Borrie Commission look like?[21] A collaborative programme of social development could be devised. A Labour government must act internationally in the first instance to protect economic and social health. This will mean working with European allies to argue for the introduction of forms of regulations over multinational corporations; closing loopholes in cross-national taxation; protecting nationally-based companies and individual employees by means of more democratic company laws; using the European Union Social Chapter to improve labour law; promoting international links between trade unions; facilitating the internationalization of democratic pressure groups; encouraging cross-national links between city authorities; and, in particular, taking new initiatives to foster relationships between the First and the Third Worlds. To such a strategy must be added measures to monitor the development of multinational companies and to democratize the IMF and the World Bank in ways which will raise the representation of Third World populations and also the social interests of poorer groups in the rich countries. The problem with existing institutions of the international financial community is not just their exclusion of Third World countries, but also their exclusion of the poorest fifth or two-fifths of the populations of the rich countries. The treatment of refugees seeking asylum and of temporary workers in Europe are prime examples of this lacuna. Action along the lines indicated above could halt and reverse widening inequality, growing poverty and social instability. That action would have to be simultaneously national and international. It would be one part of an alternative approach to that set out in the Borrie Report.

How would the approach be worked out at national level? First, it would depend on an economic strategy attuned to raising rather than restraining demand. It would increase public-sector employment – for instance, through the enlargement of social services and developing new initiatives to conserve energy, improve transport and communications, reduce environmental pollution and recycle waste. It would encourage labour-intensive private-sector employment and define minimally acceptable employment rights, earnings and benefits as the basis for nationally productive activity. Second, the distribution of resources would need to be reorganized on more equitable lines to ensure the revenue necessary for economic investment and social development. Opportunities for tax avoidance would be severely diminished; tax allowances greatly reduced; the taxation of wealth increased; and the principles of remuneration exposed to more democratic control through, say, a consultative incomes policy.[22] Some taxes would become unnecessary because of fuller employment and – because of incomes policies – more equitable earnings. Reorganization of revenue along these lines would greatly reduce the need for additional personal income taxes, but the tax rates of top earners should be raised, certainly to the average level of fellow members of the European Union. Third, anti-discrimination legislation and the positive rights of women, children and minorities, including disabled and elderly people, must be aligned. This would mean extending national insurance, care allowances, child benefit and disability income according to severity of disablement. It would mean positive legislation and administration on behalf of groups excluded from equal access to jobs and services. In short, there has to be a convincing plan to halt and then reverse social polarization, impoverishment and unemployment. It would cost more but cost is a political question. It is viable, affordable and could be very popular.

**Endnotes**

[1] Commission on Social Justice, *Social Justice: Strategies for National Renewal*, Vintage, London 1994.

[2] 5 July 1995. See the published version of the speech, *Let Us Face the Future*, Fabian Pamphlet 571, London 1995; and see also T. Blair, *Socialism*, Fabian Pamphlet 565, London 1994.

[3] In general this is conceded in many current publications by the international agencies, particularly United Nations Research Institute for Social Development, United Nations Development Programme and UNICEF, and by non-government organisations like Oxfam, One World Action, War on Want and Christian Aid, although the connections to international economic policies alike of both the agencies and multinational companies are rarely made. See in particular the text of the UN Summit for Social Development held in Copenhagen in March 1995, *Declaration and Programme of Action: Outcome of the World Summit for Social Development*, Report of the Secretary General, New York 1995. There have been increasingly savage indictments of the adjustment policies of the IMF and the World Bank, sometimes from unexpected quarters. See the editorial in *The Lancet*, 'Structural adjustment too painful?', vol. 344, no. 8934 (1994), pp. 1377–8; and the sharp commentaries over a long period from UNICEF (for example, G.K. Helleiner, G.A. Cornia and R. Jolly, 'IMF adjustment policies and approaches and the needs of children', *World Development*, vol. 19, no. 12 (1991), pp. 1823–34) and UNRISD (for example, *Structural Adjustment in a Changing World*, Geneva, December 1994, and D. Ghai and C. Hewitt de Alcantara, *Globalization and Social Integration: Patterns and Processes*, Geneva 1994). The arguments for a world economic policy which would be different from the neo-monetarist policies increasingly dominant since the 1960s are gathering momentum. See for example T. Lang and C. Hines, *The New Protectionism: Protecting the Future Against Free Trade*, London 1994, and N. Chomsky, *Global Policies: A New World Order*, Cambridge 1993. New Labour seems to be some way from recognizing this trend, though some figures in traditional Labour, like Denis Healey, make interesting exceptions; see his 'Global Forces', *New Statesman and Society*, 16 June 1995.

[4] This deserves to be at the forefront of public and political attention. Increasing inequality and poverty during the 1980s and 1990s have been documented extensively. For the Third World see, for example, I. Jazairy, M. Alamgir and T. Panuccio, *The State of World Rural Poverty*, International Fund for Agricultural Development, Rome and New York 1992. For the United States and the United Kingdom see for example, P. Townsend, *The International Analysis of Poverty*, Hemel Hempstead 1993, chapter 1. In addition there is new evidence for members of the European Union other than the UK; see D. Robbins, *Observatory on National Policies to Combat Social Exclusion*, Third Annual Report, Commission of the European Communities, Directorate General V Employment, Social Affairs and Industrial Relations, EEIG, Lille 1994.

[5] G. Esping-Andersen, *After the Golden Age: The Future of the Welfare State in the New Global Order*, UNRISD, Geneva 1994, p. 23.

[6] Ibid.; S. Leibfried, 'Towards a European welfare state? On integrating poverty regimes into the European Community', in Z. Ferge and J. E. Kolberg, eds, *Social Policy in a Changing Europe*, Frankfurt am Main and Boulder, Colorado 1992; S. Leibfried and P. Pierson, 'Prospects for social Europe', *Politics and Society*, vol. 20, no. 3 (1992), pp. 333–66; S. Leibfried and P. Pearson (eds), *European Social Policy: Between Fragmentation and Integration*, Washington D.C. 1995; A. Pfaller, I. Gough and G. Therborn (eds), *Can the Welfare State Compete? A Comparative Study of Five Advanced Capitalist Societies*, London 1991; and, for earlier examples, R.M Titmuss, *Social Policy*, London 1974; I. Gough, *The Political Economy of the Welfare State*, London 1979.

[7] For example, J. Saville, 'Labour income redistribution', in R. Miliband and J. Saville (eds), *The Socialist Register*, London 1965, and I. Gough, *The Political Economy of the Welfare State*, London 1979.

[8] T. Skocpol and E. Amenta, 'States and social policies', *Annual Review of Sociology*. vol. 12 (1986) p. 5.

[9] G. Esping-Andersen, *The Three Worlds of Welfare Capitalism*, Cambridge 1990.

[10] M. Harloe, *The People's Home*, Oxford 1995.

[11] P. Taylor-Gooby, G. Bonoli and V. George, 'Welfare futures: the views of key influentials in six European countries on likely developments in social policy', in *Squaring the Welfare Circle in Europe*, a conference of the International Sociological Association in Pavia, September, 1995 (forthcoming). See also J. Hills, *The Future of Welfare*, Joseph Rowntree Foundation, York 1993.

[12] Commission on Social Justice, *Social Justice in a Changing World*, IPPR, London, 1993.

[13] *Social Justice*, p. 95.

[14] Ibid., p. 41.

[15] Ibid., p. 96.

[16] Ibid., pp. 104, 112.

[17] Central Statistical Office, *Social Trends*, 1995, p. 94.

[18] F. Field, *Making Welfare Work: Reconstructing Welfare for the Millennium*, Institute of Community Studies, London 1995. See also F. Field and M. Owen, *Private Pensions for All: Squaring the Circle*, Fabian Discussion Paper no. 16, London 1993.

[19] Ibid., p. 20.

[20] Ibid., p. 4.

[21] Alternatives were described in evidence to the Commission, for example, P. Townsend, *International Social Policy: The Case for a National Social Development Programme as an Integral Component of a Collaborative International Strategy*, Department of Social Policy and Social Planning, University of Bristol 1994.

[22] Detailed exposition of the possibilities can be found in J. Hills, *Changing Tax: How the System Works and How to Change It*, Child Poverty Action Group, London 1988. See also J. Hills, *Joseph Rowntree Foundation Inquiry into Income and Wealth, Volume 2, A Summary of Evidence*, Joseph Rowntree Foundation, York 1995; and, for incomes policy, P. Hirst and J. Zeitlin, *An Incomes Policy for the 1990s*, Department of Politics and Sociology, University of London 1992.

# 56

# Using human rights to defeat ageism

[...]

Most of us are assaulted by the day-to-day pressures of finding our way, and we look down at our desks or our feet rather than over the rooftops and fields or at our immediate and far away social surroundings. We come to learn that the here and now is a fragment in an awesome sweep of life before our birth and after our death. We can be lucky to capture some sense of what shapes social and not just individual life; and convey, even if only to a few, and to them for only a few weeks or years, a reasoned account of predestination, so that they may join in the difficult and usually unsuccessful task of putting continuing and emerging wrongs right.

[...] This chapter, initially prepared to celebrate many years' work of British social gerontologists, provides an excellent opportunity to stand back and assess the 'big picture' and to review not only previously influential ideas, but also ideas that may not yet have found a place in the sun.

## Rise of social development policy

What is the nature of the problem? The volume of research studies, pamphlets and media programmes about the maltreatment of older people grew steadily after the war of 1939-45. A number of social and economic historians (see, for example, Macnicol and Blaikie, 1989) have traced the commissioning of surveys explicitly on old age, the emergence of geriatric medicine after the inauguration of the NHS, the looming prospects of population ageing and so-called 'dependency ratios', and the way in which state pensions were given new priority in the political interest generated after the 1939 war. Because of the respective histories of sociology and social policy, as newly arrived major disciplines, the shock-horror of the most extreme conditions, rather than cause, attracted greatest attention. Theories or explanation of poor conditions and maltreatment were over-weighted towards the demographic, or supposedly naturalistic, on the one hand, or fragmented into the convenient sub-divisions of policy subject-matter – housing, mental or physical health, education, institutional or family care, and social insurance and social assistance, on the other.

---

Townsend, P. (2007) 'Using human rights to defeat ageism: dealing with policy-induced "structured dependency"', in M. Bernard and T. Scharf (eds) *Critical perspectives on ageing societies*, Bristol: The Policy Press, pp 27–44.

Where theory had a part, and that part summary or undeveloped, it occupied a middle level designed to be immediately practical to the locations and individuals immediately at issue. Larger statements about the record of governments and of policies as instruments of cause were not much attempted. The connections between themes or subjects, and their possibly common antecedents, were not seriously addressed. The achievements of the welfare state in the early years of the 20th century and then again in the immediate post-war situation of 1945, were not hammered home, and the theory of success sustained by continuing political education. The door of public service accessible to all was not slammed shut on interlopers and thieves. In Harold Macmillan's famous comment on one of Margaret Thatcher's privatisations, assaults on public ownership and public service could be likened to 'selling the family silver'.

The gains of 'welfare' could be expressed in many ways. Certainly collective, or universal, interests, public service, interdependence and redistributive rights and responsibilities would figure largely. The recent language of 'reform' from the critics has in some measure found the advocates of welfare embarrassed or defenceless. I would want to suggest that the critics have gained ascendancy mainly because defence has been neither multidimensional nor multinational. When Friedrich Hayek published his far-right book *The road to serfdom* (Hayek, 1944), Barbara Wootton comprehensively dismembered it less than a year later in her book *Freedom under planning* (Wootton, 1945). The post-war influence of Keynes prevailed for nearly 20 years, as did the European forms of advanced or undeveloped welfare states, but then Hayek's ideas made a comeback, supported by Milton Friedman and many successor economists. In the UK senior intellectual figures began to lend themselves to the seemingly vacuous ideas of people like Lord Harris and Arthur Seldon, who set up the Institute of Economic Affairs in 1955. For two decades most social scientists dismissed the ideas as unrealistically extreme and poorly supported, and they were not taken seriously until the 1980s.

Several European Union countries have put up a steady defence of welfare. Many have maintained substantial levels of social transfers on behalf of social services, measured by percentage of Gross Domestic Product (GDP). Redistribution of income to pensioners remains considerable in all member countries. However, discussion of the European social model has become heated, and some individual governments have sought to curtail expenditure on pensions. In the UK, in particular, schemes with final salary pensions are declining rapidly, plans are being put in place to raise retirement and pension ages and comprehensive state second pensions are being phased out. The battle both to preserve, and to raise to a reasonable level, basic state pensions continues.

## Formulation of theory: 'acquiescent functionalism'

Twenty-five years ago I was one of those trying to make sense of the poor conditions being experienced by many older people. By good fortune I had worked on different national and cross-national projects before that time in residential homes[…], hospitals and nursing homes, and in private households (much of this work reflecting conditions in the US and Denmark as well as the UK). It became inevitable that I should reflect on the wider as well as immediate causes of the problems that were recognisably severe in particular locations as well as scattered more widely across the general population (see Townsend, 1981, 1986). Connections had to be made.

What could then be called the 'liberal-pluralist' tradition, now referred to as the 'neoliberal' or even Washington Consensus, was dominant. There existed a 'family' of theories – like neoclassical economics, democratic pluralism, sociological functionalism and certain theories in social psychology – that not only reflected but tended implicitly to approve the staged development of the capitalist democracies into and through the processes of industrialisation. By accepting as givens the changing structural inequalities of a competitive market, this 'family' reinforced individualistic and not social values and gained spurious authority. The continuities of economic individualism within classical economic theory, neoclassical theory, monetarism and neoliberal economics, and on the way even Keynesianism, had to be traced to reveal better what came to be built into social policies.

This 'family' of theories came to be applied to the emerging conditions of rapidly increasing numbers of older people. This can be followed in the wake of many of the social gerontologists of the earliest generation, including Donahue and Tibbitts (1957), Parsons (1942, 1964) and Cumming (1963) (see Townsend, 1986, pp 16-19). Their work, I considered, could be characterised as 'acquiescent functionalism'. This was a body of thought about ageing that attributed the causes of the problems of old age to the natural consequences of physical decrescence and mental inflexibility, or to the failures of individual adjustment to ageing and retirement, instead of the continuing as well as new exertions of state economic and social policy partly to serve and partly to moderate the play of market forces. Social inequality was thereby 'reconfigured' in the language that is now being applied to universal social services.

[…]

And still today there are features of that institutionalised ageism that have to attract our primary attention if, along with other forms of discrimination by gender, 'race', class and disability, it is to be radically reduced and dispersed so that our whole attention may be turned to the more practical fine-tuning of policy.

## Alternative theory: structured dependency

In demonstrating the value of new policies in the 1970s the consequences of conventional theory had first to be exposed. I came to understand the debt I owed to social anthropologists like Radcliffe-Brown and economic sociologists like Marx and Weber (especially Weber's *Theory of economic and social organisation*, 1947) for putting concepts of social structure, class and economic and social change at the heart of scientific analysis of society and therefore of ageing and the conditions experienced by the third, and fourth, generations.[1] Retirement, poverty, institutionalisation and restriction of domestic and community roles are the experiences that help to explain how the dependency of older people came to be artificially structured or deepened. Each of these required extensive investigation and assessment.

A great deal of evidence relevant to these forms of dependency emerged in the 1960s and 1970s. There were the examples of: a fixed age for pensions; the minimal subsistence afforded on the state pension; the substitution of retirement status for unemployment; the near-compulsory admission to residential care of many thousands of people whose faculties were still relatively intact; the enforced dependence of many residents in homes and of patients in hospitals and nursing homes; and the conversion of domiciliary services into commodity services. By the 1980s "an artificial dependency [was] being manufactured for a growing proportion of the population at the same time as measures [were] being taken to alleviate the worst effects of that dependency" (Townsend, 1986, p 43). A critical view has to be taken therefore of welfare – weeding out elements that had at the time infiltrated the concept, like parsimony and coercion. But a critical view cannot be allowed to become dismissive or override the massive evidence for extensive national, and now international, 'welfare' action.

Historically, planning as a determinant of social structure and therefore of 'welfare' had seeped into the consciousness of generations in the mid-20th century. This was the end-result of the work of theorists like Marx but also of policy advocates, like Sydney and Beatrice Webb, in European countries. I became acutely conscious of the events leading up to the establishment of the British welfare state after 1945 and understood policy as cause. I was influenced too by early 'planning conscious' social gerontologists like Yonina Talmon, who wrote revealingly about the experimental collective settlements, the *Kibbutzim*, and their value to older people, then being set up in Israel (Talmon, 1961). She understood the importance of maintaining extended family relationships in a new society struggling to introduce egalitarian values, and was especially sensitive about the values of reciprocation and location, as well as organised support for severely disabled people (Talmon, 1961, pp 288, 290, 294).

[…]

## Human rights and welfare

First, some general arguments. The language of human rights has particular virtues of *moral obligation*. Each of the rights is 'universal'. Non-fulfilment is a 'violation'. Rights are 'human' and not only civil or political. Rights are multiple and interdependent. Corrective anti-discriminatory measures have to be directed not at the separate existence of racial, religious, gender, disability or ageist discrimination but in a comprehensive, connected and proportionate manner against all forms of discrimination.

Second, the *methodology* of human rights is in its infancy. The operational definition of rights and therefore violations demands imaginative and sustained quantitative, but also qualitative, methods of investigation. The violations are not those only that end life, or involve extreme abuse, the scale of which have to be assembled in statistical handbooks, but those that represent affronts to human dignity and identity. For older people, the Quality of Life research studies carried out in the UK under the auspices of the Economic and Social Research Council's (ESRC) Growing Older Programme offer rich contributions to this objective (see, for example, Walker and Hennessy, 2004; Walker, 2005). In operationalising a definition of rights for people of all ages perhaps there has been too much readiness to adapt familiar indicators of human development or health, or economic growth, as single indicators of sometimes complex conditions or entitlements rather than build requirements for survey data about extreme conditions from scratch.

The 'indivisibility' of human rights seems to have deterred some social scientists – I include lawyers – from developing *multiple* indices of certain general conditions or priorities. And the seeming inflexibility in defining a threshold or line between satisfaction and non-satisfaction of each right listed in the Articles of rights – either the individual has a right or she or he has not – creeps into the use of a single indicator testing whether that right has or has not been fulfilled (because selecting multiple indicators raises a lot of questions about multiple criteria in agreeing a threshold when different individuals are in reality on a point in the scale from extreme non-fulfilment to generous fulfilment).

Only in recent years have serious efforts been made to organise operational definitions in a form that allows multiple non-realisation of rights to be measured reliably and relatively unambiguously. [...]

Third, the *politics of rights*. This is crucial in the choice of methodology, investigative priorities and persuasive assessment of needs and policies. As many as 191 nations have ratified the Convention on the Rights of the Child (CRC) and numbers of signatories are almost as high for the original Universal Declaration of Human Rights and still impressively high for other human rights instruments. Access to rights plays a crucial role in public discussion about economic and social developments – for example in responses to conflict, anti-terrorism measures and different types of discrimination. Acknowledgment of the influential role of human rights has spread rapidly among campaigning organisations, departments of state and international organisations of every kind. To base both research and action on human rights instruments is to apply the leverage of accepted authority and democracy.

To traditional positive national arguments for welfare can therefore now be added the perceptions as well as revelations of cross-national agreed rules of a quasi-legal kind – a growing number of which have been and are being incorporated into domestic laws. Knowledge of that process can now enthuse those concerned with domestic disputes of a familiar kind that affect older people, and not only inflame those like Hayek and his successors who have been attached to an older, and inevitably more discriminatory, ideology.

## Human rights from a UK and European perspective

I am arguing that a new analytical framework has evolved very rapidly, with which social scientists must necessarily engage. A good witness is David Feldman, author of *Civil liberties and human rights in England and Wales* (2002) and until late 2003 the legal adviser to the UK parliamentary Joint Committee on Human Rights (JCHR). Based on the European Convention on Human Rights (ECHR), the Human Rights Act of the UK dates from 1998. The rights are not guaranteed against repeal or amendment by Parliament, and the courts cannot strike down incompatible primary legislation. Nonetheless, following precedents elsewhere, the expressed rights are beginning to have a substantial impact on the law, and also on the activities and thinking of administrators, lawyers and politicians.

[...]

The UK Act incorporates the ECHR, but the emphasis is on civil and political rights and not also on economic, social and cultural rights. The rights to life, to not being subjected to torture, or inhuman or degrading treatment, or forced labour, to an effective remedy and to non-discrimination raise questions of social protection and reconstruction, and therefore stray into a range of possible social and economic rights, but this cannot be pressed strongly in law. However, the counterpart of the ECHR is the European Social Charter (ESC) (Council of Europe, 2002; Samuel, 2002). As many as 30 of the member states of the Council of Europe had signed and ratified the Charter by 2001. After the Amsterdam Treaty of 1997 came into force the revised Charter has become an integral part of the structure of the European Community. The newly elected Labour government signed the Charter in 1997. Many of the Articles reflect European agreement on the 'European Social Model' and several are relevant to conditions for older people. In particular, Article 4 of the additional protocol of 1988 spells out the right of older people to social protection....

## Violations of the rights of older people in the 21st century

Both the ESC (Council of Europe, 2002; Samuel, 2002) and the ECHR can be widely used in the analysis of conditions experienced by older people and necessary alternative policies. For example, Age Concern and Help the Aged have given worrying contemporary evidence on lack of rights. Help the Aged explained that "older people whose human rights are violated are often not in a position – or do not choose – to take action themselves" (JCHR, 2003, II, Evidence 310). Few staff, and few members of the public were yet informed about the 1998 Act. Older people subjected to abuse rarely complained.

## Failure to accept Sutherland

[...] In Britain, perhaps the most authoritative review so far in this century is the Sutherland Commission on Long-term Care (Sutherland Report, 1999). The Commission argued that the long-term costs of care should be split between living costs, housing costs and personal care. Personal care should be available after assessment, according to need and paid for from general taxation; the rest should be subject to co-payment according to means. A National Care Commission had to be created. Private insurance would not deliver what is required at an acceptable cost, nor would the industry want to provide that degree of coverage. The recently evolving private infrastructure of residential and nursing home care had grown rapidly in cost and "the 'market' was shaped in a particular way, driven by what could be paid for rather than what people needed". [...]

Partly prompted by a querulous note of dissent from two of the Commissioners, the government set aside the recommendations of the Royal Commission. With hindsight it is perhaps unfortunate that the Royal Commission did not strengthen its powerful case by formal reference to human rights generally and the new UK Human Rights Act in particular, and to the rapid developments in the treatment of both the ECHR and the ESC, together with the momentum in Europe and elsewhere in the world in favour of linking current concerns about particular problems of the day that gain wide publicity with human rights. [...]

## Practicality of human rights

... [M]ultiple material and social deprivation must be acknowledged and investigation based on identifying and then counting different types of deprivation, or abuse. One type of horror, and the identification of horror in one location, must be placed into a context that is national, multigenerational, applicable to public and private sectors, and international. I have taken the view for many years that specialised research can only carry force if there is generalised research as well, and vice versa. The best national work is that which is also international or cross-national. Of course it is never easy to ride two horses and improvisations and shortcomings will exist. But that is the first necessity. The effort remains crucial and will allow what is truly international and objectively scientific to emerge. It is vital in authenticating priority – in analysis as well as treatment. It is a value that can be lived and rehearsed at every level. [...]

Let me give two examples of the methodology. One is old-style multiplication of material and social deprivation. [...] After setting aside certain overlapping indices there remain 31 items representing commonly agreed necessities of life. As many as 37 per cent of people of pensionable age were deprived of at least one necessity, but as many as nine per cent deprived of five or more, including a third of these deprived of ten or more necessities. These nine per cent represent more than one million older people. That figure does not include half a million older people who are in hospitals, nursing homes and residential care. Severe multiple deprivation is therefore a common experience, and one that raises acute questions about human rights.

[...]

The second example arises from indexing human rights. This derives from recent work on children, in which I participated. A research team based in the University of Bristol found that different Articles of the CRC lent themselves to measurement from familiar survey data, graded from extreme violation through severe and moderate to slight and non-existent violation of different forms of material and social deprivation. The problem was to find data of a relatively standardised kind from many countries. Only in recent years have many relatively standardised surveys been carried out in a large number of countries – key examples being the Demographic and Health Surveys and the Multiple Indicator Cluster Surveys. Fortunately, serious material and social deprivation – reflected in a number of the articles of the CRC – could be categorised and measured, including malnutrition, inadequate shelter, no access or poor access to minimally adequate drinking water, sanitation, healthcare, education and forms of information. The results proved more reliable, and certainly less disputable, than the crude estimates of dollar-a-day poverty estimated by the World Bank. The next stage has been to apply Articles of human rights to the measurement of multiple deprivation among adults. For older people we can move in successive stages from the ECHR, through the ESC to the International Covenant on Economic, Social and Cultural Rights. I cannot yet offer the statistical results. What I can do is outline the stages of research.

The first is to show ways in which the ECHR can be illustrated. Table 3.2 [see Table 2: Part A, p 483 in this volume] gives an example. Additional use could be made, of course, with other Articles, like the right to marry (Article 12) and some of the Protocols, such as Articles 1 and 5 of Protocol 7, respectively on safeguards in the expulsion of aliens, and on equality between spouses.

The next step is to do the same for the ESC, which opens the door to a more sophisticated set of measurements. An outline is given in Table 3.3 [see Table 2: Part A, p 483 in this volume]. A third step in anticipating the growing acknowledgement of economic and social rights, and partly through the slow influence of the ESC on the UK government, is to examine the International Covenant on Economic, Social and Cultural Rights.

One method developed lately of accelerating progress in developing countries with the measurement of multiple violation of human rights, has been to focus on violations representing different features of material and social deprivation so that priorities in policy may be identified (Gordon et al, 2003). Another method would be to focus on the twin rights to social security and an adequate standard of living – Articles 22 and 25 of the Universal Declaration of Human Rights, Articles 26 and 27 of the CRC and Articles 9 and 11 of the International Covenant on Economic, Social and Cultural Rights (Table 3.4). The advantages to be derived from building afresh on these two rights are especially promising.

## Globalisation and the human rights of older people

In deciding the future direction of the work of social gerontologists, the growing inequality within countries as well as between poor and rich countries must provide the structural context (Townsend and Gordon, 2002). The globalisation of market, technology and communications (see, for example, Walker and Deacon, 2003) affects the organisation of all societies, including the conditions and prospects of older people. Recent failures of privatisation schemes, and even of major transnational corporations such as Enron and WorldCom and parts of the financial services industry, have led to calls for radical new policies. Fresh reports of instances of corporate corruption have paved the way for new calls for collective approaches through law and regulation that go a lot further than the minimal and highly variable expressions so far of 'corporate social responsibility'.

On globalisation, support for a change has come from unexpected sources. For example, the former chief economist at the World Bank, Joseph Stiglitz, has written revealingly about corporate greed (Stiglitz, 2002a, 2002b). Again, in the wake of the $4 billion (£2.1 billion) WorldCom scandal in 2002 Digby

**Table 3.4:** International Covenant on Economic, Social and Cultural Rights and 1995 World Summit Action Programme

| International Covenant on Economic, Social and Cultural Rights (1966-76) | Article 9: The States Parties to the present Covenant recognise the right of everyone to social security, including social insurance | Article 11 (1): The States Parties to the present Covenant recognise the right of everyone to an adequate standard of living for himself and his family, including adequate food, clothing and housing, and to the continuous improvement of living conditions |
|---|---|---|
| Copenhagen World Summit for Social Development (1995) relevant decisions by 117 countries | Action Programme 38: Social protection systems should be based on legislation and ... strengthened and expanded ... to protect from poverty people who cannot work ... | Action Programme 8: Equitable and non-discriminatory distribution of benefits of growth among social groups and countries and expanded access to productive resources for people living in poverty |

Jones, the then Director-General of the Confederation of British Industry, called for new forms of business leadership and for stronger statements about corporate responsibilities in accountancy and administration (Jones, 2002).

Public faith in agreements reached at World Summits to deal with the world's needs has begun to dwindle. Public expectations raised by the announcement of the Millennium Development Goals in 2000 and the closing statements of successive World Summits since then – including those of Monterrey on financial developments and New York on the needs of children – have been disappointed. Some of the earlier international agreements – such as that at the 1995 Copenhagen World Summit for Social Development – had a more lasting impact. The Copenhagen Declaration and Programme of Action followed a coherently organised summit and the recommendations were more specific than in other similar events (UN, 1995). The programme of action has begun to have constructive results and has considerable potentiality for the future, if governments and interest groups, including international bodies, are held regularly responsible – and accountable – for widely agreed objectives in establishing human rights and reducing inequalities and poverty. Compared with diminishing confidence in World Summits, public trust in the charters and conventions expressing human rights has continued to grow. Public support for the values upholding human rights and legally backed action remains strong.

## Universal rights

The world has seen only mixed success for the declared objective in the past 50 years of reducing the violations of human rights, including those that address different forms of severe deprivation that were selected earlier in this chapter for special attention. Our findings prompt re-examination of the links between 'universalism' or human 'rights', and both comprehensive public social service and social security. 'Targeting' as a strategy in developing countries to reduce poverty has become highly controversial and the forms of targeting that have been adopted are increasingly criticised. Reports of persisting poverty and deepening inequality in many countries outweigh the modest results that at best reflect the structural adjustment programmes and their successors, including the social funds that were introduced. In developing countries, the Programme of Action to Mitigate the Social Cost of Adjustment was set up in the late 1980s to correct the excesses of structural adjustment programmes, but was criticised for being underfunded and lacking direction (Donkor, 2002). Success for programmes intended both to restrict public expenditure and yet relieve extreme poverty by targeting resources has turned out to be elusive. Action on behalf of children is a priority, but huge numbers of older people will also continue to suffer unless comprehensive, and principled, action is taken on behalf of society as a whole.

## Conclusion

The idea of 'structured dependency' helps to explain the box before death within which many older people are placed. Unintentionally, as well as for deliberate reasons of economy and profit or convenience on the part of the state and of other institutions, their dependency is created in market, residential and hospital care and private and public social care policies. There are exceptions from which lessons can be learned about countervailing policies. […]

The various problems of 'structured' dependency persist. And those problems seem set to grow in many parts of the world. Human rights offer a framework of rigorous analysis and anti-discriminatory work. Success depends on good operational measurement – for purposes of producing reliable evidence of violations and monitoring progress – and the incorporation internationally as well as nationally of institutions and policies that reflect those rights. Human rights instruments offer hope of breaking down blanket discrimination and of using resources more appropriately, and more generously, according to severity of need. But investment in human rights is not only a moral and quasi-legal salvation from things that are still going depressingly wrong. Used best, human rights offer a framework of thought and planning early in the 21st century that enables society to take a fresh, and more hopeful, direction.

**Endnote**

[1] Among examples of sociological work on organisations that have influenced my thinking are books by Brian Abel-Smith on hospitals (1964) and the nursing profession (1960), and by Joe Jacob on the medical profession (1999). My book on residential institutions for older people, *The last refuge* (1962), had also been written at a time when there had been immense interest sociologically in the 'total institution'.

**References**

Abel-Smith, B. (1960) *A history of the nursing profession*, London: Heinemann.

Abel-Smith, B. (1964) *The hospitals: 1800-1964*, London: Heinemann.

Council of Europe (2002) *European Social Charter: Collected texts* (3rd edn), Strasbourg: Council of Europe.

Cumming, E. (1963) 'Further thoughts on the theory of disengagement', *International Social Science Journal*, vol 15, no 3, pp 377-93.

Donahue, W. and Tibbitts, C. (1957) *The new frontiers of aging*, Ann Arbor, MI: University of Michigan Press.

Donkor, K. (2002) 'Structural adjustment and mass poverty in Ghana', in P. Townsend and D. Gordon (eds) *World poverty: New policies to defeat an old enemy*, Bristol: The Policy Press, pp 226-8.

Feldman, D. (2002) *Civil liberties and human rights in England and Wales*, 2nd edn, Oxford: Oxford University Press.

Gordon, D., Nandy, S., Pantazis, C., Pemberton, S. and Townsend, P. (2003) *Child poverty in the developing world*, Bristol: The Policy Press.

Hayek, F.A. (1944) *The road to serfdom*, Chicago, IL: University of Chicago Press.

Jacob, J. (1999) *Doctors and rules: A sociology of professional values* (expanded 2nd edn), New Brunswick, NJ and London: Transaction.

JCHR (Joint Committee on Human Rights) (2003) *The case for a Human Rights Commission*, Sixth Report of Session 2002-3, vol I and II, HC 489-I and II, London: The Stationery Office.

Jones, D. (2002) Business and media supplement, *Observer*, 30 June.

Macnicol, J. and Blaikie, A. (1989) 'The politics of retirement, 1908-1948', in M. Jefferys (ed) *Growing old in the twentieth century*, London: Routledge, pp 21-42.

Parsons, T. (1942) 'Age and sex in the social structure of the United States', *American Sociological Review*, vol 7, no 5, pp 604-16.

Parsons, T. (1964) *Essays in sociological theory* (paperback edn), New York, NY: The Free Press.

Samuel, L. (2002) *Fundamental social rights: Case law of the European Social Charter* (2nd edn), Strasbourg: Council of Europe Publishing.

Stiglitz, J. (2002a) 'Corporate corruption', *The Guardian*, London, 4 July.

Stiglitz, J. (2002b) *Globalisation and its discontents*, London: Allen Lane.

Sutherland Report (1999) *With respect to old age: Long term care – rights and responsibilities. A report by the Royal Commission on Long-term Care*, Cm 4192-1, London: The Stationery Office.

Talmon, Y. (1961) 'Ageing in Israel: a planned society', *American Journal of Sociology*, vol 67, no 3, pp 284-95.

Townsend, P. (1962) *The last refuge – A survey of residential institutions and homes for the elderly in England and Wales*, London: Routledge and Kegan Paul.

Townsend, P. (1981) 'The structured dependency of the elderly: a creation of social policy in the twentieth century', *Ageing and Society*, vol 1, no 1, pp 5-28.

Townsend, P. (1986) 'Ageism and social policy', in C. Phillipson and A. Walker (eds) *Ageing and social policy: A critical assessment*, Aldershot: Gower, pp 15-44.

Townsend, P. and Gordon, D. (eds) (2002) *World poverty: New policies to defeat an old enemy*, Bristol: The Policy Press.

Walker, A. (ed) (2005) *Understanding quality of life in old age*, Milton Keynes: Open University Press.

Walker, A. and Deacon, B. (2003) 'Economic globalisation and policies on ageing', *Journal of Societal and Social Policy*, vol 2, no 2, pp 1-18.

Walker, A. and Hennessy, C.H. (eds) (2004) *Growing older: Quality of life in old age*, Milton Keynes: Open University Press.

Weber, M. (1947) *Theory of economic and social organisation* (revised and edited edn), London: Palgrave.

Wootton, B. (1945) *Freedom under planning*, Chapel Hill, NC: University of North Carolina Press.

# 57

# We have got a fair way to go

Peter Townsend explains how, if Labour is to win the next election
and rebuild Britain, it must link social justice to social and economic
development.

Time is running out for Labour Party's social development programme
– a better term for what is needed than a "social justice" or "welfare state"
programme. Choices will have to be made within the next 12 months or so,
in the run-up to the next general election. Labour faces a quite a different
set of options from those available only 20 years ago – in the days of Harold
Wilson's "social contract" – principally because the UK is tied far more
tightly into an international economic and political hierarchy.

The big question is whether Labour should go along with the free-market
ideology of international monetarism and make the best of a very bad
social job, on the grounds that we cannot on our own do much to change
that ideology and its practices. Or, on the contrary, should Labour expose
monetarism for the hollow sham that it is and go for a radically different
approach from both national and international development?

That would mean filling an international leadership vacuum. It would
mean organising different democratic alliances overseas (sympathetic overseas
governments; socialist parties; city governments; trade unions; pressure groups
and non-governmental organisations), overhauling democratic institutions
at home and re-establishing public services and utilities – all of these in
order to exert more control over international market forces and thereby
secure a better deal for the working population and the poor of the UK
and, indirectly, other countries across the world.

The choice is international before it is domestic. The power of
multinational corporations, international agencies such as the World Bank
and the International Monetary Fund, new regional associations such as the
European Union, and the newly ascendant G7 countries, with the United
States at their head, is immense. It is this network that is determining the
social conditions and destinies of nation-states.

The edicts of monetarism – deregulation, cuts in public expenditure,
cuts in personal income taxation, privatisation, centralisation through the
deliberate weakening of local government as well as trade unions and the

---

Townsend, P. (1994) 'We have got a fair way to go', *New Statesman & Society*,
25 March, pp 18-19.

substitution of subservient quangos, and "targeting" to conceal substantial withdrawal from the welfare state – are not producing a higher rate of economic growth. Nor are they producing even proportionate social access to that growth – still less the "good life".

What they have produced are higher long-term rates of unemployment, a shortage of industrial plant and skills, homelessness, inner-city deprivation and widespread environmental blight, higher rates of burglary, theft and crimes of personal violence, social insecurity, wider and deeper poverty, and peoples at odds with each other. In short, monetarist ideology and practices have simultaneously produced social polarisation and disintegration.

This ideology is writ large in the activities of multinational conglomerates in the policies of the Major government, the Maastricht treaty, the undemocratic constitution of the European Union, the leading national economies, the international agencies and the institutions dealing with overseas aid. It is, for the 1990s, a familiar example of capitalism over-reaching itself to the brink of self-destruction.

Take the example of the European Union and the Maastricht treaty. The public is familiar with the split in Tory ranks, though it may not appreciate that the Tory right does not just want to shed the Social Chapter. It wants to remove all democratic controls from the "free" operation of capitalism, thereby adding to the power of the multinationals to reduce wages, casualise and relinquish labour, and create inequality of a far more extreme kind than that under John Major's government.

Many in Labour's ranks have reservations about Maastricht of a completely different kind. They want European governments to strengthen the relatively weak social protection and employment creation measures of the Social Chapter, or conditions in the UK and the rest of the world will deteriorate even more quickly.

In too many countries in the world, both rich and poor, inequalities have been growing fast during the 1980s and 1990s. The latest reports from the United Nations Development Programme, the General Agreement on Tariffs and Trade, and the International Fund for Agricultural Development show that a majority of the poorest countries in the world are experiencing an increase in poverty not explained by population changes or the flagging growth of those parts of their economics that they still control.

Countries such as Bangladesh, the Philippines, Kenya and Mexico have experienced both an absolute and a proportionate increase in the extent of poverty.

The depressing story is captured in Tables 1 and 2, one showing the declining access of poor countries to global resources, the other giving the latest evidence of the growing affluence of the richest countries in the late 1980s and early 1990s.

**Table 1:** Percentage share of poorest 20 per cent of world population

|  | 1960-70 | 1990 |
|---|---|---|
| World GNP | 2.3 | 1.3 |
| World trade | 1.3 | 0.9 |
| World domestic investment | 3.5 | 1.1 |
| World domestic savings | 3.5 | 0.5 |
| World commercial credit | 0.3 | 0.2 |

*Source:* UNDP 1933, annual report, p 27

**Table 2:** GDP per person (relative to US = 100)

|  | 1987 | 1991 |
|---|---|---|
| Richest 22 countries | 74 | 79 |
| Next 22 countries | 34 | 34 |
| Next 43 countries | 20 | 20 |
| Poorest 40 countries | 5 | 5 |
| (Eastern Europe and former Soviet Union) | 27 | 22 |

*Source:* World Bank annual report 1993

This already unequal picture is compounded by increasing inequalities between rich and poor within most rich and poor countries (Table 3). "Trickle down" is no longer allowed to work. The compendious evidence assembled in the annual *Green Books* published by the US Committee on Ways and Means (in 1993, running to 1,800 pages) demonstrated that polarisation of gross and disposable incomes in the US. Among the poorest 20 per cent of the US population, real earnings are lower than they were in 1979.

**Table 3:** GDP per person (richest and poorest 20 per cent) relative to US average = 100. 1991 or nearest year.

| Richest 20 per cent in richest 22 countries | 146 |
|---|---|
| Poorest 20 per cent in richest 22 countries | 21 |
| Richest 20 per cent in poorest 40 countries | 11 |
| Poorest 20 per cent in poorest 40 countries | 2 |

*Source:* World Bank annual report 1993

In the UK, social polarisation has taken a similar course. The latest evidence from the Central Statistical Office (*Social Trends*, 1994) shows that the richest 20 per cent had a disposable income, after housing costs, in 1979 amounting to 35 per cent of the national total. By 1990-91, this had swollen to 43 per cent (Table 4). The richest 20 per cent have thus gained £35 billion a year

(£6,000 per household) more than they would have if policies had stayed the same as in 1979.

By contrast, the disposable income of the poorest 20 per cent fell from 10 per cent to 6 per cent of the national total (Table 4). This fall represents a loss to these 11.5 million people of £17 billion a year (or £3,000 per household).

**Table 4:** Rich and poor in the UK

| a) Percentage share of disposable household income (after housing costs) | | | |
|---|---|---|---|
| | 1979 | 1987 | 1990-91 |
| Richest 20 per cent | 35 | 40 | 43 |
| Poorest 20 per cent | 10 | 8 | 6 |
| b) Change in real median income (as percentage of income of poorest 20 per cent in 1979) | | | |
| Richest 20 per cent | 312 | 406 | 467 |
| Poorest 20 per cent | 100 | 99 | 97 |

*Source:* Central Statistical Office, *Social Trends*, No 24, 1994

**Table 5:** 'Absolute' poverty in the world

| | 1965 | 1988 |
|---|---|---|
| Percentage of rural population below absolute poverty line | 35 | 33 |
| Number | 511m | 712m |

The quasi-monetarist policies of deflation, deregulation, privatisation, cuts in public expenditure, cuts in personal income taxation and withdrawal from the welfare state are being applied in rich and poor countries alike. Mounting evidence from many Latin American, African and south-east Asian countries, Russia and eastern Europe portrays the damaging effects of such policies on health, rural agriculture, the environment, education, health and other social services, and social cohesion.

The effects can be seen at local and regional level. Cuts in direct taxation have added enormously to the incomes of the already rich. Privatisation of public services has added to the costs of the poor. Deregulation has reduced employment rights and increased casual, low-paid and unsafe employment. All three have fuelled unemployment.

Thousands of redundancies in particular areas are due to the closure of plants in rich countries, to be reopened in countries where labour costs are lower. Government intervention to moderate the damage is inhibited by state policies of deregulation and the abandonment of employment rights, as well as reduction of resources – like the proceeds from the sale of council housing and the cash limits imposed in local authority spending – from the state.

The loss of pension rights provides another example. The growing number of company mergers and takeovers by multinational companies has revealed gaps in national laws, which do not provide full protection for occupational pension rights and have had a devastating effect on the pension expectations of thousands.

The UK has already cut its social state security budget more savagely other European countries. The most substantial was the change from earnings-related to price-related state pensions. Had the formula not been changed in 1979, the basic pension (for a single person) would today be £19.25 a week more than it is. For a married couple, the pension would now be £30.55 a week higher. There have also been huge cuts in unemployment benefits – particularly for those aged under 25, and in income support.

What can be done to halt the international and national slide? A Labour government needs to act internationally, in the first instance, to protect economic and social health.

This will mean working with European allies to control the excesses of multinational corporations, partly by introducing more comprehensive international company law, controlling transfer pricing and asset-stripping resulting from takeovers and mergers; closing loopholes in cross-national taxation; protecting home-based companies and individual employees by means of more democratic company laws nationally and internationally.

It will also mean protecting small farming interests and the environment; promoting international trade-union links; facilitating the internationalisation of democratic pressure groups; facilitating cross-national links between city authorities; and, in particular, taking new initiatives to foster first-/third-world relationships. To such a strategy must be added measures to democratise the IMF and the World Bank.

In 1995, a UN summit on social development is to be held in Copenhagen. The UK can take a lead – as the Netherlands is already doing – in guiding international and national attempts to establish a common infrastructure and services.

In the UK, universality is at a crossroads. The problem is not that benefits and services should be made more selective, but that their role should be greatly improved to complement, and offset, modern market forces. This means better provision for interruptions in employment, part-time employment, migratory labour and populations, and strong public-sector employment. It means universal rights of access to health and education. And it means a universal system of child benefit and coverage for the hard work of those involved in the care of children, disabled and elderly persons.

The problem is not to defend an old institution for the sake of tradition and familiarity, but to use an efficient, economical and socially integrative mechanism to new advantage. Take retirement pensions. The latest evidence form the European Observatory on older people shows that, among member countries, the UK, with Ireland, provides at retirement the lowest pensions relative to previous average earnings. Even when occupational pensions are added to the state pensions, the UK still compares unfavourably with the rest of Europe.

Elderly women are at a particular disadvantage, with the evolution of the costly mishmash of occupational and personal pensions. They are also predominant among the more than a million elderly people who are entitled to, but do into get, income support. The basic state pension has already fallen from 20 per cent to 15 per cent of average male earnings, and will fall to 8 per cent early in the next century, unless government policies are changed.

The immediate objective must be to raise the basic state pension relative to earnings, and then to reintroduce the annual earnings-related formula. Later, the State Earnings-Related Pension Scheme – which initially had all-party support, and would still provide the only guarantee of a secure and minimally adequate standard of living in retirement for half the men and more than two-thirds of the women in the population – should also be restored.

The additional costs of a modernised and revitalised scheme for social insurance could be met, partly by extending the national insurance contribution to the top of the earnings scale; selective cuts in tax expenditures (for 1992-93, the cost of mortgage interest tax relief was £5.2 billion, the married couples allowance £4.6 billion and personal pension subsidy £1.6 billion) and selective increases in corporation and inheritance taxes. At the present time, the government estimates tax expenditures at £114.1 billion (1992-93), and there are good grounds for reducing it sharply, say, by 10 or 15 per cent (that is, £11-16 billion).

A necessary part of the strategy would be on wages. Schemes for a minimum wage have to be related to the evolution of the national (and international) wages system. There is a hierarchy of earnings. Action at any level will be effective only if it is taken – by corporations not less than by governments – to modify the entire structure. This applies especially to the topmost earnings – which set the pace for the entire structure.

Any UK government must resist the over-hasty demolition of national services, benefits and utilities in these fluid times of Europeanisation and internationalisation. One illustration makes the point. In 1988, the cost of the Social Fund and the Regional Development Fund within the then European Community amounted to 20 ecus per person, whereas social protection costs provided by individual member-states amounted to 3,028 ecus per person. But social "protection" is not enough – the big challenge is to evolve a strategy for social development.

# 58

# Human rights, transnational corporations and the World Bank

This book finds that the UN's aim to free the world of poverty sits uneasily with the current reality of unremitting social polarisation and persisting mass poverty. This is not just one of those familiar ironies about the difference in the relationship between government and governed, over tub-thumping promises and delivery of those promises. It is a paradox consistently revealed in countless shapes and sizes. Therefore, the abasement of many millions of people in the world's increasingly unequal hierarchical social structure stands in sharp contrast to the plans agreed by the overwhelming majority of countries to establish universal human rights. If the violation of those rights is to be understood, and acted upon, the scale and severity of the violation of different kinds of rights – especially economic and social rights – has to be explained in relation to policies being applied at different levels.

In Parts I to III of this book the principal thrust of current international anti-poverty policies has been described, and the anti-poverty policies as well as trends in poverty of rich and poor countries laid out for comparison and appraisal. The case for an alternative approach to policy has been made. How can some of the lessons that may be drawn be put into international and national practice? In this part of the book some of those specific as well as general lessons are explained.

## Theoretical context

This chapter picks up three elements of an alternative strategy for particular scrutiny:
1. the theoretical basis of social and economic development, including human rights;
2. the future role and functions of the major transnational corporations in relation to social as well as economic objectives;
3. the necessary recasting of the role and social and economic actions of the international financial agencies, particularly the World Bank.

---

Extract (pp 351–60) from Townsend, P. (2002) 'Human rights, transnational corporations and the World Bank', in P. Townsend and D. Gordon (eds) *World poverty: New policies to defeat an old enemy*, pp 351-76.

Inevitably a theory has to be put forward to explain the extremes of human conditions and experiences, not as if these conditions and experiences were fixed but as a rapidly evolving, and deepening, reality. Providing such a multidimensional theory is not the purpose of this chapter. However, one reminder is relevant. The evolution of global capitalism must necessarily be a key theme of theory.

Samir Amin, a major theoretician of the 'Third World', or 'the South', insists on treating capitalism as a concrete historical reality that does not lead to 'development' in the meaning currently given to that word. He argues that the expansion of capital is not to be confused with human development. For example, capitalism, he writes,

> does not imply full employment, or a pre-determined degree of equality in the distribution of income ... [or by those who control such possibilities and are] endowed, for this purpose, with the monopoly represented by private property.... Actually existing capitalism does not work as a system of competition.... [To work] it requires the intervention of a collective authority representing capitalism as a whole. Therefore, the state cannot be separated from capitalism. [The expansion and contraction of employment] are not the expression of abstract 'market laws', but requirements of the profitability of capital under certain historical conditions. (Amin, 1997, pp 14–15)

Expansion is guided by the search for profit by companies.

## The powers behind the scene

Historically, therefore, the state was the principal agent in setting the scene, and any conditions, within which companies had to operate. That situation has rapidly changed. Since the late 20th century increasing numbers of writers have pounced on the 'disjuncture' between the formal authority of the state and "the spatial reach of contemporary systems of production, distribution and exchange which often function to limit the competence and effectiveness of national political authorities" (Held, 1995, p 127). Transnational corporations (TNCs) have helped to organise the globalisation of production and of financial transactions. Investment and production decisions do not invariably reflect local or national conditions. Information technology has transformed the mobility of economic units like currencies, stocks, shares and 'futures'. Companies locate, produce and manage manufactured goods and services in different countries with an eye to deriving benefit from different production and marketing conditions across the world. The most powerful companies can determine and change those conditions directly.

TNCs have become major institutional players, along with states, in organising production, employment and trade in large constellations of countries, and therefore necessarily influencing the collective as well as individual living standards and social conditions of the great majority of people making up national populations. This has of course seized the interest of social scientists and commentators; accounts of their growth and functions are to be found in an increasing number of books (for example, Scott et al, 1985; Lang and Hines, 1993; Kolodner, 1994; Korten, 1996; Stichele and Pennartz, 1996; Kozul-Wright and Rowthorn, 1998; Madeley, 1999; Monbiot, 2000; Sklair, 2001; George and Wilding, 2002). The growth of TNCs has been spectacular by any standards in the last three decades. According to one analyst "Corporations have become behemoths, huge global giants that wield immense political power" (Hertz, 2001, p 6). One hundred of the largest corporations now control about 20% of foreign assets. Fifty-one of the world's largest economies are now corporations and the rest nation states. The scale of financial power was described in Chapter One.

The pace of their growth is testified by the continuing phenomenon of 'mega-mergers'. In 2000 Vodaphone, the communications corporation, merged with Mannesmann; SmithKline Beecham, the pharmaceutical conglomerate, merged with Glaxo Wellcome; the internet service provider AOL merged with the media corporation Time Warner. Mergers between huge companies are frequently reported on the business pages of the press.

In absorbing the full significance of the development a number of the features of corporate action have to be explained. One is the creation of mergers and subsidiaries in 20, 30 and many more countries. Such a system or network overpowers competitors. It has a snowball effect. It reduces costs and increases profits. Another feature is the location of production and services. Transfer of working capacity and labour to a new country can attract subsidies from the government of that country to boost jobs and economic viability, just as the threat to withdraw activity from another country can cause a government to reduce its taxes and offer other deals to reduce corporation costs and persuade the TNC to reconsider its plans for relocation.

A third feature is taxation. Operating in scores of different countries TNCs find it convenient to invest off-shore or arrange accounts of production and distribution to avoid or greatly reduce taxable profits, income and expenditure. One method of handling taxation is 'transfer pricing'. TNCs have subsidiaries in different countries. The parent corporation sells materials to one of its subsidiaries in another country at an artificially high price. When these materials are turned into final products profits are thereby reduced and less tax has to be paid. The price has been transferred to the overseas country and the untaxed 'excess' profit pocketed in the headquarters country. Transfer pricing is a form of tax avoidance. In Colombia local subsidiaries reported a 6% profit when the real profit was estimated to be more than ten times higher (Madeley, 1999, p 12). The extent of transfer pricing is not known and evidence is hard to assemble.

Another feature is access to the law. Corporations have the resources to command the highest-paid counsel. This provides a huge advantage in dealing with smaller competitors but also in dealing with governments. Most important of all is the ramifying issue of political power. Scale of operations can mean that local councils and governments try to please incumbent plants and labour forces, and attract others. Sponsorships can deliver good names for companies. Rough justice can be passed off as unavoidable adjustment.

## The reassessment of the power of transnational corporations

The corporations are closely linked with the international financial agencies and with states. Samir Amin has cast the Bretton Woods international financial agencies – the World Bank and the International Monetary Fund (IMF) – as "managerial mechanisms protecting the profitability of capital" (Amin, 1997, p 17). A big problem is that different UN agencies – IMF, World Bank, World Trade Organization, United Nations Conference on Trade and Development, and the UN itself – offer little or no information either about their own links with the biggest corporations or about the economic, labour and social policies followed by the corporations – whether these are internal policies for their own employees working in many different countries, or are policies affecting consumers and the general populations of particular countries in which they operate.

Secretary General Boutros Boutros-Ghali presided over the UN's demolition of three modest-sized monitoring units of TNCs at the beginning of the 1990s. A small stream of information at the time (represented in, for example, UN, 1988) virtually dried up. The corporations were scarcely even mentioned in the proceedings of successive World Summits. Examples are the Copenhagen World Summit on Social Development in 1995 and the 2002 summit at Monterrey. As a consequence, there is all too little standard public information from public sources about the activities and developments of huge corporations.

Some information can of course be extracted from the publicity that has been given to the flow of court cases and protest campaigns involving the TNCs. Damaging revelations surface frequently in relation to McDonalds, Nestle, Nike, Gap, Exxon, Shell, Unilever and Enron, for example. At the time of the collapse of Enron in 2001 caustic testimony was given by Arundhati Roy, among others, about the 1993 agreement of Maharashtra state to let Enron build India's biggest, and first private, power plant. After considerable opposition the state government was defeated in elections in 1995 and the contract was scrapped – only to be revived when intervening political pressure was exerted (for example by the US ambassador, who was subsequently appointed a director of Enron). A minority government in office for only 13 days in 1996 took the step on its last day to approve the contract that had provoked prolonged opposition. The contract for 695 megawatts in the first stage involved payments to Enron of $210 million annually. In the second stage (2015 megawatts) the state electricity board was legally bound to pay back a total of $30 billion. It was estimated that $210 million per year would be needed for the next 40 years, constituting "the largest contract ever signed in the history of India" (Roy, 2001, p 3). "Experts … have called it the biggest fraud in the country's history. The project's gross profits work out at between $12b and $14b" (Roy, 2001, p 3). The Maharashtra State Electricity Board had to set aside 70% of its revenue to pay Enron. The fixed charges were destroying the board – which was trying to crack down on local companies providing electricity far cheaper. Their prices were being forced up to the Enron level and this was putting them out of business.

Extreme practices have been vilified but information about standard practices is difficult to find. The general merits of the loans made to poor countries by the international financial agencies are widely debated but the general merits of contracts awarded to TNCs are given small attention. By 2001 the World Bank was awarding some 40,000 contracts annually to private firms. The US Treasury department calculations also show that for every $1 contributed by the US to the international development banks, US corporations receive double that amount in bank-financed procurement contracts (www.corpwatch.org; and see also Karliner, 1997).

There is no global code of conduct for TNCs. There have indeed been attempts to introduce binding codes of conduct, without success (see van der Pijl, 1993). There is the International Labour Organization code to regulate labour issues (ILO, 1998) and OECD Guidelines for Multinational Enterprises (OECD, 2001), but these are general statements and contain injunctions rather than powers or even universally agreed norms of conduct. While the courts certainly have powers over law breaking, they tend only to be used as measures of last resort, as they are extremely expensive. Activities short of law breaking can be shown to have serious consequences for society and are not in any serious sense 'accountable' (for example, see Korten, 1996; Madeley, 1999; Sklair, 2001). Many of the biggest TNCs have established codes and collaborative institutions under the concept of 'global corporate governance'. In the US a movement for 'caring capitalism' was led by Business for Social Responsibility (BSR), operating from Washington in 1992. By the mid-1990s, BSR had a national membership and affiliations of 800 (Sklair, 2001, p 159). Sometimes such corporate initiatives are good attempts to face up to new problems; but they can also be cynical attempts to sidestep costly issues by constructing images on the cheap.

## International financial agencies

The international financial agencies have played an increasing role in developing social policies favourable to TNCs – and other UN agencies have lamely followed suit. World Bank conditional loans have given the impetus to social security reforms that have privileged private company business – especially for pensions. "The privatisation of social security has benefited international corporations that become partners with local business elites" (Armada et al, 2001, p 729). Analysts have also shown that by endorsing the privatisation of health services, for example in Latin America, the WHO has converged with these policies (Armada et al, 2001, p 729). Other international agencies than the World Bank and the IMF are supporting their interpretations of current social policies. The alliance between transnational corporations, international financial agencies and the richest states is posing the major problem for the satisfaction of human rights and objectives like the elimination of poverty.

Privatisation of the kind promoted by the agencies seems to be impelling an increase in inequality and making much more difficult the reduction of poverty. Certainly this seems to be the view of no less an authority than Ravi Kanbur, director of the World Bank's World Development Report on Poverty, until his resignation in May 2000. Later in 2000 he revealed that poverty was often greater than the figures given in the Bank's handbooks of statistics. Among the reasons "it is quite possible for public services to worsen considerably and yet for this effect to not show up in the income-expenditure based measures of poverty incidence" (Kanbur, 2000, p 10). Technically this means that if the measure of income were to include the value to families of goods and services received in kind, many more people in countries that were privatising public services would be found to be below the poverty line. Effectively, Kanbur's explanation is also an admission that structural adjustment policies, giving priority to privatisation and cuts in expenditure on public services, had counteracted some if not all of any benefits from economic growth that had accrued to many poor countries. Kanbur's post-resignation account of the ideological and technical context of the work of the World Bank shows the central importance he attaches to the definition and statistical measurement of the extent of poverty. Unwittingly, his retrospective analysis justifies renewed concern about the construction of a poverty line and the value of fresh investigation of its scientific basis.

In 1990 the problem of poverty was given top billing on the world's agenda for action. Since then, however, as in the previous three decades, its reduction and eradication has proved to be elusive. This was due partly to economic and social policies that were shown to move trends in poverty in the wrong direction. However, it was also due partly to explicit and implicit explanations of the causes of the problem adopted alike by governments and international agencies that have been shown to be misplaced. The overhaul and substitution of previous entrenched conceptions will be a long and bitterly resisted process.

## The World Bank

The difference between what the governing structures of the IMF and the World Bank are, and what they might be, can be illustrated from their history. Keynes was a central figure in the creation of the Bretton Woods institutions in 1944 but the result was not what he wanted. He had advocated the creation of an international credit-creating institution and in the early years of war he called attention to the serious financial liquidity problems that would arise at its end, that needed concerted action if dangerous forms of instability were to be avoided. The industrialised countries of Western Europe had been devastated. They were obliged to restrict imports, devalue currencies, maintain tight price controls and cut public expenditure because they had insufficient resources combined with inevitably high levels of debt. In addition, their recovery would be long-delayed and economic growth kept low. This would worsen economic prospects of growth, and indeed restrict the US economy itself. On top of the need of these countries for post-war reconstruction was the problem of ensuring enough liquidity to finance the growth of world trade. The governments should not be forced by fluctuating balance of payments problems into cycles of deflation and competitive devaluation. That would depress employment and living standards in economically strong and not only weak countries.

Keynes therefore argued for a kind of world central bank or 'Clearing Union' that created a deposit of new currency for every country in the world which it could count on at times of difficulty to pay creditor governments. The big countries would create a giant fund from which countries in demonstrable financial adversity could draw – up to a sizeable minimum level – without strings. Up to that minimum level they would not have to justify their policies. The total amount of currency deposited would rise steadily in rough proportion to world trade. In fact what materialised was a pale shadow of Keynes' intentions. Total resources were less than a third of what he advised. Countries were not awarded an allocation. They had to contribute to the total fund to be eligible for membership and hence the opportunity to apply for loans – to which stringent conditions could be attached. Membership was conditional rather than universal; debtors had less independence, aid had strings, and the US remained predominantly in charge of those strings. And a system intended to promote the post-war recovery of the industrialised countries was soon converted into an instrument providing loans to the poorest countries.

Created at the Bretton Woods Conference in 1944 as an adjunct of the IMF – and broadly taking on the programme for long-term development while the IMF dealt with short-term financial stability – the World Bank Group is made up of five agencies making loans or guaranteeing credit to the 180 member countries. The five are:

- the International Bank for Reconstruction and Development (accounting for more than half the Bank's lending and $10.5 billion in 2001);
- the International Development Association (accounting for about a quarter, and $6.8 billion in 2001);
- the International Finance Corporation ($3.9 billion in 2001);
- the Multilateral Investment Guarantee Agency ($2 billion guarantees in 2001);
- the International Settlement of Investment Disputes.

Total Bank lending in each year has to be set against loan repayments – but also the value of contracts arranged with corporations. In 1993 net disbursements by the World Bank, that is, gross disbursements minus repayments to the Bank, totalled just over $7 billion – a miniscule amount by comparison with World GDP and less even than the expenditure of most *single* departments of state in the OECD countries. However, the borrowing countries paid out nearly as much in that year – $6.8 billion – to corporations from the OECD countries, leaving only a marginal positive cash flow into the treasuries of the recipient countries (Karliner, www.corpwatch.org, 1 December 1997).

The redefinition and remeasurement of poverty is a necessary part of the process of justifying, and constructing, international loans, and cannot be separated from the choice of theory required to explain the problem and specify the action required to resolve it.

## The World Bank's measure of poverty

The World Bank has been under increasing pressure about the persistence of mass poverty. In the early 1990s the Bank conceded a "loss of momentum during the 1980s" in reducing poverty (World Bank, 1993a). Yet ten years later the research development group conceded the same for the 1990s (Chen and Ravallion, 2001). A succession of World Bank reports trace the story (World Bank, 1990, 1993a, 1993b, 1995a, 1995b, 1996, 1997a, 1997b, 2000, 2001). On 28 April 1993, Lewis T. Preston, the president of the World

Bank at the time, had stated "Poverty reduction is the benchmark against which our performance as a development institution must be judged."

That 'benchmark' has to be explained. It was a 'global' standard – a "universal poverty line [which] is needed to permit cross-country comparison and aggregation" (World Bank, 1990, p 27). Poverty was defined as "the inability to attain a minimal standard of living" (World Bank, 1990, p 26). Despite acknowledgement of the difficulties of capturing the contribution to standards of living of public goods and common-property resources in any measure of poverty the World Bank settled for a standard which is 'consumption-based'. This standard comprises "two elements: the expenditure necessary to buy a minimum standard of nutrition and other basic necessities and a further amount that varies from country to country, reflecting the cost of participating in the everyday life of society" (World Bank, 1990, p 26).

For operational purposes the second of the two elements said to be necessary in the definition of poverty was set aside. Twelve years later it has still to be systematically examined in relation both to the distribution of income and the results of applying only the first element in the definition to the incidence and depth of poverty worldwide. This serious omission is highlighted in the discussion below. It is argued that data from surveys of material and social deprivation could be used constructively to restore the original scope of the Bank's definition.

## Technical limitations of the World Bank's 'partial' poverty line

How well was the first element of the Bank's definition in fact operationalised? This element of the definition was assessed as Purchasing Power Parity (PPP) $370 per year per person at 1985 prices for all the poorest developing countries (World Bank, 1993a, p 4; and see also World Bank, 1990, especially pp 25-29). For 1990 this produced an estimate of 1,133 million of poor people in the developing world. The fact that this was a rough and ready measure adopted – by implication temporarily – for the purposes of simplicity and convenience can be illustrated best by a further statement made at the time. "An extra $0.70 per day added to the poverty line implies a doubling of the number of people counted as being poor" (World Bank, 1993a, p 4). This alternative statistic suggests that research needed to be undertaken to find whether people with incomes higher than the threshold adopted were also exposed to unacceptably high levels of deprivation, poor health and lack of access to basic services. While a measure that is rough and ready can be accepted for a time pending further investigation, it cannot be accepted indefinitely. The circumstances of those just above the threshold have to be compared with those on, or just below, the threshold to justify and confirm its adoption.

In 1990 the World Bank had argued "the case for basing international comparisons" on this threshold (World Bank, 1990). However, its argument was inconsistent. First, later measures differ from earlier measures put forward by the Bank and, second, separate references are made confusingly to definitions of 'absolute poverty' and the 'poverty line' in the same report. Therefore in a 1993 report absolute poverty was defined as "the position of an individual or household in relation to a poverty line the real value of which is fixed over time"; and the poverty line was "the standard of living (usually measured in terms of income or consumption) below which people are deemed to be poor" (World Bank, 1993a, p vii).

The Bank began to be challenged on technical grounds. The 'primary conclusion' of the World Development Report for 2000 that the world was on the right track to reduce poverty was challenged, because the Bank's estimates "should not be accepted" (Reddy and Pogge, 2001, p 2). There was a "lack of a well-defined poverty line that permits of meaningful and reliable inter-temporal and inter-spatial comparisons, and relatedly, the use of a misleading and inaccurate measure of purchasing power 'equivalence', that may systematically distort estimates of the level and trend of global poverty" (Reddy and Pogge, 2001, p 1). For example the 1985 Summers and Heston PPP conversion factors were varied in the 2000 exercise, without precise specification of what had now been done and why (Reddy and Pogge, 2001, pp 3-7). These criticisms did not extend to challenging the Bank's overall conception of a poverty line, or why the 'second element' of the Bank's definition could not be included operationally, but they are nonetheless damaging.

The World Bank has continued to argue for a fixed poverty line. The standard below which people are deemed to be poor is supposed not to change. This seems to have been applied inter-temporally but not inter-spatially. For Latin America and the Caribbean the World Bank actually adopted a different poverty line of $2 per day (World Bank, 1993a, p 6). Subsequently a standard of $4 a day was adopted for Eastern Europe and the republics of the former Soviet Union. It would be hard to claim that these figures are not arbitrary and that relativity can stand the test of time. Different countries and regions have experienced different trajectories of growth and distribution and such variation is likely to persist.

Nonetheless, the Bank had given an impression in its 1990 report that its conceptualisation of poverty could be extended to all countries including the industrial countries. As emphasised above, poverty had been defined as "the inability to attain a minimal standard of living" (World Bank, 1990, p 25). This could have been a good starting point for consistent scientific and international definition. What exactly was this standard of living? "Household incomes and expenditures per capita are adequate yardsticks" (World Bank, 1990, p 25). The Bank admitted that there were drawbacks because income and expenditure measures did not capture dimensions of welfare like access to public goods and services, clean drinking water and other 'common property' resources. However, historically, wider definitions of income have included monetary equivalents to free or subsidised goods and services. The World Bank's definition, accordingly, could have included the same, and thereby could have solved the problem of comparing countries, and rural versus urban regions in those countries – with different mixes of cash and goods in kind.

So the World Bank's admission that 'common property' was not included in its measures of income does not seem to have prompted scientific enquiry to produce a more consistent or 'objective' poverty line. The procedure developed at the time was not clear. The drawbacks specified had only to be examined in relation to 'some norm' – namely a 'consumption-based' poverty line (World Bank, 1990, p 26). At the time, as noted above, the Bank made a case for measuring two elements, the expenditure necessary to buy a minimum standard of nutrition and other basic necessities, and an additional amount reflecting the cost of participating in the everyday life of society (World Bank, 1990, p 26).

The first was believed to be unproblematic. The cost of calorific intakes and other necessities could be calculated by "looking at the prices of the foods that make up the diets of the poor". The second "is far more subjective; in some countries indoor plumbing is a luxury, but in others it is a 'necessity'" (World Bank, 1990, pp 26-27). This is a very odd statement. In what sense is the need for indoor plumbing, as distinct from the need for food, 'subjective'? And when is it a 'luxury' and when a 'necessity'? Does not the cost of food, as much as the cost of plumbing, reflect participation in the everyday life of society? If plumbing is a 'luxury' in some societies does that mean that food never is in any society?

This chapter does not provide an exhaustive account of the World Bank's procedures. We have sought only to provide some of the steps that have to be questioned, in order to call attention to the unexplained, and un-researched elements in the specification. Otherwise the World Bank is left to fulfil a false prospectus on false premises. There are illustrations in different Bank reports for the period. For example, at one point the text explains that country-specific poverty lines are plotted against per capita consumption "for thirty-four developing and industrial countries", but the figure on the same page shows only the plotted figures for the poorest 12 countries among them. For the 22 richer countries country-specific poverty lines are not plotted. The need to move towards clearly formulated international standards of poverty that provide the right basis for cross-national comparison, analysis and formulation of more effective policy has now existed for much longer than a decade.

## The Bank's definition of poverty assessed

In reaching this severe conclusion it is only fair to acknowledge the particular strengths in what the World Bank did initially. In the early years the Bank's standard was simple to comprehend and apply. It did not depend on the arduous and continuous collection and compilation of data about types as well as amounts of resources, changing patterns of necessities and changing construction of standards of living.

At the same time there were, and are, major weaknesses in the Bank's approach. It is fixed in time. It ducks any acceptance that 'need' is fundamentally a social construct as well as having specifically social elements. As a social construct it is international in scope and therefore has to be open to scientific investigation and accreditation – as well as challenge. It turns out to be not in fact a 'global' poverty line at all. It is not assumed to be applicable to countries other than the poorest. On the Bank's own admission an international poverty line that is more than 'consumption-based' should, ideally, be constructed. No cost is in fact estimated for the second 'participatory' element of the definition. So the logic of the Bank's own argument is not followed: the minimum value of the poverty line is therefore underestimated and the number of poor in the world also underestimated. These criticisms gain force if it is accepted that, as time goes on, social polarisation in many countries is making the construction of an international poverty line ever more necessary, because the poorest conditions in the world now apply conspicuously to some sections of the population in middle-income and even high-income countries.

As noted above, the second element of the World Bank's 1990 definition of the poverty line was set aside. Surprisingly, the first was not much investigated or defended. The type, number and amounts of necessities other than food, for example, are not tracked down and discussed. And questions of diet – and especially thresholds of under-nutrition, in relation to income – are not rigorously investigated. Variations in the sheer quantity of the diet required among populations with widely varying work and other activity obligations and customs, as well as in the types of diet socially preferred or indeed available in local markets, and at what cost, are left unexplored. These points apply in particular to children.

In the World Bank's huge programme of research, one recurring problem has been the lack of quantitative illustration of the poverty problems of different types of family or household. Information was collected about average consumption of calories or protein by males and females of different age, including children, but the distribution by income or occupational status, or by reference to other features of standard of living, such as housing, conditions of work, environmental and sanitary facilities and access to health and education has not comprised an essential part of the investigative strategy.

There have been certain exceptions. More varied information for particular countries is to be found in the Bank's Living Standards Measurement Study surveys. The survey is a multi-topic instrument in which information is collected from all members of households. It covers a wide range of subjects, including, for example, housing, family demography, education, health, migration, economic activity, expenditure and time use.

[...]

The data are elaborate and informative. They are still placed in the approved framework of definition, analysis and policy formulation advocated by the Bank. However, by virtue of giving some exposition of the experiences of different groups in the population, concessions are made to strategies other than the trio of economic growth, human capital formation and safety nets. Therefore in the case of the elderly "only about 4% belonging to the poorest 30% of the population are covered by any pension.... The best risk prevention strategy ... is to implement a social security reform, which increases coverage to all population in the future".

The high point in the attempts to justify the World Bank's technical approach to the definition and measurement of poverty perhaps arrived with a report on trends in poverty during the 1990s (Chen and Ravallion, 2001). The report came from its Development Research Group. [...]

At face value these results offered little demonstration of the success of World Bank policies. The research group said they drew on 265 national sample surveys in 83 countries to conclude that there was a "disappointing rate of poverty reduction" (Chen and Ravallion, 2001, p 1). The 1990s "did not see much progress against consumption poverty in the developing world" (Chen and Ravallion, 2001, p 18). Yet the overall rate of growth in real consumption per person for low- and middle-income countries during the first eight years of the 1990s was 2.6% per year. "Even assuming no growth from 1987 to 1990, an annual rate of growth in mean consumption of 2.6% over 1990-97 alone would have virtually halved the aggregate poverty gap, as long as overall inequality did not worsen" (Chen and Ravallion, 2001, p 18). What went wrong? They admit that "There is now evidence of quite sharply rising inter-personal income inequality in the world during this period" (Chen and Ravallion, 2001, p 18). They referred to work by Milanovic (1999) that showed that, on average, inequality in the world as measured by the Gini coefficient had increased by 5% between 1988 and 1993. "This could easily wipe out the gains to the world's poor from global economic growth" (Chen and Ravallion, 2001, p 18). There was no reference to the responsibility of World Bank growth and structural adjustment policies for increasing inequality. The furthest that the authors were prepared to go was to admit that "there is evidence that initial inequality is too high in some countries to assure poverty-reducing growth even when the fundamentals are conducive to growth" (Chen and Revallion, 2001, p 19, referring to Ravallion, 1997, and Ravallion and Datt, 1999).

[...]

## Approaches by other agencies

Although other international agencies adopt their own programmes they compound the problem. The poverty line is defined by UNDP as "that income level below which a minimum nutritionally adequate diet plus essential non-food requirements are not affordable" (UNDP, 1993, p 225). The steps by which a minimum nutritionally adequate diet, and 'essential non-food requirements' can be defined as appropriate for different countries, and the criteria according to which these can be said to be 'affordable', are not investigated.

The specialised work of the International Fund for Agricultural Development has resulted in reports that resemble the World Bank's approach but introduce some flexibility into a 'fixed' poverty line by taking note of measures which originate nationally, and which depend on more sophisticated investigation of changes in consumption as well as consumption prices. The poverty line is defined as "a commodity bundle tied to the minimum requirement (calories and protein for food, and some notional minimum for non-food items), and the determination of an appropriate set of prices to be applied to individual commodities to calculate the poverty expenditure and income" (Jazairy et al, 1994, p 461).

The ILO has contributed over the years to a more 'structural' interpretation of poverty and its causes (International Institute for Labour Studies, 1993; but also see, for example, Franklin, 1967). In particular, its work on the structure of the labour market and questions of access to that market help to balance the monetarist perspectives of the IMF and World Bank. The ILO began in the 1970s to show the part to be played in explaining poverty by lack of community utilities or infrastructure – water, sanitation, health centres, primary schools, and transport. The development of measures of collective or community need, as distinct from individual need, as a contribution to understanding poverty, and its alleviation, deserves renewed attention. Therefore, some commentators have pointed out that the World Bank's 1990 report on poverty:

> ... represents a step away from neoliberalism and back toward the Bank's attitude of the 1960s: that the continuing existence of the poor in poor nations is the development problem. Indeed, the insistence [in the Bank's annual development reports] on remedying water and air pollution resembles nothing more strongly than 20-

year-old strategies aimed at satisfying developing countries' basic needs. (Taylor, 1992, p 57)

The ILO preoccupations of the 1970s are back in fashion (Townsend, 1993, Chapter 2).

When many governments agreed the report on the World Summit for Social Development at Copenhagen the international agencies were slow to follow up the recommendation, among others, to measure 'absolute' and 'overall' poverty separately – as a means of making comparisons between countries, and especially between rich and poor countries, more feasible. Prior to the five-year review of the programme of action in July 2000 UNDP was the first to collect reports from countries. The reports covered work to establish definitions and estimates of poverty, set targets for poverty reduction or eradication and formulate national plans (UNDP, 1998, pp 28-30). Estimates were given for some countries of the extent of 'extreme' and 'overall' poverty. In the case of India, therefore, the two figures were 6% and 36% respectively; for the Republic of Moldova 21% and 43%; for the Central African Republic 36% and 63%; for Malaysia 2% and 9% and for Panama 22% and 37%. Results on both measures were available only for 11 countries although 75 of a total of 130 countries had officially endorsed operational definitions of extreme poverty and 69 of overall poverty (UNDP, 1998, pp 22, 30).

In 2000 UNDP reported that 64 countries now provided information about the extent of both forms of poverty. Other countries provided information on one or the other (UNDP, 2000, pp 24-9). But UNDP offered no prescriptions for standardisation internationally. Its position is admittedly difficult. In successive reports on poverty it has simply reproduced data at $1, $2, $4 or even $14.40 per person per day as measures of convenience for countries in different regions (see, for example, its *Human Development Report* devoted to the eradication of poverty, 1997, pp 32-3).

The World Bank's measures have also become more diffuse. The Bank accepts measures of a 'national' poverty line put forward by individual governments, and also gives two alternative measures of an 'international' poverty line – $1 and $2 per person per day (World Bank, 2000, 2001). During these years the problem of ambiguity in international debate has multiplied because little guidance about a 'core' international or scientific measure has been offered, and a puzzling general distinction between 'income' poverty and poverty has been introduced.

## Developing an alternative poverty line

The general shortcomings of the World Bank's approach to measurement would have been evident sooner if the question 'Who is poor?' had been systematically investigated in relation to the dollar-a-day information produced, and efforts made to make strict comparisons between countries and examine trends over a number of years.

Once the distributional structure of poverty is correctly identified in different countries then both causes and anti-poverty strategies become easier to discern. Therefore in countries as diverse as India, Kyrgyz, Tanzania, Kenya and the Yemen it can be shown that poverty is above average among women, the elderly and disabled – especially women, the unemployed, lone parents, households with children, particularly households with lone parents, and households with several rather than one or two children. Poverty is also above average in rural areas and among most ethnic minority groups and most groups with low occupational status, including, for example, day labourers (see, for example, Hashem, 1996). This structural 'bias' cannot be remedied by economic growth governed only by market considerations but by 'redistribution with growth'. High priority in anti-poverty policies, according to such evidence, plainly has to be given to children, elderly and disabled people who cannot gain paid employment, and those in the labour market whose earnings are insufficient to ensure a household income adequate for health, wellbeing and social viability.

A strategy of 'redistribution with growth' to eradicate absolute poverty is not something new. It has been put forward for many years, for example in the Indian government's national five-year plans from 1961-66 onwards. Therefore an influential Planning Commission report of 1962 stated that "the time has now come when we should sharply focus our efforts on providing an assured minimum income to every citizen of the country within a reasonable time. Progressively this minimum would itself be raised as development goes apace" (Appasamy et al, 1996, p 10).

Two improvements to measurement can be made. First, existing data about incomes of households with and without children can be reviewed and an account given of the extent and severity of material and social deprivation among adults and children, with information about access to necessary services and the kinds of policies that had improved conditions of people in other countries or in the previous history of particular countries. This would be an exercise in which existing information would be reassembled for the purpose of reviewing policies as prime causes of consequential conditions. The second would be to devise improvements to the national surveys introduced as a result of the 1995 World Summit and the country studies issued by the international agencies, and collect information directly about poverty. This could pave the way for a renewed determination to restore the two-part treatment of the poverty measure originally put forward in 1990.

The World Bank constructed graphs which were supposed to show the rising real per capita value of 'country-specific' poverty lines in relation to average per capita consumption. The graph did not in fact fulfil this intention; it merely showed an upper and a lower poverty line fixed by the Bank in dollars at 1985 prices for a small number of poor countries in relation to the average per capita consumption in those countries.

## Conclusion

World anti-poverty policies have been shown to be ineffective, and need to be recast. This chapter has sought to show that a plan of action is best constructed by linking the growing international consensus in favour of the fulfilment of human rights to the analysis of the activities of powerful TNCs and the related policies of the international financial agencies, especially the World Bank.

### References

Amin, S. (1997) *Capitalism in the age of globalization*, London and New York, NY: Earthscan.

Appasamy P., Guhan S., Hema R., Majumdar M. and Vaidyanathan A. (1996) *Social exclusion from a welfare rights perspective in India*, Research Series no 106, Geneva: International Institute for Labour Studies.

Armada, F., Muntaner, C. and Navarro, V. (2001) 'Health and social security reform in Latin America: the convergence of the World Health Organization, the World Bank and the transnational corporations', *International Journal of Health Services*, vol 31, no 4, pp 729-68.

Chen, S. and Ravallion, M. (2001) 'How did the world's poorest fare in the 1990s?', Development Research Group, World Bank, *Review of Income and Wealth*, pp 1-33.

Franklin, N.N. (1967) 'The concept and measurement of "minimum living standards"', *International Labour Review*, 95, (January-June), pp 271-98.

George, V. and Wilding, P. (2002) *Globalisation and human welfare*, Basingstoke and New York, NY: Palgrave Macmillan.

Hashem, M. (1996) *Goals for social integration and realities of social exclusion in the Republic of Yemen*, Research Series No 105, Geneva: International Institute for Labour Studies.

Held, D. (1995) *Democracy and the global order: From the modern state to cosmopolitan governance*, London: Polity Press.

Hertz, N. (2001) *The silent takeover: Global capitalism and the death of bureaucracy*, London: William Heinemann.

ILO (International Labour Organization) (1998) *The ILO tripartite declaration of principles concerning multinational enterprises and social policy – ten years after*, Geneva: ILO.

International Institute for Labour Studies (1993) *Poverty, inequality, exclusion: New approaches to theory and practice*, Geneva: ILO.

Jazairy, I., Algamir, M. and Panuccio, T. (1994) *The state of world rural poverty*, London: IFDA.

Kanbur, R. (2000) 'Economic policy, distribution and poverty: the nature of disagreements', Paper presented to the Swedish Parliamentary Commission on Global Development, 22 September.

Karliner, J. (1997) *The corporate planet: Ecology and politics in the age of globalisation*, San Francisco, CA: Sierra Club Books.

Kolodner, E. (1994) *Transnational corporations: Impediments or catalysts of social development?*, Occasional Paper no 5, World Summit for Social Development, Geneva: UNRISD.

Korten, D.C. (1996) *When corporations rule the world*, London: Earthscan.

Kozul-Wright, R. and Rowthorn, R. (1998) *Transnational corporations and the global economy*, Helsinki: UNU World Institute for Development Economic Research.

Lang, T. and Hines, C. (1993) *The new protectionism*, London: Earthscan.

Madeley, J. (1999) *Big business, poor peoples: The impact of transnational corporations on the world's poor*, London and New York, NY: Zed Books.

Milanovic, B. (1999) 'True world income distribution, 1988 and 1993: first calculations based on household surveys alone', mimeo, World Bank.

Monbiot, G. (2000) *Captive state: The corporate takeover of Britain*, London: Pan Books.

OECD (Organisation for Economic Co-operation and Development) (2001) *The OECD guidelines for multinational enterprises 2001: Focus: global instruments for corporate responsibility*, Paris: OECD.

Ravallion, M. (1997) 'Can high inequality developing countries escape absolute poverty?', *Economics Letters*, vol 56, pp 51-7.

Ravallion, M. and Datt, G. (1999) *When is growth pro-poor? Evidence from the diverse experience of India's states*, Policy Research Working Paper WPS 2263, Washington, DC: World Bank.

Reddy, S.G. and Pogge, T.W. (2001) 'How not to count the poor', Unpublished paper, Departments of Economics and Philosophy, University of Columbia.

Roy, A. (2001) 'The biggest fraud in India's history', *The Guardian*, G2, 30 November, extracted from A. Roy (2002) *Power politics*, London: South End Press.

Scott, J., Stokman, F.N. and Ziegler, R. (1985) *Networks of corporate power*, London: Polity Press.

Sklair, L. (2001) *The transnational capitalist class*, Oxford: Blackwell.

Stichele, M.V. and Pennartz, P. (1996) *Making it our business – European NGO campaigns on transnational corporations*, London: CIIR.

Townsend, P. (1993) *The international analysis of poverty*, Hemel Hempstead: Harvester Wheatsheaf.

UNDP (United Nations Development Programme) (1993) *Human Development Report, 1993*, New York, NY and Oxford: Oxford University Press.

UNDP (1997) *Human Development Report 1997*, New York, NY and Oxford: Oxford University Press.

UNDP (1998) *Overcoming human poverty*, UNDP Poverty Report 1998, New York, NY: UNDP.

UNDP (2000) *Overcoming human poverty: UNDP Poverty Report 2000*, New York, NY: UNDP.

van der Pjil, K. (1993) 'The sovereignty of capital impaired: social forces and codes of conduct for multinational corporations', in H. Overbeek (ed) *Restructuring hegemony in the global political economy: The rise of transnational neo-liberalism in the 1980s*, London: Routledge.

World Bank (1990) *World Development Report 1990: Poverty*, Washington, DC: World Bank.

World Bank (1993a) *Implementing the World Bank's strategy to reduce poverty: Progress and challenges*, Washington, DC: World Bank.

World Bank (1993b) *World Development Report 1993: Investing in health*, Washington, DC: Oxford University Press for the World Bank.

World Bank (1995a) *Advancing social development: A World Bank contribution to the Social Summit*, Washington, DC: World Bank.

World Bank (1995b) *Investing in people: The World Bank in action*, Washington, DC: World Bank.

World Bank (1996) *Poverty reduction and the World Bank: Progress and challenges in the 1990s*, Washington, DC: World Bank.

World Bank (1997a) *Poverty reduction and the World Bank: Progress in fiscal year 1996 and 1997*, Washington, DC: World Bank.

World Bank (1997b) *The state in a changing world: World Development Report 1997*, Washington, DC: World Bank.

World Bank (2000) *World development indicators*, Washington, DC: World Bank.

World Bank (2001) *World Development Report 2000/2001: Attacking poverty*, Washington, DC: World Bank.

# Index

Note: Page numbers followed by *tab* and *n* refer to information in a table or a note. Titles at the Townsend entry refer to texts authored or co-authored by him from which extracts have been taken. Articles and other papers are as listed in the Contents.

## A

Abel-Smith, Brian 130, 131, 242, 339, 385
Abrams, Philip 11
absolute poverty measures 400, 638*tab*, 655
  and child poverty 258-9, 266-7
  Copenhagen Agreement (1995) 92, 96-9, 320, 326, 327-8, 329
  definitions and problems of 97, 194
  theoretical debate on 237-48
abuse
  and older people in care 457-8
    as human rights violations 478-80, 628
  public inquiry into care of mentally disabled 529-30
accountability
  TNCs 32, 79, 92, 108, 117, 644-6
  *see also* corporate social responsibility
Acheson Report 335, 338-9, 395-402
acquiescence
  'acquiescent functionalism' 450, 557, 624
  problem of 19-21
Advisory Committee on Legal Aid 567
Africa
  diet and poverty in 49-50
  élites in post-colonial countries 46-7, 52
  rural/urban population divide 48
  and social security 594
  *see also* developing countries
Age Concern England 478, 628
ageing population 406-7, 428-30, 622
  *see also* older people
ageism and human rights 557, 622-33
  'institutionalised ageism' 473, 624
aid to developing countries 71, 104
  alternative funding proposals 119-25
  and benefits to donor 67, 645
  and child poverty 258
  international minimum level 107, 120
  *see also* anti-poverty programmes; international agencies
*Airey v Ireland* case 555-6
Alcock, P. 4
Almond, G.A. 45
Amin, Samir 642, 644
Anderson, Martin 62
Annan, Kofi 122
anti-poverty programmes 64, 572-6, 577, 591, 597, 632, 656
  European Community 78
  Minority Report on World Bank 102-3
  national and international planning 65-8
  need for international agreement on poverty measures 82-3, 96-9, 101-2, 109

need for monitoring 109-10
  orthodox funding strategies and alternatives 119-25
  *see also* aid to developing countries; international agencies
anti-social behaviour 401
Armada, F. 646
artefact explanation of health inequalities 348
Association of Her Majesty's Inspectors of Taxes 292
Atkinson, A.B. 121, 196, 289, 308, 467-8
Attendance Allowance 493, 513
authoritarianism and travellers 302-3

## B

Bawkin, H. 439
Baxi, Upendra 558
Beattie, Alastair 133, 337
Beeching Committee 564
behavioural explanations of health inequalities 352-5
benefit fraud 303, 313
benefits *see* child benefit; means-tested benefits; social security
Bernstein, B. 354-5
Bethnal Green study of older people
  and family care system 407-8, 413-27
  men in retirement 408, 430-7
Beveridge, William/Beveridge Report 104, 158, 467
  review ten years after report 130, 136-47
  subsistence standards 137-46, 151, 153-4, 176, 192
Black, Eugene 67
Black Report 334-6, 337, 338, 341-56, 374, 386, 395, 402
  measures to reduce health inequalities 396-7
Blair, Tony 608
Blue Books 11, 278, 291-2
bonuses 312
Booth, Charles 148, 158, 176
Booth, T. 455
Booth Centenary Survey of Life and Labour in London 132
Borrie Report 557, 608-21
  alternative approach 618-19
Bosanquet, Nick 296-7
Bourdieu, Pierre 26
Boutros-Ghali, Boutros 644-6
Bowerbank, M. 158
Bowley, A.L. 192
Boyle, Lord 288
Brandt Report 70-1

## Index